M000318374

GOING TO THE MOVIES

From Manhattan nickelodeons to the modern suburban megaplex, and from provincial, small-town or rural America to Istanbul and the shanty-towns of Southern Africa, *Going to the Movies* analyses the diverse historical and geographical circumstances in which audiences have viewed American cinema, and the variety of ways in which these audiences have been constructed by the American film industry.

The book examines the role of movie theatres in local communities, the links between film and other entertainment media, non-theatrical exhibition and historical trends toward the globalization of audiences. Two novel features of the book are the emphasis on movie-going outside the metropolitan centres of the American North-East and the manner in which several of the chapters analyse the complexities of race and race formation in relation to cinema attendance.

Many of the leading researchers in this rapidly-developing field of cinema history have contributed to this collection, which showcases the range of issues and perspectives being examined by film scholars and historians who are exploring the complexities of the social experience of movie-going.

Editors: Richard Maltby is Professor of Screen Studies at Flinders University, South Australia. **Melvyn Stokes** teaches at University College London. **Robert C. Allen** is Professor of American Studies, History, and Communication Studies at the University of North Carolina at Chapel Hill.

Exeter Studies in Film History

Published by University of Exeter Press in association with the Bill Douglas Centre for the History of Cinema and Popular Culture.

Series Editors: **Richard Maltby,** Professor of Screen Studies, Flinders University, South Australia and **Steve Neale,** Professor of Film Studies and Academic Director of the Bill Douglas Centre for the History of Cinema and Popular Culture, University of Exeter.

University of Exeter Press also publishes the celebrated five-volume series looking at the early years of English cinema, *The Beginnings of the Cinema in England*, by John Barnes.

GOING TO THE MOVIES

Hollywood and the Social Experience of Cinema

edited by

Richard Maltby, Melvyn Stokes and Robert C. Allen

UNIVERSITY
of
EXETER
PRESS

First published in 2007 by
University of Exeter Press
Reed Hall, Streatham Drive
Exeter EX4 4QR
UK
www.exeterpress.co.uk

© Richard Maltby, Melvyn Stokes and Robert C. Allen,
and the individual contributors 2007

The right of Richard Maltby, Melvyn Stokes and Robert C. Allen,
and the individual contributors, to be identified as authors of this
work has been asserted by them in accordance with
the Copyright, Designs and Patents Acts 1988.

British Library Cataloguing in Publication Data
A catalogue record for this book is available
from the British Library.

Paperback ISBN 978 0 85989 812 6
Hardback ISBN 978 0 85989 811 9

Typeset in 10½ on 13 Adobe Caslon
by Carnegie Book Production, Lancaster
Printed in Great Britain by Short Run Press Ltd, Exeter

Cover image: An African American moviegoer climbs the stairs to the 'Jim Crow
roost' in a motion picture theatre in Belzoni, Mississippi, 1939.

Contents

CONTENTS

Illustrations

ILLUSTRATIONS

Notes on Contributors

Richard Abel is Robert Altman Collegiate Professor of Film Studies in the Department of Screen Arts & Culture at the University of Michigan. Most recently he edited the award-winning *Encyclopedia of Early Cinema* (2005) and published *Americanizing the Movies and 'Movie-Mad' Audiences, 1910–1914* (2006). Currently he is co-editing *Interrogating the National and Early Cinema* (forthcoming) and completing research for *Trash Twins Making Good: Newspapers and the Movies, 1911–1915*.

Charles R. Acland is Professor and Concordia Research Chair in Communication Studies, Concordia University, Montreal, where he teaches media and cultural theory and history. His books include *Residual Media* (2007), an edited collection of research on the aging of media and culture, and *Screen Traffic: Movies, Multiplexes, and Global Culture* (2003). Currently, he is working on a history of popular ideas about media manipulation called *Hidden Messages*.

Robert C. Allen is James Logan Godfrey Professor of American Studies, History, and Communication Studies at the University of North Carolina at Chapel Hill. He is the author of *Horrible Prettiness: Burlesque and American Culture* (1991), which was awarded the Theatre Library Association's George Freedley Memorial Award, and of *Speaking of Soap Operas* (1985). He is the co-author with Douglas Gomery of *Film History: Theory and Practice* (1985), and the editor of two editions of *Channels of Discourse: Television and Contemporary Criticism* (1987, 1992). His most recent book is *The Television Studies Reader* (2004), which he co-edited with Annette Hill.

Charles Ambler is Professor of History at the University of Texas at El Paso. His publications include *Kenyan Communities in the Age of Imperialism* (1988), *Liquor and Labor in Southern Africa* (1993, with Jonathan Crush), and (with Emmanuel Akyeampong) a special issue of the *International Journal of African Historical Studies* on leisure in colonial Africa (2003). He is currently working on a study of *Alcohol and Empire* as well as a general book on Popular Culture and Mass Media in Modern Africa.

Daniel Biltereyst is Professor in Film, Television and Cultural Media Studies, Ghent University, Belgium, where he leads the Working Group Film and TV Studies (www.wgfilmtv.ugent.be). His work is on screen culture as sites of controversy, public debate and moral/media panic, more specifically on film censorship and the historical reception of controversial movies and genres. Recent essays can be found in: *Understanding Reality TV* (2004), *Rebel without a Cause: Approaches to a Maverick Masterwork* (2005), *Communication Theory and Research* (2005), *Youth Culture in Global Cinema* (2007), *Historical Journal of Film, Radio and Television* (2007).

Richard Butsch is Professor of Sociology, American Studies, and Film and Media Studies at Rider University. He is author of *The Making of American Audiences from Stage to Television, 1750–1990* (2000) and *The Citizen Audience: Crowds, Publics and Individuals* (2007); and editor of *For Fun and Profit: The Transformation of Leisure into Consumption* (1990) and *Media and Public Spheres* (2007).

Thomas Doherty is a Professor of American Studies at Brandeis University. He is an associate editor of *Cineaste* and the author of *Teenagers and Teenpics: The Juvenilization of American Movies in the 1950s* (1988), *Projections of War: Hollywood, American Culture, and World War II* (1993), *Pre-Code Hollywood: Sex, Immorality, and Insurrection in American Cinema, 1930–1934* (1999), *Cold War, Cool Medium: Television, McCarthyism, and American Culture* (2003), and *Hollywood's Censor: Joseph I. Breen and the Production Code Administration* (2007).

Jane M. Gaines is Professor of Literature and English at Duke University, where she founded the Film/Video/Digital Program. She is author of two award-winning books, *Contested Culture: The Image, the Voice, and the Law* (1991) and *Fire and Desire: Mixed Race Movies in the Silent Era* (2001). Currently she is working on *The Documentary Destiny of Cinema* and *Fictioning Histories: Women in the Silent Era International Film Industries*.

Mark Glancy is a Senior Lecturer in History at Queen Mary, University of London, where he teaches courses in American and British film history. His publications include *When Hollywood Loved Britain* (1999), *The 39 Steps: A British Film Guide* (2003), and, as co-editor, *The New Film History: Sources, Methods, Approaches* (2007).

Ahmet Gürata is Assistant Professor of Film and Media Studies at Bilkent University, Ankara. He has written on Turkish cinema and cross-cultural reception. He is currently researching on local film culture in Turkey.

Mark Jancovich is Professor of Film and Television Studies at the University of East Anglia. He is the author of several books, including: *Horror* (1992); *Rational Fears: American Horror in the 1950s* (1996); and *The Place of the Audience: Cultural Geographies of Film Consumption* (with Lucy Faire and Sarah Stubbings, 2003). His edited books include: *Approaches to Popular Film* (with Joanne Hollows, 1995); *Defining Cult Movies: The Cultural Politics of Oppositional Taste* (with Antonio Lazaro-Reboll, Julian Stringer, and Andrew Willis, 2003); and *Film Histories: An Introduction and Reader* (with Paul Grainge and Sharon Monteith, 2006).

Jeffrey Klenotic is Associate Professor of Communication Arts at the University of New Hampshire-Manchester. His essays on cinema history and historiography have been published in the *Communication Review*, the *Velvet Light Trap* and *Film History*, as well as in several edited anthologies and encyclopedias. He is currently developing a research tool on moviegoing and cultural geography using Geographic Information System (GIS) software to construct interactive maps from multiple databases.

Barbara Klinger is a Professor in the Department of Communication and Culture at Indiana University in Bloomington, Indiana, where she teaches film and media studies. Her research focuses on reception studies, fan studies, and cinema's relationship to new media. Along with numerous articles, she is author of *Melodrama and Meaning: History, Culture, and the Films of Douglas Sirk* (1994) and *Beyond the Multiplex: Cinema, New Technologies, and the Home* (2006).

Annette Kuhn writes and teaches on films, cinema history, visual culture, and cultural memory. She is co-editor of *Screen*; Visiting Professor at Queen Mary, University of London; Docent in Cinema Studies at Stockholm University; and a Fellow of the British Academy. Her books include *An Everyday Magic: Cinema and Cultural Memory* (2002); *Family Secrets: Acts of Memory and Imagination* (2002), and (co-edited with Kirsten Emiko McAllister) *Locating Memory: Photographic Acts* (2006). Her book on Lynne Ramsay's film *Ratcatcher* is forthcoming in the BFI Modern Classics series.

Terry Lindvall holds the endowed C.S. Lewis Chair of Communication and Christian Thought at Virginia Wesleyan College in Norfolk, Virginia, and is the author of *Sanctuary Cinema* (2007), *The Silents of God: Silent American Film and Religion* (2001) and other works. He has been executive producer of over 50 award-winning films (*Cradle of Genius*, 2003) including several Student Academy Awards (*Bird in a Cage* 1986), and has taught at Duke University and the College of William and Mary.

Christopher J. McKenna is a Ph.D. candidate in English and American Studies at the University of North Carolina at Chapel Hill, where he is completing a dissertation concerning the history of moviegoing in Robeson County, North

Carolina (focusing on issues of race, censorship, and entrepreneurship). After nearly twenty years in the financial-technology industry, he currently serves as Senior Vice President and Chief Information Officer at Smith Breeden Associates, Inc., a global investment management firm.

Richard Maltby is Professor of Screen Studies and Head of the School of Humanities at Flinders University, South Australia. His publications include *Hollywood Cinema* (2nd edition 2003), *Dreams for Sale: Popular Culture in the Twentieth Century* (1989), *Harmless Entertainment: Hollywood and the Ideology of Consensus* (1983), and *'Film Europe' and 'Film America': Cinema, Commerce and Cultural Exchange, 1925–1939* (1999), which won the Prix Jean Mitry for cinema history in 2000, as well as numerous articles and essays.

Anne Morey is an associate professor in English at Texas A&M University. Her book *Hollywood Outsiders: The Adaptation of the Film Industry, 1913–1934* (2003) deals with Hollywood's critics and co-opters in the later silent and early sound periods. She has published in *Film History*, *Quarterly Review of Film and Video*, and *Tulsa Studies in Women's Literature*, among other venues. She is presently at work on a history of religious film-making in the United States from the late nineteenth century to the present.

John Sedgwick is a film economic historian who lectures at London Metropolitan University. He is particularly concerned with the measurement and interpretation of film popularity and has developed a methodology (POPSTAT) for estimating the former. His publications include *Film-going in Britain during the 1930s* (2000), an anthology of articles on the *Economic History of Film* (2005) edited with Mike Pokorny, and essays in *Cinema Journal* (2006) *Explorations in Economic History* (1998), the *Journal of Cultural History* (2001), the *Journal of Economic History* and the *Economic History Review* (2005).

Melvyn Stokes teaches at University College London, where he has been principal organiser of the Commonwealth Fund Conference on American History since 1988. His edited books include *Race and Class in the American South since 1890* (1994), *The Market Revolution in America* (1996), and *The State of U.S. History* (2002). He has co-edited, with Richard Maltby, four volumes on cinema audiences: *American Movie Audiences* (1999), *Identifying Hollywood's Audiences* (1999), *Hollywood Spectatorship* (2001) and *Hollywood Abroad* (2004). His book *D.W. Griffith's 'The Birth of a Nation': A History of 'The Most Controversial Motion Picture of All Time'* has just been published by Oxford University Press.

Judith Thissen is Assistant Professor in Media History, Utrecht University, Netherlands. She is the author of several essays on the politics of popular entertainment in the immigrant Jewish community of New York City. Her most recent publications include 'Film and Vaudeville on New York's Lower East

Side' in *The Art of Being Jewish in Modern Times* (2007), 'National and Local Movie Moguls: Two Patterns of Jewish Showmanship in Film Exhibition' in *Jews and American Popular Culture* (2006), and 'Reconsidering the Decline of the New York Yiddish Theatre in the Early 1900s,' *Theatre Survey* (2003).

Gregory A. Waller is Professor and Chair of the Department of Communication and Culture at Indiana University. His publications on American film include *Moviegoing in America* (2002) and *Main Street Amusements: Movies and Commercial Entertainment in a Southern City, 1896–1900* (1995), which won the Katherine Singer Kovacs Award from the Society for Cinema Studies and the Theatre Library Association award. He is currently completing two projects: Movies on the Road, a history of itinerant film exhibition, particularly in the 1930s, and Japan-in-America, a study of the representation of Japan in American culture, 1890–1915 (http://www.indiana.edu/~jia1915/).

Haidee Wasson is Assistant Professor of Cinema at Concordia University, Montreal. She has previously taught at the University of Minnesota and Harvard University. She is author of *Museum Movies: The Museum of Modern Art and the Birth of Art Cinema* (2005), and co-editor of *Inventing Film Studies* (2007), on the history of the discipline of film studies. She has published numerous articles in journals such as *Film History, Convergences, Continuum, Frameworks,* and *The Moving Image.* Her research interests include extra-theatrical film culture, historiography, museums and cinema, and emergent screen technologies.

Acknowledgements

THIS BOOK has its origins in a large conference on 'American Cinema and Everyday Life' held at University College London in June 2003. Most of its chapters are revised, expanded and updated versions of selected papers that were first delivered at that conference. We would like, in particular, to thank the four keynote speakers (Richard Abel, Jane Gaines, Barbara Klinger and Richard Maltby) for their contribution to the success of the conference as a whole.

The editors wish to thank the Commonwealth Fund, Graduate School and Friends Programme of University College London for helping to making this conference financially possible. They would also like to acknowledge financial support from the Cultural Affairs Office of the US Embassy in London, the British Academy, the Royal Historical Society, the London University Institute for United States Studies (now Institute for the Study of the Americas), W. W. Norton and Co. and the Film Studies programme of King's College, London.

This book has been published with the help of grants from the late Miss Isobel Thornley's bequest to the University of London, from Flinders University, and from the Australian Academy of the Humanities. The editors are very grateful to these organisations for their support.

We would like to offer our thanks to Simon Baker, Anna Henderson and Vicky Owen at the University of Exeter Press for their work on the book, to Ian Christie for his help and support on the project, and to Leigh Priest for preparing the Index.

Richard Maltby, Melvyn Stokes and Robert C. Allen

Introduction

Richard Maltby and Melvyn Stokes

D URING the last ten years, researchers have increasingly acknowledged that cinema cannot be comprehensively studied merely by studying films, and that in order adequately to address the social and cultural history of cinema, we must find ways to write the histories of its audiences. In part, this redirection of research interest forms part of what some scholars have called the 'historical turn' in cinema studies.[1] To some extent, the change of emphasis reflects a growing recognition that psychoanalytically derived theoretical models of 'the spectator' have, in the end, little more to tell us about cinema's audiences and their reception of movies than do pseudo-scientific laboratory-based studies of media 'effects.' More broadly, however, this reorientation addresses what one 1970s theorist has recently called 'the weaknesses and insularity' of contemporary film studies by challenging its intellectual isolationism and developing accounts of cinema that place audiences, rather than films, at their centre.[2] The work in this collection endeavours to address the evidential and methodological issues in writing historical studies of cinema that are not centrally about films. It represents what may well come to be seen as being among the most important research in the study of cinema in the last decade, not least because of the opportunity that studies of the social history of reception offer for cinema studies to converse with other disciplines in the humanities and social sciences.

In the second edition of *Global Hollywood*, published in 2004, Toby Miller and his co-authors suggest that screen studies has so far failed 'to engage political and social history and social theory on the human subject, the nation, cultural policy, the law and the economy.'[3] 'What would it take,' they ask, 'for screen studies to matter more?' Part of their answer is to avoid the 'reproduction of "screen studies" in favour of work that studies the screen, regardless of its intellectual provenance.'[4] One aspect of such a project may be to recognise that in order to make connections to other disciplines, the study of cinema must abandon its preoccupations with medium-specificity and with the centrality of the film text. As James Hay has argued, film histories written under the assumption of the centrality of the film text have tended to produce 'self-contained, self-perpetuating' aesthetic accounts of 'film as a distinct "language" or set of formal conventions ... without a clear sense of cinema's relation to other social sites.'[5] Histories of reception, on the other hand, must begin by acknowledging that for most audiences for most of the history of cinema, their primary relationship with 'the cinema' has not been with individual movies-as-artefacts or as texts, but with the social experience of cinemagoing.[6] An historical examination of the ways in which the cinema has provided a site and an occasion for particular forms of social behaviour, or of the ways in which individual movies have specified the nature of the site, the occasion, and the behaviour, is an enquiry into the production of meaning, but that meaning is social, not textual.

We are proposing a distinction between what might be called film history and cinema history: between an aesthetic history of textual relations between individuals or individual objects, and the social history of a cultural institution. Film history, the history of textual relations and stylistic influence, borrows its methods and rationale from the practices of art and literary history. It is predominantly a history of production and producers, concerned with issues of intention and agency underpinning the process of cultural production, usually at the level of the individual, and relatively little interested in anything, other than aesthetic influence, that happens after the point of production.

Writing the history of the American cinema is by contrast a project engaging with economic, industrial, institutional history on the one hand—in accounts of how the commercial institution of cinema operated—and the socio-cultural history of its audiences on the other. These two histories are, we believe, far more closely bound together than either of them is to a film history of textual relations. This book is concerned in the main with the socio-cultural history of audiences (in the plural) and their relationships (in the plural) to American cinema, attempting to specify both Hollywood's audiences and their behaviours. Such audiences have never been homogeneous. In consequence, writing the history of American cinema involves setting aside an idea of 'the audience' as a unitary entity, and detailing some of the ways in which tastes and practices varied markedly from region to region, between small towns and cities, between racial, ethnic and gendered groups. It also involves analysing the ways in which the industry knew this and accommodated it in its product.

2

For cinema history to matter more, it must engage with the social history of which it is a part, not through the practices of textual interpretation, but by attempting to write cinema history from below; that is, to write histories that are concerned not with the 'great men' and women of Hollywood but with their audiences and with the roles that these performances of celebrity played in the ordinary imaginations of those audiences. Histories that concern themselves with the conditions of everyday life as they are experienced by ordinary people require, as George Iggers has argued, new conceptual and methodological approaches that see history not as 'a grand narrative in which the many individuals are submerged, but as a multifaceted flow with many individual centers,' and 'an epistemology geared to the experiences of these many that permits knowledge of the concrete rather than the abstract.'[7] The aim of such histories, which we are only now beginning to write, is in part 'to reconstruct the lives of individual men and women from the popular classes of the past,' in order to reconstruct 'the relationship (about which we know so little) between individual lives and the contexts in which they unfold.'[8] As such, the work involved here forms part of a broader historical turn that seeks to restore agency to the 'undistinguished' classes by recognising 'the degree to which they contributed by conscious efforts to the making of history' and historical meaning.[9] As E.P. Thompson famously sought to 'rescue the poor stockinger, the Luddite cropper ... and even the deluded follower of Joanna Southcott, from the enormous condescension of posterity,' the goal of such histories will be to rescue the undistinguished membership of cinema's audiences from the condescension of a posterity that has so far been more concerned to contemplate 'its own desires, criteria, and representational structures' than it has been to construct a meaningful account of the past.[10]

Ironically, this book's concern with reception and with the social context and consequences of moviegoing involves an historical return to the prevailing concerns of the earliest studies of cinema, as an object of sociological and psychological enquiry, rather than the object of aesthetic, critical and interpretive enquiry that has ensued from the construction of film studies as an academic discipline in the humanities. These earlier studies, from Hugo Münsterberg to the Payne Fund research, concerned themselves with what Frankfurt School theorist Leo Lowenthal called 'the underlying social and psychological function' of cinema as a component in the modern urban environment; their methods were those of the 'human sciences,' and their objects of enquiry were people, rather than artefacts.[11]

The contributions to this collection all respond to the call by David Bordwell and Noël Carroll for 'middle-level research' and piecemeal theorising, although the principal object of their enquiry—the conditions of cinema exhibition and reception—is significantly different from Bordwell and Carroll's own concerns.[12] All these essays are firmly grounded in empirical research among primary historical sources. None of them, however, is 'empiricist' in a naive or unthinking way. To argue that what Lawrence Stone called the 'dirty and tedious archival work' of digging evidence out of sources can produce an account of the past bearing a plausible relation to an historical reality does not involve naïvely assuming that the relationship between evidence and reality is transparent or unmediated.[13] On the contrary, the very task of constructing something so unremarked and unrecorded as the quotidian experiences of ephemeral communities requires a conscious attention to the methods of discovery, criteria of evidence and modes of telling not always evident in more solipsistic studies of cinematic textuality.

Part one of this book deals with the history of cinema exhibition sites. In the first chapter, Robert C. Allen argues that our understanding of the social history of moviegoing has been retarded by broad generalisations that have greatly simplified actual exhibition experience, such as 'the nickelodeon era,' and by a focus on particular areas and groups. He points to the as yet largely unexplored complexities of cinemagoing in the South as a good illustration of what is lacking. More rural than other areas of the United States, the South had fewer immigrants, especially from Europe, and film-going there was inflected more by issues of race. For Southern blacks, watching film was deeply influenced by segregatory practices: Allen notes that the landmark Supreme Court decision of 1896 recognising the lawfulness of segregation came just three weeks after the first successful commercial exhibition of motion pictures at Koster and Bial's music hall in New York. Given the restraints on their moviegoing, Allen suggests that, for many Southern blacks, visiting the cinema may have been for many decades an occasional experience rather than a regular habit. For whites, by contrast, cinemagoing had more to do with factors such as where they lived (movie houses tended to be part of the fabric of town life, whereas few farming families went to picture shows), wider attitudes within the community (many Protestant churches were suspicious of the movies), and even the season (many theatres traditionally closed during the heat of summer).

A further complexity of moviegoing in the South, according to Christopher J. McKenna, was the existence of multi-racial as well as bi-racial communities. Based on a local study of Robeson County, North Carolina, from the 1890s to the Second World War, McKenna maps out the complex geography of moviegoing in a community with both white inhabitants and two subaltern cultures (blacks and Lumbee Indians). Segregation itself, he notes, worked both ways: 'whites only' houses were balanced by 'colored

4

theaters.' Yet Indians, with a social and cultural identity of their own, often resisted simply being treated as 'non-whites.' They refused to go to the movies at all—or sometimes tried to pass themselves off as white. Equally, they frequently insisted on having their own section of balcony space and resisted sharing it with blacks. Tri-racialism in Robeson County during the 1920s involved showing Community Service pictures to different racial groups on different nights or in different locations; by the 1930s it had influenced theatre design to the point that there were three separate entrances to some theatres and, finally, separate ticket booths for each race. Jane M. Gaines extends McKenna's thesis about the complexities of race in early twentieth-century Southern moviegoing by speculating that there may have been a white audience for black 'race' movies. This would, of course, have involved breaking segregation laws, since Jim Crow controlled where whites could go as well as blacks. African Americans, Gaines observes, often preferred black-only theatres to avoid separate entrances and condescending ushers. Yet there is tantalizing evidence that whites not only attended late-night shows that were intended for both races, but that they may also have sometimes used the darkness of night-time showings to attend supposedly all-black theatres. In transgressing racial boundaries, these spectators were prefiguring the much later phenomenon of the cross-over audience.

Whereas Allen notes Protestant suspicion of movies in the South, Terry Lindvall's local study of Norfolk, Virginia, in the period leading up to 1920, finds local churches and their middle-class congregations far more supportive of the cinema. Movie theatres were often used for non-cinematic purposes, including religious gatherings, while the churches themselves at times showed films to their congregations. There was little enthusiasm on the part of ministers in the city for movie censorship. The only matter that did concern them was the controversial issue of Sunday exhibition, covered by local 'Blue Laws.' Otherwise, Norfolk's religious leaders perceived moving pictures as offering more worthwhile and wholesome entertainment than the saloons and dance-halls of their seaport city. This increasing alliance between motion picture exhibitors and the fundamentally conservative Protestant establishment was symbolised by the mission to the city in January and February 1920 of revivalist preacher Billy Sunday. A former baseball player, Sunday was close to many Hollywood celebrities and had a generally positive view of the possibilities of the movies, which he regarded as 'the handmaiden of religion.'

The next three studies of local exhibition shift the focus of examination to the North. Richard Abel laments the lack of a survey in the U.S. similar to Emilie Altenloh's 1913 survey of German movie attendance, but believes that there is sufficient evidence available to demonstrate that the experience of moviegoing varied from place to place.[14] When and where people went to the cinema was influenced in some states and cities by 'blue laws.' Citing local studies, Abel finds different patterns of attendance in Lynn, Massachusetts, and Toledo, Ohio. Toledo had a much larger range of venues, hours of opening, programme lengths and frequency of programme changes. In the second part of his chapter, Abel turns to analysing the history of one local theatre, the Star, in Central Falls/Pawtucket, Rhode Island, from December 1911 to October 1913. The managers of the Star, as Abel reveals, had to change tactics a number of times. At the beginning of the period, they presented cheap vaudeville acts and Motion Picture Patent Company (MPPC) films. In 1912, they switched to better-quality vaudeville and films provided by Harry and Roy Aitken's Mutual Film Company. In 1913, they abandoned vaudeville completely in favour of feature films from Adolph Zukor's Famous Players and Mutual shorts. From time to time, they also offered 'specials,' with varying success. After months of experimentation, the Star finally hit on a strategy of showing multi-reelers that proved both profitable and popular. It appealed, in particular, to working-class and immigrant patrons who lived close to the theatre. Movie attendance varied throughout the year in accordance with variables such as holidays and the weather but, generally, was highest on Saturdays. It also peaked on Monday and Wednesday evenings, when programmes were changed. The value attached to seeing films as soon as they arrived, Abel notes, suggests the importance that motion pictures had by this point attained in the lives of working people.

Judith Thissen observes a similar phenomenon in the New York Jewish working-class community. By mid-1908, there was a greater density of movie houses in the Jewish areas of Manhattan and Brooklyn than anywhere else in the city. This created problems for the community's self-elected cultural leadership, notably represented by Abraham Cahan's newspaper, the *Jewish Daily Forward*. Jewish newspapers, out of ethnic solidarity, rallied to the defence of Jewish exhibitors when Mayor George B. McClellan closed all the movie theatres in New York on Christmas Eve 1908. Yet the city's Jewish cultural elite only became really engaged with the question of moving pictures in 1909–10, when Adler's Grand Theater—a live theatre specialising in Yiddish performances—was taken over by Adolph Zukor and Marcus Loew and transformed into a venue for vaudeville and motion pictures. Yiddish papers ignored the fact that Zukor and Loew were both Jewish, and presented the change as a threat to Jewish identity. With legitimate Yiddish theatre in sharp decline, they adopted a cultural strategy that involved elevating the vaudeville that they had previously derided into the mainstream of Jewish culture, and assigning motion pictures the low

6

status formerly assigned to vaudeville. Cultural gate-keepers in the Jewish community, regarding themselves as people of the book rather than the image, criticised the moral dangers posed by movies to young people. In reality, however, the popularity of the cinema amongst immigrant Jews can be seen as an expression of participatory democracy that won out in the end. By 1913–14, motion pictures were increasingly regarded as culturally acceptable. Leading Jewish stage actors were starting to appear on film and movie news had become a common feature of the Yiddish press.

It is not only film historians who have, as Robert C. Allen suggests, advanced normative ideas of what the experience of moviegoing was like. Hollywood itself was eager to advance the view that the characteristic cinematic experience of the 1920s was to patronise the movie palace. With its downtown or suburban location, the palace set out to appeal to a primarily bourgeois audience by offering a complete range of customer services. This notion of a 'middle-class accent' to moviegoing is, however, challenged by Jeffrey Klenotic, who argues that a wide range of social groups continued to patronise more traditional film theatres. He illustrates his claim with a local study of the Franklin Theater in Springfield, Massachusetts. Built cheaply in 1929, the Franklin offered a palpably different experience of moving-going to the palace. Under Lebanese ownership, it integrated well with the stable but heterogeneous population of the surrounding area. In the recollection of former patrons, it played a major role in the social and recreational life of local children. Its efforts—as a 'daily grind'—to identify enough films to fill its schedules led to the use, from time to time, of ethnic programming. Throughout the Depression of the 1930s, it offered raffles and giveaways as a means of ensuring that its working-class clients continued to patronise the theatre. The Franklin, Klenotic concludes, was not a poor imitation of the movie palace; instead, it offered a genuinely different type of moviegoing, foregrounding the social and collective experience of cinemagoing.

That experience is discussed further in the chapter by Mark Glancy and John Sedgwick. Rather than looking at the history of one cinema and its relationship with its community, Glancy and Sedgwick analyse the material on a wide range of first-run houses that appeared in the pages of *Variety*. They find that a film's local success was often the consequence of a combination of factors: pricing strategy, the regional appeal of specific actors and actresses, and endorsements by local worthies (including ministers). There was indeed, as Hollywood believed, a clear difference between metropolitan and provincial tastes. While 'double billing' was a Depression-era innovation, designed—along with engineered 'events'—to keep audiences coming to movie theatres, the division between 'A' and 'B' films was at times not clear. Double billing also created an opportunity for foreign films, especially

British ones, to be incorporated into programmes. Gregory A. Waller has already pointed out the symbiosis between country music and small-town cinema in south-central Kentucky during the Depression.[15] Using evidence from *Variety*, Glancy and Sedgwick question the conventional assumption that the coming of sound and the Depression brought about the end of live performance in cinemas, concluding that almost half the movie theatres involved in their survey were 'combination' houses that offered live entertainment together with films on the same bill. In some cases, the live performances were tailored to encourage the success of a particular film. What constituted an evening's entertainment at the movies in many places in the mid-1930s could, therefore, include an eclectic range of live acts (mainly derived from vaudeville) and specific events.

Variety was one of the sources also consulted by Thomas Doherty. In June 1963, the entertainment trade bible finally published an editorial condemning the racial segregation of Southern moviegoers—the issue previously analysed by Allen, McKenna and Gaines. Doherty's chapter examines the long-delayed but ultimately surprisingly fast desegregation of Southern movie houses. As communal spaces, cinemas were affected by growing demands for integration in the wake of the Supreme Court's landmark *Brown v. Topeka Board of Education* decision of 1954. Initially, civil rights organisations focused their efforts on desegregation in education, employment and housing, and the first specific agitation for desegregating cinemas did not appear until 1961. The favourite tactic of the movement was the 'stand-in'—a version of the sit-in used in drugstores and other social spaces. Civil rights activists queued up at the box-office to demand tickets admitting African Americans to anywhere in the house. When refused, they simply rejoined the queue to try again. Understandably, movie house managers hated the tactic, which ate into their profits. Generally, in fact, the movie industry seemed embarrassed by the publicity and controversy that surrounded protests against segregation, disliking them as bad for business. From early 1961, it collaborated with local civic leaders in a slow, controlled integration of theatres, beginning in Nashville, Tennessee. This process speeded up in the early summer of 1963 when the Kennedy Administration, concerned that continuing segregation would undercut the international fight against communism, weighed in. After Attorney-General Robert F. Kennedy met with the representatives of theatre chains in May, over twenty-five Southern theatres voluntarily desegregated within days. There was still some resistance in the Deep South, but this was broken, first with the reaction to the assassination of President Kennedy and then with the passage of the Civil Rights Act of 1964. By the end of 1964, motion picture theatres everywhere in the South were open to all races.

Underpinning most cinema history is the notion that cinema itself is synonymous with the public space of the movie theatre. This has been true from the age of the nickelodeon to the era of the modern multiplex. Yet the movie theatre has never been the only place at which films could be seen. In the earliest days of American cinema, from 1896 until the rise of the nickelodeon, films were shown by itinerant showmen in a wide variety of venues, including churches, stores, exhibition halls, YMCAs, opera houses, schools, cafés, and fairs. Even with the rise of the nickelodeon after 1905, films continued to be exhibited in other places. By 1933, as Haidee Wasson points out below, the number of 'non-theatrical' film projectors in the U.S.—including equipment for home projection—outnumbered the number of projectors in commercial movie theatres by more than ten to one. Showing of films of various types in the home was, of course, destined to grow vastly as the decades passed. Some were 'home movies' in the truest sense of the term: amateur productions intended to preserve cherished images of family life.[16] With the rise of television, more and more Americans watched movies at home on the national networks. Subsequent changes, from cable television to the video-cassettes, laser discs and DVDs of the 1980s and 1990s, have ensured that the characteristic experience of film on the part of most Americans is now a domestic one. Cinemagoing in the U.S., which reached an all-time peak of 82 million admissions per week in 1946, collapsed to around 20 million admissions by the 1960s, and averaged 28 million a week between 1996 and 2005.[17] Yet, while watching films in movie theatres did not really happen until after 1905 and has been in decline for over half a century, 'theatrical' exhibition continues to be regarded as the norm by most film historians. The next part of this book discusses aspects of 'non-theatrical' exhibition or what might perhaps be described, more accurately, as 'other cinema.'

Haidee Wasson argues that privileging movie theatres as the main centres for watching film was a product of the normalising efforts of the early twentieth-century American movie industry. There were many who sought to resist those efforts, however, fighting for a cinema that would be culturally superior and/or intended for more specialised audiences. Wasson analyses the history of one such effort: following the introduction of 16mm film by Eastman Kodak in 1923 (the industry-dominated standard gauge for theatres was 35mm), a number of people tried to transform the mass medium of the movies into a type of elitist and educational activity suitable for the middle-class American home. Following the successful introduction of the Book of the Month Club in 1926, a 'Reel of the Month Club' was launched in 1927 to bring pictures of key world events to subscribers' homes. Whereas commercial movies themselves were public, short-lived and entertaining, these films were supposed to be private, enduring and educational. They reflected the 1920s drive to make the American home an expression of upwardly mobile ideals, filled with symbols of education and refinement. Like books, these films were meant to be collected and displayed (Kodak sold faux-leather bindings to store them on shelves). Although the experiment did not last—16mm was swept away for home use by the introduction of an 8mm gauge in 1932, followed by the later emergence of television—it prefigured the modern notion of cinema as a mainly domestic experience, with most film viewing taking place in the home.[18]

While Wasson explores the early history of one alternative to theatrical exhibition of the Hollywood variety, Anne Morey examines another: an early movement towards 'art house' or independent cinema. From approximately 1925 to 1929, a 'little cinema' movement existed, with its principal focus in New York. As a symbol of public revolt against mainstream film-making, it pioneered different textual practices (preferring European to American film aesthetics) and distinct institutional structures (patterns of distribution and exhibition that repudiated the Hollywood 'norm'). Symon Gould was a major influence on the movement in New York, running first the Cameo Theatre and later the purpose-built 500-seat Film Guild Cinema. Gould sought out little-known European—and especially German—films for his theatres and pioneered the use of themed retrospectives. By 1929, however, with the coming of sound (and the additional costs this represented), the little cinema movement was running out of steam. There were too many independent little cinemas and too much cut-throat competition. What doomed the movement finally was the lack of domestic art films that prompted an over-dependence on foreign imports.

Gregory A. Waller discusses a third variety of 'other cinema': the free films shown in rural America during the 1930s. Although farm families seem to have gone less frequently to commercial movie theatres than city folk, they did attend free film shows organised under the auspices of churches, schools, business service organisations and government agencies. There was often a directness and immediacy about such films lacking in Hollywood product: farm families were more likely to see their own environment and concerns displayed in free films. Tractor-making companies such as International Harvester and John Deere exhibited films about their products at dealerships and in other locations. The American Farm Bureau Federation (AFBF), which began producing and distributing films in 1921, claimed that within two years it had supplied motion pictures for over 3,500 screenings in 35 states. By 1931, the AFBF claimed that the eleven films it had itself produced had been seen by an audience of over half a million. Most of these screenings took place in town halls, schools, churches or private homes. The

U.S. Department of Agriculture (USDA), which had been involved in the production of documentaries since the 1910s, claimed in 1933 that more than 4,700 films had been exhibited for free in schools, churches, Rotary Club meetings and similar venues to a total audience of ten million people.

The chapter by Barbara Klinger deals with a somewhat different issue: not the existence of alternative types of venue and alternative kind of film to that provided by 'Hollywood,' but the manner in which Hollywood films have been transformed through ancillary, non-theatrical exhibition. Many films, she argues, circulate well beyond their initial release. As a process, this involves considerable textual amendment and adaptation. Between the 1930s and the 1950s, many movies were adapted for radio, sometimes with the same stars in the leading roles. Inevitably, of course, this required much abridgement of the film's narrative. Moreover, different movie versions were produced for different audiences: films were adapted for Northern (or Southern) release and for foreign audiences. This has not always involved permanent changes to the film's text. In 2002, for example, an audience of school-children in an Afghan refugee camp were entranced by a showing of *The Wizard of Oz* (1939). In deference to the susceptibilities of local Islamic culture, the projectionist simply fast-forwarded through the shots of singing Munchkins to avoid the display of too much bare skin. Actual textual amendments to films, moreover, have involved additions as well as subtractions: 'remedial' re-releases have restored footage eliminated by censors or studio editors. Perhaps most crucially of all, with theatrical exhibition now responsible for only a quarter of Hollywood's revenues, movies have been 'repurposed' for home delivery. Meanwhile, non-theatrical exhibition, often ephemeral, has continued outside the home—Klinger cites a range of venues including schools, factories, prisons, hospitals and aircraft.

The third part of this book deals with the diverse ways in which audiences have been conceptualised and negotiated, with special reference to the questions of globalization and censorship outside the U.S. Hollywood's role in a more global process of Americanization—that of 'sell[ing] America to the world with American motion pictures,' as Will H. Hays proselytised in 1923—has long been asserted by both enthusiasts and detractors alike. Whether 'every film that goes from America abroad,' has correctly portrayed 'the purposes, the ideals, the accomplishments, the opportunities, and the life of America,' as Hays claimed it would, has been a subject of contention ever since.[19] Viewed from abroad, where the concept of Americanization has long carried fewer positive connotations, recent evidence of the catastrophic failure of the ideological project encapsulated by Hays might lead us to suggest that the imaginary 'American' culture of the movies became 'everyone's second culture' far more successfully as an agent of commerce than as an instrument of ideology.[20] As Victoria de Grazia has argued,

> it is not at all clear how as elusive a force as consumer culture, being the sum of myriads of marketing strategies, second-order decisions of government, and mundane choices about getting and spending, was converted into great power. Nor is it clear how the United States exercised this great power to promote democracies of consumption elsewhere, much less to advance global concord.[21]

The chapters in the final part of this book also inevitably engage with questions of textual as well as social meaning, since they are concerned with the ways in which audiences have understood and interpreted their experiences of cinema. Throughout its history, academic enquiry into the social meaning of cinema has been enormously constrained by a preoccupation with an agenda of harm, which has proposed that the primary public interest in the social institution of cinema is in minimising its 'capacity for evil.'[22] This proposition has continued to determine a research agenda constructed around a model of uni-directional flow, in which some aspect of cinema—the darkened room, 'media violence'—has been identified as a putative cause or stimulus, and some viewer behaviour—eyestrain, attention span, 'aggressive play'—has been identified as a response, a prospectively measurable effect.[23]

Models of viewer behaviour, and perceptions of the audience as either passive recipients of predetermined textual meaning or as agents in the construction of social meaning have, in many respects, been at the heart of debates over the regulation of cinema. The underlying relationship between movie and viewer proposed by the long, expensive, often excessive history of effects research is remarkably similar to that proposed by the emphasis on textual meaning: by one means or another, movies are alleged to cause viewer effects, textual meaning to create social meaning. In such formulations, the viewer in the act of viewing is understood to be the passive recipient of an at least theoretically measurable stimulus. In the words of one of the godfathers of the Production Code, Daniel Lord, 'people go to the theatres; sit there passively—ACCEPT and RECEIVE; with the result that they go out from that entertainment either very much improved or very much deteriorated; and that depends almost entirely upon the character of the entertainment which is presented.'[24] Such a framework directs attention principally to textual meaning, and determines that the regulation of cinematic meaning takes place at the point of production, with public debate circulating principally around producers' intentions.

In the early 1930s, the industry commonly relied on the protections offered by the moral narratives of melodrama, arguing that if the movies told stories in which good and evil were clearly distinguished and good seen to triumph, then the audience's moral principles would be reaffirmed. The evidence then emerging from the Payne Fund studies cast doubt on the claim that narrative was the primary influence on young audiences, suggesting that the cinema's power to corrupt lay in the potential pleasure of its spectacle. In *Movies, Delinquency and Crime*, Herbert Blumer and Philip Hauser argued that young viewers failed to construct an 'organized interpretation' of a movie's narrative. Instead, they appeared 'to have a wide range of scattered and unorganized interests, and, in addition, to be particularly responsive to incidents which are dramatic, exciting, and tempting.' As a result, they were likely to find 'details or elements of the picture' more significant than the moral contained in the movie's resolution.[25] The increasingly strident debate over the relative interpretive status of narrative and spectacle became the central point at issue in the debates over movie censorship in the early 1930s, and led to Classical Hollywood's formulation of strategies of indeterminacy, elision, enigma and suggestion as the means by which Classical Hollywood's movies provided the material for a mode of exhibition and a mode of consumption that accommodated the viewer's agency in constructing narrative, without at the same time actually acknowledging the existence of that agency.[26]

Arguably the most valuable piece of research undertaken through the Payne Fund project was never published: Paul Cressey's draft of *Boys, Movies and City Streets*.[27] Although Cressey never completed that work, he did summarise his conclusions about the sociology of the motion picture experience in a 1938 article in *American Sociological Review*—a piece that reads like a research agenda for a path unfortunately not taken. Summarising what he took to be the demonstrable findings of the Payne Fund Studies, Cressey noted that

When the motion picture is viewed only 'externally,' it certainly appears to be only unilateral, i.e., the patrons are wholly passive agents who are merely 'played upon' through the arts and skills of cinematography. We have, however, abundant evidence that this is an erroneous conception. Through imaginative participation, identification, random reflection, phantasy before and after cinema attendance, and through the impact of prior interests and values, the cinema experience is redefined in many ways and may affect the patron in forms only incidentally associated with film content.[28]

13

Cressey's proposed agenda was to examine these processes and behaviours from a position that recognised that 'the cinema's "effect" upon an individual, a community or a society never can be gauged accurately if the motion picture experience is studied only segmentally and never in its essential unity.' Any programme of research that failed to acknowledge 'all essential phases of the motion picture experience,' he argued, could 'offer little more than conjecture as to the cinema's net "effect" in actual social settings and communities.' Cressey further contended that it was

> a serious misconception of social process to assume that accurate knowledge of the cinema's 'contribution' can be deduced from particularistic studies of the motion picture experience ... Social causation is entirely too complex a problem to be explained by any such simplistic interpretation of incomplete data.[29]

The media effects research tradition initiated by the Payne Fund Studies, as David Buckingham has argued, has 'remained stubbornly tied to behaviourist assumptions,' conceiving of the social and cognitive dimensions of viewer behaviour only as 'intervening variables' mediating between the stimulus on the screen and the response in the viewer.[30] Insofar as this research has addressed Cressey's questions, its best methodological energies have been devoted to the construction of elaborate mechanisms to control for 'variables' such as 'family background, preferences, interests and social circumstance' in order to eliminate the noise they create in establishing the stimulus-response, cause-effect mechanism between content and behaviour. No amount of rhetoric suggesting that effects research is now a form of 'risk analysis' that has replaced simplistic 'hypodermic' hypotheses of cause and effect with a probabilistic account borrowed from epidemiology changes the core research paradigm.[31] What Graham Murdock has termed the 'medical model' continues to underpin the 'unbroken line of banal science' which has 'failed to ask awkward questions, to pursue other possible lines of enquiry or to place "effects" in their social contexts.'[32] The effects research tradition has yet to devise any empirical procedures that might allow us to fulfil Cressey's ambition of studying 'the cinema's "contribution" under various circumstances and social situations and to perceive more fundamentally its role in the growth of attitudes and personality.'[33]

Perhaps the project that Cressey proposed was just too hard. More probably, its conclusions were unlikely to support either of the financially well-endowed camps in the media effects debate, and thus we find ourselves, nearly seventy years later, hardly better informed about the mechanisms and processes of 'the motion picture situation' and its creation of 'imaginative states.' As Richard Butsch observes in his chapter, however, the debate over media effects has significantly changed the conception of what constitutes a 'bad' audience. In the nineteenth century, audiences for the theatre (especially lower-class melodramas) were often perceived as an unruly and potentially dangerous crowd. Late in the century, efforts were made to contain this threat: amongst other things, benches gave way to numbered seats and electric lights permitted the house to be darkened during performances. From being a crowd, threatening in its unpredictable collectivity, audiences were transformed into individuals sitting in the darkness engaged with the performance. Increasingly, reformers, sociologists and psychologists all came to believe that such individuals were weak and highly susceptible to suggestive messages from films. This belief, which underpinned the Payne Fund studies, resurfaced during the 1950s, when there was increased concern about the link between movies and delinquency. In modern times, it has influenced perceptions of fans—ignoring the idea of them as communities to foreground the notion of them as neurotic and fantasizing individuals. Butsch notes, however, that most of the 'weak-willed' people who make up 'bad' audiences are drawn from subordinate social groups. Constructing them in this way justifies efforts to control them.

The same principle of suggestibility lay behind the effort to attack 'morally unhealthy' movies. The campaign of the Legion of Decency has been explored by a number of recent scholars, but it was not only in the United States that such movements emerged.[34] Catholic attempts to clean up the movies occurred in other countries and, at least in the case of Belgium, preceded the Legion's activities. Daniel Biltereyst explains that Belgian Catholics were entrusted by the Pope with the job of co-ordinating other national Catholic film movements. The Catholic campaign to clean up the movies in Belgium was greatly affected by the division of the country along various axes. American movies themselves were more popular in the northern part of the country, Dutch-speaking Flanders; in mainly French-speaking Brussels and Wallonia, French films kept their appeal, and increased their market share after the coming of sound. Catholicism was an important force in most of Belgium but it found itself increasingly fighting for influence in French-speaking areas against socialist and liberal organisations. From 1928 onwards, Belgian Catholics engaged in various initiatives designed to influence the content of films and in 1931—two years before the Legion of Decency was formed in the U.S.—they introduced a Catholic board of classification. Although the Belgians praised the achievements of the Legion, they felt that they had pioneered where Americans followed in terms of censorship and press action.

The Belgian Catholic crusaders on film were, of course, particularly concerned about the effect of movies on suggestible children. Annette Kuhn traces the growing parallel concern over children's moviegoing in 1930s Britain. The British Board of Film Censors, set up in 1913, had developed a system of classification whose basic division was between 'U' films (for universal exhibition) and 'A' (no one under sixteen could be admitted unless accompanied by an adult guardian). As public and political pressure for stricter censorship grew, the period 1931–32 witnessed a shift of focus from the issue of children's access to 'A' films to questions arising from the actual content of films. The catalyst for this process was the arrival in Britain of a new cycle of Hollywood horror talkies, heralded by *Dracula* (1931) and *Frankenstein* (1931). Originally passed by the BBFC as 'A' films, the new label 'H' (horrific) was invented in 1932 to distinguish such films. This was an advisory classification: despite all the concerns expressed at the time over the effect of such films in frightening or horrifying children, it left the final decision on children's attendance up to their parents. In 1937, the 'H' label became a certificate, banning children under sixteen from seeing the films involved. Also by 1937, the thrust of the movement concerned with protecting children had changed: instead of protecting children from 'unsuitable' films, it recognised them as a distinct audience with particular needs who needed pictures produced specially for them.

The chapters by Biltereyst and Kuhn could each be regarded as local European responses to aspects of Americanization. 'Americanization' itself, of course, is a contested term. Both Janice Radway and Richard Ellis have recently argued that concepts of 'the American' in American Studies must always be relationally defined, in acknowledgement of the fact that the culture of the United States is multicultural and inevitably fissured in its identities.[35] Just as concepts of 'the American' are relationally defined, so, too, are concepts of 'Americanization.' The term addresses a different conceptual field once it leaves American shores, losing its positive connotations to become, instead, a term of something between critique and abuse: Hollywood as the seducer of the innocent, 'over-paid, over-sexed, and over here,' the representative here, now, of the Great Satan. In thinking over once again what is now an eighty-year history of exchanges over Hollywood's imperialism and cultural protectionism, what strikes the observer most of all is the mutual incomprehension of the parties involved, and the failure to construct a common cultural ground—a middle ground.

American historian Richard White has provided an extraordinarily powerful description of what he calls the 'middle ground' between cultures. White's description is of the cultural interactions between Europeans and Native Americans in the Great Lakes region during the eighteenth century, and is concerned with the face-to-face interactions of the frontier. Yet he does provide a powerfully suggestive model of how what he calls the 'search for accommodation and common meaning' between cultures takes place, and his model has much broader applicability than the case he considers:

> On the middle ground diverse peoples adjust their differences through what amounts to a process of creative, and often expedient, misunderstandings. They often misinterpret and distort both the values and the practices of those they deal with, but from these misunderstandings arise new meanings and through them new practices—the shared meanings and practices of the middle ground.

The middle ground that White describes developed from people's needs to find a means to gain the cooperation or consent of foreigners. In order to achieve this, they had to attempt 'to understand the world and the reasoning of others, and to assimilate enough of that reasoning to put it to their own purposes.' The middle ground was 'a realm of constant invention, which was just as constantly presented as convention.' Instead of being specific negotiations of agreed-upon differences, exchanges on the middle ground were struggles over images, often taking place within rather than between groups.[36] It is on a version of the middle ground that 'nous sommes tous Américains.'[37]

While Americans themselves might present American-ness 'as the very signifier of universal human evolution, subsuming under it all the local currencies of cultural exchange, a limitless melting pot of mores, nations and classes,'[38] non-American cultural élites, particularly in Europe, have frequently viewed American mass culture as a threat to both the security of their own cultural nationalisms and to their own cultural authority over the definition of national culture. They have also constructed the consumers of American culture as being simpler than they were, not only in the sense of being comparatively intellectually retarded, but also as being monolithic in their adoption of an American monoculture. In practice, as Ahmet Gürata demonstrates in his chapter, foreign audiences constructed a middle ground on which they made sense of Hollywood in their own cultural terms, according to their own cultural points of reference, domesticating the America of their imaginations.

In the beginning, Gürata argues, this process of adaptation was relatively easy. Film exhibitors used local lecturers, intertitles, music and sound effects to 'indigenize' American films to suit the cultural preferences of Turkish audiences. With the coming of sound, this process became more difficult.

Films were instead re-titled to meet local susceptibilities, scenes were cut, sometimes additional scenes with local stars were added, and speech was dubbed—first into French, later into English (Laurel and Hardy were very popular on Turkish screens in the 1930s, speaking broken Turkish with an American accent). So effectively was this done that spectators joined in the fiction that, for example, the Marx brothers 'lived' in Istanbul (some local people claimed to be 'relatives' of Groucho). Hollywood's product was appropriated, transformed and to some extent naturalized as part of 'Turkish' cinema, which may help to explain why, given the strict censorship of films that existed in Turkey after 1934, relatively few American films were ever banned.

Gürata's work adds to the growing accumulation of evidence for the semantic malleability of Hollywood's products, and their susceptibility to what Philip Rosen has called 'local meanings, practices, social rituals and even politics.'[39] Charles Ambler uses the evidence provided by his account of the 'Copperbelt Cowboys' of Northern Rhodesia and audiences elsewhere in Africa to argue that while 'the often disjointed and exotic images of the "Wild West" ... comprised a crucial repertoire of images' through which the young urban population could 'engage notions of modernity,' theoretical models of media or cultural imperialism offer too schematic an explanation of the complex and contested dynamics of the interpretive process. Ambler argues that 'at the same time that audiences were drawing on films to develop a lexicon of modernity, they were reinventing the films in their own cultural and political terms,' investing their characters and action with indigenous qualities. The movies those audiences watched, at almost the farthest extreme of the global distribution chain, had been subjected to a panoply of physical deconstructions, to a point where their plots would have been barely discernable to an audience equipped with the linguistic and cultural competences to 'follow' them—which Ambler's protagonists were not. To make these artefacts make sense, local audiences had to reconfigure them into patterns of symbol and behaviour which might mean something in the context of their viewing. An American film focusing on health care, for example, was disliked by Africans who assumed that disease had more to do with religion and distrusted what they saw as arrogant, corrupt nurses. Equally, Westerns appealed because men used 'Jack,' the universal cowboy figure, to help define their own perceptions of masculinity—and the freedom of watching someone ride across open spaces may have provided a degree of relief and compensation for Africans' own oppressed status.

The spread of the Internet, with its prospect of alternative modes of distribution, has recently provided Hollywood with a dramatic challenge to its existing business practice, which maintains the major distributors' control over product at an acceptable level. As in 1921–48 over issues of anti-trust and in 1976–82 over the threats and opportunities provided by domestic video-recorders, the industry has initially sought to resist technological change in an attempt to preserve its existing commercial model. In the process, the major companies have also sought to preserve the existing model of viewing conditions and its assumptions about the viewer's expectations of the viewing experience. To comprehend the existing business model, we have to reconsider the major companies' behaviour since the mid-1980s, in which we have seen—as Charles Acland's chapter describes—not only the vertical re-integration of distribution and theatrical exhibition in the U.S., but also the greatly increased internationalisation of these vertically integrated structures through the majors' extensive investment in the development of the megaplex, 'showcase screens,' and the re-building of the theatre stock in Europe, Latin America and parts of Asia. The media marketplace is now characterised by high concentration of ownership and virtually no regulatory constraints, and, as Jennifer Holt argues, this situation is in fact very similar to the business conditions of Classical Hollywood.[40] Five companies now own all the U.S. broadcast networks, four of the major movie companies, forty-five of the top fifty U.S. cable channels, and provide 75 per cent of all U.S. prime-time programming. It is arguable that the re-establishment of vertical integration, and the present sequential arrangement of distribution, has been of much greater economic—and therefore cultural—significance than the much more vaunted pursuit of synergy through mergers and convergence.[41] Unlike Classical Hollywood's distribution system of runs and zones, where the majors' profits were concentrated in first-run exhibition, subsequent release windows in the current system carry a substantially higher profit percentage than theatrical exhibition does—typically 40 per cent of the profit on videos, 45–50 per cent on DVDs and a rumoured target of 60 per cent on digital distribution via Movielink.

Acland himself draws attention to the growing international synchro-nisation of new films—the trend to release them simultaneously in many parts of the world. This has happened, he points out, not only because of the increasingly powerful international theatre chains mentioned above, but also as a means of fighting piracy and securing economies of scale. Concessions too are increasingly internationalized, although local social and cultural differences persist: Germans like sweet popcorn, Spanish moviegoers prefer salty. As this example indicates, while globalization has fostered an international sense of 'the new' and perhaps also a feeling of community between moviegoers across continents, it has not completely eliminated national or local idiosyncracies. The rise of the multiplex, according to Acland, has had a major impact on certain zones of particular cities. As Mark Jancovich argues in the final chapter of this book, however, to see the rise of the multiplex as an especially problematic illustration of Americanization—something that promotes a world with no sense of place and reduces most social activity to the level of consumerism—reduces to clichéd simplicity what is often really the product of complex negotiation and reinterpretation. As Jancovich demonstrates, the Cornerhouse multiplex in Nottingham was part of a government-sponsored strategy designed to regenerate the centre of British cities, increasingly seen as afflicted with traffic, crime and social problems. It was planned by local developers, eager to prove that their city could attract global brands of commerce and entertainment. The fight over its building had little to do with concerns over Americanization, which only emerged as a discourse near the end of the struggle. It had much more to do with the alienation of the elderly from city and local politics and their desire to preserve what remained of the city of their youth. After its opening, moreover, the Cornerhouse adopted a policy of showing not just American films: it offered independent films and, as a concession to the local Indian community, a weekly 'Bollywood' presentation. Not simply an outpost of globalization or Americanization, therefore, the Cornerhouse shows that the supposed homogenization of such processes is far from being a one-way street.

Our present understanding of how cinema functioned as an agent of consumerism can usefully be reconsidered through the experience of consumption in different places at different times in the last century. Writing about the differential spread of consumer durables in different parts of Europe in the 1970s and 1980s, Victoria de Grazia argues that the grand narrative of how household goods came to be possessed 'was in large measure indifferent to variations in class, local cultures, and history.' At any given historical moment, however, what these goods meant, socially and culturally, varied from nation to nation and region to region depending on how far each locality had progressed through the reiterated narrative of 'technological change, rise in family incomes, and revolution in outlooks, all sanctioned and pushed by a new cross-Atlantic standard of living.'[42] While in one sense (primarily a textual sense) the movies that have articulated and spread an Americanized global culture around the world since 1916 have been similarly indifferent to local variation, they have also been subject to the specific geographic and historical conditions under which their performances have been viewed—at this cinema in this neighbourhood with these people and with these detailed local understandings of social distinction.

The histories we envisage might, then, ask: to what extent did cinema, as a social agent in the promulgation of 'consumptionism,' require pre-existing economic conditions, including a level of discretionary spending among its potential audience? Where these conditions did not exist, did cinema exhibition remain a marginal activity not simply because people were too poor to attend frequently, but also because the pleasures of cinema—the aspirational pleasures of viewing consumption and viewing-as-consumption that were part of what economist Simon N. Patten had called the surplus or pleasure economy—were insufficiently engaged with or integrated into their daily lives?[43] Can we correlate patterns of cinema exhibition to the markedly variant patterns of retail sales in the U.S. and Europe for much of the century? And if we can—or, for that matter, if we cannot—what will that tell us about the social function of cinema? Did cinema represent a sort of half-way house between access to 'Americanized' consumer culture and the practicalities of economic possibility, both for poorer communities in the U.S. and for much of Europe in the first half of the twentieth century and beyond? To what extent, where, and when, did the cinema provide a substitute for consumption—a placebo—rather than an aspiration to consume and a guidebook or practical manual in the development of the practice of consumption? To put it most simply, why did people go to the movies?

If the answers to these questions are not yet plain, what is somewhat clearer is that such explanations as we may be able to offer will require different historical methods and tools from those that have so far predominated in film history. Instead, these tools are likely to be drawn from the methodological dialogues of social and cultural historians. To begin with, we will need detailed historical maps of cinema exhibition, amplified by evidence about the nature and frequency of attendance. This data then needs to be combined with broader demographic information derived from census data and other surveys to amplify our understanding of cinema's audiences. Such detailed quantitative information is vital if we are to progress beyond our current broad-brush knowledge based on trade figures, diplomatic accounts and grand theories of classical cinema as vernacular modernism to a more exact sense of who made up cinema's audiences. With this knowledge will come the means better to understand cinema's cultural function: to consider, for example, whether the geography of cinema produced new forms of social differentiation at the same time that the images its audiences consumed projected a dissolution of 'the sumptuary lines between classes.'[44]

Just as vital as this demographic history, however, is the inclusion of experience that will ground quantitative generalisations in the concrete particulars of micro-historical studies of local situations, effects and infrastructure, based perhaps around the records of individual cinemas or small chains. The heroes of these micro-histories—the Menocchios of the cinema—will be the small businessmen who acted as cultural brokers, navigators and translators of the middle ground constructing a creolised culture out of their community's encounters with the mediated external world.[45] One of these micro-histories may become the *Montaillou* of cinema history, through what it may reveal about how its citizen consumers explained themselves and their place in the world through their encounters with the forces of global and globalising culture.[46] Such histories, self-consciously acknowledging their own constructions and mediations, may also form part of comparative local histories, and, finally, may underpin attempts to consider the cultural function and performance of individual movies in more secure social and cultural detail than we can presently achieve. The work in this collection points the way to the achievement of this goal.

PART I

Studies of Local Cinema Exhibition

1

Race, Region, and Rusticity

Relocating U.S. Film History

Robert C. Allen

Before I see a movie it is necessary for me to learn something about the theater or the people who operate it, to touch base before going inside ... If I did not talk to the theater owner or the ticket seller, I should be lost, cut loose metaphysically speaking. I should be seeing one copy of a film which might be shown anywhere and at any time. There is a danger of slipping clean out of space and time. It is possible to become a ghost and not know whether one is in downtown Loews in Denver or suburban Bijou in Jacksonville. So it was with me.

> Binx Bolling, protagonist and narrator of Walker Percy's 1961 novel *The Moviegoer*.[1]

I N 2004, an issue of *Cinema Journal* featured a special colloquium entitled 'Film History, or a Baedeker Guide to the Historical Turn.' In the introduction to this section, Sumiko Higashi asks whether the field of film studies has experienced a '"historical turn" based on empirical research' over the past twenty years or so. The title of her essay would seem to anticipate an affirmative answer to this question. In fact, however, she argues that the historical turn in film studies has led not to an intellectual turnpike but a narrow country lane, and a road less taken particularly by younger scholars. Why is it that a quarter of a century after scholars began revising the existing unscholarly, schematic, and largely undocumented histories of movies in America, historical research today still represents only a 'slowly accelerating movement in film studies?' Higashi's explanation is that most academics who train students in film studies have not themselves been trained to do empirical research.'[2]

The terminological slip from historical to empirical might be confusing to some, who could be forgiven for expecting the operative term to be 'historical' or 'historiographic' rather than empirical. Although Higashi does not actually explain the relationship between what she calls 'empirical' and 'historical,' I take it to mean anything existing or posited to exist outside of the cinematic text and the inferred conditions of its reception as they are understood by the analyst. Higashi is right to locate the realm of the empirical as being at the center of the problem of film history, but the glacial momentum of the historical 'turn' today is not the result of an entire generation of film scholars all sleeping late on the day in 1985 when empirical methods were discussed in their first-year graduate course. The ambivalence toward the historical that is manifest in Higashi's analysis of the 'historical turn' is, rather, symptomatic of an even more pervasive uncertainty that has hovered over film studies since its academic institutionalization in the 1970s: what place does anything outside of the film 'itself' and its analysis by the film scholar have in film studies? What constitutes the universe of the non-textual empirical relevant to film studies? How would this realm be investigated and to what end?

This ambivalence is apparent in the realm of film studies most associated with the 'historical turn': what is variously called historical spectatorship, the audience, reception, or the social experience of moviegoing. Higashi's overview of the 'historical turn' overlooks important work being done on the history of moviegoing, but that very elision reflects the extent to which the impact of this work has been vitiated by a complex of factors peculiar to film study, among them the conventionalism of film study's theoretical heritage, its suspicion of the empirical and tendency to confuse intellectual engagement with the empirical world outside the film text with empiricism, the academic and intellectual alignment of film studies with the study of literary texts, and the concomitant distancing of film studies from the work of our colleagues in cultural and social history.

Despite a number of very important recent studies of the role of movie culture in local communities, our national road map of the history of the social experience of moviegoing is schematic, conceptually primitive, geographically distorted, not drawn to historical scale, and hence, and of limited epistemological utility. Both geographically and diachronically, this map still bears an uncomfortable resemblance to the *New Yorker* map of the U.S.: with New York, Chicago, and Hollywood looming over and barely separated by mostly ill-defined intervening terrain, and with the foregrounded satellite dishes of post-classical cinema thrown into relief by the vast flat plateau of bourgeois cinema, and not quite obscuring the charmingly picturesque working-class nickelodeons along the far historical horizon. There are very interesting and ambitious research projects underway in the U.K., the Netherlands, Germany, and Australia to document patterns of movie exhibition, audiences, and moviegoing. These will no doubt lead to much more detailed maps of the history of moviegoing in those countries, and the example of this work may spur the development of comparative and transnational historical studies of moviegoing. My hope for the future of the historical study of moviegoing is, however, tempered by my apprehension that when these local, regional, national, and transnational maps are compared, the ones that scholars around the world have to rely upon for the U.S. will remain seriously misleading.

At a pre-conference symposium held in conjunction with the 2003 Commonwealth Fund Conference on the history of moviegoing, I suggested that it might be productive to shift our historiographic and geographic perspective on the social experience of moviegoing in the U.S. in order to foreground regions, spaces, communities, audiences, and historical periods that, despite pioneering work by some resourceful scholars, remain marginalized, unintegrated, or simply unexamined. I also suggested that, as part of this project, we pay attention not only to avid movie fans and communities in which moviegoing was embraced, but also to social groups that resisted the incorporation of moviegoing into everyday life and groups whose access to moviegoing was limited or denied.

In pursuit of this goal, this chapter considers the history of moviegoing in the American South, particularly in the decades of film history which have received the most attention from the 'historical turn' in film studies: roughly, the period between the advent of commercial cinema in the U.S. in 1896 to the full industrialization of film production, distribution, and exhibition in the 1920s. The history of moviegoing in the American South troubles and complicates our assumptions about the role of movies and moviegoing in American life in the early decades of the century more generally. In what follows, I am drawing on the published work of other scholars and on research that my graduate students at the University of North Carolina have done over the years. My remarks also reflect my own reengagement with this area of research, particularly the history of the social experience of moviegoing in North Carolina, the state in which I was born and raised and where I have lived and worked for the past twenty-six years. Although I have only just begun to explore the history of moviegoing in N.C., I would propose as a working hypothesis that three interlocking factors help to explain the particular character of the experience of moviegoing in North Carolina, and in the South more generally, and to differentiate this experience from that which has achieved premature historical normative status in American film historiography: region, race, and what we might call rurality or rusticity.

One of the most enduring and striking features of American film historiography is its assumption of a particular and in some accounts determinative connection between the experience of metropolitan urbanity and the experience of cinema. To the empirical fascination with early moviegoing in New York City, which began in the late 1970s and revived in the 1990s, has been added a theoretical justification: that the experience of early cinema is inextricably tied to the social, sensory, physical, and psychological experience—what Ben Singer refers to as the 'hyperstimulus' of metropolitan modernity.[3]

Although the early audience for the movies in the U.S. might have been disproportionately centered in large urban areas, and moviegoing there certainly received a great deal of contemporaneous public notice, most *people* living in the U.S. in 1910 did not encounter the movies in anything resembling such metropolitan settings. About two-thirds of Americans lived in towns, villages, or settlements smaller than 2,500 inhabitants, or on farms in the countryside. There were only nineteen 'metropolitan' centers in the U.S. in 1910 (cities of at least 100,000 and their suburbs). About a quarter of the U.S. population, then, were 'metropolites,' and less than 10 per cent lived in cities of one million or more.[4]

The metropolitan focus of U.S. film historiography is sometimes supported by the claim that American society was urbanizing at a furious pace in the early decades of the century. By the 1920 census, it is pointed out, a majority of all Americans lived in cities. But the Census Bureau rather generously set the threshold for 'city' and 'urban' at any town of at least 2,500 people. In 1920 a majority of Americans still lived in places with fewer than 5,000 people, and in 1930 and 1940, most people were still living in places with fewer than 25,000 people. A majority of the U.S. population did not become metropolitan until the 1950 census, and this did not occur in the South for another twenty years. Even this still does not mean that most people experienced the movies as a part of everyday life amidst the 'hyperstimulation' of big city life: most of the metropolitan growth in the U.S. over the twentieth century actually occurred in the suburbs and not the central city. In fact, the percentage of the total population living in cities of over one million remained relatively constant between 1910 and 1940.[5]

There were huge regional disparities in urban density and contiguity and huge differences in historical patterns of urban development in the U.S. Roughly half the population of the Northeast was metropolitan in 1910;

fewer than one in ten Southerners lived in or around big cities. And urban growth—whether in towns of 3,000 or 300,000—did not result in the hollowing out of rural America. There were 50 per cent more potential rural moviegoers when *Gone with the Wind* was released than when *Uncle Josh at the Moving Picture Show* was made.[6] Keeping the metropolitan experience of moviegoing at the center of our historical map of American cinema squashes a complex and dynamic cultural and social geography into a simplistic binary grid of city/country. It also reproduces Hollywood's hierarchical ordering of movie audiences, movie theaters, and theater locations, with 'metropolites,' 'deluxers,' and 'big keys' at the top and 'hicks' 'dime houses,' and the 'Silo Belt' on the bottom.[7]

Film history's obsession not just with the urban experience of cinema but the metropolitan experience bespeaks a more general exaggeration of the role of the metropolis and a concomitant devaluation of the rural in contemporary historical and cultural inquiry. In his 1998 review of the field, Timothy Gilfoyle complains that American urban historiography remains stubbornly 'Gothamcentric.'[8] Steven Hahn and Jonathan Prude note that 'the whole swath of varied and methodologically innovative enquiries whose appearance marked the authentic coming of age of "the new social history" … have found urban settings most congenial. … Many of the most sophisticated, intelligent, and energetic forays into American social history during recent decades have tended to bypass the countryside.'[9]

Although there is certainly much that we do not know about whether, how, where, and to what extent movies were a part of the lives of people who lived in the American countryside, writing the 'rural' experience of moviegoing into American film history is not merely an exercise in empiricist comprehensiveness. Rather it is necessary if we are to adequately conceptualize the relationship, past and present, between cinema and place more generally. Barbara Ching and Gerald Creed draw a productive distinction between rurality and rusticity. While the former might be assayed in terms of population density and geography, rusticity is a social and a cultural construction describing the lived experience of place in the modern world in relational terms. One's relationship to any given social and cultural place is conditioned by the relationship of that place to other social and cultural places which it is understood not to be. Here Ching and Creed are not reproducing the tired structuralist binary: country/city. Rather, they are calling attention to the cultural hierarchies and social distinctions that inform the relationship between identity and place: to my stepfather growing up on a farm in the foothills of the Appalachian mountains in the 1920s going 'into town' meant experiencing the decidedly urbane place that was Rutherfordton, North Carolina. Ching and Creed argue that not only has contemporary cultural studies largely ignored the rural, but also that the difficulty of imagining a culturally productive rusticity prevents the field from adequately theorizing place in relation to other modes of social identity.[10]

What is required, I think, is a much more nuanced understanding of the relationship between the experience of urbanity, rurality, and rusticity, and the spatial and social emplacement of movies and moviegoing across the country and throughout film history. For example, the pace of urbanization was more rapid in the South at the turn of the century than in some other regions. But the nature of that process; the scale, character, diversity, and density (human, phenomenal, semiotic) of urban life; and the relationship between any given urban space and what lay beyond its political and social boundaries varied from one region of the country to another and within a given state.

In 1938, the *Motion Picture Herald* found 365 theaters in 196 towns in North Carolina, 40 per cent of them in towns of fewer than 2,500 people and two-thirds of them with fewer than 500 seats. In all but twenty-four of these nearly 200 towns, there was but a single movie theater.[11] One of those 24 towns with two movie houses was my hometown, Gastonia, N.C. It was in some key respects typical of hundreds if not thousands of towns which sprang up around the turn of the century as a part of the massive industrialization and urbanization of the South. Like many other cotton mill towns from Virginia to Alabama, Gastonia was a collection of separate mill villages connected by a central business district. Hacked out of pine forests or thrown up over cotton fields, these villages consisted of the mill surrounded by rows of cheap, quickly built shotgun houses, built and owned by the mill and rented to the families who worked in them: each room had to have at least one worker living in it for the family to qualify for residence in the mill village. In many cases, including that of my own great-grandfather, the families had been driven off surrounding farms and recruited into what they called 'public work' by periodic crashes in commodity prices As cultural historian Jacquelyn Hall has noted, 'urban' life in the mill village was produced through the dynamic tension between fundamentally rural social structures and values and the demands of first paternal and then corporate industrial capitalism, not by the elimination of the former by the latter.[12]

In U.S. film historiography, the term nickelodeon has come to stand not merely for early store-front exhibition venues and their attendant eponymous pricing policy, but for the interrelationship among specific physical circumstances of early movie exhibition, a particular social site of movie encounters, and a particular set of social identities marked by class, urbanity, geographic displacement, and ethnicity. The term 'nickelodeon era' has been made to cover not only metropolitan moviegoing between 1906 and 1912, but is now shorthand for the national experience of cinema in what is regarded as the formative period of American cinema. The nickelodeon, in Miriam Hansen's account, attracted a 'distinct class profile' of the urban, working-class, including 'millions of people,' principally European immigrants with little or no disposable income, who had never been regarded as a potential audience for mainstream commercial entertainment. Nickelodeons tended to be located in the same tenement neighborhoods in which their urban audiences lived and worked. They were a 'space apart' from bourgeois culture where 'older forms of working-class and ethnic culture can crystallize' and be 'articulated in a communal setting.' This sense of the nickelodeon as a socially liminal space applied, Hansen argues, with particular force to working class women, for whom it functioned 'as a particularly female heterotopia.'[13]

Quite apart from the question of whether this account of early moviegoing is adequate for people living in Manhattan around 1907, it does not apply to the majority of people living in the United States, and it certainly does not apply to any city, town, audience, neighborhood, or movie theater in the South. As in every other North Carolina town my graduate students and I have looked at, when permanent movie exhibition came to Gastonia in 1907, it started out and remained for a long time anchored in the town's central business district. Early theaters in these Southern towns were not located where accounts of nickelodeons in Manhattan or even Roy Rosenzweig's history of commercial leisure in Worcester, Massachusetts, might suggest they would be: in the mill villages themselves. Rather, they operated as a part of the commercial, social, and civic hub, alongside the other institutions of Southern urban life: the town bank, hotel, drug store, department store, and municipal administration.

Who might have attended these first movie theaters? From fire insurance maps, newspaper accounts, and photographs, it appears that the first permanent movie theaters in cities and small towns in North Carolina were frequently unprepossessing spaces, but this does not mean that their audiences had a 'distinct' class profile. The fact that as late as 1938 so many towns in North Carolina still only had one theater, combined with overwhelming tendency for theaters to be located not in working-class neighborhoods but in the central business district, suggest that the white audience for movies in these towns was, of economic necessity, socially heterogeneous. Furthermore, as Stuart Blumin and other social historians have suggested, we cannot simply assume that the metropolitan experience of class operated in smaller cities and towns beyond the shadow of the big city, and this experience certainly does not tell us much about the rural experience of class.

Ethnicity and immigration status were not important features of the Southern experience of moviegoing, and even during the nickelodeon period the significance of both factors decreased steeply outside the metropolis and beyond the Northeast quadrant of the country. Although recently arrived European immigrants, most of them from Southern and Eastern Europe, represented nearly half the total population of Manhattan in 1910, the demographic group whom the Census Bureau called 'foreign-born whites' made up less than 15 per cent of country's total population, about the same proportion as in 1860.[14] If the first movie theaters in the American South had had to rely upon recently arrived immigrants—from anywhere —to fill their theaters, there would not have been a single viable movie theater south of Baltimore and east of New Orleans for most of the history of American cinema. In the South, immigrants made up only 2.5 per cent of the total population, and in North Carolina only 0.3 per cent: 6,092 out of 2,206,287.

What is striking about the social status of small town movie theaters in North Carolina, and, I suspect, in other parts of the country as well, is not how removed or obscured they were from what Hansen would call hegemonic culture or how alternative or autonomous they were as public spaces, but rather how tightly woven they were, or aspired to be, into not just the town's social and cultural life but its civic life as well. The Theatorium, the first permanent theater in Concord, N.C., a cotton mill town north of Charlotte, opened its doors on 25 January 1908. The advertisement on 29 January announced that 'Our shows are run under the auspices of and for the benefit of the firemen of Concord.'[15] Small town movie theaters in North Carolina arranged special screenings or offered concessionary prices to school groups, served as a venue for local musical talent, and routinely organized or participated in charity drives. Sometimes movie theaters were the only or the largest secular public meeting spaces in town. They hosted high school graduations, town meetings, beauty pageants, and, during World War I, bond rallies. As Terry Lindvall argues in his chapter in this book, in Norfolk, Virginia, a not so small southern city, theaters quickly established themselves as civic institutions by forming an unusual strategic alliance with local mainstream Protestant and Catholic denominations to steer sailors on shore leave away from brothels and saloons and into the less morally dubious space of the movie theater.[16]

Where would white Southerners have experienced movies prior to 1907? Hansen says the first audiences for the movies were as varied as the venues in which movies were shown: vaudeville theaters, penny arcades, and amusement parks. A new 'public sphere ... eluding the control of cultural and religious arbiters' was constituted, she says, through a range of commercial entertainment forms around the turn of the century and was built around the 'new urban middle class.'[17]

This account of the historical context of early movie exhibition has very limited salience with respect to small towns in the South, and, again I suspect, elsewhere in the country as well. Most towns in the South were too small and too far from a main rail line to sustain a vaudeville theater. Amusement parks were features only of cities large enough to have streetcar or trolley systems. In hundreds and hundreds of small towns throughout the South, the only permanent venue for commercial entertainment between 1896 and 1907 was the local opera house.

Far from being a social space eluding the control of cultural and religious authorities, it typically was not only constructed by order of the town's political authorities, but was frequently also a part of the same physical structure that housed the town's executive and judicial operations. When a town achieved sufficient commercial and political density to warrant the construction of a court house or a town hall, a building was designed to accommodate civic authorities on the first floor or floors with space left on the uppermost floor for an auditorium, which might have simply been an open space with a small stage erected at one end. The Opera House in Concord, N.C. was located above the fire department. In Hendersonville, films were first shown in its opera house, located above the town's public library. The history of commercial entertainment in small towns was thus intertwined with the development of local power structures. Opera houses were typically leased to a local manager, who arranged for the appearance of traveling theater companies, minstrel shows, variety ensembles, and, at some of them at some point after 1896, movie showmen.

The role of the opera house in the circulation of culture in America cries out for further study. In 1900, only 26 per cent of the U.S. population lived in the 160 cities large enough (25,000 or more) to have had vaudeville theaters. There were, however, nearly 3,000 (2,960) towns of at least 1,000 but fewer than 5,000 residents, and two thirds of the U.S. population lived in places with fewer than 5,000 people.[18] We do not know how many small towns across the country had opera houses at the turn of the century, nor do we know how many of these hosted the visit of traveling movie showmen or with what frequency. But it is a credible hypothesis that most white Americans living at the turn of the century had their first encounters with motion pictures not in a vaudeville theater, nickelodeon, amusement park, or penny arcade, but in a small town opera house. In some communities the irregular scheduling of visiting movie showmen at the local opera house might well have been their only opportunity to see movies at all until sometime after 1906, when and if the town was large enough to support a separate dedicated venue for movies.

The most important aspect of the history of moviegoing in America that is illuminated by a change of geographic perspective and that, conversely, is most obscured by the fixation on the metropolitan experience of cinema is race. The African American experience of moviegoing in the early decades of the century has received only a parenthetical mention in most accounts, completely overshadowed by the focus on class and ethnicity in narratives of the metropolitan nickelodeon phenomenon. Although it by no means justifies the marginalization of race in these accounts, African Americans were still demographically marginal populations in the American metropolis of that time. As late as 1920, African Americans made up only 2.7 per cent of the population of New York City. By contrast, one out of every three New Yorkers had been born in Europe.[19]

Jacqueline Stewart's recent *Migrating to the Movies* sets out to correct both the empirical elision and theoretical marginalization of the black experience of film spectatorship in American film history. Challenging the 'familiar paradigm of immigration,' in accounts of early moviegoing, she organizes her account of African American moviegoing around the internal migration of Southern blacks to the urban North between 1890 and 1930, noting that this 'Great Migration' also coincides historically with the institutionalization of cinema. Focusing specifically on African American life in Chicago in the years during and after World War I, she finds there evidence for 'Black spectatorship as the creation of literal and symbolic spaces in which African Americans reconstructed their individual and collective identities in response to the cinema's moves toward classical narrative integration, and in the wake of migration's fragmenting effects.' Stewart's reconceptualization of black spectatorship is predicated upon the lived experience of race; the psychic and social dislocations of rural to metropolitan migration; the experience of metropolitan modernity; and the particular social, cultural, and physical circumstances of metropolitan moviegoing, as they relate to the experience of watching the 'self-enclosed film texts[s] on the screen' available to African American Chicagoans around 1920.[20] Stewart's points of reference in the construction of black spectatorship are other figurations of American and European metropolitan modernity in relation to a received notion of bourgeois cinema: 'I would argue that Black spectatorship is elaborated within the contradictions of the modernist promise of urban mobility, and the persistence of racial hierarchies and restrictions impeding smooth transitions into and through urban modernity. African American spectators share with the flâneur, the surrealist, and the ... [Neapolitan] "streetwalker" a kind of cultivated distance from the immobile spectator-in-the-dark position imposed by the classical cinematic apparatus and its attendant theories of the gaze.'[21]

Although Stewart's work offers a rich and densely textured account of black movie culture in Chicago in the teens, the explanatory reach of her construction of black spectatorship is limited. Despite the image we have of the great racial migration of Southern African Americans to Northern cities in the early twentieth century, in 1910 nine out of ten African Americans still lived in the South, and seven out of ten lived in the rural South.[22] The complex geographical displacement and relocation that has been summed up in the term Great Migration was one of the most significant social and demographic phenomena of twentieth century in the U.S., but it did not result in the wholesale evacuation of African Americans from the South to the North, and it certainly did not result in an exchange of rural modalities of social life for metropolitan modernity for most African Americans alive in the first decades of the twentieth century. Between 1900 and 1920, the number of African Americans living in the South rose by nearly 12 per cent, from roughly 7.5 to 8.4 million. The black population of Chicago in 1920 was 110,000, still only about 5 per cent of the city's total population of 2.7 million. Between 1900 and 1920, the black population of North Carolina increased by 139,000 (22 per cent) to more than 763,000. In 1920, one out of every three North Carolinians was African American.[23] The black migration of the early twentieth century was not just from the South to Northern cities, but to and between Southern towns and cities as well. By 1920, blacks made up a much larger proportion of Southern urban population than was the case for any Northern city: Birmingham, Memphis, New Orleans, Wilmington, and Gastonia were all more than 30 per cent black.

For most African Americans in the first half of the twentieth century, moviegoing was a part of the experience of Southern urban modernity, not Northern or Midwestern metropolitan modernity. That experience was profoundly shaped by the rigorous and systematic organization of space and place in every Southern town of any size, as sanctioned by the U.S. Supreme Court in 1896. It is worth keeping in mind that the court's decision in *Plessy v. Ferguson*, authorising the organization of social and economic life into separate spheres according to race, was handed down on 16 May 1896, only three weeks after the debut of 'Edison's' Vitascope at Koster and Bial's Music Hall in New York City.[24] By the time permanent exhibition came to Southern towns and cities a decade after that decision, urban spaces throughout the South already had been ruthlessly remapped according to the 'hyperterritoriality' of Jim Crow Moviegoing did not cease being a direct expression of the apartheid logic of Jim Crow in the

South—for all moviegoers there, black and white—until the early 1960s.[25] For nearly seventy years, then, the history of moviegoing and the history of racial segregation in the U.S., particularly in the South, were not only co-terminus but conjoined.

Jim Crow was not the delayed victory of agrarian traditionalists, nor was it merely the hardening into *de jure* writ of an unwritten system of power relations and *de facto* social arrangements emerging from reconstruction. Rather it was itself quintessentially modern—a 'new and powerful force ... as revolutionary and progressive in its transforming powers as the railroads that crisscrossed the region.'[26] As it would have been experienced in everyday life by white and blacks—to vastly differential effect, of course—Jim Crow was the racing of space—all space—but particularly Southern urban space. Its exquisite division of the world into separate neighborhoods, schools, prisons, hospitals, orphanages, funeral homes, cemeteries, hotels, brothels, telephone booths, blood supplies, toilets, drinking fountains, waiting rooms, textbook warehouses, courthouse Bibles, and theater seating was no less an expression of modernity than window shopping, metropolitan hyperstimulation, or the 'panoramic perception' of train travel.[27] Zygmunt Bauman makes clear just what is at stake in understanding the complex relationship between race, space, and modernity:

> [A]s a conception of the world, and even more importantly as an effective instrument of political practice, racism is unthinkable without the advancement of modern science, modern technology and modern forms of state power. As such, racism is strictly a modern product. Modernity made racism possible. It also created a demand for racism; an era that declared achievement to be the only measure of human worth needed a theory of ascription to redeem boundary-drawing and boundary-guarding concerns under new conditions which made boundary-crossing easier than ever before. Racism, in short, is a thoroughly modern weapon used in the conduct of pre-modern, or at least not exclusively modern, struggles.[28]

We know very little about the ways or the extent that movies and moviegoing figured in the everyday lives of most African Americans during the Jim Crow period, and we know least about the role of movies and moviegoing in the lives of African Americans in the South. Greg Waller's pioneering work on black theaters and moviegoing in Lexington, Kentucky, and Charlene Regester's recent article on black theaters in *Film History* are exceptions.[29] We do know that they are not likely to have shared the same space or 'intermingled,' as it was sometimes expressed, in movie theaters with whites: the spatial segregation of blacks in theaters was underwritten by state statute in Virginia and by municipal ordinances and coercive social practice elsewhere in the South. Where Southern theaters did admit blacks, they were consigned to what was called the 'Crow's Nest' or the 'Buzzard's Roost': a balcony reserved exclusively for African Americans. This seating arrangement obtained in Southern theaters through the 1950s in many towns and cities.

The spatial segregation of African Americans in white theaters was not simply an assertion of white consumer privilege and political authority and the concomitant relegation of blacks to a physically separate and patently unequal viewing position. Jim Crow laws and practices were a reaction against the increased visibility of blacks in the urban public sphere as well as their increased economic and spatial mobility within that sphere. Restricting black mobility and regulating their physical and economic access to the institutions of urban consumer culture was an attempt to curb what was perceived by whites as 'a dangerous assertiveness on the part of African Americans, especially the generations born since emancipation.' In John David Smith's analysis, the spatial isolation of blacks was designed to protect whites from physical and social 'contamination.'[30] The perceived 'danger' of black assertiveness and the fear of contamination were most pronounced in those urban spaces where the possibility of both racial and gender 'intermingling' was greatest. In Atlanta in September 1906, provoked by newspaper accounts of alleged black assaults on white women in public spaces, a mob of 10,000 white men began beating every black person they could find, killing twenty and seriously injuring hundreds more. Movie theaters were, like steamboats, streetcars, railway cars and railroad station waiting rooms, especially sensitive Southern 'urban' spaces in which racial separation had to be assured and most vigilantly regulated in the early decades of Jim Crow. As Barbara Welke has argued with respect to the railroad's 'place' in the history of racial segregation in the South, 'statutory Jim Crow provided an absolute protection of white womanhood and thus of white supremacy in the South by protecting the enclave of white women from encroachment by women and men of color.'[31]

Although accounts of the picture palace era of American moviegoing rarely point out the 'colored' balconies of many Southern theaters, the racing of movie theater space was not improvised or provisional by the 1920s, but rather, as a visitor to a Southern railroad station remarked about the rod separating white from black waiting rooms, it was as 'fixed as the foundations of the building.'[32] As Southern movie theaters outgrew their first downtown storefront locations and aspired to larger and more imposing quarters, the racing of the space of moviegoing was built into the very architecture of the theater itself. Architectural drawings for Southern movie theaters from the 1920s and 1930s show plans not only for 'colored' balconies, but also for separate box offices and (frequently exterior) stairways, which were the only means that blacks had to entering and exit the theater.[33] The architecture of racial separation in Southern movie theaters was designed not only to prevent blacks from occupying the same space as whites—particularly white women—but wherever physically possible and economically feasible, to efface them from the scopic and social moviegoing environment experienced by white patrons. One consequence of the architecture of raced space in Southern movie theaters is that some older white moviegoers with whom I've spoken have no clear memories of black viewers being present in theaters at all.

The absence of raced spaces in architectural drawings for Southern theaters signals an even more extreme racing of the space of moviegoing: excluding blacks from the space of white moviegoing altogether, or at least when white moviegoers would have been present. Without further research, we simply do not know what proportion of Southern theaters excluded blacks or whether this strategy tended to be employed more in larger or smaller towns. Certainly, it would have been the case in the opera houses and converted storefront theaters in which a balcony was not an architectural possibility. It seems also to have been a common practice that long outlived architectural exigencies. The first theater to admit blacks in Durham, North Carolina, was not built until the late 1920s, and was the only segregated white theater in town until the desegregation of all theaters in the early 1960s. Both downtown white theaters in Chapel Hill excluded blacks until August 1961, when a fourteen month protest sparked by the exclusion of blacks from screenings of *Porgy and Bess* eventually resulted in the grudging admission of two black UNC students to the Carolina Theater. The film playing that week was *The Dark at the Top of the Stairs*.[34]

The authority of Southern theater owners to exclude blacks from movie theaters derived from the legal status of the space of moviegoing. Unlike streetcars, railroad cars and station waiting rooms, movie theaters in the South were regarded not as public spaces but as private spaces. This crucial legal distinction gave racial exclusion the force of law and helped to deflect the desegregation struggle away from movie theaters and toward public transportation until after the Woolworth lunch counter sit-ins in Greensboro, North Carolina, in February 1960. The particular distinction at issue here was between commercial enterprises operating public accommodations or serving as common carriers and those that were not. By the time of the advent of moviegoing, common carriers—inns, coaches, trains, and other modes of public transport—had a long-established common law 'duty to serve' that, while not absolute, regulated and restricted the conditions under which admission or service could be refused. The issue in *Plessy v. Ferguson* was not whether a black ticket holder could be refused passage in a public conveyance, but whether the state of Louisiana could pass a law requiring railroad companies operating in the state to provide 'equal but separate' accommodation for passengers on the basis of race. The federal Civil Rights Act of 1875 actually included theaters among its list of public accommodations, but key provisions of the law were struck down by the Supreme Court in 1883.[35] Eighteen states drafted civil rights legislation to restore public accommodations protections to theater-goers; none of those states was in the South. There the essentially private status of theatrical space was reasserted with a vengeance by post-reconstruction legislatures and courts. Some states passed laws specifically immunizing theater owners from liability for excluding anyone for virtually any or no reason. The Tennessee law gave 'keepers of places of amusement' a right to control access or exclusion 'as complete as that of any private person over his ... private theater or places of amusement for his family.'[36] In the twentieth century the 'classical statement' of the legal status of theatrical space is to be found in the court's opinion in *Tyson & Brother v. Banton* (1927): although there is a sufficient public interest to warrant the licensing and regulation of theaters by state or municipal governments, a 'license is not a franchise which puts the proprietor under the duty of furnishing entertainment to the public or, if furnished, of admitting everyone who applies.'[37]

One thrust of recent critical legal studies has been a reconceptualizing of the relationship among space, place, and the law. As Nicholas Blomley argues, the law does not simply impose itself upon pre-existing legally empty space, but rather the legal apparatus actively produces, organizes, and reorganizes space. By the same token, law is always produced in relation to the 'local' places in which it operates: 'Law is, as it were, produced in such spaces; those spaces, in turn, are partly constituted by legal norms. Either way, law cannot be detached from the particular places in which it acquires meaning and saliency.'[38]

The legal definition of theatrical space as private space in the South not only helped to structure the social experience of moviegoing for whites and blacks in segregated theaters, it also help to create the social space in which black theaters operated in the South for nearly sixty years. To date most of what little scholarly attention that has been paid to black theaters has focused on the experience of moviegoing in black theaters in Chicago.[39] And yet, as Thomas Doherty notes in his chapter in this book, most black theaters were located in the South. There has been no systematic, comprehensive mapping of black theaters anywhere, including in the South, by film historians, and black moviegoing was largely ignored by the Hollywood film industry. Doherty quotes a 1963 *Variety* article claiming that the industry possessed almost no information on the number or location of black theaters, the proportion of white theaters that were segregated or 'Southern communities in which there are no film theaters of any sort to which Negroes have admission.'[40] A 1937 *Motion Picture Herald* survey found that only 1.5 per cent of the nation's 17,000 movie theaters were black theaters. Complicating the argument that black theaters might have represented an alternative public sphere for African American moviegoers, particularly in the South, is the likelihood that most 'black' theaters were owned and managed by whites.[41]

Furthermore, as Stewart has noted, the black movie audience was not homogeneous. In towns where blacks could 'choose' to watch movies either from the balcony of segregated theaters or at a black (though not necessarily black-owned) theater, class and other social fractures in the urban black community sometimes became evident. Charlene Regester notes a 1930 cartoon in a black newspaper in Durham, N.C. showing black patrons attending the city's only segregated theater. The caption read: 'The common people look on with amazement as the professionals and leaders climb upstairs to the Jim Crow buzzard's roost.'[42] On the other hand, Janna Jones notes that in the 1930s and 1940s blacks in Atlanta either sat in the balconies of white theaters or attended the city's one black theater. In 1940 the newly arrived president of Morehouse College, Benjamin Hays, made his position pretty clear: 'I wouldn't go to a segregated theater to see Jesus Christ himself.'[43]

There is so much that we do not know about the cultural and social complexities of black moviegoing, particularly in the South, and the historiographic challenge represented by its reconstruction is especially daunting. Establishing which white theaters admitted blacks at all is difficult. Black theaters did not advertise in white newspapers, which were much more likely to have been preserved than local black newspapers. As a result, it is extremely difficult to know what films actually played in black theaters, or when they played. We have a few published first-hand accounts of black moviegoing and some oral histories, but in my limited experience, many African Americans in their 60s and 70s who grew up in the South are not particularly eager to recall or recount the very ambivalent 'pleasures' of going to the movies.

Given the rural character of the South and the concentration of African Americans there, the likelihood that most opera houses and storefront theaters in the South excluded blacks altogether, the continuation of the policy of racial exclusion in many theaters in many towns for decades, the sparseness of black theaters (only fourteen in North Carolina in 1937 for a black population of nearly a million, for example), and the social humiliations associated with relegation to the buzzard's roost, it is likely that most African Americans were not a part of the 'moviegoing audience' at all during the pre-bourgeois period of American film history. It is also likely that for the first sixty-five years of American film history, moviegoing was occasional, rather than regular or habitual, for most African Americans, and that, as a consequence, what we might call movie culture was not a prominent feature of the lived experience of most African Americans for most of the twentieth century.

Our interrogation of the relationship among region, race, and moviegoing should, however, also involve reconceptualizing the relationship between whiteness and moviegoing in the South. Legal scholar Cheryl I. Harris has proposed looking at whiteness in American history as a form of property. Inscribed in statutes and enabled by case law, the law's 'construction of whiteness defined and affirmed critical aspects of identity (who is white); of privilege (what benefits accrue to that status); and of property (what /legal/ entitlements arise from that status).' One of the key 'rights' exercised in relation to property is the right of exclusion:

> The right to exclude was the central principle, too, of whiteness as identity, for mainly whiteness has been characterized, not by an inherent unifying characteristic, but by the exclusion of others deemed to be 'not white.' The possessors of whiteness were granted the legal right to exclude others from the privileges inhering in whiteness; whiteness became an exclusive club whose membership was closely and grudgingly guarded.[44]

Through the creation and enforcement of a separate and devalued cinematic experience for African Americans and their literal exclusion from the places of cinematic exhibition, Southern whites claimed the movies and moviegoing as their property. Whether it was purposive in this respect or even rose to the level of consciousness (which it probably only did when challenged), the very act of moviegoing was for white Southerners an exercise of their property right to whiteness.

If growing class awareness helped to fracture the black movie audience in the South, the class-transcendent nature of whiteness suppressed class difference as a variable in the experience of moviegoing for whites. What even the poorest white cotton mill worker possessed and shared with the mill owner was precisely what the most affluent African American lacked: the property of whiteness. As Harris and others have noted, European ethnic difference in America has been assimilable into whiteness. What the Russian or Italian immigrant eventually acquired—however problematically—by coming to the U.S. was ownership of whiteness.

It is arguable that, as a region, both the black and the white South stood in a different, more complicated, and, probably, more distanced relationship to movie culture than other parts of the country. More than thirty years ago, Thomas Cripps exploded the 'myth' of the Southern box office: Hollywood's disingenuous exaggeration of the size and economic importance of the Southern movie audience in order to justify its marginalization of black actors and its timidity in dealing with racial themes. Before air conditioning, he argues, some Southern theaters simply closed their doors between June and September. Movie theaters also competed not only against other forms of indoor commercial leisure, but also against outdoor pursuits for much of the year. In the 1920s a single large New York theater could take in more in a given week than an entire good sized Southern city.[45] As Greg Waller points out, Depression-era government studies of rural life found that most Southern farm families seldom went to the movies. He has also noted that in rural communities in the South and elsewhere in the U.S. what Barbara Klinger has called 'extra-theatrical' moviegoing may well have been a much more prominent feature of movie culture than in more urban communities.[46]

The role that movies and moviegoing played in many communities in the South was mediated by a deep institutional suspicion of moviegoing among members of the Protestant sects whose theologies encouraged renunciation of secular values and adherence to codes of social behavior as a sign of conversion. Norfolk, as examined by Terry Lindvall elsewhere in this volume, may be the exception that proves the rule. This strand of religious belief had a particularly strong hold among rural and urban working-class white Southerners. There is reason to believe that religious acceptance of moviegoing was an issue for all Southern exhibitors, and that for many Southerners moviegoing fitted awkwardly into the fabric of their social and moral lives.[47] As late as 1966, an article in *Christianity Today*, the magazine founded in 1957 by North Carolina evangelist Billy Graham and circulated to more than 200,000 Protestant ministers and laypersons, noted that 'Christians, as a rule, do not attend the movies.'[48]

In response to a request for materials on local movie theaters and moviegoing sent out to all public libraries in North Carolina, I was contacted by a librarian in Burlington, N.C., a cotton mill town about 25 miles west of Chapel Hill. She asked if I would be interested in looking at a 1934 day book kept by her grandmother, Bertha Burgess Frye, who was then a 29-year-old cotton mill worker employed at the Cannon Mill in Kannapolis, North Carolina Her husband, Henry, drove a truck for a local heating oil company. Their daughter would be born the following year. Each night before she went to bed, Bertha recorded the day's events in a small 4″ × 3″ leather daybook, a week filling each double page. As a part of this chronicle, Bertha made note of every time she went to 'the show,' as she and many other Southerners referred to the movies Bertha was an avid moviegoer. Most weeks she went at least twice, although never on Sunday. Sometimes, if there was no work for her at the mill, she saw two different films in one day. Although Kannapolis had several theaters, she frequently would travel to neighboring Concord or even the ten miles to the larger city of Salisbury just to see a movie.

What was striking to me as I read through her account of everyday life for that year is that even for someone for whom moviegoing meant a great deal, particular films seldom registered enough to warrant a specific mention, and only a few stars are noted. Even when specific films are noted, they had to share these tiny pages with other aspects of everyday life:

Saturday, 6 January 1934: Went to town this evening got Howards shoes and mailed them. Went to the show tonight at YMCA. Saw *The Gallant Fool* with Bob Steele.

Saturday, 21 April: Took Ada to Concord to get teeth. Got Henry tie 2 shirts. Went to Concord to the show tonight saw *The Big Shakedown* with Bette Davis and Charles Farrell.

Bertha's day book reminds us that moviegoer and audience are not ontological categories, that movies and moviegoing do not define subjectivity or social identity.

For her book on British movie culture of the 1930s, Annette Kuhn interviewed nearly one hundred people old enough to have been moviegoers in the 1930s. She found that the films they remembered most vividly were not those film historians have singled out as being the most popular or most important. A number of her interviewees were, like Mrs. Frye, avid moviegoers, but even their recollections of specific films were sketchy and unreliable. Many of her respondents, however, remembered the social spaces of moviegoing from their childhoods with remarkable specificity. Some respondents could produce detailed mental maps of 1930s cinemas in a given neighborhood, complete with ticket price differences, social particularities (this one was where courting couples lined the back row), décor, sounds and smells, and even the shops that surrounded them, despite the fact that all of these cinemas had long since been torn down or converted to some other use. 'For the majority,' Kuhn observes, 'going to the pictures is remembered as being less about films and stars than about daily and weekly routines, neighbourhood comings and goings and organizing spare time. Cinemagoing is remembered, that is, as part of the fabric of daily life.'[49]

For the past thirty years or so in the U.S., the audience to whom movies have mattered most are those of us who get paid to watch them, write about them, and persuade our students of their importance It is we who have the greatest stake in keeping movies at the center of social experience and at the center of film history. Cultural historian James Hay comes at this issue from a somewhat different perspective, but he, too, proposes a decentering of the object of film studies, or at least its dispersal within a wider spatial and social field. Such a redefinition of would begin 'by considering how social relations are spatially organized … and how film is practiced from and across particular sites and always in relation to other sites. In this respect, cinema is not seen in a dichotomous relation with the social, but as dispersed within an *environment* of sites that *defines* (in spatial terms) the meanings, uses, and place of "the cinematic."'[50]

Ironically, film studies' insistence upon the centrality of the experience of particular films and the psychological and ideological effectivity of the filmic text have helped to marginalize the 'empirical' dimensions of the experience of cinema that might well have mattered most to most people for most of film history: those associated with the social experience of moviegoing.

Tri-racial Theaters in Robeson County, North Carolina, 1896–1940

Christopher J. McKenna

THIS CHAPTER is a study of moviegoing in Robeson County, North Carolina, from the beginnings of American cinema until the eve of U.S. participation in the Second World War. Focusing on the social history of moviegoing, it validates historian Lee Grieveson's claim that cinema historians are engaged 'in delineating the multiple forces that have shaped cinema and, in turn, the way cinema has participated in the shaping of culture.' Grieveson argues that such historical enquiries are part of a larger 'history of cultural regulation' which demands 'that historians traverse other histories—of class formation, sexuality, immigration, racial discrimination, for example—to situate aspects of cinema history as parts of social, political, and cultural history.'[1] What insights or lessons can we find in an evaluation of early moviegoing in Robeson County? First and foremost, Robeson County matters because it contains physical artifacts (some still available) that undeniably confirm the segregationist role that movie-houses served in the Jim Crow South. Although most of the concrete vestiges of that dismal era have largely disappeared through the removal of 'Whites Only' signifiers such as store-window placards, distinct rest rooms and drinking fountains, race-specific transportation and eating facilities, the psychological effects of the color bar nevertheless remain, and these sites still resonate unpleasantly for specific cultural groups even today.[2] This may account for why, in 2003, the local Robeson community was virtually silent on the occasion of the seventy-fifth anniversary of the region's premier movie theater, the Carolina Theater in Lumberton, when many of the region's political and social elite had been so active in executing and celebrating its painstaking and expensive restoration two decades earlier. Since the 1980s, the Robeson community has been increasingly affected by non-white political movements, and the cultural dominance of its former key white participants has diminished as those individuals have aged.[3] In the eyes of more than a few Robesonians, the Carolina Theater today no longer merits celebration. For many, indeed, perhaps it never did.

Robesonian moviegoing also confirms the argument made by a number of film historians, that movie audiences never responded universally and identically to the siren call of motion pictures, nor did they react in the same ways to the social event of moviegoing. Moviegoers were as much constructed by what happened to them on the way to, during and after viewing a film as they were by film content or by the phenomenological effects of the film experience. In particular, it would be socially and culturally myopic not to recognize that in the American South race, which so profoundly affected everyday life, must have ranked high in any list of factors affecting motion picture reception. Consideration of the artifacts of Robeson County's exhibition history suggests how multiple moviegoing experiences can manifest themselves within multi-racial communities.

Historical moviegoing in Robeson County acts in particular as a prism through which we can study the cultural experiences of the Lumbee Indians, a group representing the fifth largest Indian people in the United States, the nation's largest non-reservation Indian tribe, and the largest Indian group in the Southeast, particularly as they participated in mass-market social entertainments with members of other racial groups.[4] Very little work has to date been done on the moviegoing experiences of Native Americans, and while the Lumbees may not represent 'typical' Native Americans (if such a thing exists), their moviegoing experiences, like their very cultural definition, remained problematic.[5] Although yoked to a Jim Crow social order, the Lumbees' racial distinctiveness could be difficult to determine at a glance.[6] Despite a century-long prohibition on mixed marriages, the region's long history of racial intermixing had marked Lumbees with a wide variety of physical features and colouring that confounded stereotypical notions of African, White, and Indian racial identity. Treating blood or skin 'colour' as a cultural determinant was a notion foreign to Lumbee conceptions of social identity. When, however, they interacted with white business owners in towns like Lumberton, where most of the county's movie houses were located, identity conflicts arose as Lumbees were forced to accept socially limiting identity labels such as 'Indian,' or worse, the region-specific derogatives 'Croatan' and 'Cro.'

In a culture involving not one but two 'subject' minorities, racial negotiations have historically fuelled the region's cultural dynamics. Lumbees especially interest cultural historians because their existence challenges dualistic views of Southern racial ideology. As an 'interstital' people historically claiming social allegiance with neither blacks nor whites, Lumbees and the tri-racial environment in which they have lived justify ethnologist Karen Blu's claim that 'if Southern racial ideology appears rigid and unyielding, its workings are far more flexible and complicated than has generally been acknowledged.'[7] As well as illuminating a particular social experience of cinema, this chapter's examination of the ways in which the region's racial complexities played themselves out within Robeson County's moviegoing spaces may encourage other historians to interrogate similar 'exceptions to the rigid biracial system in the South' in order to discover what they have to tell us about the performative nature of race.[8]

The type of historical research documented in this chapter is informed by Robert C. Allen's call for film historians to challenge certain biases that have crept into historical motion picture exhibition studies. Because these biases oversimplify more complicated and contingent experiences than those documented previously, Allen proposes 'a more thoroughgoing historiographic and conceptual *decentering*' of reception studies, one paying closer attention to the importance of factors such as 'race, class, gender, community, religion, urbanity' and ethnicity on the social experience of moviegoing.[9] As Allen argues, race was the single most important factor determining exhibition practices, and moviegoing experiences more generally, in the American South. As we analyze the relationships between race, popular entertainment, and public spaces, however, we must remember that 'race' cannot be, nor ever has ever been, defined as a simple matter of black and white. The experience of Robeson County ought to encourage the use of more conspicuously multi-racial and multi-ethnic perspectives in exhibition studies, since several racial groups faced distinctive segregationist treatment and responded to segregationist treatment differently.

Located along the Carolina border in the state's coastal plain, Robeson County encompasses a population divided fairly evenly across three racial groups (Caucasian, African American, and Native American).[10] During the period covered by this study, the white proportion of the county's population held steady at approximately 45 per cent, while the proportion represented by blacks fell from 43 to 33 per cent as the Indian population correspondingly rose to 22 per cent.[11] Although the combined non-white population in Robeson always outnumbered its white population, white residents held virtually all economic, political, and social power in this rural farming region, principally by acting as leaseholders for non-white tenant farmers. Until the 1930s, very few non-whites lived in Robeson's main towns, including the county seat, Lumberton, and the centre of the area's Indian population, Pembroke. Steadily growing numbers of non-whites seeking motion picture entertainment, however, meant that theatre managers had to decide how best to serve Robeson's non-whites, whose patronage must have tempted local exhibitors, particularly during tough economic times.

From the earliest days of motion pictures, Robeson's exhibitors incorporated racial thinking into their attendance policies as well as into the physical design of their theatres. As exhibitors struggled with the complexities of implementing a kind of American 'tripartheid,' their solutions included outright disenfranchisement for non-whites, race-specific movie houses, midnight 'race' shows, multi-racial sites that required all non-white groups to share a single segregated space, and finally, in the mid-1930s, the institutionalization of the 'three-entrance' theatre.[12]

The first itinerant motion picture exhibition in Robeson County occurred on 27 May 1897, at a benefit for a local militia group in the Maxton armoury. Four days later, it moved to what became (for approximately two decades) the centre of cultural life in Robeson: Lumberton's Opera House, a two-storey, gabled, metal-clad structure that housed a stage and an auditorium on its second floor and was located at the northernmost end of Lumberton's four-block business district. Although we know very little about its interior appearance or even the date of its initial construction, we do know that race relations influenced its physical composition. A preoccupation with preventing race-mixing determined the first two generations of Robeson moviegoing, leading to changes in physical exhibition spaces involving multiple galleries, staircases, partitions, entryways, and ticket booths, and resulting in physical site modifications that both reflected and executed local race-based social policies. In 1908, six months after the Lumberton Lyceum Bureau took over its management primarily for commercial movie exhibition, an item in the local newspaper, the *Robesonian*, reported that:

> Improvements are being made at the opera house which will add greatly to the comfort and safety of its patrons. A stairway will be built to the room on the left of the entrance and from this room an entrance for colored people will be cut to Elm street [sic]. Another stairway will be built to the gallery, making four stairways in the front of the house, which will provide better means of entrance and exit and will also provide for complete separation of the races ...[13]

48

Segregation of white and black patronage was the likely focus of the Opera House's early remodelling efforts but we might also wonder what complications these changes introduced.[14] Clearly, one set of 'non-white' facilities was insufficient to 'provide for complete separation of the races' in such a racially complex site as Robeson County. Perhaps to avoid the additional financial (and potentially social) costs involved in catering to non-whites, many Robeson motion picture exhibitors excluded both blacks and Indians by restricting theatres solely to white patrons. Having grown up a Lumbee in the middle years of the twentieth century, Ruth Dial Woods recalls that theaters often carried the 'Whites Only' signs common to many Robeson County establishments.[15] Mr. F.X. LeBeau, manager of Lumberton's third movie house, trumpeted the comparative advantage of his site when, in his first public announcement of the virtues of his site at a time when the town possessed at least three moviegoing options, he declared that in the Star Theater, 'none except white people will be admitted.'[16]

LeBeau's bald interdict implies that other theatres, and possibly previous managers of the Star, had catered to multiple racial groups. Evidence of non-white interest in moviegoing in the early days of Robesonian exhibitions proves that non-whites did go to the movies, and not always in segregation-enforced settings like the Opera House. At least two early 'colored' theatres operated briefly, probably catering to just African Americans, since in Robeson County the label 'colored' typically signified 'African American' only. Newspaper archives record the existence of the A-Mus-U Theater, a white-owned site opened in an old automobile garage in September 1914,[17] and an unnamed 'colored' theater operated (but most likely not owned) by a black man named Charley Morrisey in the African American neighborhood referred to as 'The Bottom' in 1919.[18] Moreover, perhaps to the chagrin of local whites who fondly recalled youthful evenings attending its various 'high-class' shows, the Opera House itself was converted into a coloured movie house for a few months in the fall of 1919, prior to its eventual transformation into a hotel.[19] Nevertheless, most evidence suggests that until the early 1930s, non-white patrons were either prohibited by theatre managers from attending 'white' houses, or else were relegated to second class seating and late-night 'colored' show exhibitions.

It seems plausible that neither Robeson's African nor Native Americans acquired a taste for moviegoing through the region's fixed-site theatres. Instead, from late 1919 until well into the mid-1920s, most non-white moviegoers were generally limited to the single exhibition option of Community Service Pictures (CSP). A joint venture between various local, state, and federal health organizations, these itinerant-style shows targeted rural audiences by visiting schools, churches and fairs in the area, advocating

FREE! · **SPECIAL** | **FREE!**

ANNOUNCEMENT

By Unanimous Endorsement and Vote of County Commissioners, and Through Concerted Co-Operation of Robeson County Cotton Mill Owners.

Extended Two Weeks!

MONDAY, OCTOBER 18. Centenary.	**FRIDAY, OCTOBER 22** East Lumberton Cotton Mill, Lumberton.	**WEDNESDAY, OCTOBER 27.** Prospect, (Indian)
TUESDAY, OCTOBER 19 Purvis.	**SATURDAY, OCTOBER 23.** Jennings Cotton Mill, Lumberton.	**THURSDAY, OCTOBER 28** Rennert.
THURSDAY, OCTOBER 21 National Cotton Mill, Lumberton.	**SUNDAY, OCTOBER 24.** St. Pauls Cotton Mill, St. Pauls.	**FRIDAY, OCTOBER 29** Jimmy Dial's (Indian)
		SATURDAY, OCTOBER 30 Lumberton (Colored)

U. S. GOVERNMENT'S

Marvelous Educational

SOCIAL HYGIENE EXHIBITION

Auspices U. S. Public Health Service, American Social Hygiene Association, North Carolina State Board of Health.

WONDER PRODUCING MOVING PICTURES!

Never Before Seen in Robeson County

Free Books! For Men, for Boys, for Girls, for Women, for Parents, for All. Get one.

SEPARATE MEETINGS FOR WHITE, INDIAN AND COLORED

TWICE DAILY! Afternoons, 3:30 p. m. Women Only Evenings, 8:00 p. m. Men Only

LOOK FOR THE BANNER!

See the Social Hygiene Field Car!

2.1 Community Service Pictures' Special Announcement, *Robesonian*, 21 October 1920, shows separate sessions in segregated sites for each of the three main racial groups.

improved health and hygiene via films depicting ills common to agricultural communities, such as dysentery, pellagra, and the boll weevil. Mixing one or two educational reels in with four or five reels of family-oriented entertainment, these shows offered many non-white Robesonians their first regular exposure to motion pictures.[20] Although they served a multi-racial community, CSPs were not multi-racial events. The sponsors of the plan realized that in Robeson County, they would have to divide their exhibition capacity three ways in order to serve the county's racial groups. The first announcement for CSP exhibition shows included two specifically non-white locations: 'Union Chapel (Indian) and Shannon (Negro).'[21] During their roughly decade-long run, CSP exhibitions were publicized through weekly advertisements containing similar racial markers to signify what amounted to the county's non-white motion-picture exhibition schedule.

The accounts that we have of these shows indicate that not only did the dominant white racial group seek to separate itself from non-whites through them, but also that African Americans and Indians might choose deliberately to defend their respective 'turf' from one another. Of the two non-white groups, Indians tended to be more vocal, being ever more uneasy about their position in the area's cultural hierarchy. Across the region's socio-political, economic, and spatial topographies, Indians represented the variable element within every racially charged situation, and since the initial response of exhibitors was to force all non-white groups to share a single segregated space (a move contrary to common custom in other social events), inadequately segregated spaces could offend Indians to the point of public protest, and even to threats of boycott or violence. Two weeks after the initial announcement of CSP exhibition sites, a letter to the local newspaper, unambiguously titled 'Union Chapel is Indian,' suggested that improper racial coding of CSP announcements might result in unwonted consequences. Thinking that Union Chapel had been identified as a Negro site, the letter's author warned that 'if the show will be expecting to show for coloreds they better not come. I hope the mistake will be corrected before it comes.'[22]

News accounts of CSP's shows not only demonstrate that all three races attended movies in Robeson in one fashion or another, but also hint at particular troubles facing all local movie exhibitors. In a nation largely divided along two racial axes, Robeson County's social and commercial institutions faced the need to account for a third major racial group in reasonably practical and not prohibitively costly ways. Social custom required that three groups of racial identities be accommodated, and a facility's management and exhibition staff would be called on to prevent 'deviant' racial self-identifications. In spaces that could only physically segregate two groups, contention arose over what facilities were made available to Indians. As several theatres began to admit non-whites (if only to their balconies), critical race-management issues arose, including whether or not Indians could or would accept the 'second-class' treatment afforded to blacks. Anecdotal evidence suggests that, when faced with such a choice, many Indians chose not to go to such theatres at all, while some, like Ruth Dial Woods, might try to pass themselves off as white. Some individuals were forced into even more conflicted positions; the manager of one theatre hired an Indian boy to point out 'seating violations' to the management.[23]

Doubtless the most unpleasant episodes in the racial negotiations during exhibition attendance involved primarily black and Indian patrons, for whom racial identity became a performative act albeit, perhaps, one of defiance. Alternatively, identity might be determined in the eye of the beholder, which could prove to be especially complicated in Robeson. In daily practice, Lumbees characterized by particularly dark features may have been judged as black, and therefore steered to an 'incorrect' balcony division. Light-skinned blacks may have been judged to be Indian. As a result, balcony residents may have wondered (or worse) about some of their neighbours. Finally, confusion might arise over the placement of white patrons, too. Judge Henry A. McKinnon, for example, recalls that once during his 'high school days, ca. 1935–39, I had spent most of the summer at the beach and was deeply tanned. I went to the Carolina for an afternoon show, and the lady cashier directed me to the [colored/Indian] door. Fortunately, I was with my classmate, Russell Beam, Jr., son of Dr. Beam [one of the Carolina's co-founders], and he vouched for me to get into the white section.'[24]

If, in retrospect, such confusion has a comical element to it, daily subjection to race prejudice was no laughing matter for non-whites. During the 1930s, in particular, unhappiness concerning Indian placement in facilities of all kinds exploded into public view. Contemporary sociologist Guy Johnson noted that, by 1939, Robeson's Indians were pursuing an increasingly active resistance to attempts to push them out of their position as 'the middle caste in this triracial society.' Suspecting that the 'keystone in this [caste system] is, of course, the white man's determination not to accept the Indian as his equal and, as far as possible, to put him into the same category as the Negro,' Johnson regarded movie houses as a fundamental and unusually visible symbol of the region's underlying racial ideology. Johnson knew from firsthand observations that, as the late 1930s approached, 'if he [an Indian] attends a theatre, he has to choose between one which provides a three-way segregation and one which seats him with Negroes.'[25] Either solution made many Indians uncomfortable, but steady population growth in the Indian community, as well as increased access to the towns in which movie houses were located, all contributed to an increasing non-white patronage demand that commercial exhibitors struggled variously to cater to, reject outright, or otherwise manage in a socially acceptable manner.

When tripartite accommodation could not be made or was not available, racial tensions resulted in an active battle for balcony space. In 1926, Lumberton's Pastime Theatre, the oldest nickelodeon-style theater in Robeson and its primary commercial movie-exhibition site for fifteen years, added a 140-seat balcony. Two years later, the opulent, two-and-a-half storey Carolina Theatre opened a few blocks away, dooming the Pastime to serve thereafter as a second-run house, open intermittently until 1950. Prior to one of its periodic 're-openings' in 1934, the Pastime Theatre advertised a 'balcony of 100 seats exclusively for Indians.'[26] Only a few weeks later, however, the theatre's 'entire balcony' was advertised as being 'for colored'

2.2 The newly reopened Pastime Theater in Lumberton first catered primarily for Indians. From *Robesonian*, 16 August 1934.

2.3 A few weeks later (*Robesonian*, 13 September 1934), the theater changed to cater mainly for African Americans, prompting considerable Indian outrage.

people.[27] Exactly what led to this seating-policy shift remains unclear, but since Indians tended not to be town-dwellers in Robeson County, they represented a less 'regular' or 'weekday' audience. Ernest Hancock's mid-1930s sociological study of the county noted that, according to the 1930 census, only six of the county's 12,405 Indians lived in Lumberton town; in other words, a mere 0.14 per cent of that racial group's population could be considered, in census terms, 'urban.'[28] Therefore, given the relative black and Indian populations living in or near town, switching the balcony orientation from Indian to black was probably an economically sensible step to take, especially if we assume that Indians and blacks could not coexist easily in the same balcony.[29]

Two weeks after the policy shift, the *Robesonian* printed a letter of protest from an Indian named Hansel Holmes:

I was in Lumberton with some other Indians recently and we went to the show at the Pastime theatre, which was opened some time ago as a theatre for the white and Indian people and no one else, but now negroes [sic] are allowed in the indian [sic] department. We are not going in there anymore. The theatre was working up a good trade with Indian people, but we do not want to be mixed up with the negroes. We couldn't even get in that afternoon, for the house was running over with negroes.

We have to work on the farm all through the week and could come to the show only on Saturday, when many of the negroes are in town all week and could go any time they get ready. We don't have to club up with Negroes and we don't have to go to the show at all. We won't go in there any more as long as the negroes are allowed to go.[30]

No responses to this letter appeared in the paper, and we can only speculate as to how different racial groups reacted to Holmes' letter, and what the newspaper publisher's motivations may have been in airing this grievance publicly. Its appearance, however, demonstrates that some Indians, at least, were sufficiently upset by perpetual co-equal treatment with blacks, and disappointed at the failure to attain a more socially acceptable moviegoing prospect, to risk publishing a race-inflected letter in a white-owned newspaper because they were being denied an alternative to the experience they probably faced at the town's other exhibition site, the elegant Carolina Theatre.

Confirmation of the Carolina's policies comes, ironically, through a photo of Walter S. Wishart, the original manager of the Pastime, and a frequent contributor to the local newspaper.[31] Wishart, who had left Lumberton in 1917, announced in late 1931 that he was returning to reopen the old nickelodeon-style Pastime, which had been driven out of business for a time by the opening of the newer Carolina. When this initiative failed, he landed work at the last remaining theatre in town during the Great Depression, where he became the cashier and manager for the Carolina's 'colored' (and, later, its 'colored and Indian') balcony.

This segregated balcony area was accessed by non-whites via a separate door and staircase on the theater's north side, and did not permit access into the whites-only auditorium. Containing wooden partitions that physically separated non-white groups from each another and from white patrons, it represented a tri-racial space in which Indian and black patrons were segregated yet still placed together via facilities that they alone shared. Among the Carolina's exhibition staff, Wishart and the 'white' entrance cashier probably composed the front-line group most directly charged with enforcing racial seating codes and with ensuring that non-white patronage was funnelled up the separate staircase to a tri-sectioned balcony. Nevertheless, possibly because of protests like Holmes', and possibly because the Carolina's side door failed to provide for the 'complete segregation of the races' desired even in the old Opera House, theatre managers in the county understood that the Carolina was not a wholly tri-racial facility, since it had only two entrances and only one ticket office. Having experimented with many different segregationist alternatives, from the exclusion of non-whites (at the Star and other venues), to 'colored' theaters like the A-Mus-U (usually owned and operated by whites), to race-specific shows like the CSPs, and to the relegation of all non-whites to separate and unequal seating facilities, Robeson's exhibitors took what must have seemed to be the next logical step: to provide for complete racial separation in movie exhibition facilities, all the way from the sidewalk to the seats.

Lumberton's Riverside Theater, which opened in 1939, was the exemplar of Robeson's tri-racial exhibition separatism, but it was not the first to experiment with multiple crow's nests, balconies, and ticket-booths. By 1937, renovations at the Red Springs Theatre had spread the house's 475 seats across a main floor and two balconies, while its patrons accessed the theatre through one of its three separate entrances. This tripartheid configuration appeared to pay off. The theatre manager reported that at first 'some of the Indians objected' to the 'separate seating arrangements for the whites, Indians, and Negroes ...', but 'more are beginning to attend.'[32] The renovations in Red Springs may have been a response to the same conditions that had provoked Hansel Holmes' letter about the inadequate balcony at the Pastime.

The renovations at Red Springs and its increasing business with Indians may have been noticed by other exhibitors, particularly those in the town of Rowland. Upon opening the restructured Rowland Theater in 1937, its management proudly explained that the site's configuration included

> three entrances to serve three races. The main entrance, at the front under a new marquee, will admit white patrons to the lower floor, which has 338 seats. Another front entrance will accomodate [sic] Indians, who have a section in the balcony, and a side entrance is provided for negroes occupying another section of the balcony, which has a total of 140 seats.[33]

This provides yet another instance in which a theatre's main entrance and auditorium seated twice as many white patrons as non-whites combined,

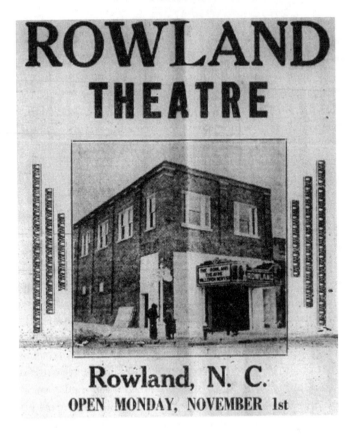

ROWLAND
THEATRE

Rowland, N. C.
OPEN MONDAY, NOVEMBER 1st

2.4 The Rowland Theatre reopened in 1937 with three race-specific entrances. From *Robesonian*, 29 October 1937.

and shuttled all non-whites up to the balcony via separate entrances and staircases.

Theatres in Rowland and Red Springs kept racial groups strictly segregated once they had purchased their tickets, but their ticket booths nevertheless exposed patrons to potential racial mixing. One final development remained: to provide each race with its own ticket booth. That happened in the county's next major theatre project. Completed in April 1939, Lumberton's Riverside Theatre was, as long-time Lumberton lawyer John Campbell remembers, 'designed for this town.' In describing its three ticket booths, news accounts of the opening noted that the 'downstairs of the theatre building will seat approximately 500 patrons, with a gallery on the west side … to seat approximately 250 colored patrons and a gallery on the east side to seat approximately 250 Indians.'[34] In order to educate the public as to how these facilities were to be accessed in an appropriately tri-racial fashion, Riverside management included segregated seating and ticket-pricing information in their advertisements for about two months.

Six months later, however, perhaps because of a boost in out-of-town attendance accompanying the harvest-time crowds unfamiliar with the rules of the house, or possibly because non-whites had attempted to sit in the auditorium, the management found it necessary to remind its patrons of the house's very deliberate human traffic control policies:

The Main Auditorium Is For The Exclusive Use Of Our White Patrons At All Times ...

The Indian Entrance Is To The Right Of The Theatre, And The Colored Entrance Is To The Left.[35]

With the Riverside in place, local theatre managers had finally realized the original Opera House modification goal of 'complete separation of the races.'

In retrospect, we can wonder why the Riverside's management bothered to reaffirm a seating policy that was no doubt common knowledge and increasingly common practice since tripartheidism had become the rule rather than the exception in the region, typified by the Robeson County courthouse's three sets of lavatories and drinking fountains. While many of those tri-segregated facilities and their attendant control mechanisms no longer exist, the movie-houses of Robeson County—oversized public spaces like the Carolina which, along with churches, remain the most architecturally impressive buildings in the region—represent permanent, indelible, and undeniable artifacts of tri-racial segregation. Robeson's movie houses reinforced, rather than challenged, cultural racial codes, even while their owners suffered financially from additional costs in theatre construction and maintenance as they sought to capture as broad-based a patronage as possible.

These tripartheid sites, and the policies they introduced or reified, suggest that exhibition histories need to examine more closely the traces of multicultural and regional difference, and insert them into otherwise dualistic scenarios of racial hegemony and resistance across the broad history of film exhibition and reception studies. Robeson County's example represents a gloomy counterpoint, for instance, to the conclusions drawn by Mary Carbine in her study of the ways in which black Chicagoans co-opted movie exhibition space, resisting cultural elision by incorporating traditional African American entertainment elements into an exhibition experience produced primarily by whites for white consumption.[36]

Chicago and Lumberton were, however, two vastly different places, and no such optimistic tale of cultural resistance can be told of Robesonian

2.5 A race-specific multi-tiered pricing structure accompanies this advertisement from the Riverside Theater for the film *Topper Takes a Trip*. (*Robesonian*, 3 April 1939)

moviegoing. By 1940, everything in Robeson—every social event and public location, from churches and schools to cafés and barbershops, from county homes and prison camps to local shops and county fairs, from medical and dental clinics for children to cemeteries and golf courses, from police and health service personnel to libraries and sports clubs, from public restrooms and telephone directories to 4H and home demonstrations clubs, and from PTAs and Memorial Day committees to beauty pageants and want ads—was segregated, indeed tri-segregated.

This narrative of theatre modifications in Robeson County demonstrates how fully racial ideology determined theatre design there. In her 1994 study of movie theatre architecture, *The Show Starts On the Sidewalk*, Mary Valentine acknowledged that movie theaters represent 'a separate architectural type, distinguished by program, emphasis, imagery, and history; one must read [the movie house] as an architectural type, rooted in popular culture with its own symbolic program.'[37] Robeson County's development of three-entrance theatres reinforcing its tri-racial social code lends Valentine's claim a special resonance. In contrast to the Chicago sites that Carbine describes, it is difficult to imagine how movie houses in Robeson could offer performative racial alternatives to non-white patrons, except for those patrons able and courageous enough to attempt to pass as a member of a racial group with higher social status. These sites fundamentally required a public affirmation of often-painful racial labels, and represented the physical embodiment of a racial dogma developed over centuries in a region that still struggles to negotiate racial difference today. When we consider the lengths to which Robeson's movie houses were modified in order to perpetuate or respond to racial dogma, when we recognize the potential economic and social costs facing each group as they participated in Robeson County's motion-picture exhibition (most obviously the humiliating, second-class experiences endured by blacks and Indians), and when we examine other exhibition histories in areas deeply impacted by racial or ethnic divisions, we must be willing to acknowledge the more disturbing narratives, and their unpleasant implications, alongside those which may flatter liberal-humanist sensibilities.

What is perhaps most remarkable about moviegoing in the Jim Crow South in general, and about Robeson County in particular, is not that non-whites occasionally resisted attending segregated theatres, or that, as in the case of Hansel Holmes, they might have tentatively voiced a public protest over their treatment in them. Given the second-class status that these theatres physically imposed on their non-white patrons through architectural designs that forced them to perform racially defined roles in order to participate in a leisure activity, the wonder is that they attended these exhibition sites at all.

3

The White in the
Race Movie Audience

Jane M. Gaines

I N her recent book, *Dust: The Archive and Cultural History*, British historian
Carolyn Steedman refers to the difficulties of constructing an entire
society from a surviving relic, which in her case is a butter churn.[1] Her
book is an ode to impossibility, a theorization of the conditions of historical
research in which we create a world out of a scrap, make something out of
the nothing that stretches before us when we first enter the archive. The
book is a boon to our resolve, a balm to our frustration. Yet some may
find it disturbing for calling attention to the way that we so confidently
bring into existence a world that never existed, or at least never existed in
exactly the way that we reconstruct it. For all that we can know about it,
our concerted efforts to find more sources to supplement existing sources
can do no more than produce the illusion of a more perfect recreation of
what happened in a past that we will never know.

Influenced by Steedman's slightly heretical but nevertheless charming
and incisive meta-history, I began to think differently about the dog-eared
photocopies of bad microfilm copies of original documents in the George P.
Johnson collection at UCLA that I was then studying, under the assumption
that original documents can tell us something about what for us is the
crucial originatory moment: the moment of reception. In particular, I was
studying the questionnaire forms that Johnson, head of distribution for the
Lincoln Motion Picture Company, had sent to theatre owners and managers
who were likely to rent the Lincoln product, a new kind of feature film for
what was emerging as the 'race film circuit.' With his brother Noble and
several other backers, Johnson had started the company in 1916. By 1918,
when this questionnaire was circulated, they had produced three films: *The
Realization of a Negro's Ambition* (1916), *The Trooper of Troop K* (1916), and

The Law of Nature (1917). A night postal clerk in Omaha, Nebraska, George promoted and booked these titles by day The questionnaire seems to have been designed to assess the competition, to compare methods of advertising, to evaluate the Lincoln service and, ultimately, to push their films. In addition, George Johnson was promoting his brother as an emerging black star who was then being featured in motion pictures produced by Lubin and Universal as well as by the Lincoln Company.

3.1 Lincoln Motion Picture Company distribution survey form (1918) from Palace Theater, Louisville, Kentucky. Source: George P. Johnson Collection, Department of Special Collections, Young Research Library, University of California-Los Angeles.

Analyzing the form filled out with a flourish and returned by A.B. McAfee, general manager of the Palace Theatre in Louisville, Kentucky, I noticed that this theatre, seating 625 people, was on West Walnut St. and that the separate blanks for ownership and management were both filled out 'colored.' Obviously, the Palace was a good Lincoln customer. The theatre had shown *Trooper* and *The Law of Nature* to 'capacity' crowds; *Realization*, on its first run, had experienced a 'good' house, but this improved to 'capacity' on a return engagement. On line 7, where the form politely asked: 'Do you cater to any colored trade?', the respondent was given the options 'partially' and 'entirely.' McAfee responded that 'yes' the theatre did cater to the 'colored trade' and, in the blank by 'partially,' wrote: 'get some whites.' Suddenly, I realized that although I had completed a study of American 'race' movies in the silent era, I had missed something interesting.[2] This one line on an eighty-year-old questionnaire ('get some whites') became the fragment out of which, I began to believe, an entire world could be constructed.

Steedman is right about the 'nothing' from which we create our historical accounts. This is especially the case with the historical spectator whose moviegoing is among the most ephemeral of phenomena to track; whose 1918 dental records might, indeed, be easier to find. Film scholars write about historical spectators from the standpoint of not knowing—and being unlikely *ever* to know—*who* these people actually were. The anonymity of the object of our study, the spectator defined by our statistics, tells us next to nothing. In spite of the certainty of never knowing, I find that I still want to know who it was who in 1918 dared to go into a black movie house to see an all-black cast film. And I do mean 'dared,' since in this chapter I will be writing about the South where, as Gregory A. Waller told us in his seminal study of the earliest African American nickelodeons in Lexington, Kentucky, the taboos against 'intermingling' were the strongest.[3]

Many, of course, will pose the question: why study more white persons, particularly given the impressive record of publication of new research on the African American founders of race movies in this period?[4] The issue of 'why white people' takes on a new meaning when whites begin to thin out in the audience and become anomalous. Situations of this kind underline the fact that research and publication on race in America has over time become strangely segregated. Black studies have been separated from white studies in a way that parallels the segregation of the facilities we have been examining. If truth be told, our research and publication is more segregated than the lives of moviegoers living in the South in the early decades of this century. And what of the companion question about who studies whom, a question that resonates in American studies from within the U.S., where the racial identity of the researcher has been so carefully matched with that of the subjects of study? Once again, Carolyn Steedman has thought through the situation of the historian who seeks tell about those inaccessible others, unreachable across class, race, and time, the historian who wishes to tell 'somebody else's story.'[5] It is an 'obscure desire,' she says, one that 'means you understand—and write—the self through others, who are not like you.'[6] We do resign ourselves to the conditions of the search for others whom we know are nothing like us, but we start, of course, from the premise that we are writing them and not us, even though there is no way to access them except through us. Who I *find* will never be who was *there*, so the burden is on us to ask why it is that we want to find whoever it is that we want to have been there then. And this resolves itself, ultimately, into the question of who it is that we want each other to be at this time in history.

There is one caveat here. Entering into the project of researching the white who went to see race movies, I may have an image of whom I want to find. But this would seem to contradict the entire reason for doing archival research in the first place. As I define it, the reason for doing historical research, the entire rationale for going to so much trouble, is not so much to recreate a world as it is to uncover what I call 'counter-ideological phenomena,' which has the power to change the versions of the world that have historically held consciousness captive. A good example would be Southern historian Jacquelyn Dowd Hall who, some years ago, documented references to the women and children who attended lynchings, a phenomenon that significantly altered our image of the Southern community en masse, and taught us an emphatic lesson about how much we rely upon gender assumptions in the reconstruction of our image of the historical past.[7] The discovery of a significant number of black women who were, for however short a time, managers of all-black theatres, should similarly alert us to the subtle influence of the gender assumptions we all carry.

I would not wish to give the impression that there were no white people in the history of race movies. White people were, in fact, everywhere—as stockholders in the Lincoln and Micheaux Companies, as patrons of white theatres who didn't want to sit next to blacks, as local censors, as theatre owners and managers, and, as Dan Streible tells us, in the case of the black-owned Harlem Theatre in Austin, Texas, as projectionists before the union was integrated.[8] White people seem to have been everywhere except as paying customers for race movies in the seats of black movie houses. There are a few exceptional white supporters such as Harry Gant, Noble Johnson's childhood friend from Colorado Springs, cameraman on the Lincoln Company films, and a few friends also in the race film business, such as Richard J. Norman, owner of the Norman Film Manufacturing

3.2   Noble Johnson and Harry Gant, Lincoln Company cameraman.
Source: George P. Johnson Collection, Department of Special Collections, Young
Research Library, University of California-Los Angeles.

Company in Florida, producer of *The Flying Ace* (1926), and a friendly correspondent of Oscar Micheaux. But whites figure most predominantly as the competition.

As George Johnson's form, with the blank distinction between 'colored' and 'white,' tells us, the distinction between white and black-owned was everything to the race film pioneer. His papers, especially the typescript histories of the Lincoln Company and his brother Noble's career, are full of race designations, 'white' or 'colored' appearing in parentheses before or after the names of various figures, telling this whole history in carefully raced terms. I derive my term, the parenthetical white, from Johnson's practice of pencilling in the distinction. In the early years of both the Micheaux and the Lincoln Company, there was a special category of whites—the white audience who would, the producers believed, see their films. The very notion of 'respectable' entertainment, an exhibitors' code word for films that would appeal to middle-class patrons, perhaps also, by implication in this case, meant films designed to some degree to 'play to whites,' even though these would be the films that never exactly did succeed in playing to a

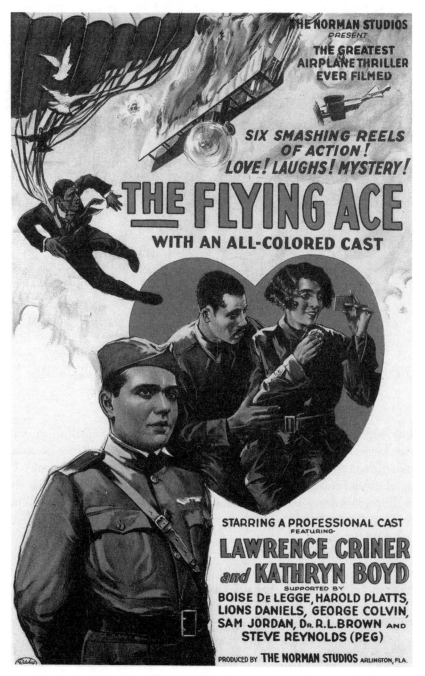

3.3 *The Flying Ace* poster (Norman Manufacturing Company, 1926).
Source: George P. Johnson Collection, Department of Special Collections, Young
Research Library, University of California-Los Angeles.

3.4   The Ebony Motion Picture Company. Source: Library of Congress, Motion
Picture, Broadcasting, and Recorded Sound Division.

white audience. What is remarkable here in the history of film exhibition
is the class of films that never found a segment of their audience because it
was an imaginary or hypothetical audience of receptive white people. For
the white audience that 'race' companies wanted was an audience that they
sought to convert to another point of view—the point of view not of black
people as a whole but of the aspiring, educated, industrious black—the
black middle class.

In her recent book on early black criticism in the black press, Anna
Everett notes Micheaux's 'evangelical approach' to black cinema in these
years. In 1919, he wrote that without cinema produced by race men, 'the
white race will never come to look upon us in a serious light, which
perhaps explains why we are always caricatured in almost all the photoplays
we have even the smallest and most insignificant part in.[9] What I have
elsewhere called the 'facializing mission' of race movies was an attempt to
put sympathetic faces on respectable black characters, to show particularly
the men as honorable in the case of Lincoln, and in the case of Micheaux,
the women also as virtuous.[10] Thus, for example, in the Lincoln production

Law of Nature (1917), which the manager informed George Johnson 'took on like wildfire' at the Palace Theatre in Louisville, Johnson is the father who must rear the couple's baby when his wife is lured to the city.[11]

Both Micheaux and the Johnsons were optimistic that they could break into the white market. Perhaps this optimism was based on George Johnson's early achievement in renting out white theatres in Omaha, Nebraska, and Micheaux's success in selling his books to white farmers in South Dakota and Iowa.[12] Certainly, their early promotional efforts targeted whites. Micheaux, for instance, advertised an ambitious marketing scheme for smaller towns where the existing black film circuit did not reach. He offered to mail advertising heralds for free to every resident listed in the town directory and to advertise in the papers.[13] Yet neither Lincoln nor Micheaux ever penetrated the white market. The Lincoln Company was out of business by 1921 and although Micheaux continued production until 1948, he increasingly produced popular genre films (musicals, urban crime drama) solely for the race movie circuit.

My own position is oddly like that of aspiring race film producers in the late teens and early 1920s. Like them, I want to find those white people who would plunk down their money to see a new phenomenon—black 'uplift' drama. Their approach was aggressive ballyhoo. Mine has to be somewhat more subtle. I have to work back and forth between the spectator I want to find and the traces of the historical spectator who may have been many things but was probably not what I am looking for at all. Thus, I come to one of the other methodological divisions that defines our field—the relation between the empirical and the theoretical spectator.[14] As I work back and forth between the document that points to 'some whites' at the Palace Theatre in Louisville and the parenthetical white, the *white in parenthesis*, I realize that there is something pristine about this formulation of whites identified as white on paper—that is, paper whites. Without referring to any particular people, it seems to encapsulate the race consciousness of the period, exhibiting features of both the theoretical and the empirical. It is abstract enough to refer to all white people yet offering somewhat more precision in the descriptive modifier 'paper,' but the apparent precision turns out to be a further abstraction. A 'white on paper' or a parenthetical white is race, in theory, only in theory. Before encountering the frustrations that I know will follow from not finding, knowing I will never really find, the formulation gives hope in its abstraction as well as its precision. The paper white trail encourages my illusion that I am discovering and not creating the history of people who went to the movies. I am encouraged despite knowing that I will never *really* know 'who they were' and why they went.

Thus painted into a corner, the aggressive researcher takes another tack. When in doubt about the spectator, film scholars know to reconstruct the conditions under which he or she viewed. In this case, the conditions of the reception of race movies in the South would have been qualified by the conditions of Jim Crow rule. The first defining feature of the white race movie paper spectator is that he has transgressed the tawdry spirit of Jim Crow.

The Jim Crow Condition

Segregation in the American South controlled whites as well as blacks. As black exhibitor Clarence Muse observed in his book, *Way Down South*: 'Jim Crow law works both ways in the South and just as colored folks may not mix with whites in places of entertainment, so also whites are prohibited with equal sternness any social intercourse with their darker brethren.'[15] Although whites were prohibited from going to the movies with blacks, there are many indications that they did go. We have no idea whether this was out of defiance or indifference. What we can say is that the system of compartmentalization set up in the Jim Crow South worked because of an internalization of 'one's place' enforced by the ushers and managers who policed the system. More interestingly, the invisible boundaries of time and space conspired to create the perfect illusion of two distinct societies.

This was not, however, without some juggling and sorting. Actually, the films themselves (white Hollywood product as opposed to all-black cast films) worked in combination with theatre seating policies to sort people out. It was never so simple as white films/white theatre, black films/black theatre, however, as the chart I used in order to 'locate' viewers shows:

American Segregation Era Motion Picture Theatre Seating Chart
- whites to all-black cast film in a black theatre—fewer
- whites to white film in a black theatre—few, but the majority of cases in a Jim Crow House
- whites to all-black cast film in a segregated theatre
- whites to white film in the black section (balcony) of a segregated theatre
- blacks who preferred segregated white theatres (ie. who did not want to sit with blacks only)
- blacks who only went to black theatres (preferably owned and managed by blacks)

As Charlene Regester has argued in her work on moviegoing in Durham, North Carolina, the black theatre was a refuge for black audiences who wanted completely to avoid the insults of the separate entrances and the snooty ushers of the segregated white theatres.[16] The Atlanta *Independent*, in 1920, urged patrons to 'Go where you will not be jim-crowed.'[17] What we will need to ask about the white patron who went to the black movie theatre is whether he too sought to escape the Jim Crow condition. The problem here is that the question of this spectator forces us to see how very differently the quarantine worked for the two groups. Although there was enforced separation, whites would not have been legally banned from entrance to a black theatre. Local custom was thought to be quite enough.

As Douglas Gomery observes in one of the most comprehensive overviews of Jim Crow moviegoing so far published, where there were few theatres in a Southern town, facilities were segregated by time.[18] From the notoriety of the 'midnight ramble,' where blacks came in after the white screening, we have come to think that the late night show was the exclusive purview of blacks. Midnight shows in the 1920s, however, were set aside for whites as well as blacks. At the white-owned 81 Theatre in Atlanta, Thursday night was 'whites only.'[19] There is evidence that around 1922, the black-owned Attucks Theatre in Norfolk, Virginia had reserved Friday night for whites to see black-cast films, 'an opportunity for such white people as were interested in colored shows to visit the theatre.'[20]

It goes almost without saying that these Southern theatres were segregated by space. We know about the separate entrances and exits, and the reputation of the 'crow's nest,' 'peanut heaven,' 'buzzard's roost' and 'nigger heaven,' has been well established. What is so striking about the photo 'The Opening Night of the "Rex" Theatre' in Hannibal, Missouri, on 4 April 1912, is the apparent orderliness of the arrangement—the agreement that we sit here and you there. The town pride is on view on this special occasion in which young boys, possibly ushers, wear bootineers and some women wear hats. The white crowd, facing forward, is oblivious to the black patrons in their 'roost.' They share the same film but not the same section of the house, at such a distance from the stage and the center of the house. Blacks recede into facelessness while some whites, those with privileged front row seating, have faces. How innocently they show their faces to the camera. How innocently they had learned their entitlement, the lesson that Lillian Smith described: 'your skin color is a Badge of Innocence which you can wear as vaingloriously as you please because God gave it to you and hence it is right and good. It gives you priorities over colored people everywhere else in the world, and especially those in the South, in matters where you eat, the theatres you go to, the swimming pools you use, jobs, the people you love …'[21]

3.5 Opening Night of the Rex Theater, Hannibal, Missouri (4 April 1912). (*Below*): detail of the balcony. Source: Museum of Modern Art Stills Collection.

In Mark Twain's home town, however, and in other towns and cities in the South, the race experience was not as orderly as the photograph implies.[22] Hannibal, in the formerly slave-holding section of a state that was not entirely slave-holding, was the scene of throbbing tensions and dissatisfactions. New research on interracial mingling in the South suggests the permeability of the boundaries. It is reasonable to assume that the awkward juggling of time and space produced some mistakes. One imagines a sleepy white viewer dozing off during a late film and waking up at midnight to find himself in the black show. Another, enamored of movies in general, would just stay on after 11:00 pm to watch another show. A white might be out of place under cover of dark; what interests me in this is the way in which the dark of the race movie theatre offered the means to express a desire to be out of place.

White Camp/Black Camp

In his introduction to *A Separate Cinema: Fifty Years of Black Cast Posters*, Donald Bogle suggests that Oscar Micheaux talked white Southern theatre managers and owners into showing his films at special matinées or at midnight shows for 'white audiences interested in black camp.'[23] While I have no quarrel with his assertion that black films for white people was a special situation and finding, as we have, the Friday midnight show for whites at the Attucks Theatre in Norfolk, I wonder about his definition of camp. It seems to me that it is white camp that he should be talking about and not black camp. Camp is, of course, always relational, contextual, a question of when and for whom. In Esther Newton's *Mother Camp: Female Impersonators in America* (for me the *locus classicus* of the notion of camp), incongruity, theatricality, and humor define camp.[24] Camp 'inheres' not in the thing itself or even in the person, but in the 'tension' between person and thing, and always in relation to context.

So the problem is one of understanding at what point and for whom all-black cast movies become camp. In the early decades of the century, the situation of black films might seem to generate a multiplicity of incongruities, beginning with the very idea of blacks being larger than life on screen, filling out all of the roles. For blacks to be seen doing the things that white people do—blacks as cowboys, doctors, dentists, and aviators, blacks in unimaginable situations and circumstances—is incongruous (to whites), unimaginable because as yet unimagined by a Jim Crow society. Camp is about substitutions, and blacks not in their place is camp. What race movie pioneers saw as 'just like' might have been seen by incredulous whites as something out of place.

71

The 'when' question in relation to the camp reception of race movies is one for present-day audiences who, in my experience, have responded in distinctly different ways, depending on their assumed racial make up. Predominantly black audiences find more things to laugh at in race movies from the silent era than white audiences, perhaps because they have both more distance and more knowledge than whites. That is, they have more inside knowledge, and this contributes to the distance, the knowledge-of-black culture effect producing the 'collision of interpretations' that Noël Carroll has theorized as the production of humour.[25] But let us look at the production of humor question historically. The bane of the existence of the race movie 'uplifters' were, of course, the 'chicken licking' black comedies, programmed so often and so offensively (to the black press) by whites who owned and/or managed black theatres. It is significant that the Lincoln Company produced no comedies and that Micheaux did not add comedy until the sound era. Jacqueline Stewart discusses what she calls the 'Black people are funny' assumption, epitomized by white-owned Ebony Pictures and apparently endemic among white exhibitors who programmed black theatres.[26] We can also reverse this assumption, however, by asking how white people were funny to those blacks who flocked to see the white fare in race movie theatres—almost always second run features and action pictures. In my new formulation, black camp is not what 'interested' whites saw at midnight in Norfolk in 1922. They saw 'white camp' (camp for white folks). Black camp—camp for black people—involves blacks looking at white movies and thinking 'what fools these white folks be.' While white audiences looking at Ebony Pictures comedies were encouraged to take a 'what fools these black folks be' position, white audiences looking at race ('uplift') movies might, given a 'white camp' sensibility, take a different position, something like 'what fools these black folks are making of whites.' This is, of course, given the white situations which these films dramatized—and also given a sense of the incongruity of blacks in white circumstances during this era of separation.

Eric Lott's study of black face minstrelsy is among the most influential work done in American Studies on the white working-class reception of all-black entertainment. It is perhaps the doubleness of his thesis in *Love and Theft* that has produced its utility, for the mixture of fascination, envy, and self-derision he describes serves many purposes, not to mention the welcome importation of a British cultural studies model into American Studies.[27] Lott's assertion that white working-class people did not live so comfortably with their whiteness, after all, makes it possible to imagine a spectator whose dissatisfaction verged on revolt and thus whose attraction to race movies might just be not that they were black but that they were not-white.[28]

But Lott's thesis requires significant revision in its application to silent film reception, and not just because race movies were never the popular phenomenon that minstrelsy had been in the previous century. There are two other caveats: Firstly, there is the wish-fulfilment behind the phenomenon of the White Negro that so interests Lott, and builds to a degree on Norman Mailer's understanding of the hipster who 'had absorbed the existential synapses of the Negro' and was so envious of black male sexuality.[29] Although the phenomenon of jazz clarinetist Mezz Mezzrow, who crossed over to black society as much as he could, initially because he felt that he never really fit into white society, offers a preferable example, even here, the White Negro seems too much of an urbanite and not native to the American South.[30] It remains for us to discover a different kind of race traitor, a concept opened up by new studies in white cultural recalcitrance such as Mab Segret's work on race traitors.[31]

The second caveat is that we would want to factor in the phenomenon of movies (still) as an attraction in and of themselves, particularly in the early part of the twentieth century. Beyond the minstrelsy effect, we would want to look at the lure of the movies which brought wonders never before seen to small towns as well as larger cities in the South. We would want to look at a double attraction: the technology that made things move and people doing things on the screen that they were not seen to do in everyday life. (That is, for whites, blacks were not seen—yet—as aviators or detectives.) This second part of the attraction, the things previously unseen part, leads me to my modification of Lott's 'fascination,' to a spectator motivated by 'interest,' a curiously curious person, about which we know only one thing: He was a night owl.

Cross-Race Curiosity

New work on the history of curiosity has rescued it from the low opinion in which it has been held in more traditional humanities research. The features of this theory allow us to take curiosity-seekers seriously, to listen to their discontent, to understand their appetite for empirical phenomena, and to appreciate the way that they might themselves become curiosities.

There would be, argues Barbara Benedict, a visual dimension to the transgression.[32] Married to the idea of cinema's curious spectator, this visual transgressor would have been someone who dared to look and wished for more where daring to look means wanting things to be different—perhaps without even knowing it.[33] The curious spectator is one whose empirical appetite leads him to seek out counter-ideological phenomena—although this is, of course, our term, not his.

To go to see a race movie in the South in the 1910s, one would have to be sufficiently curious about black life to cross town into the wrong neighborhood, perhaps under cover of night. One had to dare to be in the wrong place and to dare to look at the wrong things on the screen. The crossing-over of this particular white spectator was almost certainly not systematic enough to constitute what the race movie pioneers hoped for: a cross-over audience. This dream would not become a reality for several decades Not until the advent of race records would we see the phenomenon of a popular culture performed by blacks and first popular with them being picked up by white consumers.[34] Thus, I want to stress the isolation of the phenomenon that interests us—a one time crossing, perhaps, maybe not followed by another. For the phenomenon of genuine fandom we would need to look at genres and stars. Discussing a somewhat later period, after the advent of sound, Arthur Knight suggests that the attraction of all-black cast musical films for whites was that of 'blacks as musical,' a popularity expressed as a preference for the genre over the black stars of the genre.[35] Although the existing literature suggests that the first cross-over black star was Sydney Poitier, my sense is that we need to look much earlier.

3.6 Noble Johnson, early 'cross-over' star. Source: George P. Johnson Collection, Department of Special Collections, Young Research Library, University of California-Los Angeles.

74

We may, in fact, need to look at the aborted 'cross-over' stardom of Noble Johnson, hints of which are there in the 1918 survey. At the white-owned Alamo in Washington, DC, where the audience was 'partially' white and where *The Law of Nature*, the *Trooper of Troop K* and *The Realization of a Negro's Ambition* had done 'BIG' business, Noble Johnson was identified as 'the one best bet.' Although I have no evidence of the relative popularity of the Universal serials in which Johnson first starred, it is clear that films such as *The Red Ace* and the eighteen-episode *The Bull's Eye* (1918) were marketed to a predominantly white audience, with the black audience an added bonus following Johnson's discovery by owners of black theatres, who then advertised his performances in the black press. Pearl Bowser and Louise Spence note this concerted effort to find black actors in white films, producing them as stars through advertising even when they had minor parts. Eddie Polo might have been the star of *The Bull's Eye*, but when it played at the white-owned Owl Theatre in Chicago in 1918, the theatre ran an ad in the *Chicago Defender*: 'COME AND SEE THE RACE'S DAREDEVIL MOVIE STAR.'[36] Indeed, one of the reasons for Noble Johnson's forced resignation from the Lincoln Company in 1918 had to do with an early short-sightedness about the cross-over effect on the part of exhibitors who thought that his appearance in Lincoln Company films hurt the business they were doing with the Universal serials.[37] In this short period, roughly 1916 to 1918, we may find that Noble Johnson exemplified an early kind of cross-over where white as well as black fans followed a star from white product to black product and back again.

I hope here to have dramatized the position we find ourselves in, between the theoretical attraction of the cultural studies paradigm with its challenge to the system and the industry history that must find what it finds. To add to our challenge there is the inevitability of always finding who we want to find, invariably what we want each other to be at any time in history. Despite this, and as an antidote to it, let there be no detail too inconsequential in our attempts to tell a story that we can never completely tell. Even after we determine *that* people went to the movies we may still have no idea why they went and what they did with what they saw. As for the white who went to race movies, I never did find him. Let me correct this. I did find one, but I'm not sure that he counts. At least, he doesn't quite fit my theoretical profile of the curious spectator, the race traitor who spontaneously learns to be critical of white culture at the juncture of two cultures: as a white watching race movies with an all-black audience. And this is to demonstrate the way in which our empirical spectator is supplemented by, eclipsed by, and even may come to be supplanted by a theoretical one.

4

'Sundays in Norfolk'

Toward a Protestant Utopia Through Film Exhibition in Norfolk, Virginia, 1910–1920

Terry Lindvall

O N 5 May 1916, *Variety* reported that evangelist Billy Sunday's arrival in Kansas City for a seven-week revival meeting had had an immediate economic impact on local picture houses: 'His opening sermon drew an audience of 37,000, while the theaters reported a slump in attendance.'[1] A similar assault on movie attendance occurred later the same year in Boston, where Sunday drew 54,000 to the Tabernacle on his first day, and *Variety* lamented that he was to be around for ten weeks.[2] Well into the 1920s, *Variety* frequently reported the baleful effect that evangelical missions led by preachers 'of the Billy Sunday type' had on movie attendance.[3]

Sunday was, however, not only a symbol of the apparent competition between moving pictures and mainstream, conservative Protestants. He was also a remarkable indicator of an emerging symbiosis between them. In both the style and structure of his own performances, and in his well-publicized camaraderie with Hollywood celebrities, the conservative, saloon-fighting, former baseball star provided middle-class Protestants with a demonstration of how to embrace the new technology's blend of entertainment, edification and uplift. Sunday directly engaged the moving picture industry, both as a consultant and as a moral guide for those who were hesitant to frequent theaters. His embrace of movies as worthwhile amusements stood in sharp contrast to his condemnation of the saloon, the dance hall and 'the rottenness … on the stage.'[4] In several sermons, he declared that movies were much more acceptable to Christians than the legitimate theaters which had been corrupted by their content. The moving picture trade establishment

4.1 Billy Sunday not only endorsed motion pictures, he appeared in one. Courtesy of Library of Congress (*Motion Picture News* 11:9, 6 March 1915, p. 60).

The World's Renowned Evangelist

THE REV. BILLY SUNDAY

See Him in Motion Pictures

ONE SOLID REEL
LIFE THROBBING ACTIONS
Each gesture appropriate to his striking sayings

The Billy Sundaygrams have reformed thousands
The livest Reel you have shown on your screen.

Block One and Three Sheets
WRITE OR WIRE FOR TERRITORY
IT'S GOING FAST!

LEWIS-WOLFF CO., 110 West 40 St., New York

noted his support as early as 1912. In a *Motion Picture News* column, reviewer William Lord Wright listed several things to be grateful for during that Thanksgiving season. Topping the list was 'that evangelist Billy Sunday says picture shows are all right.'[5]

As historian John Tibbetts has suggested, Billy Sunday and the movie industry 'preached' to the same audience of the emerging, American middle class.[6] William McLoughlin, one of Sunday's biographers, described a typical member of this audience as being married with children, commuting by car to work, spending leisure time at his lodge meetings, playing cards, drinking an occasional glass of beer, and going to church regularly.[7] Courted by the movie industry, this same audience financed the transition from the nickelodeon to the middle-class movie house of the 1910s and 1920s through their ticket purchases.[8]

Norfolk's local exhibition conditions support the arguments made by Robert C. Allen and Russell Merritt for the existence of a bourgeois audience actively attending nickelodeons before 1910.[9] In 1908, Jake and Otto Wells, proprietors of the most extensive film exhibition circuit in the South, moved from Richmond to base their exhibition operation in Norfolk. Viewed by the local press as upstanding and socially involved citizens, they became a vital part of the middle and upper classes that brought together social respectability and moviegoing.[10] The management of the Colonial, a vaudeville and moving picture theater, took out an advertisement in 1909 that thanked the 'press, the public and members of the pulpit' who had been 'good enough to openly compliment the character of our entertainment, to commend its worth and merit and to comment with co-operative spirit upon the class and volume of our patronage.'[11] While such self-promotion could be an engaging strategy for attracting such an audience, Norfolk's theatres had already drawn considerable numbers of religious leaders and their congregations into their environs, and apart from periodical upheavals regarding amusements on the Sabbath, churches in Norfolk enjoyed a remarkably accommodating relationship with the theaters.

Studies of the reception of silent American cinema have generally focused on the social and economic constitution of movie audiences, particularly those in urban centers. An emphasis on issues of class, race and gender has been essential in identifying the contours of early movie exhibition practices. A key variable missing from these studies, however, has been religion, which was a determining factor in shaping the everyday experiences of middle-class American audiences. In a 1932 study on the Protestant church and moviegoing, University of Idaho Professor Carl D. Wells articulated the contrast between these two institutions when he noted that 'the church has an immediate *rural* heritage while the movie has a distinct *urban* heritage.'[12] A contextual history of film must acknowledge the dominance of Protestant perspectives on amusements, education, and social life in the popular discourse of the silent film era.[13] Local newspapers, particularly in rural communities, testify to the impact of such concerns. The nature of cinematic exhibition in Norfolk, Virginia, for example, was in large part constituted by religious communities and religious sensibilities.

In contrast to the prevailing historical accounts that have suggested that the 'most vociferous opponents of moving pictures were usually Protestant clergymen,' I shall argue that in smaller cities like Norfolk the churches practiced a vibrant, progressive attitude toward the cinema in the period from 1906 to 1926, and sought to harness the potential of filmmaking for religious ends.[14] In doing so, I hope to show not only that the boundaries of spectator participation expanded into the religious realm, but that the Church was itself a site of contested views about the nature and role of film in the life and health of religious communities.

In 1910, Norfolk was a prospering, progressive Mid-Atlantic community of over 67,000 citizens. It was a busy seaport city, a thriving small metropolis that provided an all-year playground. Much like Gregory Waller's description of Lexington, Kentucky, Norfolk was a southern city in temperament and attitudes, marked by a spirit of boosterism, a substantial African American community (37 per cent of the population was black), and a long-standing sense of being 'southern.'[15] By 1920 the population had doubled, while the ratio of whites to blacks remained constant.[16] Known as the economic and cultural 'gateway to the South,' Norfolk was strategically situated, both geographically and socially, to welcome the novelty of nickel madness. As first and foremost a 'Navy town,' however, Norfolk was also less flatteringly known as 'the City of Vice' and 'the wickedest city in the US.' In a 1919 meeting considering the legislation of Sunday entertainments, one speaker reminded the city council that because Norfolk was 'a seaport town,' it faced 'conditions that few other American cities had to contend with,' namely the saloons and brothels that served the naval base.[17] At the end of the nineteenth century, Norfolk contained an area known as 'Hell's Half-Acre' which spawned over 200 saloons, gambling parlors, brothels, and 'social clubs.'[18] In this community, moving pictures offered a conspicuously more virtuous alternative to less wholesome amusements provided for young sailors away from the moral constraints of home.

A significantly Protestant community, Norfolk hosted twelve white and twenty-three 'colored' Baptist churches, eleven Episcopal churches and missions, fifteen Methodist churches, nine Presbyterian churches and congregations, and twelve 'colored' Methodist Episcopal churches in 1910. Alongside three Roman Catholic churches and four Jewish congregations, several other smaller Protestant sects existed. By 1920 the Baptists had tripled the number of their houses of worship, the Methodist doubled theirs, and other new congregations had appeared.[19] Many of the mainline churches joined forces through the ecumenical Church Federation of Norfolk to coordinate the city's religious and moral concerns, including Sabbath showings and the ministry to military personnel.[20] Often joining them in dealing with social issues was the elite colored Interdenominational Ministers' Meeting, whose concerns for uplift paralleled the Church Federation.

Norfolk's social elite, and particularly its religious leaders, championed the role of film in helping to stem a tide of what they saw as true wickedness. In 1894, itinerant Prohibition preacher Sam Small launched a reform crusade against vice-ridden neighborhoods and corrupt local government. With the help of both black and white associations of the Women's Christian Temperance Union (WCTU), Small and the reformers castigated Norfolk's city council, police corruption, and inadequate school system, claiming that it was the only city in the nation with a population over 5000 to have no high school, while eighty-one brothels were allowed to operate within 'the circle of the shadow of one church spire' alone.[21] Small's old-fashioned religious revivals, heavily spiced with politics, reportedly 'drove his audiences at the Academy of Music theatre into righteous frenzy,' and led the Drys into control of the city.

The location of Small's revival in the Academy theatre was a precursor to the growing collaboration of churches and the movie theaters. As historian Charles Musser observed of the early days of the moving pictures, one 'could be a religious person and not only go to a vaudeville house, but one could even find religious inspiration there.'[22] In Norfolk, one was even likely to

4.2 Judged by their formal attire in this cartoon, members of the social elite did attend motion pictures. T.E. Powers, 'Our Moving Pictures,' *The Virginian Pilot*, 10 July 1910, p. 29.

worship in such houses. Throughout the period, church leaders appropriated movie theatres for their own purposes, adapting the auditoria of theatres for religious ends, and, to a degree, sanctifying the sites. Unlike the local Aldermen, who complained of the nuisance of the use of phonographs for attracting attention to the moving picture theatres on the main streets of the city, Norfolk's clergy seemed to embrace the motion picture as a potentially positive alternative to the city's more insidious vices.[23] As Tom Gunning has observed, American cinema's transition from 'attractions' to narrative involved an engagement with codes of morality and a 'conscious movement into a realm of moral discourse.'[24]

Secular and sacred cultures were remarkably intertwined during the early part of the twentieth century. As early as 1906, ministers and exhibitors in Norfolk were making common cause together: theaters and churches frequently exchanged buildings in forging a mutually beneficial relationship. Under the auspices of the Church Federation of Norfolk, various religious services and social actions were held in local theatres between 1911 and 1921.[25] Like opera houses at the end of the nineteenth century, several of

4.3   The Granby Family Theatre in Norfolk (1907). Courtesy of Sergeant Memorial
Archives. Norfolk Kirn Public Library.

the theaters, especially the Academy of Music, the Granby, the American, the Colonial, and the newly constructed Wells Theater (1912), provided the largest and most commodious auditoria in the city. As such they became the main venues for everything from high school graduations to special religious events, and it was not unusual for revivalists and preachers to proclaim their messages at the best auditoria in the city.

During the season of Lent, exhibitors usually noted a slump in attendance, as church-goers gave up various leisurely activities and pleasures such as the movies.[26] Those denominations such as the Episcopalians and Lutherans that celebrated Lent, however, conducted noonday services for businessmen at the Granby and American theatres, reportedly drawing

4.4 The American Theatre (1913). Courtesy of Sergeant Memorial Archives. Norfolk Kirn Public Library.

capacity crowds.[27] The Brotherhood of St. Andrew recruited prominent speakers, such as the Rt. Rev. A.M. Randolph of the Diocese of Southern Virginia, to address the male business community at the noon devotions in the Granby, considering it 'advisable to obtain a larger auditorium than that used heretofore.'[28] Exhibitors seemed to realize that good public relations during holy seasons would bear fruit in terms of future attendance.[29]

The theatrical venues attracted audiences not only because of their spacious roominess, but also because of the dramatic backdrop they provided for stirring or sensational sermons. In 1918, the itinerant evangelist C.E. Heard of New York City intrigued his audience with his strategically timed lecture at the American Theatre on 'The Fall of Babylon' soon after D.W. Griffith's *Intolerance* had played at the theatre.[30] Seats were free and he promised to take no collections. Evangelist Irwin D. Richardson also appeared at the Colonial to speak on how the Great War was predicted in biblical prophecy.[31] Across the Elizabeth River in 1911, Pastor William Burleigh of the Park View Christ Church preached on 'The Sins of Portsmouth, and How To Cure Them' at the Orpheum Theatre.[32]

Churches often adopted theatrical methods to attract worshipers, even with 'posters advertising services at some hall or theatre,' and others 'luring non-churchgoers' through illustrated sermons.[33] Not only did advertisements for the theaters appear on the same pages as church news, but theaters also advertised that they were sites for religious activities. In 1915, the Crosman Theater announced that the Rev. Frank Pratt would speak Sunday nights on such themes as 'The Way Our Bible Came to Us.' The Arcade promoted Salvation Army evangelists, like Colonel John Dean who traveled to Norfolk to lecture on crooked women and purity of living, while a citywide Baptist revival occurred in the 'sacred' halls of the Majestic theater, where the union services 'were marked by intense feeling and deep spiritual power.'[34] After their initial success, the revival meetings were relocated to the First Baptist church, while the Majestic provided a venue for the Norfolk colored Baptist conference's 'simultaneous campaign for the uplift and betterment of its race.'[35]

Co-operation between church and theater even extended to conservative evangelistic meetings and moral uplift. In 1908, Rev. Joseph Rennie preached on 'If Not Christ—Whom? Or What?' at the Wonderland theater while the theme of Rev. G.E. Booker from the Y.M.C.A. and Epworth Methodist was 'Self-Control.'[36] The same year, the proprietor of Barton's Theatre permitted a fiery evangelist, Mr. Asher, to conduct services in his variety theater:

This place of amusement, known to Norfolk citizens as a variety house, where questionable women sing and others perform and allow men to buy them drinks, was filled last night not by the usual type of citizens that patronize the place, but by some of the best and most prominent men in town. Up in the boxes ordinarily used as a place where drinks are served ... were gathered prominent citizens and the women who sat beside them knelt in prayer and joined in the singing of religious songs and hymns. It was a joyful sight to see every man and every woman kneel for ten minutes on the dirty floor of this same place and beg God's forgiveness for sin and promise to mend their lives.

About forty men signed coupons declaring their intention of becoming church members. Even James M. Barton, the proprietor, had his hands uplifted, declaring that he would 'get out of this business' of salooning.[37]
Protestants were not the only ones to cooperate with the local theaters. Roman Catholics promoted a St. Vincent de Paul Conference at the Victory Theatre, with proceeds going to the unfortunate, 'so that persons attending this show can feel that a part of their admission price paid will go towards relieving need and distress in Norfolk.'[38] Mayor Albert L. Roper joined Otto Wells and the elite of Norfolk in a mass meeting at the Colonial theatre to raise money for Starving Children in the European Relief Fund.[39] Not all civic events involved the exhibition of pictures. At the American Theatre, S. Frankel held what was called the first Zionist Meeting in Norfolk while the Young Men's Hebrew Association congregated at the Colonial.[40]
Many Norfolk churches incorporated cinema into their evangelism, instruction and worship. As historian Kathy Fuller has pointed out, traveling exhibitors such as Lyman Howe gained the imprimatur of churches and other respectable social institutions to promote their wares, and Norfolk was no exception.[41] As early as February 1906, the conservative South Street Baptist Church announced that it was exhibiting Edison Moving Pictures, charging adults twenty-five cents and children fifteen cents.[42] Other churches followed a tradition of using illustrated sermons with stereopticons, usually accompanied by hymn singing.[43] *The Passion Play*, the latest New York 'spectacular sensation ... from the hands of the finest artists of France,' was presented as early as 1907 to crowded houses at the Lyceum Theatre, with local baritone soloist, C.S. Carr, rendering hymns as accompaniment.[44] When a film of the Oberammergau Passion Play was advertised that season by the Colonial Theatre as 'Sacred Drama,' audiences were assured that there is 'nothing in this grand performance that will be sacrilegious or irreverent, or any pictures presented offensive to any Christians of any denomination.'[45]
Missionary pictures were especially appealing, combining the biblical injunction of the Great Commission with the novelty of the travelogue.[46] In 1908 the Memorial Methodist Church coordinated with social ministries to present films on preventing bubonic plague, fever and other 'dreaded maladies.'[47] Two years later, the Disciples of Christ Church endorsed the moving picture as a means to enable the church to understand the 'heathen rites' of people it was evangelizing, when films secured by the Foreign Christian Missionary Society were shown as part of a church lecture on

'Strange People of Many Lands.'[48] Dr. Adams at the Freemason Church of Christ showed moving pictures 'portraying in a vivid manner the manners customs and habits of the inhabitants of the heathen world, showing how they had been brought under the saving and sanctifying influences of the Gospel of Christ and the number of preachers, doctors and professors have been sent out by our missionary, who were converts to the Christian faith. Some of these have been converted from cannibalism.'[49]

A 1914 newspaper advertising campaign admonishing readers to 'Go to Church Sunday' was designed not to promote church attendance but to prepare the religious community for the discovery of a series of religious films produced by the International Bible Students' Association, telling the 'Story of the Creation.' Under the banner of 'Using Motion Pictures to Save Souls,' Otto Wells coordinated this free, four-week Sunday program at the New Wells theatre, with special appeals to the church community. The spectacle of 'colored lantern slides, tinted moving pictures and synchronized phonographic lectures' sought to 'harmonize science, history and the Scriptures [in] a very plausible manner.'[50] Its clerical sponsor, Charles Taze Russell, believed that he had divine sanction for visual communication through the Bible's use of 'parables and in the symbols of Revelation, which are word pictures.' Russell was one of many members of the clergy who argued that that within a few years high school educators would be using film to bring general knowledge of religious truth to all people with the 'greatest efficiency.'[51]

The success of the Creation series at the Wells helped to generate interest in the churches' using films 'for evangelism, outreach, and community service.' In 1914, the Calvary Baptist Church exhibited 'Sacred films on Sunday nights,' such as *Queen Esther* or *Joseph of Egypt*, in what they claimed was a 'first in the South.'[52] The church fully approved its use 'for evangelism, outreach, and community service, a pattern successfully tested by churches in Chicago and New York City.'[53] While local Blue Laws forbade theaters from exhibiting their films on Sundays, the Cumberland Street Methodist Church announced in February 1916 that it would show moving pictures illustrating religious subjects at its Wednesday evening services 'for some time to come.'[54] The same week, the Church of Christ, South Norfolk, announced that on Sunday night, 'in connection with the services, feature films will be shown depicting the Life of Our Saviour,' explaining that 'while this is a new departure in church worship in the East, the feature films are being widely used in the West, and are meeting with popular favor.'[55]

The Christ and St. Luke's Episcopal Church, built in 1909–10, installed a Moviegraph Stand and projector, along with a screening auditorium on its upper floors, to explore how moving pictures might preach messages.[56] The parish house of Christ Episcopal Church, opened in December 1919, had a large auditorium with a fully equipped moving picture booth and a seating capacity of about 500 on its top floor.[57] Methodist churches followed recommendations set down by the 1919 Centennial Conference in Ohio and incorporated 'attractive programs' for its series of Friday evening community entertainments given in their churches.[58] Interspersed with songs and stories were Ford Weekly motion pictures, Burton Holmes travelogues, Bray Pictographs and odd comedy pieces like 'Honeymooning on $18.75' and ice cream socials. Dr. E.L. Bain often would add a seven-minute talk, with Mrs. Bain telling the children the stories. Inspired by his neighbor's experiment the year before, the First Christian Church inaugurated its own 'annual open air movies' out on the church lawn under the stars. The Greek Orthodox Church conducted their services at the Arcade theatre, hosting a viewing of *The Life of Moses*, as a means for both religious instruction and civic sponsorship.[59] Under the auspices of the Church Federation of Norfolk and Roman Catholic Organizations, churches in Norfolk had undertaken an active moving picture program by 1920.[60] What is significant about the variety of lectures and sacred concerts at the various theatres was a pervasive sense that theatres enhanced the quality of life and virtue in the community. If one could sing the Messiah, hear an evangelistic sermon or attend charity benefits in a theater, then perhaps other activities in the same place were not too profane.[61]

Religious leaders such as the Reverend Luther Tesh envisioned the spiritual opportunities that film would provide for the church, arguing that either the 'Church or Devil [would] … Entertain [the] Young of This Century,' and that 'If the people of God do not furnish that entertainment, the devil will.' The real question, Tesh and others believed, was who would commandeer the available technology and sundry means to entertain and instruct youth.[62] Movies frequently provided didactic texts for local ministers. Moving picture dramas on the evils of drinking and the problem of the fallen woman took on local significance in the context of Norfolk's struggles with saloons and prostitution, as ministers would use the films as material for their sermons.[63] In 1914, Methodist minister J.A. Thomas used movies as part of his sermon attacking the saloon.[64] By enlisting ministerial support for 'social dramas,' exhibitors could inoculate themselves against charges that they were merely appealing to prurient interests. In 1917, for example, the Rev. Thomas B. Gregory praised *Idle Wives* for being 'true to nature, men and women as they actually are in the world. *Idle Wives* takes no text but it preaches a sermon greater than any that was ever heard in a pulpit.'[65] A cultural alliance between exhibitors, like the Wells brothers, and various Protestant ministers developed, enabling them to pit their ideal of uplifting and wholesome entertainment against exploitative alternatives. In February 1916, when Norfolk was again seeking to clean up its suspect streets, the Colonial Theatre focused attention on the plight of 'these unfortunates,' the 'magdalenes.'[66]

In 1918, Rev. H.R.L. Shephard declared that the 'way in which the cinema might be used for benefiting lost people is perfectly amazing to anyone who has thought at all.'[67] Films such as *The Wanderer* and George Loane Tucker's *The Miracle Man*, both bringing 'uplift,' took Norfolk by storm in 1919.[68] Such sermonic photodramas were viewed as a way of drawing people to church. Some argued that 'one of the developments of the future will be the church cinema ... where such films as *The Miracle Man* or *The Sign of the Cross* are exhibited in churches.'[69] In 1921 Lois Weber's *The Blot*, a film addressing the pitiful wages of teachers and preachers, received high praise when it was shown at the Granby.[70] An invitation to a private showing was sent to all the lawyers, doctors, preachers, school teachers, and city officials as an act of community service: 'Throughout the story moves the pity-impelling figure of a threadbare young minister of the gospel, hopelessly underpaid and hopelessly in love with America.'[71] Its central message of the need for increased pay for poor clergy and educators did not hurt the theaters' campaign for positive public relations. Clerical support was not restricted to dramas of uplift. In 1923, Methodist Episcopal Reverend B.G. Houghton sent Harold Lloyd a handbill showing himself playing a Lloyd picture whenever his church gave an entertainment, and informing Lloyd that 'we are using considerable of your pictures.'[72]

Whatever rhetorical fire sparked from church folk in Norfolk during the first two decades of the twentieth century, it was rarely ignited by issues of censorship. Near the end of the 1910s, the citizens of Norfolk noted that their neighbors in North Carolina were considering censorship but, considering themselves more sophisticated, resisted it themselves.[73] Incendiary debate over movies and over the social habit of going to the movies did not fully materialize until the early 1920s, when both the modernist/fundamentalist divorce in theology and numerous Hollywood scandals occurred.[74] What did stir the ire of the Norfolk faithful during cinema's first two decades, however, was the national issue of Sunday moving-picture exhibitions, an issue rooted in an objection to Sunday being exploited as anything other than a sacred day of rest.[75] The resulting Blue Laws were attempts to exert religious influence over social and economic relations in towns throughout the country, especially in the South. As the early trade journals and historians have documented, Sabbatarian campaigns focused on protecting Protestant concepts of Sunday against the encroachment of amusements.[76]

In the year of cinema's invention as a public amusement, Bishops of the Episcopal Church felt compelled to publish their view that the day of rest and worship 'cannot be disturbed without grave evils to the individual and the family, to society and the State.'[77] Similar sentiments were expressed a decade later by Methodist minister John Wesley Hill, who complained that 'the red laws of riot, carnival and immorality' had supplanted 'the blue laws of Puritanism.'[78] The often strident, consistently unyielding call for a 'Blue Sunday' underlay almost all local religious objections to the cinema.[79] Voicing the sentiments of the Methodist churches in Norfolk in 1910, preachers issued a pastoral address on behalf of their female constituency, deploring 'growing tendencies to worldliness.' They called on other Methodists 'to refrain from all participation in theatre-going and card-playing, Sabbath desecration, and like worldly practices.' The Norfolk conference of the M.E. Church condemned what they saw as the creeping growth of 'worldly amusements' that desecrated the Sabbath. Their emphasis was clearly on the need to protect the sanctity of the Lord's Day, rather than on any religious opposition to cinema as such.[80] Norfolk's religious community rarely protested the apparatus or content of moving-pictures. Even when a controversial film like *Traffic in Souls* (1914) appeared, it was framed as a 'modern movie melodrama' with a salutary 'moral lesson' that particularly 'prudish' New York censors had sought to suppress. In fact, a Norfolk critic found it ironic that the film had 'attained considerable free advertising on the strength of the New York censors' action in forbidding the presentation.'[81]

The prime object of Methodists in promoting the Christian Sabbath in Norfolk was to educate public sentiment in 'bringing Sunday work down to the minimum of mercy and necessity, checking the Sunday amusements and securing as great and thoughtful a day as possible.'[82] Even as nickelodeons were proliferating in the Norfolk area, judges and politicians were joining clergy in warning against all kinds of Sabbath breaking. At the end of the second decade of the century, Presbyterians and Baptists joined with Methodists to affirm their stance against Sunday film showings. A Presbyterian pastor, ironically speaking at the Colonial Theatre, declared that 'The law of the Sabbath was written in the statute book of Almighty God, Himself, and who shall dare to abrogate it.'[83] The same day, Rev. Sparks W. Melton, pastor of the Freemason Street Baptist Church, spoke resolutely against opening picture shows in Norfolk on Sundays, condemning the movement in no uncertain terms.[84] In 1919, Rev. Frank Robertson warned that 'The project to throw open the doors of the theatres may possibly conceal an ulterior design. If we let the bars down to provide entertainment for the service men, have we any assurance that things will not gradually widen until the first thing we know we shall have a continental Sunday.' A principal fear was that moviegoing would become a commercial 'wedge' for a variety of amusement activities on Sunday. According to Robertson, the real purpose of Sunday showings was not to provide local service men with entertainment, but 'to provide commercialism with a chance to "pillage" on the Sabbath. They have six days in which to make money, ... and if they can't make enough on those days they ought to go out of business.'[85] While, as Charles Musser has pointed out, some exhibitors really did view 'religious subjects as a crafty device to evade Sunday blue laws,' the fact that churches had been using theaters for Sunday schools and special educational and revival services complicated the clergy's attitude toward the possibilities of exhibiting religious and educational films for soldiers and sailors.[86]

Since movies were generally seen as a source of virtuous enlightenment, the issue did not concern the moral vice of moving pictures, but whether the Sabbath would be kept holy. By 1912, a survey of Ministers of the Methodist Episcopal Church found that two-thirds of them went to the theaters without regarding it as being sinful. They felt that 'John Wesley's injunction leaving the amusement question to the conscience of individuals was the wisest regulation for Americans of the twentieth century.'[87] In 1920 one minister expressed the view that women parishioners preferred not to hear sermons delivered against 'modern shows because the majority of them probably like to go.'[88] For Norfolk clergy, however, an overriding problem was how to minister to the military personnel during their free hours of leisure. Numerous churches sought to attract entertain and uplift the young people, especially the military men.[89] The Cumberland Methodist Church made a concerted effort to lure sailors with their big screen show and provide moral uplift for the young men away from their homes. In September 1917, the church showed *Samson's Betrayal* to a group of sailors ushered by the Methodist Church's volunteer staff of young single women, who 'heavily laden with roses presented a flower to each man in uniform.'[90] Other targeted audience groups included orphans, who were often invited to free entertainment. The church made every Thursday night a gathering place for the children and tired mothers of the community, where they could see pictures of a high moral tone and also enjoy good music.[91]

Sunday movie showings were consistently rejected in Norfolk throughout the 1910s, and the police demonstrated their willingness to arrest any violators.[92] In 1918, however, one local issue, the opening of the Red Circle Theater on a local military base for the benefit of service men, ignited specific community-wide arguments over the desirability of showing films to local sailors and soldiers in order to keep them from more nefarious activities.[93]

The Red Circle operated on the Sabbath with lecturers who gave illustrated talks without charge. Such an educational tactic was deemed acceptable, but not Sunday movies. A fierce debate among city council members centered on whether Sunday amusements could be provided for the service men.

The moral and religious forces of Norfolk supported any city council action 'for the eradication of the evils complained of. The armory building must not be used on Sunday for any purpose other than the holding of illustrated talks on travel, health or "such other educational" lectures as may be given from time to time. [But] Norfolk will not permit the opening of any other place of amusement on Sunday in violation of the laws of the state of Virginia.'[94] The issue was well defined in an article that asked: 'What is the moral difference between seeing a static or a moving picture?' The editorial suggested that Sunday pictures would not draw people from church. They found it 'monstrous to suggest that the churches and the cinematograph are two rival organizations competing as attractions for the masses. Such a view is fundamentally irreligious. A man who wishes to go to church will go there, whatever other ways of spending his time may be open to him. A man who goes to church because he can go nowhere else is not likely to derive any edification from his religious exercises.'[95]

Black clergy in Norfolk enthusiastically joined their white equivalents in this protest, aligned in a common cause: both feared the danger of introducing a secular wedge into the Christian community. Voicing their opposition as a way of protecting the colored youth of the city, the ministers gave their 'support to those brave and wise white ministers who see an "entertaining wedge" for the introduction of the "Continental Sunday.' They argued that this 'wedge' would 'curse the Negro youth of Norfolk as well as our white youth,' because the Sabbath is intended for worship and if 'the church, the Sabbath school, the young people's societies, the Y.M.C.A., the Knights of Columbus, the community Centre, reading rooms, and the Red Circle theatre can not save him from sin, bootleggers and the red light district, neither will the Sunday movie deliver him.'[96] By 1922, however, a liberalizing tendency that approved 'uplifting and inspiring' religious films on Sunday had grown significantly stronger, and as far as the local newspaper was concerned, the tide had turned against Sunday 'blue laws.'[97]

In January and February 1920, Billy Sunday's revivalist mission to Norfolk was reported in detail in the local press. The *Virginian-Pilot* covered pages of print with Sunday's sermons and reports of every meeting he held with community leaders. In his sermons, the popular evangelist decried the demoralizing influence of card playing, dancing, the saloon and some aspects of the legitimate stage, but he saw cinema as a 'handmaiden of religion,' and an effective instrument of uplift and edification.[98] His name was even appropriated to recommend certain films. In a full-page advertisement, Sunday recommended D.W. Griffith's *Orphans of the Storm* as a 'sermon of the highest value.' 'The power of the moving picture,' he argued, 'should be used to inculcate warnings and lessons that the world needs ... would that every story carried on the screen might have a lesson as powerful, and as useful, a motive as praiseworthy.'[99]

Billy Sunday was no stranger to the entertainment business. Before becoming a minister, he had been a professional ballplayer for 'Pop' Anson's Chicago Whitestockings. During his baseball career, he had a religious experience in a Chicago rescue mission, and subsequently gave up baseball to devote his life to preaching the Gospel. According to his biographers, Sunday's preaching style paralleled the energy and theatricality of actors. One did not simply attend a Billy Sunday crusade; one experienced it, watching it almost like a motion picture:

He races to and fro across the platform. Like a jack knife he fairly doubles up in emphasis. One hand smites the other. His foot stamps the floor as if to destroy it ... No posture is too extreme for this

4.5 Billy Sunday to Mae West: 'If you ever quit acting and wanted to, you could be a sensation in the pulpit' (1933). Courtesy Culver Pictures.

restless gymnast. Yet it all seems natural. Like his speech, it is an
integral part of the man. Every muscle of his body preaches in accord
with his voice.[100]

Sunday was renowned for his friendly relations with Hollywood celebrities:
he was the brother-in-law of Essanay owner George K. Spoor, and an
acquaintance of Douglas Fairbanks, Mary Pickford, Charlie Chaplin,
William S. Hart and Cecil B. DeMille. In his 1917 Los Angeles crusade,
he played baseball against a team of motion picture personalities organized
by Fairbanks. Two years earlier, he had acted as technical advisor to director
Alan Dwan for *Jordan Is A Hard Road* a picture about an evangelist played
by Frank Campeau. According to Dwan:

> We put up a huge tent over in Hollywood across from the studio
> and filled it full of extras—not professional ones—just people off the
> streets. Now, in the story, [lead actor Fred] Campeau is supposed to
> harangue them about religion and make them come to God, but I
> got Billy Sunday up there and he let them have one of his best hot
> lectures, and I had about three cameras filming only the audience.
> And pretty soon these people began to feel it, and the first thing
> you know, they were crawling up the aisles on their knees, coming
> up to Billy Sunday to be saved, hollering 'Hallelujah' and going into
> hysteria. A terrific scene. No bunch of million-dollar actors could
> have done it. You could see the frenzy in their faces. And after we cut,
> he actually went on with the religious revival right there. Then I was
> able to put Campeau up there and let him go through the gestures
> of talking, cutting back all the time to these people I'd already shot.
> The effect was astonishing.[101]

Sunday was viewed as an ally to the moving picture in attracting all
social and economic classes:

> Billy Sunday dispenses religion. Yet is his audience confined to
> Methodists? No, people of all sects and creeds jostle and elbow
> their way into an auditorium to hear him. He mixes religion with
> entertainment without distorting values. He preaches to you and
> makes you like it. Whether or not you believe in his doctrines you
> are impressed by what he says. The same effect is produced by the
> skillfully handled religious picture. By 'religious picture' I do not
> mean a palpable effort at preachment nor the dramatization of a
> sectarian creed. I refer to a picture which derives its drama from

some broad principle of religion to which all systems subscribe, such as belief in the Divine Power, piety and morality.[102]

Sunday's arrival in Norfolk in 1920 marked a culmination of Protestant middle-class relations to film, and his famous sermon on 'Amusements' reaffirmed local Protestant attitudes toward moviegoing. His moral authority on numerous subjects, including motion pictures, resonated with the community. As a spokesperson for conservative Protestants, he augmented the credibility of the motion picture industry, particularly in relation to its more controversial stars such as Chaplin and the remarried Fairbanks and Pickford, by appearing in publicity photographs and staging sports events with them. His views mollified a cautious mass of conservative Protestants and, perhaps unwittingly, enabled films to find an opportunity for Sunday exhibition, even becoming a wedge for commercial exploitation.

A year and a half after Sunday's visit, an editorial in the African American *Norfolk Journal and Guide* echoed Sunday's hot moral sermons, lambasting the Tidewater community's ongoing vice problems and castigating a spreading menace of the 'Red Light district,' and 'dance halls' as doing 'as much harm as anything else.'[103] Soon afterward, prominent black Baptist minister R.H. Bowling decided to determine the most serious vices in Norfolk and so polled his congregation. Of over 3600 votes cast, theater attendance came in last of all the vices, with only 2 per cent selecting it as the most serious, lagging far behind lying, bootlegging, gambling, and non-support of the church. Movies were not even mentioned.[104]

Throughout the decades, churches had used and 'sanctified' theatre sites for religious services, musical concerts, and old-fashioned revivals.[105] Churches exhibited films in their own sanctuaries and integrated films as sermonic material for uplift and education. Even after the evangelistic apologetics of a Billy Sunday, changes were forthcoming after 1920, however. The Hollywood scandals of the early 1920s, the drift of film content toward the end of the silent era, the emergence of radio, a new medium favoring the spoken word of Protestant preaching, and the escalating influence of the Roman Catholic hierarchy in propagating moral standards in the public sphere would ultimately foster a divisive relationship between all religious groups and the film industry, and in part provoke the establishment of the Production Code. Yet historically, as a contested site for articulating its own mores and values, moving picture exhibition in the silent era in Norfolk, Virginia, shared more in common with the dominant Protestant establishment than has so far been imagined.

5

Patchwork Maps of Moviegoing, 1911–1913 [1]

Richard Abel

IMAGINE you are a 'picture fan' in the textile mill town of Central Falls, bordering Pawtucket (Rhode Island), in September 1912. You're one of several single young working women—a recent Polish immigrant training on the looms in a nearby silk thread mill, a second-generation French-Canadian operating the winding machines in a cotton mill weave room, or a Jewish grocer's daughter working behind the store counter on Pulaski Square in the Polish neighborhood.[2] You and several friends are looking forward to going to the movies Saturday evening, 14 September, but you haven't decided where. After reading the *Pawtucket Times* the night before, you know what's playing at several downtown theaters.[3] At the Music Hall, there's a variety program that includes *The Unseen Enemy* (by the un-named D.W. Griffith), *A Romance of the Coast*, *Live Wire*, and a *Pathé Weekly* newsreel. At the Star, there's a special screening of Selig's three-reel *Coming of Columbus*, along with two other films and two vaudeville acts. There you might even encounter some of the Italian immigrants (you may want to, you may not), who live just across the river. But a new theater, the Pastime, also is opening that day, and one of the four films scheduled is a 'Bison feature,' the two-reel *Battle of the Red Men*, plus several illustrated songs. Which theater you choose could depend on several factors, but, as a frequent moviegoer, you could count on the familiarity and relative quality of the variety program at the Music Hall. Or you might be attracted just enough by a 'special feature' like *The Coming of Columbus*, which you had wanted to attend, but couldn't, when it played in nearby Providence three

94

months earlier. Or you could simply be tempted by the novelty of a new theater like the Pastime, whether you like westerns or not, especially since you've heard that in the past it was a burlesque house.

This snapshot of a quasi-fictional moment in the everyday life of an 'ordinary' picture fan can serve to introduce some of the issues and debates about movie audiences and moviegoing in the early 1910s. Unfortunately, no study apparently exists in the USA comparable to Altenloh's groundbreaking 1913 sociology dissertation, in which she sought to describe and explain the large and still growing audience for moving pictures in Mannheim, a major industrial city in Germany.[4] In surveys of 2,400 people, she found that nearly one third went to one of the city's fourteen cinemas 'once or even several times a week.' Not only did she come up with familiar reasons for that—low admission price, the possibility of going 'at any time one chooses'—but she also posited others that would assume greater prominence in later theories of modernity—for instance, cinema epitomized the 'nervous restlessness' that more or less synchronized modern leisure and work.[5] For my purposes, Altenloh extrapolated from her surveys 'certain regularities' about when and how often various people went to the movies.[6] Seasonal events such as holidays and unexpected variables such as weather impacted attendance, but the most consistent factor was the weekly routine of different social groups. In downtown cinemas, the lowest frequency of attendance fell on Fridays, partly because that 'traditionally [was] cleaning day in multi-room apartments, when the women of the petite bourgeoisie and middle classes [were] busy with domestic duties.'[7] Yet in working-class *faubourgs*, the lowest frequency fell on

5.1 Mutual Movies ad, *Minneapolis Journal*, 3 January 1914.

Thursdays, perhaps because money was tight just before the Friday payday.[8] By contrast, attendance was highest at these outlying cinemas on Sundays, whereas it was highest downtown on both Saturdays and Sundays.

Despite the lack of comparable studies, it is still possible to make some conjectures about moviegoing in the U.S. during this period, as I have tried to suggest in my opening quasi-fictional snapshot. For surviving documents provide enough material (however mediated) to let us sketch the spatial and temporal conditions of moviegoing in specific cities, summarize the habits of particular groups of moviegoers, construct a map of 'certain regularities' whose patterns could differ from place to place, and hazard some explanation of those patterns. My own contribution to such a project, admittedly daunting even if one focuses on just two or three years of the transitional era, perhaps inevitably is a work-in-progress. But it does seek to break new ground by drawing on sources other than the relatively familiar discourse of the trade press, urban recreational surveys, and so on. Instead, for the first part of this chapter, my primary sources are daily newspaper ads, columns, and stories in selected cities (from New England to the Upper Midwest), official local documents in those cities, and specific historical urban studies. The second part relies on similar sources for the joint cities of Pawtucket/Central Falls, including a recent study of immigrant working women in the area and, most important, a long-lost weekly accounts book from the city's second largest moving picture theater.

Sketch Patterns of Exhibition

By now, it is no longer surprising to hear that, during the early 1910s, the temporal conditions of moviegoing were not always the same from one city to another or even within one urban center. But the range of differences could be significant. In most cities, picture theaters tended to be open every day of the week. In those such as Youngstown and Canton (Ohio), where 'blue laws' forbade live entertainment on Sundays, vaudeville theaters and 'opera houses' also turned into picture theaters on Sunday afternoons and evenings. In New England industrial cities such as Lowell or Lynn (Massachusetts), where similar laws were in effect, however, 'Sunday concerts' of moving pictures were restricted to evening hours; yet in others such as Pawtucket, there were no Sunday moving picture programs at all. Daily opening and closing hours also varied widely. In some cities, downtown picture theaters opened their doors in the morning and ran until late at night. Typical were those that began their programs at 10:00 or 11:00 am: the Grand Photoplay (Rochester, New York), the New Dome (Youngstown), or the Colonial (Des Moines, Iowa).[9] Among those with the longest hours were the Cameraphone

(Cleveland), which opened at 8:30 am, and the Empress (Toledo, Ohio), which opened at 9:30 am (but 10:00 am on Sundays). Yet, in a surprising number of cities, downtown theaters were open only in the afternoons and evenings. In Lowell, for instance, all the theaters opened at 1:00 pm and closed at 10:30 pm, Monday through Saturday. The same was true of Canton, for vaudeville houses and picture theaters, as well as Minneapolis, where the Seville opened at noon, the 575-seat Crystal at 1:00, and the 1,700-seat Lyric at 2:00. In Pawtucket, the Bijou, the Star, and the Pastime had similar hours, but their doors were closed between 5:00 or 5:30 and 7:00 or 7:30 pm (dinner hours), except on Saturdays. Neighborhood picture theaters, already numerous by the early 1910s, also had business hours that varied considerably. Some, like the New Park (Minneapolis) and Namur's University Place (Des Moines), were open weekday afternoons as well as evenings. Most operated only on weekday evenings, with added weekend matinees, but not all of these were small and/or cheap, for they could include elegant suburban theaters like the 1,200-seat Knickerbocker (Cleveland) and 650-seat Laurel (Toledo).

Other factors besides operating hours also affected when, where, and how often people went to the movies. As late as 1912, a great number of picture theaters across these regions still changed their programs daily, a practice supported by the release schedules of licensed as well as independent

5.2 Advertisement for 'Iowa's Most Beautiful Photo Play Theatre', *Des Moines Register and Leader*, 4 December 1912.

manufacturers, which now averaged four to five reels of film a day. This was the case with downtown theaters from Youngstown to Des Moines, even in newly constructed theaters like Youngstown's 1,000-seat Dome or Des Moines' 650-seat Casino. It also held true for some neighborhood theaters, again, like the New Park (Minneapolis) and University Place (Des Moines). Yet as many, if not more, picture theaters changed their programs less often, and sometimes staggered those changes for competitive purposes. In Lowell, the Voyons changed its first-run licensed films on Monday and Thursday, with an added special program on Sunday, whereas

5.3 Advertisement for the Canton Odeon, *Canton News-Democrat*, 1912.

The Jewel presented four weekly changes of first-run independent films. In Pawtucket, the Star changed its programs on Monday and Thursday; the Pastime, its programs on Monday, Wednesday, and Friday. In Canton, the Odeon (where recently I discovered that my grandfather played the clarinet in a small orchestra) offered four weekly changes of first-run licensed films: Monday, Wednesday, and Friday, with another new program on Sunday. In Minneapolis, the Seville changed its independent first-run films on Sunday, Tuesday, and Thursday; the Crystal did likewise, except its third change came on Friday. In Des Moines, the Family and Golden, both independent theaters, changed their films three times a week, but on alternate days. Yet, whatever their frequency of changes, most of these theaters ran 'continuous shows,' which encouraged the kind of 'drop-in' clientele familiar from the nickelodeon period. Only a few picture theaters sought to present programs more characteristic of 'legitimate' theaters, beginning and ending at set times. One was Keith's Bijou (Boston), where Josephine Clement ran five daily shows of two hours each (changed twice a week), with licensed films, a one-act play, classical music, and a short lecture. Another was the Lyric (Minneapolis), where S.L. 'Roxy' Rothapfel initially ran four daily shows of an hour and half each (also changed twice a week), with licensed films and special musical arrangements.

In other words, the constantly changing variety package, averaging an hour or so in length around 1911–12, still served as a major means of attracting most moviegoers. The regularity of the variety program allowed exhibitors to promote their more popular films in consistent ways: the Orpheum (Cleveland) had its 'good Essanay' (usually a western) every Sunday; the New Grand (Minneapolis), 'Monday's Biograph release'; the Alhambra (St. Paul, Minnesota), a new *Pathé Weekly* every Monday; and the Cozy (also Cleveland), its 'Vitagraph night' every Thursday.[10] This kind of promotion continued when multiple-reel films were introduced in 1912 and 1913: the Crystal (Minneapolis), for instance, presented its celebrated Kay-Bee Indian pictures and Civil War films every Sunday through Tuesday; yet the Unique (Des Moines) featured them on Friday and Saturday. On the one hand, in many cities (certainly downtown, but even in some neighborhoods), the variety program could draw a heterogeneous audience over the course of a week or even a day, and give impetus to what *Nickelodeon*, in 1910, was perhaps first to call 'picture fans.'[11] On the other, the routine patterns of attendance that it encouraged also could differentiate those fans according to their 'taste' for a particular brand of film or 'personality,' such as Essanay's Broncho Billy Anderson or Vitagraph's Florence Turner. By contrast, in seeking to 'elevate' the variety program or multiple-reel feature, the Keith Bijou (Boston) and Lyric (Minneapolis) set out to attract a more exclusively middle-class clientele. Here, as in the Saxe brothers' theater chain (which acquired the Lyric in 1912), the ambiance of the theater served to lure 'regular patrons.'[12] For their 'comfort and convenience,' the Bijou offered 'well-appointed reception room[s] ... with checking facilities, writing desk and telephone service,' maid service, and a 'men's smoking room.'[13] Among its amenities, the Lyric had 'a playground for the children with all kinds of toys' and a 'rest room ... for shoppers where hot tea and cocoa [were] served by colored matrons after the matinee free.'[14]

Sketch Patterns of Moviegoing

Specific traces of moviegoers' daily or weekly habits during this period are more difficult to puzzle out. The trade press and moral reformers showed great interest in who attended picture theaters and what kinds of pictures were preferred, but paid less attention to where they went and when. Still, tantalizing observations did crop up, especially about women and children, because they came under greater scrutiny for enjoying the benefits of increasing leisure time at the turn of the last century[15]—yet few of those confirmed the cliché that men predominated at downtown theaters and women and children at neighborhood theaters.[16] A 1913 survey of Waltham, a small factory town on the western outskirts of Boston, showed that single working women were more likely than men to attend downtown Boston picture theaters once a week, probably on weekends.[17] About the same time, in Worcester, an industrial city farther west, a reporter complained that women used picture theaters as lunchrooms: at noon: 'half of the women patrons [are] nibbling lunch biscuits, cakes, or sweet meals of some kind.'[18] Even earlier, 'taking in the movies [had] become a regular noon habit' in Providence, but a local newspaper was surprised to find the patronage included 'a considerable number of prominent Providence [as well as Pawtucket] businessmen.'[19] According to recreation surveys, children and adolescents everywhere remained frequent moviegoers. If, in New Britain (Rhode Island), 50 per cent of school children went to the pictures once a week, in Portland (Oregon), 90 per cent under the age of fourteen attended at least once a week, and 75 per cent went at night.[20] Moreover, 'a considerable number of boys and girls under eighteen years of age' (especially girls aged 16–18) went 'unaccompanied by adults.'[21] Indeed, more than two-thirds in Cleveland were 'unaccompanied' at night.[22] Yet no one in that city seemed unduly alarmed because generally 'young people [were] well cared for while in the theaters'—as they were too at the Princess, in Peoria (Illinois), where unattended school children allegedly received special attention at afternoon screenings.[23]

Research on specific cities also can yield a better sense of the weekly habits of moviegoing. Take Lynn (Massachusetts), for instance, a city famous for its shoe factories and electrical works, with a 1910 population of 90,000.[24] Although divided into ethnic neighborhoods (Irish, French-Canadian, Greek, Italian, Polish, Jewish, Swedish), this population was concentrated in three-decker multi-family buildings and lodging or boarding houses, most of them within a half mile of the main square.[25] This partly explains why moviegoers had no more than a half-dozen downtown picture theaters from which to choose, all of which charged ten cents admission and were open from noon or 1:00 to 10:30 pm, six days a week, except for special screenings (mostly second-run films) from 5:00 to 10:00 pm on Sundays. Using mass transit, of course, anyone who could afford the fares also could go into Boston for weekend shows, much as did the young working women of Waltham. Not unexpectedly, several of Lynn's theaters were huge: Central Square seated 1,500, and the Olympia, with its 3,200 seats, briefly may have been the largest in the world, until the Gaumont-Palace opened in Paris in late 1911. Programs of first-run licensed films changed just twice a week at the Olympia and Comique, as did programs of first-run Universal films at the Central Square. Only in the fall of 1912 did Dreamland introduce a thrice-weekly change of first-run Mutual films. In short, moviegoing in Lynn was relatively regimented in terms of time and limited in terms of venues and subjects. If this encouraged moviegoers to become fans of a particular brand or regular customers one day of the week rather than another, special attractions featuring vocal performers could lead them to prefer one theater over another. In late 1912, for instance, Geoffrey Whalen was recognized as a 'spellbinding' lecturer at the Olympia, and Prof. Hammon, a 'well known picture talker,' performed at the Central Square; by contrast, 'lifelike effects' accentuated the pictures at the Comique, and, as late as the fall of 1913, alternated with illustrated songs.[26]

For a sharp contrast to Lynn, take Toledo (Ohio), with a 1910 population of 170,000, a city much more diversified in its industries (shipping, glass, steel, automobile parts).[27] In the early 1910s, Toledo had more than forty picture theaters, with a dozen located downtown (of various sizes, and charging from five to ten cents) and the rest spread out in secondary shopping districts, industrial areas, and ethnic neighborhoods.[28] There were several in East Toledo, a Hungarian immigrant community, several more close to a near south side Polish immigrant community, and far more in the suburban residential area of South Toledo. At least four downtown theaters appealed to working-class moviegoers by advertising in the leading labor weekly, and one, the Hart, encouraged its readers to 'get in the habit of dropping in ... when you are downtown.'[29] Here, as already noted, was a much wider range of venues, operating hours, program lengths and changes, and subjects to support a variety of picture fans. Yet an especially revealing bit of evidence about moviegoing comes from an early 1911 contest sponsored by the *Toledo Blade*, asking readers to submit short pieces of moving picture criticism for weekly cash prizes.[30] Initial announcements assumed a generic reader, but several indicated that males were to be the chief contestants. Yet, over the first three weeks, the majority of winners were young women, and the final week's 'prizes [were] won by girls.'[31] What pictures these women (all apparently unmarried) saw and where they saw them hardly fit the expectations of the trade press. Some did attend neighborhood theaters, on the near south side (a Polish immigrant community) or in South Toledo, but others saw their films downtown. This suggests that Toledo's downtown picture theaters appealed to young women as well as the working men hailed by the Hart, whether they were lunching shop girls and typists or weekend shoppers and pleasure-seekers. Moreover, three chose to write about westerns, and not merely cowboy girl pictures. This further suggests that surveys in which children and adolescents still preferred Wild West pictures as late as 1913 were not off the mark, for young women apparently shared those preferences.

Patchwork in Pawtucket/Central Falls

Finally, let me turn again to Pawtucket/Central Falls and one specific downtown theater, the Star, whose weekly accounts book covers a two-year period from December 1911 through October 1913.[32] The information in this rare document reveals much about the weekly operation of a relatively large downtown cinema during this period in an industrial city in New England. Although the weekly payroll for personnel (among which was a small orchestra of union musicians) is only rarely included, and figured as a lump sum (ranging from $80 to $155), other expenses are listed in some detail.[33] Here it is worth noting that a $10-a-week salary was well above average for a young single working woman. Most costly was the building's weekly rent, which remained $76.93 throughout the period. Next was the weekly film service fee, which initially ran as low as $10 (for older General Film releases), later increased to $42 and then $55 (for Mutual releases), and could reach more than $100, with special features. Then there was the city's aggregate weekly charge of $35 for a license and apparently the on-site presence of a policeman and fireman (a police station was located within 100 yards of the theater). Another $10 to $20 each week went for posters and newspaper advertising. A weekly average of $20 also went for electrical lighting; during the winter months, the same amount could be spent on coal for heating. Renting a piano cost $10 per month; liability insurance came to $50 a year. The charges for maintaining or upgrading equipment could vary widely: $15.60 one week for 'repairs on machine,' $30.15 another week for tungstens, $120.18 for 'mirror screen repairs,' and $218 for a new Simplex projector. Consistent low-cost items included cleaning supplies, towels, railway express charges and tickets, telegrams, long distance telephone calls, typewriter ribbons, stationary paper and envelopes, postage, and (my favorite) tins of food for the house cats. Interestingly, the Star's weekly expenses generally exceeded its weekly receipts for nearly a year, until October 1912—and the questions that discrepancy raises will be addressed shortly.

By itself, this accounts book suggests little about the Star's audiences and their moviegoing habits. However, within the context of other sources— newspaper ads and stories, local city records, and Louise Lamphere's study of immigrant working women in the area—its unique record of daily receipts becomes more revealing. So, what information is available about Pawtucket/Central Falls that could be relevant to an investigation of moviegoing at the Star? Sometimes described as 'the birthplace of the American industrial revolution,' Pawtucket was one of a series of Rhode Island textile mill towns situated along the Blackstone River. With a population of slightly more than 50,000 by 1910, it bordered the larger city of Providence (nearly 400,000 people) on the south and Central Falls (22,500 people) on the north.[34] The largest immigrant groups initially were English, Scottish, and Irish, and it was they, along with the later Germans, who came to control most of the city's manufacturing base and political offices. Other groups soon followed: French-Canadians, Germans (among them some German Jews), and Swedes (after 1875); Italians (after 1885); Russian Jews, Poles, and Portuguese (after 1895); and Greeks, Syrians, and Armenians (after 1905). Except for French-Canadians (concentrated in woodworking jobs) and Swedes (heavily involved in machinists' trades), the more recent immigrants tended to be employed by textile companies handling cotton and silk. An equal number of men and women worked in such industries as cotton yarn and thread, braids and lace, and silk and rayon piece goods; more men than women worked in dyeing and finishing textiles, and more women than men, in knitting cotton, woolen, and silk goods. Although most working women were young and unmarried, according to Lamphere's study of Central Falls, only Polish women tended not to drop out of the labor force after marriage. By contrast, the sons and daughters of earlier immigrants, by 1900–10, were taking up the new clerical, teaching, and other white-collar jobs, many of which were in the central business district.

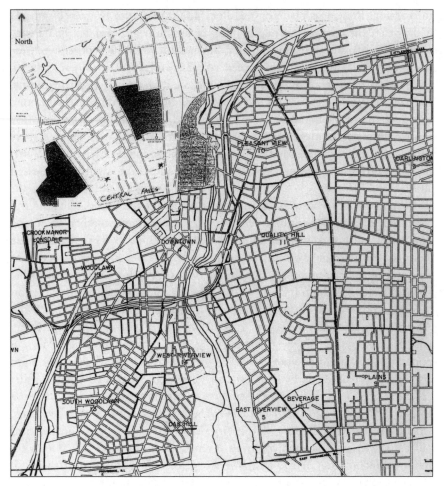

5.4 Pawtucket/Central Falls, Rhode Island.

Like most industrial cities at the turn of the century, Pawtucket was relatively segregated according to ethnic neighborhoods. The wealthier second- and third-generation English, Scots, and Germans, now defined as 'native-born Americans' by the census office, tended to live in Oak Hill (south of downtown), in Quality Hill (on the bluffs above the Blackstone River east of downtown), and on the eastern outskirts, in Darlington. French-Canadians and working-class Irish dominated Central Falls to the north; Poles were concentrated in an area of Central Falls bordering Pawtucket, along the river (their numbers had reached 2,500 by 1915); Italians tended to congregate along the eastern edge of the river and to the north in Pleasant View (there were about 1,000 by 1915); Russian Jews were concentrated on the northern edge of Pawtucket[35] and also mixed into the Polish neighborhood around Pulaski Square; other immigrant groups were more scattered, but the Portuguese (there were 1,000 by 1915), Greeks, Armenians, and Syrians seemed to migrate into and around the Italian areas on the east side of the river. Most of the recent immigrant families or single men and women (especially Poles) lived in tenement buildings with multiple apartments or in older two-family dwellings. Many of these were clustered near the textile factories along the river or in the area that stretched from the Coats thread mills in Central Falls through Church Hill west of downtown Pawtucket and into South Woodlawn, along the railroad tracks. No matter where their tenement was located, according to Lamphere,[36] it was not unusual for recent immigrant workers (including women) to walk a mile or more to their jobs, which suggests that they could

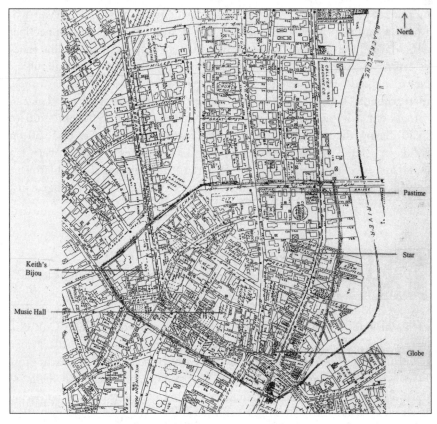

5.5   Downtown Pawtucket, c. 1913.

walk into the downtown shopping district as well. Moreover, an extensive network of trolley lines could ease the journey.

Pawtucket's downtown formed a lop-sided ellipsis on the west side of the Blackstone, anchored on the south and west by Main and Broad (the central business district), on the east by High Street and North Main (closest to the river), and on the north by Exchange Street, which curved southwest to connect with Broad (near the old rail station). As in Lynn, all of the city's moving picture theaters were located within this area, and adjacent to the main trolley lines: the Music Hall and the Globe on Main, Keith's Bijou and the Scenic on Broad, the Pastime on the corner of High and Exchange, and the Star on North Main. Along with the 1,200-seat Keith Bijou (the former Grand Opera House), the 900-seat Star was the largest and best-appointed theater in Pawtucket; by contrast, the 500-seat Pastime was located in a former burlesque theater. Owned and operated by the Star Amusement Company, the Star opened on Thanksgiving Day, 1907, in the renovated former Masonic Temple, for several years a warehouse for a prominent downtown department store. The company was run by Walter S. Davis, a former printer who operated several other theaters in Connecticut and Massachusetts, and his recently widowed mother-in-law, Julia Reid, described as 'one of the most successful lady financiers throughout ... New England,' who served as the company's treasurer—in other words, that accounts book was hers. Much like the other downtown theaters, throughout this period the Star was open from 1:30 to 5:00 and 7:00 to 10:30 during the week, 1:30 to 10:30 on Saturdays (and noon to 10:30 on holidays). There were no Sunday shows. Ticket prices normally were ten cents for evenings (five cents for children) and five cents for matinees; programs lasted approximately an hour and a half each and changed just twice a week, on Monday and Thursday.[37]

5.6 Advertisement for the Pawtucket Star, *Pawtucket Times*, 23 November 1907.

For its first two and a half years, the Star offered programs of Motion Picture Patents Company (MPPC) moving pictures and illustrated songs. In April 1910, through an affiliation with the Keith circuit, the theater switched to vaudeville and MPPC pictures, in parallel with the Bijou. Surviving documents in Pawtucket shed little light on this change, yet it is not unlikely that the Star was adopting the 'pop' vaudeville format established the year before by Marcus Loew and Adolph Zukor in their theaters in New York City and elsewhere in the Northeast. Whereas Keith's big theater in nearby Providence (relatively accessible by trolley or train) booked the top performers in 'high class' vaudeville, the Star offered less expensive acts, accompanied by MPPC films. If this format was successful at first, it certainly was not by the first weeks recorded in Julia Reid's accounts book, in December 1911. Within a month, according to newspaper ads, the Star abandoned the 'pop' vaudeville format and, in its stead, began to present special 'state rights features,' still accompanied by MPPC films. This new format ran from January through August 1912, with mixed results. Profitable weeks were few and far between and included the holidays of Christmas and New Year's, Decoration Day, and Labor Day. The only other good weeks came in early February, when ticket prices were doubled for a three-day screening of the five-reel *Dante's Inferno*, and in March, when a three-reel sensational melodrama, *The James Boys from Missouri*, proved unusually attractive. Several other special multiple-reel films during those months, from Kalem's *Arrah-Na-Pogue*, specially lectured by Charles Edgar Pelton, to Pathé-Frères' *Passion Play* and Great Northern's *Temptations of a Great City*, also did well enough for the Star to come close to breaking even. Most 'specials,' however, were disappointing. In March, the *Durbar in Kinemacolor* was nearly disastrous (perhaps due to unusually hefty ticket prices of twenty-five and fifty cents and a screening in Providence earlier that week);[38] in May, the response was lukewarm to efforts to rebook Pelton as a lecturer for such second-run pictures as Selig's *Two Orphans* and *Cinderella* and Pathé's *In the Grip of Alcohol*.

Beginning in early September 1912 (the moment I chose for my opening), Davis and Reid changed their programming in two ways. First, they reinstated vaudeville, but began booking more expensive acts; second, they switched to the Mutual Film service. These were risky moves in that their costs escalated and their only profitable weeks for the next month came from scheduling General Film specials, including Selig's *The Coming of Columbus*, on the first two weekends. That the Star continued to lose money through the middle of October meant that the more costly of those moves, the vaudeville acts, simply could not justify the expense. But there was another reason. In mid-September, the Pastime Theatre opened just two blocks

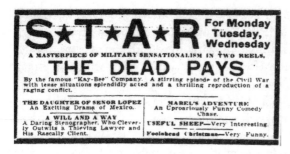

5.7 Advertisement for the Star Theatre, *Pawtucket Times*, 4 January 1913.

away, on the north edge of downtown, with programs presenting five reels of motion pictures, along with illustrated songs, and changed not twice but three times a week. Moreover, the Pastime's major attractions were multiple-reel sensational melodramas that had been popular elsewhere months before but had not yet played in Pawtucket: Bison-101 westerns such as *Battle of the Red Men* and *The Lieutenant's Last Fight*, 'Copenhagen dramas' such as *The Two Sisters* and *Almost a Tragedy*, and Gaumont historical thrillers such as *Written in Blood*. Within a month of the Pastime's opening, Davis and Reid must have cottoned on to the popularity of such films and, in a blatant competitive move, once more switched their programming entirely to moving pictures supplied by Mutual, which was distributing multiple-reel as well as short films. Now the Star too could offer sensational melodramas on a regular basis, beginning with Kay-Bee's three-reel *Custer's Last Fight*, along with the new Keystone comedies. This move immediately proved profitable, and by December, the theater's receipts had more than doubled (with profits averaging $100–$200 a week), sustained by a steady stream of multiple-reel Indian pictures, Civil War films, and sensational crime films such as *The Auto Bandits of Paris*—some of which reportedly provoked wildly enthusiastic applause.[39]

For the next seven months or more, Reid's accounts book indicates that only once did the Star lose money and only twice did it take in less than seventy-five dollars in profits.[40] For the most part, the Star's weekly profits averaged an incredible $200–$300, except for two consecutive weeks in January and another in mid-March when they reached $400, and twice—once during the week that culminated in New Year's, and again in late March—when they topped $500. In January, the four-reel *Resurrection*, starring Blanche Walsh, 'packed [the theater] to the walls' just as did such sensational melodramas as Warner's *Tracked by Wireless*, Kay-Bee's *The Burning Brand*, and Éclair's French thriller, *Tom Butler*. In March, the hit films had more topical subjects: *Lieutenant Petrosino* (which dramatized the recent killing of an Italian-American detective in Italy), paired with

The Inauguration of President Wilson, and *Shipwrecked in Icebergs* (which exploited the Titanic disaster of the year before). In May, personal one-night appearances by Scout Younger the 'Reformed Outlaw' and the Thanhouser Kid further added to the Star's success. In August, shortly before the Bijou reopened with programs exclusively of moving pictures, Davis and Reid took another risk and contracted with Famous Players to supply the Star with a regular schedule of three feature-length films a week, accompanied by Mutual's basic service of its own newsreel, Keystone comedies, and other short films.[41] Although this required a more frequent change in programs (Monday, Wednesday, and Friday), the level of the Star's receipts remained about the same as before, and then began to decline slightly. Partly due to the increased costs of renting Famous Players features, however, the weekly average of profits declined even more, eventually falling to around $100. In the midst of this change in program format, Davis and Reid also booked the Italian epic, *Quo Vadis?*, for a full week in mid-September, running just two shows a day and charging twenty-five to fifty cents admission. Although the receipts that week totaled a record of nearly $2,000, 60 per cent of that went to the distributor, George Kleine.

There may be no direct evidence of exactly who frequented the Star Theatre and made it part of their everyday life, but its location, programming, and other scattered bits of information are suggestive. In late 1909, the business weekly, *Pawtucket Chronicle and Gazette* credited the theater with having turned North Main Street into a 'busy thoroughfare.' What else may have made the street 'busy' is difficult to tell, beyond what contemporary maps indicate were textile factories several blocks up river, small office buildings, furniture stores, a police station and 'Central Garage,' as well as tenements that began immediately north of the theater. Although relatively distant from the central business district, where the Bijou was located, the Star was still within two blocks or so of city hall, the main post office, the city library, and the local telephone company. More importantly, it had the advantage, along with the Pastime, of close proximity to French-Canadian, Irish, Jewish, Polish, Italian, and other immigrant neighborhoods (hence my choice of those three fictional young women).[42] That these groups were among the city's biggest movie fans, and probably formed a significant portion of the Star's audience, is suggested by the fact that, in 1913 and 1914, the only new cinemas opened just across the city's border in Central Falls: one on the western edge of the Polish and Jewish neighborhoods; the other near an Irish neighborhood adjacent to the Coats thread mills. Comprised chiefly of westerns, Civil War films, other sensational melodramas (including French crime thrillers), and Keystone comedies, the Star's successful programming in 1912 and 1913 suggests a largely working-class audience (including many women), but certain profitable films, according to the accounts book, exhibited a definite ethnic appeal. Initially, that appeal was Irish, as in Kalem's *Arrah-Na-Pogue* or even Solax's *Dublin Dan*, booked for New Year's. More consistently, it was Italian, and not just for 'art films' such as *Dante's Inferno* and *Quo Vadis?*, but for a variety of titles, from *The Coming of Columbus* to *Lieutenant Petrosino* and *Garibaldi, or a Sicilian Heroine*.[43] Finally, recent immigrants must have frequented the Star enough for a reformist 'Civic Theatre Movement,' led by a Congregational Church pastor in Central Falls, to select and screen moving pictures in the theater on Sunday evenings, beginning sometime in 1913, in order 'to educate and familiarize foreign speaking people with the customs, principles, and institutions of our American life.'[44]

But what can Reid's accounts book tell us more specifically about the weekly moviegoing habits of these audiences? Again, indirect evidence is available, if one does a little number crunching with the weekly receipts. Between the beginning of January and the end of May 1913, weekly receipts ranged from a low of $575 (in early February) to a high of $945 (in late March), and averaged between $750 and $800. If one assumes that on average each week the Star sold half of its tickets at ten cents (to adults in the evening) and the other half at five cents (to children anytime, and adults at matinees), an average of 11,000 to 12,000 tickets were sold each week during those five months. Because some of those tickets may have been sold to people attending more than once a week, of course, the Star's pool of regular customers may have been slightly smaller than that weekly figure of 11,000 to 12,000. However, one can conclude that the Star probably was attracting up to 15–20 per cent of the combined population of 75,000 people in Pawtucket and Central Falls, and perhaps (although at this point this can be only hypothetical) closer to a third or a half of the population residing in the areas north and east of the theater—predominately, Poles, Italians, Russian Jews, and other recent immigrants. How these 'movie fans' may have been distributed by age—among children, adolescents, young male or female workers, adult workers—or by social grouping—families, shoppers, groups of young men or young women, couples—remains unknown.

And when exactly did all these fans of the Star tend to go to the movies? In April 1910, the *Providence Sunday Journal* reported that the noon hour was one of 'three periods of the day when the attendance [was] especially heavy' at downtown theaters.[45] In Pawtucket, however, the hours of operation at the Star and other theaters precluded moviegoing at that time. This left the weekday afternoons and evenings for what the *Journal* called 'regular playgoers,' as well as Saturday, when the Star ran continuous shows from noon to 10:30 pm. Not unexpectedly, the accounts book reveals that Saturday consistently drew the largest crowds (from 15 to 25 per cent of the weekly total), with receipts often double or triple those of any other day. What is surprising is that the next highest days, in order, usually were Thursday and Monday, precisely when the Star changed its programs, and the lowest almost always was Friday.[46] Not only did the Star's fans tend to make Saturday their principal day to go to the movies, but nearly as many seemed eager to attend the opening day of their three-day runs. Throughout the period of 1912–13, that pattern remained unchanged, except that attendance increased dramatically, especially on the opening day of Mutual's first-run multiple-reel pictures and Keystone comedies. This routine only deviated when an unusually popular film—e.g., *Tracked by Wireless*; *Quincy Adams Lawyer*; *In the Bishop's Carriage* (starring Mary Pickford)—drew even larger audiences on Tuesday than on Monday. Indeed, the weekly routine of attending the Star on Mondays, Thursdays, and/or Saturdays was so ingrained that it persisted during the first months that the Star booked Famous Players films, beginning in August 1913. Despite the change this booking required, from three-day to two-day programs, audiences continued to attend the Star in larger numbers on Thursday rather than on Wednesday, no matter the film. Unfortunately, the accounts book breaks off in October, and leaves unanswered the question of whether the Star's audiences eventually adapted to the new schedule and to a new routine.

Later newspaper stories and ads, however, do contain traces of further changes at the Star. In early January 1914, Davis also took on the job of managing the Bijou, which had the effect of making him and Reid the dominant figures in Pawtucket's moving picture business. Interestingly, during the last four months of 1913, the Bijou had been competing with the Star by offering two-day programs headlined by Warner's Features (most of them, however, running no more than three reels). As a result of his move, Davis shifted the Famous Players features from the Star to the Bijou (and dropped Warner's altogether), opening the initial January performances with Mary Pickford in *Caprice*. Whatever the alignment between the Star and the Bijou, and the Keith circuit's measure of control over either in late 1913, this shift is suggestive. Apparently, Davis and Reid concluded that it had been a mistake to book Famous Players features into the Star, hoping that these film adaptations of prestigious plays and players would appeal, at such low cost, to its nearby immigrant working-class neighborhoods. Instead, as the Star's receipts declined, they realized that the features would be more profitable if screened in the city's largest theater located centrally in the business district, finally accepting Famous Players' own assumption that they were meant to attract a more middle-class clientele (from shoppers to businessmen) or those aspiring to that class status (white collar workers).

As for the Star itself, the Mutual service continued for several months into 1914, but then, in late March, the theater switched to Universal programs, kicked off by a full-week run of *Traffic in Souls* (with three shows a day, at fifteen and twenty-five cents a ticket). Reversing the usual patterns of exhibition just this once, the Star extended its appeal for customers beyond Pawtucket to Providence, where the film had not been screened. In short, the Universal programs, heavy with sensational melodramas, allowed the Star to continue catering to what seems to have been its usual clientele.

Certain variables—holidays, bad weather, unusually popular or highly promoted films—produced anomalies, of course, in the daily receipts of the Star's accounts book. And the 'regularities' of the audiences' perceived weekly routine (like those of my fictional young women) still leave a host of questions unaddressed: when were wage earners generally paid, if not on Friday; what were the shopping hours for most businesses; did specific ethnic groups attend the Star on particular days; when did children most frequently attend, when did adults; when did women most frequently attend, when did men; how did religious practices (Pawtucket and Central Falls were predominantly Roman Catholic) affect moviegoing; what were the attendance patterns at other Pawtucket picture theaters? Yet whatever answers one might posit to these questions, they probably would not contradict at least that one surprising conclusion about the eagerness of the Star's fans, in 1912–13, to see Mutual's first-run multiple-reel films (and Keystone comedies) on the very first day of their release. If so, that eagerness would be an equally telling testament to the hold moving pictures now had on working people's weekly habits of planning and spending their leisure time as the rare settlement house finding, in May 1912, that 'the moving picture show allowance [was] as much a part of the expense for necessities as ... the rent and the grocery bill.'[47]

Next Year at the Moving Pictures

Cinema and Social Change in the Jewish Immigrant Community

Judith Thissen

O N 22 March 1912, in the week that Loew's Delancey Street Theater, the first picture palace on New York's Lower East Side, opened its doors, a comic Yiddish weekly satirized the future of the Yiddish theater: a jester, more precisely, a moving picture manager in the costume of a jester (so we learn from the inscription on his collar) takes the Yiddish actors, dramatists and the theatergoing crowd to the ten cent cinema. The title of the cartoon—'Next Year at the Moving Pictures' (*leshono habo' bimuving piktshurs*)—makes a pun upon the wish 'next year in Jerusalem' (*leshono habo' birusholaim*), a wish that Jews, then and now, exchange at the conclusion of the Passover feast (seder) and the Yom Kippur service which entertains the hopes that the Jewish people in Diaspora will eventually return to the Land of Israel. The legend comments: 'Moving picture manager: This way, this way, Jews! Cheap, cheap, cheap! all stars for ten cents! (A scene from next season, according to the prophecy of the best theater prophets).'

The cartoon not only hints at cinema's far-reaching influence (clearly, the moving picture manager—do we recognize Marcus Loew?—pulls the strings), but also implies cinema's ascending cultural and social currency in the immigrant community of Eastern European Jews. The following years indeed witnessed significant developments in the direction of the medium's broad acceptance. At first sight, it seems that by the mid 1910s, film exhibitors in Jewish neighborhoods had successfully transformed the cinema from a *goyish* entertainment scorned by the leaders of their community, into a form of entertainment appropriate for Jews as much as for Gentiles—just

6.1 'Next Year at the Moving Pictures,' *Groyser kundes*, 22 March 1912.

as on the national level, cinema had been transformed from a cheap, somewhat disreputable amusement into the nation's favorite entertainment pastime, suitable for Americans of all classes. However, a closer look at the cartoon challenges this view. Cinema might have been accepted but it was not necessarily respected, because the moving picture manager remains a *nar* (jester). Worse yet, in the cartoonist's view, everybody becomes a *nar* by going to the moving picture theater.

This chapter discusses why, in the Jewish context, the cinema could not but remain a contested site of Americanization. The community's self-declared leadership of newspaper editors, writers, labor organizers and political activists felt a fundamental discomfort toward the film medium and the Jewish involvement in the American motion picture business. Cinema's popularity among the Jewish 'masses' not only undermined their cultural and moral authority, but, more importantly, also threatened the Eastern European Jewish social hierarchy which they had transplanted to the New World. The Jewish masses, for their part, took full advantage of American democratic culture and sought to redress the traditional balance of power between the educated and the uneducated. It was in this context that the cinema became an important arena for the articulation of a new social order, in which the men of the books no longer pulled the strings.

Cinema's Initial Reception

During the 1905–06 season, the first nickelodeons appeared on East Fourteenth Street and the Bowery, the two main arteries of nightlife in downtown Manhattan. The following year, five-cent movie theaters were also opening up in the densely populated tenement district east of the Bowery, an overwhelmingly Jewish neighborhood. One of the first film exhibitors to venture into the area was Adolph Zukor. In late 1904, he and his business partners launched a penny arcade on Grand Street. The location was perfect: right in the heart of the 'ghetto' and next-door to Jacob P. Adler's Grand Theater. Two years later, the place was doing 'a rushing business' with 'moving pictures that could be seen for five cents.'[1] Zukor's success was rapidly emulated by other Jewish immigrant entrepreneurs. The recession of 1907–08 further fueled the demand for inexpensive entertainment and the concomitant expansion of five-cent theaters specializing in moving pictures. Yiddish music hall managers, who suddenly saw a falling-off of business because many of their regular customers could no longer afford to pay a dime or a quarter for admission, lowered their ticket prices and switched to film as their main attraction. Others with no prior experience in the field also tried their luck in the booming nickelodeon business. The Jewish masses eagerly incorporated the *muving piktshurs* into their everyday lives. By mid-1908, Jewish working-class neighborhoods in Manhattan and Brooklyn had the highest density of motion picture shows in New York City.[2]

How did the community's leadership respond to this cheap 'American' amusement invading the Jewish streets? Were the proliferating nickelodeons perceived as a threat to the cultural or moral fabric of the Eastern European Jewish immigrant community? An examination of the representations of moviegoing that circulated in Yiddish-language newspapers might help us to answer this question. Due to the relative weakness of traditional community structures, the Yiddish press had developed into a major cultural, political and social institution, an agent of Americanization and ethnic community enhancement, and a powerful vehicle for radical as well as conservative ideas.

Outstanding in this respect was the socialist *Jewish Daily Forward* (*Forvertz*), which had become the most widely read Yiddish newspaper in America under the editorship of Abraham Cahan.[3] It was the principal organ of the Jewish labor movement and the Russian-Jewish intelligentsia. A day-by-day examination of the *Forward* reveals that the paper largely ignored the nickelodeon boom when it hit the Lower East Side during the 1907–08 season. Between the summers of 1907 and 1908, only a handful of human interest stories covered the entertainment revolution caused by the rapid proliferation of moving picture shows in the Jewish district.[4] Over the next year, the *Forward* became a little more interested in the cinema, but it was not until the East Side mourned the first victim of the 'nickel madness'—the casualty of a balcony crash in a Rivington Street nickelodeon in December 1908—that Cahan devoted an editorial to the *muving piktshur pletser*, centering on the physical threats the storefront shows posed to the masses of moviegoers:

> The masses that are squeezed together in the tenements do not know where to go during the cold evenings. In the gloomy buildings where they sleep and have their sacred homes, there is no space to live. They are forced to go outside. They cannot afford real amusement, so they pass their time for five cents in a moving picture show. This business is booming thanks to the sorrowful life of the masses. These places are crammed like the rooms where they live. Who cares when this human merchandise is crushed? One more person squeezed inside, one more nickel earned. The result is that a railing is pushed and that those who went inside to amuse themselves are taken out dead or injured. Ah, woe to the masses of workers, how they live, how they work, how they rest, and how they amuse themselves! Death is lurking everywhere: in their work, in their food, in their sleep, in their breath and even in their entertainment![5]

Neither Cahan nor his fellow socialists perceived the moving pictures as threatening Jewish cultural identity. In fact, most early *Forward* reports on moviegoing revolved around the economic consequences of the nickelodeon boom, especially for the Yiddish vaudeville business.[6] Significantly, cinema's ideological impact upon the Jewish working-class was not an issue at all, although *Forward* articles devoted to the East Side picture shows frequently underscored how spellbound audiences were by the events on the screen. While Progressive reformers embraced the movies in their efforts to Americanize immigrant Jews and their children, and while the American Federation of Labor realized that socialist pictures could help the labor movement and urged workers to boycott theaters that showed anti-labor films, Jewish socialists failed to see cinema's potential as an agency for edification, acculturation or class struggle.[7]

At the other end of the political spectrum, the conservative *Tageblatt* and *Morgen zhurnal* also adopted a neutral stance on the new film medium. Their targeted readers were predominantly (lower) middle-class immigrants who were politically moderate and emotionally bound to the Jewish way of life.[8] This reading public included many small businessmen, peddlers, storekeepers, contractors, and the like. Both papers played on the traditionalism of these immigrants in the realm of religion and politics, and hence supported the Orthodox and Zionist causes in their editorials. At the same time, they served their readers' upwardly mobile aspirations by publishing the latest business news. While the *Tageblatt* and *Morgen zhurnal* rarely captured the atmosphere of moviegoing on the East Side in human interest stories, they provided extensive coverage of what was happening in the motion picture business at large, on the national as well as on the local level. For instance, they gave their readers up-to-date information about such topics as the formation of the Motion Picture Patent Company and the introduction of a new system for colored pictures.[9] Both papers also closely followed Mayor McClellan's actions against the nickelodeons and the exhibitors' responses.[10] Inclined to defend the interests of small Jewish businessmen, they consistently rallied to the side of the film exhibitors in times of crisis. After the fatal nickelodeon accident on Rivington Street, for instance, both papers insisted on more stringent rules for picture shows, but at the same time defended the proprietors of the theater, who were charged with homicide.[11] In the opinion of the *Tageblatt*, none other than the excited audience was guilty of the deadly accident:

> If the hot-heads that jumped down last Saturday [from the balcony], would have left [the theater] quietly through the side-exits that are indicated with red-lights which even a blind man can see, a lot of trouble would have been spared. The managers wouldn't have had all the heartache and anxiety about an accident for which they were not responsible.[12]

In fact, even the *Forward* did not accuse the proprietors of the Rivington Street nickelodeon outright. With the usual share of socialist rhetoric, Cahan concluded that the capitalist system alone was to be held responsible for the accident.[13]

As these examples illustrate, a broad range of descriptions of East Side picture shows, their owners and audiences circulated in the Yiddish press—descriptions which sometimes contradicted each other, but generally overlapped. What is striking is that, in sharp contrast with the reception of the nickelodeon boom in the mainstream English-language press, the Yiddish press did not define the cinema as a contested site of Americanization. Regardless of their orientation, almost no Yiddish newspaper article touched on the subject of the moral influence moving pictures had upon immigrant Jews. Until late 1909, this was not a subject for debate within the Jewish immigrant community.

The Revitalization of Jewish Ethnic Identity

The popularity of moving pictures only became a source of concern at the beginning of the 1909–10 season. All of a sudden, Yiddish newspapers on the left and right felt the need to address what the *Tageblatt* would later define as '*di muving piktshur frage*' (the moving picture issue).[14] The immediate cause was the take-over of Adler's Grand Theater by Adolph Zukor and Marcus Loew. For several years, Zukor had operated a small nickelodeon next to the 2000-seat playhouse, which was the first theater in New York City especially built for Yiddish performances. For the Grand, the pride of the East Side and the only Yiddish playhouse where literary drama remained a visible part of the repertoire, to be turned into a movie theater scandalized public opinion. Many immigrant intellectuals, Cahan at the forefront, found it difficult to put up with the idea that their 'Temple of Art' was falling in the hands of some uptown *alrightniks* (nouveau riches) and moving pictures were to replace Jacob P. Adler starring in Gordin's *Jewish King Lear*. But both Cahan's *Forward* and the theater unions were defeated in their attempt to retain the playhouse for Yiddish performances. In the first week of September 1909, brightly colored posters in Yiddish and English announced that the Grand Theater ('formerly Adler's theater') would reopen as a five-ten-fifteen cent moving picture and vaudeville house.

The take-over of the Grand Theater came at a pivotal moment in the relation between the Jewish community and the American mainstream. In April 1908, the word had begun to spread in certain uptown, German-Jewish circles that a new era was dawning in which 'New York is about to repent assimilation and seeks to be conservative in all things Jewish.'[15] A month later, at a conference of Jewish Charities, Louis Marshall, a prominent member of the German-Jewish elite, offered a new perspective on Jewish social life. The effort of Jewish communal institutions, he said, 'should be, not to strive for a minimum, but for a maximum of Jewishness.'[16] The following years would indeed be characterized by a revitalization of Jewish ethnic identity in all spheres of Jewish social life: in the realm of education, religion and philanthropy; on the work floor and in the realm of leisure.

The season of 1909–10 witnessed a course of events that marked a turning point in the American experience of the Eastern European Jews.

In particular, it was the year that the Jewish labor movement gained a firm foothold among immigrant Jews. As the depression of 1907–08 came to an end, tens of thousands struck for higher wages, shorter hours, and improved working conditions. In November 1909, twenty thousand shirtwaist makers, mostly young Jewish women, left their work to walk the picket lines. Five months later, the 'girls' handed on the torch of Jewish labor activism to their male colleagues in needle trades: in July 1910, 70,000 cloak makers declared a general strike—the largest in the history of New York City. The labor movement helped immigrant Jews to formulate a new sense of collective identity and forge a more explicit place for Eastern European Jews in the American public sphere. On the eve of World War I, the United Hebrew Trades, a federation of Jewish unions, encompassed more than one hundred unions with approximately 250,000 members.[17]

On the Lower East Side, the mobilization of the Jewish proletariat—as Jews and as workers—was not only played out on the work floor. During the 1909–10 season, Yiddish vaudeville, which had almost vanished from the bills of five and ten cent theaters, made a remarkable come-back. Yiddish music hall managers, who had switched to moving picture exhibition during the depression of 1907–08, returned to their original format. In their footsteps, local nickelodeon managers began to add more and longer Yiddish vaudeville acts to their bills. Until now, they had used songs and brief sketches merely as 'fillers' to amuse their patrons while the reels were changed. The revival of Yiddish vaudeville might be understood as a grass-roots response to the 'Americanization of early American cinema' (in Richard Abel's words).[18] To counteract the increasing influence of mainstream American culture via the film medium, Jewish immigrants demanded more 'home-made' entertainment on the bill of their neighborhood movie theaters. As I have argued elsewhere, Yiddish vaudeville acts 'reinforced feelings of belonging to an ethnic community with shared values and pleasures, based upon a communal language and history.' More importantly, programmed in between moving pictures, live entertainment in Yiddish shaped the reception of these movies, thus reducing their Americanizing agency.[19]

Loew and Zukor: Goyim or Alrightniks?

The rise of nationalism within the American film industry not only gave rise to sharp debates between immigrant Jews and the American host society over the nature of 'American' cinema, but also led to internal conflicts over cinema's contribution to the Jewish experience in America. While never expressly thematized, at stake was whether or not cinema could be made compatible with a continued Jewish identity.

Although the leading Yiddish newspapers disagreed about Adler's motives to sell the lease of the Grand Theater, there existed a virtual consensus on the question of who was ultimately to blame for the fact that the playhouse was lost for Yiddish performances. As the Grand drama unfolded, Loew and Zukor were exposed as the true villains. At the same time, however, the editors of the Yiddish dallies did not wish to antagonize their readers by blaming upwardly mobile Jews for destroying the community's cultural heritage—the Grand Theater had been the home of Yiddish literary drama almost since its opening in 1903—and, hence, they carefully avoided revealing the Jewish identity of the Grand's new proprietors. At first, commentators insisted that the theater had fallen into the hands of *'American* theater managers' [my italics]. Eventually, the Yiddish newspapers got so caught up in their efforts to hide the truth that they stripped Zukor and Loew of their Jewishness. The leftist *Warheit* repeatedly used the term *goyim* in association with the new proprietors of the Grand. For instance, a few days before the reopening of the Grand Theater, it described the people behind the moving picture company that had secured the lease of the playhouse as 'goyim' and 'Yankees.'[20] *Forward* readers too were made to believe that Gentiles had gained control over the Grand.[21] Even the Orthodox *Tageblatt*, which at first hushed up much of the commotion around the take-over, eventually joined in with its competitors.[22]

The Grand Theater affair was a moment of crisis in which attitudes crystallized, defining a 'we' and a 'them.' So horrified were the editors of the Yiddish newspapers by the realization that their authority over the immigrant community was challenged by two *proste jidn* (people without learning, taste or spiritual virtues), that they decided to repress this social and cultural upheaval by redrawing the boundaries of the ethnic group. They outlawed Loew and Zukor by defining them as 'goyim' rather than 'alrightniks,' the sneering Yinglish term that the East Side's intelligentsia normally used for the allegedly uneducated Jews who had done economically well in America.[23]

How did the Jewish immigrant audience respond to the affair? There is no indication whatsoever that they boycotted the new moving picture temple on Grand Street. Jewish masses had embraced Yiddish vaudeville anew, but without jettisoning the film medium. They liked the entertainment of the American movies enough not to want to do away with them as an act of ethnic correctness. Moreover, while sympathetic and responsive to the message of ethnic solidarity, they did not oppose acculturation into the mainstream. On the contrary: to many of them, Loew and Zukor were role models of upward mobility, and the stories of their success functioned as Horatio Alger novels. Marcus Loew, in particular, presented the East Side Jews with a symbol of Jewish success in America and an incentive to pursue the American Dream. In 1913, he built the palatial Avenue B theater on the very site of the dingy tenement in which he had been born. At the time, Loew made a clear statement of his commitment to America by commissioning a large patriotic painting for the proscenium. The painting was a belated but unequivocal answer to the Grand Theater affair. Its unmistakable message was that the Jewish road to success began at Loew's 'million dollar theater' under the watchful eye of George Washington, and not of Abraham Cahan's. Radical dreams about a socialist revolution were reduced to the image of the Revolutionary War (War of American Independence). The cinema itself was the new battle field.

Fighting the Movies

In the years following the Grand affair, the Yiddish press responded to the crisis in two ways. The *Forward* sought to provide the immigrant workers with a suitable home-made alternative for the *goyishe* movies. Yiddish 'legitimate' drama, which the socialists had long considered the civilizing agency *par excellence* for the uneducated masses, was in a deep crisis and they therefore had to look elsewhere. Endorsing the revival of Yiddish vaudeville seemed the solution, but the trouble was that, for years on end, the *Forward* had treated it as a stupid and vulgar form of entertainment, an appropriation of the wrong aspects of American culture. Cahan himself had been the driving force behind several campaigns against the Yiddish music halls. In the end, however, Cahan's desire to maintain his leadership position was stronger than his aversion to Yiddish vaudeville. In an attempt to secure consent for the existing distribution of power, he decided to incorporate—or rather 'assimilate'—Yiddish vaudeville into the mainstream of Jewish culture. In December 1909, the *Forward* began to promote Yiddish vaudeville as an authentic expression of Jewishness (*yidishkayt*).[24]

While Yiddish vaudeville was legitimized by the *Forward* critics, the cinema, for its part, was constructed as the new 'low-Other' and relegated to the bottom end of the cultural hierarchy, a position which had previously been occupied by Yiddish vaudeville. In the process, prostitution, white slavery and loose sexual behavior—urban American vices that had been associated with the Yiddish music hall business—became more and more linked with moviegoing. From late 1909 onwards, the *Forward* frequently reported about the moral dangers that the nickelodeons held for young people. Short back-page news items with titles as 'break into a home because of moving pictures' and 'movies turn children into gangsters' depicted local movie theaters as schools of crime where murder, shop-lifting, robbery and holdups were illustrated.[25] Highly sensational stories about the connection between movie houses and prostitution made the front pages. On 13 May 1910, the white slavery hysteria gained momentum. The paper's headline screamed: 'Don't let your children go alone into the moving picture houses: Mothers beg the *Forward* to save their children from ruin and shame.'[26] Articles highlighting the moral dangers of moviegoing were also commonplace in the English-language press of the period, but in the mainstream press, cinema's critics often used these stories to illustrate the need for regulation, arguing that if immoral movies could turn children into criminals, moral subjects might just as well turn them into good citizens. This type of reform discourse remained absent in the commentaries of the *Forward*.

Cahan's competitors shared his concern about the corrupting influence of moving pictures, but they were less convinced that Yiddish vaudeville was the right answer to the *muving piktshur frage*. Rather than offering an alternative to the movies, they merely outlined the potential dangers of the cinema to their readers. For instance, in an editorial entitled 'Moving Pictures and Children,' the editor of the Orthodox *Tageblat*, warned parents that the establishment of the National Board of Censorship offered no guarantee that all movies were suitable to *Jewish* children.[27] A remarkably blunt example of the strategy to discourage moviegoing was 'Abie's moving pictures,' a series of cartoons published in the leftist *Warheit* in 1912. More than any other Yiddish newspaper, the *Warheit* displayed the tendency toward eye-catching illustrations typical of the American yellow press. Not unexpectedly, then, the paper chose to fight fire with fire. The 'Abie's moving pictures' cartoons depict the misadventures of little Abie and Izzy after their return from the picture show. The boys imitate what they had just seen at the movies. Every cartoon concludes with a punitive ending, usually their mother beating them. In the most revealing episode in the series, Abie and Izzy harass their old grandfather after watching a Christmas movie, tearing his beard like two *pogromchiks*. They want him to buy them Christmas presents, but he drags his grandsons back home to read the Torah, accusing them of behaving like converts to the Christian fate (*geshmad*).

Toward Acceptance?

The 1913–14 season marked a turning point in the battle between the intellectual elite, amusement entrepreneurs and the moviegoing masses over cinema's position in Jewish immigrant culture: motion picture news became a permanent feature in the Yiddish press. In October 1913, *Israel der*

6.2 'Abie's moving picture' cartoons, *Warheit*, 1912.

yenki [sic], the theater critic of the Orthodox *Tageblatt*, launched *Theater un muving piktshurs*, a Yiddish-language weekly devoted to the Yiddish stage and the world of moving pictures. In January 1914, the *Forward* started a regular film column entitled 'Interesting facts about moving pictures.'[28] Although both initiatives were short-lived, it was the beginning of a process in which film news became integrated, little by little, in the weekly theater pages of the Yiddish dailies.

Around the same time, the leading actors of the Yiddish stage began to make moving pictures. In 1914, Jacob P. Adler, who had always prided himself as an ardent promoter of 'true art,' starred in the title role of the five-reel feature *Michael Strogoff* (*The Courier to the Czar*), the first production of Popular Plays and Players. 'Note the Jacob P.—this is the great Adler, one of America's foremost romantic actors,' the company boasted in the

Moving Picture World.[29] That same year, his wife Sarah Adler made her film debut in *Sins of the Parents.*[30] A year later, Boris Thomashefsky, another well known Yiddish theater star, set up his own production company to make films based on Yiddish plays.[31]

It appeared that the traditional tastemakers, from Abraham Cahan to Jacob P. Adler, had decided to go along with the tide. If moviegoing had become a permanent part of Jewish immigrant life, then let the *Forward* be respectful of this leisure habit. If the Jewish masses wanted to see the great stars of the Yiddish stage for five or ten cents, then why not make movies to satisfy their demand? Tellingly, however, when *Michael Strogoff* premièred on the Lower East Side—of all places, at the Grand Theater (formerly Adler's)—Adler put a special notice in the *Forward*, warning the public that he was only performing at the People's Theater on the Bowery.[32] An unease with cinema was also still evident in the *Forward*'s movie columns. Whereas 'What is going on in the world of the theater' dealt exclusively with the local Yiddish theater, 'Interesting facts about moving pictures' only related to what happened on a (inter)national level. The paper's cinema column never dealt with local news. No attention whatsoever was given to films running in Jewish neighborhood theaters, to the openings of new movie theaters on the Lower East Side, and the like. The cinema remained something profoundly *unheymish* for Cahan and his staff.

As Yiddish theater historian Nina Warnke points out, the unease of the community's cultural elite with popular amusements like Yiddish vaudeville and moving pictures was rooted in a 'deep seated distrust of commercial entertainment which was thought—by American social reformers as well as immigrant intellectuals—to exploit working people's need for cheap urban recreation, to corrupt the innocent, and to break up family life.'[33] There is, however, also something else at work here. The ways in which the Eastern European Jews responded to the cinema in America were structured by deeper levels of ideology, and in particular by the ideology that Jews are a People of the Book rather than a People of the Image. In exploring this proposition, I am aware that I tread on dangerous ground. Jewish attitudes toward visual culture in general, and the understanding of the Second Commandment in particular, are sensitive issues and should perhaps be left to colleagues in the field of Jewish studies.[34] The problem is that these scholars, who come from a profoundly text-centered tradition, have only recently begun to explore the visual components of Jewish culture and have focused their research almost exclusively on expressions of high art.[35] It may be a long time before they venture into cinema studies.

Next Year in Jerusalem

'Next year at the moving pictures,' the title of the cartoon with which I opened this essay, refers directly to a crucial moment in the history of the Jewish people: the departure from Egypt, which the Jews commemorate during the Seder, the home service on the eve of *Pesach* (Passover). In the Diaspora, the Seder concludes with the recitation of the wish 'Next year in Jerusalem.'[36] But that is not all there is to it. The Exodus was the beginning of a journey that was to lead the Israelites to the Promised Land under Moses' guidance. Unexpectedly, this journey took forty years, in punishment for their disobedience to Moses and to God.

The rebellion is recounted in Exodus 32–34.[37] While Moses remained at Mount Sinai to receive the tables of the Law, the Israelites at the foot of mountain grew impatient. They doubted that their leader would return and requested a visible god to lead them to the Promised Land. On their request, Aaron created the statue of a calf out of golden ornaments willingly donated by the people. By worshiping this calf, the Israelites rebelled against their leader and directly transgressed the order of the Ten Commandments to have no other gods but the Lord. After God revealed to Moses what was happening, Moses came down from the mountain, caught the people in the act of worshiping the calf with feasting and merriment, and in a burst of anger smashed the tablets of the Law on the ground, thereby effectively canceling the covenant with God. He subsequently obtained a pardon for his people and carved the tablets anew. Thereafter, Moses led the Israelites for forty years through the wilderness, until those who had rebelled and worshiped the idol had died and a new generation had grown up, the generation which was allowed to enter the Promised Land.

The cartoon depicts a man leading a crowd to a temple. Considering the title and the time of publication (two weeks before Passover), there is little doubt that the cartoonist alludes to Israel's journey to the Promised Land. In the American context, however, it is a moving picture manager who is the liberator of Israel and leads the Jews through the wilderness of the New World. Tellingly, the crowd is a crowd of actors and actresses, followed by their fans—all dressed as jesters. To fully understand what this allusion means in terms of cinema's relationship to the process of Americanization, we have to make yet another excursion outside the discipline of film studies.

Despite the fact that the 'guilty' generation was not allowed to enter the Land of Israel, the anxiety about yet another rebellion and lapse in idolatry remained strong. In the book of Deuteronomy, the fifth and last book of the Torah, Moses takes leave of his people, warns them of their frequent disobedience and lack of faith in God, and exhorts them to fidelity. Deuteronomy is generally understood as the 'book of law.' It recapitulates the main religious principles and legislation, including the Ten Commandments, and insists on the absolute rejection of idolatry.[38]

Conventional wisdom holds that Judaism is suspiciously hostile to the visual arts because of the Second Commandment. Artifactual evidence amassed by archeologists, ethnographers and art historians reveals a different reality. Alerted by this material evidence, Jewish historian Kalmen Bland recently analyzed a number of medieval texts and concluded that, throughout the pre-modern period, Jewish society affirmed the legitimacy of Jewish visual images. As late as the sixteenth century, according to Bland, 'neither Jews or Gentile ever understood the biblical law to be a prohibition against the production, use or enjoyment of *all* visual images.'[39] In his view, it was not until the nineteenth century that German-Jewish intellectuals, following Kant and Hegel, began to ascribe to Judaism a comprehensive aversion to the visual arts.

In contrast to what is generally believed, Jewish opposition to visual representation might well have been restricted rather than comprehensive. There is, however, one mode of artistic expression that has long been regarded unequivocally idolatrous: the theater. In the Talmud and later writings, rabbis condemned the theater, which they associated with the pagan worship of gods, the 'theaters and circuses' of the Romans, and later with medieval mystery plays. Well into the nineteenth century, theatrical performances were prohibited in Eastern European Jewish communities, with the exception of the so-called *purimshpiln*.[40] An examination of this exception provides further insights into the rabbinical distrust of the theater.

During the holiday of Purim (the 'Jewish carnival'), young artisans and yeshiva students, dressed as non-Jews and women, paraded down the streets and performed sketches in courts of synagogues and in wealthy Jewish homes—sketches that laced the biblical story of Esther with coarse parodies of both the local dignitaries and the biblical heroes of the story. In many respect, Purim resembled the medieval Feast of Fools and the Renaissance *Fastnachtspiel*. However, while in the Christian context, the carnivalesque (in the Bakhtinian sense of the term) was primarily about freedom from official order and social status, in the Jewish context there was more at stake. In Diaspora, as theater historian Michael Steinlauf points out, 'the characteristic reversals of the carnivalesque concern not only high and low, but also inside and outside.'[41] The unique danger of the *purimsphil* in particular, and the theater more generally, Steinlauf argues, was that it allowed Jews to let the ultimate Other, the non-Jew, inside them.[42] In

Eastern Europe, the potential social criticism embedded in the Purim plays increased as the tradition was appropriated by the *proste yidn*, the lowest social orders among the Jewish population; those men who, by the norms of traditional Jewish society, were considered most like the *goyim*.[43] Tellingly, nowhere was the rabbinical objection to theatrical performances more vigorous than in the Russian Empire. In fact, legal prohibitions against acting and unceasing efforts to contain it to Purim seriously hampered the development of a professional Yiddish theater.

In turn-of-the-century New York, the Jewish immigrant intelligentsia sought to make the Yiddish theater compatible with the spirit of Jewish elite culture. Socialist intellectuals in particular were a driving force behind a relentless campaign to uplift the Yiddish stage from its origins in folk theater. Not theater *per se*, but historical operettas and spectacular melodrama—so-called *shund* (trash) theater—was the object of their criticism. In the radical press, they attempted to teach their 'uneducated' readers an appreciation of true art (*emese kunst*), meaning literary drama.[44] Popular theater was condemned as *purimshpil*; *shund* plays were considered '*nareshe zokhen far 'n prosten theater bezukher*' (stupid things for the ignorant theater-goer).[45] Typically, *shund* was depicted as a *nar*—which adds yet another layer of meaning to the figure of the moving picture manager in our cartoon.

Rabbinic tractates regulating Jewish intercourse with Gentiles in the socio-cultural sphere often played on a conception of 'low' and 'Other' against which to construct a Jewish difference. Similarly, the theater reviews written by the Jewish immigrant intelligentsia frequently constructed the popular theater as a 'wrong' American influence. Around 1900, Jacob Gordin, a prominent socialist intellectual and the foremost writer of Yiddish realist drama, defined the corrupting influence of the American stage on the Yiddish theater as follows:

The American stage asserts itself in the growing belief that the most important thing is not the play but who plays; not the literary value but the degree of piquancy; not the content but the attractions; not the idea but the accessories and the sceneries. Closely resembling the American theater in its mercantile character, its unliterary influence, and its exclusive management by speculators and gamblers, the Yiddish theater, too is conducted mainly as a *geschäft*. To gain profit, every attempt is made to attract the public, either by sensational shows, or by pretended brilliancy of historical 'trash,' or by sentimental, tearful, pseudo-romantic 'harrangue'—just as it is done in the 'serious' theaters of uptown. Sometimes, however, the practices of 'less serious' theaters are imitated, and the Yiddish public is treated to dramatizations of criminal cases, to exhibition of limbs, to various stage effects and devices, or to coarse pugilistic and athletic trickery.[46]

What strikes me most in this stab at the mainstream American stage and the Yiddish popular theater is not so much the distrust of commercial entertainment, but Gordin's suspicion of the spectacular: 'the most important thing is ... not the content but the attractions; not the idea but the accessories and the sceneries.' Clearly, as men of the Word (if no longer God's Word), the secularized offspring of the rabbinate remained opposed to a culture of the Image. This helps to explain why the immigrant intelligentsia fought so hard to bring literary drama on the Yiddish stage. It also helps to explain why they vetoed cinema's integration into the American-Jewish experience. Within their belief system, the spectacle of the movies represented an almost ontological threat to the survival of the Jewish people, and certainly to their own position as newspaper editors, journalists and writers. Time and again, the Yiddish newspaper editors sought to bring their readers back to the text-centered tradition of the rabbis. In this respect it is significant that, unlike American social reformers, immigrant intellectuals never came to consider the movies as a possible means to uplift the Jewish masses.

Conclusion

Let us return a final time to the *leshono habo' bimuving piktshurs* cartoon. It was published during the month of Adar, in between Purim and Pesach. What it basically represents is an Eastern European Purim parade. Typically, Purim parades were headed by a *loyfer* (runner) dressed in the costume of a medieval jester, just like the moving picture manager in the cartoon.[47] Purim plays were filled with reversals, mocking biblical heroes and parodying local worthies. In the cartoon, the moving picture manager—someone who is most like a *goy*, by the norms of the immigrant elite—changes places with Moses, the man who the bible portrays as the greatest of all prophets. In short, a *proste yid* is leading the Jewish masses, instead of *moyshe rabeyne* (Moses the teacher).

In the Old World, the reality of everyday life under oppressive conditions left little room for social and political action. Purim was an annual eruption of carnivalesque freedom into the normative cycle of the Jewish year, but it reinforced the existing social order more than it suggested alternatives.[48] In the New World, where immigrant Jews lived separated from traditional community structures and moral authorities, the carnivalesque could erupt everyday and give birth to a culture of opposition. Street protests, rent boycotts and strikes were among the more obvious forms of collective action that aimed at redressing social injustice.[49] The popularity of moviegoing among immigrant Jews, I would argue, was yet another public display of participatory democracy. It was a carnivalesque revolt of the Jewish masses against the persistence of long-standing social hierarchies, against the elite's efforts to maintain traditional distinctions that privileged the men of the written word. Rather than be led by the immigrant intelligentsia, the Jewish masses preferred the moving picture manager—alias the jester, the very figure who turns the world upside down—to guide them on the way to Americanization. That the moving picture temple represented the New Jerusalem may have been a horror scenario for the community's leadership, but for the Jewish masses it proved to be a promising perspective, because if Jerusalem was the cinema, then the Promised Land was just around the corner, and thus much closer than either the socialist 'land of milk and honey' or the Zionist dream of a return to Erets Yisra'el.

'Four Hours of Hootin' and Hollerin''

Moviegoing and Everyday Life Outside the Movie Palace

Jeffrey Klenotic

R ESEARCH on the history of urban film exhibition after the nickelodeon has amply documented Hollywood's efforts to add a normative middle-class accent to the theater experience of an increasingly diverse, cross-class audience.[1] These efforts culminated during the cinema's late silent and early sound eras, when major studios invested heavily in the ownership, renovation and construction of motion picture palaces.[2] The picture palace was typically found in downtown areas or prosperous suburbs. In both locations, the key to success was access to established lines of mass transit and proximity to 'bright light' centers of shopping and social activity. Unlike the many smaller theaters it sought to eclipse, the movie palace assumed no distinct tie to the ethnic, racial or class specificities of the immediate community. Instead, palaces courted patrons from around the city, as well as from smaller towns on the outskirts where luxurious picture houses were seldom found. As Peter Stead has observed:

> The big show-piece cinemas were built to pull in the fashionable trade but they were not designed for the exclusive use of a social elite ... To attract the best patrons the movie-houses had to ape the conventions and the standards of theatres and opera-houses but very quickly the whole industry realized that the appeal of the movie palaces was not unrelated to the fact that all customers had to be treated the same and so they became temples of a new classlessness.[3]

As 'temples of a new classlessness,' picture palaces provided an intense experience designed to attract the largest, most heterogeneous audience possible. That experience began with the electric signage that lit up the night while ticket-seeking patrons queued excitedly in long lines or lost themselves in amorphous crowds. The experience then proceeded through the exotic foyer where paintings and musicians occupied moviegoers waiting for a show to finish, to reach the multimedia format of the entertainment presentation itself—stage shows, short films, musical performances, ambient or even atmospheric lighting, and a first-run feature film.

Inside the theater, patrons were ushered to seats and expected to uphold polite standards of decorum. As Richard Testa discovered, employee manuals instructed palace ushers to enforce decorum in a diplomatic manner:

> If a patron is creating unnecessary noise say, 'I beg your pardon, sir. You are annoying those around you,' and then leave immediately. (Do not wait for an answer in this case as it might lead to an argument and this is to be avoided at all times.) If the patron persists in making a noise, call an executive at once. Intoxicated patrons, petting couples, degenerates and morons should not be handled by you without first calling a member of the management, unless the circumstances demand immediate attention.[4]

Under duly monitored conditions, patrons were invited quietly to immerse themselves in the film experience, which worked with the opulent, stunning architecture to hold them 'in the dark somnambulism of celluloid fantasy.'[5]

Perhaps the most important aspect of the picture palace formula was the policy of complete and uniform customer service. Staffed nurseries were provided for families with children. Theater employees were trained to treat patrons as royalty and to show no favoritism or familiarity toward any individual moviegoer. This was because managers 'believed that if service staff members held conversations with some people, other patrons would feel less important; the goal of management was to make everyone feel that they were as valued a customer as everyone else.'[6] Staff were instructed to be 'Salesmen of Happiness,' and in keeping with the 'chain store' model of American Big Business in the 1920s the happiness they sold was predicated on giving standardized service for money.[7] Where in earlier times a moviegoer might have known the proprietor of the theater and her or his family, who might have also served as staff, now there was a quasi-personal 'exchange' relationship. If the social experience of some forms of urban moviegoing had once been informal and prone to vary by neighborhood, the new style picture palace was not only 'a vision of wealth, a touch of royalty,' but also a 'reprieve from community.'[8]

When viewed as a prominent landmark of social progress and architectural grandeur in 1920s America, and taken as a powerful symbol of Hollywood's own capacity for progress and transformation, the movie palace casts a long shadow in cultural memory and historical imagination. Maggie Valentine, for instance, contends that 'movie palaces replaced nickelodeons the way talkies replaced silent movies—quickly and irrevocably.'[9] Palaces did not, however, constitute the typical moviegoing experience of the 1920s. It is important to keep in mind how rare movie palaces were, and how often they may have operated at less than full capacity, even at the height of what has often been perceived as the 'movie palace era.' As Richard Koszarski has documented, '*Film Daily Yearbook* noted sixty-six major first-run houses in 1927, only seventeen of which grossed as much as $1 million annually. It would appear that a great many Americans were still patronizing neighborhood and subsequent-run houses.' Miriam Hansen makes a similar point, estimating that picture palaces amounted to roughly 5 per cent of all American movie theaters between 1915 and 1933.[10]

Although movie palaces projected a social vision of classlessness and upscale egalitarianism, the actual experience of class mixing remained limited, as Roy Rosenzweig found in his case study of workers and leisure in the industrial city of Worcester, Massachusetts: 'many working-class people continued to view movies within their own neighborhood theaters, which more closely reflected the behavior patterns, conditions, and ownership of the early movie days.'[11] The neighborhood vitality that Rosenzweig found in some Worcester theaters has been echoed by more recent research on Depression-era moviegoing by Thomas Doherty, as well as by studies on film exhibition in 1920s and 1930s Chicago, where both European immigrant and African-American audiences maintained largely insular modes of neighborhood moviegoing, drawing on residual traditions of cultural practice.[12]

Given the diversity of audiences and moviegoing experiences represented in the growing scholarship on the social history of exhibition, it seems important not to identify the cinema's institutional and cultural development only in terms of 'forces of standardization.'[13] This chapter's case study of moviegoing at the Franklin Theater in Springfield, Massachusetts, seeks to contribute to our understanding of the meaningful role that non-dominant forms of film exhibition continued to play in the everyday lives of many Americans who found themselves on the economic and cultural outskirts as a result of their structural positioning within marginalized working-class, racial and ethnic spaces. My study focuses on the late 1920s and early

7.1 The Franklin Theater, c. 1940.

1930s, arguably the peak of the movie palace phenomenon, in the hope of illuminating vestigial moviegoing practices otherwise eclipsed by the shadow of these palaces. In the process, I hope to capture a sense of the rich social experience that we might overlook if we were to define exhibition in Springfield during this period exclusively in terms of a 'movie palace era.'

Theoretically, this study assumes that like all acts of cultural consumption, moviegoing is part of a wider process of social communication; it is a sign.[14] Like all signs, what going to the movies communicates, what it means or can mean for those who practice it and through their social and interpretative competencies encode and decode it, is fundamentally subject to multi-accentuality, the property by which a sign carries the potential to signify multiple, even contradictory, meanings contingent on the conditions of its use.[15] The meanings that audiences produce for and through the activity of moviegoing take shape as a consequence of physical, economic, social, and discursive contexts that are subject to varying ideological interests and intersect in variable ways to form historically specific conditions of reception. While these conditions can and should be analyzed for what they tell us about the interpretive processes of specific audiences in relation to particular films,[16] it is vitally important to recognize that these conditions are themselves a meaningful part of the cultural experience of moviegoing as it has been practiced over the past one hundred years. Our understanding of the intersection of film history with the wider history of American society and culture is greatly enriched by taking into account the variable, yet still structured, ways in which Americans have used their local movie theaters and made sense of their countless moviegoing experiences.[17]

Parameters of Springfield Movie Exhibition

Where in Springfield could one see a movie between 1926 and 1932? What types of theater ownership were evident? How much of the overall exhibition market fell into each type? These questions can produce a snapshot of the full range of movie exhibition in Springfield that will give context to the specific case of the Franklin Theater, which first opened in 1929 in the middle of this period. Equally important, answering these questions will heighten awareness of the empirical complexities—not to mention the theoretical and ideological ones—that emerge in the search for even rudimentary forms of generalization about the social history of moviegoing.

At the start of 1926, Springfield had twelve theaters that presented movies. These were, in ascending order by seat capacity, the Cleveland (350), the Garden (500), the Grand (690), the Strand (746), the Bijou (900), the Phillips (900), the State (900), the Jefferson (1,036), the Fox (1,444), the Broadway (2,200), the Capitol (2,200), and Poli's Palace (3,000).[18] Of these, all but two were devoted to screening motion pictures as the primary attraction. The two exceptions were the State, devoted to burlesque but occasionally home to scandalous films of a sort 'banned in Boston,' and Poli's Palace, where feature films regularly shared the bill with live vaudeville. If the State is excluded due to the extreme rarity of its films, the remaining eleven theaters provided a total 13,966 seats. Mean seat capacity was 1,270 seats. Four theaters exceeded the mean, seven failed to reach it.

By 1932, the total number of theaters showing movies had increased to sixteen. One theater, the Cleveland, had gone out of business but five new theaters had opened. In addition, the State had new ownership and in September 1931 switched from burlesque to a movies-only policy.[19] Overall, the movie exhibition market in 1932 included: the Pine Point (386), the Garden (500), the Grand (690), the Strand (746), the Franklin (800), the State (900), the Bijou (900), the Liberty (960), the Jefferson (1,036), the Arcade (1,100), the Phillips (1,200), the Fox (1,444), the Broadway (2,200), the Capitol (2,200), Fox-Poli Palace (2,500), and the Paramount (3,200).

Together, these sixteen theaters provided 20,762 seats. Mean seat capacity was 1,298; five theaters stood above the mean while eleven fell below it.[20]

What types of ownership were represented among these theaters and did the pattern change? In 1926, Springfield had one theater integrated into a national, studio-owned chain: the Fox Theater, owned by the Fox Theater Corporation. In addition, there were two theaters that were part of two different regional chains. The Broadway operated under the Goldstein Brothers Theater Corporation, which controlled several theaters throughout New England and was owned by Springfield residents Samuel and Nathan Goldstein. Poli's Palace was part of a New England chain of vaudeville–picture houses owned by Sylvester Poli of Connecticut. Springfield also had a budding local chain. The Winchester Amusement Corporation had been formed in 1925 by local residents Harry Cohen and Louis Cohn, who at that time owned the Phillips and Jefferson theaters respectively. By 1926, the chain had grown to four, as the previously independent Strand and Garden theaters joined the fold. Finally, the remaining theaters in the city—the Bijou, the Capitol, the Cleveland, and the Grand—were independent, non-chain operations.

We can begin to gauge the prominence each type of ownership had within Springfield in 1926 by tallying the number and percentage of movie seats in each category: National chain = 1,444 seats (10 per cent); regional chain = 5,200 seats (37 per cent); local chain = 3,182 seats (23 per cent); and non-chain = 4,140 seats (30 per cent).

By 1932, ownership patterns had changed considerably. The city no longer had any regional chain theaters, as these were absorbed by Hollywood studios during the normalization phase of vertical integration that commenced after 1926. Hollywood's real estate in the city thus grew larger, at least in the downtown business district, which is where the studios made all their acquisitions. Warner Bros. introduced Springfield to sound pictures in 1927 at the Capitol, then bought that formerly independent theater themselves in 1929. Fox Corporation, which already owned the Fox, bought Poli's regional circuit and thereby added Poli's Palace to its holdings, changing the theater's name to Fox-Poli's Palace in 1928. In 1929, Publix bought the Goldstein chain and so acquired the Broadway. That same year, Publix also constructed the city's largest theater, the Paramount.

At the level of local ownership, Winchester Amusement added another theater in 1928, when it built the Liberty, which joined the Garden, the Jefferson, the Phillips, and the Strand as part of the Winchester chain of neighborhood theaters (all but the Garden were located outside downtown, and the Garden itself sat close to the south side of downtown, which was home to a large Italian-American community). The number of locally owned independent theaters grew as well, from four to six. The Bijou and Grand remained independent, the former downtown and the latter in an outlying neighborhood. In addition, three new independent theaters were built. The Pine Point (1927) and the Franklin (1929) went up in two separate neighborhoods, while the Arcade (1931) was constructed downtown. The State, also downtown, was purchased by a local independent owner and converted from burlesque to movies in 1931. The independent Cleveland Theater was no longer in business, having closed in 1927.

By 1932, then, the relative distribution of movie seats by type of ownership was greatly altered: National chain = 11,544 seats (56 per cent); regional chain = 0 seats (0 per cent); local chain = 4,442 (21 per cent); and non-chain = 4,776 seats (23 per cent).

The changes between 1926 and 1932 can be summarized as follows:

	1926	1932
Movie theaters:	11	16
Total seats:	13,966	20,762
National chain seats:	10%	56%
Regional chain seats:	37%	0%
Local chain seats:	23%	21%
Non-chain seats:	30%	23%
Mean seats:	1,270	1,298
# Above/below mean:	4/7	5/11

These figures document the overall growth that occurred in Springfield's exhibition market, and point to the centrality of moviegoing as a form of leisure during this period. The numbers also show the redistribution of seats as a result of increased national chaining, lending support to Gomery's finding that regional chains were important precursors to national chains and that 'when Hollywood came to bid and buy, the founders of these great [regional] operations sold out.'[21]

At the same time, there is evidence of the persisting importance of local chain and independent movie theaters. Although the percentage of seats owned by local chain and independent theaters decreased slightly, the actual number of these theaters increased from eight to eleven. Vertical integration apparently did not close off local interest in theater ownership, although studios did capture and control a majority share of the city's total available seats. This control was accomplished by buying and renovating, or constructing from scratch, the largest first-run houses in the city, all located downtown. Hollywood laid claim to, and sought to make normative, a new 'movie palace era' in Springfield, a flattering development, perhaps, to a city staking its own claim to cosmopolitanism. What remains of interest, for present purposes, is determining to what extent, and in what possibly divergent ways, moviegoing at the growing number of local theaters—in this case the Franklin Theater in Springfield's North End—was integrated into the social experience of everyday life in surrounding neighborhoods.[22]

The Transformation of Springfield

Before one can hope to know what it was like to attend a neighborhood theater, let alone begin the even more humbling task of understanding what this activity might have meant in the subjective experience of people, it is first necessary to consider what it may have meant to live in a particular neighborhood. To ask, 'What did it mean to go the Franklin Theater?' would minimally seem to require as a prerequisite an answer to the question 'What did it mean to live in Springfield's North End?' This question might itself be less daunting if the North End existed in a social and historical vacuum but, of course, it did not. Indeed, we can begin to comprehend the subjective meanings of life in the North End only after we have a general understanding of the social, cultural and economic history of the broader city within which North Enders located their identities and defined their senses of place and community.

Springfield sits in Western Massachusetts, about sixty miles south and west of Worcester and a hundred miles west of Boston. In the 1920s the corporate city encompassed thirty-three square miles of land, just under half of which was farmland or woodland.[23] The full length of Springfield's western border was formed by the Connecticut River. The city's central business district became most densely concentrated along the middle of this riverfront. City neighborhoods eventually fanned out from the central business district in northerly, easterly and southerly directions. From the heart of downtown, near the river, it was approximately six miles to the eastern border of the city, and about 2.5 miles to either the northern or southern borders.

According to historian Michael Frisch, Springfield changed from small New England town to industrial city between 1840 and 1880.[24] During the following fifty years, the city experienced its greatest growth. In 1880, Springfield's population numbered 33,340. By 1900, it reached 62,059. By 1920, total population had doubled again, reaching 129,614. During the 1920s, roughly 30,000 residents were added, and population in 1930 stood at 158,129. Growth was so steady that in 1923 the Springfield City Planning Board envisioned a population of 225,000 by 1940.[25] That projection never materialized—indeed, estimates for the Depression years of the early 1930s showed a population decline of roughly 10,000—but Springfield had nonetheless grown at a rate nearly three times faster than comparably sized cities in New England, and by the 1920s had become the third largest city in Massachusetts, behind Boston and Worcester.[26]

Nationally, there were sixty-eight American cities that the 1920 census found to have a population of more than 100,000, and Springfield was one of forty-three to fall between 100,000 and 250,000. In terms of the number of people living within what the census specifically designated as the 'urban district' surrounding a city, Springfield ranked above many cities with higher total populations. As H. Paul Douglass reported in his 1926 social survey, 'Springfield ranks fifty-first in size among American cities, but thirtieth if the aggregate urban population of which it is a center is considered.'[27]

The engine driving Springfield's rapid urbanization was industrialization. The railroad system that was developed during the 1830s and 1840s made downtown Springfield the principal rail gateway between New England and the rest of the country; by the 1920s over a hundred trains passed through the city each day. The railroad was a large industry itself, employing thousands, but it also facilitated the growth of other manufacturing interests, both downtown and in outlying districts. By the turn of the century, Springfield had over 500 manufacturing plants. Many were small machine shops, but there was also a diversity of large-scale industries that served as important sites of employment into the 1920s and 1930s (unlike some New England cities, Springfield's economy was never dependent on textiles).[28] In his social survey of the city in the 1920s, Douglass classified the employed labor force as follows: Manufacturing and mechanical industries—46.8 per cent; Trade—13.9 per cent; Clerical occupations—12.7 per cent; Domestic and personal service—9.9 per cent; Transportation—7.5 per cent; Professional service—6.3 per cent; Public service—2.4 per cent; All other occupations—0.5 per cent.[29]

Urbanization and industrialization accelerated immigration, and although city directories from 1920 to 1932 consistently reported 75 per cent of the population to be 'native born,' this figure obscured the fact that a large percentage of the native-born were second-generation immigrants.[30] According to Douglass, 'the displacement of the original stock by the children of foreign or mixed parentage has proceeded until this element nearly equals the purely native one.' By 1920, 35.9 per cent of the city's total population was 'native white of foreign and mixed parentage,' which combined with 24 per cent foreign-born meant 60 per cent of city residents were first- or second-generation immigrants. Douglass classified the composition of this 60 per cent into (rounded) percentages: 13 per cent

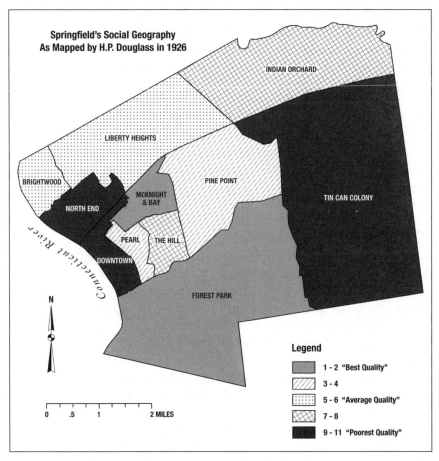

7.2 A map of Springfield showing the 'social quality' rankings put together in H. Paul Douglass's church survey of 1926.

Irish, 10 per cent British (English, Scotch, Canadians of English heritage), 9 per cent Italian, 9 per cent French Canadian, 6 per cent Hebrew (primarily Russian and German), and 13 per cent other (Polish, Greek, Syrian, Armenian, Lebanese, Swedes, Chinese). African Americans accounted for 2 per cent of the total population.[31]

As the size of the 'new stock' grew, its composition changed. In 1890, the Irish constituted nearly half the total foreign-born in Springfield, but by 1920 they constituted only 18 per cent of that population. The fastest growing groups of foreign-born were from Southern and Eastern Europe, with Italians jumping from 1.9 per cent in 1890 to 14 per cent in 1920, and Russians increasing from 1.4 per cent to 12 per cent. Polish, Greek, Syrian,

Lebanese, Armenian, and Turkish immigration also increased dramatically during this period.[32] From the perspective inscribed in the *Springfield Church Survey*, the new patterns of immigration created confusion and were cause for concern. If the city's 'old stock' Anglo-Americans had grown resigned to the Irish, despite that group's 'never having come to an entirely good understanding, so far as culture and civic ideals are concerned, with the original New England stock,' by the 1920s, the larger and more difficult problem had become 'the changed character of foreign population with its increasing preponderance of elements much more remote in tradition and culture from the ideals and standards which the city developed for 250 years.' As Frisch puts it, 'an older leadership that had helped turn government and business into an engine of growth now feared that they were losing control ... and that this powerful engine now could be turned against them as different hands reached for the throttle.'[33]

Whatever retrograde feelings of cultural stress the 'old stock' experienced by the 1920s as a result of Springfield's transformation, the city as a whole remained committed to growth. In fact, Springfield was caught in an intense drama of relative standing in which increasingly regional and national frames of cultural and economic reference became the yardstick by which local self-definition was measured. Frisch explains:

> Cities like Springfield were subject to what has to be called a kind of frantic peer pressure in the competition for survival and growth in industrializing America. Keeping up with the Worcesters and the Hartfords (and pulling far ahead of the Northamptons and the Westfields) was not just a matter of status—it seemed a matter of survival. And as the city grew, so did its frame of reference: a piping system that might have seemed appropriate in one year suddenly came to appear provincial and pedestrian the next.[34]

Driven in part by this 'frantic peer pressure,' Springfield entered a boom of institutional building after World War I. Historian Frank Bauer has chronicled the numerous public works construction projects that were initiated at enormous expense in the name of enhancing Springfield's cosmopolitan image. The construction of the ornate Memorial Bridge over the Connecticut River in 1922, for example, cost the city three million dollars.[35]

In the domain of non-public institutional building, city businesses such as Massachusetts Mutual Insurance and the Federal Land Bank moved into massive new structures that testified architecturally to the grandeur of Springfield's new status among cities in New England. Downtown movie theaters such as the Broadway (Paramount-Publix), the Capitol (Warner Bros.), and Poli's Palace (Fox) were bought by major studios in the late 1920s and underwent extensive renovations that upgraded their architectural status and as a bonus made way for talking pictures. In September 1929 Springfield's image as a cosmopolitan 'big city' that had truly arrived was capped off by the construction downtown of the 3200-seat Paramount Theater at a cost of nearly 1.2 million dollars.

Springfield's North End as Context for Moviegoing

Less than two months after the Paramount premièred to great fanfare downtown, a new 800-seat movie house opened rather furtively in the North End, at a cost of only $45,000 dollars.[36] The Franklin was built less than one mile north and east of the Paramount, on the other side of a wide line of Boston and Albany railroad tracks that marked the boundary between downtown and North End.[37] To understand the meanings that may have been contained in and expressed through moviegoing at the Franklin, it is necessary to grasp the cultural logic and social geography of the North End. By describing the sense and sensibility of everyday life there, and then drawing out the social dimensions of theater experience at the Franklin, it becomes possible to see how permeable the border could be between a neighborhood movie theater and its surrounding community. In fact, what seems most precisely definitive about life in the North End was that it afforded scant reprieve from community—not in the home, not in the school, not in the streets, not in the stores, not in the movies. Despite its many deprivations, or perhaps as a consequence of them, what the North End at its best had to offer was a social environment—and theater experience—marked by openness, familiarity, reciprocity, spontaneity, outgoingness and informality.

The grand architectural boom that hit downtown in the 1920s did not spill over to the North End, but the more fundamental changes that had occurred in the city certainly made a dramatic impact. The North End became a densely condensed microcosm of wider patterns of industrialization, urbanization and immigration. A highly industrialized, polyglot urban space that presented an inescapable heterogeneity, the North End bore the full intensity of Springfield's historical transformation and symbolized its most dramatic changes, more so perhaps than any other part of the city except the central business district. Not surprisingly, social perceptions of the North End sometimes evinced the ambivalence, fear, anxiety and concern that many residents felt about the 'new' city itself. This perception of Springfield's changing social geography is deeply etched into Douglass's

Springfield Church Survey, which ranked the North End ninth out of the city's eleven districts in overall 'social quality.'[38]

The North End was the initial stop for many immigrants—some with neighborhood sponsors—newly arrived to the city. In the 1920s its population of roughly 21,000 residents was 35 per cent foreign born, compared to an average of 23 per cent across all districts in Springfield. An additional 41 per cent of North End residents were native born of foreign or mixed parentage. The predominant ethnic groups were: 1) Russian Jewish, 2) Irish, 3) Polish Jewish, and 4) Greek. There were a significant number of Syrians, Russians (non-Jewish), African Americans, and Chinese.[39] Given its relatively high proportion of first generation immigrants, the North End had the second highest level of English language illiteracy in Springfield (more than twice the mean for all districts), with 6 per cent of its residents unable to read or write in English.[40]

Unlike downtown, which had the highest rate of intra-district mobility in the city, residents of the North End tended to inhabit the same dwellings for good lengths of time, and the North End had the lowest rate of intra-district mobility in Springfield. As Douglass observed, the North End 'shows a very much smaller than average number of changes within a district in which few homes are owned, perhaps reflecting the racial conservatism of the Jewish population, which does not change without reason.'[41] The low number of address changes may also be attributable to the predominance of extended family living arrangements, common in the North End even into the 1920s and 1930s. As Mary Annese remembers of her old North End neighborhood, 'Kids got married, they stayed home ... They'd go live up in the attic.'[42] Douglass reported 5.5 persons per dwelling in the North End, compared to an average of 4.88 across all eleven city districts.[43]

Given the North End's diversity, the tendency of families to stay in the same residences over time meant strong inter-ethnic bonds could be forged between families living in the same tenement or neighborhood. While inter-ethnic relationships between children might, in the end, weaken the insularity and endurance of ethnic and religious traditions within a particular family, these relationships afforded opportunities for children to share cultural traditions and leisure time experiences with each other in productive ways. Former North End resident Richard McBride,[44] for example, recalls that:

> When I was growing up, the family that lived upstairs was Schwartz; I've never forgotten them. They were a Jewish family, a real Jewish family, and they had a couple of kids that were part of our group ... And I used to love their holidays, because I used to love matzo, matzo

crackers, and we'd get them and cover them with peanut butter. And then above the Schwartzes lived a family, I can't remember if they were Polish or Italian, but they spoke a foreign language. They spoke English too. They had one boy. We were never gangs, we were groups, and we played together.[45]

He adds:

At that time you made your own sports, you played your own. In school, you played normal playground games, because that was all the land that was available and generally, it was paved or concrete asphalt. But you played there. You didn't have big parks and recreation. You had ball games, but they were always pick-up ball games on empty lots around the town. [We] and the eighth graders down, we had to make our own sports.[46]

The lack of park space identified by McBride was partly a consequence of the North End's saturation with multiple family homes and tenement housing, with some single family homes in the mix, as well as its status as a heavily industrialized zone of the city. Indeed, only the downtown area ranked lower on the *Survey's* index of industrialization.[47] With the Boston and Albany train station and freight house located on its southern edge, the North End was home to many industries that relied on the railroad for obtaining raw materials or shipping out finished goods.[48] From the cultural perspective of Douglass's *Survey*, industrialization in the North End 'created undesirable conditions for human habitation' that went hand-in-hand with the low level of fortune that marked districts with dense ethnic populations. 'In general,' Douglass concluded, 'the degree of industrialization corresponds very closely to the areas occupied by population of foreign-born antecedents or by Negroes. The most American districts are least industrialized, indicating the general ability of the American population to get away from undesirable environment.'[49]

However, as Richard McBride's earlier comments indicate, an environment perceived as undesirable by some on the outside is not necessarily experienced or defined as such by those who inhabit it. To be sure, industrialization put limits on the amount of park and recreation space available to North Enders, but residents still found space—if only on porches, stairwells, street corners and city lots—for social interaction and creative cultural production. Within the North End, the cultivation of inter-ethnic, peer group consciousness was a tangible asset, particularly in an environment defined by pervasive scarcity. From this perspective, the privatized, status-oriented way of life found in ostensibly better parts of the city would be a decided liability. As Mary Annese remembers:

> We lived down in the 'ward,' and that was from Armory Street all the way down to Main Street and … all the way down Chestnut street. That's what they called the 'ward.' Then, from Armory Street up, I don't know what they called it … I guess they were the ones who thought they were a little better than the rest of them. And down in the 'ward,' there were Jews, there were Blacks, there were Chinese, there were Poles, French, Irish, … Greeks, Italians, and I'll tell you, everybody helped each other, but not up on the hill … There were a lot of good people there, but they weren't as outgoing.[50]

Clearly, one could not live in the North End without encountering culturally divergent languages, traditions and practices, and at their best, residents remained open to mixing and sharing these resources in creative, reciprocal and outgoing ways. Such openness and creativity made a virtue of necessity and helped address problems of scarcity—of money, food, space, and time. Everyday life in the North End thus provided conditions amenable to the maintenance of residual cultural practices and linguistic traditions, as well as to the expansion of new cultural horizons through inter-ethnic exchange and a sharing of common problems attendant to everyday working-class life.

In this type of community context, the numerous saloons and ethnic-based social clubs that sprung up in the North End, as well as front porches, tenement stairwells and the streets themselves, could be mobilized as 'alternative public spheres' where people might gather to explain, validate, escape and transcend the shared experience of cultural dislocation and displacement brought about by immigration and conditions of wage labor.[51] It is also quite possible that the social space of the Franklin Theater, a space emerging from within the cultural logic of the community itself, could have been mobilized to serve these purposes as well.

The North End's Franklin Theater

The 800-seat Franklin Theater was a free-standing, single-story, plain brown brick structure with modest architectural detail on its façade. It had a concrete floor and offered only floor-level seating.[52] The theater was located near the geographical center of the North End, on Chestnut Street just north of the intersection with Franklin Street. It sat adjacent to Kasser Israel Hebrew Church and was surrounded by a variety of small businesses, manufacturing industries, single and multiple family homes, and tenement apartments. Boston and Albany's railroad lines and freight stations were less than one-half mile due south of the Franklin.

Although the theater was near a temple and a variety of small neighborhood businesses, it was also just a few blocks north of Congress Street, considered one of Springfield's major vice areas by political leaders and social reformers. In fact, the day before the Franklin first opened, the *Springfield Daily News* reported the comments of Independent mayoral candidate Charles W. Louis, who criticized incumbent Mayor Ferris C. Parker for having 'permitted Congress Street vice and crime to become a notorious and disgusting municipal landmark.'[53] Given the theater's proximity to Congress Street, it seems unlikely that residents living outside the North End would have attended the Franklin very often, if ever. Rita Soplop, for instance, who lived just above the North End in the Brightwood district, remembers that the Franklin 'was restricted, so we didn't go there ... To us, it was in kind of a bad section, we thought, [so] we stayed within our own.'[54]

The Franklin was licensed to Barbara and Wadie Semanie, who both came to America from Lebanon and settled in Springfield, where they met and married.[55] The theater's building permit, filed in April 1928, identified the 'owner's address' as 823 Armory Street, which the 1928 *Springfield City Directory* listed under Barbara Semanie. Armory Street was 1.5 miles east of the Franklin and formed the eastern boundary of the North End. The 1928 *Directory* listed a separate residence for Wadie Semanie—The Liberty Apartments at 250 Liberty Street. This residence afforded an easy walk to the theater, less than one-half mile away. After 1928, Barbara Semanie was listed with Wadie as residing at 250 Liberty. Another Semanie, George, lived nearby at 310 Liberty Street. Mary Annese remembers that Semanie family members staffed the theater, although she cannot recall exactly which family members worked there because 'there were so many of them there, the Semanie family was a big family.'[56]

The Franklin advertised only sporadically in city newspapers, and by far the most concentrated burst of advertising came the first two weeks after the theater opened. At that time its small ads typically carried the slogan 'Any Seat 10c Any Time' and promoted 'continuous' shows from 1–10:30 PM with 'programs changed daily.' Audiences were further informed that the theater was 'Locally Owned and Managed' and had 'Sound Tone Installed.'[57]

The Semanies no doubt wanted to get their business off to a smooth start, but the Franklin's opening was met by protest from Springfield's Central Labor Union. On 25 October 1929, a 'Special Notice' appeared next to the Franklin's advertisement in the *Springfield Daily News*:

Do not be mislead by barkers and rumors that the Franklin Theater is unfair to organized labor. Persons found guilty of circulating such literature will be prosecuted to the fullest extent of the law. The operators of this theater are members of the 'Knights of Labor, Inc.,' a recognized labor organization. We wish to thank our many friends and patrons for their continued support during the circulation of false statements sponsored by unfair business methods of a union committee.[58]

In a district as heavily industrialized and unionized as the North End, the Central Labor Union's actions against Franklin owners Barbara and Wadie Semanie could have resulted in disastrous consequences, as would be the case two years later, in 1931, when the Union mobilized protests against Max Tabackman's use of non-union projectionists at the State theater in the downtown district, thereby helping to ensure Tabackman's ownership of the theater would be short-lived.[59]

As indicated in the 'Special Notice,' however, the family-operated Franklin claimed affiliation with the Knights of Labor, at one time a national federation of labor assemblies, particularly known for gender-inclusive and gender-neutral policies, whose history in Springfield pre-dated the formation of the Central Labor Union in 1887.[60] By the 1920s, the more aggressive and better-organized Central Labor had become the most powerful labor organization in Springfield, but it was perhaps still possible for the Semanies to demonstrate allegiance to labor through affiliation with the once-prominent Knights of Labor.[61] Although it remains unclear exactly how (or even whether) an accord was reached, the Franklin's success in defusing the 'unfair to labor' allegation lodged by the Central Labor Union is perhaps suggested by the disappearance of the 'Special Notice,' which stopped running in subsequent editions of local newspapers.

In 1929, the Franklin was the only theater in Springfield to offer daily program changes, and in this it may have encountered some of the difficulties common to a type of theater known in the trade papers as 'the daily grind.' As Paul Seale points out, vertical integration meant that studios focused their run-zone-clearance distribution pattern around urban first- and second-run, chain-owned theaters, a move that signaled the studios' willingness to reduce their role serving 'daily grinds' in favor of only the greenest of urban pastures.[62] This situation put 'daily grinds' in a precarious position in terms of securing enough film product to meet the demands of everyday program changes, forcing them to rely on the output of small, independent, 'Poverty Row' studios to supplement the larger studios' 'B' pictures and, subsequent runs of 'A' pictures, if they were allowed to procure them. Additionally, an urban exhibitor with strong ethnic patronage could use an occasional foreign-language film, tailored to the local audience, to help meet the demands of everyday program changes.

Nonetheless, the writing was on the wall for the 'daily grind,' as the stranglehold that vertical integration achieved over film distribution coalesced with the worsening effects of the Depression to make daily program changes impossible to sustain. It is not surprising, then, that in 1931 the Franklin switched from seven daily program changes to four programs per week, with changes on Monday, Wednesday, Friday, and Sunday. Soon thereafter, the Franklin also raised prices to fifteen cents for children and twenty cents for adults, with weekday matinée tickets for children and adults priced at a flat rate of ten cents. By 1932, ticket prices had changed again, stabilizing at fifteen cents for adults and ten cents for children.

The typical program at the Franklin consisted of two feature films, a comedy short, a serial, a newsreel, and other short subjects such as cartoons and travelogues. A review of feature titles advertised in the *Springfield Daily News* between 21 October 1929 and 26 November 1932 suggests the theater's favored genres were the marriage melodrama (such as *Virtuous Husbands*, *Obey Your Husband*, which was promoted as 'a dramatic story of modern marriage,' and *Seed*, which was billed as 'the inside story of married life'), the gangster picture (such as *The Gangster*, *The Perfect Crime*, *Bullets and Justice*, and *Smart Money*, the last of which starred Edward G. Robinson), the comedy drama (such as *Ladies Must Play*, *Girls Gone Wild* and *Chiselers of Hollywood*), and the western (such as *The Big Trail*, starring John Wayne, and *One Way Trail*, with Tim McCoy).

Broadway-centered musicals, so popular at downtown Springfield's first-run movie palaces during the early sound era, were almost totally absent from the Franklin's programming schedule. A definitive reason for the absence of Broadway-centered musicals remains elusive, but one possibility may be that such musicals were simply not targeted toward, nor very appealing to, the North End audiences that typically gathered at the Franklin.[63] To fill out its schedule of features, the Franklin periodically programmed pictures of special ethnic and political interest to the North End's immigrant, working-class patrons. Indeed, within one month of its grand opening, it was the only theater in Springfield to have shown *Guilty*, 'a German special production,' and *Russia*, which depicted the 'overthrow of Csarism' and was accompanied by a comedy short featuring 'Toots and Gaspar.' Likewise, the theater showed the occasional silent film of enduring interest to North Enders, as was the case on 1 April 1930, when Chaplin's *Gold Rush* (originally released in 1925) was screened.

In addition to a regular program of film entertainment, the Franklin also offered a variety of raffles and merchandise giveaways, beginning in early 1930. These practices were adopted by all neighborhood theaters located outside downtown in attempt to gain advantage over the city's first-run and second-run theaters in the competition for the patronage of neighborhood moviegoers. At the Franklin, promotions were offered Monday through Thursday, which most likely were the theater's slower nights for box office. Thus, Monday night was 'vanity ware night,' Tuesday night was 'gift night,' Wednesday night was 'china night,' and Thursday night was 'bargain night at reduced prices combined with country store.'[64] Live turkeys and chickens were raffled in conjunction with Easter, Thanksgiving, and Christmas holidays. As Richard McBride recalls, such promotions were often tied to neighborhood businesses, and the merchandise given away often had immediate use value: 'They used to raffle off turkeys around the holidays, or they'd raffle off gift certificates for Santos market down the street. You could get $5 or $3 or $2 gift baskets of stuff. They gave away just about everything ... [including] pencils, they gave away a lot of pencils ... Two pencils would last you a year at school.'[65]

While promotions like China Night and Vanity Ware Night might be taken as signs of the cinema's larger stake in promoting consumer culture as a whole, these practices may also be understood, in Pierre Bourdieu's terms, as being rooted in the cultural habitus corresponding to the working-class experience of economic necessity. For Bourdieu, the experience of economic necessity produces a 'popular' cultural disposition marked by an insistence on the practical utility of cultural goods, on the 'affirmation between art and life, which implies the subordination of form to function.'[66] Although this disposition might possibly have applied to the manner in which working-class audiences related to particular films, it may have also helped shape the relation between working-class audiences and particular movie theaters. Because giveaways at the Franklin were directed toward a neighborhood audience for whom there was little reprieve from the experience of scarcity and necessity, a free turkey, perhaps in combination with the china plates on which to serve it and the silverware with which to eat it, represented a tangible, objective measure of the cultural use value of moviegoing at the neighborhood theater, as opposed to moviegoing at the first-run, studio-owned movie palace. What the neighborhood theater lacked in formal architectural niceties, it may have made up for in functional terms by becoming a locus of distribution for material goods helpful in the ongoing struggle with economic necessity.

The pursuit of a complete set of china or silverware may have reinforced the consumption ethic being promoted through the mystique of the tastefully arranged 'ensemble' that was cultivated in advertising discourse of the 1920s.[67] The articulation of an 'ensemble' mentality to moviegoing undoubtedly served the neighborhood theater owner's objective of securing repeat attendance, as moviegoers pursued the goal of completing a set of china or silverware. Nonetheless, working-class moviegoers may have made sense of the giveaways less through an 'aesthetic' disposition emphasizing the formal qualities of the distributed merchandise, than through a 'popular' disposition that transposed economic necessity into the cultural virtue of 'getting more for your money.' On this basis, it would not be uncommon for giveaways to become the prime reason for attendance. Indeed, Mary Annese recalls 'a lot of people went cause they were trying to make a set of dishes,' a sentiment echoed by Richard McBride, who points out that 'lots of people would go pay the dime and go watch the travelogue, or whatever it was, and maybe one of the pictures. If it was lousy they'd leave, they got their plate, you know?'[68]

On some occasions, merchandise giveaways moved beyond the realm of practical utility to add an air of informality and interactivity to the immediate moviegoing experience at the Franklin. Richard McBride recalls how the dropping of a china plate or saucer could precipitate widespread audience response. As he puts it,

> The women were always given these plates, and invariably, they might go in and get a dinner plate, a saucer, a cup, a soup bowl, a cake stirrer, and invariably, you'd listen during the movie, and all of the sudden you'd hear 'crash,' where someone had the plate on their lap [and dropped it], ... and everybody would clap, yeah, yeah, one down, or that's the third down, cause generally it was never one it was two or three. Sometimes if the theater didn't have a big crowd, they'd replace it, you'd pick it up, so the sweeper didn't have to sweep it, and take it on the way out the owner or manager would replace it. Lots of times, they would say 'break this you don't get another, because I only got so many.'[69]

McBride also describes how the raffling of bags of candy could reinforce a sense of collectivity among hungry audience members, who as a group shared the winner's rewards: 'For the kids, they had these candies with the candy corn in them or the milk balls, and everybody would get a ticket and they'd [theater staff] stand up and call these tickets off. And if you had the number you'd go up and get it, and of course if you got it, about once around the crowd and it was all gone.'[70]

While feature films and merchandise giveaways no doubt had great appeal for both adults and children at the Franklin, it was the serial shorts that held the greatest attraction for child audiences, who often attended the theater in groups on Saturday afternoons.[71] As Richard McBride remembers,

> Most of the time, the group at that period of time, the seventh or eighth grade, we'd all walk to it [the Franklin], a whole crowd, and as we'd walk along, a couple more would join us, and sometimes you'd end up walking and there'd be 12, 15, 20, 30 even. And for the good ones, we'd say 'come on, this is going to be a good one,' [maybe one that] Richard Arlen played in. I'll never forget those serials, there was always boat chases in there. It was quite a thing ... [Neighborhood] theaters were the thing, because you got so much for the money. And then you'd go back home, and then that night, or during the week, you'd sit on the stoops at night after supper and talk about the movies, as to what went on, and what's the serial now. [We'd say] 'this is what's going to happen,' 'no it ain't, you're wrong,' and everybody had their ideas, because they knew they were going to get another 15 episodes, and they'd always start another one, about 8 or 10 episodes into this one, so you always got two going, one almost finished and a new one starting.[72]

McBride also points out that the serial film's low production values provided children with another kind of enjoyable game—trying to spot continuity errors:

> They didn't put that kind of money into making them. We'd always like to watch to see if we could find, ah, all of the sudden it's a sedan being chased by the cops, then all the sudden you're looking at a touring car being chased by the cops. We used to always try to pick out the mistakes. That was the fun, trying to find the mistakes, as well as watching the pictures.[73]

While the film interests of child audiences centered on the use value of the serial form for generating public discussion and youthful games, it was also true that the informal social environment provided by the neighborhood theater itself contributed greatly to the overall pleasures of their moviegoing experience. As McBride remembers, the Franklin gave great value for the money because 'you generally got about four hours of hootin' and hollerin' ... especially if there was too much lovey-dovey in the movie.' He also points out that 'everybody always sat in one area ... And you'd always hear, "you savin' that seat?" "Yeah." "Who for?" "No you're not!"'[74]

150

During the early years of the Depression, the Franklin's child audiences found innovative ways to secure admission. Mary Annese points out that, during the Depression, children of working-class families often did not have money for movies. She remembers, however, that 'they would go down to the railroad tracks, and some of the factories would leave their copper out in the field. And then they'd light a match to it so as to get all the coating off the copper, and you know, after the fire went down, you'd pick up a few pennies there to get to the movies.'[75]

Another common strategy was to search for discarded milk bottles to return for deposit value, which could be used to fund a couple of children's admission to the theater. Once inside, these children could take advantage of the darkness of the theater and the sympathetic attitude of attendants by popping open the fire doors, thereby admitting other children from the group into the theater. As Richard McBride describes this practice:

> In the early thirties, salaries were not big ... Store bought milk bottles were five cents a deposit, so you were always trying to find milk bottles. You'd probably get one or two [kids] who you'd give money, everybody would chip in, you know, 2 or 3 cents here or there, and they'd go in the theater and go down the side aisles and they'd hit the safety doors. The doors would pop open, and when they did a whole mess of us would run in. You might get caught, you might not, but you didn't consider it would be too bad. That was part of the game. And of course the attendants knew ... [The theater] had attendants because it was dark. You didn't have all the big lights on the doors that said exit so that you could read a newspaper ten feet away, 'cause it wasn't required. You had doors, and the painted exit across the doors. [The attendants] had flashlights, but they were busy. [Sneaking in] used to be a game, but they knew it! They all knew. We'd go out, and we'd always say, 'thanks a lot for the free movies.' They knew, they knew what was going on![76]

It is difficult to imagine such practices having been possible, let alone knowingly tolerated, at Springfield's 'better' theaters, where good lighting, carefully managed ushering, and daunting architecture set conditions for a more controlled and formal accent to the moviegoing experience. But at the Franklin, the material features of the theater, combined with the close relation of the owners to the North End community, provided structural conditions amenable to formation of a public sphere marked by unpredictability, informality, familiarity, reciprocity, and even an openness toward 'illegal' social practices born from economic urgencies magnified by the

151

Depression. The cultural logic of the North End spilled into its movie theater: a scarcity of money creatively addressed by hunting for copper down by the railroad tracks or by sneaking in a theater; a scarcity of food solved by mixing peanut butter and matzo crackers or by passing around a bag of candy won at the theater; a scarcity of private space ameliorated by taking pleasure in sharing one's porch, or the streets themselves, with neighbors to talk about movies and other happenings.

Like the North End itself, the Franklin became an important landmark in the cultural geography of the city. It helped mark a unique, if marginalized, space. It also helped mark time; serials parceled out in a rhythm that prompted neighborhood kids to look backward and forward with excitement and anticipation. 'Dish nights' and other giveaways dutifully counted the days and nights of the week as well as any clock or calendar. Beyond this, as a form of consumption, moviegoing at the

7.3 One week's programming at the Franklin theatre, 9–15 May 1937.

Franklin not only captured and communicated the status and informal social conditions of the North End, but also served as a type of creative expression as well. The porch stoops, empty lots, streets and spaces of the neighborhood were articulated to the physical and cinematic space of the Franklin itself, and together these became the imaginative and expressive medium out of, and into which were carved the shapes and meanings of everyday life.

Conclusion

Springfield's North End was a largely insular, if not homogeneous, working-class environment marked by heavy industrialization, extensive multi-family housing, a large and diverse ethnic population, a vice district, a high level of English language illiteracy, and high rates of juvenile delinquency relative to the city's 'better' districts. For better or worse, it was a microcosm of the intense changes behind the 'new' industrial city and had all the characteristics of an area of low 'social quality,' at least as defined by Douglass's *Springfield Church Survey*.

Given these community conditions, it would have been unlikely for residents outside the North End to attend the Franklin Theater, although as Mary Annese points out, children from other neighborhoods occasionally patronized the Franklin 'if grandma brought 'em or something like that.'[77] By the same token, although North Enders certainly had occasion to attend the 'better' movie theaters, especially as adults, they were perhaps likely to choose the Franklin as their primary theater, supplementing this with visits downtown when they could afford it. Still, from the standpoint of the working-class experience of economic necessity, which according to Bourdieu produces a cultural disposition that defines cultural value in pragmatic and often quantitative terms, the ostensible 'added values' the movie palace provided in terms of architecture, service, and status might have held little attraction. Richard McBride, for instance, recalls:

> We liked the local theaters 'cause you would get so much more! Sometimes you went to the big ones, and you'd get a new Pathé, or RKO, or whatever, and you'd get maybe a travelogue of what the movies to come, and then you'd get a cartoon, one cartoon, and then maybe a double feature if they had double features there, or maybe a real class 'A-1.' And that was it! Two and a half hours and you were out of there. Where if you went to the local ones, you generally got about four hours ...[78]

153

With local ownership, low prices, continuous shows, films tailored to the surrounding community, and an unpredictable and informal theater environment, the Franklin was the site for a mode of moviegoing and theater experience that was more open to residual working-class and ethnic traditions of interactive sociability than was the formal and privatized mode of film reception often found at movie palaces. Although the normalization of vertical integration did influence the Franklin's programming, helping to force a shift from daily changes to four changes per week (dropping down to three changes per week later in the 1930s), the theater's overall operations were hardly standardized according to the normative dictates of the movie industry.

The moviegoing experience at the Franklin was not a 'poor imitation' of the experience found at a studio-owned movie palace, nor was it a defining realization of an 'essential' neighborhood theater experience. It was, simply, a uniquely meaningful and distinctly accented mode of reception that took root in palace shadows and grew in accord with the social geography and cultural dispositions of Springfield's North Enders.

8

Cinemagoing in the United States in the mid-1930s

A Study Based on the *Variety* Dataset

Mark Glancy and John Sedgwick

THROUGHOUT the 1930s, the entertainment industry trade journal *Variety* published extensive information on the North American exhibition market in each of its weekly issues. The 'Pictures' section of *Variety* included weekly box-office reports from as many as 200 cinemas in 30 cities.[1] The cinemas included were mainly 'first-run' venues with a large seating capacity, but there were also some smaller, second-run and specialty cinemas. The reports were organized by city, and they provided general comments on the trading conditions, audience preferences and promotional strategies seen in each city during the previous week, as well as more specific reports from a selection of the city's cinemas, indicating the box-office results for the week, and listing the items on each cinema's programme. In the 1930s, the standard running time for a cinema programme was just under three hours, and programmes could include one or two feature films, a live stage performance, cartoons, newsreels, short films, as well as 'bank nights' or 'giveaways.'[2] *Variety's* comments on these programmes would consider if one half of a double feature was regarded as a greater attraction than the other, whether the stage show interested audiences more than the film, or if in fact it was the bank night or a newsreel that drew the crowds. The overwhelming impression given by the reports is that the cinemagoing experience was seldom if ever limited to a single film in this era. Rather, the cinema offered a diverse range of attractions and entertainment forms, in which a single feature film might be a secondary or even an incidental consideration.

Altogether, the array of information available in *Variety* constitutes a valuable historical source, and one that offers a highly revealing and often fascinating glimpse into both the film industry and its audiences during the Depression era. That it remains largely unexploited by scholars is most likely due to the density of information in each issue as well as the manner in which it is presented on the page; it is not easily or readily digestible. This paper has been designed as a pilot study of the *Variety* data, demonstrating the range of information available and how it can be used. However, even within our designated time frame, October 1934 to October 1936, it is not within the scope of the study to utilise the reports from all of the 200 cinemas and all of the 30 cities. Instead, we have drawn data from tables that were published monthly in *Variety*, which presented a selection of the data from the previous four weeks. These tables offer a condensed and more easily digested overview of each month's box-office activity, and they include reports from 100 first-run cinemas in 23 cities across the United States plus another four cinemas in Montreal, Canada.[3] In addition to the weekly box-office grosses, the *Variety* tables also list each cinema's seating capacity, admission price range and its record box-office 'high' and 'low.' These cinemas and attendant statistics are listed in Appendix One. This condensed sample of the data involves a substantial body of information: the 104 cinemas represented in the tables played 967 films on 8,694 separate programmes during the twenty-five month period.[4] In addition to the tables of data, we have also drawn upon the weekly textual reports for further information on exhibition conditions and practices, at least insofar as they relate to the data sample, in order to offer a fuller picture than that provided by the box-office grosses alone.

The data will be used here to investigate four aspects of cinemagoing during the Depression. The first centres on audience preferences and film popularity, although it will be argued that, even with extensive box-office data, judgements in this area often require careful qualification. The second is a consideration of the diversity of films shown in these mainstream cinemas, with particular attention to the presence of foreign films and the extent to which the major Hollywood studios dominated this sector of the exhibition market. It should be noted that the specific time period chosen for this study, October 1934 through October 1936, coincides with a concerted campaign by one foreign producer, Gaumont-British, to market its films in the United States, and the data sample offers one means of assessing the success of that campaign. The third concerns the practice of 'double billing,' which proliferated in the early 1930s. Of the 8,694 programmes recorded in the dataset, 6,384 are single bills and 2,310 are double bills, and we will consider which films played on double bills and the circumstances in which they were paired.[5] The fourth aspect is the use of live stage shows to accompany feature films in cinemas. In the mid-1930s, this remained a common feature of cinemagoing in the first-run cinemas of major cities. Approximately 18 per cent of all programmes in the sample combined a feature film with a live stage show, and the *Variety* data offers an opportunity to examine the nature and success of this now largely forgotten aspect of Depression-era exhibition practices.[6]

The Validity of the Data

Given that there were approximately 15,000 cinemas operating in the U.S. during the mid-1930s, and that most films received between 2,000 and 10,000 bookings, it is clear that the dataset sample for this pilot study is a highly select one.[7] It includes reports from just 104 cinemas, and only 14 per cent of the films (134 films) in the sample have more than twenty bookings, while 55 per cent of the films (533 films) have ten or fewer bookings. Hence, questions as to the validity of the sample should be addressed. On what basis can a survey of cinemagoing practices and preferences at such a small sample of cinemas be said to represent the cinemagoing experiences of Americans more generally? The answer lies in the fact that the cinemas in the sample represent a large proportion of the first-run sector of the exhibition market.[8] The Motion Picture Producers and Distributors of America, Inc. calculated that in 1941 there were approximately 450 first-run cinemas in cities with over 100,000 inhabitants, and so the sample represents approximately one-quarter of the cinemas in this sector.[9] These cinemas were at the top of the exhibition hierarchy. They tended to be located in the most populous areas, typically on the main streets of city centres, and they tended to be the largest cinemas. They played films first, they played them exclusively (within their area), and they charged the highest admission charges. As this profile suggests, they were not entirely typical as cinemas and they had some distinctive exhibition practices; for example, they were more likely to have live entertainment and less likely to have double bills. However, the size and scale of this market, and the large number of patrons that it drew, make it an important one to examine and understand. In regard to cinemagoing preferences, the fact that *Variety* focused its reports on this sector of the market is itself revealing. These showcase cinemas provided the first test of a film's popularity before it went on to subsequent runs (the 'second-run,' 'third-run' and so on) in cinemas that tended to have fewer seats, to charge less for an admission, and to be located away from the main streets and in outlying neighbourhoods or small towns.[10]

The pattern of popularity experienced in the set of first-run cinemas and reported in *Variety* would not necessarily be replicated exactly in the lower orders of cinemas. Sedgwick's study of cinemagoing in Britain during the 1930s noted distinctive patterns of preferences between metropolitan and regional audiences, and in particular between audiences attending cinemas in London's West End and those attending cinemas in Brighton and in Bolton. It was noted, too, that the lower-order cinemas exhibited films not seen in the higher-order tiers.[11] Maltby's study of American cinema audiences also suggests that the notion of a single 'undifferentiated' audience is a misleading one, and that audience preferences were fragmented along class, gender and geographical lines. The divide between rural and metropolitan tastes is said to have been particularly pronounced, with a wide gap existing between the preferences of metropolitan audiences attending first-run cinemas on Broadway and those of provincial American audiences.[12]

Yet the reports in *Variety* do not promote the notion of a single, homogenous audience, and they came from much further afield than Broadway and New York City. The cities in the data sample include the five largest cities in the United States (New York, Chicago, Philadelphia, Detroit and Los Angeles) and also much smaller cities such as Birmingham, Indianapolis, New Haven, St. Louis and Tacoma. All regions of the country are represented, and in fact divergent tastes are readily apparent in the data. Nevertheless, the fact of local, regional and other distinctions in taste is not sufficient to explain the overall level of popularity of a film. Or, to put it differently, films that were the 'hits' of their day needed to perform extremely well across the first-run sector, and it is apparent that, for the greater part, those films that did so were also relatively popular amongst audiences attending lower-order cinemas. This can be demonstrated with reference to the studio ledgers unearthed by Glancy and Jewell.[13] Among the figures reported in the Eddie Mannix (MGM), William Schaefer (Warner Bros.) and C.J. Trevlin (RKO) ledgers are 'domestic earnings figures' that represent the sum of all exhibition revenues received by these studios for each of their films. These revenue figures included all earnings accrued by the studios from every stage of exhibition and throughout all regions of the United States and Canada. An analysis, comparing the *Variety* dataset grosses and the ledger grosses for all MGM, RKO and Warner Bros. films released in this period, indicates a very strong correlation between the two sets of figures, from which it is possible to conclude that, in the vast majority of cases, films that proved popular in the first-run market were similarly popular across all exhibition sectors.

The issue of the validity of what was reported in *Variety* should also be addressed. Were the figures reported each week truly an accurate measure of the gross earnings of films? That question simply cannot be answered with absolute certainty. However, there is an apparent emphasis on accuracy in the reports: projected grosses were reported in each weekly issue and then followed by confirmed grosses in the following week's issue. Furthermore, and as argued elsewhere, some confidence can be taken by the fact that the trade treated *Variety* with respect. It told a story about the relative and absolute popularity of films that accorded with the experience of those whose livelihood was bound up in the film business. This is most important, because without such veracity it seems highly unlikely that *Variety* would have continued to serve as the industry's principal trade publication.[14]

Film Preferences

The weekly box-office reports in *Variety* offer a rich source of information for reception studies centred on the tastes and interests of local audiences, as well as studies centred on the reception of stars, genres or individual films across different locales. The value of the source lies not only in the financial figures themselves, but in the textual reports that accompany them. It is these reports that reveal the influences behind the figures, and the comments regularly discuss local pricing strategies, promotional campaigns, critical views expressed in the local press, and the age, class and gender of those attending a film. For example, the success of *The Gay Divorcee* in Cincinnati was said to stem, at least in its first week, from the excellent reviews the film received in the local papers.[15] In Brooklyn, *The Crusades* was reported to have benefited from endorsements by local ministers, who had been given a special preview screening of the film and then urged their congregations to see it.[16] *A Midsummer Night's Dream* was reported to have had limited success in St Louis because ticket prices were set as high as $1.50 and 'locals won't pay top price.'[17] In Kansas City, *The Story of Louis Pasteur* did not attract a sizeable audience because the biopic was 'too classy for this town'[18] In Minneapolis, *The Painted Veil* was a hit because audiences considered its star, Greta Garbo, to be a 'Scandinavian luminary,' but in Birmingham the same picture failed because 'Garbo doesn't mean anything here and this film means less.'[19] As some of these comments indicate, there was a remarkable gap in regional tastes; a gap between 'classy' metropolitan audiences, who paid 'top price' for biopics, adaptations of Shakespeare and exotic melodramas, and the more provincial audiences, who preferred their entertainment to be decidedly less expensive and less exotic. This divide is particularly apparent in the reception given to the populist dramas of film star Will Rogers, whose homespun values and common sense celebrated the virtues of small town, middle-America. His films were merely routine releases in eastern cities such as New York, Boston, Philadelphia and

Washington, D.C. Yet the further west and south they travelled, the more their fortunes improved. In Birmingham, Rogers was actually the city's top star, and his *In Old Kentucky* and *Steamboat Round the Bend* were by far the two top-earning films of the period in this city.[20] He had a similar status in cities such as Indianapolis, St. Louis and Tacoma. In these cities, as in Birmingham, the preference for Rogers' films was accompanied by a predilection for Westerns, the family entertainment of Shirley Temple's films and the small-town dramas *Ah, Wilderness* and *The Country Doctor*.[21] More sophisticated fare, meanwhile, did not last long, and metropolitan favourites such as Chaplin's *Modern Times* and the costume drama *The Barretts of Wimpole Street* had a much more limited drawing power in these smaller, provincial cities.[22]

A comparison of local and national film preferences is one of the interesting opportunities the data offers. However, the comments that accompany the box-office reports consistently indicate that levels of attendance were governed by an array of factors, some of which had no relation to a single film's individual qualities or popularity. The notion of 'audience preferences' thus becomes problematic, or at least in need of careful scrutiny and qualification. Box-office takings in individual cities were often reported to have been affected by competition from alternative entertainment forms such as circuses, sporting events and state fairs. Games, giveaways, bank nights and raffles, on the other hand, were said to attract audiences who otherwise were reluctant to attend, not least because the first-run houses offered prizes as substantial as a new car and, in one instance at least, a fully furnished four-bedroom house.[23] Good and bad weather was frequently reported to have affected box-office either positively or negatively. And establishing audience preferences is further complicated by the fact that a single feature film was often only one item in a programme that had other attractions. Even minor items such as short films were sometimes said to be the primary attraction for audiences. The most notable example of this was a film made of a boxing match between heavyweights Max Schmeling and Joe Louis. The match took on a particular significance because Schmeling was representing Nazi Germany while Louis was a black American, and the short film, which circulated in the week after the match, was reportedly a more important draw than the feature films it preceded.[24] In some instances newsreels were also cited as significant attractions for audiences. A *March of Time* segment on the Nazi persecution of the Jews, for example, was said to have garnered considerable interest, and in some cinemas more interest than the feature films it accompanied.[25] It was exceptional, though, for such short items to be cited as a more significant attraction than the feature film. Much more frequently, the issue of a single film's popularity was clouded by its inclusion on a programme with another feature film or with live entertainment.

On their own, most feature films simply could not fill these capacious theatres for several showings a day throughout an entire week-long engagement, and so they were often paired with other features or with live entertainment. However, there was a distinct minority of films that needed little or no support. These were the top-earning films, and, as Table One indicates, it was common for these films to enjoy runs of several weeks in a single city. They rarely appeared on double bills during their first-runs, and when they did it was usually in one of the smaller cities. In the larger cities, an additional feature simply was not necessary to draw audiences. Paradoxically, these top-earning films were actually more likely to appear on programmes with live entertainment. This is because they played in the largest cinemas of New York City and Chicago, and many of these venues regularly featured live entertainment, regardless of the film that was showing. Outside of these cities and that type of venue, they played without the support of a live show. *San Francisco*, for example, had engagements recorded in twenty-two of the twenty-four sample cities for a total of seventy-nine weeks. It never appeared with live support and it only played on a double bill during an unusually long three-week engagement in Denver. Similarly, *Top Hat* had engagements recorded in twenty cities for a total of fifty-four weeks. It appeared with live entertainment only during its three-week engagement at New York's Radio City Music Hall, where the stage show was a regular feature, and it played on a double bill only once, in Tacoma. The exceptional popularity of such films is evident in the fact that a small number of films took a disproportionately large amount of the box-office. The ten top earning films, for example, represent only 1.0 per cent of the films in the sample, but they account for 7.5 per cent of the box-office gross for the period; and the fifty top earning films represent just 5.2 per cent of the films in the sample but they took 25.3 per cent of the total earnings.

The most popular films in the sample have some striking similarities. All of the ten top-earning films are either costume dramas or musicals, and the film that earned more than any other, *San Francisco*, belongs to both categories. The popularity of costume dramas was not reliant upon any single studio or set of stars. Those that rank among the fifty top-earning films of the period, as listed in Table One, include a wide array of performers and were produced by several different studios. If there is a dominant strand of the genre, it is the tasteful or 'culturally elevated' strand, represented by such films as *Mutiny on the Bounty*, *Anthony Adverse*, *David Copperfield*, *Lives of a Bengal Lancer*, *The Gorgeous Hussy*, *The Barretts*

of Wimpole Street, *Becky Sharp*, *Anna Karenina* and *A Tale of Two Cities*
These were films that were set within a relatively modern historical period
(the eighteenth or nineteenth centuries), and films that were either adapted
from canonical literature or centred on the lives of key historical figures.
Another type of costume drama, centred on medieval or ancient times, and
favouring spectacle over literary values, was far less prominent, as is evident
in the poorer performance of films such as *Cleopatra*, *The Crusades* and *The
Last Days of Pompeii*.[26] In contrast to the costume drama, a large measure
of the popularity of the musical can be attributed to the phenomenal success
of a single star team. Fred Astaire and Ginger Rogers made five films at
RKO during this time period. Four of their films (*Top Hat*, *Swing Time*,
Roberta and *Follow the Fleet*) appear among the ten top-earning films in the
sample, and the other (*The Gay Divorcee*) is not far behind. These distinctly
contemporary, witty and sophisticated musicals, which combined singing
and dancing, were broadly popular across audiences and in all regions.
MGM's three-hour extravaganza, *The Great Ziegfeld*, was another musical-
in-costume that was exceptionally popular. The operettas of Grace Moore,
and Jeanette MacDonald and Nelson Eddy were also successful, but none
was in quite the same league as Astaire and Rogers.

Only two other stars came close to matching Astaire and Rogers. One
was Clark Gable. Altogether, Gable's films earned more than those of any
other star in the sample period, but this was partly the result of the sheer
number of films that he had in cinemas over these twenty-five months.
They include the highly successful costume dramas *San Francisco* and
Mutiny on the Bounty, the romantic dramas in which he starred with Jean
Harlow (*China Seas*, *Wife Versus Secretary*) and Joan Crawford (*Forsaking All
Others*, *Chained*), and a few new releases that must have been considered
commercial disappointments (*After Office Hours*, *Cain and Mabel*, *The Call of
the Wild*). They also include re-releases of three of his earlier films (*Dancing
Lady*, *It Happened One Night* and *Men in White*). The latter are particularly
noteworthy as there were only twenty-five re-releases in the data sample,
and the fact that three of Gable's films were chosen for re-release offers
another sign of his box-office standing. The other leading star was Shirley
Temple, and she too made an impact at least partly as a result of the sheer
volume of her films. Over the twenty-five months, she starred in no fewer
than eight new releases, some of which were markedly more successful than
others. This was an era in which audiences were able to see their favourite
stars in several films each year, and they were apparently willing to pick
and choose among the films.

With costume dramas and musicals as the most consistently popular
genres, it appears that escapism was a key aspect of cinemagoing for most

people in this period. Indeed, it is notable how very few of the most successful films bear any significant traces of the harsh economic climate of the 1930s. Among the 50 top earning films, those that come the closest are Frank Capra's *Broadway Bill* and *Mr Deeds Goes to Town*, the Warner Bros. crime drama *G-Men* and the comedies *Modern Times* and *My Man Godfrey*, but their engagement with contemporary concerns is oblique at best. Nevertheless, the decade is often characterized as one in which a significant number of films engaged with social issues and problems, and did so in a realist manner.[27] Many of the films chosen by historians to demonstrate this view were notably poor performers within the data sample. The grosses for both *Fury*, the story of small town prejudice and injustice, and *Black Fury*, the story of a labour dispute, fell short of $250,000. So, too, did the gross for *Bullets or Ballots*, another Warner Bros. crime film. *The Informer*, John Ford's account of 'the troubles' in Ireland, and the political drama *The President Vanishes* fared even worse, with grosses below $200,000. *Our Daily Bread*, meanwhile, was almost uniquely unpopular and grossed only $51,250. This film, directed by King Vidor, centres on an impoverished young couple who struggle to work a farm as a collective. It was shown throughout the country, but it had the dubious distinction of ranking among the lowest grossing films in almost every city it played. It is apparent that such films were perhaps the least representative of audience preferences in the period, as social relevance and box-office failure invariably went hand in hand.

Film Diversity

In some respects the data sample may seem to cover a narrow range of films. Not only does a disproportionately large amount of the earnings go to a minority of very popular films, but, as Table Two indicates, the vast majority of earnings are attributed to films made by the major Hollywood studios. Altogether, the sample includes 741 films made by MGM, Paramount, Warner Bros., RKO, Twentieth Century-Fox, Fox, Columbia, Universal and the independent American companies that produced for these studios and for United Artists, and these films account for 94.6 per cent of all of the earnings recorded in the sample. However, there is greater diversity than this figure would seem to suggest, because the remaining 5.4 per cent of earnings was derived from 226 films made by a further 52 production companies. Double billing undoubtedly facilitated this diversity. As Taves has argued, the proliferation of double billing in the early 1930s created a demand for feature films that the major studios could not fulfil, and that demand was met by smaller studios.[28] This is borne out by the data sample, which includes films produced by Republic (twenty-five films), Monogram (twenty-four), Chesterfield (fifteen), Mascot (thirteen), Invincible (eleven), Liberty (ten), Atherton (eight), Buck Jones (four), Majestic (three), and an additional twenty-five companies that had only one film listed. These films rarely appeared on single bills. For the most part, their entrance into the first-run market was a result of the need for 'second features.' This was particularly true in the smaller cities, where double billing was much more common and engagements were shorter, thus intensifying the demand for additional films.

Foreign films also benefited from double billing. The Department of Commerce reported that 190 foreign films were released in the United States during 1935 alone, and that German and 'Spanish' films were the leading imports.[29] Very few of the films from non-English speaking countries appear in the data sample, but when they do it is always as one feature within a double bill. The Swiss travel documentary *Wings Over Ethiopia* was released in the month that Italy invaded Ethiopia, and curiosity about the conflict enabled the film to garner engagements on double bills in eleven cities. The intriguingly titled *Legong: Dance of the Virgins* was actually an anthropological documentary from the Dutch East Indies, and it played on double bills in three cities. The German film *Mädchen in Uniform* and the Mexican film *She-Devil Island* were in the sample only by virtue of (separate) one-week engagements on double bills. Of course, a distinct market for foreign films and for 'poverty row' films existed beyond the first-run cinemas, and their appearance in the data sample is only sporadic and marginal. Yet it demonstrates the increased exhibition opportunities offered by double billing, which appears to have opened at least some of the first-run sector's cinemas to a wide range of films.

British films benefited from double billing to a much greater extent than other foreign films. Of the seventy-five British films in the data sample, thirty-one played only on double bills, and in fact many had their original running time cut to facilitate this.[30] Other British films were much more significant releases, which played widely and mainly as single features. London Films was the most successful of all British companies, and *The Scarlet Pimpernel*, with data sample earnings of nearly $335,000, was by far the top-earning foreign film of the period, followed by the same company's *The Ghost Goes West* (with $255,000) and *Things to Come* ($205,000).[31] It is notable, though, that these films took an unusually large share of their earnings from their highly successful New York City engagements. *The Scarlet Pimpernel* earned a staggering $162,500 in the two weeks that it played in Radio City Music Hall, but that level of success was not maintained throughout the country. In fact, those earnings represented 49 per cent of the film's earnings throughout the country, whereas the average film took 21 per cent of its earnings from New York. *The Ghost Goes West* took 44 per cent of its gross from four weeks at New York's Rivoli Theatre, and *Things to Come* took 37 per cent of its gross from three weeks at the Rivoli. It is also notable that, beyond New York City, these films were most likely to be held over for additional weeks in large cities such as Boston, Chicago, Philadelphia and Washington, DC, while engagements elsewhere did not last for more than a single week and yielded comparatively small sums. In the divide between metropolitan and provincial tastes, British films landed firmly on the metropolitan side.

London Films held a relatively privileged place among the British production companies seeking access to American audiences. Its films were released through United Artists, a major American distribution firm, and that ensured that they received a high profile and extensive playing dates. Yet the company produced only eight films within this period, and so its impact was limited. Gaumont-British had much more ambitious plans. It intended to release most, if not all, of its British-made films in North America, and in 1934 it established its own American distribution company to facilitate this. Some success in this endeavour is apparent: no fewer than twenty-four Gaumont-British productions appear in the data sample, and many of these played in one of New York City's largest first-run houses, the Roxy Theatre. There, in one of the country's largest and most lucrative venues, films such as the Alfred Hitchcock thrillers *The 39 Steps* and *The Secret Agent*, the musical *It's Love Again*, the futuristic drama *Transatlantic Tunnel*, the historical adventure film *Rhodes of Africa* and the melodrama *Little Friend* were popular enough to be held-over for a second week, and each earned between $60,000 and $80,000 in this venue alone. These notable successes undoubtedly helped the company to gain playing dates further afield, and the films all showed in major venues throughout the country. A familiar pattern emerged, however, in which the box-office takings dropped markedly outside of New York City and particularly in the smaller and more provincial cities. The company's other films, meanwhile, did not enjoy such wide releases and were more likely to be seen on double bills wherever they did play. This intermittent success was clearly not enough for Gaumont-British, which ceased film production in 1937.[32] Nevertheless, it is apparent that for a time in the mid-1930s the company was able to release more British films in the United States than any other company, and to distribute them widely. In doing so, Gaumont-British came close to matching Hollywood's Columbia and Universal studios (in both total revenues and per-film averages), and achieved a status that was far above the 'poverty-row' level. The same cannot be said for the other British companies, including major concerns such as British International and

British and Dominions, which, by any measure, languished at the bottom of the rankings.[33]

Double Billing

The question of how to attribute the earnings of a programme that includes two feature films is a difficult one. One option would be to attribute the earnings to both films, on the grounds that audiences saw both, and earnings levels are meant to reflect the size of the audience. However, this method would double the revenue recorded for some programmes and thereby distort the true levels of earnings within the data sample. A second option rests on the notion that double bills were formed by combining a popular 'A' film with a more obscure 'B' film, and that, because audiences were primarily drawn to the 'A' films, all or most the earnings should be attributed to the 'A' film. This combination of 'A' and 'B' films is evident in some double bills. For example, the only double billing recorded in the data sample for MGM's *San Francisco* was in Denver, where it was accompanied by another MGM film, *The Three Godfathers*, which had a much lower level of earnings and played most of its engagements as a double feature. It therefore seems reasonable to assume that audiences in Denver were drawn primarily to see *San Francisco* and that the earnings should be attributed accordingly. However, in many other instances the 'A' and 'B' divide is not so clear. For example, *The Three Godfathers* also played on double features with RKO's *The Witness Chair*, Columbia's *Meet Nero Wolfe* and Warner Bros.' *The Case of the Velvet Claws*, and it is impossible to determine which might be the 'A' or 'B' film in these cases. All of these films played most but not all of their engagements on double bills, and they were usually paired with similarly low-profile films. The majority of double billings, in fact, seem to be various combinations of what Taves refers to as 'shaky A films,' 'programmers' from major studios, and 'B' films from smaller studios.[34] That is, most double bills did not have a strong and weak component, but were combinations of relatively weak films. Hence, the third option, to divide the earnings evenly between the two films, seems to be the fairest and most appropriate method of dealing with double bills, and it is the one that we have adopted here.[35]

Gomery states that the 'trend for double features' began in 1930 as a result of economic hardship. In the year following the Wall Street crash, and as the economy spiralled downward, the public were increasingly less inclined to spend money on a leisure time activity such as cinemagoing unless they were offered the greater value of seeing two films for the price of one.[36] By 1934, the number of cinemas that regularly showed double features was estimated to be between 50 per cent and 75 per cent.[37] Within the data sample, it is apparent that practices varied widely and were set according to local conditions. In the smaller cities, such as New Haven and Tacoma, double billing was the norm within the first-run sector, and single features were a rarity. In larger cities, double billing was used selectively and to support films that were not perceived to fit clearly into either the 'A' or 'B' category. The fact that *Variety* often reported on double bills by commenting on which film was the greater attraction is indicative of this uncertainty.[38] Many of the very largest cities, meanwhile, did not have double bills at all within the first-run sector. Exhibitors in Chicago, Minneapolis, New York, Philadelphia and Washington, DC, held to mutual agreements that banned double billing in these venues. One reason for this was that the practice increased costs for the exhibitor, who had to pay for two films rather than one, but another and perhaps a more important reason was to protect the special quality of the first-run cinemas, which were meant to be movie palaces rather than bargain cinemas. Audiences paid a higher admission fee to attend these cinemas and they may have welcomed the change of pace that a single-feature programme provided. This is evident in the fact that, although double bills were appreciated as a good value, there were also many objections to them.

A survey conducted by Warner Bros. in 1936 indicated that 78 per cent of those polled preferred single bills, and an array of complaints about double bills explained this preference.[39] Among them was the length of programmes, some of which were extended to four hours in order to include a second feature. Conversely, there were complaints that some programmes were kept within three hours by cutting the films to the point where they became noticeably 'jerky.' It was also said that 'a good picture is invariably coupled with a bad one' This complaint did not necessarily refer to the aforementioned divide between 'A' films and 'B' films, but could also reflect the often haphazard method of pairing films. Audiences complained that the films on a double feature did not 'match' one another.[40] This complaint was voiced separately by exhibitors, who pointed out that films were not planned as double bills at either the production or distribution stage, to ensure that they would complement one another on a single programme.[41] Instead, they were often combined simply on the basis of availability. Thus, odd pairings abounded. Within the data sample, these include double bills that combined *The Informer* with the society farce *Going Highbrow*; Fritz Lang's *Fury* and the children's musical *Let's Sing Again*; Robert Flaherty's documentary *Man of Aran* with the crime serial *Charlie Chan in Paris*; an adaptation of Dickens' *Great Expectations* and the dating agency comedy *Bachelor Bait*; and the German film *Mädchen in Uniform* with *Dealers in*

Death, a documentary expose of the munitions industry in the First World War. As intriguingly odd as some of these combinations appear to be, it is plain to see that an audience paying to see one of the films was unlikely to find the other as appealing. Of course, the Warner Bros. survey also found a minority of 22 per cent who favoured double bills, and one commonly cited reason for preferring them was that second features replaced vaudeville stage acts in many venues. Or, as one patron put it, 'If you only have only one feature at the movies you'll have vaudeville, and vaudeville is lousy.'[42]

Live Acts

Many of the theatres in the data sample had been built as vaudeville houses rather than as cinemas, and in earlier decades films had been only one item on programmes dominated by vaudeville acts. Films then gradually pushed the vaudeville acts off the programmes. By the mid-1930s the decline of vaudeville was frequently discussed in the trade papers, and it was termed the 'orphan child of show business' by *Variety*.[43] One major factor was the expense of live entertainment, which many venues could not afford in the depression. Another factor was said to be that vaudeville had relied upon the same material and formulae for too long, and the familiar range of acts, including acrobats, magicians, comedy sketches, dancers, vocalists, impersonators and animal acts, was said to have lost its appeal.[44] The most significant factor, however, was undoubtedly the advent of 'talking pictures,' which allowed films to take up vaudeville's staple entertainments: spoken comedy, tap-dancing, and music in a variety of forms. Films could not duplicate the excitement of a good live performance, of course, but they could record the best performances of some of the world's greatest performers. They could be distributed more widely than even the most extensive stage tour, and they could do all of this at less cost to the exhibitor.

Many of the most popular films of this period borrowed from vaudeville even as they replaced it. Fred Astaire and Ginger Rogers, for example, began their careers (separately) in vaudeville, and their films typically foreground their status as stage entertainers. While the films do not adhere to a 'revue' format, they nonetheless offer a variety of entertainment forms, including a range of singing and dancing styles as well as comedy in the form of both verbal 'gags' and situational sketches. Moreover, the stage is frequently foregrounded within their films. *Swing Time*, for example, begins with a shot of the proscenium arch in a large theatre. On stage, a team of dancers can be seen, but it is a long shot from the perspective of the theatre audience, and so it is difficult to discern the individual performers, or even to see that Astaire himself is leading the team. This opening shot thus offers only the limited vantage point of an audience watching a stage performance. The shots that follow demonstrate the advantages of cinema. They offer not only much closer views of Astaire, but they also allow the audience to see the spaces backstage and in the dressing rooms, and they reveal musical performances that are private (or 'integrated' into the film's story). Furthermore, the subsequent stage performances are freed from the constraints of the proscenium, once again demonstrating the privileged position available to the cinema audience. The only blatant reference to vaudeville comes in the very first lines of dialogue, in which an ageing magician stands just off-stage complaining that his act has been cut from the show because it was 'too old-fashioned.' He attempts to perform a card trick for a stage hand, but the stage hand is too captivated by his close view of Astaire dancing on stage to notice the old-timer's routine. It is a brief scene, but the camera's backstage view, the stage hand's privileged position, and the notion of new and old entertainment forms can serve as a succinct demonstration of the decline of vaudeville and the triumph of musical cinema.

Another key film of this period, the musical *The Great Ziegfeld*, demonstrates a different type of self-consciousness toward vaudeville. The film seems designed to satiate the audience's appetite for staged entertainment. As a 'biopic' of the showman Florenz Ziegfeld, it offers a veritable history of popular staged entertainments, at least within its subject's lifetime. It begins with carnival attractions and culminates on Broadway with the spectacular Ziegfeld Follies stage show, and throughout it features all manner of acts and performances. It is essentially a very long and varied 'revue' programme, and one that is linked together rather thinly by the biographical story line. Its extraordinary 170-minute running time may have been a canny strategy on the part of MGM, which produced the film. Very little time was left for anything else on the programme. An abbreviated newsreel, a cartoon or a trailer may have been possible, but there certainly could not have been a stage programme or second feature. And that, of course, meant that the box-office earnings would not have to be shared with any other attraction. It is clear that audiences did not feel cheated, though, as *The Great Ziegfeld* earned one of the top grosses of the period, and in fact its fifteen-week engagement at the Carthay Circle in Los Angeles was the longest recorded in the data sample.

Even if vaudeville was being eclipsed in the mid-1930s, it was not yet time to sound the death knell for live entertainment in combination with films. One of the most striking aspects of the data sample is the extent to which live entertainment was still used as an accompaniment to film screenings in the 1930s. Of the 104 cinemas represented in the data sample,

45 were what *Variety* referred to as 'combination houses,' or theatres that combined live and film entertainment on the same bill. For the most part, these were the largest theatres in the largest cities. The two largest, New York's Radio City Music Hall and the Roxy, had approximately 6000 seats each, and each regularly combined film and stage shows. The stage shows were a key part of their identity and appeal, and they were also crucial to the theatres' ability to draw in thousands of patrons at advanced prices and for several daily shows. Of the other New York venues in the sample, the Capitol (5,486 seats) and Paramount (3,664) had live shows in most but not all weeks, while the Center (3,700), Strand (2,758), Rivoli (2,092) and Rialto (750) theatres never did. A similar pattern held in other large and medium-sized cities, with the larger venues more likely to offer live entertainment and the smaller venues very rarely offering it. In the smaller cities 'combination houses' were rare, and cinemas offered a 'double bill' of two feature films rather than combining stage and screen entertainments. Even in these cities, however, the occasional live performance could be extraordinarily successful. Throughout the country and in cities large and small, the appeal of live entertainment in combination with films was often remarkably strong.

In some rare instances, live performances were tailored to fit with or to celebrate a film. This was reserved for the most important releases, such as *Top Hat*, and it was done only in the grandest venues, such as Radio City Music Hall. There, *Top Hat* was preceded by a stage show that featured a projected backdrop of the film's title designs, a recreation on stage of the film's ballroom set, dancers in top hats and tails, and an all-male choir with twenty-four members singing the film's signature song, 'The Piccolino.'[45] In most other instances, if a strong 'A' film was accompanied by a live attraction, it would not be a particularly prominent one. When MGM's *Wife Versus Secretary* was shown at the Loew's State in New York City, for example, *Variety* commented that the 'strong screen fare' meant that the theatre was offering only a 'routine' live programme.[46] It was the weaker 'A' films and 'B' films playing as single features that needed to be coupled with a strong live programme in order to improve or maintain audience numbers. One particularly notable example of this concerns Paramount's *The Scarlet Empress*. Directed by Josef Von Sternberg and starring Marlene Dietrich, *The Scarlet Empress* is now considered a classic film, but when it was first released in the autumn of 1934 it met with dismal box-office returns. It was not held over for a second week in any of the thirteen engagements represented in the data sample, and it earned its four highest box-office grosses in the cities where it was accompanied by a stage show. In one of those cities, Pittsburgh, the Stanley Theatre postponed its engagement of the film for several weeks, waiting until it could book a stage show that would 'carry' the film through its one week engagement. Hence, *The Scarlet Empress* was screened on a programme that also included a variety show led by the popular Fred Waring Orchestra, and the box-office gross for the week was a remarkably high $26,000. This would make it seem as though *The Scarlet Empress* was one of the leading attractions in Pittsburgh during the 1934–6 period, and yet according to *Variety*, it was the live act that drew audiences to the theatre that week and the live act that compensated for the '100 minutes of dull celluloid.'[47]

While traditional vaudeville was seldom seen as a key attraction in the mid-1930s, stage shows led by a prominent 'headline name' often drew remarkable results. These appearances could add considerably to the venue's overhead costs. Top-rated performers such as Jack Benny, Eddie Cantor and Milton Berle were able to earn between $7,500 and $15,000 for a one-week engagement, as well as garnering a percentage of the box-office takings.[48] Exhibitors were willing to pay such sums only during the weeks in which the main feature film was thought to be a weak attraction. Pittsburgh offers further examples of the effect that prominent live acts could have in cinemas, as well as examples of the way in which 'combination houses' operated outside of New York City. The two largest venues in Pittsburgh, the Penn and Stanley theatres, regularly used headline acts to support minor feature films. As Table Three indicates, this strategy was at times highly successful. Films such as *Behold My Wife*, *Exclusive Story*, *Hide Out*, *Dangerous*, *O'Shaughnessy's Boy*, *Sequoia* and *Hands Across the Table*, which had a much lower profile in other cities, were among the twenty top-earning attractions in Pittsburgh during this period, and in each case a live performance was credited with drawing the crowds. When more prominent films played in these theatres, however, stage shows were not usually offered and there was no need for shows with an expensive 'headline' act. A similar pattern is also seen in other major cities, and Table Four and Table Five demonstrate the impact that live performances had in Detroit and Minneapolis, respectively. Live appearances by performers such as Amos 'n' Andy, John Boles, George Burns and Gracie Allen, the Marx Brothers, Stepin Fetchit, Ed Sullivan, and the orchestras led by Cab Calloway, Eddie Duchin and Guy Lombardo, were able to draw audiences to see films that did not fare nearly so well on their own.

Many of these performers had begun in vaudeville, but by the mid-1930s they were known primarily for their work in radio and films. That they could return to the stage as vital support for struggling film exhibitors is one indication of the cross-fertilization that allowed vaudeville, radio and film to intermix and evolve. At this point, radio was of course much more important to their drawing power than vaudeville. Radio ownership doubled over the course of the decade, and although there was initially some suspicion and hostility in Hollywood toward the new medium, by the middle of the decade the relationship between film and radio had become a mutually beneficial one.[49] Nationally syndicated radio programmes promoted and publicized film stars and the latest film releases. Films such as Paramount's *The Big Broadcast of 1936* and *The Big Broadcast of 1937* portrayed the backstage operations of a radio station and offered the dramatic rationale for a succession of comedy and musical acts. Crucially, they also gave audiences the opportunity to see the performers they normally only heard. There was also at least one instance of a syndicated radio programme forming the basis of a touring stage show that played in cinemas. This was the 'Major Bowes Amateur Show,' an amateur talent contest hosted on the radio by Major Bowes. The winners of the radio competition were placed in Bowes' stage revues, which toured the country playing in combination houses. These stage shows were essentially amateur vaudeville hours, featuring the usual mix of singers, tap dancers, magicians and comedians, and yet they drew audiences into cinemas in a manner that standard vaudeville no longer could. They could even support 'B' films playing as a single feature in a major venue.[50] Their popularity was so remarkable that in 1935 the shows were also filmed as 'short subjects' so that they could be distributed more widely and to smaller venues.

The persistence of vaudeville—albeit in various guises—is one of the most notable characteristics of this period of cinemagoing, but the combination houses were always searching for new and different acts. Among the many other stage acts that preceded film screenings in this period were acrobats, roller skaters and, for a brief time, some venues even tried staging badminton or basketball games before showing a film.[51] These were short-lived phenomena. Nevertheless, they offer further evidence that notions of what constituted an evening's entertainment at the cinema continued to include a surprisingly wide array of different attractions in the 1930s.

Conclusion

Today, *Variety* continues to offer its readers information on box-office grosses in North America, but its reports focus entirely on the national level and little (if any) attention is given to individual cities or to specific cinemas. This is undoubtedly appropriate in the contemporary context. Audiences today usually go to the cinema to see a single film rather than a programme of attractions. The majority of cinemas lack individual character and a distinct identity. And films are promoted through national rather than local campaigns. In the 1930s, by contrast, there was apparently little interest among *Variety's* readers in national box-office grosses; the box-office earnings that were reported so carefully each week were not added together to form a national gross. The national level simply was not important. Rather, it was important to report what was happening in individual cities and cinemas, and how audiences were responding to specific programmes, promotions and pricing strategies. The cinemagoing experience itself varied widely, even at the local level, and the task of *Variety* was to report on the success or failure of any number of variations. Thus, the reports allow film historians to observe changes in industry and exhibition practices, to study the context in which films were shown and how that changed over time, to assess audience preferences and compare the tastes of different cities or regions, and, of course, to examine the journey of a single film as it makes its way across the country and through various exhibition contexts. Its focus on a representative selection of the exhibition market means that the *Variety* dataset is not a comprehensive source. Yet it is a remarkably detailed and informative source and, to date, it is one that has been largely overlooked or under used.

Table 8.1   The fifty top earning films in the data sample

A ranking of the fifty top earning films, based on all of the earnings recorded in the data sample, with indications of how many engagements were recorded, the total number weeks that each film played, and the number of weeks that it appeared on a double bill and the number of weeks it appeared with a stage show.

Film (Studio, director, year)	Sum of all box-office earnings	No. of cities played	No. of weeks played	Weeks on a double bill	Weeks with a stage show	Top-billed stars
1 *San Francisco* (MGM, Van Dyke, 1936)	1,147,650	22	79	3	0	Clark Gable Jeanette MacDonald
2 *Top Hat* (RKO, Sandrich, 1935)	1,132,550	20	54	1	3	Fred Astaire Ginger Rogers
3 *The Great Ziegfeld* (MGM, Leonard, 1936)	966,700	22	66	0	0	William Powell Myrna Loy
4 *Swing Time* (RKO, Stevens, 1936)	964,650	21	48	6	8	Fred Astaire Ginger Rogers
5 *Mutiny on the Bounty* (MGM, Lloyd, 1935)	939,100	21	53.5	0	0	Clark Gable Charles Laughton

Film (Studio, director, year)	Sum of all box-office earnings	No. of cities played	No. of weeks played	Weeks on a double bill	Weeks with a stage show	Top-billed stars
6 *Roberta* (RKO, Seiter, 1935)	873,650	19	51	0	10	Irene Dunne Fred Astaire
7 *Follow the Fleet* (RKO, Sandrich, 1936)	806,600	20	47	0	0	Fred Astaire Ginger Rogers
8 *Anthony Adverse* (WB, Leroy, 1936)	793,000	20	47.5	0	1	Fredric March Olivia De Havilland
9 *David Copperfield* (MGM, Cukor, 1935)	738,450	23	48	2	2	W.C. Fields Lionel Barrymore
10 *Love Me Forever* (Col, Schertzinger, 1935)	731,900	21	43	3	9	Grace Moore Leo Carrillo
11 *One Night of Love* (Col, Schertzinger, 1934)	711,300	21	47.5	5	8	Grace Moore Tullio Carminati
12 *The Gay Divorcee* (RKO, Sandrich, 1934)	661,500	21	41.5	2	3	Fred Astaire Ginger Rogers
13 *China Seas* (MGM, Garnett, 1935)	644,900	23	45.5	0	0	Clark Gable Jean Harlow
14 *Rose Marie* (MGM, Van Dyke, 1936)	634,100	22	44	0	0	Jeanette MacDonald Nelson Eddy
15 *The Barretts of Wimpole St* (MGM, Franklin, 1934)	623,700	21	40	0	5	Norma Shearer Fredric March
16 *Broadway Bill* (Col, Capra, 1934)	620,850	22	41	8	6	Warner Baxter Myrna Loy
17 *G-Men* (WB, Keighley, 1935)	613,650	23	39	3	8	James Cagney Ann Dvorak
18 *Modern Times* (Chaplin, Chaplin, 1936)	608,270	18	40.5	5	0	Charles Chaplin Paulette Goddard
19 *Lives of a Bengal Lancer* (Par, Hathaway, 1935)	605,200	22	37	1	6	Gary Cooper Franchot Tone
20 *My Man Godfrey* (Uni, La Cava, 1936)	605,050	22	45	12	1	William Powell Carole Lombard
21 *The Gorgeous Hussy* (MGM, Brown, 1936)	598,450	23	48	9	4	Joan Crawford Robert Taylor
22 *Mr Deeds Goes to Town* (Col, Capra, 1936)	591,150	21	48.5	10	2	Gary Cooper Jean Arthur

Film (Studio, director, year)	Sum of all box-office earnings	No. of cities played	No. of weeks played	Weeks on a double bill	Weeks with a stage show	Top-billed stars
23 *Mary of Scotland* (RKO, Ford, 1936)	589,800	21	34	7	6	Katharine Hepburn Fredric March
24 *The Big Broadcast of 1937* (Par, Leisen, 1936)	567,950	20	32	5	5	Jack Benny George Burns
25 *Under Two Flags* (TCF, Lloyd, 1936)	567,150	21	33	1	3	Ronald Colman Claudette Colbert
26 *Belle of the Nineties* (Par, McCarey, 1934)	564,825	19	31.5	1	3	Mae West Roger Pryor
27 *The Broadway Melody of 1936* (MGM, 1935)	530,400	22	43	0	0	Jack Benny Eleanor Powell
28 *Wife vs. Secretary* (MGM, Brown, 1936)	529,300	23	39	2	2	Clark Gable Jean Harlow
29 *The Littlest Rebel* (TCF, Butler, 1935)	527,800	21	29.5	7	4	Shirley Temple John Boles
30 *Libeled Lady* (MGM, Conway, 1936)	517,275	19	43	13	0	Jean Harlow Myrna Loy
31 *Poor Little Rich Girl* (TCF, Cummings, 1936)	512,450	22	35	9	7	Shirley Temple Alice Faye
32 *The Green Pastures* (WB, Connelly & Keighley, 1936)	509,350	21	34	5	0	Rex Ingram Oscar Polk
33 *The Little Colonel* (Fox, Butler, 1935)	507,800	19	27	1	5	Shirley Temple Lionel Barrymore
34 *Show Boat* (Uni, Whale, 1936)	505,950	20	45	4	1	Irene Dunne Allan Jones
35 *Forsaking All Others* (MGM, Van Dyke, 1934)	503,145	21	39	2	2	Joan Crawford Clark Gable
36 *The Little Minister* (RKO, Wallace, 1934)	500,500	19	30.5	2	11	Katharine Hepburn John Beal
37 *His Brother's Wife* (MGM, Van Dyke, 1936)	492,850	23	34	8	1	Robert Taylor Barbara Stanwyck
38 *Becky Sharp* (Pioneer, Mamoulian, 1935)	490,550	20	33	1	2	Miriam Hopkins Frances Dee

Film (Studio, director, year)	Sum of all box-office earnings	No. of cities played	No. of weeks played	Weeks on a double bill	Weeks with a stage show	Top-billed stars
39 *Naughty Marietta* (MGM, Van Dyke, 1935)	488,450	20	44	3	6	Jeanette MacDonald Nelson Eddy
40 *The Country Doctor* (TCF, King, 1936)	486,350	22	32.5	2	4	Dionne Quintuplets Jean Hersholt
41 *Anna Karenina* (MGM, Brown, 1935)	485,400	21	34	1	1	Greta Garbo Fredric March
42 *A Tale of Two Cities* (MGM, Conway, 1936)	481,200	21	33	1	0	Ronald Colman Elizabeth Allan
43 *Little Lord Fauntleroy* (Selznick, Cromwell, 1936)	476,300	21	31	6	2	Freddie Bartholomew Dolores Barrymore
44 *Curly Top* (Fox, Cummings, 1935)	475,500	21	33	3	0	Shirley Temple John Boles
45 *No More Ladies* (MGM, Griffith, 1935)	474,050	22	39	4	6	Joan Crawford Robert Montgomery
46 *Strike Me Pink* (Goldwyn, Taurog, 1936)	466,600	20	37	2	0	Eddie Cantor Ethel Merman
47 *Trail of the Lonesome Pine* (Par, Hathaway, 1936)	450,250	21	36	5	5	Sylvia Sidney Henry Fonda
48 *Les Miserables* (TC, Boleslawski, 1935)	447,600	15	30	2	3	Fredric March Charles Laughton
49 *The Bride Comes Home* (Par, Ruggles, 1936)	446,650	21	26	6	7	Claudette Colbert Fred MacMurray
50 *Captain Blood* (WB, Curtiz, 1935)	444,650	22	34	2	1	Errol Flynn Olivia De Havilland

Table 8.2   The leading production companies

A ranking of the leading production companies in the data sample, based on the sum of all box-office earnings.

Rank	Studio/ Production company	Box-office total ($)	Percentage of total box-office earnings	Number of releases	Average box-office per film ($)
1	MGM	23,179,352	19.14	107	216,629
2	Paramount	19,631,855	16.21	131	149,861
3	Warner Bros.	17,526,849	14.47	123	142,495
4	RKO	13,715,798	11.32	82	167,266
5	Twentieth Century-Fox	8,250,675	6.81	45	183,348
6	Fox	8,210,000	6.78	60	136,833
7	Columbia	7,875,432	6.50	89	88,488
8	Universal	6,623,519	5.47	69	95,993
9	Goldwyn (UA)	3,121,066	2.58	9	346,785
10	20th Century (UA)	2,677,500	2.21	8	334,688
11	Gaumont-British	1,805,935	1.49	24	75,247
12	Reliance (UA)	1,201,950	0.99	6	200,325
13	London Films (UA)	1,021,925	0.84	8	127,741
14	Republic	908,355	0.75	25	36,334
15	Chaplin (UA)	608,270	0.50	1	608,270
16	Pioneer (RKO)	582,175	0.48	2	291,088
17	Selznick (UA)	476,300	0.39	1	476,300
18	Pickford-Lasky (UA)	395,450	0.33	2	197,725
19	Principal	366,850	0.30	5	73,370
20	Monogram	311,690	0.26	24	12,987
21	Gainsborough	272,190	0.22	8	34,024
22	Mascot	270,750	0.22	13	20,827
23	Roach (MGM)	266,175	0.22	3	88,725
24	British & Dominions (UA)	252,300	0.21	7	36,043
25	Hecht-MacArthur (Paramount)	195,767	0.16	3	65,256
26	Liberty	143,985	0.12	10	14,399
27	Atherton	122,850	0.10	8	15,356

Rank	Studio/ Production company	Box-office total ($)	Percentage of total box-office earnings	Number of releases	Average box-office per film ($)
28	Invincible	93,700	0.08	11	8,518
29	Chesterfield	79,650	0.07	15	5,310
30	British International	77,000	0.06	12	6,417
31	Van Beuren	73,800	0.06	2	36,900
32	Select	68,966	0.06	3	22,989
33	Mr & Mrs Martin Johnson	68,750	0.06	1	68,750
34	Lianofilm	67,085	0.06	1	67,085
35	Howard B Franklin	64,450	0.05	1	64,450
	35 other companies	503,550	0.42	48	10,491
	TOTAL	121,111,913	100.00	967	125,245

Table 8.3   The top attractions in Pittsburgh

The top attractions in Pittsburgh, ranked by local earnings and with a comparison to national ranking.

Film/ studio	Local earnings	Local ranking	National ranking	Local cinema	Weeks played	Live artist/ headline name
G-Men (WB)	$52,500	1	17	Stanley	2	Folies Bergere
Anthony Adverse (WB)	$47,500	2	8	Stanley	2	none
Mutiny on the Bounty (MGM)	$44,200	3	5	Penn	1	none
				Warner	2	none
Green Pastures (WB)	$35,300	4	32	Penn	1	none
				Warner	1	none
Behold My Wife (Par)	$34,500	5	217	Stanley	1	Jack Benny
The Gorgeous Hussy (MGM)	$33,000	6=	21	Penn	2	none
San Francisco (MGM)	$33,000	6=	1	Penn	1	none
				Warner	1	none
Top Hat (RKO)	$33,000	6=	2	Penn	2	none
Rose Marie (MGM)	$32,700	9	14	Penn	1	none
				Warner	1	none
The Great Ziegfeld (MGM)	$32,500	10	3	Penn	2	none
Broadway Melody of 1936 (MGM)	$31,500	11	27	Penn	1	none
				Warner	1	none
Exclusive Story (MGM)	$31,000	12=	215	Stanley	1	Jack Benny
Hide Out (MGM)	$31,000	12=	210	Penn	1	Ted Lewis Orchestra
China Seas (MGM)	$30,500	14	13	Penn	1	none
				Warner	1	none
Dangerous (WB)	$30,000	15=	176	Stanley	1	Major Bowes
O'Shaughnessy's Boy (MGM)	$30,000	15=	242	Stanley	1	Major Bowes

Film/ studio	Local earnings	Local ranking	National ranking	Local cinema	Weeks played	Live artist/ headline name
Devil Dogs of the Air (WB)	$28,500	17	106	Stanley	2	none
Sequoia (MGM)	$28,000	18	251	Penn	1	Eddie Cantor
Hands Across the Table (Par)	$27,600	19	114	Stanley	1	Guy Lombardo
Swing Time (RKO)	$27,000	20=	4	Stanley	1	none
				Penn	1	none
Follow the Fleet (RKO)	$27,000	20=	7	Stanley	1	none
				Warner	1	none

Table 8.4   The top attractions in Detroit

The top attractions in Detroit, ranked by local earnings and with a comparison to national ranking. All of the films played as the single feature film.

Film/ studio	Local earnings	Local ranking	National ranking	Local cinema	Weeks played	Live artist/ headline name
The Littlest Rebel (TCF)	$60,000	1	29	Fox	2	Molasses'n' January
Roberta (RKO)	$54,000	2	6	Fox	2	none
Curly Top (Fox)	$53,000	3	44	Fox	2	none
In Old Kentucky (Fox)	$50,000	4	81	Fox	2	vaudeville
Life Begins at Forty (Fox)	$49,500	5	97	Fox	2	Dorsey Brothers
The Country Doctor (TCF)	$49,000	6	40	Fox	2	Phil Baker
Love Me Forever (Col)	$47,900	7	10	Fox	2	none
San Francisco (MGM)	$45,000	8	1	United Artists	4	none
Mutiny on the Bounty (MGM)	$44,500	9=	5	United Artists	3	none
Private Number (TCF)	$44,500	9=	58	Fox	2	Eddie Duchin

Film/ studio	Local earnings	Local ranking	National ranking	Local cinema	Weeks played	Live artist/ headline name
King of Burlesque (TCF)	$40,000	**11**	123	Fox	2	Clyde Beatty
Poor Little Rich Girl (TCF)	$39,500	**12**	31	Fox	2	Ed Sullivan Unit
His Brother's Wife (MGM)	$39,000	**13**	37	Michigan	1	NBC Radio Unit
Modern Times (Chaplin)	$38,800	**14**	18	United Artists	3	none
Libeled Lady (MGM)	$37,500	**15**	30	United Artists	3	none
Charlie Chan in Shanghai (Fox)	$36,000	**16**	262	Fox	1	Cab Calloway
Anthony Adverse (WB)	$35,500	**17**	8	United Artists	3	none
The Little Minister (RKO)	$35,000	**18**	36	Fox	2	vaudeville
The Bride Walks Out (RKO)	$34,000	**19=**	168	Michigan	1	Major Bowes' Amateurs
Rhythm on the Range (Par)	$34,000	**19=**	53	Michigan	1	Bob Ripley Unit

Table 8.5   The top attractions in Minneapolis

The top attractions in Minneapolis, ranked by local earnings and with a comparison to national ranking. All of the films played as the single feature film.

Film studio	Local earnings	Local ranking	National ranking	Local cinema(s)	Weeks played	Live artist/ headline name
Roberta (RKO)	$34,000	**1**	6	Orpheum	2	none
The Bride Comes Home (Par)	$32,000	**2**	49	Minnesota	1	Burns & Allen
One Night of Love (Col)	$30,500	**3**	11	Orpheum	2	none
San Francisco (MGM)	$29,000	**4**	1	Minnesota	2	none
Libeled Lady (MGM)	$28,000	**5**	30	Lyric	2	none

Film studio	Local earnings	Local ranking	National ranking	Local cinema(s)	Weeks played	Live artist/ headline name
				Minnesota	1	none
Top Hat (RKO)	$27,800	6	2	Orpheum	2	none
Broadway Bill (Col)	$27,500	7	16	Orpheum	2	none
My American Wife (Par)	$27,000	8=	170	Minnesota	1	Eddie Duchin
Trail of the Lonesome Pine (Par)	$27,000	8=	47	State	2	none
				Minnesota	1	none
Follow the Fleet (RKO)	$26,500	10	7	Orpheum	2	none
Goose and Gander (WB)	$26,000	11	221	Orpheum	1	Folies Bergere
Swing Time (RKO)	$24,500	12	4	Orpheum	2	none
Mr Deeds Goes to Town (Col)	$23,500	13=	22	Orpheum	2	none
My Man Godfrey (Uni)	$23,500	13=	20	Orpheum	2	none
Cain and Mabel (WB)	$23,000	15	178	Minnesota	1	John Boles
The Great Ziegfeld (MGM)	$22,500	16	3	Minnesota	1	none
				State	1	none
Wife vs Secretary (MGM)	$22,000	17	28	Minnesota	1	none
				State	1	none
The First Baby (TCF)	$21,000	18	522	Minnesota	1	The Marx Brothers
The Gay Divorcee (RKO)	$20,000	19=	12	Orpheum	2	none
Two in the Dark (RKO)	$20,000	19=	370	Orpheum	1	Wayne King Orchestra
Walking on Air (RKO)	$20,000	19=	216	Orpheum	1	Folies Parisienne

Appendix:
The sample cinema set for the period October 1934 to October 1936.

Cinema	City	Affiliation	Seats	Price range (cents)	Box-office over the period ($)[a]	Regular live acts? (yes/no)	Films screened	Best week's film/act	Best wk's box-office ($)	Worst wk's box-office ($)	Best run film/act	Best run box-office ($)	Best run weeks
Alabama	Birmingham	Publix	2,800	30–40	743,950	No	117	Steamboat Round The Bend	8,700	3,000	Steamboat Round The Bend	8,700	1
Empire	Birmingham	Acme	1,100	25 only	285,100	No	112	Devil Dogs	5,500	1,300	Mr Deeds Goes To Town	7,300	2
Strand	Birmingham	Publix	800	25 only	187,000	No	135	In Old Kentucky/ Keeper Of The Bees	3,000	500	In Old Kentucky	4,250	1.5
Boston	Boston	RKO	2,900	25–50	1,690,625	Yes	144	Folies Bergeres Unit/Hot Tip	38,000	3,100	Folie Parisienne Unit/Walking On Air	58,500	2
Memorial	Boston	RKO	3,212	25–55	1,509,180	Occ.	89	Top Hat	40,000	5,000	Top Hat	111,200	5
Metro- politan	Boston	Publix	4,331	35–65	2,803,200	Yes	112	Jack Benny/ Private Worlds	49,000	2,500	Paul Lukas/ Trail Of The Lonesome Pine	58,000	2

Cinema	City	Affiliation	Seats	Price range (cents)	Box-office over the period ($)ᵃ	Regular live acts? (yes/no)	Films screened	Best week's film/act	Best wk's box-office ($)	Worst wk's box-office ($)	Best run film/act	Best run box-office ($)	Best run weeks
Orpheum	Boston	Loew's	2,900	25–55	1,529,450	No	126	Mutiny On The Bounty	24,000	6,000	San Francisco	67,900	4
State	Boston	Loew's	3,700	30–55	1,501,550	No	151	Barretts Of Wimpole Street	24,500	4,000	San Francisco	55,000	4
Albee	Brooklyn	RKO	3,245	25–50	1,301,500	No	138	Swing Time	25,000	2,500	Swing Time	43,000	2
Fox	Brooklyn	Independent	4,075	25–50	1,479,100	Occ.	141	stage show/ One Night Of Love	29,000	8,900	stage show/ One Night Of Love	72,500	3
Metropolitan	Brooklyn	Loew's	3,618	25–50	1,658,500	Occ.	115	Eddie Cantor/ Transatlantic M-G-R	36,000	13,000	San Francisco	85,000	6
Paramount	Brooklyn	Publix	4,156	25–65	1,581,500	No	102	Captain Blood	40,000	5,600	Captain Blood	65,000	2
Strand	Brooklyn	WB	2,870	25–50	565,200	No	198	Show No Mercy/$1000 A Minute	13,000	2,500	Show No Mercy/$1000 A Minute	31,000	3
Buffalo	Buffalo	Publix	3,489	30–65	1,566,000	Occ.	113	Ted Lewis Orch/Ladies In Love	25,000	5,700	Ted Lewis Orch /Ladies In Love	25,000	1

Cinema	City	Affiliation	Seats	Price range (cents)	Box-office over the period ($)[a]	Regular live acts? (yes/no)	Films screened	Best week's film/act	Best wk's box-office ($)	Worst wk's box-office ($)	Best run film/act	Best run box-office ($)	Best run weeks
Century	Buffalo	Publix	3,076	25 only	643,350	No	204	Don't Turn 'em Loose/Old Hutch	10,000	3,200	Robin Hood Of El Dorado/Widow From Monte Carlo	14,300	2
Hippodrome	Buffalo	Publix	2,089	25-40	742,500	No	146	David Copperfield	22,000	3,100	David Copperfield	13,500	2
Chicago	Chicago	Publix	3,861	35-75	3,652,000	Yes	97	Veloz and Yolanda/Bride Comes Home	59000	14,000	stage show/Belle Of The Nineties	95,900	2
Oriental	Chicago	Publix	3,217	25-40	1,805,600	Yes	111	Vaudeville/One-Way Ticket	27,600	10,300	vaudeville/One-Way Ticket	27,600	1
Palace	Chicago	RKO	2,500	25-55	2,280,300	Occ.	80	Swing Time	34,700	5,900	Top Hat	141300	6
State Lake	Chicago	Jones	2,734	20-35	1,375,400	Yes	107	Vaudeville/Iron Man	19,200	9,800	vaudeville/Iron Man	19,200	1
UA	Chicago	Publix	1,696	35-65	1,523,500	No	47	Mutiny On The Bounty	28500	7,000	Great Ziegfeld	95900	5
Albee	Cincinnati	RKO	3,317	35-42	1,377,950	No	108	Follow The Fleet	26,000	5,500	Libeled Lady	32,000	2

185

Cinema	City	Affiliation	Seats	Price range (cents)	Box-office over the period ($)[a]	Regular live acts? (yes/no)	Films screened	Best week's film/act	Best wk's box-office ($)	Worst wk's box-office ($)	Best run film/act	Best run box-office ($)	Best run weeks
Keith's	Cincinnati	Libson	1,500	30-42	547,300	No	98	Flirtation Walk	10,500	2,100	Flirtation Walk	15,000	2
Lyric	Cincinnati	RKO	1,432	35-42	503,900	No	107	Night At The Opera	16,000	1,800	Night At The Opera	16,000	1
Palace	Cincinnati	RKO	2,614	35-42	1,171,900	No	103	San Francisco	22,000	3,750	San Francisco	36,000	2
Denham	Denver	Cooper	1,392	25-50	659,500	Occ.	110	Belle Of The Nineties	16,000	1,000	Cleopatra	22,500	2
Denver	Denver	RKO	2,525	25-50	899,900	No	115	Mutiny On The Bounty	15,000	4,000	Mutiny On The Bounty	15,000	1
Orpheum	Denver	RKO	2,600	25-50	732,400	Occ.	118	**Ben Bernie Orch** /Romance In The Rain	16,000	2,000	San Francisco	31,500	3
Paramount	Denver	RKO	2,096	25-40	319,925	No	160	Bride Of Frankenstein	7,000	1,000	Bride Of Frankenstein	9,000	1.5
Fisher	Detroit	Publix	2,975	30-40	85,350	No	37	David Copperfield	6,200	3,100	David Copperfield	6,200	1
Fox	Detroit	Independent	5,500	25-55	1,929,600	Yes	78	**Cab Calloway Orch** /Charlie Chan In S'pore	36,000	12,000	Littlest Rebel	60,000	2

Cinema	City	Affiliation	Seats	Price range (cents)	Box-office over the period ($)[a]	Regular live acts? (yes/no)	Films screened	Best week's film/act	Best wk's box-office ($)	Worst wk's box-office ($)	Best run film/act	Best run box-office ($)	Best run weeks
Michigan	Detroit	Publix	4,038	25–55	1,852,200	Yes	86	NBC Radio Unit/His Brother's Wife	39,000	10,000	NBC Radio Unit/His Brother's Wife	39,000	1
UA	Detroit	Publix	2,070	25–55	656,800	No	45	Mutiny On The Bounty	20,000	3,500	San Francisco	45,000	4
Apollo	Indianapolis	Fourth Avenue	1,171	25–40	327,950	No	59	Steamboat Round The Bend	9,800	1,300	Steamboat Round The Bend	19,900	3.5
Circle	Indianapolis	Monarch	2,638	25–40	318,350	No	99	Swing Time	10,500	1,900	Swing Time	14,700	2
Loew's	Indianapolis	Loew's	2,431	25–40	517,050	No	112	Mutiny On The Bounty	14,000	2,500	Mutiny On The Bounty	19,600	2
Lyric	Indianapolis	Olson	1,896	25–40	724,800	Yes	83	Major Bowes' Amateurs/Pepper	14,000	5,000	Major Bowes' Amateurs/Pepper	14,000	1
Main Street	Kansas City	RKO	2,500	25–40	1,046,000	Yes	99	Folies Bergere Unit/Case Of Lucky Legs	25,000	3,000	Top Hat	38,000	3
Midland	Kansas City	Loew's	4,000	25–40	1,222,345	No	101	China Seas	24,000	2,400	San Francisco	47,500	3

Cinema	City	Affiliation	Seats	Price range (cents)	Box-office over the period ($)ª	Regular live acts? (yes/no)	Films screened	Best week's film/act	Best wk's box-office ($)	Worst wk's box-office ($)	Best run film/act	Best run box-office ($)	Best run weeks
Newman	Kansas City	Publix	1,800	25–40	800,100	No	108	Belle Of The Nineties	18,000	2,700	Both Belle Of The Nineties and Goin' To Town	25,000	2
Uptown	Kansas City	Fox	2,045	25–40	460,375	No	108	Steamboat or Poor Little Rich Girl	11,000	1,200	Steamboat Round The Bend	19,400	3
Carthay Circle	Los Angeles	Independent	1,518	55–165	298,800	No	2	Great Ziegfeld	19,500	8,100	Great Ziegfeld	201,600	15
Chinese	Los Angeles	Fox	2,020	30–55	982,080	No	129	Modern Times	26,230	4,200	Modern Times	37,530	2
Down Town	Los Angeles	WB	2,500	30–40	655,800	No	131	Captain Blood	14,500	2,200	Captain Blood	27,500	3
Hollywood	Los Angeles	WB	2,758	30–55	768,760	No	100	Roberta	15,000	2,200	Dodsworth/Case Of The Velvet Claws	33,000	3
Panatges	Los Angeles	RKO	2,812	25–40	669,250	No	134	My Man Godfrey/Yellowstone	23,700	1,500	My Man Godfrey/Yellowstone	45,200	3
Paramount	Los Angeles	Patmar	3,347	30–55	1,922,160	Occ.	105	Eddie Cantor/Paris In Spring	33,860	8,400	Big Broadcast Of 1937	56,200	3

Cinema	City	Affiliation	Seats	Price range (cents)	Box-office over the period ($)a	Regular live acts? (yes/no)a	Films screened	Best week's film/act	Best wk's box-office ($)	Worst wk's box-office ($)	Best run film/act	Best run box-office ($)	Best run weeks
RKO	Los Angeles	RKO	2,916	25–55	807,700	No	99	My Man Godfrey /Yellowstone	20,300	2,600	Top Hat	42,000	4
State	Los Angeles	Fox	2,422	30–55	1,311,700	No	139	Mutiny On The Bounty	24,300	5,100	Mutiny On The Bounty	38,900	2
Capitol	Manhattan	Independent	5,486	35–110	3,665,300	Occ.	64	Mutiny On The Bounty	75,300	7,000	David Copperfield	235,000	5
Center	Manhattan	Independent	3,700	25–110	564,500	No	21	Ah, Wilderness	37000	6,000	Thanks A Million	86,000	4
Paramount	Manhattan	Publix	3,664	35–85	3,264,900	Yes	60	Cleopatra	68,000	8,500	Big Broadcast Of 1937	156,600	4
Radio City Music Hall	Manhattan	Independent	6,200	40–165	8,952,500	Occ.	78	Top Hat	134,000	48,000	Top Hat	348,000	3
Rialto	Manhattan	Publix	750	25–65	411,200	No	26	Lives Of A Bengal Lancer	21,800	5,000	Lives Of A Bengal Lancer	39,200	2
Rivoli	Manhattan	Independent	2,092	35–99	2,692,800	No	39	Modern Times	74,500	10,200	Modern Times	230,500	6
Roxy	Manhattan	Independent	6,000	25–65	3,492,910	Yes	90	Stage show/If You Could Only Cook	62,500	16,000	Sing Baby Sing	141,800	3
Strand	Manhattan	WB	2,758	35–85	2,366,900	No	57	G-Men	61,300	6,500	Anthony Adverse	200,000	5

Cinema	City	Affiliation	Seats	Price range (cents)	Box-office over the period ($)	Regular live acts? (yes/no)[a]	Films screened	Best week's film/act	Best wk's box-office ($)	Worst wk's box-office ($)	Best run film/act	Best run box-office ($)	Best run weeks
Lyric	Minneapolis	Publix	1,126	20–25	224,400	No	112	Kelly The Second	7,000	900	Libeled lady	10,000	2
Minnesota	Minneapolis	Publix	4,024	25–55	477,000	Occ.	37	Burns and Allen/Bride Comes Home	32,000	6,500	San Francisco	29,000	2
Orpheum	Minneapolis	Singer	2,600	25–40	1,095,000	Occ.	100	Folies Bergere Unit/Goose And The Gander	26,000	2,200	Roberta	34,000	2
State	Minneapolis	Publix	2,290	25–40	761,900	Occ.	110	Major Bowes' Amateurs/Redheads On Parade	17,000	2,500	China Seas	19,800	2
Capitol	Montreal	Famous Players	2,603	50 only	841,950	No	200	Lives Of A Bengal Lancer	18,000	3,000	Lives Of A Bengal Lancer	28,000	2
Loew's	Montreal	Loew's	3,200	50 only	995,100	Occ.	149	John Boles/Public Enemy's Wife	20,000	6,000	John Boles/Public Enemy's Wife	20,000	1
Palace	Montreal	Famous Players	2,582	50 only	929,800	No	105	Mutiny On The Bounty or Roberta	16,000	6,000	San Francisco	60,200	7

Cinema	City	Affiliation	Seats	Price range (cents)	Box-office over the period ($)	Regular live acts? (yes/no)[a]	Films screened	Best week's film/act	Best wk's box-office ($)	Worst wk's box-office ($)	Best run film/act	Best run box-office ($)	Best run weeks
Princess	Montreal	CT	2,200	50 only	788,800	No	160	Modern Times/Guard That Girl	15,000	3,000	Modern Times/Guard That Girl	34,500	3
Paramount	New Haven	Publix	2,373	35–50	695,600	Occ.	178	Belle Of The Nineties	11,000	2,400	Belle Of The Nineties	14,500	2
Poli's	New Haven	Loew's	3,005	35–50	955,900	No	189	Mutiny On The Bounty	15,000	2,700	Great Ziegfeld	19,300	2
Sherman	New Haven	WB	2,076	35–50	601,100	No	193	Flirtation Walk	12,000	2,600	Follow The Fleet	15,000	2
Aldine	Philadelphia	WB	1,416	35–55	618,300	No	35	Dodsworth	19,000	2,700	Dodsworth	44,500	3
Boyd	Philadelphia	WB	2,338	35–55	1,388,700	No	83	Anthony Adverse	31,500	6,500	Anthony Adverse	71,500	3
Earle	Philadelphia	WB	2,728	40–65	1,650,800	Yes	112	Eddie Cantor/One Exciting Adventure	31,000	9,500	Eddie Cantor/One Exciting Adventure	31,000	1
Fox	Philadelphia	Independent	3,457	40–65	1,875,200	Occ.	81	stage show/Thanks A Million	35,000	8,000	Vincent Lopez Orch/Private Number	75,500	4

Cinema	City	Affiliation	Seats	Price range (cents)	Box-office over the period ($)[a]	Regular live acts? (yes/no)	Films screened	Best week's film/act	Best wk's box-office ($)	Worst wk's box-office ($)	Best run film/act	Best run box-office ($)	Best run weeks
Roxy	Philadelphia	Independent	4,683	35-75	310,800	Yes	9	Jack Benny/Woman In Red	43,800	26,000	Jack Benny/Woman In Red	43,800	1
Stanley	Philadelphia	WB	3,009	35-55	1,486,800	No	84	San Francisco	31,000	7,500	San Francisco	85,000	4
Penn	Pittsburgh	Loew's	3,487	25-50	1,506,400	Occ.	103	Ted Lewis Orch/Hideout	31,000	4,000	Top Hat	33,000	2
Stanley	Pittsburgh	WB	4,000	25-50	1,722,500	Yes	103	Jack Benny+Mary Livingstone/Behold My Wife	34,500	3,200	Folies Bergere Unit/G-Men	52,500	2
Warner	Pittsburgh	WB	1,800	25-40	496,600	No	192	San Francisco	11,000	1,000	Mutiny On The Bounty	16,200	2
Broadway	Portland	Parker	1,956	25-40	556,050	Occ.	125	Libeled Lady	11,500	2,500	Libeled Lady	24,100	3
Paramount	Portland	Hamrick-Evergreen	3,066	25-40	611,650	Occ.	133	Marx Bros./Ten Dollar Raise	10,800	3,300	Curly Top	17,000	2
UA	Portland	UA-Parker	962	25-40	580,100	No	63	Mutiny On The Bounty	10,700	2,400	Mutiny On The Bounty	34,400	6
Albee	Providence	RKO	2,394	15-40	762,350	Occ.	131	Top Hat	17,000	2,300	Top Hat	39,000	2.5
Majestic	Providence	Fay	2,262	15-40	775,550	No	187	Anthony Adverse	13,000	3,800	Curly Top/Silk Hat Kid	20,000	2

Cinema	City	Affiliation	Seats	Price range (cents)	Box-office over the period ($)	Regular live acts? (yes/no)[a]	Films screened	Best week's film/act	Best wk's box-office ($)	Worst wk's box-office ($)	Best run film/act	Best run box-office ($)	Best run weeks
State	Providence	Loew's	2,500	15–40	1,149,900	Occ.	160	Great Ziegfeld	23,500	5,000	Great Ziegfeld	33,500	2
Strand	Providence	Independent	1,500	15–40	751,899	No	192	Klondike Annie/Her Master's Voice	14,300	2,000	Trail Of The Lonesome Pine	16,800	1.5
Ambassador	St. Louis	Fanchon and Marco	3,018	25–55	158,500	Occ.	21	Belle Of The Nineties	16,000	4,000	Belle Of The Nineties	31,000	2
Fox	St. Louis	Fanchon and Marco	5,036	25–55	171,500	Occ.	14	County Chairman	18,000	6,000	One Night Of Love	40,000	4
Missouri	St. Louis	Fanchon and Marco	3,516	25–40	94,700	Occ.	31	stage show/Marines Are Coming/Strange Wives	6,000	3,000	stage show/Marines Are Coming/Strange Wives	12,000	2
Shubert	St. Louis	Fanchon and Marco	1,710	25–40	160,000	Occ.	23	Gay Divorcee or Lives Of A Bengal Lancer	15,000	6,000	Lives Of A Bengal Lancer	26,000	2
State	St. Louis	Loew's	3,050	25–55	233,000	Yes	14	David Copperfield	17,000	8,000	Chained	32,000	2
Golden Gate	San Francisco	RKO	2,800	30–40	1,460,800	Occ.	80	Eddie Cantor/Last Outlaw	34,000	9,000	Top Hat	58,400	3

Cinema	City	Affiliation	Seats	Price range (cents)	Box-office over the period ($)^a	Regular live acts? (yes/no)^a	Films screened	Best week's film/act	Best wk's box-office ($)	Worst wk's box-office ($)	Best run film/act	Best run box-office ($)	Best run weeks
Orpheum	San Francisco	Independent	2,900	30–40	806,050	No	104	One Night Of Love	20,000	2,000	One Night Of Love	68,000	8
Paramount	San Francisco	Fox	2,735	30–40	1,205,800	No	152	San Francisco	28,000	6,000	San Francisco	67,000	3
Warfield	San Francisco	Fox	2,657	35–65	1,893,600	Occ.	109	Forsaking All Others	29,400	4,750	Libeled Lady/ Sitting On The Moon	54,000	4
Fifth Ave	Seattle	Hamrick-Evergreen	2,420	25–40	936,525	No	105	Rose Marie	17,200	3,800	San Francisco	35,600	3
Liberty	Seattle	Jenson & Von Herberg	1,800	15–35	542,300	No	109	Broadway Bill	12,200	1,700	Mr Deeds Goes To Town	82,700	14
Music Box	Seattle	Hamrick-Evergreen	970	25–40	411,950	No	99	Roberta	9,100	1,800	Roberta	28,500	6
Paramount	Seattle	Hamrick-Evergreen	3,000	25–35	594,650	Occ.	193	French Folies/Annie Oakley	12,800	2,300	Gorgeous Hussy/Star for The Night	17,300	2
Music Box	Tacoma	Hamrick-Evergreen	1,500	15–35	444,357	No	206	San Francisco	8,000	2,600	San Francisco	11,800	2
Roxy	Tacoma	Jenson & Von Herberg	1,200	25–35	422,837	No	168	China Seas	9,000	2,800	Broadway Bill	12,400	2

Cinema	City	Affiliation	Seats	Price range (cents)	Box-office over the period ($)a	Regular live acts? (yes/no)	Films screened	Best week's film/act	Best wk's box-office ($)	Worst wk's box-office ($)	Best run film/act	Best run box-office ($)	Best run weeks
Columbia	Washington	Loew's	1,000	25–40	486,200	No	97	In Old Kentucky or Baboonab	8,000	2,000	In Old Kentucky	14,500	2
Earle	Washington	WB	2,240	25–70	1,929,500	Yes	110	**Jan Garber Orch**/Mr Deeds Goes To Town	26,000	6,000	**Jan Garber Orch**/Mr Deeds Goes To Town	26,000	1
Fox/Capitol	Washington	Loew's	3,433	25–60	2,326,500	Yes	106	**Vaudeville**/Rendezvous	30,000	15,000	**Stage show**/Naughty Marietta	56,500	2
Keith's	Washington	RKO	1,500	25–60	1,014,100	Occ.	77	Top Hat	24,500	2,500	Top Hat	68,500	5
Palace	Washington	Loew's	2,700	25–60	1,724,500	No	68	Gorgeous Hussy or Mutiny On The Bounty	28,000	9,000	San Francisco	54,000	3
Total			282,674		121,112,628								

Sources: *Film Daily Yearbooks* for 1936 and 1937; *International Motion Picture Almanac* for 1936–7 and 1937–8, *Variety*, weekly for the period.

Notes:

a. Money values for Montreal are expressed in U.S. dollars.

b. The makers of the documentary animal drama *Baboona*, Martin and Osa Johnson, were present during the week of the film's screening.

Race Houses, Jim Crow Roosts, and Lily White Palaces

Desegregating the Motion Picture Theater

Thomas Doherty

O N 28 October 1963, nine years after the United States Supreme Court ruled that separate but equal school systems were inherently unequal, Attorney-General Robert F. Kennedy addressed the annual convention of the Theater Owners of America. Kennedy called on the exhibitors to abolish all kinds of racial segregation practiced in American movie-houses. 'I know that there are pro-segregationists among you—theater owners who question the government's right to regulate the way you conduct your business,' he acknowledged, implying that in his mind, at least, the right of the Department of Justice to regulate this particular business conduct was a settled issue. Yet he came to persuade, not browbeat, and tempered the prospect of federal coercion with a flattering call to civic responsibility. 'Even where community opinion is opposed to integration, theater owners have found that they can safely desegregate as long as they do so in unison with their competitors,' he pointed out. 'You, as influential and responsible men in your community, are well qualified to be leaders.' At the close of Kennedy's remarks, scattered among the polite applause, the sounds of low hissing and angry boos rumbled up from the audience.[1]

To think of the great battles over equal access to public accommodations during the civil rights era is to conjure up images of stoic activists forcibly claiming seats in diners, classrooms, and city buses. Yet no less than other racially restricted areas, the communal space of the motion picture theater—where white Americans and black Americans might sit shoulder to shoulder partaking not of food but of film—was a resonant site of conflict in the campaign for integration. Besides shedding light on a dark corner of American history, to recall the struggle over something as seemingly innocuous as shared spectatorship also illuminates the always tight and tangled kinship between Hollywood and American culture.

Viewed through a racial lens, motion picture exhibitors in America had traditionally practiced three distinct color-coded policies, each arrangement reflecting the idiosyncracies of local law, custom, and history. In some regions, enforcement was casual and haphazard; in others, sternly monitored and fiercely enforced.

First, strictly segregated venues on both sides of the color line duplicated the legal and social apartheid of the culture at large, with separate and unequal status in architecture and programming alike. For blacks, the so-called race houses, all-black theaters catering to an all-black clientele, located largely but not exclusively in the South, exhibited a program of marginal independent films featuring an all-black cast in rotation with mainstream Hollywood films that had long since 'played out' in priority white markets.[2] For whites, the grand motion picture palaces of the classical Hollywood era screened prestigious A pictures while enforcing a lily-white policy that denied admission to 10 per cent of the audience pool. The exclusions and delays in programming are well remembered by a generation of African American motion picture fans. In *Chuck Berry Hail! Hail! Rock and Roll* (1987), a documentary celebration of the life of the classic rocker, Berry stands in front of the Fox Theater in St Louis, Missouri, and recollects how, as a child during the Great Depression, he and his father had been refused entry to a first-run screening of *A Tale of Two Cities* (1935). 'It took *two years* to come to our theater in our neighborhood,' Berry snarls.[3]

The second strategy was what might be called 'the house divided,' where segregated seating was cordoned off for African American audiences, often in the balcony (referred to as 'Jim Crow roosts' by civil rights activists, and 'nigger heaven' in the vernacular). Stamped tickets, designated entranceways, and alert ushers prevented black patrons from trespassing into the off-limits white sections on the ground floor. For 500-seat movie-houses in small markets, the restricted balcony was the 'difference between profit and loss,' a lucrative arrangement that reconciled Jim Crow and good business sense. 'It is impossible to operate successfully in the Deep South—in a small town—without the revenue from a colored balcony,' an exhibitor admitted in 1957. 'Say what you please, but when your box office is closed and you are counting your money, it is impossible to identify the Negro share of the receipts—so now we let them walk upstairs for a reduction of 15 cents and all is well.'[4]

9.1   Separate entrance, separate seating: an African American moviegoer climbs
the stairs to the 'Jim Crow roost' in a motion picture theater in Belzoni,
Mississippi, 1939.

Sometimes too the segregation was by time not space, with a special day
or screening time designated for 'colored audiences.' In another variation, if
a Hollywood film were thought to possess special 'Negro appeal,' exhibitors
reserved extra seats in normally white sections of the house to accommodate
the anticipated overflow audience. 'This sort of piffling relaxation of Jim
Crow policies in segregated theaters used to be quite common and was
supposed to forestall Negro protest,' recalled a commentator in the *Crisis*,
the official weekly of the National Association for the Advancement of
Colored People (NAACP), in 1953.[5]

The third option—a colorblind admissions policy—was practiced by a
small subset of nominally integrated theaters outside the South, though
these venues too were often *de facto* segregated because of custom, pricing,
or housing patterns.

Unfortunately, precise statistical information about the patterns of racial
restriction in motion picture spectatorship is elusive: what is customary is
seldom noted.[6] In 1963, writing for *Variety*, pioneer film historian Robert
J. Landry, one of the few trade-wise commentators consistently sensitive to

racial issues, labeled 'theaters which relate to Negro patronage' as 'one of the little-known and least reported segments of the American motion picture exhibition industry.' Landry lamented the fact that 'nobody seems to possess any data on the total number of (a) Negro-only situations, (b) Negro-balcony situations, and certainly not as to (c) Southern communities in which there are no film theaters of any sort to which Negroes have admission.'[7]

Only when a curious anomaly in segregation practices erupted did the Hollywood trade press take bemused notice. For example, in Memphis, Tennessee, two first-run movie palaces, the Warner Theater and the Strand, each practiced different kinds of normative segregation, both in accord with local custom. Whereas the all-white Strand was totally segregated, the 2000-seat Warner Theater maintained a 'colored gallery' of 300 seats. In 1952, when RKO released a special newsreel compilation of the championship bout between Joe Walcott and Rocky Marciano, the notorious Lloyd T. Binford, head of the Memphis Board of Censors, forbade the film to be shown to the racially mixed audience at the Warner Theater but okayed it for the all-white Strand.[8]

The film also played unimpeded at the all-black Daisey Theater on Beale St. 'The censor [Binford] said we couldn't show the fight picture here because of our colored gallery,' said the perplexed manager of the Warner Theater, who had lost his booking to the Strand despite being the higher bidder.[9] Watching an evenly matched interracial dual in an interracial venue—even a segregated one—was judged too combustible for comfort by the censors.

Of course, among the countless galling humiliations and sometimes lethal consequences of Jim Crow, the denial of equal access to Hollywood cinema ranks low on the scale of injustice. Yet the emotional residue of this ritualized reminder of subaltern status seems to have rankled with a special force. Few African American memoirs of the segregation era fail to mention a moviegoing experience where embarrassment at the images being projected on screen is matched only by the humiliation of gaining access to them. 'But most of all, I remember that we had to sit upstairs, in a balcony section set aside for "Coloreds." We called it the Buzzard's Roost, and I hated it,' recalled civil rights activist John Lewis of his boyhood in Troy, Georgia. 'It was an insult to have to sit up there. I felt it intensely. To this day I rarely go out to the movies. The memory of sitting up in that balcony is just too strong.'[10]

In 1955, Antoinette S. Demond shared a searing motion picture memory in a poignant article entitled 'On Sitting' written for the *Crisis*. A Northerner studying at Fisk University in Nashville, Tennessee, Demond was introduced to the codes of Southern moviegoing while enjoying a night out on the town in the early 1940s. After her date purchased the correct tickets, the couple walked to their designated seats—but not through the theater lobby:

> We went half way down a cobblestone alley and walked up five flights of stairs to the small gallery situated above the main floor, above the mezzanine, above the balcony. I have no recollection of the film. I felt so bitterly ashamed to be sitting there. I felt ashamed too that other Negroes in the gallery were so conditioned to sitting there that they did not seem to feel the same shame I felt.[11]

But even as Nashville's swank motion picture palaces were forcing African Americans to enter via the fire escape, the rising expectations wrought by World War II were overturning the venerable seating arrangements that had been standard exhibition practice since the dawn of cinema. Emboldened by the egalitarian credo that fortified the national mobilization against two racist regimes overseas, the crusade for racial integration accelerated in the postwar era: in professional baseball, which integrated in 1947; in the armed forces, which integrated in 1948; and, not least, in a series of Hollywood social problem films which foregrounded the evils of racism: *Pinky* (1949), *Home of the Brave* (1949), *No Way Out* (1950), and *Bright Victory* (1951). By the early 1950s, the spectatorial status quo was also being challenged by court decrees, state laws, civil rights activists, and—eventually—the motion picture industry itself.

On 17 May 1954, the debate over equal access to public space reached a tipping point with the landmark Supreme Court decision in the case of *Brown v. the Board of Education at Topeka*. Despite the mandate to act 'with all deliberate speed,' the implications for American culture radiated out slowly, in motion picture theaters very slowly. Not until the close of the 1950s did the connection between public education and public entertainment begin to rewrite the codes of Jim Crow exhibition.

In the immediate wake of the Brown decision, *Variety* consulted the NAACP and found that 'no theatre segregation cases are pending anywhere in the country' nor were any contemplated: 'Theatre men in the South are sitting tight for the time being. In most states segregation is decreed by state law. Should exhibiters terminate [segregated seating], they would be subject to prosecution under these statutes.'[12] The state of Virginia, for example, required anyone operating a theater or other public hall to segregate the races; patrons who refused to take assigned seats were charged with a misdemeanor offense.[13]

For the motion picture industry, the event that placed the issue of segregated spectatorship into heightened relief was the crisis over public school integration in Little Rock, Arkansas, in September 1957.[14] A critical mass of media attention—newspaper headlines, magazine features, and, most vividly of all, television images showing terrified black schoolchildren beset by howling white mobs—forced a belated confrontation with the decision of 1954. Compelled at last to act, President Eisenhower sent in National Guard troops and, in a nationally televised address on 25 September 1957, the executive branch finally put its enforcement authority behind the Supreme Court decision At the center of the storm, the connection between the preservation of Jim Crow culture and the power of American cinema was highlighted by an exhibitor in Little Rock who showed his colors by booking D.W. Griffith's *The Birth of a Nation* (1915).

To be sure, in the broad scheme of things, and within this venomous and violent milieu, motion picture theaters were tangential arenas of combat. In many communities, they enjoyed a kind of benign neglect—insulated from on-site protests, almost like unofficial safe houses. Husbanding their resources and focusing their firepower, the NAACP and other civil rights activists concentrated on acquiring the more valuable entry tickets to education, employment, and housing. As late as 1959, civil rights activist Marian A. Wright bracketed motion picture theaters with golf courses and parks as 'fringe areas of the segregation problem.'[15]

Even so, by the 1950s, segregated spectatorship could no more operate under the cultural radar than segregated schooling, housing, or employment. The same postwar media focus that spotlighted the sorry options for African Americans on the Hollywood screen also directed attention towards the status of African Americans before the Hollywood screen. As an added incentive—or provocation—motion picture theaters contained two additional sites of volatile social interaction: rest rooms and concession stands. In short, along with other monuments to Jim Crow culture, it was inevitable that motion picture theaters would be given a due measure of regard by the civil rights movement.

Once the battle was joined, the level of protest against segregated seating and the relative ease or difficulty of the transition to integrated spectatorship varied depending upon the location of the theater. As if switching over a film title on a marquee, some communities adapted readily, almost imperceptibly, with no fanfare or nasty incidents. Other communities fought as fiercely for Jim Crow at the box office window as at the school-house door.

In most Northern and 'border' states, desegregation proceeded quickly, smoothly and unobtrusively, well in advance of coercion from the Department of Justice or federal legislation. In 1952, New York passed a state law forbidding discrimination in public accommodations. In 1954, theaters in Washington, DC, desegregated so quietly and completely that local civil rights activists were unaware that a goal they were even then organizing to achieve had already been attained. A bemused columnist for the *Interracial Review* interpreted the sudden open door policy as a reaction to a postwar phenomenon more disturbing to exhibitors than civil rights. 'Since juvenile delinquents have been wantonly slashing theater seats with sharp instruments, annoying other customers, necking, dropping their bubble gum here and there, and causing minor riots on occasion ...,' he wrote, 'I am convinced that movie theater managers are hoping that Negro patronage will improve the low moral, cultural and aesthetic climate now prevailing in many of their battered and tarnished establishments.'[16]

Of course, the year-round roosts of Jim Crow in the Deep South housed the main sites of contention and witnessed the most serious action. There the campaign to desegregate motion picture theaters occurred in the wake of, and appropriated the tactics of, the campaigns to integrate restaurants, department stores and other public facilities: boycotts, pickets, and sit-ins. In time, as the civil rights campaign gained momentum, the tactics grew more aggressive. Protesters went limp, staged mass sit-downs in front of theaters, locked arms to block entrances, and forcibly entered theatrical spaces[17] Interestingly, civil rights activists almost never disrupted an actual screening, as if to impede the viewing of the desired spectacle would be a unforgivable transgression. The opposition, however, did not practice the same restraint. Before theaters, as elsewhere, protestors endured scuffles, beatings, and intimidation. 'We came down to the theater to buy tickets,' a white member of the Congress of Racial Equality testified after a stand-in at a theater in High Point, North Carolina. 'We were refused. When people started hitting us, we stood there and took it.'[18] In Savannah, Georgia, robed Ku Klux Klansman first picketed and then tear-gassed the interior of a recently integrated motion picture theater, closing it down for several days.[19]

The theater-specific agitations began in earnest in 1961, after the widespread and successful deployment of sit-in tactics against downtown stores and diners in Nashville, Tennessee, in 1959–60. The protests gained steady momentum over the next year, reached a crescendo of intensity in the summer of 1963, and, with the passage of the Civil Rights Act of 1964, ultimately achieved total victory. That the actions paralleled the arc of the administration of John F. Kennedy is not coincidental.

The preferred protest tactic for activists targeting motion picture theaters was a clever variant on the sit-in appropriately dubbed the 'stand-in.' Whereas the sit-in was stationary and stubborn, the stand in was mobile and active. 'Under the theater stand, participants line up in single file, approach the ticket window, and request tickets admitting Negroes to any seat in the house,' *Variety* explained in 1961, noting that the technique was 'characterized by the quiet approach' wherein protesters 'infiltrate the ticket queue.'[20] After being refused service, the activists would then return to the back of the line and repeat the process. The stand-ins clogged lines, confused ticket sellers, frazzled ushers, angered moviegoers made late by the delays, and in general disrupted the smooth flow of a schedule-sensitive business.

Stand-ins were especially widespread in college towns, where the combination of a progressive student body and a vibrant motion picture scene created hotbeds of protest against Jim Crow seating in Austin, Texas; Lexington, Kentucky; and Chapel Hill, North Carolina.[21] Sometimes, white students fronted for black classmates by buying two tickets and then attempting to enter the theater with their black companions.[22] Conversely, black students would buy tickets to the colored balcony for their white companions.[23] Black students who defiantly sat in the segregated main floor would be arrested for trespassing; upstairs, their white allies who defiantly sat in the colored balcony would be arrested for refusing to vacate seats reserved for blacks.[24] In some college towns, harried theater managers bowed half way to the protests by permitting African American students to enter the main floor in a 'controlled' integration policy limited to 'students only,' providing they presented a valid student identity card.[25]

University faculty followed in the footsteps of their undergraduates. In Durham, North Carolina, hundreds of professors from Duke University and the all-black North Carolina College joined together to picket and stand-in at segregated theaters. In a resolution issued to the press, the professors declared: 'Recognizing racial segregation and discrimination in all forms as morally indefensible, contrary to democratic principles and harmful to American prestige, we the undersigned members of the faculties of Duke University and North Carolina College, jointly express our interest in, and our support of, our students and others who peacefully demonstrate against the practice of segregated seating in the Center and Carolina Theaters here in Durham.'[26]

Though any Jim Crow theater offered an affront sufficient to attract protest, activists slyly targeted theaters playing films whose themes resonated with the cause. In 1957, in Greensboro, North Carolina, the local branch of the NAACP urged a boycott of movie houses after an African American minister had been ordered to a segregated balcony at a preview screening of Cecil B. DeMille's *The Ten Commandments* (1956). 'The humiliation of segregation should certainly not be at our own expense,' said an NAACP official, who linked one flight from bondage with another. 'To attend segregated theaters in Greensboro, particularly during the showing of *The Ten Commandments*, would be a sacrilege.'[27] Likewise, when *King of*

Kings (1961) was playing at the segregated Tower Theater in Dallas, Texas, students from nearby Southern Methodist University seized the occasion to picket the theater and stage stand-ins because, said a theology student from SMU, the life of Christ expressed their basic convictions.[28] Another opportune protest erupted in Louisville, Kentucky, when the all-white Brown Theatre booked *Porgy and Bess* (1959), the Sam Goldwyn production of the George Gershwin play. Fifteen members of a local Negro youth group ordered tickets over the phone and then showed up to seek admission. All were turned away, whereupon pickets paraded in front of the theater with signs reading 'All Negro Cast' and 'This Theater Admits No Negroes.'[29]

Not incidentally, Hollywood released its own transparent statement on racial tolerance and segregated seating in *To Kill a Mockingbird* (1962), the popular motion picture version of Harper Lee's classic novel. The centerpiece sequence of the film, set in the South in the 1930s, depicts the trial of a black man falsely accused of rape. The southern courtroom on screen is conspicuously segregated—whites sweltering on the ground floor, blacks sweltering in the balcony—a mise en scène that mirrored the set design in at least some of the theaters playing the film.

The drive-in theater, the exhibition innovation most associated with the 1950s, presented a unique problem for segregationists and civil rights activists alike. Initially, the novelty of the phenomenon opened a brief window of opportunity in the wall of Jim Crow. 'Among the "new" audiences which drive-ins are said to be creating, one large segment is represented by Negroes,' *Variety* reported in 1949. 'In many sections of the south where segregation in regular houses is strictly enforced, the rule is not applied to ozoners Because of this, Negroes flock to the open-air theaters which are attractive deluxe affairs as compared to the second-rate flickeries generally available to them.'[30] In 1954, an NAACP official concurred, noting that 'to avoid humiliation or segregation, most Negroes in Las Vegas [Nevada] sit in their cars to see a movie—the drive-in theater being the only place where they can be certain of non-segregation.'[31]

Though caught unaware by the motor vehicle violations, Jim Crow soon closed the loophole. By the end of the decade, drive-ins in the Deep South were as segregated as the hardtops and no less vehement about staying that way.[32] Civil rights activists responded by mounting a suitably vehicular form of protest against drive-in segregation—what might be called a 'drive-in' at the drive-in—by organizing caravans of black motorists to drive to segregated drive-ins and attempt to gain entrance.[33] Predictably, drive-ins in Dixie also mimicked the racial policies of the hardtops by devising an automotive version of the colored balcony: a segregated parking section for blacks.[34]

The other major exhibition trend of the postwar era tended to be as open-minded in seating policies as film programming. Catering to a clientele of university students and urban intellectuals, the art house also cultivated an un-American sensibility in admissions. 'Should you consider some form of entertainment the legitimate theater will sell you a ticket,' reported the *Interracial Review* in 1955. 'So will a few movie houses that feature foreign films and carefully selected Hollywood products. Other houses will not admit you.'[35] Though forced by state law to abide by Jim Crow, art houses in the Deep South bristled against segregation and often defied it at the first opportunity.

Exemplifying the independent spirit of the art house was a feisty exhibitor named Maggie Dent, the manager of the New Rialto Theater in Durham, North Carolina, a venue serving the emergent cultural oasis of the Research Triangle area. Aligning her democratic principles with her cinematic sensibilities, Dent proudly declared that as of 27 May 1963, the New Rialto was the first integrated theater in Durham. 'I've thought from the beginning that a successful art house in this area needed the additional attendance from the North Carolina College students and faculty and that of the Negro professional cultural, and art groups,' she wrote in *Variety*; 'This in addition to the decided views I have that any public business, so run, should be open to anyone … and that I have always thought segregation and discrimination based on race [or] religion were morally and constitutionally wrong.' With financial support from local cinephiles—faculty members from surrounding universities made $100 contributions—Dent managed to refurbished the venue and open her establishment as a shining example of business-wise community relations. 'The fund-raising, the many congratulatory calls and letters I have received,' Dent commented, 'indicate to me that because we wanted to integrate and [became] the first theater to do [so], we will have a more interested and faithful patronage than we otherwise would have had.' Ever optimistic, she concluded that 'Except for the bomb threats … our integration proceeded quietly.'[36]

Though the civil rights campaign concentrated its forces on venues in the Deep South, the protests in Dixie were sometimes coordinated with actions against prominent Northern theaters—integrated venues owned by national circuits that practiced Jim Crow in affiliated theaters south of the Mason Dixon line. On 12 February 1961, the Congress of Racial Equality chose Abraham Lincoln's birthday to organize marches on theaters in San Francisco, Chicago, Boston, and New York.[37] Picketing of integrated theaters in the North owned by chains that maintained segregated theaters in the South seriously embarrassed big-name corporations seeking to cultivate a progressive profile. 'Racial picketing in Northern situations assumes a considerably broadened political implication,' commented *Variety* meaningfully. 'Theatermen don't like it at all.'[38]

Yet no motion picture theater, north or south, ever welcomed picket signs obscuring the marquee and repelling potential moviegoers. After all, the movie-house had always represented itself as a zone of comfort and escape from the tensions and controversies of the outside world. Any unrest, disruption, hassle, or unpleasantness at the box office window diminished the allure and depleted the profits.

The unfavorable publicity and economic effects from pickets, stand-ins, and other civil rights protests ultimately persuaded the executives of the national theater circuits and even the managers of many locally owned venues in the South to negotiate a surrender. In the major cities of what was not yet the late twentieth-century 'New' South, political and business leaders seeking to attract northern companies and international investment saw racial segregation—or rather the well-publicized agitation against racial segregation—for what it was: bad for business. Bankers, real estate developers, and other community leaders understood that to resist the rising tide was to be swept under. Hoping to avoid further economic costs and social upheaval, they decided to integrate motion picture theaters—but quietly, with a minimum of fuss.

The preferred method of unobtrusive integration was first implemented in the civil rights flashpoint of Nashville, Tennessee. In 1959–60, Nashville had been the scene of an incendiary series of sit-ins and boycotts aimed at downtown department stores, restaurants, and drug stores. After months of bruising conflict and huge financial losses for businesses, the city finally surrendered. Having won that battle, local activists moved on to another contested arena: public accommodation. Remembering the humiliations of the Buzzards Roost in Troy, Georgia, movement leader John Lewis, then an undergraduate at Fisk University, set his sights on motion picture theaters. 'And this time we would not be sitting in,' Lewis promised. 'This time we would be standing.'[39]

The Nashville stand-ins targeted the downtown Loews and Martin Theaters, the city's flagship motion picture palaces. Descending in force, and emboldened by the previous sit-in successes, dozens of veteran protesters were arrested for standing-in. A harried theater manager blustered that 'there is no chance of a change of policy concerning the seating of Negroes,' but in order to avoid a protracted and costly struggle, city fathers in Nashville opted for a discreet capitulation on this next civil rights front.[40] What would turn out to be an unconditional surrender, however, had to be negotiated in secret.

In April 1961, the behind-the-scenes maneuvering began with the quiet introduction of a single black couple into audiences at selected screenings. Then, after a few days, the number of couples was gradually increased. For protection, the first couples were shadowed by plainclothes white policemen, and all of the pioneering moviegoers were chosen for their well-mannered deportment and respectable attire. So as not to alert segregationists and precipitate an ugly incident, the plan proceeded without any advance publicity, with local police and media cooperating in the silent conspiracy.

The plan went off without a hitch—whereupon, after having surreptitiously integrated the theaters, the city announced that the theaters had, in fact, been successfully integrated. 'If a responsible, conservative, propertied leadership of a southern city gets together and decides to end racial segregation in film theaters, apparently what happens is simplicity itself. Overnight, Jim Crow "tradition" is abolished!' enthused Robert J. Landry in *Variety*. '[Nashville] has successful[ly] desegregated its film houses without publicity, without announcement in advance and without one single reported "incident."' [41] With so easy an implementation and so happy an outcome, the Nashville plan would become a model for social change in other southern cities.

Monitoring the situation from further South, Atlanta was next to emulate the prudent Nashville example. The city hosted three midtown first-run theaters (the 1000-seat Rialto, the 1000-seat Roxy, and the 2200 Loew's Grand), none of which admitted blacks. Located about a mile from downtown, the 4400-seat Fox Theater maintained a 174-seat colored balcony, which was closed in 1961 in response to the agitation for integration. Thereafter, Atlanta theaters were 100 per cent segregated. [42]

As in Nashville, Atlanta's civic leaders had planned to sneak an advance guard of black moviegoers into theaters and then announce the news of integration as a fait accompli. Also according to the Nashville precedent, the conspirators had hoped to secure the cooperation of the police and to keep the local newspapers quiet. However, in April 1962, the *Atlanta Journal* broke the news that Negro couples were soon to be infiltrated into the all-white venues downtown.

With the secret exposed, community leaders and civil rights activists braced for a backlash against the now transparent scheme. After the plan was put in operation, however, *Variety* described the anticlimactic outcome:

Then, Monday [14 May 1962] the Negroes made their move. According to plan—and agreement—two showed up at each of the four designated theaters, Loews Grand, Fox, Rialto, and Roxy, purchased tickets and entered. They were not treated any differently than any other ticket purchaser. Their arrival time (3 o'clock) was the same at all four houses and, as noted, there were no 'incidents,' the bugaboo that haunts a Southern locality any time such a move is made.[43]

Thereafter, African American patrons faced no restrictions and the plan proceeded progressively to outlying theaters in the suburbs. 'Just when it looked like the matter of integrating Atlanta's motion pictures had developed into a stalemate, the move was made, without fanfare, fuss or feathers and became a fait accompli without "incidents,"' concluded the pleasantly surprised *Variety*.[44]

'Controlled integration'—the quiet introduction of African American couples into low-attendance matinées, followed by gradually increasing numbers at prime screening times—became the method of choice for big cities eager to avoid trouble and get the necessary unpleasantness over with as quickly as possible.[45] Negotiated by interracial Community Relations committees, conducted in harmony with a close-mouthed press and a cooperative police department, the tactic of controlled integration made a potentially explosive situation seem matter of fact and inevitable.

Meanwhile, offstage, the federal government was encouraging the transition, though with a velvet glove rather than an iron fist. As a concession to Confederate pride, the Department of Justice held back from coercive action and permitted localities to 'voluntarily desegregate'—a charade perhaps, but an expedient one. Southern communities 'take more kindly to desegregation if it is clear that the principal sponsors of this move are respected local businessmen,' counseled the *Motion Picture Herald* 'Opposition would assuredly be more vocal—and perhaps even violent—if disaffected elements got the notion that any element of federal pressure were involved."[46]

Not that civic responsibility and progressive impulses were the main motivations. Unlike the small town neighborhood theater, the big city theaters paid for the privilege of racism. Whereas segregated seating in a small theater with one ticket window and one entrance could be a low-maintenance, cost-efficient enterprise, a large metropolitan theater with a 'colored balcony' needed to maintain a level of racial etiquette befitting the palatial surroundings. Employing separate cashiers, ticket-takers, and ushers to operate a 'black shelf' (as it was called) cost an estimated $100 to $200 in added weekly wages in 1961; yearly overhead could run an additional $5,000 to $10,000.[47] Moreover, the returns on the investment were proportionally diminished because black patrons typically paid only half as much for their tickets as white patrons (fifty cents for adults, fifteen cents for children).[48]

If integration in some major cities of the Deep South proceeded relatively smoothly, negotiated by interracial community groups and backed by city fathers, white moviegoers in other communities, especially in smaller cities and rural hamlets, were more stubborn about relinquishing their reserved seats. The 'controlled integration' schemes depended upon the anonymity of the metropolis; in a tightly knit community, such infiltration tactics would be an open secret. 'Neighborhood theaters, generally, are evading integration,' *Variety* conceded in 1963. 'Catering to residents in the immediate vicinity, with race prejudice harder to sterilize, these situations hope to remain segregated, and for the time being are playing a waiting game.'[49] Even at that late date, the high profile integrations in some big-name Southern cities were not yet commonplace.[50]

In fact, as the civil rights movement gained adherents and momentum, and as protests became more volatile and aggressive, some Southern theater managers and their white clients dug in their heels. An exhibitor in Durham, North Carolina, retaliated against the stand-ins by closing his segregated balcony and forbidding admittance to all blacks 'in view of the obvious fact that our separate facilities for Negro patrons are no longer acceptable to many.'[51] In Thomasville, North Carolina, over forty African American protesters were jailed for blocking the entrance to the town's only motion picture theater, a segregated venue with a colored balcony. The manager counterattacked by declaring that Negroes might take seats on the ground floor but that the price of admission would be five dollars Likewise, whites who wished to sit in the colored balcony would also be charged five dollars. The normal admission price was under one dollar[52]

But like their colleagues in the big cities, many small town theater owners wanted only the peace and quiet that drew crowds inside rather than gawking at the pickets outside. 'I don't know what would happen if I opened the entire theatre to Negroes, and I don't know what would happen if I don't,' moaned the manager of a 400-seat theater in Oxford, North Carolina. 'I'm just a small businessman.'[53]

The self-styled spokesman for such small businessmen was *Motion Picture Herald*, the exhibitor-oriented weekly serving the independent theater owner. Founded in 1930 by Martin Quigley, a guiding hand behind the Production Code, and edited either by Quigley or his son until the magazine folded in 1972, *Motion Picture Herald* mixed conservative values and commercial interests, ladling out moral probity with no-nonsense advice on exploitation stunts, advertising campaigns, and concession-stand items. It sought to nurture a homey sense of community among independently owned neighborhood theaters ('nabes' in trade parlance) located in small towns and urban enclaves across the nation. The issue of segregated spectatorship was sensitively registered—or rather not registered—in its pages.

Though priggish on matters of screen content, the Quigleys were reliable advocates of progressive social policies, not least equality for African Americans. The problem they faced was that a goodly portion of the journal's subscriber base resided in the South. As a result, throughout the 1950s and early 1960s, as the civil rights movement simmered and boiled over, the news and editorial pages of *Motion Picture Herald* were studiously silent on the issue of segregated spectatorship. 'Better Theaters,' a monthly feature that lovingly celebrated the lavish interior designs of motion picture palaces, also failed to note racial restrictions in the architectural blueprints. By 1963, however, even *Motion Picture Herald* could no longer ignore the financial-cum-moral quandary facing certain of their subscribers. Gently at first, and with increasing boldness as the months wore on, Martin Quigley, Jr. advised theatermen to open their doors to any customer, black or white, with the necessary dollars.

In coaxing exhibitors towards integration, Quigley's initial editorial comments are case studies in mealy mouthed equivocation. 'In many places the theater owner finds himself as an unwilling bystander caught in the middle of the race struggle,' he reflected in June 1963, ignoring the fact that the theater owner who practiced segregation had already placed himself smack in the middle of the situation. Quigley suggested that exhibitors put their fingers to the wind and play a waiting game:

> The best thing a theater owner can do is to open up channels of communication with opinion leaders in his community. In this way he will be prepared, if an emergency should arise, to work with the moderates on both sides and find acceptable answers.[54]

But where Quigley was equivocal, hardcore segregationists were determined and single-minded. Nothing less than the coercive intervention of a federal government worried about more than the equal protection clause of the Fourteenth Amendment to the U.S. Constitution would compel racist theater owners to serve all comers. As the summer of 1963 loomed, and as emboldened civil rights protesters organized to call in the marker on a dream deferred, the shadow of Jim Crow threatened to undercut the reputation of the U.S. in its long twilight struggle against communism. On both the international and domestic front, the Kennedy administration viewed racial segregation as more than a public relations débâcle: it cut to the very core of American moral capital in the Cold War.

Characteristically, this most media-savvy of presidents was acutely conscious of the geo-political backfire from motion picture segregation. 'Kennedy, according to associates, sees the Negro-only balconies and no-Negro one-floor theaters on the hominy grits circuits as possibly triggering violence,' commented *Variety* in its trademark blend of glib rhetoric and blunt analysis. 'The Kennedy administration is avowedly frightened that with summer recess from the schools the nation may be disgraced by race riots, a political liability in the United Nations and in the ideological war with Soviet Russia.'[55] In the spring of 1963, as police dogs and fire houses were being unleashed on Martin Luther King, Jr. and civil rights demonstrators in Birmingham, Alabama, as the contradictions of American life were being broadcast on national television and transmitted overseas, the face of Jim Crow was the best propaganda trump card the Soviet Union held.

Foreseeing a long hot summer of violent protests, the Kennedy administration held two meetings in order to, as an official White House press release put it, 'examine some aspects of the difficulties experienced by minority groups in many of our cities in securing employment and equal access to facilities and services generally available to the public.'[56] Among the businessmen in attendance, motion picture exhibitors were singled out and double teamed by the two Kennedy brothers, first by Robert, then by John.

On 27 May 1963, Attorney General Robert F. Kennedy called together at the White House executives from forty theater chains representing 80 per cent of Southern operations. In the sternest terms, he urged the exhibitors to desegregate voluntarily. 'It was evidently made clear that the government—though it asked for no promises and gave none—would look favorably on those [exhibitors] who followed the "straight road" to desegregation,' reported *The Film Daily*. 'No alternative was presented, it is understood.'[57]

The Attorney General informed the exhibitors that the administration's pending civil rights bill—the bill that would become the Civil Rights Act of 1964—would contain a public accommodations provision requiring theater circuits to desegregate. The *Motion Picture Herald* reminded any readers in need of a lesson in law and the motion picture business that 'the distribution of film to theaters has been held by the courts to be interstate commerce; hence, theatres are clearly involved'[58]

The exhibitors got the message. Kennedy's blunt warning resulted immediately in what one theater owner delicately referred to as 'certain crystallized results.' Within days, an estimated twenty-five to thirty theaters had voluntarily desegregated. Theaters throughout Virginia—within easy driving distance of the Department of Justice in Washington, DC—quietly took down their segregation signs 'with no notice or comment but with no ill-effect.'[59]

On 4 June 1963, RFK's instructions were seconded by the President himself, who included theatermen in a closed meeting with prominent business executives also attended by Vice-President Lyndon Johnson and the Attorney-General. Suddenly eager to please, the theatermen presented the Kennedys with a lengthy list of recently desegregated theaters. According to a motion picture executive in attendance, once the press had been ushered out of the meeting, the president argued for theater desegregation in a 'most persuasive' manner and reaffirmed the administration's commitment to equality. The 'temper of the meeting,' reported an exhibitor, was 'general endorsement' of the president's goals.[60]

As if on cue, another powerful voice rallied behind the full court press from the Kennedy administration. For decades, *Variety* had confined its comments on Jim Crow to snide asides about colored balconies and Dixie obtuseness. After the signals from the Kennedy brothers, however, it published a rare editorial, set off in black borders and headlined with a blunt imperative: *Desegregate*. 'Why all the timidity?' the show business bible asked. 'The dangers [of desegregation] are slight and perhaps imaginary. Such is the moral to be drawn from those Dixie cities which have so far been "bold" enough to sell tickets to all who approached the box office.' As usual, the ethical argument was laced with a commercial sweetener stressing 'the practical dollars and sense reasons for making a gesture to an important segment of the audience by doing everything possible to remove the section[al] disadvantage with its symbolic affront.'[61] After all, in the age of television, an African American family could watch white folks on the home screen without enduring the humiliations of Jim Crow seating to watch white folks on the big screen.[62] Quite simply, in the postwar buyer's market, exhibitors no longer had the luxury of picking and choosing among their customers

Though so far only rhetorical, the pressure emanating from the Department of Justice and the White House had a measurable effect. 'Quickened by recent demonstrations and Federal government pressures, the pace of desegregation of film houses in Southern cities has apparently increased,' reported *Variety* in June 1963, adding self-reflexively that 'where two years ago, and less, it was streamer news in *Variety* that Nashville had removed the racial restrictions at the box office, this has now become, if not commonplace, at least a repeated decision.'[63] That autumn, the trade weekly noted with satisfaction that 'only in cities of the real "deep south" are balconies for colored still found.'[64]

Yet despite growing pressure from the Kennedy administration, despite the progress of high profile integration in Nashville, Atlanta, and other big southern cities, and despite the regular appearance of platoons of disruptive stand-in demonstrations, motion picture segregation in the deepest regions of the Deep South was still tenacious and difficult to uproot.[65] In August 1963, a progress report on theater desegregation prepared for Congress by the Department of Commerce found much cause for optimism—some former southern flashpoints such as Kansas City, Missouri, Memphis, Tennessee, and Houston, Texas had lately integrated fully and peacefully. Nonetheless, high-profile cities in a four-state belt comprised of Louisiana, Mississippi, Alabama, and Georgia continued to resist the general trend. 'No efforts have been undertaken to desegregate theater facilities, legitimate stage, or cinema in Birmingham, Alabama,' reported the survey. Similarly, theaters in New Orleans 'still operate on a segregated basis, and there has been no move to change this situation.'[66]

What changed the situation was another Kennedy-related pressure: the assassination of John F. Kennedy. Stricken by the assassination, Martin Quigley, Jr. penned a forthright and emphatic editorial. 'President Kennedy directly and through his brother, Attorney General Robert F. Kennedy, did everything he could to encourage theatres in the United States voluntarily to cease discriminatory admissions policies,' Quigley wrote. 'The President helped exhibitors and their communities to realize that a merchant—such as a theater operator—must treat all patrons equally.' Remembering the shameful outbursts after Robert Kennedy's speech to the Theatre Owners of America less than a month earlier, Quigley argued that 'it is a bitter memory to recall that a minority booed the Attorney General's calm exposition of the effects of racial policy on theatre admissions at the Theatre Owners of America dinner.' By way of eulogy and tribute, he declared that 'the best service exhibitors can do in memory of a great President is to push on in an orderly and intelligent fashion toward the goal of nondiscriminatory admission in every theater in the land.'[67]

Yet far more important than the transformation of attitudes within the motion picture industry was the new law on the books. In the wake of the Kennedy assassination, the United States Senate finally mustered the political will to pass civil rights legislation that had for years been bottled up in committee or blocked by filibuster. On 1 July 1964, the passage of the Civil Rights Act made denial of equal access to public accommodations illegal throughout the land. It ended the charade of 'voluntary desegregation' and spelled out the legal consequences of defiance. Southern theaters—palaces, nabes, and drive-ins—had no real option now but to comply with the public accommodations section of the law.

In even the most virulent of segregationist outposts, federal law forced a decisive change Among the die-hard citadels of Jim Crow seating was the city of New Orleans, which had steadfastly refused to heed Kennedy administration calls voluntarily to desegregate. 'Pressures are believed to originate in Washington with the Attorney-General and a desire to eradicate one conspicuous southern city holdout, but New Orleans so far just won't budge, Kennedys or no,' *Variety* reported in a front page story published just two weeks before the Kennedy assassination.[68] With a law on the books and an executive branch with the will to enforce it, the new Johnson administration compelled New Orleans—and any other defiant district—to budge. 'Negroes testing the new Federal Civil Rights Law Monday [6 July 1964] found doors opened at previously all-white downtown and nab theaters, drive-ins, restaurants, and hotels,' *Variety* reported in a front-page follow-up published the week after the passage of the Civil Rights Act.[69]

So transformed was the cultural atmosphere and so rigorous the enforcement regime that nationally owned chains felt no need to send out special instructions to guide local theater managers. 'None are necessary,' said an executive. 'All our people will obey the law.' Asked about the possibility of a recalcitrant local theater manager offering wildcat resistance on his own, the same executive promised, 'If that happens, he won't be our manager very long.'[70] Later that summer, the Congress of Racial Equality, which monitored the compliance of theaters and other public accommodations, confirmed that no theater had refused to abide by the law. By the end of 1964, as the result of an at-times mysterious and usually uncommemorated change, Hollywood motion pictures were living up to their time-honored billing as universal entertainment for the American public.

Today, as with so many customs and codes of the Jim Crow era, the rituals of segregated spectatorship—separate entrances, colored balconies, and race houses—are remembered, if at all, as the primitive folkways of a remote and inscrutable past. Yet more than most battles of the civil rights era, the campaign to integrate motion picture audiences has faded from popular memory. Given the provenance of the images projected on the Hollywood screen, breaking through the turnstiles of the local Bijou might have been expected to exert a special evocative power and photogenic attraction. At the time, perhaps, the reputation of the motion picture theater as a romantic refuge for nuzzling couples may have caused civil rights activists, wary of defying a social taboo sterner than shared spectatorship, to fight one battle for equality at a time. In the years since the fight to gain admittance to motion picture theaters may also have seemed trivial compared to the weightier and more deadly campaigns for education and voting rights. Doubtless too the preeminent presenter of the pictures of American history—Hollywood itself—has been reluctant to recall that moviegoing was not always an all-American activity.

PART II

Other Cinema

Alternatives to Theatrical Exhibition

The Reel of the Month Club

16mm Projectors, Home Theaters and Film Libraries in the 1920s

Haidee Wasson

S TUDIES of exhibition and reception have demonstrated the crucial role that movie theaters, changing technologies, practices of distribution, regulatory efforts, popular discourses, and other forces play in shaping the wider cultural meaning of films and the experiences of audiences who watch or otherwise engage them. Articulating the broad field in which questions of culture claim their due alongside studies of form and aesthetics, this scholarship maps the transformation of film-as-medium into cinema, a complex of social, cultural, industrial, and aesthetic phenomena. Histories of particular theaters, analysis of emergent public spheres, and investigations of projects to control film audiences enhance our understanding of the dynamics endemic to showing, watching, thinking about, debating, and otherwise making sense of movies. Thinking through the multiple factors that constitute the matrix of film exhibition and reception helps us to understand better the conditions of modern vision generally—whether linked to celluloid, video, print, computers, painting or other visual forms. As the fluidity among these media increases, work on the socio-cultural dynamics of moving images will only become more indispensable to the vibrancy of film, cultural, visual, and media studies.

By and large, research focusing on film exhibition and reception has tended to position the movie theater as the primary nexus or fulcrum for such histories. The best of this work demonstrates that movie theaters are complex sites, interwoven with the struggles that constitute the socio-political contests undergirding public life and leisure more generally. Movie theaters, this work inveighs, are not autonomous entities nor are they simply venues for the transcendental appearance of films but rather serve both to reflect and enact varied ideas about race, class, gender, and of course, about cinema itself.[1] Individual films are but one element in what we think of as the institution of cinema; they exist inside and never outside the currents of history. Movie theaters—semiotically dense spaces and regulated zones of public life—are another such element.

While there can be no doubt that the movie theater occupies a privileged and crucial position in the history of cinema and its institutions, the precise place of the theater on a much wider map of film exhibition and reception needs to be more fully considered. Recent work on contemporary exhibition argues persuasively that, since the mid-1980s, movie theaters function as multi-mediated entertainment zones, dedicated not just to films but to food, video games, and shopping. When considering the life cycle of particular films, movie theaters now function as expensive advertisements for, and indices to, future consumption of moving images in the more lucrative media that constitute the composite technology of television: broadcast, cable, video and DVD.[2] Such theaters are but temporary way stations in the long, widely disseminated life of movies. Arguments such as this nuance our understanding of cinema by reorienting us away from thinking about the movie theater as the primary organizing site for the performance of cinematic texts and its attendant rituals, and sending us on a sprawling search through video stores, mail-order catalogues, satellite systems and, most importantly, homes.

When thinking about earlier phases of film and media history, one of the reigning conceptual dichotomies that underscores the place of the movie theater in our understanding of exhibition and reception is a division between what is termed theatrical and non-theatrical exhibition. This split depends on some reasonably straightforward assumptions: the primary destination of films for the bulk of the medium's life has been large, darkened auditoria where audiences pay to watch projected celluloid images. The shape and size of the screen is generally standardized, as is the quality of image, sound, seating and over-priced refreshments.[3] Films, we assume, are in fact made to be shown in precisely such venues. As a result, it is also widely assumed that theaters are the natural home for movies. In short, there is a widely held tacit agreement that, on the whole, film has historically happened first and foremost in commercial movie theaters. Thus, the cultural experience of watching movies, when considered at all, has consequently been understood as coincident if not coterminous with the event of theatrical projection. All other venues are considered secondary, tertiary, and residual, supplying diminishing returns on film's primary remit.

Non-theatrical, then, tends to refer to everything that does not satisfy this ideal—movies that are shown or happen everywhere else. The term performs a seemingly limitless task, as it designates not only a vast range of films (among them instructional and educational shorts, stag films, feature-length religious films and sometimes Hollywood features) and indexes an equally expansive set of spaces (including boardrooms, department stores, union halls, classrooms, and homes). In short, I suggest that the 'non' of 'non-theatrical' should strike us—after even the smallest amount of due consideration—as notably non-sensical, a term stretched so thin as to hinder rather than help understanding.

Dividing the history of exhibition and reception by invoking the categories of theatrical and non-theatrical inevitably designates a vast range of film and cultural practice in the negative, defining it first by what it is not. This split enforces a highly constructed and powerful industry-sanctioned norm, successfully secured since the second decade of cinema, and forwarded by self-described educators, filmmakers, amateurs and Hollywood moguls alike. By defining movie theaters as the central and primary stage for moving image performance and experience, the American film industry effectively stabilized a diverse field. It established the norms by which a whole medium would be measured, providing one of many formidable barriers to entry which served to limit challenges to its oligopoly. The theatrical/non-theatrical split has also, to repeat, been upheld by film scholars, who have overwhelmingly focused on excavating the history of commercial movie theaters rather than the ostensibly less important but far more numerous *other* sites of exhibition. This focus on movie theaters must be understood as a sensible beginning to what is clearly an inchoate but expanding interest in moving image cultures and practices. This work investigates the histories of what are widely understood as authoritative institutions and their norms. As such, it makes good sense. Yet, as Barbara Klinger and others have noted, there is also a certain lag or resistance among film scholars, in particular, to accept the changing conditions for moving image aesthetics, distribution and exhibition. Many cling to a dated and industry-sanctioned hierarchy: darkened theaters, filled with projected celluloid, still constitute the film-ideal. Watching moving images on televisions or VCRs or DVD players involves a troubling deterioration of cinema-proper.[4]

There is an emergent body of work scratching away at this hierarchy, exploring the ways in which the entertainment industry, the home, and activities such as collecting transform our baseline understandings of what cinema is and where it happens.[5] Yet, despite these important strides, there remain some noteworthy ellipses requiring fuller consideration. While the relatively recent fact that VHS and DVD rentals have eclipsed box office

219

revenue serves as a lightning rod for those of us interested in the current cinema, I want to assert that cinema's past is equally in need of such reconsideration. Indeed, long before the VCR, DVD and the internet, portable film projectors participated in an equally fundamental transformation of what it meant to watch, think about, write about, love and hate movies. For instance, one 1933 study issued by the Department of Commerce reported 190,000 'non-theatrical' projectors were in use, including home sets.[6] When compared to the roughly 17,000 to 18,000 commercial movie theatres operating in this period, this figure provides a striking counter-example to the film circuits dominated by Hollywood, gesturing toward a network of distribution and exhibition that was potentially ten times bigger. The sheer size of this network requires careful tempering as it includes a range of film gauges, rental systems and exhibiting institutions, not to mention films that were silent and sound, short and long, international and domestic. It nonetheless serves as a poignant reminder of the arguably innumerable ways in which moving images—Hollywood and other—have long found their ways into a vast range of spaces, necessarily requiring us to rethink the ways in which cinema itself has long been part of an everyday common sense about what it means to see in the spaces between movie theaters. That is, the fact of 190,000 film projectors, issuing images in homes, museums, school, hospitals, prisons, libraries and so on, constitutes a dramatically under-considered venue for the generation of a common sense about the place of moving images in everyday life, a common sense that has long been generated not just in movie theaters but also just about everywhere else.

This chapter maps out a series of questions that mark the beginnings of an effort to break up this vast field of film practice. It is a small part of a larger project that seeks to explore the specific institutional and material networks of 16mm technologies of exhibition, the dominant technological infrastructure for what I will provisionally refer to as 'extra-theatrical' film exhibition and reception. For over fifty years, portable 16mm film projectors provided a means by which the industry-dominated standard of 35mm film gauge and theatrical moviegoing was circumvented and perhaps circumscribed. This constitutes a qualitatively different mode for the generation and elaboration of film culture, one that has long been standard and taken for granted. Accepted knowledge about 16mm-as-exhibition apparatus is implicated most clearly in the widespread institutionalization of moving images after World War II. Despite its roots in nationalist wartime strategies, this was an international cultural network, through which ideas about nation, good and evil, coexisted with ideas about film as art, history, and education. Many of our most basic concepts of cinema were generated within such networks.

Yet, the significance of 16mm as idea and practice begins long before the war, and resides in an equally important set of generative ideas and practices that pre-exist the standardization of the gauge in 1923, and were catalyzed by its rapid spread throughout the interwar period. On the one hand, 16mm was central to a range of utopian discourses about images-on-demand, access to yesterday's films (repertory), alternative film networks based on open exchange, aesthetic exploration, and political debate. On the other hand, this enthusiasm for new ways of thinking, writing, and watching movies was also coincident with very particular and often class-based discourses about moral uplift, disciplined behaviors, and affirmative consumption. 16mm became the preferred gauge for an ascendant cultural force seeking to wrest mass media away from its threatening populist and commercial power, to tame cinema by campaigning for better films, specialized audiences, and a repertoire of prescribed methods and manners for engaging movies.[7] These histories are much larger than can be tackled here. Nevertheless, as a way of demonstrating the rich and suggestive trajectories of one piece of these histories, this chapter addresses the ways in which 16mm was imagined early on in its development as a new revolution less in institutions of public or civic purview and more in the tasteful, safe, and ordered salon of the middle-class American home.

A New Reel Monthly

In the fall of 1927, William Ganz announced the formation of the *Reel of the Month Club*, a subscription service promising regular and timely motion pictures of the world's key news events 'almost' as they happen. Once monthly a film that had been carefully selected for what was termed 'quality' and 'relevance' would appear on that magically abundant site—the home doorstep—alongside the milk, newspapers, packages and envelopes that constituted the day's mail. In theory, these films would be eagerly watched by the growing body of home movie fans and then promptly placed on the library shelf, alongside the Encyclopedia Brittanica, the leather-bound Shakespeare, and the family photo album, as part of the ordered and tasteful home library.

Ganz had been in the film business since 1919, but his most recent ventures, including *The Reel of the Month Club* and *Peerless Cine News* (promising 'Highlights from the News, the World in Your Home') had taken a particular turn.[8] Spurred by the proliferation of 16mm projectors and films facilitating movies in the home, bolstered by the recent vogue for simultaneity encouraged powerfully by radio and inspired by the marketing genius of The Book of the Month Club (1926), Ganz sought to accelerate an ongoing and lasting trend in film culture. Like his contemporaries, he attempted to use the mail and the ascendant empire of advertising, newspapers and middlebrow magazines to broker a key shift in how movies would be packaged, sold, circulated, and seen. Ganz tried to make the mass medium of the movies into a polite and edifying activity, transforming cinema into a consumable object for the leisured and affluent middle class, providing an evening's entertainment away from the roaring crowds of the picture palace or the neighborhood theater by relocating it to the inner sanctum of the bourgeois salon and, eventually, the home library.

From surviving evidence, The Reel of the Month Club was never the sweeping success Ganz imagined. It does, however, provide a compelling if humble index to a much larger shift brought about by the spread of portable film projectors and the domestication of cinema. Until the introduction of the 16mm standard, the field of home movie-making and watching was a small field of hobbyists, amateurs and elite enthusiasts.[9] From 1923 onward, 16mm-as-apparatus effectively consolidated, coordinated and accelerated these activities, and during the 1920s, home movie theaters moved from the relatively small domain of the hobbyist to the expanded discursive realm of the mass media.[10] Like the concurrently and similarly transforming field of radio, format standardization, techniques of mass marketing, equipment automation, and direct address to the home and to women made home movie theaters viable as a mass mediated and commodified ideal. Ganz's business was intimately tied to these shifting conditions, as well as to the more general ways in which electrified home entertainment was taking root across a range of media forms: radios, phonographs, and of course, movie projectors.

Sixteen millimetre technology was an amalgam of cameras, projectors and film stock, introduced in 1923 by Eastman Kodak, world leader in the manufacture of celluloid. The gauge was bolstered by industry agreements established with Bell and Howell, prominent film equipment firm, and later with Victor-Animatograph, a leading stereoscope manufacturer.[11] A rebuff to the dominance of Pathé's 28mm system, and a contemporary of the same company's 9.5mm system, 16mm reduced the costs of previous formats, continued to increase portability, and maintained the non-flammability of its rival formats by exclusively using Eastman acetate stock. Previous literature on the emergence of 16mm technologies has focussed on the changes introduced by the new gauge to ideas and practices of filmmaking.[12] Yet, the *idea* of 16mm exhibition or self-operated theatres—as distinct from amateur or do-it-yourself movie-making—had a far greater and more lasting impact, spreading quickly both nationally and internationally. By 1930, the new gauge was associated with a feverish enthusiasm for the

Descriptive Catalogue
of

KODASCOPE
LIBRARY

16 m m

Motion Pictures

Some in Color

Seventh Edition

10.1 Catalogue for Kodak's 16mm Kodascope Library Service (cover, 1930). Note that mother is operating the projector and thus orchestrating the show.

promise that it would extend the cinematic frontier everywhere. Commercial film libraries proliferated to deal in the new gauge. A vast library of titles was made available through an international rental and purchase system: Bell and Howell's Filmo Library, Kodak's Kodascope Library, Pathé's Pathéscope Library and a series of smaller agencies entered the fray. By 1928, an estimated 22 such libraries targeted the American home.[13] These libraries functioned occasionally as stand alone rental agencies, but mostly made use of department stores, drug stores, camera shops, and mail order systems, creating vast networks of moving image circulation and exchange. Listed subjects ranged from slapstick to animation, travel, sports and nature films—clearly reflecting a middlebrow disposition. Titles ranged from the offerings of defunct production companies to films that had only recently concluded their theatrical runs. For instance, Kodascope Libraries had

10.2 An advertisement for Pathégrams, Pathé's short film service. The text emphasizes the variety and the 'sparkling' nature of the monthly subscription service. (*Movie Makers*, 1930).

contracts with Paramount, First National, the U.S. War Department, Fox Films, Warner Brothers, and even rival Pathé. It also circulated films from long-departed production companies such as Biograph, Triangle, World, Mutual, and Essanay.[14] Films were often chosen explicitly for their propriety and advertised as quality films, appropriate for all family members.[15]

Specialty services were also founded within these larger lending libraries, designed to accent the simultaneity indexed earlier by the *Reel of the Month Club*. These services were designed to bring connectedness and timeliness into the home film market, turning the parlor into a window on the world. In the presidential election year of 1928, as a part of the Pathégrams series, Pathé advertised 'glimpses of the Democratic and Republican candidates ... See your favorites in public and home life. Know and understand them better through their "action" before the lens.'[16] Kodak Cinegraphs were similarly designed to provide recordings of 'the most important events of the world as they take place,' keeping spectators in touch with current world news events.[17] These films were often shorter than regular standard rentals, making them more affordable for outright purchase. They were, then, also an important element of the next stage in the gradual expansion of extra-theatrical moving images into the middle-class home, not just in the form of exhibited moving images but also in the form of the home film library. As the Cinegraph catalogue read: 'Most Cinegraphs you will want to buy and keep permanently—just as you collect worthwhile books for your library.'[18]

In terms similar to modern discourses attached to home computers and home theaters, Cinegraphs crafted their films as purveyors of a privileged form of knowledge and experience. Advertisements positioned Cinegraph films as a transparent link to distant and past events that could now be dramatically 'lived' and 'relived' in the home. One ad for the *World War Movies* read:

A vast panorama of war ... now revealed with stark realism. This is not a motion picture in the usual sense. It is a chapter of your life brought back to live over again. [...] Words simply cannot describe these pictures. You must see them to appreciate them ... They will become priceless 'heirlooms' to be passed on in any family ... increasing in value as years go by.[19]

Kodak sold a new kind of historical experience, one brokered by rolls of celluloid and stored on a shelf alongside other 'great adventures of modern times' in the form of books, magazines, and photo albums. Cinegraphs were sold as valuable items for the home library—precious objects to be collected and cared for—an integral part of a proper family's pedigree, suitably enhancing the family's wealth, in part, by expanding their worldly knowledge-as-visual experience. Moving pictures of the world-in-the-home were likened to the virtues of the library, a comprehensive store of living knowledge whose very possession and endurance through time increased the virtues of family and home. Kodak designed a cinema notably distinct from that of the commercial movie theater. Rather than public, ephemeral and entertaining, they crafted a domestic theater infused with precisely the opposite characteristics: private, familial, enduring and educational. While the home was clearly being linked to the world through discourses of relevance and simultaneity, these quintessentially modern ideas about rapid time and diminished space were counter balanced by the prospect of moving images whose value—under the protective shelter of the home library—not only endured but appreciated over time. In short, moving images were sold

225

as a means by which the changes wrought by modern life would be made slower, safer and more easily contained.

Hollywood Homes

The enthusiasm for 16mm as a domestic technology was not only the purview of technology and celluloid manufacturers such as Kodak or diversified global media companies such as Pathé. Hollywood also noticed the growing field. The recent reorganization of industry structure surely facilitated this interest. The 1920s was a period in which film production interests began to merge aggressively with film exhibiting interests, forming vertically and horizontally integrated corporate structures. Indeed, there was a noteworthy increase of investment among the film, recorded music, radio and publishing industries as well. As Donald Crafton has noted, the movie industry by 1929 'had become a huge tentacular structure with healthy interests across media forms, and with equally close ties to the paradigmatic shifts ushered in by electricity conglomerates.'[20] The American film industry had made clear material and imaginative connections with corporations that had set their sights on capitalizing on the growing affluence of American homes and the synergistic value of cross-media entertainment networks.

In 1930, *Variety* declared that these collective ventures into the 16mm field constituted the next entertainment revolution.[21] Estimating that 200,000 American homes were already equipped, the trade paper predicted that there were at least two million more homes that could afford to be efficiently served by 16mm film libraries. With traditional modesty, the industry organ exclaimed that through 16mm 'the film industry sees itself in a position to dominate the entire peoples of the world'—bypassing theaters and directly targeting people everywhere else.[22] Synchronized sound also came quickly to home units, shadowing trends in theatrical exhibition. That Christmas, *Variety* reported that 48 'Home Talker Sets' were available for consumer purchase.[23] Film libraries followed suit. In 1930, Bell & Howell's Filmo rental service announced the addition of 120 German films produced by Ufa, available in silent or sound-on-disc version. Sound-on-film rentals were available from 1934 forward, shortly after the introduction of its Filmosound projector.

Despite the hyperbole attached to 16mm homes, its position as the specific tool of Hollywood's home conquest was, it must be said, never realized. Indeed, the utopian home-life of 16mm was relatively short-lived, swept away by the introduction of 8mm in 1932 and the rise of television shortly thereafter. Concerns about unauthorized copies of films that might serve to weaken the functional monopoly of movie theaters on admission revenue also persisted. The enthusiastic energies attached to 16mm migrated to other locations. It became the primary gauge for schools, churches, libraries and universities from the mid-1930s forward. Yet, throughout the 1920s, 16mm held brief if frequently maniacal promise of forever changing home entertainment. It is to the specificities of this promise that I now turn.

Electric Domestic

The 1920s witnessed sizable changes both in the middle-class American household and in federal policy pertaining to the home. The elevation of the single, self-owned family dwelling as the standard currency of economic policy begins in the first years of this decade, providing the basic building blocks for the massive suburbanization we tend to associate with the post-war period. Home ownership was refashioned as the generative

10.3 This advertisement for a 'home-talkie' unit featured 'America's foremost entertainers' and 'operatic stars' appearing in the parlor every night, a pre-televisual idea about liveness and simultaneity. (*Movie Makers*, 1930).

site of American nationhood in presidential speeches and publications, conceptualizing the home owner as the epitome of individual prosperity and moral accomplishment. The American Dream was grafted onto the American Home giving birth to the notion of the 'Dream House.'[24] It was through idealized figurations such as the Better Home and the Dream House that material changes to the American home took on fuller meaning: electrification, central heating, hot/cold indoor plumbing, convenience foods, and electrical appliances constituted highly visible elements of a widely disseminated and highly commodified domestic ideal.

The new and better dream house was also inseparable from the gendered economy of the household. Taylorist principles were matched with the automation of domestic labor through the electrical home appliance in a series of widespread discourses that linked efficiently run homes to the moral rectitude of the consuming housewife.[25] These discourses formed most fully and were spread most widely in women's magazines such as *The Delineator, Better Homes and Gardens, Ladies Home Journal,* and *Good Housekeeping,* on the pages of which one could find prescriptive literature about cooking, sewing, beauty and shopping alongside ads for electric stoves, vacuum cleaners, phonographs, radios, encyclopedias and—importantly— home movie theaters.[26] In one typical campaign, seen widely in Kodak's own literature but also in its national advertising campaigns, Kodak simply imported its 'You push the button, we do the rest' slogan—previously used to sell its cameras—and attached its projectors, crafting images of calm housewives showing movies to enraptured children, husbands and houseguests. In short, the home movie projector attained solid footing in the popular imaginary through pictures that were consistently circulated in mass-distributed magazines (and newspapers) throughout the period. In the pages of women's magazines, these machines became resolutely gendered.[27]

In venues such as *Ladies Home Journal* and *Good Housekeeping,* movies in the home and home theaters were inextricably linked to discourses about automated, efficient homes and housewives. To be sure, the home movie theater was an industry ideal not to be mistaken for an empirical reality. The prices of home movie systems were prohibitive even to the affluent middle class of the period, comparable to top-of-the-line home theater systems today.[28] Yet, it is clear that companies such as Kodak initially set out to market movies and projectors as part of the contemporary explosion of electrical appliances and domestic euphoria endemic to the period. A contemporary study by advertising firm J. Walter Thompson, which held the Kodak account from 1928 onwards, confirms the presumed link between prosperity, gender, electrified appliances and movies in the home. The

10.4 'A click of the Switch...' Kodak promised to automate home theaters by making projectors easy for mother to operate. (*Ladies Home Journal*, April, 1927).

survey co-articulated camera and projector ownership with the acquisition of toasters, radios, vacuum cleaners, coffee pots and stoves, as well as other Kodak equipment. According to this one and admittedly very partial study, J. Walter Thompson concluded that the owners of home motion picture equipment were predominantly women, who consistently owned more home appliances than owners of all other photographic equipment (e.g. point-and-shoot cameras).[29] This at least confirms that there was an identifiable industry-sanctioned idea about home movie systems in general. Cameras and projectors were being gendered as feminine, a configuration that is markedly different from the ways in which, as Barbara Klinger's work has demonstrated, the technophilic and masculinized home theater unfolds in contemporary discourses.[30]

The idea of movies in the home was a beneficiary of the ascendant means and methods of the modern, electrified, commodified home. Their appearance in the burgeoning body of middlebrow women's magazines alongside other domestic appliances is but one symptom of this. Yet another is the way in which the film projector-as-machine and the growing body of films were marketed. In short, watching movies in the home was also linked to the discourses addressing middle-class homemakers, and their ascribed need to differentiate themselves by selectiveness of consumption, announcing prosperity through particular strategies of home decoration that made active use of culture-as-object.

In her discussion of the Book of the Month Club, Janice Radway has argued that culture was being transformed throughout the 1920s into a 'characteristically modern business,' employing speed, quantity, and efficiency and geared toward increasing consumption. The proliferating objects of culture reflect the growing preoccupation of the middle class to accumulate and display the signs of upward mobility, education, prosperity, and refinement. The ideal home became a site dense with the signs of accumulating knowledge and erudition. Books, for instance, became standard elements of the middle-class home, not only as the gears for good reading habits but as objects imbuing the home with the status offered by literature, whether they were read or not. One critic of the time described the books circulated through the Book of the Month Club as 'furniture books,' due in part to the founder's insistence that all of his books be leather bound in order that they look good on shelves. Their outward appearance was as or more important than anything written or read inside their covers.[31]

For films, these Bourdieu-inflected strategies of distinction hold a particular twist as the titles available for rental and purchase did not necessarily share the readily accepted and respectable status of literature, poetry or history. Nor did film watching easily call forth the appeal of the book to nineteenth-century ideals of the slow, meditative or the private. Moreover, the grey metal cans that held these films did predictably little to compensate for these supposed shortcomings. Thus, arranging films in the home was harnessed to the indices associated with other objects of edification. The unsightly film can was made discreet and respectable by placing it in faux-leather book casings, thus facilitating its smooth integration with its more visually appealing brethren on the book shelf. Kodak, along with other companies, sold a range of faux-leather bindings and other such tasteful storage devices. Resonating with the contemporaneous trend to subsume the technological apparatus of the radio and turn it into furniture, large entertainment centers were crafted to house both films and projectors, and sometimes screens. In 1927, Kodak marketed 'The Library Kodascope,' an expensive oak unit in 'moderne' style that allowed for regular projection or self-contained viewing (rear-projection). Happy

Harmonious With Any Period is This
Smart Ensemble Cabinet in Walnut
that makes home movie projection easier than ever before

10.5
Advertisement
for Kodak's
line of film
furniture,
making cinema
harmonious
with modern
domestic décor.
(*The Cine-
Kodak News*,
March 1930).

TO most people the introduction of Ciné-Kodak home movie outfits meant the opening of a new field of entertainment and pleasure. But to interior decorators everywhere, these several pieces of home movie equipment presented a problem in furnishing.

They, ever seeking to combine beauty with utility, and both with convenience, requested a projection case and cabinet which would not only make home movies easier to show, but would provide ample storage space for films, camera and accessories. Equally important, they declared, each should be a lovely piece of furniture harmonious in design with any period.

To supply this want, the Eastman Kodak Company engaged an internationally famous designer, a man of outstanding ability, to create just such a case and cabinet. Illustrated on this page is the result... an exquisite ensemble in walnut, fashioned by the hand of an artist.

Beauty Harmonious with Any Period

Exquisitely beautiful is the Library Kodascope and its accompanying case, in the lustrous finish of its fine-grained, hand-rubbed walnut, in its rich marquetry and

polished ebony trimming. No less lovely is the cabinet to match. Conservatively modern, the design is harmonious with any period. Distinctive, yet unobtrusive, the Library Kodascope and cabinet add charm to any home.

New Projection Convenience

The Library Kodascope is instantly available for showing home movies. Con-

sisting of the Model B Kodascope, a handsome case, a self-contained screen and one-inch and two-inch projection lenses, together with a 400-foot aluminum reel, spare lamp, connecting cord, splicing outfit and oiling outfit, it provides everything necessary for showing movies but the film.

The cabinet has ample storage space. There are compartments for twenty-six 400-foot reels, and a roomy drawer for accessories. Hinged on the inside of the cabinet door is a shelf, which, when swung into a horizontal position, gives generous room for reel containers when films are in use, and for editing and splicing. Secured to the door under this shelf is a detachable, walnut-mounted Kodacolor Screen. The top of the cabinet revolves, permitting the self-contained screen of the Library Kodascope to be extended in any direction, or permitting the showing of movies on a larger screen without moving the cabinet.

The Library Kodascope is $300; the cabinet is $150. They may be purchased separately or as a unit. *Ask a Ciné-Kodak dealer for a demonstration.*

EASTMAN KODAK COMPANY,
Rochester, N. Y.

couples and sometimes families were shown gathered around small and smaller screens, sometimes as small as roughly 6 × 6 inches. Such diminutive screens were easily obscured by the furniture meant to conceal them. More discreet and less expensive versions of the Library Kodascope were designed to sit on tables, and were often pictured beside books, or neatly arranged to compliment other household objects.

The problem of where to house the unsightly projector was only magnified by the problem of where to place the large and awkward film screen. While budget screens or no-frills units were sold that could easily collapse and be hidden in a closet, another model paired a film screen with a card table. Entitled The Kodacarte, the table was hinged on one side, quickly swinging open to provide ready access to a mobile projector's wares. More sleek were upscale screens that were permanently and conveniently mounted but obscured by tasteful tapestries or pastoral scenes that pulled down like a blind to quickly reveal or cover a frequently used and centrally located screen. In the context of the idealized home, the modernity of cinema's machine—projectors, films and screens—was muted by ideals of contained, safe, and enduring domesticity, its threatening powers subordinated to a feminized moral housekeeper equally schooled in the efficient operations of other domesticated, commodified machines. Images of family togetherness persisted throughout these pictures, reaffirming a bourgeois sociality, markedly distinct from the sprawling, polyglot and charged crowds of the public movie theater.

Enduring Vestiges

Anne Friedberg, Tom Gunning, Anna McCarthy, Vanessa Schwartz, Barbara Klinger, Michelle Hilmes and many others have implored film and media scholars to rethink the phenomena deemed relevant when investigating the current and the past of film and television as both aesthetic media with distinct formal properties but also as experiences, spaces, and technological and material networks. Examining the home theater of the 1920s and 1930s suggests interesting departures from contemporary domestic film cultures, implicating home theaters less in amateurism and cinephilia and more in a set of discourses about the modern home, automation, and domestic rituals of affirmation—and in a set of ideas about turning the home inside out without threatening its privileged and autonomous site. Moreover, movies in the home were presented as an ideal to the growing body of women magazine readers, linking home theaters unmistakably to discourses of efficiency, gendered labor, and moral housekeeping. Film programming as home entertainment was shaped as women's work.

Marketing films to the home in the 1920s belies a certain anxiety about importing moving images into the increasingly central site for announcing moral propriety and individual success under capitalism and its commodified home stage. Screens were only welcomed with ambivalence, carefully directed away from the lurid and sensual appeal of the popular movie theater and made safe by reassuring images of feminized oversight and general containment. Commercial film libraries attempted to connect that home and those screens to an ever-expanding world, but they did so clearly within the constraints of a particular cultural stance, crafting films as news or as educational objects that maintained value through time—clearly differentiating them from the ephemeral pleasures of public entertainments. The home became one of the many sites imagined as a generative mechanism for a new kind of film audience, familial or individual—brokered by the efficiently laboring 'lady of the house.'

The commercial film library (similar to Blockbuster today) was the imagined and material stage where the cinematic world came together and was stored, reorganized and redistributed along specific logics to newly atomized film audiences. The home film library further privatized these activities, linking them firmly to the familial and the domestic. Seeing and saving films in the home was likened to the function of reading and collecting books. The film library was designed as a way to rein in the world of news, entertainment and travel, connecting home viewers to audiences, places, events, natural wonders and even historical periods far away. Long before the director's cut and the 'collector's edition,' the home film library of the 1920s reflected the attempt to negotiate the position of film within a rapidly transforming and highly gendered domestic arena, in a manner that presaged some of the debates surrounding television by 20 years.

The idea manifest in The Reel of the Month Club was clearly a prescient one, applied effectively today by companies such as Netflix, WalMart, Blockbuster and others. The application of this idea has transformed cinema into a phenomenon that primarily addresses a domestic audience, even as the spectacular and the global are increasingly central themes of mainstream film culture. The Reel of the Month Club marks a telling cultural ideal in a much earlier incarnation of domestic film culture, embodying the vestiges of preceding domestic entertainments such as stereoscopes, and bearing relevance for the impending arrival of television. To be sure, images from everywhere have long been reorganized by institutions of domesticity, whether still or moving, educational or entertaining. More pertinent for this discussion is this: homes have long mattered for making sense of cinema. Elaborating precisely how they matter for cinema is a major and necessary project on the horizon.[32]

During the 1920s, the idea of a monthly film in the home coincided with contemporaneous changes to home entertainment, signaled by the transformation of a range of media into electrified commodities: radios, phonographs, and film projectors. Watching and owning these films was co-articulated with class-specific ideas about edifying leisure, gendered labor, and consumption as a sign of (in Bourdieu's term) 'distinction.' Also relevant was a noteworthy increase of the domestic address by Hollywood and other film technology industries through amateur and fan magazines, novelizations, radio programs, star product endorsements, and other movie-related material artifacts. Inquiring about cinema—exploring other domestic entertainments and media forms—provides one of the many starting points for future work. Consulting the vast body of television scholarship will, of course, be another.

Examining domesticity in the context of cinema is important for several reasons. The home theater has long been crafted as the counterpoint to public commercial moviegoing. Each shaped the other and thus tells us much about the way in which industry discourses (including but not limited to those of Hollywood) have long negotiated the integral links between public and private moving image realms. Organizations such as the Reel of the Month Club also index a period during which the ephemeral moving images of the movie theater were transforming into enduring and material objects, integrated alongside other objects of domestic life and commodity culture. This phenomenon resonates loudly with current DVD trends, providing continuity to this practice but also key points of departure from it. Lastly, it is clear that as the American film industry became increasingly organized, the home early on became at least a faint but visible blip on the emergent radar charting the explosion of residual markets for film product. For all of these reasons, homes matter for making sense of cinema. This basic fact will only be amplified as emergent technologies continue to privatize cinema and spread the signs and experiences of moving images throughout both imagined and real domestic spaces.

11

Early Art Cinema in the U.S.

Symon Gould and the Little Cinema Movement of the 1920s

Anne Morey

T HE archaeology of pre-World War II art cinema in the United States has remained largely unexplored. One reason for this neglect is the understanding that the content of such a cinema was largely European and is thus best studied in the context of a particular film's national cinema. Another is the belief that American art cinema institutions could not come into full existence before the monolithic control of the studio system was broken by the effects of the 1948 Paramount Decree. Suggesting that any understanding of art cinema must comprehend institutional structures as well as a set of textual practices, David Bordwell argues that the post-Second World War appearance of art cinema in the United States is attributable to Hollywood's diminished control of its own market.[1] Steve Neale also implies that art cinema is typically understood relationally, with the structuring binary being that of Hollywood v. non-Hollywood film practice.[2] Both Bordwell and Neale suggest the existence of a kind of prehistory of the art cinema, but it is not of major interest to them because it does not appear to be continuous with postwar practice—if only because the institutional landscape is so radically different on either side of the Second World War. Yet not only did the pre-war American art cinema exist, in the shape of what was then known as the 'little cinema' movement, but it also has much to tell us about a long-running dissatisfaction with both Hollywood films and exhibition circumstances in the 1920s and 1930s.

To be sure, even viewed exclusively as an exhibition context, the little cinema movement in the United States did not influence the rest of the industry, in part because its heyday was very brief, running only from 1925 to 1929, with an afterglow that ran, in some communities, into the 1930s. Little cinema is a collateral relative of later American art cinema rather than a direct ancestor, because the movement was effectively ended by the coming of sound. Moreover, from the standpoint of showcasing American filmmaking, the little cinema movement never resulted in particularly close cooperation with American avant-garde filmmakers or with amateur filmmakers working outside of Hollywood. While its theaters welcomed works such as *Manhatta* (1921, Sheeler and Strand), such films were simply not numerous enough to represent a distinctive piece of the market, a segment that was anyway later captured by museum film collections such as that of the Art Institute of Chicago or the Museum of Modern Art in New York. Yet what was distinctive about the little cinema movement was an urgent (if unpopular) understanding of an underserved audience, in some instances 'movie-phobes,' who could be claimed for the right kind of cinema.

The little cinema movement is thus of greatest value to the film historian in representing a socially significant manifestation of public revolt against mainstream filmmaking. While movements for children's matinees or the dismantling of collusive economic structures such as block booking and blind selling were similar outbreaks of consumer dissatisfaction in the 1920s and 1930s, the little cinema movement attracts our attention because, as Bordwell suggests of art cinema generally, it unites both textual practices and institutional structures in a way that many other rejections of Hollywood did not. The little cinema, in other words, used some of Hollywood's own products against it (older films were opposed to newer ones). It also systematically opposed German, French, and Soviet filmmaking styles to domestic narrative practices, and it combined this textual critique with the promotion of distribution and exhibition structures that explicitly rejected Hollywood's business methods.

The National Board of Review's correspondence files in the New York Public Library manuscripts division reveal that it was the clearinghouse for most American efforts associated with the little cinema or little theater movement from 1922 through the 1930s. Appeals for information and assistance, usually taking the form of letters requesting information on the location of hard-to-find foreign films or American comedies, came to the Board from as far afield as Denver, Colorado and Beaumont, Texas. Entrepreneurs or film enthusiasts in relatively more sophisticated Cleveland, Ohio and Newark, New Jersey considering the establishment of little cinemas would frequently write to the Board for advice. In turn, the Board would trumpet their successes in its house organ and exchange cooperative advertising between *The National Board of Review Magazine* and program notes or leaflets distributed by the little cinemas. On occasion, the Board would hold meetings in successful little cinemas in New York and its environs; sometimes it would be the only avenue through which to find a print of an important foreign film, such as *Siegfried* (1924, Lang). Even a hardened veteran of the Film Society in London such as Iris Barry found herself needing to consult the Board for help in locating prints of films once she took up her curatorial duties at the Museum of Modern Art in New York.

The National Board's centrality makes it necessary briefly to contextualize its philosophy of film-going and filmmaker/audience relations. The National Board was an artifact of Progressive Era interest in the social role of entertainment in a modern urban environment. From 1909, when it was founded, to 1915, when it changed its name from the National Board of Censorship, the National Board of Review cooperated closely with the film industry (then more or less concentrated in New York), hoping to demonstrate that self-regulation was a method by which the film industry might avoid national and local censorship. Despite the absence of any legal authority to regulate film content, Daniel Czitrom notes that 'by 1914 the N.B.C. [National Board of Censorship] claimed to be reviewing 95 per cent of the total film output of the country: it either passed a film, suggested changes, or condemned a movie entirely.'[3] In 1915, however, the turmoil over *The Birth of a Nation* divided the membership of the Board, and the Supreme Court decision authorizing prior restraint of films (*Mutual* v. *Ohio*) laid the judicial groundwork for a series of attempts to control film content by figures outside the film industry, some of whom were, unlike the Board, notably unsympathetic to it. 1915 also saw two other significant institutional changes in the film industry. The court decision against the Motion Picture Patents Company effectively dismantled the Board's local industrial partner, while production facilities had, of course, already been gradually moving westward to Hollywood, and the resulting consolidation of film production in California also diminished the Board's sense of connection to the film industry.

In some respects, the Board's new lack of authority did not become completely evident until 1922, when, as Mike Budd observes, 'industry leaders withdrew their support from the National Board of Review and formed ... a new self-regulatory organization,' the Motion Pictures Producers and Distributors Association (MPPDA).[4] Nonetheless, the National Board might have found itself in a political backwater by the early 1920s even without this array of court decisions. Francis Couvares argues that the career of the Board demonstrated considerable contrast between liberal, metropolitan (specifically New York) film culture and that of the more conservative interior. As early as 1913, Couvares notes, 'the Motion Picture Exhibitors' League of America condemned the National Board of Review for passing pictures that predictably ran into trouble with local police or censoring committees and voted instead for state censorship as the only means of guaranteeing exhibitors a measure of peace in their home communities.'[5] In part, of course, the discrepancy in viewpoint visible in this example between that of the Board and a trade association stems from a conflict between definitions of film as, on the one hand, a new, popular art form that must be given room to mature, and, on the other, a national commodity that must be rendered inoffensive in order to fit a wide variety of local communities immediately.

While the most urgent manifestation of the friction between New York, and, say, Dubuque, Iowa was what was or was not considered censorable in each community, there were other manifestations of divergence that might be categorized as significant differences in taste. In short, there was dispute over acceptable films, and, beyond that, dispute over pleasurable films. David Pratt and Mike Budd have investigated the American reception of the films of the 'German Invasion' of the early 1920s, and, since a number of those films (preeminent among them *The Cabinet of Dr. Caligari* [1920, Wiene]) become the enduring fodder of little cinema movement film programmers for the remainder of the decade, it is worth discussing their findings briefly. Pratt examines the reviews meted out to a wide variety of German films appearing in American cities in 1921 and argues that films such as *Caligari*, *Deception* (1920, Lubitsch), *Shattered* (1921, Pick), and *The Golem* (1920, Wegener) found virtually no purchase among audiences outside the country's largest cities or a few smaller cities, such as Milwaukee, with notable concentrations of German-Americans.[6] Pratt discounts the influence of systematic anti-German sentiment fostered by organizations such as the American Legion as the cause of disaffection with such films. Rather, he argues that even when American distributors such as Samuel Goldwyn made an effort to place these films, they simply did not find favor with audiences in the less populous and less cosmopolitan segments of the market that provided the majority of Hollywood's revenues. More crucially, Pratt notes that the initial *urban* success of *Passion* (1919, Lubitsch) proved to be punishing for the films that followed it, inasmuch as it caused an increase in film rental rates, later generating considerable resentment among exhibitors who wanted a box office draw commensurate with their expenses and the risk they were taking by exhibiting a foreign novelty.[7] These observations introduce one of the first leitmotifs of the little cinema movement, namely that would-be operators will have to control costs ruthlessly.

Budd puts the difficulties *Caligari* encountered outside New York in 1921 in somewhat more general terms when he observes that 'although the advertising apparatus attempted to recuperate its difficult modernist qualities in various ways, and although the film received substantial publicity, it remained too transgressive to succeed within the commodity culture.'[8] What *Caligari* did do, however, was attract the notice of commentators who typically ignored film, garnering reviews and commentaries in periodicals as far afield as the *Journal of the American Institute of Architects*.[9] Budd focuses his attention particularly on the sympathetic review received by *Caligari* in the house organ of the National Board of Review, *Exceptional Photoplays*, because it exposes what he sees as the National Board's reduction in power from a body with significant authority over what could be released to an organization with power beyond the encouragement of particular kinds of film taste. As Budd puts it, 'By 1921, its power quickly diminishing to the symbolic, the board began more explicitly to shift what was left of its cultural capital away from Hollywood toward an international canon of artistic films, which would include but not be limited to Hollywood productions.'[10] While there is considerable justice in Budd's categorization of the interests of *Exceptional Photoplays* as increasingly directed toward foreign films, I think it is possible to overstate the sense of loss the Board may have felt over its waning power. Its more active, political role was to some extent wished upon it, and, since it always viewed itself as a clearinghouse for any organization hoping to secure the betterment of the cinema, it could hardly have hoped to operate in anything more than a mild, advisory capacity.

What does need to be acknowledged is the Board's consistent opposition to censorship, the steadfast belief in selecting and presenting excellent, even daring, cinematic work at the price of offense, and concern with underserved audiences, such as children. We might also note that the emphasis on the daring is unexpected, given the Board's allies. The organization yoked together, loosely and at times uneasily, such disparate groups as the Daughters of the American Revolution, the Parent-Teacher Association, the Church and Drama Association, the Federal Council of Churches of Christ, assorted trade unionists, sociologists, and public figures such as Fannie Hurst. The range of interest and attitude displayed there is simply enormous. Finally, it should be noted that the Board's opposition to censorship was grounded in a fervent belief in the primacy of the well-prepared citizen's right to choose and to shape his or her entertainment, which, of course, made support of the little cinema movement a natural extension of the Board's other endeavors.

As a consequence of the Board's large variety of interests, the little cinema movement was only one method of securing better films and better audiences pursued in the pages of *Exceptional Photoplays*, at conferences, and in its correspondence with groups such as women's clubs and church groups. Indeed, precisely because the Board was interested simultaneously in religious filmmaking, junior matinees, helping to support character education through film programs, developing museum collections of film, and the like, the little cinema movement was perhaps starved of some of the attention it might otherwise have received. The Board, in other words, never had the unitary (and more purely aesthetic) agenda of a *ciné* club in France, or the Film Society in London, and this may be one of the reasons that the little cinema movement became rather attenuated by the end of the decade. Nonetheless, the Board presented itself as a prime mover in little cinema circles from 1922 onward. As Wilton Barrett, executive secretary of the Board, observed in a letter to A.W. Newman of the Little Theatre of the Movies in Cleveland, 'The National Board, as you know, is greatly interested in the Little Photoplay Theatre movement and properly so, since we sponsored this movement many years ago [presumably in the pages of *Exceptional Photoplays*] and were the first here in New York to undertake private invitation showings of unusual films in order to build up a nucleus audience.'[11]

The major figure outside the National Board of Review associated with the first appearance of a little cinema in New York was Symon Gould, and his efforts will accordingly be the focus of the remainder of this chapter. New York remained the epicenter of the movement, able to support more than one such theater when many communities found it difficult to develop even one. Gould began a recognizable 'little cinema' with a subscription repertory program at the Cameo Theatre at 42nd Street and Broadway beginning in 1925. Because the Cameo Theatre was featured (under the alias The Century Theatre) as a representative case in a volume of the Harvard Business Reports dedicated to the film industry,[12] we know a certain amount about the ins and outs of the business done by Gould. The B.S. Moss Company initially owned the theater, which, owing to its location, was conceived at the time of its construction in 1920 as an obvious venue for premières of first-run pictures. From 1923, the theater gradually ceased to play that role as distributors gave the pick of new titles to theaters more closely allied with particular film producers.[13] It experienced a further loss of business attendant on still greater consolidation in the film industry and competition from bigger, newer theaters in the same part of town. Gould then stepped into the breach with his repertory program for the 500-seat theater and succeeded in increasing the weekly revenue, which was typically $3,000 over the previous, unmentioned average.[14] In a letter to the National Board of Review, Gould claimed total attendance figures of 1,500 to 3,000 for his first showings late in 1925.[15] Moreover, demand was evidently stiff enough to sustain prices that started at twice those the Cameo had charged for its pre-Gould program ($1.00 to $2.75).

Gould's organization, the Film Arts Guild, then maintained a relationship with the Cameo until 1927, when, as Howard T. Lewis delicately observed, 'the ... Theater became affiliated with a large chain of theaters located in the Atlantic seaboard states, [and] the entertainment policy ... reverted to ... showing the best American films available, including wherever possible the first-run showings of films produced by a large motion picture company for which the theater chain served as a distributing outlet.'[16] This policy change evidently occasioned a drop in gross revenue for 1927, suggesting that the Cameo had a loyal following and that the change disappointed its regular customers. Later the same year the management reversed itself again and went back to European films, but not necessarily to revivals or the selections made by Gould's organization. Lewis's list of the reasons undergirding the last policy change is revealing: 'In relation to other theaters in the chain, the Century [Cameo] Theater was much smaller in size; it maintained a program without vaudeville; it drew its audience from an ever-changing public [in other words, it was not the neighborhood theater of a particular population]; and it did not share the common name of the chain.'[17] In effect, showing contemporary imported silent films was the best option for the theater owing to size, location, and, I suspect, the patronage established by Gould's organization. Gould evidently then moved operations to the Times Square Theatre for Sunday showings of Film Arts Guild programs, but this was clearly a stopgap, being considerably less elaborate than the subscription programs at the Cameo had been.[18]

The loss of the relationship with the Cameo in 1927 clearly did not quench Gould's ambitions. Evidently the success of his programming emboldened him to enter theater construction. Gould's desire for more complete control of a theater dedicated to film revivals was realized with the erection of the Film Guild Cinema on Eighth Street between Fifth and Sixth Avenues. The architect of the 500-seat cinema was the Viennese Friedrich Kiesler, who probably came to Gould's attention through his connections with the Theatre Guild, the Neighborhood Players, or the Provincetown Players, who invited him to New York to exhibit contemporary European theatrical design in 1926.

Kiesler's designs may have smacked of pretentiousness, but his conception of the first purpose-built little cinema in New York suggests that the organizers of the little cinema movement were not only rejecting contemporary film *texts*. In an article in *The National Board of Review Magazine* (the retitled *Exceptional Photoplays*), Herman Weinberg elaborated on the new conception of the temple to film art, clearly intended as a distinct contrast to the film palaces otherwise available on Broadway and elsewhere in New York:

> Everything which belongs to the stage, which is extraneous to the *purpose* of a motion-picture theatre, which is false, pseudo-arty and merely precedent, has been abolished by him. The proscenium has been done away with. The seats are arranged in 'stadium fashion' so that there does not exist a sea of dark silhouetted heads between the spectator and the screen. The screen is the center of attention since the auditorium is not festooned with coloured lights and the architectural lines of the auditorium are determined by the position of the screen in that they *converge* with the screen as the apex of a triangle whose other two sides are formed by the two walls. Radical changes and improvements have been made in projection. The music has been hidden and subdued, to allow a subjective emotional contemplation. … Even the facade—at once—gives the function of the building in which the screen has been used, i.e., its colour scheme being black and white—the fundamental colours of cinema.[19]

This wholesale rejection of the glories of the movie palace may surprise us now, but it was hardly unique to Gould and Kiesler in the 1920s and 1930s. Clearly, what irritated the little cinema organizers was distraction from the film as film; hence their rejection of anything that smacked of the stage or even conventional theater design. Nothing was to come between the viewers and their films, neither the dead hand of the theatrical past, nor the architectural distractions of the movie palace such as twinkling lights resembling stars in the ceiling, nor fellow cinephiles. In effect, the ideal little cinema experience was one of pure, even private, engagement with a primarily visual medium. Weinberg even used the word 'hidden' of music, which suggested that it too was an unwelcome *visual* feature, a stray from some other medium with the unwanted power to detract from the experience of cinema as such. Gould evidently experimented with exhibiting films in total silence even before the move to 8th Street, offering his audience in 1926 'nine reels of Dostoievski's 'Raskolnikov' done by the Moscow Art Players. With the stillness of the tomb.'[20]

Finally, the theater's exterior signaled the artistic purity of the new medium, its color scheme the severe but modern black and white. Kiesler's architecture insisted on film's autonomy and freshness (the theater's association with *art moderne*, for example, rather than the faux-archaic design of Grauman's Chinese Theater or the many Egyptian-style theaters that were the rage in the 1920s). Arguably, his austere *art moderne* design was more *foreign* than were Chinese or Egyptian theaters, which had been thoroughly domesticated to American tastes. Kiesler's work, on the other hand, arrived with the whiff of Bauhaus or late Viennese Secession architecture, and, as we shall see below, appeared to some observers designed to appeal most to cultural groups maintaining strong affiliations with European developments.

In his discussion in *The National Board of Review Magazine*, Harry Alan Potamkin made the motivations for the rejection of movie palace architecture more explicit than Weinberg did. In 'The Ritual of the Movies,' Potamkin described the organization's roots in a movement designed to return participation in commercial leisure back to audiences:

> In the building of these large temples and cathedrals—and I say they are rightly called temples and cathedrals—everything has been done to merchandise the show. ... Have they improved the pictures? They have done things to the stage show which is part of the ritual. They have done things to the basement: into the women's room there may have been introduced a Helena Rubenstein demonstration of preparations, cosmetics; in the men's room there may have been set up billiard tables and demonstrations of golfing. ... Everything has been done to inveigle the audience, and it is my contention that not until the audience ceases being part of the ritual does it become an audience.[21]

Potamkin wanted to see the anodyne and ancillary attractions (or distractions) of the movie palace replaced with films that demanded and received complete audience attention.

Like the Film Guild Cinema, the Lenox Little Theatre similarly touted its rejection of characteristic theater architecture: 'The Lenox Little Theatre will be happily free from all the oppressive trappings of the typical motion picture "palace."'[22] Sadly, the circular did not elaborate on the particular trappings that oppressed, but informality and neighborliness appeared to be the other watchwords. Possibly the sheer scale of the movie palace offended, as may have the prospect of attending films with too heterogeneous a downtown audience. What is fascinating about these remarks, however, is the unexpected return of concern about the venues of film exhibition. Received wisdom suggests that the appearance of the movie palace starting in 1910 incontrovertibly signaled film's arrival as a middle-class entertainment and moved the locus of external attempts at control from theater to narrative. Here, however, we find a variety of commentators expressing a desire to take back from the chain retailer not only the film narrative, but also the film theater itself.

Gould's theater architecture evidently became a bone of contention in the overcrowded field of Manhattan little cinemas, which would, by 1929, include the Fifth Avenue Theatre, the 55th Street Playhouse, the Little Carnegie, the Greenwich Village Theatre, and the Little Picture House, along with others in outlying communities such as Brooklyn and Newark. As early as 1928, the competition may have verged on the cutthroat, as a letter from Alfred Kuttner (secretary to the Exceptional Photoplays committee of the National Board) to Montgomery Evans of Film Associates suggests:

> New York City seems to have reached the saturation point as regards little theatres, and there is practically no new film material available, while too many repeated showings of *Caligari*, *The Last Laugh*, etc., are immediately razzed by the critics and the public. ... The 55th Street Theatre as well as the St. George Theatre in Brooklyn are running at a steady loss. There has also been an unfavorable local development. Gould has broken ground in West 8th Street for a new theatre. Frederick Kiesler, Viennese Architect of considerable reputation, has designed an entirely new form of cinema house, which having [been] carried out will have a novelty appeal for the public and especially for the Jewish intelligencia [sic] which will undoubtedly draw the crowds away both from the Greenwich Village Theatre and from the Fifth Avenue Playhouse.[23]

In this climate of scarce film resources, limited audience numbers (particularly in the summer months), and too plentiful theaters, Gould's attempt to introduce architectural novelty appears to have been well calculated. In considering the many factors that brought about the end of the heyday of the little cinema movement, one must note the remarkable mutual hostility expressed in the correspondence of these showmen. There was typically much jockeying for position as the innovator of the movement, the first exhibitor of a given picture, the originator of more complete program notes, and the like—all of which points to both the prestige and precariousness of the enterprise. Gould proved to be exceptionally resourceful, linking his project to as many other satellites of the little cinema movement as he possibly could. Starting in 1928, he positioned himself as the American distributor of the modernist British film magazine *Close Up*. This strategy may have signaled the failure of his hopes of developing his own little magazine devoted to cinema at the same time it manifested Gould's allegiance to European film movements and perhaps also to a critical coterie that rejected Anglophone cinema, both European and American. As Anne Friedberg observes, '*Close Up* remains distinct from its French predecessors because of its strong distaste for the Hollywood film.'[24] Although Gould may have subscribed to that philosophy personally, he did not program his theaters in accordance with that approach, but wherever he could emphasize the European, he did.

When it became clear that the obvious plums of German cinema, the darling of all little theater operators, had been presented to audiences too many times (as Kuttner complains of above), Gould went further afield to more obscure works such as *Slums of Berlin* (1925, Lamprecht), which he retitled and edited for American tastes. He turned this effort on his part into the occasion for a meditation on the differences between American and German viewer psychology:

> In presenting 'Slums of Berlin' at the Cameo commencing this Sunday, the Film Arts Guild makes no claims of another 'Variety' or 'The Last Laugh' for it. 'Slums of Berlin' is an average German program film and it will be interesting to note to what extent the usual New York public will favor a foreign motion picture built, to an appreciable degree, along the usual sentimental lines of the Hollywood product, with the exception that when it touches life its interpretive realism is uncompromising.[25]

Gould likewise pioneered thematically unified retrospectives, built around the work of a single director or even a single star, as in the case of Emil Jannings, whose brief American sojourn Gould thus capitalized upon. And even though Gould was in some respects the most dogmatic of all New York little cinema managers about the necessity of showcasing the artistic and the unusual, American films of note consistently had a place in his programs, including *Blood and Sand* (1922, Niblo), *Salome* (1923, Bryant/Nazimova), *The Sea Hawk* (1924, Lloyd), *Humoresque* (1920, Borzage), *Beau Brummell* (1924, Beaumont), and *Dr. Jekyll and Mr. Hyde* (1920, Robertson), which suggested a range of interests outside the lasting fascination with both the foreign and domestic work of Ernst Lubitsch. Gould's approach to American film suggests that the little cinema was a place for important films of whatever origins to be kept in circulation in the days before organized museum collections, which did not appear in the United States until the mid-1930s. Again, this trend runs counter to much of the contemporary lore of the film industry, which dismissed the economic value of its vaults until television revealed what might be made of them. Gould harbored hopes that the Film Arts Theatre would in fact serve as museum and 'asylum for superb foreign films which we are so eager to deport the moment they arrive.'[26]

Gould's ability to see ways in which to package and repackage his product was impressive. It became clear to a number of shrewd observers by the end of the 1920s that the capture stream for the little cinema might well prove to be the children's matinée. Children were a still underserved audience that all agreed must be served, and they were relatively easy to program for. The sense that Europe was not yet producing innovative sound films and that its best silent films had been tapped out may have caused programmers to look again at American films of note, particularly comedies. More to the point was the support of the National Board, which was increasingly turning its attention to ways and means of serving the child audience. By the beginning of the 1930s, we find the Little Picture House and the Lenox Little Theatre both addressing themselves primarily, if not exclusively, to the child audience, typically with retrospectives of suitable American fiction films, documentaries, and educational films.

Gould saw the trend and in 1929 produced a slick flyer and series of press releases trumpeting the formation of a Junior Film Guild, clearly designed to appeal to the membership of the Board, which had been informed for many months about the prospects for junior matinées at regular theaters. In the same year he also formed a Science Film Guild, which, somewhat mysteriously, proposed to show *La coquille et le clergyman* (1927, Dulac, and mistakenly translated as *The Coquette and the Clergyman* on the flyer) as a 'psychoanalytical production.' Perhaps somewhat desperately, Gould was attempting to create carefully segmented subscription audiences; sales of seats by subscription were particularly effective for capturing children, whose parents wanted something for them to do every Saturday morning or afternoon, and who could be given subscription books as gifts by relatives. But Gould was also reasoning by analogy from the success of the recently instituted Junior Literary Guild, which did for the child reader what the Book-of-the-Month Club was doing somewhat more pretentiously for the adult reader. If the Book-of-the-Month Club in part promised to expose its subscriber to the fiction he or she should be reading but was too undisciplined to go out and get otherwise, the Junior Film Guild promised to keep the juvenile audience away from the films it should *not* be seeing, a major concern of the subscribers to *The National Board of Review Magazine* during this period. And, as further evidence for the thesis that the children's matinée became the capture stream of the little cinema movement, there was Gould's clever play upon the anxieties of parents: 'If you have taken the time and trouble to listen to a "speakie," most of which purvey "crook" language, musical comedy slang, off-color talk or banal theatricalities, you will agree that the talking film has nothing to offer to the psychology of the child except corruption of a highly penetrating quality.'[27] Little cinema's desire to remain in the silent film era is thus made to betoken moral as well as artistic purity.

Gould's interest in children's matinées did not signal the abandonment of adult fare, as the simultaneous formation of the Science Film Guild attests. As late as November 1929, he approached his patrons with a solicitation to become shareholders in an organization of National Film Art Guilds, whose board of directors was headed by novelist Theodore Dreiser. Investors would receive shares of stock, ticket books (including tickets to Junior Film Guild shows) and various other rewards.[28]

The files of the National Board of Review do not reveal the fate of this attempt to raise capital for the National Film Art Guilds, but Gould's adaptive strategies of packaging films and segmenting audiences may have been running out of steam. The creation of both the Junior Film Guild and the Science Film Guild suggests, however, a major trend in the evolution of the little cinema movement, a progression from the aesthetic to the institutional, with the emphasis shifting from film text to exhibition circumstances. Little cinemas were initially motivated by a desire to see films other than the typical Hollywood fare, even in an environment of Hollywood's making, such as the Cameo Theatre. By the end of the little cinema movement, that wish had been transformed into the hope, however forlorn, of maintaining exhibition structures outside of Hollywood's purview and aesthetically opposed to Hollywood's practices of merchandising and distraction.

In some respects, the lack of indigenous art films made this shift in emphasis from text to theater inevitable. Without an adequate flow of films, product differentiation inevitably followed from novel exhibition circumstances rather than from textual innovation. As Budd's comment about the failure of *Caligari* within early 1920s American commodity culture suggests, even the European art film could not succeed in a vacuum. The film texts of the little cinemas were simply less autonomous than competing Hollywood fare—they required able showmen to fit them into an appropriate framework. Gould, therefore, might best be understood as a throwback to the showmen of nickelodeon days, who had considerable discretion in the ordering of films within an evening's program, the provision of program notes to audience members, and even the editing of films (think of his efforts with *The Slums of Berlin* in this context). Gould's outlook and architectural program, together with his fervent insistence on the film medium's freedom from the claims of theater, music, and other art forms, also suggest that the most important artists of the little cinema movement, America's first art cinema, were in fact the exhibitors rather than the filmmakers.

12

Free Talking Picture—
Every Farmer is Welcome

Non-theatrical Film and Everyday Life
in Rural America during the 1930s

Gregory A. Waller

I N 1932, as part of the marketing of its 16mm projectors and its Filmo Library of motion pictures, the Bell & Howell Company released a directory of available films 'in the field of Agriculture,' claiming that 'many individual agriculturalists, who to an increasing extent are adding the 16 mm. movie projector to the radio, iceless refrigerator, and similar up-to-date furnishings of the modern electrified farm home, will find the directory decidedly useful.'[1] The electrified farm home-as-movie theater may have been just another advertising executive's pipe dream, but Bell & Howell was not totally off base: the 1930s saw the increased availability of 16mm films and equipment, the circulation of a significant number of films concerned with agriculture, and the existence of a sizable rural audience for film exhibition.[2] To get a better sense of this audience, the motion pictures they watched, and the producer/distributors who serviced this market, I will look outside both Bell & Howell's electrified farm home and the local movie theater in search of other exhibition sites where 'agricultural' motion pictures were publicly screened in rural America.[3] In so doing, I hope to contribute to several histories of the 1930s that in significant ways remain to be written: histories of free shows and target audiences, of the place of the movies in rural everyday life, of the discourse concerning commercial and government-sponsored film production and distribution, of the ways that rural America was represented in film for rural Americans, and of the

Free Show!

Come---Bring the
Family!

At Courthouse

Tuesday, Dec. 17

7:0₀ P. M.

Educational—entertaining w i t h
Amos 'n Andy on screen. All colored, about farm feeding presented
by Arcady Feed Co.

Shipp & Warner
AGENTS

12.1 Advertisement for a Free Show in
Campbellsville, Kentucky, in 1940.

non-theatrical film industry during an era when it underwent particularly
substantive transformation and growth.[4]

Moviegoing and Rural America

This chapter's focus on non-theatrical venues and what were in period
parlance called 'free shows' is not intended to underestimate the cultural and
social importance of the Depression-era Main Street movie theater, a venue
that I have examined at some length elsewhere.[5] Theaters were intimately
connected with what sociologists J.H. Kolb and Edmund de S. Brunner of
the 'President's Research Committee on Social Trends' called in 1933 the
'villageward trend of rural life.' By this they meant that improvements in
transportation and communication technologies had increasingly made the
village or small town 'the center for much of rural social life.' That center
was marked by its many ties to the urban/national scene, including the
increasing presence of chain stores—and, of course, by the movies screened
in those local theaters that remained in business despite the costly conversion

to sound and the deepening Depression.[6] In such theaters, audiences might have experienced Hollywood's take on the agricultural, whether in homespun fare such as *State Fair* (1933) and Chic Sale's shorts for MGM, animated barnyard antics, B-westerns concerned with the property rights of beleaguered individual ranchers, small town-iana like the *Andy Hardy* series, or the parched-earth drama of *The Grapes of Wrath* (1940). The principal concern of this chapter, however, is to examine how, apart from Hollywood productions or Pare Lorentz's acclaimed New Deal documentaries, rural America figured in or became a target audience for motion pictures.

Depression-era exhibition practices and programming strategies at small-town theaters can be charted, at least partially, through advertisements in local newspapers. There is, however, little information available about how frequently townspeople, farmers, and other rural residents actually attended the movies. One valuable source is a 1935–36 federal Works Projects Administration (WPA) study of family income and expenditures that relies on data collected by the United States Department of Agriculture's Bureau of Home Economics from more than 14,000 families in a range of sites across the nation. Although this multi-volume 'Consumer Purchases Study' has certain obvious limitations and biases—most notably, it takes 'families' to mean only native-born, 'unbroken' families that have not received government relief (thereby omitting the poorest people in rural America), and it considers African American families only in the South—it remains noteworthy both for how it conceptualizes moviegoing as a type of purchase and also for the conclusions it offers about the leisure-time consumption patterns of certain farm families in the mid-1930s.[7]

The Bureau of Home Economics placed adult and child attendance at the movies (together with plays, fairs, spectator sports, circuses and dances) under the category of 'Paid Admission.' This, in turn, was a subdivision of 'Recreation,' which also covered expenses related to non-spectator games and sports as well as to radio, musical performance, toys, photography, and pets. By this rubric, 'farm families ... spent less than did the urban for recreation,' particularly for moviegoing, 'perhaps because the bright lights of the moving picture theaters were less temptingly near and perhaps because other forms of recreation were preferred'—hardly a surprising finding.[8] Thus we learn, for example, that no more than one-third of the farm families (again, meaning white, native, unbroken families not on relief) in the rural Ohio-Pennsylvania region attended movie theaters, and those that did spent an average of $2.00 annually on admissions, while Chicago families of comparable income spent $11.00.[9]

Correlating region, race, and economic status with moviegoing, this mid-Depression survey also pointed to certain distinctions among non-urban consumers. Nationally, motion picture admissions accounted for almost one-third more of the recreational dollars spent in small cities and villages than in farm regions where, at all income levels, far fewer families used their discretionary income on moviegoing.[10] Some 59 per cent of the farm families surveyed in Iowa and Illinois reported some expenditure for movie admissions, ranging from $3.00 a year for families in the $750–999 annual income bracket to $14.00 a year for families making $4,000 annually.[11] Attendance rates were lower in the South: 50% of the white farm families and 20% of the African American farm families (whether sharecroppers or independent 'operators') in North Carolina and South Carolina bought tickets to go to the movies. Smaller annual amounts allocated for moviegoing across all income groups in North and South Carolina probably indicate that trips to the picture show for rural Southern farm families were few and far between. Over the course of a year, how many movie tickets would $3.00 buy for a white Carolina farm family earning $1,500–1,749 annually?—or fifty cents, which was the average amount spent per year on moviegoing by African American sharecropper families in Mississippi and Georgia?[12]

Farm families had opportunities to see motion pictures at familiar, accessible venues other than the movie theater, however. The most memorable Hollywood image of the rural non-theatrical moviegoing experience comes from Preston Sturges's *Sullivan's Travels* (1941), where, in an isolated African American church deep in a swampy Southern backwater, a Disney cartoon projected on a sheet provokes peals of communal laughter from white chain gang convicts and rural black families alike. During the 1930s, newspapers in agricultural areas often advertised film screenings outside the local theater(s). The occasional amateur picture or recycled studio product might be mentioned but, more often, newspapers referred to professionally produced, non-Hollywood films usually shown for free under the auspices of a church, school, business, service organization, or government agency. Such free shows made motion pictures generally (that is, beyond what we typically think of as 'the Movies') that much more culturally visible and potentially available on a daily basis for rural Americans, who would be more likely to see their own workaday concerns and familiar landscapes in non-theatrical fare than in Hollywood productions.

One form of non-theatrical programming strategy and rural motion picture attraction was the 'free farm movie' produced by agricultural equipment companies such as International Harvester, Allis-Chalmers, and John Deere. These free films promoted and participated in what is arguably the major shift in American agriculture in the first half of the twentieth century: the 'powering' of the farm.[13] Widely available in certain regions of the United States, especially in the later 1930s, free farm films were sponsored by local merchants and typically screened at retail sites, though they could also be shown at schools, public halls, or even temporary outdoor facilities. To situate the merchant-sponsored free show and its cinematic paeans to 'power farming' in historical terms, this chapter will examine the role of motion pictures within the social and cultural programs of the American Farm Bureau Federation (AFBF) and the extensive film activity of the United States Department of Agriculture (USDA), before concluding with a brief look at motion picture related discourse in *Country Gentleman*, self-styled as 'America's foremost rural magazine.'

Attention! Mr. Farmer!

Given that farm families would, according to a study conducted in 1930, drive into their 'home town' for 'groceries, machinery, furniture, dry goods, banking, marketing their products, high school, movies, church, social affairs, and library services,'[14] it is not surprising that they would also come to town for free motion picture shows, whether sponsored by churches, farm supply companies, or—perhaps most prominently—by automobile dealerships. For instance, in Winamac, Indiana (with a population under 2,500) on the same day in 1936, Zellars Motor Company screened a four-film 'Free Talking Picture' program in its showroom, while Duggleby Motor Sales offered a 'Big Double Feature Talking Picture Show' that included *The Frame-Up*, 'an interesting comedy-drama produced by Oldsmobile under the supervision of Hollywood directors.'[15] Winamac was also one stop for the Chevrolet Traveling Theatre, a self-contained mobile screening facility on tour in the summer of 1938.[16]

Another form of the free show was aimed more specifically at farmers. 'Free Talking Picture ... Every Farmer is Welcome,' declared a newspaper ad (23 January 1935) for the McFarland Implement and Seed Company in Bowling Green, Kentucky, whose population then topped 12,000. 'Ladies and children' were also invited to attend the special Friday afternoon screening inside McFarland's Main Street store. Though neither the title of the film nor the company that sponsored it were mentioned in this ad, there is no doubt about the commercial motivation behind McFarland's venture into on-site sound film exhibition, for the ad promised that 'in addition to being a most entertaining "talkie," this picture also has a high educational value because it shows and describes the importance of tractors and power farming equipment in reducing the cost of crop production.'[17]

Cinematic celebrations of 'power farming' remained something of a stand-by in Bowling Green. In February 1936, McFarland advertised another show—a 'big double bill' of talking pictures (*Sheppard & Sons* and *Murphy*

Delivers the Goods) provided by John Deere.[18] Free farm films also came to this small Kentucky city under the auspices of other local merchants, including the American Hardware Company (as part of 'Power Farmers Day') and a feed supply firm, which sponsored a screening at the state Teacher's College of *Hidden Harvest*, a 'two hour talking' picture from the Checkerboard feed company that was billed as a 'farm life movie.' Judging from the following promotional notice, this dramatization of agricultural progress also seems to have been a model of economical construction and product-driven narrative:

> Walter Conway, a collegiate son of an industrialist, is injured in an automobile accident and is taken into the farm home of the Allens. During convalescence, he takes a deep interest in Mary Allen. The film ends with Conway marrying Mary Allen after the Allen farm has been greatly improved by a 'hidden harvest' plan with which the young couple become acquainted while attending a movie entitled, *Animal Checkers*, depicting sequences of work in the barnyard.[19]

It ought not to be surprising that free farm films were available in the relatively 'urban' small city of Bowling Green, which served as a retail center for area farmers and staked its economic faith in agriculture. 'The state of the country's prosperity is in direct ratio to the thickness of the farmer's purse,' declared one of Bowling Green's newspapers in 1938.[20] The same editorial 'credo' informed weekly newspapers from much smaller towns in the region, where farm supply companies, tractor dealerships, and even hardware stores sponsored screenings. In Campbellsville, Kentucky (1930 population: 1,923), one firm offered a 'Big Power Farming Show and Entertainment' at the county high school, while another staged a 'Free Show' at the courthouse that promised to be 'educational—entertaining with Amos 'n Andy on screen. All colored, about farm feeding.'[21] In Columbia, Kentucky (1930 population: 1,195), 'John Deere Day' meant a free program of four different motion pictures, including *Friendly Valley* and *What's New in Farm Equipment*.[22] In Winamac, Indiana, Hoch Hardware invited all to a Friday night show with live entertainment and 'talking pictures of a beautiful romance of pioneer days up to the introduction and use of the Allis-Chalmers All-Crop Harvester.'[23]

Local newspapers rarely indicated whether a company sales representative was on hand to participate in the show. Tracking these newspaper ads over different localities, however, reveals not only a sizable number of examples, but also a range of variation in the programming of free farm movies. Whereas the incorporation of live entertainment could possibly 'localize'

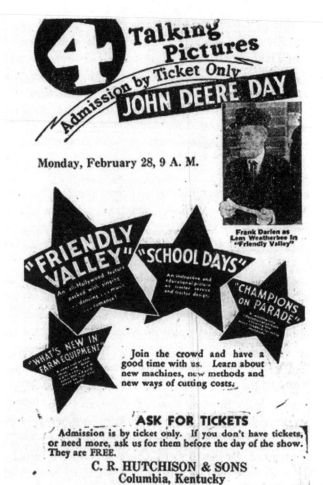

12.2 Ad for John Deere Day, 1938.

any given show, ads indicate that the John Deere Day multi-film program cited above was constant from place to place. Describing a tractor film as a 'talkie' or as part of a 'big double bill' attempted to blur the distinction between Hollywood's version of the Movies and non-theatrical, commercial motion pictures, as did the narrativization of farm films like *Hidden Hand*. The seed store, garage, or high school auditorium was, however, obviously not the Main Street movie theater. Unfortunately for our understanding of rural audiences, contemporary newspaper accounts provide little detail about the conditions of non-theatrical film exhibition: the behavior of the audience, for example, or the seating arrangement, screen size, and projection equipment. One thing is clear. By the mid-1930s there was nothing novel about these non-theatrical film sites, which were too familiar and mundane to merit newspaper coverage, and there was nothing surprising about John Deere and International Harvester being in the business of funding and circulating motion pictures.

Tractor Films and Power Farming

International Harvester, the largest farm equipment company, had been active in film production and distribution since the early 'teens and had released at least eight 'industrial and educational subjects' such as *The Power Farmer* and *Uncovering Earth's Riches* by 1926.[24] International Harvester relied heavily on advertising during 1921–27 as it struggled with Ford in what agricultural historian Robert C. Williams calls an 'epic in industrial competition' to see which company would dominate the tractor market.[25] According to film historian Anthony Slide, 'no company was as important as International Harvester in pioneering the use of sponsored production and film as an advertising medium,'[26] but other commercial firms also funded motion pictures intended for the rural market in the late silent era. Ford promoted its Fordson tractors in *Farm Progress*, while General Electric offered *The Yoke of the Past*, a 'pictorial record of a century of progress in agriculture.' And the Caterpillar Tractor Company circulated six 'industrial subjects' promoting earth-moving machinery.[27]

Among the more than 200 motion pictures that the United States Department of Agriculture had available in 1926 was a one-reel film entitled *Should I Buy a Tractor?*[28] In its celebration of 'power farming,' International Harvester—like Ford, John Deere, and its other competitors—had a ready answer. Widely distributed International Harvester films like *The Progress of Power* and *The Power Behind the Orange* stood as professionally produced demonstrations of the 'innumerable ways in which modern power machinery saves labor for the farmer.'[29] Tractor films became even more numerous and more widely screened during the 1930s, spurred in part by improved 35mm and 16mm sound film technology.[30] In 1932, a spokesman for Caterpillar insisted that his company was 'the largest user of motion pictures for business purposes,' since 'practically every Caterpillar dealer throughout the world is equipped with one or more 16mm projectors and a complete library of films on various subjects supplied free to them by the Caterpillar Tractor Co.'[31] Ford relied on a similar distribution strategy for films like *Farms of the Future*.[32]

By 1934, International Harvester was distributing forty-three free agricultural films through its home office in Chicago and its eighty-five 'branch houses' in the United States and seventeen in Canada. These were primarily one- or two-reelers promoting the general advantages of mechanized, modernized farming (like *The Horseless Farm* and *Power in the Farm Home*) or depicting the application of new technologies to a wide array of particular crops and agricultural ventures from soybeans, corn, and livestock to dairy farming, orange groves, and cherry orchards. As a result, some International Harvester films had a markedly regional focus: *Fruitland*, for instance, looked at the 'Niagara fruit belt,' which was quite distinct from the Midwestern cornbelt or the 'modern plantations' of the Mississippi Delta region, a site featured in the three-reel *Power Farming in the South* (1934).[33] Geographic specificity was also a crucial element in *Partners*, a particularly ambitious six-reel sound film produced by John Deere in 1934. Promising to show 'the John Deere tractor in actual field operation,' *Partners* was set at the Iowa State Fair and used 'a charming farm home nearby' for its location shots.[34] One of the most telling aspects of the farm film as a genre is how it contrasts the archaic with the modern, while simultaneously addressing the claims of the regional and the national, and rearticulating the relation between the rural and the urban.

The epic among early Depression-era farm films was *Romance of the Reaper*. According to *Educational Screen* in 1931, this five-reel production was 'the most widely used industrial talking picture ever produced,' with 124 prints circulating in the United States alone and numerous foreign language prints also available.[35] Shot on location in Virginia, *Romance of the Reaper* served as the centerpiece of International Harvester's centennial celebration of the McCormick reaper. Thus, the local McCormick-Deering dealer in Chesterton, Indiana, exhibited *Romance of the Reaper* as part of day-long festivities at the town's biggest hall, complete with a free lunch, live demonstrations of new products, and a working model of the 1831 machine. 'Never before has so much real history been packed into a single film of this kind,' claimed an ad in the *Chesterton Tribune*. 'From the first scene to the last, *Romance of the Reaper* is authentic. It is interesting and educational; it is romantic; it is thrilling.'[36] Long after the centennial celebration had concluded, *Romance of the Reaper*—like a great many farm films—remained readily available for use in a wide array of non-theatrical venues.

For example, International Harvester screened its motion pictures not only at small-town dealerships, but also at the annual National Conference of Visual Education and Film Exhibition in Chicago. Sponsored by the DeVry Corporation (manufacturers of projectors and cameras, including, from the 1910s, portable 35mm projectors), this event was in the mid-1930s a key site to showcase new films, including amateur pictures, instructional material tailored for the classroom, and industrials produced by, among other major companies, American Steel and Wire, Ford, Firestone, General Motors, and Household Finance.[37] International Harvester regularly participated in the conference, bringing *Boulder Dam* in 1936 and *Farm Inconveniences* in 1937, thus keeping pace with other agricultural machinery companies that were also showing off new films: Caterpillar with *Power and Progress* in 1936 and Allis-Chalmers with *Soil Builders* in 1937.[38] At the 1938 conference, which celebrated Henry DeVry's 25 years of involvement in visual education, International Harvester used the occasion to underscore its own history in this domain, screening two films: its first industrial, *Back to the Farm*, an Essanay production the company had 'sponsored' in 1911 (which it claimed to be 'the first full length reel industrial motion picture ever made in America');[39] and their 'latest rural life "talkie,"' *The Beaverton Consolidated School*, which dramatized how 'improved roads and motor buses for transportation have greatly aided the transition from the Little Red School House to the Big Modern Consolidated Country School.'[40]

International Harvester's boundless optimism about the improvability of 'rural life' was not quite unfounded. 'Both the farmers and the farm machinery industry,' claims the author of the authoritative book on the John Deere Company, 'came through the 1930s stronger than any could have imagined in the depths of the Great Depression in 1932.'[41] The same could be said of the American Farm Bureau Federation, which for a time rivaled International Harvester as a sponsor of farm films.

The American Farm Bureau Federation: Rural Motion Picture Entertainment

Organized in 1919, the American Farm Bureau Federation (AFBF)—the national umbrella group for local, county, and state Farm Bureaus—began, in historian Christiana McFadyen Campbell's phrase, as a 'crusading educational agency.'[42] It is, therefore, not surprising that this activist organization made significant use of motion pictures. According to Arthur Edwin Krows, the first historian of non-theatrical films in the United States, the AFBF had begun producing and distributing films as early as 1921, under the aegis of the 'Farm Films Service,' which sold prints, arranged for sponsored theatrical and non-theatrical screenings, and provided portable projection equipment. Among the farm films it distributed were several of its own titles including *Spring Valley* (1921), *The Homestead* (1921), and *My Farm Bureau* (1925).[43] In 1923, the AFBF claimed to have supplied motion pictures for more than 3500 screenings that attracted an audience of 670,000 across 35 states. By the end of the 1920s, the AFBF's film production and distribution had expanded even further (with as many as 50 prints of each AFBF film in circulation), a trend that Krows attributes to the

257

organization's willingness to sell 'advertising space' in its films, but also an indication of the growing national presence of the Farm Bureau.[44]

While the most publicly visible role of the AFBF during the Depression was as a key player in shaping federal agricultural policy, it continued to have an ongoing commitment at the local level to what it called its 'Home and Community Department.' Nancy Berlage convincingly argues that the AFBF's programs in social welfare, education, and recreation during the 1920s underscored 'an ideology of family farm, family production, and community' intended to 'forge a sense of group identity' for farmers as farmers.[45] The AFBF's *Community Hand Book* (1928) described more than twenty different programs designed to bring rural families together on a regular basis in order to encourage an 'appreciation of the value of rural life,' a 'satisfying rural family life' and a 'spirit of neighborliness' in the rural community.[46] Along with oratorical readings, sing-a-longs, plays, games, and debates, motion pictures were mentioned as effective 'program material,' for 'many valuable truths and lessons can be taught through the medium of moving pictures.' In addition to promoting its own 'official' productions, the AFBF recommended obtaining 'pictures suitable for farm gatherings' from the USDA, state agricultural extension offices, and commercial distributors like Homestead Films Company, the Pathé Exchange, and Universal Film (through its Division of Education). In effect, the AFBF assumed that there was enough 'suitable' material then available for any local farm bureau to arrange for what the *Community Hand Book* called 'regular motion picture service.'[47]

I have found no information indicating how many local Farm Bureaus actually sponsored *regular* motion picture screenings, but by 1931 the AFBF announced that its own 11 motion pictures then in circulation (on both 16mm and 35mm) were screened 5,898 times across the United States under the auspices of 1,435 county Farm Bureaus, attracting more than 540,000 spectators. Sometimes incorporated into vocational classes, 4-H Club meetings, and Sunday evening church services, these films played at a range of highly accessible venues: 'rural schools, town halls, country churches, private homes, outdoor natural theatres and other rural gathering places.'[48] Based on these attendance figures, the AFBF's Motion Picture Division boasted in *Educational Screen* early in 1932 that it was 'the largest purveyor of rural motion picture entertainment in America.'[49] Although the AFBF's actual membership was at its lowest point in 1932–33, its trademarked motion pictures may have been one way for the organization to maintain its visibility: 'Farm Bureau movies are made by the Farm Bureau for farm folks.'[50]

According to the AFBF's promotional material, its free farm films were top-notch two-reel productions distinct from mainstream theatrical releases principally because they were tailored 'to please farm people.' The intended result was 'interesting and educational films, professionally produced, and always with a "farm slant"' and an endorsement of the goals of the Farm Bureau. To this end, 'real actors and actresses are employed [for all AFBF productions] because it is felt that professional artists can act more like farmers before the camera than farmers can themselves.'[51] Often made in co-operation with 'outstanding commercial and industrial firms' and principally shot on location and at the studio of the Atlas Educational Film Company in Oak Park, Illinois, AFBF films were

> educational and entertaining features for farmers which are generally not obtainable in the regular theatrical releases. They are decidedly not the lecture type. Each tells a real dramatic story, packed with romance, comedy and other necessary attributes to a good photoplay. In each picture is demonstrated some Farm Bureau project, ranging from sewing and cooking for farm women to a picturization of the organization of a live stock shipping association and other kindred subjects.[52]

Contemporary accounts suggest that AFBF productions from the early Depression years mimicked theatrical films, favoring topical and even explicitly political narratives that reworked familiar tropes of action melodrama and represented the rural family or farm as always already endangered. Indeed, it was presumably the dramatic quality of these productions that also allowed the AFBF to offer 'radio versions' of its films, which were broadcast over the NBC network.[53]

Deadline (1932), for instance, pits a girl reporter for a weekly county newspaper against 'city promoters' who are attempting 'to force an expensive highway through the county in preference to adequate secondary roads for the farmers.' With the aid of the local Farm Bureau, the interlopers are foiled.[54] Similarly, *On Time* (1931), made in 'cooperation' with International Harvester and filmed partly in rural Indiana, (melo)dramatized the politics of road construction and farm property rights, as a positive review in the 'School Department' section of *Educational Screen* made clear:

> It is a 'road-building' story—of an old farmer and his daughter through whose little farm the preceding Commission had planned to run the highway. Pleas for a change in route were refused in high-handed fashion—but a new authority comes into power in the form of a young engineer-hero. He seems to see justice in the old farmer's side of the case, and is no less willing to see it after glimpsing the

charming daughter. To change the blue-prints the Commissioner's signature is required, and the hero starts over the State to locate him. The villain, foreman of the job and with a degree of authority, tries to rush through the job of tearing up the farm before the hero can return—but he failed to reckon on the spirit of the farmer, shot-gun in hand. The old fellow's threat postpones the danger until the hero—after a fast and exciting race in his auto over all sorts of roads—returns in triumph with the precious signature, and 'on time.' Then, the kind of happy ending everyone will enjoy. On Time is not only entertaining but is a realistic bit of genuine country life and rural economies.[55]

On Time would be followed by The Test, another two-reel AFBF production with a decidedly topical theme, described in the 1934–5 edition of the Blue Book of Non-Theatrical Films as 'a lively story dealing with city gangsters' attempt to prevent organization of farm cooperatives.'[56] The organization ceased producing or distributing motion pictures after 1934, although it continued to use them in its activities. It was, for example, probably affiliated with the non-profit National Farm Council for Visual Education, an organization based in Chicago that sponsored a nation-wide contest in 1934 'to develop and promote the use of agricultural motion pictures among farm people.' The winner was a Farm Bureau county agent from Indiana who managed to screen a film about the 'need for cooperation in milk marketing' to twelve different groups during the brief time the film was in his hands.[57]

Perhaps farm films came to play less of a role in AFBF local activities because, as de Brunner and Lorge suggest, Farm Bureau efforts were increasingly focused on community-building 'folk' recreation—group arts and crafts projects, dancing, music, and drama—in an effort to maintain membership and buttress rural values.[58] Especially for progressive agrarians like C.R. Hoffer (writing in Rural America in January, 1934), the motion picture show and other forms of 'commercialized recreation' were inherently problematic by comparison to pageants and other participatory, collective activities.[59] It is interesting to note, however, that the photographs of successful entertainments published in Hoosier Farmer, the official Indiana Farm Bureau magazine, in the mid-1930s showed amateur blackface minstrel shows, popular musical groups, and 'mock' weddings—precisely the same kinds of local performances that small-town picture shows favored—rather than historical pageants or topical plays.[60]

The AFBF seems to have cut back its production of motion pictures just as the number of companies distributing farm films increased. The Department of Commerce listed more than 50 sources for non-theatrical 'agricultural' films in 1935, most of which offered 'free' films in 16mm (although only one-third of those sources handled sound films). Distributors ranged from the YMCA Motion Picture Service and the National Dairy Council to a host of companies and individuals (e.g., Ideal Pictures in Chicago, Film Classics Exchange in Buffalo, Mogull Bros. in New York City, International Educational Pictures in Boston) renting various non-theatrical titles, presumably as a profit-making venture.[61]

The AFBF was not mentioned in the Department of Commerce's 1935 *Composite List of Non Theatrical Film Sources* or in *Educational Screen*'s more selective *Blue Book of Non-Theatrical Films* (1940—41 edition). The *Blue Book* identified producers and distributors who handled notable films related to agriculture and, more specifically, to 'rural life and farm engineering,' including the USDA, General Electric, and International Harvester, as well as firms based in Denver, Indianapolis, and Peoria, Illinois, home to C.L. Venard, a 'producer-distributor of agricultural films.' It is, of course, difficult to assess thematic and ideological shifts in as amorphous a category as 'agricultural film' over the 1930s on the basis solely of promotional literature and synopses, but the blend of comedy, newsreel, and human interest suggested in the following list of Venard's 1940 offerings seems a far cry from the AFB's action-packed attempts to dramatize 'rural economies':

Farming in One Lesson (2 reel): 'comedy of young city couple who try to farm'

Give the Pigs a Square Deal (2 reel): 'how a 4-H Club profits from a visit to a steel mill'

Hidden Treasures (6 reel): 'Human interest story of the soil and proper farm management'

National Farm Newsreel (2 reel)

Partner's Three (4 reel): 'a 4-H Club story about a boy's reclamation through a girl's efforts to bring him back on the farm'

A Safe Bet (2 reel): 'corn husking contests'

Steel: Servant of the Soil (4 reel): 'use of steel on the farm; proper method of erecting wire fences'

Tom, Dick, and Harry Co. (5 reels): 'How a run-down farm becomes productive through proper crop and livestock rotation'

Tunin' In (1 reel): 'comedy of a happy old farmer, after a hard day's work on the farm, tunin' in on the radio'

Under the 4-H Flag (7 reels): 'all-talking production of the story of 4-H Club work.'[62]

The rural non-theatrical market was still expanding in 1940, even with the absence of the American Farm Bureau Federation (whose earlier motion picture productions probably remained in distribution.) Quantity, however, hardly tells the whole story. Meager, if tantalizing, evidence concerning the long-orphaned films circulated by Venard, the AFBF, and firms like International Harvester suggests that farm films of the 1920s–1930s merit the attention of historians, not least because they address, narrate, and participate in rural everyday life in America. That is especially true for the major supplier of farm films, the United States Department of Agriculture, which circulated its films though more than 3,000 agricultural extension field agents and select state universities.[63]

The United States Department of Agriculture: Non-Commercial Motion Pictures for the Farming Families of America

The USDA had been the primary federal agency involved in film production since the 1910s.[64] 'Motion-picture activities' fell under the jurisdiction of its Extension Service, which was also responsible for all manner of 'cooperative extension work' and 'agricultural exhibits' at fairs.[65] The 1926 edition of *The Blue Book of Non-Theatrical Films*, for instance, lists 220 Department of Agriculture instructional films usually dealing in what seems to have been a no-nonsense, practical way with individual crops, problems afflicting farmers, and regulatory concerns, in titles such as *Cranberries—and Why They Are Sometimes Bitter*. A closer look at the USDA's own motion picture catalogues reveals that the agency's output was actually quite varied, including films like *Uncle Sam, World Champion Farmer*, which in one reel covered the gamut of U.S. agriculture from cotton and citrus fruit to cattle and sheep, and *Poor Mrs. Jones*, which took four reels to recount 'the vicissitudes of a farm woman who seeks a rest by visiting her sister in the city,' thereby gaining a 'lesson in appreciation of the advantages of country life.'[66]

Lessons in appreciation as well as solutions to problems were probably packaged quite differently across the multi-genre range of the USDA's 'educational motion pictures.' The department's official 1926 catalogue included a few animated films (like *A Tale of Two Bulls, Charge of the Tick Brigade*), various self-described 'scenics' (for example, *Vacation Days on the National Forests, Roads from Surf to Summit*, and *De Vargas Day in Santa Fe, N. Mex.*), and a surprising number of narrative films dramatizing, for instance, the capture of an elk poacher by a forest ranger (*When Elk Come Down*), the effort of a preacher in the Ozarks to convince his flock to stop burning wooded land (*Trees of Righteousness*), and the good work done by

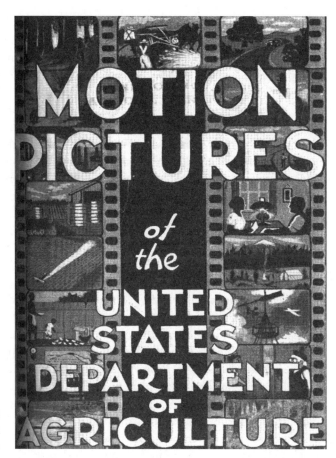

12.3   The 1926
USDA Motion
Picture Catalogue.

agricultural extension agents in the home and on the farm (*Apples and the County Agent*).[67]

Since USDA motion pictures could be purchased by the foot for a flat rate (with an additional charge for foreign language intertitles), there is no telling how many prints of *Poor Mrs. Jones* and *When Elk Come Down* were in circulation, although both of these films, and indeed, more than half of the films listed in the 1926 catalogue, were still available in 1931. In addition to describing its motion pictures according to genre and topic area (such as Domestic Animals: Beef Cattle; Federal Regulations: Food Inspection; Meteorology; National Forests, Western-Scenic, and so on), the USDA offered a fairly elaborate, if not entirely systematic categorization based on likely audiences, with certain productions designed for a quite specialized clientele and others for a broader public. Some titles were considered 'of general interest for rural communities' or simply for 'rural use,' while others were designated as being 'of general interest in the South,' 'particularly for dairyman, but of general interest,' or 'of interest to campers and nature lovers.'[68] This strategy no doubt reflected the USDA's mission as a national agency with a host of quite varied constituencies and clients, but it also complicates any simple understanding of the 'rural' audience.

By 1934, 256 of the approximately 500 motion pictures the USDA had produced were still in circulation by the agency itself (not to mention the prints that had been purchased, for example, by educational institutions). New titles were added each year, including a few sound-on-film productions in 16mm as well as 35mm.[69] Among USDA sound films from 1934 were *Highway Beautification* and *Roads to Wonderland*, both re-issued with scores performed by military service bands, as well as *4-H Club Work* (1932), a three-reel production using footage shot around the country.[70] *Poor Mrs. Jones* had been dropped from the catalogue, but her spirit remained alive at the USDA, notably in a three-reel 1940 release entitled, *Re-Creation*, which detailed 'how one family escaped the distractions of city life through a vacation to the National Forests.'[71] The catalogue as a whole was indicative of the diverse range of sponsoring agencies within the USDA, including, for instance, the Forest Service (*Forest Fire!*), the Bureau of Agricultural Economics (*The Master Farmer*), the Bureau of Entomology (*An Undesirable Alien—The European Corn Borer*), the Extension Service (*From Ranch to Ranch in California*), and the Bureau of Public Roads (*Roads in Our National Parks*). USDA catalogues also reflected the gradual diffusion of technological innovation in the non-theatrical film industry during the 1930s, even as 35mm silent films remained in distribution. In 1935, a substantial part of the USDA's list could be rented or purchased in both 16mm and 35mm, although only 10 per cent of the titles were sound films. Of the thirty new USDA motion pictures released between July 1934 and January 1936, seven were sound films, with titles like *Farm Women's Markets* and *Winter Sports* only available in silent versions.[72]

Although the USDA did address pressing contemporary concerns with *The Agricultural Crisis* in 1933,[73] the release of Pare Lorentz's high-profile social documentaries on American agriculture and the plight of the land, *The Plow that Broke the Plains* (1936) and *The River* (1937), seemed to necessitate a more purely 'instructional' focus for the Department of Agriculture's motion picture division. Lorentz's documentaries quickly attained canonical status, largely squeezing USDA productions—even titles like *The Negro Farmer* (1938) or the silent two-reeler, *Helping Negroes to Become Better Farmers and Home Makers*—out of the picture for scholars of American non-fiction film. As Brian Winston aptly put it, 'the received history of US documentary in the later 1930s becomes the story of Pare Lorentz.'[74]

The specter of 'documentary,' as well as the (false) charges that the Roosevelt administration was spending vast sums on film production, was faced directly by Raymond Evans, Chief of the USDA Division of Motion Pictures since 1927. Evans delivered what amounted to a public policy statement when he addressed the DeVry National Conference on Visual Education and Film Exhibition in June 1937. Federal government films, Evans avowed, should not be politically partisan, informed by rarified aesthetic values, or—worst of all—designed to pass for 'entertainment.' 'We do not believe,' Evans told his audience, 'that the educational field and the entertainment field have anything important in common.'[75] No doubt this was music to the ears of Will Hays and the MPPDA, who wanted no theatrical competition from government-made films.

A year later, speaking to the same gathering of educators and non-theatrical film producers and distributors, Fanning Hearon, the Director of the Division of Motion Pictures, U.S. Department of the Interior, was more willing to cede that 'entertainment has a place in the educational film.' The genre could benefit, he declared, from 'professional titling, background music with subject feeling, interesting, rhythmic narration; social implications; camera angles and special photographic effects; a little drama in the story; a little humor and perhaps a lively girl in a white bathing suit. In short, if such an expression makes sense, a factual improvement on reality.' Motion pictures made with federal funds and aimed toward what Hearon called the 'farmer families of America' were thus drawn into the Griersonian discourse on documentary cinema,[76] that tangled debate in the 1930s concerning the competing claims of facts and reality, style and transparency, social responsibility and individual creativity, information and enlightenment in the non-fiction film.[77] Grierson's 'Man of Aran is essentially a work of art,' Evans argued, 'and the government has no business spending taxpayers' dollars on forms of pure art while there remains a crying need for instructional films on the control of syphilis, of malaria, of hog worms, of the Japanese beetle or the boll weevil.'[78] USDA farm films, in other words, ought to be not so much *about* farmers or some agrarian ideal, as *for* farmers and other people who lived and worked in rural America.

The heightened attention paid to the state of U.S. agriculture during the Depression probably gave a sense of topical urgency to issue-oriented USDA films like *Salt of the Earth* (1937)—on 'the contribution of the farmer to national wealth and the body politic'—and *Farm and City—Forward Together* (1939).[79] But even the USDA's most patently instructional reels are of interest for their understanding and promotion of the 'agricultural,' whether framed in terms of the farm, the forest, the rural, the countryside, the region, and/or the nation. This discursive construction had everything to do with the intended audiences for farm films. As Richard Dyer MacCann notes in his study of U.S. government motion pictures, USDA films, while potentially serving the larger 'farming community,' were produced with 'specialized publics' in mind: 'the women, the cattlemen, the corn farmers, the western farmers, the farmers afflicted with specific pests.'[80] And, we might add, the African American farmer, the teenaged 4-H Club member, and the farmer as consumer. Clearly reflected in the USDA's own promotional publications, this strategy of addressing and serving multiple audiences in the 1930s—a clear instance of pragmatically targeted filmmaking—is one of the most significant features of the non-theatrical film industry in the period, a point of particular contrast with Hollywood.

To target 'specialized audiences,' as well as the more inclusive 'farming community,' and to be cognizant of the usefulness and cost-effectiveness of motion pictures is necessarily to be concerned with matters of distribution and exhibition. The USDA regularly publicized its success in precisely these terms, noting, for example, that in 1933 more than 4,700 agency films were exhibited at no charge to an estimated 10,000,000 people.[81] For both Raymond Evans and Fanning Hearon one obvious flash point in this regard had to do with the desirability, the cost, even the ethics of screening USDA films in movie theaters rather than non-theatrical venues, especially in the later 1930s when the availability of 16mm had significantly increased the number of potential screening sites. Paramount's successful theatrical distribution of Lorentz's *The River* only exacerbated what had at least sporadically long been on the table. Arthur Edwin Krows claims, for instance, that the USDA had attempted to 'obtain theatrical circulation of Department motion pictures' as early as 1917-9.[82] The 1926, 1931, and 1935 editions of *Motion Pictures of the United States Department of Agriculture* offered films free to theaters as well as to non-theatrical sites. (There is no such offer in the 1941 catalogue.) The USDA's *Use of Motion Pictures in Agricultural Extension Work* (1926) directly encouraged its extension agents to take advantage of local theaters, since 'theaters, especially in the smaller towns, are frequently eager to arrange special exhibitions of films for farmers,' citing one successful case in Centerville, Tennessee, where 'the business men's club raised a fund to pay a theater's actual expenses in running free shows of agricultural films on two Saturday afternoons each month.'[83]

The Department of Agriculture had long gauged its success in part on the circulation of its films, the shelf life of which was measured in years. For instance, *Out of the Shadows* (1921), a dramatized warning about how bovine tuberculosis can infect farm children, was finally retired from active service in 1931, after having been booked 1,644 times, with most bookings involving multiple screenings (and with sixty-one prints sold for use outside the United States).[84] The USDA encouraged the extension agent to make use of portable equipment so that 'he can carry his film message to any place in his county.'[85] 'While agricultural extension agents have preference in booking' USDA films, wrote Cline Koon in *Motion Pictures in Education in the United States* (1934), 'effort is made to serve also schools, especially agricultural high schools, churches, civic organizations, and other worthy agencies.'[86] Raymond Evans in 1932 enumerated a similar list of potential screening sites and sponsoring agencies: 'schools, churches, granges and scientific organizations.'[87] Furthermore, it is worth recalling when gauging the circulation of USDA films that all of the department's productions were also offered for sale, with one crucial proviso: 'no commercial advertising matter [is to] be added to or inserted in the films.'[88]

For a sense of how USDA-styled, highly localized, non-theatrical activity operated at ground level, we can consider the case of the University of Kentucky's College of Agriculture, whose Extension Service had fifty reels of motion pictures in circulation in the early 1920s. These films were exhibited by agents throughout the state, including, for example, screenings sponsored by the Rotary Club and the Men's Bible Club of the (Colored) First Baptist Church in Lexington, Kentucky. This latter exhibition also featured a professor from the university lecturing as well as live musical performances.[89] In other words, the USDA films were not only brought into non-theatrical sites that were very familiar for prospective viewers (a Rotary Club meeting, a church) but were made part of a program. In this regard, it is noteworthy that the University of Kentucky's Agricultural Extension service actually set out in the early 1920s to create its own 'balanced' five-reel program, in which three reels of USDA farm films would be combined with a comedy and a travelogue.[90] Without considerably more research into the activities of local agricultural extension agents, it is impossible to determine much about specific programming practices, although Don Carlos Ellis and Laura Thornborough reported in 1923 that state-funded 'portable operating units' mounted on trucks offered isolated rural communities in North Carolina a six-reel program 'made up from comedy, history, literature and agricultural subjects of both general and local interest,' and *Educational Screen* in 1937 described a very similar effort by the Louisiana State University Agricultural Extension Division, which sponsored a traveling motion picture show that stopped at over 250 rural communities, screening three reels of educational film and either a cartoon or a scenic.[91]

These final two examples seem somewhat anomalous, since most of the other rural non-theatrical exhibition so far examined relied little if at all on recycled Hollywood fare. (Itinerant moving picture shows and many screenings in churches, resorts, and military bases are another matter.) Programming was, however, consistently a concern for the producers and exhibitors of agricultural film. The John Deere Company not only invested in films about farm machinery, but also sponsored a multi-film show promoted as 'John Deere Day.' Programming, likewise, obviously mattered to the AFBF, which incorporated its two-reelers into community building events, and to the USDA, which took pains to inform agricultural extension agents about how to structure and pace a four-reel program into a 'harmonious whole,' integrating music and lectures with motion pictures.[92] These strategies reflected different assumptions about how rural audiences were best attracted to and influenced by free screenings. More generally, the programming of farm movies raised important questions about the relation between the theatrical and the non-theatrical: did the fact that free farm films were organized into programs (even, at times, into 'shows') work to collapse the difference between the non-theatrical and the theatrical?[93] Was the typical 1930s movie theater programming strategy (a feature with various shorts, supplemented occasionally by live entertainment) the model for the exhibition of motion pictures outside of theaters? At the very least, programming provides one way to differentiate among the broad range of non-theatrical venues, to separate the classroom (and perhaps the home, as well), for example, from the church or traveling show, the resort or YMCA hall.

The Movies in *Country Gentleman*, 'America's Foremost Rural Magazine'

Tractor films, USDA shorts, American Farm Bureau Federation productions—all these quite distinct versions of the free farm film may have reached substantial rural audiences and drawn extensive coverage in *Educational Screen*, but they seem to have been ignored by periodicals such as *Rural America* and *Hoosier Farmer*, and even by a mass-market magazine like *Country Gentleman*, which billed itself as 'America's foremost rural magazine.' This large format, heavily illustrated monthly put out by Curtis Publications (publisher of *Saturday Evening Post* and *Ladies Home Journal*) frequently editorialized on agricultural policy issues, had monthly 'farm departments,' and contained ads for work clothes, tractors, and automobile products, while devoting considerable space to the 'Country Gentlewoman' and the 'Outdoor Boy.' As might be expected considering the proclivities of Curtis's other magazines, *Country Gentleman* regularly took up the theme of the movies (Hollywood in particular) throughout the 1930s. A brief look at this mass circulation magazine helps to contextualize free farm movies and underscores the fact that film entered into rural everyday life discursively as well as theatrically and non-theatrically.

The movies were the subject of nine feature articles published in *Country Gentleman* between 1930 and 1939 (including three focusing on Disney's characters and studio practices), one short story with a movie setting, and, for three months in 1938, Jerome Beatty's 'Hitch Your Wagon,' a serialized novella about press agentry, studio politics, a temperamental starlet, and a young man from Kansas who more than holds his own on both coasts and winds up as a screenwriter for the fictitious Amalgamated Pictures. It was not, however, as material for feature articles or fiction that the movies figured most prominently in *Country Gentleman*. An issue-by-issue survey turns up a fairly wide range of movie-related material: advertisements, cartoons, jokes, free 'movie books' such as *The Virginian* or Shirley Temple dolls offered as an inducement to new subscribers, and a monthly advice column from Ruth Hogeland. Hogeland's column always featured photographs of sophisticated Hollywood stars or would-be stars, who sometimes passed on their beauty tips: 'An interesting lipstick idea comes from Bette Davis, who tells how to apply it evenly. The way to do it, she explains, is to powder the lips slightly, then apply your lip rouge, and you'll get better results with less effort. These are all useful ideas that virtually any girl or woman [urban or rural, farm or village] can profit by.'[94]

The same stars who graced Hogeland's columns reappeared in advertisements in virtually every issue of *Country Gentleman* throughout the decade, along with their male counterparts. Beginning in 1931, testimonial ads for Lux soap ran each year in March, April, May, June, July, September, and October—always starring at least one leading lady, like Irene Dunne and Loretta Young, who warn against the dangers of 'cosmetic skin.'[95] Union Leader tobacco's campaign throughout 1934–5 relied on satisfied male customers from Lee Tracy to George Brent, while Merle Oberon, Bette Davis, Errol Flynn, and Shirley Temple swore by Quaker Puffed Wheat; Joan Bennett, Claudette Colbert, and Dick Powell chewed Doublemint gum; Fritz Lang drank Maxwell House coffee; Maureen O'Sullivan and Judy Garland cooked up homemade jelly the Certo way; Ken Maynard used Listerine; and George Raft drove on Goodrich tires. Nothing in these testimonial ads specifically refers to farms, small towns, or any other aspect of rural life. In targeting readers of *Country Gentleman*, these ads brought Hollywood stars doubly into the rural everyday: firstly, by associating screen celebrities with mundane products; and, secondly, by keeping the stars so visibly in mass circulation outside the theater and the fan magazine.

Even ads that made no direct reference at all to Hollywood could underscore the deeply embedded presence of motion pictures in *Country Gentleman*'s rural America by graphically mimicking in their design a strip of perforated celluloid or a series of panels arranged like an edited scene. (Clearly, such ads were also indebted to comic strips. Indeed, Grape Nut Flakes in 1936–7 regularly ran narrative comic-strip ads in *Country Gentleman* featuring movie comedian Joe E. Brown and western star Buck Jones.) Goodrich dubbed its February 1936 ad about winter weather 'A Newsreel Short.' Lava soap combined captioned dialogue and photos of the Nissen farm family of Meservey, Iowa to create a 'Lava Soap Movie with Real People.'[96] In such ads, stars were not necessary—'real people' (even real rural people) were the protagonists of their own movie shorts, facing problems, using the correct products, achieving success frame-by-frame.

Given the theme of this chapter, the most intriguing ad from *Country Gentleman* during the 1930s was a full-page spread for Wolverine Shell Horsehide Work Shoes starring a middle-aged farmer troubled by sore feet. Frame-by-frame, the narrative unrolled: 'Can't go tonight,' the farmer tells his friend, Bill, 'chores ain't done and my feet hurt like h___!' Bill recommends a pair of Wolverine Shell Horsehides and is willing to bet five dollars that they will do the trick. Having bought a pair, fed the hogs, and plowed for fourteen hours, the rejuvenated protagonist is convinced that he's made the right purchase and tries to pay off the bet, but Bill refuses to accept the money. So the protagonist takes Bill to the 'show' instead: in the final frame the two farmers (rural adult males—hardly the sort of demographic we associate with Hollywood movie audiences during the Depression) are headed toward a movie theater where, of all things, *Top Hat* (released in 1935) is playing. Going to the 'show' is the reward for hard work and good friendship; the movie theater is within easy distance from the farm; Astaire and Rogers, not tractors, are on the bill. This farmer needs farm-ready work boots; he has no need for farm movies.[97]

An ad for Wolverine Shell Horsehide Work Shoes in *Country Gentleman* is admittedly a long way from a promotional notice in a weekly newspaper inviting Mr. Farmer to a free show. Seeing Bill and his pal head off to buy tickets for *Top Hat* at the movie theater in town rather obviously suggests that Hollywood movies were an available, accessible, and desirable part of life in rural America. Moviegoing is here the entirely fit and justified pay-off for putting in an honest day's labor, heeding friendly advice, and making smart consumer choices. The presence of the movie industry, star culture, and the movie theater in *Country Gentleman* is a corollary to the absence of tractor films and, indeed, any trace of the non-theatrical in this 'rural' magazine. What we are dealing with is a decidedly imbalanced equation, at least in the period under consideration: the Movies (made-for-profit entertainment that was widely and nationally circulated in theaters and in print discourse) had no need to acknowledge or worry about getting mistaken for non-theatrical 'free shows.' As a category of motion picture production, distribution and exhibition, the non-theatrical could, however, only construct its public identity in relation to—if not necessarily in opposition to—the theatrical: it was, after all, the *non*-theatrical. That is the tirelessly reiterated message of *Educational Screen*, the closest thing to a non-theatrical trade journal in the 1920s and 1930s. It is equally evident in Raymond Evans' argument for expunging entertainment from USDA productions and in the American Farm Bureau Federation creation of 'a real dramatic story, packed with romance, comedy and other necessary attributes of a good photoplay.'[98] Willfully resisting or willingly mimicking the movies kept the non-theatrical in the same historically bound dialectical relationship with its ubiquitous, highly public Other. The challenge for film historians is to acknowledge this relationship without reifying either the theatrical or the non-theatrical.

There is also a much more practical challenge to thinking historically about the non-theatrical. If we can now easily own a copy of *Top Hat*, it is much more difficult to track down even the most widely seen farm films, which very likely have long been 'retired' even from those university libraries that did not junk their 16mm collections. These problems of access have prevented me from including any analysis based on actually viewing motion pictures about power farming, invading pests, and public road projects from this chapter. Such textual analysis is, I believe, a necessary corollary to archival research on production, distribution, exhibition, and reception. Judging from the information gathered from catalogues, reviews, and promotional material, these films prompt a host of compelling questions: what did the electrified and tractor-powered farm look like? What constituted those 'advantages of country life' that the USDA's poor Mrs. Jones came to appreciate after a visit to the city? Did commercial and instructional films present rural America, in the words of a 1935 *Country Gentleman* editorial, both as a 'vast market for goods' and a source of 'national ideals?'[99] How did these films gauge the distance between urban and rural, small town and farm, farmer and consumer? How did they visualize and make sense of the natural, the regional, and the rural—all within the context of the agricultural?

Such questions are germane not only to the motion pictures screened for promotional purposes by farm equipment dealers, but across the range of what were in the 1920s and 1930s called 'agricultural' films. I have discussed various examples of the genre, taking into account period discourse, the institutional history of producer-distributors like International Harvester and the USDA, and the ephemeral traces of free shows and their audiences—all in service of the larger goal of exploring what free farm films can tell us about a topic that is as maddeningly diffuse as it is inescapably important: the place of film in everyday life in rural America. Ben Highmore provides a good guide to modernist and post-modernist theorizations of the everyday— which has been located in the strange or the mundane, the novel or the repetitive, the ideologically dominant or the resistant, the culture's detritus or its ubiquitous landmarks.[100] To consider the place of film in everyday life at a particular historical moment means, for me, to examine both how motion pictures represent and shape (intentionally or not) the everyday and also the accessibility and availability of motion pictures on a daily basis, including where, when, and how they were promoted, programmed, exhibited, and received, in and out of the movie theater. In exploring this topic, it is entirely possible to limit 'motion pictures' to 'movies screened theatrically.' But after following the trail prompted by a few ads for free tractor movies, I remain convinced that film historians need to at least take the non-theatrical into account before dismissing it as categorically distinct from or simply irrelevant to the study of the Movies.

13

Cinema's Shadow

Reconsidering Non-theatrical Exhibition

Barbara Klinger

I BEGIN with two stories.

Between 1938 and 1950, the words 'Last night I dreamt I went to Manderley again,' from Daphne du Maurier's celebrated novel *Rebecca* were spoken by a number of Hollywood's most fabled leading ladies. In their respective performances as the second Mrs. de Winter, Margaret Sullavan, Joan Fontaine, Ida Lupino, Loretta Young, and Vivien Leigh each uttered these remarks from the novel's introductory subjective narration. In turn, Maxim de Winter's climactic admission of his true feelings about his first wife: 'You thought I loved Rebecca? ... I hated her' was pronounced with varying degrees of passion by a succession of leading men: Orson Welles, Laurence Olivier, Ronald Colman, and John Lund. But only Fontaine and Olivier starred in a film version of the novel, the well-known 1940 adaptation produced by David O. Selznick and directed by Alfred Hitchcock.

Decades later and worlds away, school children filed into a classroom, where, once lights dimmed, a Kansas twister filled the screen. This was the first time the children had seen *The Wizard of Oz* (1939); in fact, it was the first time many had ever seen a movie of any kind. Although the film was in English, the audience was transfixed, gasping in awe when the film blossomed from black and white into color. Out of respect for the local sense of propriety, however, the projectionist fast-forwarded through the scenes with singing Munchkins in frilly pink tutus to avoid showing too much skin.[1]

In some senses, these two stories could not be more different. The first is expressly concerned with Hollywood and its successful relationship with an early rival medium. The surplus of actors and actresses who played lead roles in *Rebecca* performed in successive radio adaptations of the novel and the film. After the 1938 publication of du Maurier's novel, Orson Welles and John Houseman quickly adapted it for the airwaves for the debut episode of 'The Campbell Playhouse.' With a musical score composed by Bernard Herrmann, Welles and Sullavan assumed the roles of Maxim de Winter and his second wife. In 1941, 'Lux Radio Theater' adapted Hitchcock's version of *Rebecca* with Colman and Lupino in the leads. In 1948, 'The Screen Guild Players' broadcast another version of the film starring Lund and Young. Finally, in 1950, 'Lux' revisited *Rebecca* with Olivier reprising his original screen role as Maxim and Leigh, his real-life wife, playing opposite him.[2]

Set in 2002, the second story takes place far from the limelight. *The Wizard of Oz* was shown in a refugee camp for residents of Afghanistan displaced from their homes by the 2001 allied invasion that toppled the Taliban regime. The screening was arranged by FilmAid International, a U.S.-based nonprofit organization founded in 1999 by film producer Caroline Baron in response to the Kosovo refugee crisis. FilmAid's self-described mission is to use cinema 'to educate, entertain, and inspire … displaced people throughout the world' by providing programming that 'eases psychological suffering, fosters understanding, engages the mind, and sparks the imagination.'[3] With the collaboration of other aid agencies, including the United Nations Children's Fund (UNICEF), FilmAid offers those living in refugee camps a kind of assistance most relief organizations, focused on urgent physical and material needs, cannot supply. By furnishing education, a sense of community, diversion from tedium, and an emotional buoy, cinema is seen as a means of reaching people who often wait in camps for years, even decades. Since Afghanistan has one of the worst refugee crises in the world, it represents a particularly compelling site for FilmAid's brand of support.

The revivals of *Rebecca* and *The Wizard of Oz* clearly represent disparate deployments of Hollywood cinema: the former takes place within a past commercial, American setting, while the latter occurs within a contemporary humanitarian, global context. Yet, these examples have more in common than it otherwise might first appear. Each represents an instance of the ancillary, non-theatrical exhibition of a Hollywood film—that is, the presentation of a commercial title after its initial theatrical run in a medium other than 35mm and/or in a space distinct from cinema's official dedicated venue, the motion picture theater. Within this alternative realm, each story summons a vision of cinema in an unexpected place where, unleashed from its customary domain, it enters more intimately and expansively into the everyday experience of diverse spectators.

From the 1930s to the early 1950s, radio programs adapted hundreds of Hollywood titles, casting movie stars in lead roles. Hitchcock's oeuvre alone inspired radio productions of *The Lodger* (1926), *The 39 Steps* (1935), and most of his films from the 1940s and early 1950s, from *Foreign Correspondent* (1940) to *I Confess* (1953).[4] Through this inter-media alliance, radio sponsors and advertisers hoped to gain greater exposure for their products by exploiting the national visibility of stars appearing on their shows, while the film industry wished to capitalize on radio's ability to reach audiences in the home.[5] In the process, Hollywood's empire extended further into private space, making the studios' features accessible through the turn of a radio dial.

FilmAid International represents a more public instance of non-theatrical exhibition. Refugees often watch movies outdoors on Barco video projectors and movie screens bolted to flatbed trucks that travel from camp to camp. In Afghanistan, films have also been shown in schools and in deserted barns, where children may sit in old cow stalls appropriately prepared for the occasion. Movies screened are often educational, related to literacy and health issues, for example; but commercial shorts and feature films also have their place. Organizers regard Charlie Chaplin films and other silent fare, for instance, as 'pure entertainment' that is 'always a big hit' with audiences. In this context, such films are regarded as having a therapeutic effect, relieving boredom and the trauma of displacement by creating both diversion and spontaneous communities for spectators.[6]

While I will return to these examples, what interests me here is how vividly they inspire consideration of rarely addressed aspects of cinema's existence critical to a fuller understanding of its business, aesthetics, and social impact. Research on the exhibition and reception of Hollywood films, especially in the United States, has tended to concentrate on a film's original release period in legitimate American public theaters. Theaters may indeed influentially introduce a film to audiences during its initial run or upon the occasion of its big-screen reissue. But public theaters comprise only a moment in the life-cycle of a particular title—a life-cycle that often sees the title, Phoenix-like, rise up repeatedly from the ashes, appearing in venues as diverse as museums, airplanes, cable television, and laptops. From 16mm film to video and DVD, a succession of new technologies and media has helped to realize cinema's extra-theatrical existence in times and places far removed from first runs. Given the importance that foreign markets have long had to Hollywood, these times and places necessarily involve international, as well as domestic, contexts.

In this chapter, I shall examine cinema's life beyond the movie house, exploring what non-theatrical exhibition and recycled films contribute to reception studies and to Film Studies more generally. Without being able to do justice to the extensive history of non-theatrical cinema in private or public spheres, I hope to provide a view of its insistent pervasiveness in everyday life and its significance for the study of film and spectatorship.

I begin by sketching the history of cinema's presence in the U.S. home, focusing on the phenomenon of recycling. Recycling is a practice rooted in industry economics: the reissue is a cost-effective way to continue gaining revenue from a single property. As it inevitably results in alterations of theatrical texts, so that they conform to the characteristics of a different media outlet, this practice also has substantial aesthetic consequences worth considering. The second part of the chapter concerns cinema's more public face. While texts are subject to alteration in public exhibition as well, here I examine a different ramification of recycling: the impact of non-theatrical settings on film reception. Once films leave the theater, they are inserted into multifarious spaces, from the home to the refugee camp. What effects do these non-theatrical situations have on the film experience and film meaning? Since the question of the semiotics of setting is most pointedly raised when Hollywood products cross national frontiers, my emphasis will be on the challenges that globalization brings to analyses of exhibition. Finally, no study of the non-theatrical can conclude without addressing the question of why its exhibition sites have for so long remained marginal areas of inquiry, laboring in the shadows of their more lavishly neoned big-screen counterparts.

Although the term non-theatrical applies more familiarly to non-commercial films produced by certain companies for educational purposes, I concentrate on another species of the non-theatrical: commercial studio films appearing in non-35mm formats outside of the precincts of the motion picture theater. Without intending to marginalize other kinds of non-theatricals, my interest in the recycled studio film lies in its ability to expose clearly the breadth and depth of the relative invisibility of this alternative cinema within dominant paradigms of contemporary film theory, criticism, and history. Despite its massive presence in daily life, the non-theatrical Hollywood film has not truly entered the mainstream of academic research. Often dismissed as an inferior version of a big-screen original, the Hollywood non-theatrical hides in plain sight.

Cinema at Home

While many conceive of film exhibition in the home as beginning with network television in the 1950s and accelerating in the 1970s with the development of cable television and the VCR, commercial and non-commercial films have been shown in domestic space since cinema's invention in the late 1800s. According to Ben Singer, in 1896, two years after the appearance of Edison's Kinetoscope, manufacturers produced dozens of projectors intended for amateur use in the home and elsewhere; among these machines were Edison's own Projecting Kinetoscope and Pathe Frere's Pathoscope.[7] At the time, entrepreneurs saw cinema as another medium that could be successfully exploited for home leisure, along with an assortment of other audiovisual phenomena, including the photograph, the phonograph, the magic lantern, and the slide projector. Inventors and businesses hoped that developing a place for cinema in the parlour would compound the medium's popularity by appealing to families for whom the concept of home entertainment was gaining increasing importance.[8]

Although companies like Edison and Pathé produced films specifically for the home and educational market, they relied largely on their own previous theatrical releases to create a catalogue of titles available for home audiences. In an alternate model, companies that manufactured equipment for the home cinema market made deals with studios, including Vitagraph and Biograph, to supply subjects for their catalogues. In either case, films could be rented or purchased through the mail or through regional 'brick and mortar' outlets.[9] These early arrangements involving supply and distribution established enduring business models. Studios continued to have their own non-theatrical distribution divisions and to license their products for distribution by other media concerns; similarly, both mail-order and retail outlets have remained central means of delivering films to home viewers, from Netflix.com to Blockbuster Video.

Beyond establishing such precedents, the phenomenon of parlour cinema defines the medium's place in the private sphere as an intimate part of its total history. At the moment of cinema's birth, entrepreneurs grasped the economic incentives for developing multiple viewing contexts for the medium—signaling that cinema's invention was inextricable from its dissemination in other venues. While the early sensational success of the movies was realized in public forums like the nickelodeon and, later, the motion picture palace, studios and media businesses suspected that part of building cinema's fortunes lay beyond the silver screen, in stirring interest in the possession and experience of the new medium in the consumer's most intimate surroundings. Early experiments in home cinema suggest that efforts to 'domesticate' the medium were necessary moves toward its Manifest Destiny, with its expansion into the household conceived as a means of securing its place in American life.

After this inaugural moment, cinema's history in the home continues unbroken through a series of technological developments. The 1920s and early 1930s saw immense technical advances that affected both amateur filmmaking and the home exhibition of studio films, including the introduction of 16mm and 8mm film gauges, color cameras, and sound projectors. As the heyday of radio adaptations of Hollywood films came to an end in the 1950s, films were broadcast on independent and network television stations. In 1975, cable television and video were introduced to the consumer market, each later outstripping network TV as an ancillary venue for Hollywood. More recently, since 1997, titles have been rented and sold on DVD. Besides other methods of home cinema delivery, including satellite television and video on demand, feature films are streamed and exhibited every day legally and illegally by the hundreds of thousands—some estimate by the millions—on the Internet. Media industries have thus tirelessly and successfully managed to situate cinema within a succession of competitive entertainment technologies designed for home use, not only increasing revenues through the new distribution windows represented by these technologies, but weaving movies further into the audience's daily routines, rituals, and experiences.

The issue of non-theatrical exhibition is especially important because for the last thirty years more American viewers have watched Hollywood films at home than in the theater, causing revenues generated from the home consumption of feature films to surpass box office takes. Meanwhile, formats and systems designed to deliver movies to viewers through the TV set or computer have multiplied, indicating that the domestic sphere will maintain its central economic and cultural position in relation to cinema. As theatrical exhibition now amounts to no more than one quarter of the industry's global revenues, the home's importance as a screening venue is even more pronounced in foreign markets.[10] In countries where movie theaters are sparse and pirated videos, VCDs, and DVDs proliferate, cinema is almost totally identified with television.

The longevity and contemporary prominence of this non-theatrical market makes the home and the ancillary versions of films shown in domestic space critical to an analysis of moviegoing. Among other things, the home is the site par excellence of a deeply ingrained, pervasive practice that has become the sine qua non of the film business and experience: film recycling, known in the industry as repurposing. To generate as much revenue as possible from a film—an imperative especially important today as a means of offsetting the blockbuster's immense price tag—repurposing may result in a network of marketing tie-ins, from fast-food franchises to cartoon series spin-offs. But, repurposing also means 'taking a given property developed in one media form and repackaging it for sale in all the other forms possible,' resulting in the systematic reissue of films in ancillary exhibition venues.

After its theatrical run, a recent film will reappear according to an elaborate 'windowing' sequence that staggers its re-release in multiple venues over a number of months, providing the studios with valuable additional revenue along each step of the way. While the order is subject to change, it often begins with home video and DVD, followed by pay-per-view channels and direct satellite broadcasts, premium cable movie channels, basic cable, network television, and, finally, local television syndication.[11] Although their sequencing is not as complex, classical Hollywood and older titles are also repurposed. At times, they materialize on the big screen, such as the restored version of Alfred Hitchcock's *Vertigo* (1958) that appeared in 1996. More often, they are re-released on video and DVD or through cable channels with large libraries of old studio titles, such as TBS. In its ability to resell established properties, whether classic or contemporary, repurposing is an essential economic strategy that is enormously suggestive for the aesthetic, historical, and cultural study of cinema.

Before DVD, film academics typically regarded the repurposed film as a bad object. Panned and scanned and re-edited for length, content, and commercial interruption, the televised film, for example, was for many the equivalent of the Frankenstein monster, haphazardly thrown together with horrific results. Invariably, the films that circulate in the home are not the same as their theatrical relatives, nor do they provide the same experiences. Domesticated feature films undergo various kinds of surgery to suit the commercial and technological characteristics of their exhibition venues. Radio broadcasts of Hollywood films provide a pointed example of how extensive these changes could be.

Because radio dramas often ran either in half-hour or hour-long programming slots, were interrupted by commercials, and included the commentary of announcers and hosts, feature films were substantially abridged in the process of adaptation. 'Lux Radio Theater,' for instance, presented each film in three acts separated by framing materials. A one-hour show, 'Lux' allotted between twelve to twenty minutes for the host's comments (until 1945, the show's host was Cecil B. DeMille), commercials, and intermissions, leaving between forty to forty-eight minutes for the adaptation itself.[12] Thus, with a theatrical running time of 130 minutes, Hitchcock's *Rebecca* had to be cut to roughly one-third of its original length to fit the programming slot. Half-hour radio shows condensed the film to approximately a fifth of its original length.

Radio adaptations based on the film thus abbreviated or deleted scenes from Hitchcock's movie and excised incidental characters and subplots deemed as not absolutely necessary to the story. In the shortest of the *Rebecca* adaptations, the half-hour *Screen Player's Guild* presentation with

Loretta Young, there is no Mrs. Van Hopper, the ugly American who is the narrator's employer. Jack Favell, Rebecca's cousin with whom she has had an illicit affair, and Ben, the mentally disturbed character who hangs about the cottage on the Manderley estate, are similarly missing. Plot connections made by such incidental characters are simply forged by the major characters.

In addition to these kinds of alterations, radio writers obviously had to convert a visual into an aural medium; in the process, scenes that relied heavily on images to express narrative information were eliminated or transposed into aural counterparts. For instance, due to its literal reliance on cinema's visuality, all of the radio adaptations of *Rebecca* cut the scene in which Maxim projects 16mm home movies of his honeymoon with his second wife. The scene's function in the film—to emphasize the distance that has grown between the couple since the honeymoon—is not lost, but expressed through narration and dialogue in other scenes.

Because new performers often assumed parts originally played by other actors and actresses, character roles also underwent change. Along with an emphasis on sound effects and music, the grain of the voice would dominate the adaptation. Thus, while striving to express the shy, self-effacing nature of the second Mrs. de Winter, Margaret Sullavan, Ida Lupino, Loretta Young, and Vivien Leigh each crafted distinct variations of the breathy, anxiety-ridden, and vulnerable voice expected from this character. Unavoidably, their screen personas also entered into the mix, making strange bedfellows in the audience's mind, perhaps, between Leigh's fiery Scarlett O'Hara from *Gone with the Wind* (1939) and the ineffectual second Mrs. de Winter, who is never even given a first name. Thus, along with other alterations, recasting in radio adaptations of Hollywood films rearranged the alchemies between voice, star persona, and role established by theatrical films, providing new dimensions to old material.

Such changes help describe how feature-length films materialized in the homes of millions of listeners for more than two decades. Hollywood's extension into the private sphere meant that its products had to be transformed to suit a different medium and context. This transformation in turn produced a hybrid creature—part cinema, part radio—that served both the interests of the film and broadcast industries, a relationship that would continue influentially into the television era.

Changes in the theatrical film had, however, always been a component of off-theater exhibition. In home cinema's early days, films were often shown on substandard formats (that is, gauges smaller than 35mm), including 17.5mm and 28mm and, later, 16mm and 8mm, offering viewers images that differed in quality from those on the big screen. During the classic

Hollywood era and beyond, the major studios produced abridgements of their features for the home and other ancillary markets, customarily cutting them to less than sixty minutes in length. As it not only saved on shipping costs, but used the abbreviated form to advertise the full-length feature, this practice continued well into the 1960s and 1970s. During the height of 8mm's popularity, for example, MGM reissued scaled-down or 'reader's digest' prints of some of its major titles in this format. Thus, the sagas of *How the West Was Won* (1962) and *Doctor Zhivago* (1965) were condensed into twenty-minute mini-epics. As the educational market developed, fiction films were shortened and edited into pedagogical lessons that provided information about everything from travel and history to morality. For example, in 1937, Paramount Pictures' *Maid of Salem* (1937) became 'Seeing Salem,' a 16mm short showing what life was like in eighteenth-century New England. In 1953, Warner Bros.'s anti-Nazi film *The Mortal Storm* (1937) saw 16mm re-release as 'First Seize His Books,' a version of the film that redesigned its original message to suit the Cold War era, so that Communists, not Nazis, were the enemy.[13]

From the beginning, then, the history of home exhibition has been at the same time a history of textual transfiguration. Re-mediatized, cut, interrupted, reinterpreted, theatrical films appear to home audiences in dramatically altered forms. But the physical modification of films is not the only consequence of recycling; the non-theatrical setting itself provides another significant dimension to the encounter between spectators and films. Although the home represents the most familiar of these settings, films have been shown in public venues other than theaters for over a century, comprising a history as long and as complex as that of home cinema.

Cinema in the Public Eye

As historians such as Douglas Gomery and Gregory Waller have explained, the medium's earliest days saw public film screenings in an array of locations, including vaudeville houses, street carnivals, fairs, amusement parks, and circuses. When films found more permanent residence in nickelodeons and later incarnations of movie houses, cinema could still not be contained within the walls of these official establishments. Until the end of World War II, traveling exhibitors in the United States presented films in opera houses, tents, town halls, libraries, and schools.[14] Well before the advent of video, numerous independent companies and distribution networks leased and sold both commercial and non-commercial 8mm and 16mm films to schools, businesses, restaurants, religious organizations, museums, factories, hospitals, prisons, ocean liners, airlines, and the military. Today, through a variety of forums, including pay television and video, films are still publicly shown in many of these same places, as well as in bars, hotels, department stores, automobiles, and parks.

Certainly, these settings have a makeshift, ephemeral quality compared to the motion picture theater or even the home. But this quality is the very source of their value for study. Along with the home, the street carnivals and airplanes help comprise a history of cinema in its 'ambient' forms, to borrow a term from Anna McCarthy's analysis of television, which calls attention to the medium's pervasive presence in spaces distinct from its official outlet. Such spaces represent cinema's 'quotidian geography,' a geography that allows insight into the local tasks cinema performs, the constellation of interests outside of the film industry that attempt to define its social use, and the relationships it has forged with off-theater audiences.[15] For audiences, ambient exhibition settings operate very much like their theatrical counterparts, acting as 'signal systems,' environments that shape audiences' dispositions toward media texts through various cultural and institutional cues.[16] Just as showing a film in the 1920s in a luxurious motion picture palace had an enormous impact on the spectator's consumption of films and attitudes toward moviegoing, homes, schools, prisons, ocean liners, and other non-theatrical arenas carry their own respective institutional charges that affect the film experience. The social and historical contexts in which the non-theatrical is embedded further define the meeting of films and spectators.

To consider the potential these sites have for reception study, let us return to the case of FilmAid International and its efforts in Afghanistan. Like other exhibition sites, the refugee camp's viewing situation involves interrelated institutional, physical, emotional, and social elements. Organizers screen Charlie Chaplin shorts and *The Wizard of Oz* within the framework of a humanitarian enterprise in which films are regarded as therapeutic vessels that can relieve monotony, trauma, and isolation among diasporic peoples. As films are presented under the stars, in schools, or barns, the distinctive rhythms, sights, sounds, and smells of each setting contribute further to the film experience. Exhibition is additionally defined by the fact that, from 1996 to 2001, Afghanistan was ruled by the Taliban, a fundamentalist and anti-Western Islamic regime that, among other regulations, forbade all media, including cinema, television, and music. Thus, at least for many children, movies were novel; for female children and women, whose public presence was severely restricted under the Taliban, watching films in male company brought other new dimensions to camp screenings.

The refugee camp is also notably a space of cross-cultural or transnational reception; American films are shown to foreign audiences who have different linguistic, cultural, and historical backgrounds. In exploring the implications of this exchange, we see at first glance a resurrection of the historical function silent cinema once served for pre-literate or non-English speaking immigrants in the United States. Because of its lack of dialogue and reliance on gesture and action, the silent film was and apparently still is able to appeal to diverse cultures, races, and ethnicities. The showing of *The Wizard of Oz* raises other parallels with the past. As in cinema's early days, the exhibitor has license to alter the original film, practicing a local act of censorship in deference to the sensitivities of the audience; hence, the screening committee advises the projectionist to fast-forward through the Munchkin scenes to avoid offending Muslim viewers. Moreover, reports on the screening suggest that the sheer spectacle of *The Wizard of Oz*'s *mise-en-scène*, particularly its transformation into color, operated as a cinema of attractions for an audience new to or long deprived of the visual arts. In this sense, exhibition demonstrates the fluidity and reversibility of cinema's history when placed in a global context—that is, the ability of practices and experiences reminiscent of cinema's origins to return over a century later in new and unanticipated circumstances.

More speculatively, *The Wizard of Oz* has pointed relevance for this particular audience. Consider the affinities between the narratives of the film and the refugee. In the film, a young person is violently uprooted from home and forced to wander a strange landscape, only to find that it was all a bad dream and that home and loved ones actually lie within arm's reach. Despite obvious cultural differences and the film's fantastic proportions, this story bears a resemblance to that of the refugee, who has also experienced a sudden, tumultuous displacement, followed by mandatory roaming and a quest to return to home and normalcy. Whether plausible or not, such a vision of the film's meaning calls attention to dynamics within cross-cultural consumption that can aspire to identification across racial, religious, and social lines. Through what Ella Shohat and Robert Stam refer to as 'analogical structures of feeling,' that is, 'strongly perceived or dimly felt affinities of social perceptions or historical experience,' spectators, particularly those whose communities go unrepresented, identify with cinematic images from starkly different cultural contexts.[17] In this sense, we can imagine that those living far from home in strange and uncertain surroundings might convert films—even those as apparently far removed from their daily life as *The Wizard of Oz*—into allegories of the diasporic experience.[18]

As an instance of transnational reception, this case clearly poses substantial challenges to interpretation. For the Western observer, the labor of decoding is both an immense and a sensitive undertaking. Not only must the siren song of Orientalism be somehow evaded, but the ideological stakes involved in the globalization of Western products must be considered. Does the exhibition of U.S. films in this context represent Western imperialism—a humanitarian gesture that nonetheless results in the captivation of the imaginations of a susceptible foreign audience by U.S. cinema? Conversely, might it represent cinema's ability to connote freedom and democracy to oppressed peoples, or, more generally, to act as a powerful affective force capable of raising spirits and providing hope? Or, could it reveal how thoroughly subject Hollywood films are to massive rewriting according to the social, political, and historical coordinates of the local, destination culture? While there is insufficient information to paint an adequate picture of this exhibition scene, the circumstances and considerations involved are suggestive. At the very least, this example depicts the complexity of signal systems operating beyond the pale of theater districts and the rich role cinema's ambient manifestations should play in reaching a broader understanding of the medium's social and ideological functions.

Despite the enormity of cinema's ambience in both public and private realms, however, ancillary exhibition has so far generated little interest in Film Studies scholarship. Why has this form of exhibition occupied such a peripheral place in the field?

Big Screen/Small Screen

For film scholars and enthusiasts, cinema is fully realized as a medium in the projection of 35mm film in the motion picture theater. The big screen is implicitly regarded as offering optimum access to cinema aesthetically and experientially and, therefore, as the rightful forum for its exhibition. Many spectators, including film academics, nevertheless *watch* movies on the small screen via such media as cable TV, video, and DVD. Cinema thus attains a kind of schizophrenic identity, derived from its shifting material bases and exhibition contexts: it exists both as a theatrical medium with images registered on and projected in celluloid and as a non-theatrical medium with images often rendered electronically and shown on a TV monitor. This double identity assumes an immediate comparative aesthetic and experiential value. The big-screen performance is marked as authentic, as representing bona fide cinema, while the small screen by comparison is characterized as inauthentic and ersatz.

Although no one could deny that there are differences between theatrical and non-theatrical cinemas, the fact that these differences are frequently assessed within a value-laden dichotomy that privileges the theatrical over the non-theatrical is problematic. In continually appraising the non-theatrical

284

through a comparative lens, this dichotomy has restrained a more fulsome critical and cultural study of non-theatrical exhibition venues and of the ancillary forms of movies that have existed since the late 1800s in multiple formats from 17.5mm to Internet files. In the logic that embraces big-screen aesthetics, ancillary forms (with the exception of 16mm and DVD) are often seen as perversions or assaults on 35mm originals. As John Ford once said upon viewing the deletions that rendered *Young Mr. Lincoln* (1939) incoherent in its 1960s TV broadcast, 'Your name's on it but it isn't the thing you did.'[19] As in the colorization scandals of the 1980s and countless other unwelcome transformations of celluloid originals, alterations make ancillary versions of movies seem completely unworthy of serious critical attention.

However unseemly the changes that cinema may undergo in its post-theatrical life, the dichotomy between big and small screens has been drawn too sharply and upon some premises that require reconsideration. As Peter Krämer has pointed out in the case of home film exhibition, this is not simply a parallel history that exists separately from its theatrical counterpart.[20] The theatrical and household incarnations of cinema are financially and experientially interdependent. Particularly after the advent of video, the theatrical motion picture business has relied on the small screen to generate profits that help support the production of its extravaganzas. Conversely, home exhibition venues rely on movies for programming, while also cashing in on the drawing power of blockbusters and other noted films.

The viewer's experience is similarly defined by a continuum of theatrical and home cinemas. Viewers return home from the movie theater to find yet more movies available to them on television and computer. Today, with so many different ancillary viewing options, spectators would be disconcerted if they could not rent, own, and re-view theatrical fare at will. Moreover, although critics have complained that the allegedly sloppy aesthetics of television watching, in which viewers talk and engage in otherwise distracted and distracting behavior, have invaded movie theaters, scholars such as Roy Rosenzweig and Janet Staiger have shown that theaters have been the site of such 'misbehavior' since their origins.[21] Even if we grant the invasion of codes of viewing associated with other media into movie theaters, surely influences are reciprocal. Research on home video consumption has found that viewing dynamics commonly linked to the motion picture theater—that is, attentive watching from beginning to end without interruption—have also affected domestic spectatorship.[22] This influence has only grown through the efforts of home theater and DVD marketers to promote their products as providing the same quality of experience as the theater. Thus, although the provinces of the movie theater and the home have unique characteristics as exhibition venues, they are not radically discontinuous, but richly and unavoidably interdependent.

The dichotomy between big and small screens also presumes a kind of stability in theatrical exhibition seen as lacking in the non-theatrical situation. In this perception, the darkened establishments animated by projector beams and dedicated to celluloid comprise the ideal space of spectatorship, an ideal difficult for other institutions and settings with diverse activities and circumstances of viewing—the street carnival, the ocean liner, or the home—to realize. This view, however, minimizes the impact of the historical variability in motion picture theater technology, space, design, and atmosphere on spectatorship. Which kind of theater exactly represents the optimum cinematic experience: the converted store-front nickelodeon, the luxurious motion picture palace, the dilapidated dollar cinema, the shopping mall theater with its paper-thin walls, the modern multiplex with digital sound or the fully digital theater that lacks altogether a celluloid dimension? This flux in the concept of theaters and the experiences they provide to patrons is only exacerbated when we enter the global stage, where the type, condition, and cultural prominence of public film venues vary greatly from country to country.

Instabilities characterize the products shown in these official exhibition sites as well. As we have seen, ancillary versions of films have always been subject to multifarious kinds of alterations, including re-editing and abridgement. But the fate of the theatrical picture has not been so different. In cinema's early days, multiple versions of a title routinely circulated during an opening run, consequently giving that title a shifting identity for audiences. Exhibitors regularly edited films to suit municipal censors, the tastes of their clientele, and/or the conventions of preexisting successful forms (such as the magic lantern show). In his essay on Edwin Porter, Charles Musser establishes that, before the producer and cinematographer obtained more control, the theater exhibitor decided what would appear on screen. In fact, films were constructed for exhibition 'in such a way that individual scenes, functioning as self-contained units, could be selected and organized at the discretion of the exhibitor.' Early cinema historians have been particularly adroit in recognizing the fluctuating nature of their objects of study, not only because numerous prints have been irretrievably lost, but because what constitutes a definitive print is often a matter of intense debate (as, for example, in the case of the different circulating prints of Porter's *Life of an American Fireman* [1903]).[23]

Cinema's chameleon-like status did not end, however, after the passing of cinema's 'novelty phase.' Multiple versions of films destined for theatrical release continued to exist in the days of classical Hollywood cinema. In one common example of this, different prints of certain titles were struck for Northern and Southern audiences. To avoid alienating Southern audiences, studios produced what they hoped would be less 'offensive' cuts of films with African-American actors and actresses or racial themes (such as *The Pirate* [1948] which featured the Nicholas Brothers and *Imitation of Life* [1959], a story about racial passing and discrimination), either excising performers of color outright or otherwise editing to minimize aspects deemed controversial. In a variation of this practice, studios prepared a number of theatrical prints for foreign release. So, for instance, the British release of *Vertigo* included an epilogue that explained what had happened to the villain, providing a moralistic touch missing in the U.S. release. More recently, the orgy scene in Stanley Kubrick's *Eyes Wide Shut* (1999) was digitally censored for its first run in the United States (among other things, to disguise frontal male nudity), while the British version displayed the scene in full. Regionalism, foreign release, censorship, studio interference, and marketing decisions are but a few factors that enter into the potentially volatile modification and multiplication of prints during their initial theatrical life

Perhaps the theatrical film's changeability is nowhere more evident than in the phenomenon of the remedial release—the reissue of a film that 'remedies' in various ways the shortcomings of the first-run version. Re-releases of newly uncensored prints, re-mastered films, or director's cuts are part of theatrical practice. Theaters have screened, for example: *King Kong* (1933) in 1971 with previously censored footage included; the physically restored and digitally re-mastered version of *Vertigo* in 1996; and the director's cut of *Blade Runner* (1982) in 1992, which altered the original studio cut by removing the voice-over narration and changing the ending. With its proliferation of re-edited versions of films accompanied by extra features, the DVD market has made the remedial variant a steadfast part of the film business and cinematic experience. While alteration of the original theatrical print has been an intimate part of cinema's big screen history, the ancillary market manifests most clearly the inherent and potentially never-ending revisionism that cinematic texts are subject to through successive waves of repurposing that mark their exhibition histories.

Because many re-edits on the big screen and the ancillary market claim that they provide a definitive copy of a film, the remedial release also challenges the first-run theatrical print in a key area of presumed authority—that is, the originality and authenticity that appear to accompany its position of primacy in relation to all subsequent versions. The remedial release attempts to establish that, in thrall to industry forces, the first-run print has failed to realize its director's original designs. Along with the case of *Blade Runner*, this claim is particularly clear in the 1998 re-editing of Orson Welles' *Touch of Evil* (1958), which revises the film according to a lengthy memo Welles wrote to Universal's studio head in 1957. Although the remedial re-release is no less a commercial entity, it brings the authenticity argument full circle: reclaiming originality becomes the terrain not of primary, but of ancillary forms. Today, as industry executives increasingly conceive of theatrical exhibition as an advertisement for later DVD release, the issue of theatrical primacy becomes even more dramatically vexed.

But, even if it results in a reversal, this struggle over originality is still caught up in the push-and-pull of the dichotomy between screens. Returning for a moment to the case of *Rebecca*, we can consider an alternative solution to this conundrum. As we have seen, du Maurier's novel served as the source for Welles' radio drama. As it was presented in cooperation with Selznick International, which owned the rights to the novel, the radio drama was used as a forum to publicize Selznick's plans to adapt the novel. Both the novel and Welles' version influenced the Selznick production directed by Hitchcock. After the Hitchcock film appeared, it formed the basis of subsequent radio adaptations. With the rise of television, the novel *Rebecca* continued to be adapted—in an NBC production in 1962, a BBC production on PBS's show *Mystery!* in 1978, and again in 1997 on PBS's *Masterpiece Theater*. Thus, the story of the shy and inept heroine, her mysterious and withdrawn husband, and their twisted housekeeper enjoyed rather persistent staging and restaging over six decades in several different media.

Asking which of these is the best adaptation of the literary source or of the film is a legitimate and perhaps inevitable question. But if that question dominates the field of inquiry, it obscures a different productive approach to this flurry of repurposed narratives. As André Bazin argues, critics should 'find not a novel out of which a play and a film had been "made," ' but rather a single work reflected through three art forms, an artistic pyramid with three sides,' which should be 'all equal in the eyes of the critic.' From Bazin's perspective, the original work would 'be only an ideal point at the top of this figure, which itself is an ideal construct. The chronological precedence of one part over another would not be an aesthetic criterion any more than the chronological precedence of one twin over the other is a genealogical one.'[24]

Bazin suggests that in those studies of adaptation that regard one entity as derived from and compared to another, there is an inherently limiting dualism that prevents a more nuanced understanding of the adapting text. Through the figure of the pyramid, he advocates a different view, seeing each version as helping to constitute the work, belonging to its overall architecture and conception, with none privileged by virtue of original status. This means that rather than concentrating on fidelity as the central issue, adaptations of *Rebecca* should be regarded as valid re-articulations of the original that comprise an integral part of its overall identity. In a further revisionist move, by referring to it as an 'ideal construct,' Bazin questions the notion of the original itself. If we consider du Maurier's novel as the source, what of the novel's roots in the Gothic tradition stemming from, at the very least, the Brontë sisters' oeuvre in the nineteenth century? The line of aesthetic ancestors alone makes the attribution of a primary source problematic.

Although many ancillary versions of films are not adaptations in the strict sense, Bazin's perspective helps shed a different light on the value of re-mediated films, whether they appear on 8mm, radio, video, or other formats. Like adaptations, ancillary variants transform the source text to various degrees to suit the requirements of a new outlet or medium; like adaptations, then, these variants translate the source into a different language. Each cross-media transformation is interesting for what it can tell us about the 'work,' understood as a complex, prismatic entity subject to shifts and changes within the parameters of its re-production, re-release, and reception. Or, put in the terms of Bazin's genealogical analogy, thanks to both theatrical and non-theatrical distribution, the multiple versions of a film constitute part of its 'family tree.' No version should be dismissed, because each represents a revision that demonstrates the *realpolitik* of a film's history—not something that exists 'out there,' definitively apart from the original text. With its ties to the novel, the film industry, and radio conventions, the Welles' adaptation of *Rebecca* alone illustrates that the interests of multiple media are present in any adapted and repurposed form. This fact of textual existence further amplifies the deficits of any dualistic model of exchange, and the importance of maintaining an inclusive, nonhierarchical perspective when considering the phenomena of ancillary forms.

In this view, then, along with the film re-edited into an educational travelogue of Salem and the mangled TV print that kept John Ford awake at night, the radio adaptation of a Hollywood feature that elides its visuality and foregrounds its aural dimensions, condenses its narrative, replaces its original actors and actresses, and interrupts it with commercials, should not simply be consigned to an aesthetic rogue's gallery. As part of a film's material social history, these versions yield insight into its afterlife and its continually shifting relationship to audiences. With Hollywood's economic engine behind it, textual afterlife is in many cases inevitable. In fact, the most vigorous existence for many films lies in their revival by various institutions long after they originally circulated. These are the moments in which they often literally become memorable. Films such as *The Wizard of*

Oz and *It's a Wonderful Life* (1946), for instance, owe most of their audience penetration and fame to ritual television screenings. FilmAid International's enterprise offers a particularly keen view of the unexpected twists and turns that Hollywood films are subject to during the course of their circulation, where their significance and meaning can be utterly transformed through changes in their historical, institutional, and cultural exhibition settings.

Moreover, the non-theatrical encourages reflection about how originality itself is constructed during certain times and according to certain imperatives. Since originality is as much a commodity as an aesthetic criterion, we can trace how ancillary versions intervene in, confuse, and regulate the appearance of authenticity within a film's exhibition history. As the exhibition history of a film like *The Wizard of Oz* or *Metropolis* (1927) reveals, successive claims about presenting the most authentic and inclusive print doggedly accompany some films, making the rediscovery of their true, definitive version into a serial, steadfast component of their continued cultural circulation.

Thus, realizing the protean character of the Hollywood feature inspires more serious examination of how cinema's many screens and situations of viewing affect the manner in which its objects are decoded and enjoyed. While acknowledging the aesthetic and experiential differences of non-theatrical exhibition, we should be careful not to let those differences establish all the terms of discussion or produce a hierarchy that, in privileging celluloid, regards the non-theatrical film as a kind of 'un-cinema' or inferior proxy. As a means of analyzing non-theatrical film outside of its usual dichotomous position, we can turn our attention instead to the transformations of film identity that occur in the cinematic afterlife and the implications that such transformations have for the aesthetic and cultural study of the medium.

In conclusion, let me return to the figure I have used to describe the non-theatrical's subordinate status—that is, as 'official' cinema's shadow. In the dictionary, shadow is defined in multiple and sometimes contradictory ways. It can be construed as a derivative entity: a reflected image; an imitation; an imperfect and faint representation; an attenuated form or vestigial remnant; even a state of ignominy or obscurity. But, in a less frequent usage, shadow also connotes a force in its own right: an inseparable companion; a pervasive and dominant influence. This latter set of meanings better represents the nature of non-theatrical cinema. In its daily incarnations, it exists beyond, but intimately connected to, the motion picture theater's darkened auditoriums and silhouetted spectators who, upon leaving the theater, have no reason to expect that they will enter a world without cinema.

PART III

Hollywood Movies in Broader Perspective

Audiences at Home and Abroad

14

Changing Images of
Movie Audiences

Richard Butsch

W HAT makes a 'good' audience or a 'bad' one? For two centuries, despite dramatic transformations of entertainment media and audience styles, the conception of the 'good' audience in public discourse—in popular magazines and trade books, scholarly journals and books, and reports by reformers—has remained remarkably consistent. Uniformly, this discourse has preferred an audience that acts more like a public. The conception of 'bad' audiences on the other hand has changed. The considerable public debates about television through the second half of the twentieth century presumed a conception of audiences as isolated individuals, weak and vulnerable to the influence of the screen. By contrast, debates about live entertainments, particularly in the nineteenth century, conceived audiences as volatile and potentially violent crowds. Discourses about movie audiences were part of the transition from the one to the other type of bad audience that elites worried about. This chapter is concerned with how the discourse shifted during the first half of the twentieth century, when movies were the predominant visual entertainment.

Crowds, Audiences and Riots

One kind of bad audience is the crowd. Before movies, nineteenth-century audiences gathered in theaters were considered crowds and therefore conventionally seen as a threat to public order. Authorities and elites imagined crowds as lower-class mobs, prone to riot.

Crowds were not always seen as a danger to public order. Pre-industrial traditions, shared by elites and lower classes alike, considered crowd actions and even riots as acceptable forms of political expression. According to

Paul Gilje's epic study, *Rioting in America*, crowd actions in the eighteenth century tended to be contained within channels familiar to both participants and authorities. Riots were ritualized and directed at property rather than persons. Both rioters and authorities knew their scripts.[1] Gilje echoes one of the early statements of this interpretation of crowd history, that of English historian Eric Hobsbawm, who described 'the mob' as part of a tradition in non-republican, pre-industrial cities ruled by princes, where mobs expected authorities to make some concessions to their protests of violations of their traditional rights. It was understood by rulers and by lower classes that if their rights were infringed, the lower classes could riot to bring attention to this, and the ruler had an obligation to make concessions to them. Edward P. Thompson called this the 'moral economy' of the crowd.[2] If bread prices rose too high, crowds could legitimately riot to restore affordable prices. Crowds were not a threat to the status quo, seldom exercised violence against elites and, since there was a recognized script to this ritual, were less fearsome to authorities.

Carnival and street parades were part of another tradition of crowd behavior condoned by authorities, in this case as outlets for the lower classes. Included among these were rowdy and even riotous theater audiences. American working men, who could afford theater by the late eighteenth century, claimed sovereignty over the stage, and were granted it by managers and civic authorities. It was accepted that they had the right to call for tunes and encores by musicians and performers, and to call managers and performers before the curtain for an accounting of their behavior on and even off the stage. Authorities assented to this because they felt confident they could control such crowds.[3]

Crowds became worrisome, however, once bourgeois republican government instituted an expectation that all groups in a society express their demands through legal channels of discussion and petition rather than through crowd action. The rising bourgeoisie asserted its own voice by advancing its Enlightenment project of deliberative gatherings (publics, legislatures, republics). This project was antithetical to mobs and riots, and disapproved of them. In the transition to modern societies, authorities became increasingly concerned about their control over crowds.[4]

Discourse shifted from one of accepting crowds as exercising traditional rights and letting off steam to one of fearing crowds as sinister sources of rebellion. In 1715, in order to strengthen the power of civil authorities to stop crowds that they feared might riot, the English Parliament passed the Riot Act, which required crowds as small as twelve people to disperse within an hour of being ordered to do so by a magistrate. Throughout the eighteenth century, British authorities repeatedly attempted unsuccessfully to disperse crowds, a pattern of behavior which peaked in the 1809 OP (old prices) protests and riots at Covent Garden theater, which lasted sixty-seven days.[5] Fueled by reports on the crowds of the French Revolution, such incidents confirmed elite fears of crowds.

By the mid-nineteenth century, authorities and elites in the United States had become increasingly alarmed about crowds as they went beyond the traditional script and authorities lost control. The growing violence of crowds had coincided with the growth of theater and commercial entertainment in the Early Republic and the Jacksonian era, and the growing presence of lower classes inside these theaters.[6] Nineteenth-century theater audiences specifically came to be feared as potential rioters, and did indeed riot, infrequently but regularly. Theater audiences were increasingly characterized as dangerous. Rowdy crowd behavior in theaters was identified as a mark of lower-class status. 'Proper' ladies were cautioned not to attend theater because of the disreputable and disorderly crowd that was the audience. The withdrawal of the well-to-do to their own exclusive theaters and the parallel segregation of 'legitimate drama' from 'melodrama' was itself a statement disapproving the rowdiness of lower-class audiences.

Individualizing the Crowd

In the United States, the second half of the nineteenth century was marked by considerable efforts by theater owners and managers, and by the law, to restrict and contain audiences to prevent them from becoming mobs. The re-conceptualization of audiences as dangerous and unruly crowds threatening rational democratic or aesthetic discourse justified efforts to contain such audiences. Audience sovereignty was no longer acknowledged by managers and constables. Through the second half of the century, managers and directors imposed a new definition of audience behavior through a variety of changes. Among these were alterations in legal discourse, in the physical arrangement of the theater, and in the style of drama and acting.[7]

Legal discourse redefined audience rights. Albert Brackett, author of the standard text on theater law, summed up the development of theater law through the nineteenth century by concluding that 'The manager has full right to insist that his patrons behave in an orderly manner ... This requires propriety of deportment and silence when the play is in progress.'[8] Another standard legal text, *Bishop's Criminal Law*, citing nineteenth-century criminal cases, stated that theater audiences had no right to disturb a performance and that planning to hiss in unison constituted criminal conspiracy. Hissing and applauding was acceptable only if each individual spontaneously chose to do so.[9] These statements abrogated the old rights of audience sovereignty to direct the performance and required audiences to act as individuals rather than a crowd.

Managers made changes in theaters that not only physically restricted audiences' ability to act as crowds but also symbolically expressed the expectation that they should act as individuals. Previously the theater pit, which we now call the orchestra, was less expensive and had benches that could be picked up and moved about. More people could be crowded into the pit; and the benches could contribute to disturbances. In the second half of the nineteenth century, the pit was redesigned as the orchestra. Loose benches were replaced by single seats, ordered in rows and bolted to the floor. The shift from multi-seat benches to single seats symbolized the redefinition of audiences from crowds to individuals. Bolting made it clear that each patron was confined to a fixed space with clear boundaries between them and their neighbors, avoiding the body contact that crowd psychologists of the time believed was conducive to crowd action.

The installation of electric lights enabled managers to darken the theater while lighting the stage, making it difficult to see your neighbor, and harder to ignore the stage. Previously, candles and gas lights remained on during performances, allowing audience members to observe and communicate with each other. Darkening of lights still to this day is used as a clear message that the audience should cease conversing and silently watch the stage. New seating and lighting 'disciplined' the audience both structurally and symbolically.

This effect of darkness was complemented by the new tradition of dramatic realism and its new style of acting and staging at legitimate drama theaters. The stage was withdrawn behind the proscenium arch, which became an invisible 'fourth wall' separating the audience but allowing them to witness events portrayed. The curtain closed or opened this window. Actors no longer came to the fore of the stage to give monologues. To look at the audience, let alone talk to them, would destroy the illusion of reality. They remained 'in role,' speaking only to other actors and ignoring the audience. This new dramatic style stated to the audience that they were to see but not be heard.

These changes redefined the manner in which the audience was conceived or constructed from a unified crowd into a mass of separate individuals 'spell-bound in darkness,' as moviegoing itself would also be described For the first time, audiences were expected to be silent, isolated witnesses in theaters, instead of members of a large crowd. A few writers even began to wonder publicly what docile people legitimate theater audiences had become. An editorial in *Every Saturday* bemoaned: 'woe befall the man who had the frankness to signal his displeasure in any other manner than by leaving the house' and then described his experience at a very poor performance in a New York theater. One man of the twelve hundred in the audience hissed mildly and was ejected by a policeman, while the rest 'tamely submitted to the insult' of the performance. 'What mild creatures we are when sitting at a play!' he wrote, 'with what pitiful patience we submit to the long-drawn-out stupidity of thin melodrama.'[10]

Not all audiences, of course, complied. Whole sectors of cheap entertainment continued to allow or even encourage active audiences who hissed and hoorayed. Vaudeville, especially cheap vaudeville, thrived on dialogue between audiences and performers. But, even here, managers planned to direct audiences responses, not to allow them autonomy.[11]

Spellbound in Darkness

Darkness and the fourth wall were not stylistic choices but technological necessities of motion pictures. Movies removed a strong stimulus for audiences acting as a crowd, since there were no live actors whose performance they could alter, even though in the silent era, some audiences still demanded that projectionists and pianists change their performance. At the same time, movies substituted a realism that might draw viewers into the movie and away from their theater mates. This appeared to cement the transformation of audiences from crowds to individuals. Like dramatic realism, narrative movies also placed the audience in the role of furtive spectators, peeping through the camera, with the screen as a fourth wall allowing them to watch but excluding them from the events depicted.

In the nickelodeon era, writers also briefly promoted an image of immigrant audiences as crowds using the storefront movie houses. The loosely arranged chairs not bolted to the floor were reminiscent of the old days of theater. Patrons packed together as in the old theater pit. For a brief time magazine articles for the well-to-do about the early movie house were part of a much larger 'reformer' or 'slumming' literature that included works by Dreiser, James and other novelists, describing the teeming masses of great cities in the era of the great wave of immigration. These articles sketching the inside of urban nickelodeons uniformly attributed moviegoing to the lower classes, and especially to immigrants. They described, however, a friendly group, not the menacing crowd described by French intellectual Gustave Le Bon in his classic text *The Crowd* (1898). Writers commonly referred to these neighborhood nickelodeons as social clubs. John Collier of the New York People's Institute, indeed, called them 'family theaters,' full of women and children, rather than places of dangerous crowds. In a deeply sympathetic sketch, wealthy reformer Mary Heaton Vorse described every woman as having 'a baby in her arms and at least two clinging to her skirts ... A baby seems as much a matter of course.' In Sherman Kingsley's account, 'Father and mother, the baby, the older children, the grand parents—all were there.' While the recurring mention of mothers with many children may have invoked a common fear among upper-class conservatives that they were being overrun not only by migration but also procreation, it also provided an assurance that these were not dangerous crowds, but vulnerable people.[12]

Picturing Weak Individuals

Through the twentieth century a variety of stories accumulated about audiences as weak individuals easily swayed by media messages. Cultural critics, social reformers and political conservatives charged that media led audiences to crime and violence, copycat behavior, addiction, fanatical obsession, aesthetic degradation, civic disintegration, and also made them succumb more easily to propaganda. These tales of audiences flourished especially after the introduction of television and the rise of effects research as the dominant paradigm in both public and scholarly debate on audiences. Such stories began in the early days of movies and quickly became the central theme of public debate about movies.

Stories about movie audiences emphasized the spellbinding capability of motion pictures to exert a dangerous influence on the minds and behavior of film-goers. The idea of being spellbound was part of the crowd psychology of the time that was widely held among academics and elites ranging in political convictions from Progressives to conservatives.[13] This theory was the bridge for the intellectual redefinition of audiences from bad crowds to weak individuals, since it was based on a psychological mechanism of individual susceptibility to suggestion. At the heart of crowd psychology was the concept that people in crowds were more prone to suggestion, to being stirred up emotionally by a demagogue and then turning into rash and violent mobs. The theory of suggestibility was borrowed from widespread nineteenth-century theories of means to control the minds of others, especially hypnotism. These ideas were also linked to the corollary belief that subordinate groups were particularly susceptible to such mind controls.[14] Crowd psychology gained popularity among intellectuals and elites in Europe in the 1880s and 1890s, and was soon imported into the U.S. by some of the most prominent psychologists and social scientists of the day.

The most influential exponent of this theory was French sociologist Gustave Le Bon. In *The Crowd*, Le Bon argued that the primary characteristic of crowds is that individuals surrender their independent thinking through a process of 'emotional contagion.' Crowd leaders implant suggestions through the emotional intensity of their exhortations. The suggestion 'implants itself immediately by a process of [emotional] contagion in the brains of all assembled.' According to Le Bon, emotion bypasses reason. Le Bon claimed that the impulsiveness and emotionality that cause suggestion, 'are almost always observed in beings belonging to inferior forms of evolution—women, savages and children,' and that a nation was less susceptible when the 'spirit of the race' was strong in the upper class.[15]

Many progressive reformers expressed their belief in the powerful suggestibility of movies which they hoped to harness to uplift the masses. The terms 'spellbound,' 'implant' and 'mesmerize' were sprinkled through articles on the effects of movies. More broadly, social reformer Jane Addams called cheap theater the 'house of dreams', a powerful inducement to fantasies.[16]

One recurring story was that movies depicting crime and sex made deep impressions on teenagers and led them into juvenile delinquency. Most of this discourse focused on working-class youth as those most susceptible to this influence. Boys would engage in drinking, drugs and driving as well as minor crimes. Girls would be persuaded to engage in sex and ruin their reputations and chances for respectable marriage. Such stories were presented so often about nickelodeon movies as to suggest they were an urban myth rather than facts.[17] These claims argued that crimes were copied from movies. Allegedly unstable, highly suggestible people saw things in movies that suggested to them the idea of imitating it themselves.

Soon professors entered the discourse. George Elliot Howard, soon to be president of the American Sociological Society, writing in the *American Journal of Sociology*, used crowd psychology in order to claim audiences are very suggestible. He went on to allege that audiences of the lower sorts were even more so: children, women, striking workers more than burghers, the ignorant more than the cultured, Italians, Slavs and Irish more than Dutch, German or English. Howard proposed, therefore, to use movies as a means of suggesting the proper things to the lower sorts.[18]

Harvard psychologist Hugo Münsterberg's *The Photoplay* (1916), also argued that movies implanted ideas. Münsterberg was an important figure in the formation of American psychology at the turn of the century and a founding member of the American Psychological Association. He said about movies that 'The intensity with which the plays take hold of the audience cannot remain without social effects ... the mind is so completely given up to the moving pictures.' Münsterberg was familiar with theories of crowd psychology, as he was advisor to Boris Sidis, a Russian émigré student at Harvard, whose thesis, *The Psychology of Suggestion*, had become the single most important book in the U.S. on the subject, when it had been published in 1898.[19]

Like many of these writers, Münsterberg considered women, lower classes and certain races to be more susceptible. He held strong opinions about the inferiority of women and was an outspoken opponent of suffrage. He advocated the superiority of Anglo-Saxons and Germans, to whom he credited the creation and protection of 'civilization.' He referred to 'the millions ... daily under the spell' and exhorted reformers to use film for the 'aesthetic cultivation' of 'the masses,' emphasizing that he considered the lower classes to be the group most vulnerable to influence from the movies.[20]

Such claims continued into the 1920s. In 1921, psychologist A.T. Poffenberger of Columbia University expressed the belief that young people and adults of low mentality were led to crime by movies. In 1928 sociologist E.A. Ross, renowned for his writings on crowd psychology and social control, claimed that movies 'stirred the sex instincts into life years sooner than used to be the case with boys and girls from good homes,' suggesting the contamination of higher-class children by this low-class entertainment. Also in the 1920s University of Chicago sociologist Ernest Burgess claimed that movies countered the good influence of home, church and school.[21] In 1930, *Christian Century* published a series of five articles by Dr. Fred Eastman, religious educator and playwright, on the 'menace of the movies,' especially to youth who lived in 'congested areas,' i.e. poor neighborhoods.[22] Consistently through the silent movie era, these writers identified working-class teenagers, adults and Southern and Eastern European immigrants as especially susceptible to movies' spellbinding effects.

In 1933, the Payne Fund, a private foundation, published *Motion Pictures and Youth*, eight volumes of studies by prominent psychologists and sociologists that examined the relationship between movies and teen-age delinquency, plus a research summary volume as well as a popularized summary.[23] This was by far the most ambitious investigation into film effects on moviegoers. It was inspired by a desire to convince Americans of the power of movies over children, so they would support censorship. While studies by University of Chicago sociologist Herbert Blumer and his graduate students Philip Hauser and Frederick Thrasher tended to confirm the arousal of teenagers and claim movies encouraged delinquency, Louis Thurstone and Ruth Peterson, Frank Shuttleworth and Mark May, William Dysinger and Christian Ruckmick concluded that movies had varied effects and were capable even at times of countering delinquent tendencies. But the popular summary by Henry Forman ignored such equivocations—and evidence for the positive impact of motion pictures—in order to emphasize movies' negative influence on youth.[24] In his two Payne studies, Herbert Blumer reaffirmed the conception of movies mesmerizing audiences when he framed his reports around his concept of 'emotional possession,' which he described as one in which

> the individual identifies himself so thoroughly with the plot or loses himself so much in the picture that he is carried away from the usual trend of conduct [and] even his efforts to rid himself of it by reasoning with himself may prove of little avail.[25]

Blumer also reaffirmed the idea that the influence of motion pictures 'is less in the cultured classes' and more 'in disorganized city areas,' a euphemism for the urban poor.[26]

Ironically, although Blumer and the other sociologists working on the Payne studies were part of the University of Chicago department renowned for its ethnographic approach that emphasized community and group subcultures, all of their studies, as well as those of the psychologists, methodologically treated the movie audience as individually affected by the movies with almost no investigation into the influence from their friends or the rest of the audience watching with them.[27] Thus, from the initial conception of their research the Payne studies excluded from consideration the concept of the audience as a crowd or community, and concentrated almost exclusively on the audience as isolated individuals focused on the movie. They retained the mechanism of suggestibility but discarded the idea of the crowd, producing a picture of weak individuals vulnerable to the spellbinding influence of movies.

After the Payne Fund studies were published, public debate about movies receded. Part of the reason for this may have been that their major proponent, Reverend William Short, died shortly after publication. But policy within the industry also changed with the institution of the Production Code Administration in 1934. The Production Code of 1930 itself had discouraged much of what reformers such as Short disapproved, but the work of the PCA after 1934 also greatly reduced the controversial treatment of issues such as, for example, crime. In the 1950s, however, a moral panic again arose about the effects of movies. A new movie genre depicting rebellious teen-agers, including *The Wild One*, *Blackboard Jungle* and *Rebel Without a Cause*, was blamed for what was perceived as a rise in juvenile delinquency. The rise of a teen market served by drive-in movies and movies about teenagers contributed to debates about what movies were doing to teens. This was part of what James Gilbert called a 'cycle of outrage'

301

that also targeted comic books, and rock'n'roll. Trade books by psychiatrists and journalists and Senate hearings all fed the flames of fear about movies and other media corrupting youth. As Gilbert phrased it, echoing the language of turn of the century crowd psychology, 'the popular metaphor was one of contagion, contamination and infection.' Again, lower classes were implicated. This time, according to Gilbert, the discourse expressed fears that middle-class teens would be infected by the delinquent behavior of working-class youths represented in the movies.[28]

Such beliefs about individuals mesmerized and deeply influenced by movies have continued into more recent years, in news reports offering explanations of juvenile crimes and deaths. In the 1980s, incidents of teenagers lying in the road while cars passed over them were claimed to be copycat cases inspired by a movie in which a character did this. School shootings of the 1990s were sometimes attributed to the influence of movies and video games. A report on a trend in the new millennium of turning action movies into video games that producers hope consumers will want to play again and again conjures up images of the isolated spellbound loner, crazed by repeated viewing, who goes out and kills someone.[29]

Two other tropes duplicate this conception of audiences as spellbound individuals, but—in contrast to the focus on children by much of the discourse on suggestibility—concentrate more on adults. Children and even teens are assumed to be vulnerable, but suggestible *adults* clearly require some explanation. Adults who are heavily influenced by movies are labeled 'fans' or 'addicts' and presumed to be neurotic. Addiction discourses often consider the weak will of the addicted person as the central mechanism explaining why particular individuals are susceptible, just as suggestibility was presumed to depend on the weak will of some individuals. Like suggestibility, addiction is attributed to presumed weak-willed groups, particularly subordinate races, who are understood to be too weak to resist their compulsion to indulge in their addiction.[30]

Movies have seldom been described as addictive, but the obsession of the fan, short for 'fanatic,' is closely related to the compulsiveness of the addict. The intense attachments of fans to movies and stars was individualized and psychologized by claiming that fans were 'drugged' by movies, and comments about the hysterical movie fan proliferated in the 1920s and 1930s. Samantha Barbas notes that the image of the fan as an obsessed fanatic became so strong that many people made a point of dissociating themselves from that label. Movie fans were presumed to be immature or childlike, uneducated and unintelligent. It needed not be said that they were female, since fan and female were considered synonymous. A censorship advocate and doctor claimed that many adult movie fans possessed the 'mental age of an eleven year old.' The fan was likewise understood to be deluded about the realism of the movies, an image that was also used to deride woman soap opera fans. In 1939 Margaret Thorp characterized fans as gullible and cited a claim that their letters indicate a very limited vocabulary. Another writer, Carl Cotter, deduced from the simple writing of fan magazines that fans must be uneducated and naïve.[31]

In recent years, some fans of 'cult movies' have developed their own communities and even acted in some ways like publics to lobby the movie industry, but images of fans as communities have not been included in the dominant discourses about them.[32] When mentioned, they are instead used to confirm the psychopathology of fans, for example in news coverage of fan conventions that focus on fans dressed in bizarre costumes.

In these discourses, the predominant image is of isolated individuals with eyes fixed on the screen. Representations of different, active movie audiences were buried in infrequent newspaper reports of children misbehaving in neighborhood theaters, and were overshadowed by the image of individualized viewers.

Publics, Fans and Addictions

Jane Gaines' discussion of political mimesis suggests an underlying similarity between the discourses on the audience as crowd and as isolated individuals. Gaines discusses the intent of the 'radical documentary' to arouse the audience to collective action, to 'kick and yell' and carry on the struggle even if it means 'fighting back in physical ways that exceed restrained public demonstrations of protest.'[33] She is referring to a movie's appeal to the senses and emotion rather than reason: the movie as demagogue, as Le Bon might have presented it.

Gaines compares this response to those noted by Linda Williams: that horror films make you scream, melodrama makes you cry, and pornography makes you orgasm. Williams notes that these movies cause in spectators an 'almost involuntary' bodily response.[34] In each of these non-political instances, audiences are isolated individuals, focused on the bodily convulsions on-screen and absorbed in their own individual bodily spasms. Their responses, with the possible exception of the screams, are private and do not unite them as a crowd.

Although Williams describes audiences acting as individuals, and Gaines describes audiences acting collectively, both actions are induced by the same seemingly 'involuntary' visceral reaction to movies. Le Bon described individuals transformed into crowds by a demagogue; the discourses on audiences described individuals transformed by movies, but not into crowds. They remain individuated. Discourses on both crowds and isolated individuals thus begin with some central focus that each member of the audience attends to.[35] Both the dangerous crowd and the weak-willed individual are cast as *undesirable* audiences.

The significance of this is more evident as we notice that those who are 'bad' or weak-willed are almost always peoples who are subordinate groups. Discourses on audiences as crowd or individual consistently assert that those of 'lower' class, race, and gender are more susceptible to suggestion, especially from visual media such as movies.

Crowds, Publics and Individuals

What possibility lies between the bad crowd and the weak individual audiences? In the discourses I have discussed, implicitly or explicitly, the preferred bourgeois audience is a Habermasian 'public,' active and thoughtful but not unruly and riotous. Audiences as publics are imagined with bourgeois characteristics. They are intellectually, aesthetically, socially and politically 'cultivated.' They engage the entertainment in all these dimensions; and they employ the entertainment to engage each other in all these dimensions. They watch and think about the movie individually, come to their own conclusions, and then respond as a group joined by their individually derived opinions.

Discourses on audiences both as crowds and as individuals agree that a 'good' audience response is to act as a bourgeois public. Film scholar Miriam Hansen was perhaps the first to introduce the concept of the movie audience as a public rather than a crowd, using the Habermasian ideas of public sphere.[36] Habermas described the bourgeois public sphere as practices of public discussion in a social space where all participants were treated as equals, regardless of their status outside that space. This was thought critical to the European transition from aristocracy to democracy. He cited the English coffee house and the French salon as examples.[37]

Hansen sees in the sociality of the nickelodeon a public sphere of the working class and women that was autonomous from supervision by authorities and higher classes. Nickelodeons are, however, also limited as the ideal public space, since there is scant evidence of political discussion in this space and little evidence of diverse social statuses present. Indeed, it was the homogeneity of audiences that encouraged their sociability, and formed them as a community more than a public. In fact, a public sphere may simply be a utopian ideal. The closest that American theater audiences came to such a public sphere was in the Early Republic when Federalists and Jeffersonians 'debated' in theaters. These incidents were, however, more like shouting matches and sometimes erupted into riots. They were, in other words, more the actions of crowds than of publics. Thus, since these are the discursive terms in which their *behavior* has always been couched, it seems more consistent with the history of audiences to use the concept of crowd rather than public.[38]

In the cases of both the nineteenth-century crowd and twentieth-century individualized audiences, concern has centered on the failure of lower classes to engage in and adhere to the rules of debate and discourse within the framework of a bourgeois public sphere. Such a sphere presumed a discourse based upon the bourgeois culture of reading and education, and inevitably put lower classes at a disadvantage. Lower classes historically have been more effective as collectives rather than as individuals. Crowds, not publics, and streets, not salons were their preferred political implements.

Nineteenth-century audiences, typically the lower class segments of audiences or audiences in theaters catering to lower classes, did not abide by the decorum of public sphere debate. Instead they exercised power as a crowd. The rights of audience sovereignty vigorously exercised in the Early Republic and the Jacksonian era were rights to collective action, to command musicians and performers to perform favorite selections, to demand accounting from performers and managers by calling them before the curtain. To some degree, these practices survived in cheap theaters until their demise at the hand of movies in the early decades of the twentieth century.[39]

The dominant discourse therefore increasingly called for the containment, rather than the inclusion, of these crowds. Managers and metropolitan police embarked on a program of repression of such crowd actions. Courts seem to have upheld audience rights only when behaviors such as widespread hissing could be construed as an opinion expressed by a public.[40]

On the other hand, audiences of the twentieth century were believed to be debilitated by mass media such as movies, and thus disabled from the prospect of participation in the bourgeois public sphere Mass culture critics blamed media for undermining the enculturation of the masses into the bourgeois culture that is the prerequisite to participation in the public sphere. At first, cultural uplifters hoped that movies, radio and television would be their tools. Progressive reformers hoped that movies would teach lessons of Americanism to low income immigrants. Promoters of high culture, such as Walter Damrosch, believed that radio would make America a nation of Beethoven fans. Educators thought television would bring the world into the home of every child and make him well informed. None of these hopes was realized, as profit outbid culture for media use.

Instead, lower classes and other subordinate groups have been cast as the weak audience that bourgeois critics fear are undermining democracy by consuming too much of the wrong kind of media and neglecting civic participation, choosing consumption over citizenry.[41] The discourses defining subordinate groups as 'bad' audiences disenfranchise them by de-legitimating their expression and justifying efforts to limit or control it.[42] Until they are seen to be acting like a bourgeois public in using movies and other media, they continue to be characterized as endangering themselves and democracy in their alleged habits as audiences.

'Healthy Films from America'

The Emergence of a Catholic Film Mass Movement in Belgium and the Realm of Hollywood, 1928–1939

Daniel Biltereyst

Recreation, in its manifold varieties, has become a necessity for people who work under the fatiguing conditions of modern industry, but it must be worthy of the rational nature of man and therefore must be morally healthy.

(Pope Pius XI, 29 June 1936)[1]

T HIS quotation from Pope Pius XI's Encyclical Letter on the motion pictures, *Vigilanti Cura*, exemplifies the shifting attitude of the Catholic Church towards cinema in the 1930s. While cinema had long been considered an immoral medium and a major force of secularisation, now the highest Vatican authority openly praised the American Legion of Decency's successful efforts at improving the morality in Hollywood movies. The 1936 papal encyclical was even more determined than ever to take the offensive in encouraging Catholic film movements in other countries to increase their initiatives against 'morally unhealthy' movies.

The general drift of argument in the papal letter gave the impression that the centre of the Catholic 'moral crusade' lay in the US, an impression likely to be corroborated by the recent scholarly attention given to the role played by the Legion of Decency and individual American Catholic figures in changing the Production Code, and with it the nature of American movies.[2] This impression is, however, misleading. In fact, in many European countries where Catholicism had a major influence on society, local religious organisations had been actively trying to shape the medium for a long time.[3] In 1928, many of these Catholic film organisations were brought together in an international network, the *Office Catholique International du Cinématographe* (OCIC), while during the first half of the 1930s some local European Catholic organisations engaged in an impressive range of activities intended to influence film consumption, from production, distribution and exhibition to initiatives to create a film propaganda machinery, film news agencies, film magazines, film classification or censorship boards, and wider efforts to initiate a film mass movement.[4]

In Belgium, the Church and local Catholic film organisations succeeded in increasing pressure on various levels of the wider film culture. From the end of the 1920s onwards, the well-organised Belgian Catholic film movement grew into a forceful player on the national film scene, while trying to spread its influence on a wider, international level. Through the well-oiled information and propaganda machinery of the Brussels OCIC headquarters, and through the personal engagements of some of its leaders, Belgian Catholics succeeded in influencing Vatican views on what was commonly called the 'film problem.'[5] As John Trumpbour has argued, the Belgian Catholic film movement 'played a special role on the international plane, entrusted by the Vatican with coordination of national Catholic film movements.'[6] Trumpbour even suggests that:

> In the Catholic Church's international strategy on film, Belgium at times played a more central role than the U.S. Legion of Decency. While Pope Pius XI in his Encyclical of 1936 (*Vigilanti cura*) regarded the Legion of Decency as the national model for Catholics, the Belgian church stood out as the international command-and-control center of the movement by heading the Office Catholique International du Cinéma ... Organizing international conferences and fostering Catholic ownership and entrepeneurship in the exhibition sector, the OCIC built a films movement well in advance of the Legion of Decency and indeed served to inspire its American cadres.[7]

Much scholarly work has still to be done on the history of OCIC as well as on the strategies of national Catholic film movements in Europe.[8] This chapter, which is part of a larger research project on the history of official and Catholic film censorship in Belgium, examines Belgian Catholics' shifting attitude towards 'immoral' or 'unhealthy' films during their crucial period of growth and influence on the film market.[9] From the end of the 1920s until the Second World War, Belgian Catholics developed a clear strategy in promoting particular types of movies while heavily boycotting others. Given the dominance of American movies on the Belgian market ever since World War I, the main focus here is on the Catholic film movement's attitude towards American cinema throughout the 1930s. Through an analysis of pamphlets, reviews, and other writings from the Catholic Film Action, it will be shown how the initially negative image of Hollywood and its products gradually changed into a more positive one, distinct from the perception of some European pictures as controversial and many French pictures as immoral.

Belgian Film Market, Hollywood Hegemony and the Catholic Film Action during the Interwar Period

Since Belgium achieved independence from the Netherlands in 1830, the Church and various local Catholic organisations played a significant role in its political, economic, educational and cultural life. Probably more than in any other Western European country, the Church succeeded in developing a network of influential institutions ranging from a dominant political party, press, schools, hospitals and trade unions to youth, women's and other organisations aimed at leisure and cultural development. After World War I devastated the country, social change was intensified under the banner of modernity.[10] Universal male suffrage brought the Socialist party to government, and this growing democratisation was accompanied by mass production, industrialisation and rapid urbanisation, so that by the 1930s more than half of the Belgian population lived in major cities. These changes also brought new forms of urban cultural production and consumption—including the growth of music halls, fairs and—above all—cinema. The Church, however, viewed much of this change as threatening to their traditional worldview.

Before World War I, Brussels had already been an important centre for film trade, and distribution and exhibition activities grew further after the War.[11] International film trade overviews reported that Belgians were heavy film consumers,[12] and throughout the interwar period the small Kingdom was celebrated by the big international production centers as one of the most liberal film markets in Europe.[13] American sources reported Belgium to be a market with "no agitation" against Hollywood and no restrictions against the import of American movies. The Motion Picture Producers and Distributors of America, Inc. (MPPDA) regarded it as a free trade zone, since it placed few obstacles in the way of Hollywood's market dominance.[14] In addition to the strong position occupied by the distribution arms of American and German corporations, Belgium was seen as a 'natural' extension of the French film market. Initially, the film market was dominated by Pathé and Gaumont, but other French corporations such as Aubert, Franco-Film and Osso also had a share of the Belgian distribution and exhibition market. The gravitational force of French production also pulled Belgian creative personnel such as Armand du Plessy, Jacques Feyder, Charles Spaak or Fernand Gravey across the border. The openness of the small Belgian film market was increased by the lack of any serious state intervention to stimulate local production or quota regulations diminishing the inflow from abroad. As a result, Belgium probably showed a greater cross-section of international film output with fewer policy restrictions than anywhere else in Europe.

After 1918, American distribution corporations entered the Belgian market, opening branch offices of their Parisian distribution companies in Brussels.[15] By 1929, most American majors had a Belgian subsidiary.[16] Little information about the majors' market share is available, but only German and French movies seemed to be able to withstand Hollywood's hegemony in the interwar period. A Commerce Report by Leigh W. Hunt on the Belgian film market in 1923–24 claimed that 'of the films shown in Belgium probably 60 to 70 per cent are American,' adding that these 'generally come into Belgium through France, Germany, or England.'[17] At the end of the 1920s, this percentage had grown to 80 per cent, with the remaining market share divided between mainly French and German movies.[18] The country's cultural and language divisions meant that there were significant variations in the popularity of different national products, however. The appeal of American movies was much stronger in the northern, Dutch-language part of the country (Flanders), where Hollywood productions accounted for more than 80 per cent of the market. In the bilingual Brussels market and the French-speaking southern part of the Kingdom (Wallonia), however, French movies were much more popular, and after the introduction of sound, French productions increased their market share there to more than 50 per cent[19] This internal division of film taste and consumption patterns continued until the end of the 1930s, when in the French-speaking parts American movies were dubbed and only accounted for 30–40 per cent.[20]

At the height of cinema's popularity during the interwar period, the Church's moral and political power also reached its apex, especially in Flanders and on the countryside. In major cities and in the French-speaking parts of the country, however, its power position was increasingly opposed by Socialist and (to a much lesser degree) liberal organisations. For the

Church and many Catholic leaders, the commercial exploitation of cinema epitomized the immorality of modern urban entertainment. The Church's institutional attitude remained one of aversion to what in 1929 was still identified as one of the major 'modern diseases.'[21] Before World War I there had nevertheless been some local initiatives to integrate movies into various Catholic activities and to build a network of Catholic cinemas, often under the leadership of local priests.[22] These initiatives continued after the war, and in 1920 a Catholic film distribution company, Brabo-Films, specialising in 'morally healthy' films aimed at both parochial and commercial cinemas, was established. Brabo was also active in building film projectors and other hardware, but as the Dominican Felix Morlion, one of the leaders of the Catholic film movement, wrote later, the Church did not invest in cinema nearly as effectively as it had done in its programmes of building Catholic schools, hospitals and newspapers.[23]

At the end of the 1920s, as Brabo-Films started to break into the commercial film distribution sector, this began to change. In 1928, the Church decided to bring all local film initiatives and Catholic cinemas together under the umbrella of the *Katholieke Film Centrale* (KFC, or in French *Centrale Catholique du Cinéma*).[24] The KFC's main purpose was to act as an 'intermediary between the many pagan distribution companies and the growing number of Catholic cinemas.'[25] Under the leadership of a small group of clergymen, openly supported by the highest Belgian Church leaders, new initiatives were developed.[26] In 1930, a film educational service was launched, and in 1931 Brabo-Films was dissolved and transformed into a more forceful film distribution company (Filmavox). Filmavox 'disguised' itself as an independent commercial company amongst others, successfully trying to put more pressure upon commercial exhibition and distribution.

In 1931, a Catholic film documentation and information service was created: *Dokumentatie der Cinematographische Pers* (DOCIP) in Dutch, *Documentation Cinématographique de la Presse* in French. DOCIP soon grew into an important films news agency and a propaganda instrument for the whole movement, not only by creating its own film magazine (*Filmliga* in Dutch, *Cran* in French) but more importantly by trying to convince Catholic radio and press outlets to publish their film articles. This strategy proved very successful, and DOCIP journalists soon came to dominate the film pages of some of the most popular and elite Catholic newspapers of the country, such as *De Standaard*.[27] By 1937, the Catholic film movement played a major role in film criticism in the Belgian newspaper and magazine market.[28] DOCIP played a major role as a Catholic moral guardian, and developed an international dimension after OCIC established its headquarters in Brussels.[29]

A key instrument in this perspective was another Catholic film initiative: in 1931 the Katholieke Filmkeurraad (KFK)—a Catholic Film Classification/Censorship Board—was founded, specializing in the moral and aesthetic evaluation of all films issued in Belgium.[30] Similar to what happened in France and some other countries where Catholic film 'censorship' was organized, the KFK awarded movies a rating, from a positive 1 ('for all') to a negative 5 ('dangerous') and 6 ('to be avoided'). According to an internal guideline for Catholic censors, pictures with a 6-rate identified movies 'whose basic thesis is bad' from a moral, religious and social political perspective, or which could lead to 'debauchery,' and could be 'compared to "books on the Index."'[31] The Catholic censorship board's decisions (usually lists of accepted movies and 'black lists') were widely publicized through DOCIP articles as well as by posters displayed in church portals, parochial halls and leaflets distributed by other Catholic organizations.[32]

In 1932, other initiatives were launched by Father Felix Morlion, who turned out to be a formidable propagandist and organizer, with growing links to the highest Vatican authorities.[33] Morlion dreamed of building a

15.1   Father Felix Morlion (1904–1987) [in the middle] photographed later in Rome. Morlion was a skilled Catholic propagandist against modern mass media. Source: DOCIP, Brussels.

mass organization as well as of influencing what was considered the heart of the problem: film production. Between 1932 and 1934, leaders of the Belgian Catholic film movement frequently wrote of the need to move beyond the activities of the range of action from education, information and distribution to engage in production and establish a mass movement. In 1932, Morlion argued that while it was important to influence censorship and the programming schedules of commercial cinemas, 'the only sound solution to the film problem' was to 'guide film production itself into a healthy direction, and increase the proportion of good movies.'[34] In a similar vein, Canon Brohée wrote in 1933 that 'the solution is in the production and not elsewhere,'[35] a statement which was supported by Cardinal Pacelli's April 1934 Letter to OCIC's president.[36] After some local initiatives, however, the Belgian Catholics were soon sobered up by the difficulties of film production in a small country.[37]

The other project of building a mass film movement was more successful, however. Also in 1932, Morlion created the Catholic Film Legion (*Katholieke Film Liga*, or KFL),[38] which tried to make use of the many local Catholic youth, women's, men's and workers' organizations in order to make people more sensitive to the need for 'good movies.'[39] The KFL recruited several thousand members to spread the censorship board's decisions and DOCIP's film lists and leaflets, and in some cases to organize local protests against film theaters showing 'immoral movies.'[40] This overview indicates that by July 1932, when an international film congress was organized in Brussels, a strong Belgian Catholic film movement was in place. At this congress, Cardinal van Roey openly declared that the Belgian Episcopate recognized the significance of the movement. In June 1933, finally, the wide range of Church activities over movies were coordinated under the umbrella of Catholic Film Action (in Dutch: *Katholieke Film Actie*, or KFA, in French: *Centre Catholique d'Action Cinématographique*, or CCAC).[41]

The Belgian Catholics' promptness of action also had an international dimension, which gained attention from higher Church authorities and led to OCIC's move to Brussels and the appointment of the Belgian KFA leader, Canon Brohée, to the presidency of the international Catholic film organization in 1933.[42] Compared to the Catholic film movements in most other European countries, the Belgian KFA had succeeded in rapidly establishing an integrated approach to the cinema 'problem' which included a distribution company (Brabo/Filmavox), an exhibition network of parochial cinemas through KFC, educational activities, a film classification/censorship board (KFK), press and wider media actions, a film information apparatus (DOCIP), a mass movement (KFL). Only its initiatives in the field of film production produced disappointing results.[43]

313

This active and aggressive attitude towards the 'film problem' might appear exceptional, but its practical 'pastoral' approach embodied the idea of Catholic Action, which itself represented a wider shift of attitude towards modernity and urban culture among Catholic Church leaders in Belgium and elsewhere in the world. Belgian Catholic Action in the field of cinema was paralleled in other fields such as the press, which had a quite similar structure of censorship, information and mass mobilization. Responding to the threat of modernism, Pope Pius XI's idea of Catholic Action carried the spirit of a Catholic 'reconquista,' capturing people in their everyday activities, including cinema. In Belgium, where Catholicism had great influence over a huge majority of the population, Catholic Action stood for the idea of a moral revival. Especially after the social and economic crisis at the end of the 1920s, what had begun as a rejection of pagan modernity became a militant, more engaged attitude that evolved together with a growing discourse of conservative morality. The whole movement was built upon a clear hierarchy: clergymen organized concrete local actions, mobilizing laymen as militant soldiers, and tried to expand the Catholic network of organizations. Where the media—and cinema in particular—had previously been seen as a dangerous school for crime, socialism and immorality, the new more aggressive campaign welcomed these modern inventions as potentially a formidable tool in a new campaign of 're-christianization.'[44] This new attitude, which was translated into martial terms such as a Catholic film 'offensive,' 'action' and 'guidance,' would reach its peak of momentum with the campaign of the American Legion of Decency to promote movie morality.

Vaudevilles, Sex-appeal and the Turning Tide of Hollywood

In 1934 and 1935, the Legion of Decency's successful activities in the U.S. were regularly reported in the film pages of Belgian Catholic newspapers. In KFA publications, leaflets, letters and other internal documents, there was great enthusiasm for their American counterparts' success in turning the tide in Hollywood. Already in 1933, leaders of the Belgian KFA referred to American Catholic initiatives, such as those by the National Council of Catholic Women.[45] But, mainly from July 1934 onwards, Belgian Catholic film leaders openly supported the success of the Legion in influencing Hollywood. In several texts, including an undated internal report about the growth and strategies of the Legion of Decency, Belgian Catholics saw both clear parallels and differences between the American and European Catholic actions over film. On the one hand, 'the organization of the Catholic film action in America can be fully compared with our purposes in Europe,' while the success of this 'most powerful action group ... should be highly instructive for us.'[46] In another undated internal document, Father Morlion praised the 'clear purposes ... rapid action ... and powerful leadership' of the American Catholics' 'film offensive,' which had led to 'major victories in less than four months time.' In the same document, however, Morlion criticized the Legion's structural problems and short term strategies:

> While the protests and the general boycott cannot last for a long time, America will soon have to organize its own censorship system, documentation and press action. Otherwise the fruit of the victories will soon vanish. Here in Europe we should better start our action in a reversed manner: first we must have a technical basis and then we should risk a major offensive ... In the meantime we should try to prevent (bad) American movies, which no longer have any chance to be screened in America, from coming faster to Europe.[47]

In an August 1934 article in the leading conservative newspaper, *De Standaard*, Morlion referred to a meeting between the Pope and the Catholic film press and tried to interpret the importance of the Legion's breakthrough for the European and international Catholic film movement:

> America has started the battle with great courage and power, but it lacks any technical basis for its own work: an authoritative Catholic censorship board, a documentation and press service. In our country and in a couple of other European nations these organisms do exist, but here we do not have a big mass movement. In some countries they have nothing at all. The time has come ... that we will soon, after so many years of preparation, launch a big Legion[-style] offensive in our country too. We want to repeat in a brutal and patient manner that we, the defenders of decency, faith and humanity, are the potential masters of the game.[48]

The Legion of Decency not only inspired the Belgian Catholics to accelerate their attempts to set up a wider mass movement and to increase their offensive against local theatres and immoral productions. More generally, it also heralded an increasingly positive attitude towards American cinema. Since 1918, American movies had been associated with productions that sought 'to break with morality at large,' and Hollywood escaped none of the prejudices against the dangers of cinema.[49] In numerous articles and pamphlets, Hollywood was associated with paganism:

cinema is born in a pagan environment. Especially the American cinema during the lawless years after the war ... seemed to define evil as its basic theory. Debauchery was glorified. Women who had lost all sense of shame become the ideals of femininity and sincerity. Men with the faintest moral concerns were portrayed as heroes and winners. Dances, images and relationships became ever more suggestive in order to titillate the audience, which was demoralized and depressed by the ongoing crisis.[50]

At the end of the 1920s, when Belgian Catholics faced the film problem in a more structured manner, American cinema was perceived through the binary oppositions of America vs. Europe, industrial vs. art cinema, and immoral/pagan vs. moral/religious movies. In line with debates on growing American hegemony during the second half of the 1920s,[51] some writers opposed European cinema to American commercialism, paganism, and the use of cheap tricks, 'sex appeal' and 'bluff.' In a series of articles published in early 1929 on 'The Flemish Catholics against the Film Problem,' American film production was indicted as 'conservative' and 'rooted in easy and entertaining formulas,' while European film makers were more 'honest in searching for a pure, aesthetic and independent form of cinematography.'[52] In a 1932 pamphlet on the future of cinema, another Dominican concluded that in the U.S. most movies

> work upon the element of 'sex appeal' as the main point of attraction and upon voluptuousness as the main target of life ... Life has become a pure adventure with a pagan materialist spirit: pleasure and making fun as much as we can ... The chances of a comedian in the USA depend upon his potential to stir up a 'civilized' erotic excitement among the audience.[53]

In their criticism, Catholic film writers were extremely sensitive to movies with religious themes, Biblical dramas and films portraying clergymen. Referring to such movies as *Queen of Sheba* (1921), *King of Kings* (1927) and *The Gaucho* (1927), several authors warned that readers should not be deceived by movies with an apparently 'religious feeling or motive.' Many of these films featured 'provocative half-naked women,' while religion was 'represented as one kind of hysteria':

> American film producers are clever in this perspective; but this religious varnish and trick prove that they know nothing about these ceremonies, let alone understand the deeper sense of religion ...

Tragedy becomes a comedy of passion or even a parody ... They once heard about miracles; and they will try to work upon the sensational aspect of it, but then in an American sense: bluff![54]

The theme of Europe vs. America soon became more complicated and less relevant, because, according to KFA writers, German and French studios imitated many themes, strategies and the overall profligacy to be found in American movies.[55] In 1931 and 1932, a new batch of Catholic film writers widened the debate by beginning to write more fully about alternatives to mainstream commercial cinema, and the possibility of a truly Catholic cinema. Earlier conservative Catholic denunciations of Soviet communist cinema changed into a re-examination of the potential of a truly ideological cinema. In several speeches and in an internal document on the dangers of cinema, probably from 1934, Felix Morlion made a distinction between the dangers of communist and industrial capitalist cinema, arguing that while 'communism is of course the public enemy,' Catholics 'need to recognize two major qualities of its production: the courage to put everything in service of an idea as well as the denunciation of sex-appeal and other cheap means in order to attract audience attention'[56] The openly ideological nature of communist cinema, and its critique of cheap capitalist film techniques were enough to devote great attention to communist cinema in the first half of the 1930s.[57] Morlion claimed that capitalist industrial cinema posed 'a greater danger because it disguises its poison,' and was nothing less than 'a great hypocritical enemy,' which 'seems to attack nothing or deny nothing, but finally undermines every conviction.'[58] Referring to both French and American films but specifically citing *The Love Parade* (1929), *King Kong* (1933) and *The Sign of the Cross* (1932), Morlion went on to denounce the influences of this type of industrialist/capitalist cinema as cultivating a 'false romanticism' against the joys and duties of family life, 'the need for strong sensations' and 'eroticism' instead of true love, and 'false mysticism' rather than the deeper sense of true religious faith.[59]

By the time that the Belgian Catholics had constructed a firmer structure for their film movement, American movies were no longer the sole targets.[60] In press articles and a variety of internal documents, the Catholic film movement heavily criticized German *operette-filme* and initiated a crusade against French *vaudevilles*. Many French low-budget movies were put on the black list, dominating the categories of 'dangerous films' (rating 5) and the ultimate 'bad movies to be avoided' (rating 6). In the first years of the censorship board dozens of French B-movies, often light-hearted, quite theatrical comedies with music and songs, filled the black list. Controversial films such as *Arlette et ses Papas* (1934), *Bibi la Purée* (1934), *On a trouvé*

15.2 Lloyd Bacon's *Wonder Bar* (1934) was one of the last American films to receive
a rating of 6 ('to be avoided'). Source: Belgian Film Archive, Brussels.

une femme nue (1934) and *Sexe Faible* (1933) were criticized for not being
serious about 'marital fidelity,' for showing 'complete nudity' and for the
general 'atmosphere of immorality.'[61] In this first batch of censored movies,
a significant number of American movies were also given a rating of 5 or 6,
among them *Wonder Bar* (1934) and *Murder at the Vanities* (1934).

In the following years, however, the censorship board increased its
attack on French cinema, under the banner of a campaign against French

'vaudevillisme.' This was also linked to the fact that, since the first half of the 1930s, sound had reduced Hollywood's market share and increased the appeal of French cinema, especially in the capital and in the Walloon part of the country. In the wake of the Legion of Decency's success, the French Catholic film movement, the *Comité Catholique du Cinéma* (CCC) had started a campaign against the French film industry, but with few concrete results. Their 'anti-vaudeville campaign' in 1934 and 1935 was heavily supported by their Belgian counterparts, who tried in vain to mobilize a wider movement in order to 'encircle the Parisian pagan film industry.'[62] In this particularly vicious campaign, the French film industry was often associated with theories about international conspiracy under Jewish and pagan leadership.[63] In Belgium, this campaign lasted for several years, and in the published black lists based upon the censorships board's decisions, French movies continued to fill the 5 and 6 ratings. In a blacklist for March 1935, more than five out of six movies were French, including many which could be categorized as light-hearted comedy 'vaudevilles.' Other reasons also appear, and in this list of 'films to be avoided' can be found Renoir's *La Chienne* (1931), Allégret's *Lac aux Dames* (1934) and several Parisian Paramount movies (e.g. *Plaisir de Paris*, Gréville, 1932). The list also contained some movies adapted from books on the Church Index, such as *Jocelyn* (Guerlais, 1933, after Lamartine), which was banned by the Church for its objectionable representation of clergymen. The satirical comedy *Rosier de Mme Husson* (Deschamps, 1932), which made Fernandel a star, was boycotted by local Catholic groups. This successful boycott illustrated the power of the Catholic Film Action.[64]

Table 15.1 The Belgian Catholic Censorship Board's evaluation: number of movies by origin on the black list's code 6 ('to avoid')

	French	US	German	Soviet	Czech	total
March/April 1935	54	5	3	1	1	64
January 1937	14	0	0	0	0	14
September 1939 (three weeks)	12	1	0	0	1	14

Source: Filmliga (March/April 1935; January 1937) and De Standaard (8.9.1939; 22.9.1939; 29.9.1939)

As Table 15.1 indicates, French movies dominated the black list until the Second World War. A list issued in January 1937 contained only French movies, including some extreme 'scandal' movies, such as *La Garçonne*

(1936), *Lucrèce Borgia* (1935) and *La vie est à nous* (1936). It is difficult to measure the precise impact of this severe Catholic censorship, negative press reviews, campaigns of boycotting or picketing theaters, and pressure upon local politicians and authorities. At least in the northern part of the country, where the Catholic press was dominant and where the KFA controlled film discourse, this anti-vaudeville campaign might explain why French cinema had only a marginal market share in Flanders. The extreme instance, and a moment of glory for the Belgian Catholic film movement, was the reception of the historical movie *La Kermesse Héroïque* (1935), made by Belgian director Jacques Feyder. In this French-German co-production, Feyder went back to a Breughelian sixteenth-century Flemish setting, telling how local people 'collaborated' with the Spanish invaders. Several groups, including local extreme nationalists, considered Feyder's movie a disgrace to Flemish historical heritage and collective identity, and demanded that it be banned.[65] The Catholic film movement had first made only few objections, but soon changed its position and started a massive offensive action against the movie. For the KFA, which succeeded in dominating the public debate, the movie only demonstrated the perverted nature of French vaudevilles, in the way that it turned Flemish women into whores, men into cowards, and local priests into hypocrites. Felix Morlion took the lead:

> This movie should be boycotted ... It is a pity that our warnings have not been sufficiently heard when we talked about movies such as: *Arlette et ses Papas, Simone est comme ça, Beguin de la Garnison, Ce cochon de Morin, Chasseur de chez Maxim's, On a trouvé une femme nue, Ferdinand le Noceur, La folle nuit*, and many other French movies, which went from town to town ... Taking into account the better directions in the American production, one could say that nearly half of it can now be labeled as 'for all' or 'for adults.' In the French production though, suitable films are still a small minority.[66]

By 1935, only a few American movies were still on the Catholic blacklist. Most of the U.S. movies given a 6-rating were older pictures, still in circulation but soon to disappear, such as *Back Street* (1932), *Flying Down to Rio* (1933), *Hoopla* (1933), *Queen Kelly* (1922) and *Murder at the Vanities* (1934). For Belgian Catholics, it was clear that the Legion of Decency had proven that 'the morally healthy film can be as profitable, or even more interesting, than dirty productions.'[67] The Legion's efforts had given rise to several innocent genres such as 'adventure movies,' and one KFA critic joyfully wrote that even 'Cecil B. de Mille had finally understood that decency and good taste are indispensable in film production.'[68]

This heavy rejection of French movies as immoral, by comparison to the increasingly positive evaluation of American cinema as morally healthy, was echoed in France itself. Table 15.2 is based on a 1936 article which originally appeared in *La Cinématographie Française* and was reproduced in the Belgian Catholic magazine *Filmliga*. It shows the proportion of American and French movies placed in each of the three basic categories used by the French Catholic censors and published in French Catholic newspapers. The CCC advised French cinemagoers to avoid more than half of the national production, while praising 90 per cent of Hollywood movies. Commenting about these data, the Belgian Catholics claimed that 'only three years ago, such a comparison would have been much more negative for Hollywood.'[69]

Table 15.2 The French Catholic Church's evaluation for French and US movies: percentage of movies for three codes

	French	US
A (for all)	20 %	50 %
B (for adults)	25 %	40 %
C (to be avoided)	55 %	10 %

Source: Filmliga, November 1936, p. 4.

Conclusion

Given the relatively small size of the Belgian market, the activities of the Belgian Catholic film movement might seem of marginal importance. As I have argued, however, the Belgian film market was exceptional in its openness, in the intensity of the film trade, and the high rate of film consumption among the population. The Belgian KFA was one of the earliest and most elaborate Catholic film activities in Europe, and seems to have played a key role in the Vatican's more offensive views upon this modern medium. The demonstrable shift in its attitude towards American cinema was, from an international perspective, perhaps almost as significant in influencing Catholic action in neighbouring countries as was the American example of the Legion of Decency itself. The KFA's increasingly positive perception of Hollywood movies in the 1930s provides support for Ruth Vasey's thesis, in *The World According to Hollywood*, that Hollywood increasingly produced morally sound as well as culturally and politically acceptable products.[70] In a critical review of Vasey's book, Ian Jarvie suggested that her findings might be tested by comparing them with archival material from those who received such films.[71] The Belgian Catholics' case, at least, tends to support Vasey's thesis by demonstrating the clearly more positive appreciation of Hollywood movies as 'morally healthy' entertainment.

The Child Audience and the 'Horrific' Film in 1930s Britain

Annette Kuhn

I N Britain in the 1930s, children's cinemagoing was seen as an issue of the most pressing social concern.[1] Childhood seems to be a universal site of, and cause for, cultural anxieties; and worries about young audiences and users have surfaced repeatedly throughout the history of popular media. But the content, tenor and circumstances of such concerns are always unique, and 1930s Britain saw the emergence and evolution of a distinctive set of constructions of the child cinema audience in the context of a specific set of strategies aimed at regulating film exhibition and children's access to certain sorts of films. In particular, the first few years of the decade saw a sharp rise in the profile of the British Board of Film Censors (BBFC) and its system of film classification, along with pressures on film exhibitors to police children's access to cinemas. These circumstances eventually became focussed around a cycle of Hollywood films that were dubbed 'horrific.' An unprecedented set of events then unfolded involving the BBFC, government, a disparate array of pressure groups, and the film industry itself.

From its very earliest years, cinema's potential effects on the child audience had been the subject of considerable concern, in Britain, the U.S. and many other countries.[2] During the 1910s, British worries about the young cinema audience focussed on the danger of sexual assaults on children in or near cinemas, as well as on eyestrain and other physical damage children might suffer as a result of watching films. Thus a report by the Medical Officer of Health of the Yorkshire industrial town of Bradford could conclude in characteristic tones with the observation that:

... cinemagoing can affect the vision and mind of children, giving rise to visual and mental fatigue prejudicial to normal development which, if these displays are too frequently indulged in, is certain to lead in the end to a greater or lesser degree of organic defect.[3]

Conflation of children's 'organic' and moral integrity marked many expressions of disquiet in these early years. A *Times* leader of 1915 on the children and cinema question alludes to the 'moral and physical dangers to which young children may be exposed if they are allowed unrestricted admission to cinematograph shows';[4] and it was in fact combined such physical and moral concerns that lay behind Britain's first-ever systematic inquiry into the cinema audience: *The Cinema: Its Present Position and Future Possibilities* was conducted in 1917 under the auspices of an influential social purity organisation, the National Council of Public Morals.[5] The inquiry's prime concern was children's 'health, intelligence and morals,' all of which were seen as equally at risk from the harmful consequences of cinemagoing.

In the years that followed, anxieties about young people's cinemagoing persisted; but by the 1930s the focus on the potential moral and/or physical harmfulness of the entire activity of cinemagoing—the places where films were exhibited as much as the films themselves—had largely given way to a conviction that many of the films shown in cinemas and seen by children were simply not suitable for them. While a shift in attention from 'harm' to 'unsuitability' may have taken place in other countries as well, the British situation is distinctive in a number of significant respects.

In the period between 1930 and 1933, the British government was subjected to pressures from numerous quarters, ranging from calls to reform the existing system of film censorship in its entirety to demands to set some limits on children's cinemagoing. Britain's system of film regulation was unusual in that it came about as a result of a piece of legislation (the Cinematograph Act, 1909) that was designed to empower local authorities to license premises where films were screened. Some local licensing authorities, using their powers to lay down conditions for the granting of cinema licences, soon seized the opportunity to set conditions concerning the content of films shown in the cinemas they were responsible for licensing.

Within a year or two of the Act's passage, many authorities were imposing conditions concerning the 'morality' and 'decency' of films. At this time, film exhibition in Britain was enjoying its first boom; and like every new form of mass entertainment, cinema—with its predominantly working-class and youthful audience—immediately became a major focus for public concern. Film exhibitors sought to protect their businesses from the vagaries of local censorship by lobbying government for a 'voluntary' central scheme of film regulation, to be sponsored by the film trade; and in 1913, the BBFC, financed by fees from film companies, began its work with the promise that 'No film subject will be passed that is not clean and wholesome and absolutely above suspicion.' Films infringing this code would be subject to bans or cuts; and in a system of classification that was to remain in force for many years, those passed for exhibition would be certificated either 'U' (for 'universal' exhibition) or 'A' (for 'public' exhibition).

The BBFC had (and indeed still has) no legal powers to censor films: strictly speaking, it can only offer advice to the local cinema licensing authorities who do hold these powers. In consequence, at various points in its history the Board has found itself caught between the competing interests of its various clients—the Home Office (the government department responsible for administering the Cinematograph Act),[6] the film industry, and the local licensing authorities, as well as of various, often very disparate pressure groups. From the outset, governments of all persuasions were anxious to avoid Parliamentary accountability in the delicate area of film censorship, and the arms' length principle enshrined in the BBFC's non-governmental status has remained in place.

The public record reveals, however, that the Home Office and the BBFC have occasionally felt the need to consult with each other behind the scenes, while the Home Office's responsibility for the working of the Cinematograph Act has always meant that it was explicitly tasked with liaising with local authorities on matters concerning the licensing of cinemas. In public, the Home Office had been at pains to tread warily in its relations with the BBFC, and it was not until ten years after the Board was founded that it was publicly endorsed by the Home Office in a recommendation to local authorities that cinema licence conditions should include the rule that 'no film ... which has not been passed for "universal" or "public" exhibition by the British Board of Film Censors shall be exhibited without the express consent of the [licensing authority].'[7]

Children and 'A' Films

Six years later, the Home Office was to find itself publicly involved for the first time in the thorny issue of children's cinemagoing. In the last weeks of 1929, it circulated a private letter headed 'The Cinema and Children' to every local authority in England and Wales with responsibility for issuing licences to cinemas. This attempted to clarify the system of film classification developed by the BBFC: 'U' films were those passed by the Board for universal exhibition, while 'A' films were those passed as suitable for persons above the age of sixteen. Licensing authorities were urged to adopt the BBFC's scheme of certification and to make it a condition of granting cinema licences that under-sixteens would not be admitted to 'A' films unless accompanied by a *bona fide* adult guardian, and that the categories of films on exhibition would be clearly displayed both inside and outside cinemas.[8]

In its broad-brush way, this was explicit recognition of a need to exercise some degree of control over the sorts of films that could be seen by children; and the Home Office expressed the view that the BBFC's scheme of film classification 'has done all that could be reasonably expected ... to protect the interests of young people', but that in the end it was up to the licensing authorities to see that it was enforced. Originally intended only for these authorities, 'The Cinema and Children' at first attracted little attention outside official circles; but in the summer of 1931, the Home Office decided to publish it. How did this come about?

The intervening eighteen months had seen renewed, and increasingly heated, public debates about children's cinemagoing, as well as mounting pressure on government to reform the existing film censorship arrangements. It was brought to the attention of the BBFC and the Home Office that the recommendations regarding the exhibition of 'A' films were not being consistently enforced across the nation, and that in many places children were able without difficulty to see any and every film screened in local cinemas (it was common practice, for instance, for children to ask adult strangers to pose as guardians and 'take them in' to the cinema). At the other extreme, some local authorities were enthusiastically exercising their legal powers of censorship independently of the BBFC's advice.

In October 1930, a decision by the Liverpool licensing authority to exclude all under-sixteens from 'A' films, whether accompanied by adults or not, received nationwide publicity. Since children represented a substantial proportion of their custom, it also alarmed film exhibitors. The Liverpool decision became the subject of a test case aimed at determining the extent and limits of local licensing authorities' powers of censorship, although it in fact failed to do so.[9] In the months that followed, a number of other authorities followed Liverpool's lead. In this volatile climate, the Home Office commissioned an investigation of the local take-up of the model licensing conditions recommended in the 1929 circular, especially those concerning admission of children to 'A' films.

While two-thirds of all eligible authorities reported that they had made it a condition of granting licenses that children unaccompanied by adults should not be admitted to 'A' films, few of them felt they could deploy the resources to enforce the rule. Despite guarded official expressions of satisfaction that 'the censorship as now established meets requirements very well indeed on the whole,' the unevenness in the practice of regulating children's cinemagoing brought to light by the survey was anathema to both the Home Office and the BBFC, because it posed a clear threat to the carefully cultivated arms' length principle of British film censorship, which could only work as long as local authorities accepted the BBFC's advice.[10]

Against this background of non-compliance by some authorities, pressure group activity around the 'problem' of children's cinemagoing was mounting. Early in 1930, the BBFC had received a deputation from the London Public Morality Council (LPMC), urging greater clarity in the advertising of film classifications, expressing general concern about 'sordid themes' in films, and calling for the production and promotion of films suitable for children. In July, the Parliamentary Film Committee asked the Home Secretary to appoint a committee of inquiry into film censorship; and in the same month the Birmingham branch of the National Council of Women (NCW) made a private visit to the Home Secretary to discuss an investigation they had conducted of children's cinema matinées in their city.[11] In November that year, the Birmingham Cinema Inquiry Committee (BCIC), a body that was to become particularly vociferous on the issue of children's cinemagoing and a thorn in the side of the BBFC and the Home Office, held a meeting to voice concern about the exposure of children and adolescents to 'harmful and undesirable' films. It was agreed to mount a petition to the Home Office calling for a committee of inquiry into film censorship.[12]

This was certainly an embattled start to the new decade for both the government and the BBFC, with 1931 in particular an *annus horribilis* for all concerned. BBFC President Edward Shortt began the year with an attempt to take some heat out of the debate, issuing a warning to the film trade that films showing a 'continuous succession of prolonged and gross brutality and sordid themes' would no longer be certificated.[13] But Shortt was missing the point: the main concern was not at this stage with representational practices—the contents, sordid or otherwise, of films—but with the welfare of the children who were flocking to see them. Throughout 1931, a motley array of pressure groups, including churches, women's groups and various social purity and vigilance organisations, entered the fray. Some of these bodies conducted their own investigations into children's cinemagoing. In May, the BCIC published a substantial report of its own researches, which it used as ammunition as it continued to press for a public inquiry, sending further deputations to the Home Office during 1931 and 1932.[14]

Other reports of inquiries into children's cinema and film censorship were published by, among others, the Sheffield Social Survey, the Birkenhead Vigilance Committee, the National Council of Women and the Mothers' Union.[15] It seems clear that the Home Office decision to publish its December 1929 'Cinema and Children' circular eighteen months after its original private circulation came as a response both to internal pressure wrought by anomalies in local licensing authorities' enforcement of controls on children's access to cinemas and to external pressures from the various interest groups.

These groups were quite diverse in their objectives, and some were more supportive of existing film regulation arrangements than others. The well-organised, persistent and vociferous BCIC took the toughest line of all, and its repeated calls for a public inquiry were seen as irksome (they were dismissed by one Home Office official as 'neither impartial nor well-informed')[16] and went unheeded. By May 1931, when representatives of the BCIC called once again on the Home Secretary with a petition calling for a committee of inquiry into 'the undesirable nature of many of the films shown in picture houses' and urging the total exclusion of under-sixteens from 'A' films,[17] a course of action rather more agreeable to the Home Office and the BBFC had already been quietly decided on.

In January, the London Public Morality Council had held a private conference on cinema, calling not for a full-scale public inquiry but for the appointment of a small consultative committee on film censorship.[18] Neither were bodies such as the Mothers' Union and the National Council of Women clamouring for any wholesale change to the film censorship system. In its May 1931 'Report of an Inquiry into Film Censorship,' for example, the NCW obligingly recommended the establishment of a consultative committee which would keep the BBFC in touch with the various interested parties and look into the question of 'A' films and children.[19] In fact, by May the Home Office had already started setting up this body, and in November the newly convened Film Censorship Consultative Committee (FCCC) held its first meeting.[20] While the establishment of the FCCC by no means put an end to pressures on the Home Office and the BBFC, it did mean there was now a ready answer to further demands for government action on censorship.

'Horrific' Films and Children

At this point, the problem of children's access to 'A'-certificated films was still the main cause for concern. It was not until the following year that the more specific issue of films' contents and their effects on children began to be looked at. This shift was prompted by anxieties about so-called 'frightening films.' The BCIC had been first to draw attention to this question when one of the speakers at its November 1930 conference made passing reference to 'the fear element' as a cause for concern in films seen by children; and in its 1931 investigation, children had been asked about their responses to 'frightening pictures.' But it was some months later, with the UK releases of *Dracula* and *Frankenstein*, that a new cycle of Hollywood horror talkies began to make its presence felt across Britain, exciting concern about particular films. At a conference hosted by the BCIC early in 1932, there was mention of *Frankenstein* (which the BBFC had passed 'A' with some cuts the year before) and of *Dr Jekyll and Mr Hyde* (passed 'A' with major cuts in 1932). At this point the films were called 'thrillers.'[21]

In April 1932, the FCCC took up discussion of complaints about *Frankenstein*, noting that a number of licensing authorities, including the influential London and Surrey County Councils, had taken their own steps to restrict children's access to the film. The Committee considered a range of policy options.[22] When the question came up again at a later meeting, the committee agreed that there ought to be some arrangement whereby exhibitors could be notified of films the BBFC considered entirely unsuitable for children, so that they could 'continue to warn the public of "horrific" films by methods similar to those adopted in the case of ... "Frankenstein."'[23] This decision marks the birth of the BBFC's advisory 'H' ('horrific') label. Although not a separate certificate, the 'H' was intended to inform exhibitors and warn parents that an 'A' film that bore this label was unsuitable for children. It did not prohibit admission of children to these films, however. At the end of the year, the committee produced an internal report which looked again at arrangements for limiting children's access to 'A' films in general, and which also named several 'horror' [sic] films.

The arrangement proposed was that the FCCC secretary would keep a list of 'horrific' films to pass on to the Cinematograph Exhibitors' Association (CEA), which would in turn ask its members to post notices outside cinemas when such films were showing, warning parents not to bring in their children. This report in essence formed the text of a new Home Office circular, 'Children and A Films,' distributed in March 1933.[24] The FCCC's proposals were also endorsed in the BBFC's Annual Report for 1932, which was published after the distribution of the circular and which discussed the 'horror' film for the first time.

However, because these additional restrictions on admitting children to 'horrific' films were purely advisory, exhibitors were not obliged to enforce them. The final decision as to whether or not to take children into cinemas to see 'horrific' films was expressly left up to parents. Moreover, titles on the FCCC's 'horrific' films list appear to have been somewhat erratically selected, and the grounds for placing some films and not others on the list remain unrecorded (the first films to acquire the 'H' label were *The Ghoul*, *The Invisible Man*, *King Klunk*, *Vampyr* and *The Vampire Bat*). It seems reasonable to conclude that the purpose of launching the 'H' label was mainly to forestall further troublesome complaints from the public and from pressure groups, and so to protect film producers and exhibitors, as well as the BBFC itself.

When frightening films were first dubbed 'horrific,' calls for clarification of the term soon followed. The London County Council, a licensing authority that regularly took a leading role in film censorship policymaking, set out what was to become the standard definition of a 'horrific' film: 'one likely to frighten or horrify children under the age of 16 years.'[25] The definition of a film genre in terms not of its themes or iconographies but of the responses it is likely, or intended, to provoke in a particular audience has interesting implications. Looked at from another perspective, it suggests that the test of a 'horrific' film's effectiveness lay in its capacity to provoke a certain emotional and/or physical response. Studies of children's cinemagoing conducted during the 1930s, including those referred to above, routinely inquired into dreams and nightmares experienced after visits to the cinema; and indeed many people who were children in the 1930s remember their responses to horror films seen at the time extraordinarily vividly.[26]

By the time the 'Children and "A" Films' circular was made public, the FCCC had achieved what it was set up to do—divert demands for censorship reform. The frenzy of pressure group activity around children, 'A' films, and frightening films had largely died down, despite sporadic commotions around 'horrific' films over the following few years, when a few local authorities tried to exclude under-sixteens altogether from screenings, banned them outright, or imposed exceptional restrictions on children's entry to individual pictures.[27] By the mid-1930s a new, and more restrictive, Hollywood Production Code was in place, while Hollywood producers had yielded to pressures from Britain and other foreign markets by reducing their output of frightening films. And yet when the newly appointed BBFC President, Lord Tyrrell of Avon, attempted to 'kill' the 'horrific' category, an outcry ensued and he was obliged to back down.[28]

In June 1937, yielding to pressure from the LCC, the BBFC agreed to make the 'H' label a certificate, meaning that children were now officially excluded from 'horrific' films (the first film to be given an 'H' certificate was *The Thirteenth Chair*). It seems clear that this change was made with uniformity of cinema regulation across the nation in mind rather than in response to any fresh wave of 'horrific' films, because by this time, as Tyrrell had hinted, the film industry had come to the conclusion that horror films were 'more trouble than they are worth.'[29] In fact, the 'H' certificate was applied to only a tiny fraction of films released in Britain before being quietly withdrawn in 1951.[30] By the time the certificate was introduced, the tenor of public opinion about children's cinemagoing had in any case changed, with ideas about young people's psychological vulnerability to 'horrific' and other 'unsuitable' films giving way to calls for films produced, programmed and screened especially for children.

An Audience Apart

By the later 1930s, children's cinemagoing was increasingly becoming an issue of concern for educationalists, child psychologists and academics, rather than for pressure groups. In 1936, the newly formed British Film Institute (BFI) made a bid to shift the terms of the debate about the child audience, hosting a high-profile conference on Children and the Cinema. Speakers pointed out that only a small minority of commercial cinemas were offering special weekly matinées for children, and that children's preferences for films with movement, action, moral outcomes, heroic deeds, and happy endings were not being catered for. It was consequently resolved to look at the potential for putting together programmes of films specifically for children and presenting these at special children's performances in mainstream cinemas.[31] The BFI soon produced the first of a series of lists of films recommended for such performances; and this fresh direction in thinking about the young cinema audience also inspired further debate and renewed inquiry into children's cinemagoing habits and preferences.[32] From these beginnings, organised children's cinema matinées and film clubs were to develop.

From the mid-1930s on, then, the notion that children had specific needs in the cinema gained impetus, and this led to increasing demands for a child-centred approach to film programming. This was symptomatic of an important shift in thinking about children's cinemagoing. Children now began to be regarded as an audience apart with needs of its own, a group whose film-going—through children's matinées, special screenings, films made for children, and so on—should be segregated from that of adult audiences.[33]

In Britain, the pressures on film regulation and censorship that arose during 1930 and 1931 were in the first instance about the meaning and the enforcement of the BBFC's 'A' certificate with regard to the child audience. These pressures were grounded in, and produced, a conceptualisation of young cinemagoers as a group for whom certain films were 'unsuitable' by virtue of being morally or psychologically harmful, or simply inappropriate at particular stages of their mental development. It is against this background that the naming of a new type of film, deemed unsuitable for children because it was intended to arouse fear, must be understood. The concept of the 'horrific' film emerged towards the end of 1932 in response to a cycle of Hollywood talkies which had seen their British releases a year or two earlier; and the anxieties aroused by this type of film joined with pre-existing concerns about the meaning of the British Board of Film Censors' 'A' and 'U' classifications in relation to the child audience. These in turn touched on the question of parental rights and responsibilities in choosing the films children should see; on the problem of non-*bona fide* guardians taking children into 'A' films; and on the issue of what was and was not a film suitable for children. Significantly in this context, 'horrific' films were defined and understood not in terms of their contents—narrative themes, characters, and so on—nor even in terms of their iconographic and expressive elements, but in relation to the *response* they generated (fear) and the *audience* (children) in which it was generated.

The history of public anxieties about children's use of popular media is a long one. The introduction of each new medium—be it film, radio, comics, television, video, computer games or the Internet—has given rise to similar sorts of concerns about their impact on young people, and to consequent waves of pressure group activity, scholarly research, and even the occasional moral panic:[34]

> Each time we seem to go through the same stages ...Whenever there is a new social invention, there is a feeling of strangeness and distrust of the new until it becomes familiar.[35]

Moreover, interest—whether political, professional or academic—in children's use of popular media has invariably been quite distinctive in tone and content. While such interest is always grounded in historically and culturally specific conceptualisations and constructions of childhood, in actual instances these interact with broader and more diffuse figurations of childhood as a site for a range of often diffuse cultural anxieties. In the early 1930s, concerns about children's cinemagoing reached a peak, generating public debate, pressure group activity, official reaction and academic research in virtually every country where young people could go to the cinema.

The story of the child audience and the 'horrific' film in Britain is therefore a small episode in a much wider history. But it is significant because in it are encapsulated all the broad, varied and changing cultural concerns about childhood as a separate state and stage, as they worked their way through a very particular, local set of circumstances. This process produced not only a new film genre, but also a new—and metapsychological *avant la lettre*—understanding of what makes one genre different from others.

Hollywood in Vernacular

Translation and Cross-cultural Reception of American Films in Turkey

Ahmet Gürata

To write the international history of classical American cinema ... is a matter of tracing not just its mechanisms of standardization and hegemony but also the diversity of ways in which this cinema was translated and reconfigured in both local and translocal contexts of reception.[1]

Cinema as 'Vernacular Modernism'

THE world-wide success of classical Hollywood cinema is usually attributed to a combination of its universal intelligibility, derived from its popular and hybrid nature, and the cultural imperialism that resulted from the enormous economic power of the U.S culture industry. According to the first argument, Hollywood films developed a narrative style that different audiences throughout the world found easy to comprehend. As Will Hays, President of the Motion Picture Producers and Distributors of America, Inc. (MPPDA), recalled in his *Memoirs*, 'American films of the earliest silent picture era had to be designed to appeal to the less educated groups and to the large foreign-language sections of our own population. It was essential that the viewer should be able to follow the story whether understanding English or not. Hence our silent pictures early developed a style and form that commended them to all races and groups of people, without the aid of words.'[2] The popularity of Hollywood films in the sound era has also often been explained by reference to a comparable universalism, in which American cinema's repetition and quotation of its own images and genres proved more responsive to consumer desires than did the products of other cinemas.[3] Most accounts of Hollywood's strong global presence, however, also attribute its success to political and economic factors such as its significant mode of production, large economies of scale and the US. government's support and aggressive policies.[4]

Beyond these narrative templates and industrial strategies, however, more localised processes by which these products were adapted to suit the cultural preferences of the target audiences contributed significantly to their success, as did the specific ways in which they were exhibited. As Jacques Malthête's study of Georges Méliès' films shows, the adaptation of films into specific contexts of reception started almost with the introduction of the *cinématagrophe*. The English and French versions of Méliès' films sometimes differ significantly, and from 1900, Méliès' catalogues included a twenty-metre film aiming to thank respective spectators of his films: *Vue de remerciements au public*. In this short film, different people display the same banner, reading 'thanks' in French, English, German, Spanish, Italian, Russian and finally in Arabic and Greek. The latter, addressing Ottoman audiences, was presented by two women and a men in Oriental dress.[5]

17.1 *Vue de remerciements au public* (Méliès catalogue no. 292, 1900).
The banner reads 'Thanks' in Arabic and Greek (From Malthête, 'Méliès et le conférencier,' *Iris*, p. 128).

334

Interpreted by lecturers or inter-titles and accompanied by music or sound effects, silent movies were adapted for different culturally specific audiences. Although the introduction of sound made these kinds of modification more difficult and expensive, similar strategies were used by producers, distributors and exhibitors alike during the sound era. Altering foreign films, especially Hollywood products, helped to increase movies' popularity among local audiences. As Miriam Hansen observes:

If classical Hollywood cinema succeeded as an international modernist idiom on a mass basis, it did so not because of its presumably universal narrative form but because it meant different things to different people and publics, both at home and abroad. We must not forget that these films, along with other mass-cultural exports, were consumed in locally quite specific, and unequally developed, contexts and conditions of *reception*; that they not only had a levelling impact on indigenous cultures but also challenged prevailing social and sexual arrangements and advanced new possibilities of social identity and cultural styles; and that the films were also changed in that process.[6]

In this chapter, I would like to focus on the processes of cultural adaptation by which Hollywood films were modified and translated into the local context in Turkey between 1930 and 1970. In some cases, the movies were significantly altered for particular export markets.[7] More importantly, local distributors, exhibitors and censorship bodies modified these movies to facilitate their reception by their culturally specific audiences. Sometimes scenes were removed, or performances featuring local stars were inserted into the original prints. These transformations particularly affected the local context of reception in relation to the experience of modernisation and modernity. In her essay on the transnational currency of classical Hollywood cinema, Miriam Hansen, describes the promiscuity and translatability of this cinema as a form of 'vernacular modernism.'[8] She suggests that the American movies of the classical period played a key role in mediating competing cultural discourses on modernity and modernisation.[9] Appropriating Hansen's theoretical framework, I would like to discuss the role of marketing, programming and exhibition practices, as well as dubbing and censorship, as strategies of translation in effecting the cross-cultural reception of Hollywood cinema.

Marketing, Programming and Exhibition

Hollywood films have been an integral and naturalised part of Turkish movie culture, spreading from Istanbul's highly Westernised Pera district to the whole country. Starting in 1913 with the opening of Istanbul's *Cinéma Americain* theatre promoting Vitagraph films, American films become highly popular, outnumbering continental brands by the mid-1920s. As the movie theatre's name itself indicated, French was used extensively amongst the Ottoman elite.[10] In the late nineteenth and early twentieth centuries, French symbolised all European—or Western—networks and values. Until the mid-1940s, American films were either dubbed into French or screened in the original with French subtitles in Istanbul's Pera district.[11] As late as 1948, the U.S Department of Commerce was reporting that 'from a foreign language point of view with regard to films, French could be rated next to Turkish.'[12] This trend changed only in the 1950s, with the impact of the Marshall Plan and Turkey's growing relations with the US. Before then, American culture made its entry, if not in Turkish then in French.

American film titles were translated into Turkish, in the process often being either adapted to the local context for easy comprehension, or stripped of any offending phrases, in order to attract larger audiences. *Cheaper by the Dozen* (1950), a movie about a couple who try to conduct their lives efficiently as they have a dozen children, was translated as *Demokrat Aile* (*Democratic Family*), referring to the just and equal care given by the parents, but also connoting the Democratic Party, which was then enjoying its first years in power after the end of single party rule in 1950. Cecil B. de Mille's *The Crusades* (1935) was screened under the title *Selahattin Eyyübi ve Haçlı Seferleri* (*Salahaddin-i Ayyubi and the Crusades*), emphasising the role of the Abbasid Sultan fighting against the Crusades.[13] The movie's dialogue was probably also modified to justify this emphasis. In a practice that Robert Stam has called 'parasitical translation,' movies were sometimes also re-titled to refer to earlier box-office hits for obvious commercial reasons.[14] For example, after the success of Rudolph Valentino's *The Sheik* (Turkish title *Şeyh Ahmet*) and *The Son of Sheik* a number of movies screened under similar titles. Roman Novarro's *The Sheik Steps Out* (Irving Pichel, 1937) was screened under the familiar title *Şeyh Ahmet*, while *The Barbarian* (1933) was titled as *Peyhin Apký* (*The Lover of the Sheik*) probably because the word barbarian, a term commonly used to describe Turks in the West, was conceived as insulting.

The movies were also exhibited in locally specific ways. Movie program formats varied. The program of Istanbul's *Türk* movie theatre in 1935 included a Turkish short, a Fox Movietone newsreel and a feature film.

336

Other Istanbul theatres showed double-bills, programming two films, each approximately sixty minutes long, for the price of one.[15] Generally, however, the two-hour program of American movie theatres was standard in Turkey, although exhibitors were reluctant to go beyond this limit. If a film did not fit into this program together with the shorts and newsreels, it was automatically shortened. For example, 20 minutes out of 140 minutes of *The Story of Dr Wassell* (Cecil B. de Mille, 1944) was removed by its Turkish distributors. This type of trimming caused misapprehensions and was strongly criticised by film journals in the 1940s.[16]

Distributors also removed songs and dance scenes from some musicals. Spectacular Hollywood productions such as *Kismet* (Vincente Minnelli, 1955) and *South Pacific* (Joshua Logan, 1958) were exhibited in much shorter versions, without their songs.[17] 1940s Turkish audiences disliked musicals, despite their being the third most popular genre (after action and drama) among audiences worldwide according to a survey conducted by MGM into the relative popularity of different genres, Turkey was listed with India, Egypt, Iraq and Lebanon as being among the countries with tastes almost diametrically opposed to those of American audiences.[18] These films were further modified by inserting locally produced scenes featuring local singers or dancers into the original film. Although this method was widely used in adapting Egyptian and European films, some Hollywood movies were also altered in this fashion. As Alim Şerif Onaran, a film scholar and former member of the Turkish censorship body, explains, international films were 'not just retitled, but altered in order to give the impression that the movie was set in Turkey.' As a result, 'the movies were presented as almost like a Turkish movie.'[19]

Indigenisation of this kind was a cheap way of catering to local tastes, since film production in Turkey was limited at the time. The modification of movies gained a new momentum in 1948, when local taxes on film admissions were reduced in favour of Turkish products. As a result, the number of films produced in Turkey increased from six in 1946 to eighteen in 1948. In response, foreign film distributors released nearly twice as many dubbed and modified films in 1948 as they had in the previous year.[20] Most of these dubbed versions included inserted indigenous performances, and new film studios were established to produce them. Faruk Kenç, who started his career by shooting inserts of local dancers, singers, comedians and magicians described this process as the 'Turkification' of a movie.[21] While these inserts often replaced song and dance scenes in the original prints of musicals, dramas and other genres of films also included such performances Here, the aim was to offer something like the variety form of programming that had been highly popular among Turkish audiences during and after the silent period. As late as the mid-1930s, some Turkish movie theatres were not equipped with sound projectors, and most of these continued to use a variety programming format. For example, before the exhibition of a Turkish film, musicians performed a classical Turkish music concert in Konya's Belediye movie theatre.[22] Inserting locally produced performances or significant modification of films can be considered as an extension of this type of variety programming.

This suggests that even in the sound period the relationship between film and viewer in Turkey was 'presentational' rather than 'representational.' According to Hansen, early modes of presentation, alternating short films with live performances, borrowed their disjunctive style from other commercial forms of entertainment. 'Presentational' films address the viewer directly, with frequent asides to the camera and a frontal organisation of space. According to Hansen, 'early cinema's dispersal of meaning across filmic and nonfilmic sources, such as the alternation of films and numbers, lent the exhibition the character of a live event, that is, a performance that varied from place to place and time to time depending on theater type and location, audience composition, and musical accompaniment.'[23] Some of these practices remained quite common in Turkey in the sound era, and distributors and exhibitors transformed classical films into 'presentational' ones, by cutting different scenes into original copies or programming them together with musical numbers.

Dubbing

During the early sound years, Hollywood companies mostly dubbed their own movies into different languages, but before long they received protests from several countries about the use of unsuitable accents and intonation. This method also left little room to modify any inappropriate scenes. During the early 1930s, eleven countries introduced regulations requiring dubbing to be carried out on their home soil.[24] After the success of the first Turkish talking picture, İstanbul Sokaklarında (On the Streets of Istanbul) (Muhsin Ertuğrul, 1931), which was dubbed at Epinay Studios in France, Turkey's sole production company İpek Film decided to build a new sound film studio in Istanbul. In 1933, with equipment from Tobis-Klangfilm and under the supervision of a German engineer, İpek Film's dubbing studio was launched.[25] In its first year, the studio dubbed four movies.[26] Soon other dubbing studios were launched and, by the late 1940s, Turkish studios were dubbing more than a hundred movies a year.

The cultural adaptation and familiarisation provided by dubbing might best be exemplified by the case of voice actor Ferdi Tayfur (1904–58), who worked for the İpek Studio. He was a man of many trades, translating and dubbing films as well as acting and directing. As fellow dubbing actor Mücap Ofluoğlu recalls, he could simultaneously translate films from French and English: 'in some cases, he would just listen to the original dialogue and then translate it into Turkish. German was his mother-tongue. He had a vast knowledge of Ottoman-Turkish and was proficient in Istanbul dialect. He could imitate the dialects of [non-Muslim] minorities and Anatolian people very well. He had an appealing and natural voice.'[27] Tayfur dubbed a number of Hollywood stars, such as Roman Novarro, Spencer Tracy, Clark Gable and Gary Cooper.[28] He is, however, best known for his successful dubbing of a number of comedians, including Groucho Marx, Eddie Cantor and both Laurel and Hardy.

Comedy was one of the most popular genres of 1930s and 1940s in Turkey, and the films of Stan Laurel and Oliver Hardy were highly successful. Both characters were dubbed speaking broken Turkish with an American accent. İpek Film's studio manager, the famous poet Nazım Hikmet (1902–63), together with dubbing actor Ferdi Tayfur, thought Laurel and Hardy's gags and puns were 'too American' and did not make much sense in Turkish. The idea of Americans speaking Turkish with an accent did the trick, although the locale and the topics also had to be altered to fit into the context.[29] As Tayfur, who dubbed both characters, explained in a 1938 interview:

Question: Why did you decide to dub Laurel and Hardy in an American accent?

Tayfur: We wanted to add some extra comic elements via the characters' voice and accent. Don't you like it?

Q: On the contrary, I quite like it. But do you translate literally or do you improvise?

Tayfur: Well, at the beginning I tried to translate word by word, but later I thought it was more appropriate to lip synchronise my very own gags. For example, in one of the movies Laurel and Hardy bought the shadow (!) of the famous Galata Tower. In another one, Hardy sings a traditional folk song, while Laurel compares him to a local singer. Of course, there are similar adaptations in their movies.[30]

Similar strategies of adaptation were quite widespread. In Spain, Laurel and Hardy were dubbed as speaking in 'trick pigeon Spanish.' MGM modelled this for the French version of *The Night Owls* (James Parrott,

1930). Later, they were dubbed in French speaking with a strong English accent. Although 'poor accent and bad grammar were no hindrance to foreign success,' improper French 'reinforced the slapstick and burlesque character of comedies which were based on physical gags, incongruous behaviour, or loss of dignity.'[31] In a similar fashion, Tayfur added specific qualities to his characters' voice, such as pronunciation and accent, and used vernacular idioms. As Tim Bergfelder suggests, idioms based on class, generational or sub-cultural variations, create a nationally recognisable correspondence between language, social status, and character.[32] Through these modifications, comedy films were also assimilated into different generic traditions. In the end, these films were promoted almost like a local product, emphasising the significant role of their voice actor, as exemplified in this advertisement.

17.2 In this flyer Ferdi Tayfur is seen while dubbing a Laurel-Hardy film. The caption reads, 'Tayfur, both Laurel and Hardy' (*Perde ve Sahne* 4, 1941).

Tayfur also changed protagonists' names and transferred them into familiar locations. The Marx Brothers, who were renamed *Üç Ahbap Çavuşlar* (Three Buddies), lived in Istanbul in their films' Turkish versions. Groucho Marx, dubbed by Tayfur, was renamed as Arşak Palabıyıkyan, an Armenian from Istanbul (Palabıyık: bushy-moustache, with the suffix -yan meaning 'from the family of' in Armenian). According to Tayfur, 'this character was so well-liked that some Armenians living in Istanbul even claimed to be relatives of Arşak Palabıyıkyan.'[33] Chico was called Torik (Bonito), and Harpo was Kıvırcık (Curly) in the Turkish versions. Tayfur also transformed Eddie Cantor into a *nouveau-riche* merchant from Turkey's Kayseri region called Yani Babanoğlu, who is unscrupulously savvy —conforming to the stereotype of this region's inhabitants.

These were successful adaptations of the films' original 'ethnic role-playing' into another context. As Charles Musser notes, by the 1920s in Hollywood, 'the daily conditions of role-playing are reversed. Instead of immigrants seeking to lose their ethnic markings and assimilate, native-born performers assume ethnic identities—and yet do so without simulating specific qualities that would associate them with that group.'[34] Among the early sound comedians, the Marx Brothers and Eddie Cantor, both originating from the polyglot city of New York, used a humour that was verbal and ethnic. Cantor's *Whoopee* (1930) and Marx Brothers' *Animal Crackers* (1930) were 'quintessential New York comedies that take the city's ethnic, social, and cultural milieu as their subject and ridicule.'[35] These characters' comic appeal depended on their performances as highly adept role-players. In moving the original setting from New York to another cosmopolitan city, Istanbul, Tayfur managed to preserve the basic comic contradictions of the Marx Brothers. While Jewish Groucho Marx and WASP Margaret Dumont (Mrs. Rittenhouse in the original) are given Armenian names, Italian immigrant Chico is turned into a tough Turkish guy. In the case of Eddie Cantor, references to his Jewishness are replaced with local stereotypes. Similarly, in the 1950s, Italian comic Antonio de Curtis's popular character Toto was dubbed in a Turkish-Jewish accent in his movies' Turkish versions (by dubbing actor Necdet Mahfi Ayral).[36] Rubber-faced French comedian Fernandel (Fernand Contandin), who starred in the Don Camillo series, was also dubbed in a Kayseri accent, like Eddie Cantor (dubbed by actor Mücap Ofluoğlu).[37] The table below, adapted from Ian Jarvie's work on stars and ethnicity, shows the perceived ethnicities of these comedians both in the original and Turkish versions:[38]

Table 17.1   Comedy and ethnic role-playing in dubbed movies

Star name	Name on screen	Name in Turkish version	Where born	Ethnicity 'real'/ perceived	Ethnicity on screen	Ethnicity in Turkish version
Stan Laurel	Same	Same	Britain	British	WASP	American
Oliver Hardy	Same	Same	US	WASP	WASP	American
Julius Marx	Groucho	Arşak Palabıyıkyan	US	Jewish	Jewish	Armenian-Turkish
Adolph Marx	Harpo	Kıvırcık (Curly)	US	Jewish	—	—
Leonard Marx	Chico	Torik (Bonito) Necmi	US	Jewish	Italian	Turkish
Margaret Dumont (Margaret Baker)	Mrs. Rittenhouse	Madam Hayganuş	US	WASP	WASP	Armenian-Turkish
Eddie Cantor		Yani Babanoğlu	USA	Jewish	Jewish	Turkish (Kayseri)
Fernand Contandin	Fernandel	—	France	French	French	Turkish (Kayseri)
Antonio de Curtis	Toto	Toto	Italy	Italian	Italian	Jewish-Turkish
Ali al-Kassar	Ali Baba	Balıkçı Osman (Osman the Fisherman)	Egypt	Arab	Arab	Turkish (Black Sea)

Although accents were an asset in comedy, standardised dialect was a general requirement for other genres. Voice actors, mostly from Istanbul's Municipality Theatre, were trained to speak in an Istanbul accent, and both international and Turkish films were dubbed in this accent. In many films where accent was used to emphasise social and cultural differences, this produced an effect of cultural levelling. In this sense, dubbing functions as the effacement of the national signifier, as Mark Betz suggests. At the intra-national level, it creates the 'synthetic unity' of a shared national language. At the international level, on the other hand, dubbing may be regarded as a form of national protectionism and a different kind of nation building, since the dubbed film becomes a new, often local product once it is re-contextualised through this process.[39]

Dubbing was an important tool for cultural adaptation and familiarisation, especially in the case of comedy. Through dubbing, a film's foreign origin was at least partially effaced, giving its Turkish audience 'the chance to disavow what they really know, hence opening an avenue for cultural ventriloquism through voice post-synchronization. In doing so, the dubbed film appears as a radically new product rather than a transformed old one, a single text rather than a double one.'⁴⁰

Censorship

It was not only local distributors and exhibitors who omitted certain scenes from movies and replaced them with new ones; censors also decided how the movies should be modified, and Turkey's extremely strict censorship rules served as a straitjacket that all movies had to wear. Although there were virtually no rules on film censorship in the early days of cinema, the 1934 Law on the Obligation and Authority of the Police entrusted the duty of censorship to local governors. Under their authority, films were reviewed and censored by two police officers in each city where they were to be screened. The Regulation on the Control of Films and Screenplays was introduced in 1939. This regulation, based on an Italian model, stayed largely intact until 1985. It established two control commissions, one based in Istanbul reviewing foreign films, and the other in Ankara for Turkish films.⁴¹ The membership of these boards comprised representatives of the governor (head), the chief of Metropolitan Police, the Interior Ministry (controlling the police force), the Ministry of Education and the Directorate of the Press (part of the Tourism Ministry). Depending on the nature of the film, representatives of the army or other ministries were also to join the commissions, and eventually army officers became *de facto* members.⁴² The commissions not only reviewed all movies to be screened in Turkey, but also the scripts for movies that were to be shot. The rules of censorship were comprehensive and strict. Article 7 has been defined as the 'ten commandments of censorship' by film scholar Oğuz Makal.⁴³ This article prohibited movies deemed guilty of the following offences:

1) political propaganda in favour of a particular state;
2) degrading a race or a nation;
3) humiliating allied states and nations;
4) propagating religion;
5) propagating political, economic and social ideologies hostile to the national regime;
6) contradicting general decency and morals, and national sentiments;
7) debasing the honour and dignity of the armed forces, and propagating anti-militarism;
8) undermining the order and security of the country;

343

9)   provoking people to commit crimes;
10)   including scenes that are propaganda against Turkey.

Out of these 'ten commandments' the most controversial were numbers one and five. According to a survey by critic Nijat Özön, 30 per cent of banned foreign films fell under these clauses.[44] In the 1950s, the foreign film commission banned almost all Soviet productions, citing the two clauses. Another common basis for rejection was the fourth clause, under which a number of Hollywood epics, including *King of Kings* (Cecil B. de Mille, 1927), *The Ten Commandments* (Cecil B. de Mille, 1956), *The Bible* (John Huston, 1966), and *The Devil at Four o'Clock* (Melvyn Le Roy, 1961), were banned.[45] Decency and moral considerations were the other great concerns of the censors. Almost 25 per cent of movies were banned under clause six, according to Özön. Hollywood movies tamed by the Hays Code were not much affected by this rule, however, and the French 'New Wave' troubled the censors most in the 1960s.

The army was also sensitive about the portrayal of the military in films, whether indigenous or foreign productions. Clause seven affected a number of war movies such as *The Men* (Fred Zinnemann, 1950), *The Attack* (Robert Aldrich, 1956) and *The Victors* (Carl Foreman, 1963). Ironically, *Francis* (Arthur Lubin, 1950), the first of the series about the talking mule Francis, was also banned in 1951 because Francis befriended an army private. Scenes of revolt, riot or crime were also unacceptable under clause eight: *El Cid* (Anthony Mann, 1961), *Ben Hur* (William Wyler, 1959), *Doctor Zhivago* (David Lean, 1965), *Riot in Cell Block Eleven* (Don Siegel, 1954), and *Crisis* (Richard Brooks, 1950) were all banned under this clause. Finally, most of the international movies set in Turkey or related to Turkey, such as *Lawrence of Arabia* (David Lean, 1962), *America, America* (Elia Kazan, 1963)[46] and *Topkapı* (Jules Dassin, 1964) were banned from screening in accordance with clause ten.

The censors were also equipped with other rules that authorised them to ban movies that conformed to the 'ten commandments.' Article 8 of the Regulation permitted censors to prevent 'the screening of over-used and damaged films that might threaten spectators' eyesight.' Old classics with damaged prints and even some films with atmospheric lighting were banned under this article, which was used, controversially, to prohibit Orson Welles' *Citizen Kane* (1941) and *Macbeth* (1948), and *Long Voyage Home* (John Ford, 1940).[47]

The commission would approve the release of some previously rejected movies if certain conditions were met. These conditions, or in the terms used by the Regulation 'revision requests,' normally involved the removal of certain scenes, re-titling or dubbing. The revisions could only be carried out after the approval of the film's distributor. In most cases, distributors consented to the revisions in order to avoid financial loss. Between 1940 and 1967 the censors banned 4.5 per cent of the foreign movies they reviewed (a total of 9,097), while approving the release of some 7.9 per cent of movies with certain revisions.[48] For example, the censorship committee authorised the release of Anatole Litvak's *The Journey* (1959) with two cuts. The film was set in the 1956 Hungarian uprising, and told the story of a bus-load of passengers who were detained by a Russian major. The censorship committee requested the removal of two sentences: 'Russians are good people' and 'Men are bastards, but after 10 p.m. they become irresistible.'[49] In another instance, the censors requested the removal of blessing scenes during the war between Spanish and Arab soldiers, as well as King Ferdinand's death, in *El Cid* (Anthony Mann, 1961).[50] Similarly, all the love scenes were removed from *Love Story* (Arthur Hiller, 1970) at the censors' request, turning it into an entirely platonic affair.[51]

It would be interesting to evaluate which countries' films had most problems with censorship. According to a survey by Özcan Tikveş, only 18.9 per cent of the films imported from the USSR could be screened in Turkey without any revisions. 41.3 per cent of USSR films were banned, while 39.8 per cent of them could only be released with some revisions. French and Italian films were also most likely to be censored. 17 per cent of French films and 13.1 per cent of Italian films—mostly on the grounds of general decency and morals—were subject to modification. Censors viewed US. films quite favourably, and banned only 2.6 per cent of these between 1951 and 1966.[52]

Table 17.2   Films reviewed by Istanbul Controlling Commission from 1951 and 1966

Country of origin	Conditionally accepted (%)	Rejected (%)
US	2.2	2.6
Britain	5.6	3.5
Italy	13.1	3.8
Germany	7	6.4
France	17	7.8
USSR	39.8	41.3
Total	8.1	5.3

(From Tikveş, *Mukayeseli Hukukta ve Türk Hukukunda Sinema Filmlerinin Sansürü*, p. 154).

We should also note that, even before they sent their films to the censorship body, the distributors might have modified them while dubbing or subtitling. As seen from these examples, what is left out from these films is quite significant. As Annette Kuhn has argued, film censorship 'is not reducible to a circumscribed and predefined set of institutions and institutional activities,' and should be understood as a process.[53] In this sense, the unwritten rules of prohibition have changed with time and context. In the relatively liberal atmosphere of the early 1960s and mid-1970s, the discourses and practices about film censorship shifted, allowing some former banning decisions to be lifted. One can explore the nature of these discourses and practices by examining the individual examples that are cited here.

Conclusion: The grocer and the chief

> America is the original version of modernity. We are the dubbed or subtitled version.
>
> Jean Baudrillard, *America*

Daniel Lerner, in his classic 1964 text on Turkish modernisation, *The Passing of Traditional Society*, explains the function of movies in this process. When he first visited Turkey in 1950, Lerner's first stop was Balgat, then a village eight kilometres outside Ankara. There he met a village chief (*muhtar*) who, for him, represented the traditional, and a grocer who was much more forward-looking. Lerner used the story of these characters as a parable of modern Turkey. One of the questions Lerner asked was: 'If for some reason, you could not live in your country, what other country would you choose to live in?' The chief's answer was 'nowhere,' while the grocer wanted to live in America, because he heard that 'it is a nice country, and with possibilities to be rich even for the simplest person.'[54] In Lerner's survey, which was carried out in the mid-1950s, the answers to this question form what he calls the 'empathy index.' According to the survey, a large majority of people who could imagine living outside Turkey chose the U.S. as their preferred imagined residence.

Table 17.3   Empathy index

Ability to imagine	Moderns	Transitionals	Traditionals
Living outside Turkey	94	74	49
Living in U.S.	100	98	74

Source: Lerner, 1964, 144.

346

Lerner was also interested in the 'influence' of movies, commenting that they became a 'commodity to which the ordinary Turk gained access on the terms of closest equality with the ordinary American' in the 1950s.[55] Ticket prices were, however relatively more expensive than in the US at the time. An ordinary Turkish worker was working at least an hour for a single admission to a cinema, whereas his American counterpart need to work for half that time.[56] Lerner believed that the growth of media—movies, theatres, radio and newspaper circulation—along with the parallel growth of literacy, would bring the Enlightenment to Turkey. He asked a number of questions, such as 'What sort of movies do you like best?,' 'Which country makes this kind of movies best?' and 'What is it about their movies that is better than others?' The grocer thought that Turkish movies were gloomy and ordinary, commenting that: 'I can guess at the start of the film how it will end ... The American ones are exciting. You know, it makes people ask what will happen next.'[57] The chief did not have much of an opinion about them, and only stressed that his sons were always impressed by the movies they saw.

Table 17.4   Movie attendance

	Moderns	Transitionals	Traditionals
Attend movies	88	63	27
Prefer American movies*	68	48	23

* Among moviegoers

Source: Lerner, 1964, 139.

The most important deficiency in Daniel Lerner's study was that he conceived the modernisation process as a struggle between 'modernists,' who provided Turkey's elite with a model for the country's future, and the 'traditionalists,' who 'neither have nor seek a shaping influence over the Turkish future.' This approach has long been discarded as oversimplified in studies of modernisation.[58] Rather than merely providing a modern alternative to traditional forms, as Lerner would have claimed, Hollywood's products were appropriated and transformed in different contexts. These films were received and interpreted in ways that were bound to their local historical context, 'naturalising' them as part of Turkish cinema. Once the films entered local distribution they were subject to translations, cultural adaptations and significant modifications, which not only made them intelligible to a different language market, but also offered a vernacular version of the modern.

18

Cowboy Modern

African Audiences, Hollywood Films, and Visions of the West

Charles Ambler

I n 1948 A.M. Baeta, a young female student in England who came originally from the British colony of the Gold Coast (now Ghana), published a brief but remarkable commentary in the journal *Sight and Sound* on the impact of film in her home country. Reflecting on the contributions to a conference in London sponsored by the British Film Institute on 'The Film in Colonial Development,' Baeta took strong issue with the prevailing wisdom expressed by conference participants on colonial film reception.[1] She first disputed the general assumption that 'primitive' Africans lacked the capacity to fathom film representation and then challenged the argument, widely and persistently held among white observers and 'experts,' that even relatively sophisticated urban African audiences were unable to comprehend films that depicted unfamiliar settings and circumstances.[2] As Baeta pointed out, the moviegoing practices of urban Africans, with their deeply held affection for Hollywood epics, demonstrated very clearly that African audiences were more than ready to watch movies that featured foreign landscapes and cultures. Moreover, these films represented a very important resource for African urban residents to develop an understanding of the larger worlds into which they were increasingly drawn.

In her essay, Baeta described the surprise that she and her fellow West African students experienced when they arrived in England and found a country that was in many respects quite at odds with the 'Europe' that they had constructed back home out of the fragments of conversations with people who had been there, magazines, newspapers, and, above, all films. In particular, they were stunned to find working-class Englishmen engaged in manual labor, a phenomenon very different from their vision of the roles of whites, nurtured in colonial contexts and reinforced in the popular culture that they experienced. As Baeta noted, all films, including those that were purely for entertainment, did 'leave certain impressions on the minds of people especially where very little is known about the matter depicted on the screen.'[3] In particular, these films were instrumental in shaping popular West African stereotypes of Western cultures:

> If you ask anyone who enjoys seeing films at home to describe an American, he is sure to tell you the American carries a revolver with him everywhere he goes and shoots on the slightest provocation or that the American never wastes time planning things, but goes in for action and thinks of the results later.

When asked to describe a typical Frenchman, West Africans would 'give you the picture of a happy, carefree man—not caring what's happening around him, so long as it does not interfere with his happiness. A man who dances every night in magnificent and well-lit halls.' An Englishman, in the popular imagination, was quite different: 'a well-dressed man, sitting peacefully behind his desk and smoking a cigarette or reading a book.'[4]

This chapter explores the meanings that these impressions had for African audiences and the processes through which these cultural constructs were conveyed, received and ultimately synthesized. A deeply held and shared theory of media power governed the discussions that took place at the 1948 conference Baeta attended and, in fact, shaped most official thinking about the impact of film in the British African colonies.[5] The presumption that unsophisticated African audiences were passive recipients of film imagery and texts led colonial authorities enthusiastically to embrace both censorship and the development of film for educational and propagandistic purposes.[6] Baeta pointed out, however, that people in places like Ghana and Nigeria in the 1940s had to assemble their understandings of the larger world out of the information and images that they had at their disposal, within the contexts of their existing world views, and based on their own cultural precepts. This process had little to do with either lack of sophistication or the mesmerizing character of film. Superficial or distorted notions of the West simply reflected a lack of knowledge and experience: a phenomenon perhaps even more evident in Western representations and readings of Africa through film. 'A European trying to think in terms of the primitive African fails, and what he gets is anything but the way a primitive African thinks,' Baeta commented. 'What others think Africans think, is not necessarily what we think.'[7] Such circumstances, in which viewers grapple with plot lines and images across profound barriers of language, education, and culture, only reinforce Richard Maltby's criticism of the lack of attention to audiences in film scholarship, reflecting its tendency to focus attention 'on the relatively abstract entity of the "film-as-text."'[8]

Films in African Communities

The movies came to Africa in the first decade of the twentieth century, and by the 1920s and 1930s cinema shows were a commonplace phenomenon in urban areas across the continent.[9] Films were shown in a wide range of venues, from luxurious movie palaces in South African cities to simple outdoor theatres in the towns in Zambia's rapidly industrializing Copperbelt.[10] In the 1940s, young people like A.M. Baeta would have grown up on the movies, seeing largely the same films as audiences in England and, especially, America. This was, not surprisingly, a matter of concern for imperial policy-makers. In a 1926 article, in the British journal *The Nineteenth Century*, Robert Donald drew attention to imperial dependence on foreign suppliers for more than 90 per cent of films shown and called for action to end 'the stranglehold of the United States on the world's film supplies.'[11] Worse, the vast majority of American films were 'just hick films,' some of which were not regarded as fit for exhibition in the United States and consequently were 'dumped in overseas markets.' With unmistakable anti-Semitic undertones, Donald noted that the dominant filmmakers cared only about profits and turned out pictures 'without other motive than to make money in providing people with an entertainment.' While admitting that these films had no direct propagandistic intent, Donald argued that 'the propaganda is all the more telling because it is unconscious.'[12] In his view, these films carried no explicit message, but instead exported in broad terms the idea of America and American culture. To illustrate his point, he quoted Will Hays, described by Donald as the 'head of the motion picture industry in the United States,' making the argument that 'American films abroad create a demand for American clothes and other American products, and have been an important aid to the American manufacturers doing business in foreign markets.'[13]

Generations of censorship boards in African colonies would expend countless hours determining the impact of particular plot lines and scenes on the colonial architecture of political and racial hegemony but, as Robert Donald implied, African audiences were drawing less explicit ideas from American movies. The cultural experiences of African audiences shaped their very definition as an audience for films. In particular, as the American cultural historian Lawrence Levine has noted in his study of popular culture in early working-class communities, 'people enjoyed popular culture not as atomized beings vulnerable to an overpowering external force but as part of social groups in which they experienced the performance or with which they shared it after the fact.'[14]

In Accra, the capital of the Gold Coast or Ghana, the first established theater was the Merry Villas Cinematograph Palace, built in 1913 to seat more than 1,000 patrons. This theater and two others built during the next decade showed imported films and also offered variety shows, social evenings, and dances. Moviegoers represented a wide spectrum of the population, with both cheap and more expensive seats offered to African and white patrons alike.[15] The most well-known of the theaters, the Palladium, began life as the 'West End Kinema Palladium,' and was the creation of the local African entrepreneur, Alfred Ocansey. Having traveled to England and seen the theater and cinema there, Ocansey was determined to offer a similar kind of 'modern' entertainment in Accra.[16] In her recent book on the development of an indigenous theater tradition in Ghana, Catherine Cole documents the interplay between the films and the plays known as 'concerts' that were often performed in the very same theaters. The pioneers of concert party entertainments got their ideas from play books, sheet music, from visiting entertainers from England and America and, especially, from the American films that played in the local theaters where they performed. African actors took their cues from American movie performers, notably Al Jolson, and often blackened their faces and put white makeup around their mouths. The group that is now recognized as the original concert party troupe went by the name of 'The Two Bobs and Their Carolina Girl.'[17] Clearly, the application of black makeup was not intended as a racial marker (since the actors were all 'black' according to European and American racial categorizations), but rather was an element in a broader effort to appropriate 'American' and other modern attributes.

As the history of the concert performers and their predecessors makes clear, this was not a case of either 'cultural imperialism' or indiscriminate appropriation of American or Western culture. As early as 1915, a Ghanaian writer, Kobina Sekyi, had written 'The Blinkards,' a play for popular audiences. In that play, Sekyi took satirical aim at newly educated and well-to-do people who had become slavishly devoted to everything English. Integrating the use of English and the local language, Twi, the play essentially argued for adoption of English customs that made sense in the African context. Later concert party performers extended this tradition by rejecting a definition of modernity defined as exclusively Western and in opposition to 'primitive' culture, instead conceiving of 'the modern' as describing 'an integrative process involving conscious choices of inclusion and exclusion.'[18]

American movies continued to be a critical source of cultural vocabulary in Ghana in the post World War II period, when the under-employed 'veranda boys' who flooded Ghana's urban centers in the period leading up to independence in 1957 incorporated elements from popular films in their distinctive styles. A passage from Cameron Duodu's novel, *The Gab Boys* (1967), captures the open-ended engagement of such young men with movies: 'I love this woman, I said. And I'll go to her. What would Robin Hood have done? What did the young boy I had seen in the film *Lorna Doone* do? Didn't he climb a huge waterfall to go to his love? Didn't Romeo sleep in the house of Juliet on the night of his exile? And what did I have to fear? Only two policemen …'[19] In Accra, at the same time, groups of young men formed clubs marked by distinctive styles of playing and listening to rock 'n' roll music that they encountered especially in American rock 'n' roll movies.[20] In each of these cases, the young people who made up the mass of film audiences saw movies as sources of information about other parts of the world and, in particular, as sources of inspiration for defining styles and modes of behavior. This was quite different from superficial and indiscriminate copying. Colonial officials, and especially white settlers, were seemingly preoccupied by fears that screen narratives and images would drive African audiences to criminal behavior and immorality, but African audiences were generally more likely to criticize Western behavior than to emulate the actions that concerned censors. At the same time, however, they were anxious to enjoy and appropriate story elements, characteristic styles and behaviors, and visual images that seemed to offer guidance in the difficult work of navigating a rapidly changing social context.[21]

The remarkable and persistent appeal of American movies among African audiences both perplexed and appalled colonial observers. White officials and residents often found it hard to comprehend how uneducated Africans, who knew little or no English and who in many cases had grown up in remote rural areas, would be attracted to films set in foreign locales populated by stock characters whose fictional lives seemed to be about as far removed from the experience of residents of Ghana or of the Zambian Copperbelt as was possible to imagine. Yet the popularity of these films was unmistakable. Week after week, crowds poured in to the bioscope intent on the latest escapades of cowboy heroes.[22]

The deep affection that young women and men on the Copperbelt and elsewhere in Africa had for these films challenged deeply entrenched colonial mythologies. From the highly racialized perspectives that dominated much imperial thinking through the end of colonialism and beyond, Africans should have lacked the cognitive and imaginative capacities to comprehend and appreciate American and European feature films. In a colonial world marked by manifestations of supposedly atavistic behavior, such as the Mau Mau rebellion of the mid 1950s, how could it be that Africans would be so powerfully drawn to such radically foreign cultural artifacts as Hollywood movies? From the point of view of more progressive whites (and growing numbers of Africans), whose aspirations for the development of African societies gained increasing prominence in the 1950s, the appeal of American films was similarly disturbing and inexplicable. For them, the images portrayed in standard Hollywood fare purveyed distorted notions of life in Europe and America and undermined efforts to build the foundations of middle- and working-class respectability.

The debates that surrounded these issues and the resolution of the contradictions inherent in them involved the construction of successive or competing notions of what constituted African audiences and African audience behavior. As might be expected in the racially very stratified circumstances that defined central and southern Africa, these debates were highly theoretical in the sense that they were rooted in white assumptions about African culture and behavior—the belief that 'we know our own Bantu'—rather than any objective empirical research.[23] Whether they held deeply racist or more progressive views on the potential for African development, white observers shared a common faith in the extraordinary power of the film medium and, in particular, in its power on 'impressionable' audiences. At the same time, of course, African film-goers were defining themselves as an audience—or a series of audiences. But only very occasionally was a voice like that of A.M. Baeta raised to articulate their positions and to challenge the prevailing notion of African spectators as the passive recipients of the images and messages of film. Scholars have, by and large, failed to challenge the assumption of the inarticulate audience. In a brief chapter in her study of urban society in Northern Rhodesia, the anthropologist Hortense Powdermaker left a rich record of African film-going on the Copperbelt in the 1950s, but subsequent scholarship has tended to conceptualize film as a tool of imperial subjugation, reinforcing the passivity of the audience to the degree that it emerges into view at all.

Colonial Film Spectatorship

The paucity of scholarship addressing the global impact of popular films reflects a broad inattention in film studies to film reception across race, ethnic, national, class, generational, and gender lines.[24] Standard accounts of the history of movies in the United States, for example, typically pay little attention to audience and especially to audience diversity.[25] This apparent lack of serious concern among film historians and other scholars for the process of film consumption contrasts quite remarkably with the continuing prominence in political and moral discourse—in locations as diverse as the United States and South Africa—of the dangers that certain kinds of films supposedly represent to the social and moral order. In the first full-length study of the impact of film in Africa, historian James Burns traces the development of theories of film literacy in British Africa.[26] Burns documents the persistence of white assumptions that unsophisticated African audiences were incapable of distinguishing between reality and representation. The stock example, cited repeatedly, was the supposed confusion caused by films on malaria that featured shots of mosquitos depicted in very large scale. Ironic comments from audiences regarding the size of mosquitos in the area where the film had been shot were simply taken at face value and cited as evidence of African inability to grasp the nature of film and the related need for cinema for Africans to be produced in accordance with their supposedly limited capacity for the reception of film images. In the late 1940s, however, at the same time that A.M. Baeta raised her objections to this racist folk wisdom, such thinking was increasingly under challenge. Certainly, imperial planners were impressed that 'as a medium of education and entertainment, the cinema in African society is known to be effective, but the modes of its effectiveness are still largely unknown.' Since film production was expensive, the British government directed the Colonial Office in the early 1950s to 'conduct a proper research into the suitability of the film as a method of educating backward peoples.'[27]

In response to that directive the colonial administration funded a study in rural Nigeria that was designed systematically to address the question of African reception to film.[28] Specifically, researchers were charged with investigating a number of 'problems urgently demanding attention,' including whether 'primitive peoples' comprehended various forms of representation; whether and how comprehension varied among people of different cultures and in relationship to various types of films, especially cartoons; if the 'habitual associations of ideas of African peoples are very different from those of Europeans,' in particular with reference to the 'causes of laughter'; and, finally, whether there were clear differences in terms of reaction and understanding among people from diverse cultures to the same films.[29] This study, and other less systematic observations from the same period, demonstrated conclusively that even inexperienced rural audiences readily understood films, and that a wide range of audiences could understand the messages in propaganda or educational films—even if they did not appreciate them. In West Africa during that period, as colonies moved rapidly toward independence, a non-racialist view of cinema reception emerged, but the traditional, racially inspired assumptions remained widespread, even among film 'experts,' in the racially highly stratified societies of southern Africa.

The 1953 official study of film reception in rural Nigeria, undertaken by anthropologist Peter Morton-Williams, provides a fascinating window onto the impact of film in colonial Africa, even though it focused almost exclusively on the reception of educational films rather than Hollywood products.[30] In analyzing audience response, Morton-Williams was particularly interested in exploring the question of the relationship between 'the habitual associations of ideas' linked to members of particular African 'tribes' and their understanding of ideas conveyed in films. The research relied heavily on the observation of audiences watching films and was rooted in a presumption that consistent observable responses were a strong indicator of common interpretation of meaning. Typically for the period, the research project was developed in a framework that privileged a social order defined by exclusive and neatly bounded ethnic or tribal affiliations, and largely ignored the distinctions of generation, social standing, and gender in these rural societies.[31] Although cultural relativism strongly influenced Morton-Williams's perspective, he was nevertheless a developmentalist—looking for ways that films might be utilized to 'break into a closed system of thought.'[32] What emerges most clearly in the report, especially in the very detailed accounts of audience responses to showings of the same films in different locales, is the easy accommodation to the film medium even among people who had very little or no experience with movies. Audiences typically took the apparatus of cinema for granted and focused on the film action—although they also expressed a preference for films with dialogue, even when, as was usually the case, they did not understand the spoken words.[33]

Confounding the typical assumptions of imperial officials, the responses of audiences suggested no greater affinity or effectiveness for educational films with African locales. In fact, the preoccupation of audience members with identifying the unfamiliar styles and customs represented in such movies seemed to obscure the film topic. In some cases, for example, there were confusions regarding the gender and behavior of the film characters because they were at odds with local custom.[34] Nevertheless, audience interest in ethnic and regional cultural differences represented in films, and occasional confusion derived from them, did not translate into any preference for films with very localized settings—although the researchers themselves persisted in assuming that this was the case. In one example, the negative response of audiences to a film about the Caribbean was explained away in terms of the unfamiliarity of the topic—a fairly preposterous suggestion given the strong audience preference, expressed repeatedly, for Westerns and Chaplin movies rather than the educational fare that was being served up.[35]

With its stated objective of exploring the role of local cultural contexts in shaping film understanding, the Nigerian research project did provide some provocative insights into the readings that specific audiences made of film elements. In particular, the researchers carefully charted incidences of laughter with the objective of gaining some insight into the perplexing immunity of African audiences to certain brands of British humor and, especially, into their disconcerting tendency to laugh at scenes that European film-goers would be expected to see as serious or even tragic. At about the same time, British officials in colonial Zambia experimented with a showing of the film *Cry the Beloved Country* based on the South African novel by Alan Paton. Not only did many in the audience leave because there were no cowboys on the bill, but others laughed uproariously at the scene in which the wealthy white landowner is informed of the death of his son.[36] As the Nigerian research project and other evidence of audience reaction in Africa showed, people inevitably reacted to particular scenes and characters very much out of their own experience.

The presentation of serious issues in European and American dramatic films could often appear to African audiences preposterous or grossly inappropriate, especially as audiences had the expectation that films would be entirely for entertainment. In those circumstances, dramatic moments could provoke laughter that was as much derived from nervousness or incomprehension as amusement, although it is quite likely that politics shaped responses to *Cry the Beloved Country*.[37] More significantly, the Nigerian study pointed to the interesting ways in which local belief systems and experience shaped film readings, even as audiences often brought a broad accumulation of knowledge to their encounters with unfamiliar movie subjects. In one instance, at a film showing in the Yoruba area of southwestern Nigeria, an educational film about the value of modern health care ran up against local tendencies to understand disease in religious terms and to see hospitals as dangerous, even spiritually polluted, places. The film went to some lengths to portray the African nurses as caring and efficient, but these efforts were unconvincing to an audience which assumed that nurses were arrogant and corrupt, often demanding personal cash payments to ensure proper care.[38] It is hardly surprising, then, that audiences read Hollywood film products in contradictory and inventive ways and appropriated and invested meanings in elements and images from popular cinema that would have very much confounded filmmakers. Moreover, as the Nigerian report showed, even within a single if highly diverse territory, class, gender, and especially culture shaped quite distinctive responses to films. In such circumstances, there could be no monolithic *African* response to films.

Cowboy Culture

In a predictably brief section on 'Natives' in Thelma Gutsche's lengthy 1946 study, *The History and Social Significance of Motion Pictures in South Africa*, the author noted that 'the reaction of native audiences to the cinema was in many cases unexpected and remained constant in only one instance—affection for "Wild Westerns."' Although Gutsche's study focused almost entirely on white South Africa, she perceptively noted that in South Africa, as in many other areas across Africa, 'more than twenty years of film exhibitions' had failed to cure working-class African audiences of 'their affection for a mythical cowboy called "Jack" (no matter what his real name) and his always-successful deeds of daring.'[39] In the memoir of Zimbabwean author Shimmer Chinodya, 'those were the days of the mobile bioscope [movie theater], when the nights belonged to Mataka and Zuze and the Three Stooges and cinema was so alive you could smell cowboys' gunpowder off the big white screen.'[40] Although Westerns and other popular British and American action movies almost entirely dominated African movie screens from the 1930s through the 1960s, scholars have, with few exceptions, avoided the topic.[41]

But the cowboys were everywhere. In the French West African colony of Senegal, when the striking railway workers portrayed in Sembene Ousman's great novel, *God's Bits of Wood*, gathered to pass the time, 'their discussions were invariably concerned with the same subject—the films they had seen in the days before the strike. They told the stories of every one of them over and over again, but never without feverish interruptions ... Next to Western films, war films were their favorites.'[42] In Senegal, as in Zambia and in communities across Africa, films were savored and discussed and their elements examined. This imagined Wild West with its legendary cowboy heroes (and it is notable that the Indian 'enemies' that populated some Westerns were largely ignored) penetrated popular culture well beyond the boundaries of the moviegoing public, and in fact many people who had rarely if ever seen a movie were very familiar with the Wild West ethos. In rural eastern Nigeria in the 1940s and early 1950s, young men formed into cowboy gangs that adopted none of the outward trappings of Wild West attire but adopted the bravado and aggressiveness that they somehow associated with their notions of cowboys.[43] Everywhere across the continent, youths who were in the vanguard of defining a self-consciously modern society, linked to global political, economic, and cultural forces, shared this fascination with Western films. Often, these young men and some women were urban migrants or the town-nurtured children of urban migrants. In the urbanized copper-mining region of colonial Zambia, some of these youths strutted around town wearing ten-gallon hats and chaps. White officials and missionaries, as well as older Africans, often looked with alarm at these young men, seeing dangerous assertiveness and potential criminality in their dress and attitude. In the 1950s, when the host of a popular radio request program made a visit to mining communities that he described as 'pulsating with a noise and vitality,' he encountered one young man wearing a 'loud-check shirt and a cowboy hat' who responded to a mention of World War II with the comment 'that's what I'm like when I smoke *dagga* [marijuana] just like Hitler.' He then added, 'Jus' gimme jive!' Then 'holding his silver-studded belt with his thumbs he elbowed his way through the children, and announced, "I'm the best jiver on the whole Copperbelt."' [44] For this youth, and many of his compatriots, his 'cowboy' identity synthesized an eclectic mix of modern behaviors and qualities. The same author, however, stressed that in the vibrant urban communities of Central Africa this was simply one among numerous manifestations of modernity. Many of his listeners, for example, enjoyed making fun of the craze for Westerns and the 'unemployed juvenile delinquents of the Copperbelt dressed in cowboy clothes and living a Wild West fantasy life,' by asking questions they may well have already known the answers to: 'Are all Americans cowboys or are there some ordinary people like villagers and clerks? Are the cowboys we see in films employed people or do they look after their own cattle?' [45] At the same time, such questions quite directly illustrate the ways that movie audiences explored the cowboy world through their own, very typically Central African, lens.

The 'cowboy culture' was also very much in evidence in the capital of the British Protectorate of Tanganyika (now Tanzania). According to a 1956 survey of Dar es Salaam:

> there has grown up, as elsewhere in East Africa, the cult of the cowboy, the African equivalent of the English teddy-boy. The young man from the country, or the young man from the Town, soon acquires the idioms of tough speech, the slouch, the walk of the 'dangerous man' of the films; the ever-popular Western films teach him in detail the items of clothes that go with the part, the wide hat, neckerchief, particoloured shirt, often with tassels, jeans, and high heels, or at least the *kilipa* [the local term for crepe soled shoes]

... After the first years of direct imitation local fashions have added their own peculiarities, such as the *uchinjo* jeans drawn down tight to well above the ankle ... With such an outfit, sometimes costing as much as a hundred shillings ... goes ... an attitude of mind; it is the revolt of the adolescent, in age and in culture, against the authority of elders, of the established, of the superior and supercilious.

The survey report linked cowboy styles with the activities of gangs of youths in bars, dance halls and cinemas and asserted that 'the cult of cowboy clothes is the safety-valve of the dangerous mob element.'[46] If such alarmist claims of linkages between Hollywood films and challenges to authority were exaggerated, the report accurately placed film as a critical element in the development of local sub-cultures.

By the 1930s across urban Africa, movies had become a very important leisure activity and in South Africa, in particular, films were attracting very large audiences.[47] In the Johannesburg region, for example, by the late 1950s there were thirty-two cinemas open to the black population, attracting a weekly audience of 150,000.[48] In historian Bill Nasson's description of leisure in the District Six neighborhood of Cape Town, cinema shows emerge as community institutions, and the film-going experience spilt out into the surrounding neighborhoods and spread beyond the patrons themselves. Managers aggressively promoted film shows, organized a wide variety of promotions, and, like their counterparts in Ghana, opened their theaters to a wide range of entertainment activities and meetings.[49] In South Africa, theaters were strictly segregated by race, but in terms of the moviegoing experience and the films shown, there was perhaps a greater difference between the first- and third-run theaters located in black communities than between black and white first-run cinemas.[50] The first-run theaters showed a much smaller number of action and adventure movies and carefully cultivated an atmosphere of elegance and decorum. For better educated and more affluent black audiences, these film shows offered an opportunity to reaffirm definitions of respectability and enrich their cultural vocabularies through the films shown. For them, like moviegoers in Ghana, musicals and various kinds of spectaculars offered a means to join local cultural traditions with the sophisticated modern entertainments served up on film.[51]

Like the movie houses that catered to immigrant audiences in New York, the South African cinemas fostered intensely social experiences that reinforced collective identities.[52] This was particular evident among the audiences that returned week after week to shabby third-run theaters, encountering their friends and neighbors each week in a crowded and raucous atmosphere often redolent with the odor of marijuana, where patrons vocally engaged the B film of the week. These working-class moviegoers had no patience with heavily plotted dramas, voting with their feet for the action-oriented Westerns and gangster films whose rough and rebellious characters seemed to resonate more with their own marginal circumstances.[53] Writer Don Mattera recalled that, in the black community of Sophiatown, near Johannesburg, in the 1940s and 1950s, residents flocked to the local cinemas: 'almost everything we wore or ate was fashioned after American styles. Some gangs and gang members chose the names, habits and mannerisms of film stars such as George Raft, John Garfield and John Wayne, who was nicknamed *Motsamai* (swaggerer).' People were prepared to pay high prices for 'the privilege of wearing USA imports such as Florsheim, Nunn Bush and Jarman shoes.'[54] For these movie patrons, the images and behaviors observed on screen provided critical guidance in shaping not only their superficial appearance but their individual and group identities.[55]

In her account of the culture of moviegoing in the industrial mining communities of colonial Zambia in the 1950s, Hortense Powdermaker described film shows that attracted many hundreds of patrons to outdoor cinemas. At that time as many as half the adults living in these communities attended movies once a week, drawn by both the films themselves and the excitement of 'being part of a movie audience of more than a thousand people, constantly commenting to each other, shouting their pleasure and booing their displeasure.' In contrast to radio listening or film attendance in Europe and the United States, 'going to the movies was a social experience.'[56] Powdermaker, like most white observers, bemoaned the affection of audiences for B cowboy movies while simultaneously asserting the incapacity of unsophisticated African audiences to comprehend the products of Hollywood studios. Yet the invaluable detailed evidence of audience reaction that Powdermaker provides suggests that Zambian audiences had little difficulty distinguishing between fact and fiction, although not surprisingly they often mis-interpreted (or perhaps reinterpreted) the 'intended' meanings of dialogue and plots.

Film shows in the mining districts generally began with newsreels and other educational films, and African audiences invariably expressed their anti-white settler perspectives in reaction to any films that smacked of propaganda for the white-dominated Central African Federation.[57] Powdermaker interpreted the reactions of high school students to a film about 'The First Easter' as evidence of their incapacity to see the distinction among documentaries, docudramas and fiction films, but the students' comments can also be read as indicating an astutely skeptical engagement with the movie: one asked if there were actually records from the time of Jesus, another wanted to know why white people portrayed the characters, and a comment that the king's cape resembled Superman's was probably more evidence of the importance of Hollywood films in defining the visual vocabularies of students than any confusion between Herod and the caped crusader. A number of the students complained vocally at having to look at such a film at all, and there is a good chance that the young man who asked whether there were cameras during the time of Jesus had his tongue in his cheek. After all, another indicated his preference for Westerns by saying, 'with cowboys it is interesting, because it is all acting.'[58]

Both women and men were attracted to the action movies, with their weak plots and continual scenes of combat between cowboys and their adversaries. White censors had assembled long lists of types of scenes and plot lines that they regarded as too dangerous for Africans to see, but African audiences seemed to approach films in ways that transcended such concerns.[59] They looked in particular for the behavior of the cowboy hero, always referred to as 'Jack,' and the quality of the fight scenes. During the fight scenes, the sounds of the crowd cheering on the protagonists could be heard several miles away: 'They all fear him because they cannot fight him ... This one's a weakling ... That is the only man who can fight Jack! ... Jack is very clever, he can fight them all ... This is the kind of Jack we want.'[60] Especially for male residents of these mining towns, many of whom worked in very physically demanding jobs, cowboys represented a culture of toughness that they found appealing: 'When the people are fighting, I feel as if I am also going to fight someone ... I always want to see how strong Jack is ... I expect the hero, Jack, to beat everyone and to win every time ... He *must* always rise up after he is hit and the enemy *must* always run away. I like the way they ride and fight with their hands ... If I went to America, I would very much want to be a cowboy.' More tellingly, another audience member stated: 'I like best the cowboy films, because they teach us how to fight others and how to win lovers.'[61]

Inverting the arguments of the censors, Powdermaker was anxious to find a political explanation for the appeal of cowboy movies. The cowboys, according to Powdermaker, were white but not British and the 'cowboy hero fits into the present power relations between European and Africans.' Zambian audiences, she argued, found in the 'hard fighting cowboy' riding across open spaces some relief from their smoldering resentment of their oppressed political and social status. Certainly, residents of the mining communities were increasingly politicized during the 1950s, but there is little evidence in their affection for these heroes and their responses to these films—or the similar responses from audiences across much of Africa—to suggest a powerful political metaphor.[62] In fact, what was much more notable among film-goers in South Africa, Zambia, Ghana and elsewhere was the creativity with which they drew the action and characters off the screen and invested them with indigenous qualities. Thus, at the same time that audiences were drawing on films to develop a lexicon of modernity, they were reinventing the films in their own cultural and political terms. Cowboys, and the mythic hero, Jack, in particular, were seen as possessing supernatural powers and having important kinship connections: 'The cowboy has medicines to make him invisible. His enemies have failed to see him hiding in the bush. Jack knows he is younger than Chibale [an older cowboy who plays the part of a clown] ... So Jack has to respect him. Cowboys show respect. And Jack is also the son of a big man.'[63] At the same time, films that showed displays of affection between men and women or both women and men together at the beach or at a pool were, on the one hand, read as guides to sophisticated behavior and, on the other, observed through a local moral code that led viewers to ascribe immorality to the characters and to make negative judgements about Western society and mores.[64]

The Return of Film

In the 1960s, with independence and the advent of other forms of popular entertainment, the cinema declined in importance across Africa, as larger numbers of people gained access to radio and even television and as the cowboy genre itself lost popularity globally.[65] In West Africa especially the cultural ferment associated with decolonization inspired the emergence of a number of highly regarded filmmakers, notably Sembene Ousmane from Senegal. However important in artistic terms, these filmmakers and their works made relatively little popular impact. With few exceptions, African films were not widely distributed and most failed to find substantial audiences. Moviegoers in African urban centers continued to favor imports, but increasingly they preferred Kung Fu films from Hong Kong to Hollywood products. In the late 1980s, the availability of VCRs dramatically revived the popularity of films and a video revolution swept across the continent. In urban neighborhoods and in rural hamlets, local businessman put together the capital to buy a television set and a VCR and gain access to electricity, if necessary with a small generator, in order to open small video dens. These dens were in some cases no more than a backroom, and in others small theaters.[66] For a few cents the new and tragic 'leisure class' of under- or unemployed young men could spend hours watching pirated copies of Hollywood and Hong Kong epics. In their fathers' and grandfathers' time, cowboys had ruled the cinematic landscape; now the heroes of martial arts epics dominated, while they gathered in small groups in shabby facilities that were a far cry from the hundreds who had assembled for outdoor film shows in Zambia in the 1950s or in the grand movie palaces in South African cities. Increasingly, relatively affluent households could afford their own apparatus.[67] In the midst of bitter fighting in 2003 in the eastern Congo, video dens were virtually the only businesses that remained open in the town of Bunia as warring militias ravaged the town and the surroundings.[68] With schools shut down and few opportunities for work, boys and young men flocked to these makeshift theaters to pay about eleven cents to see movies like *Mortal Kombat* and a Chinese action feature called *Iron Angels*.

As in the earlier period, these films served as critical sources for the development of distinctive sub-cultures and the construction of self-consciously modern forms of behavior, especially during a period of time marked by growing economic despair. Ernie Wolfe III's fascinating compendium of images of hand painted movie posters created in Ghana between the mid-1980s and mid-1990s, as video dens proliferated, provides visual evidence of the cultural processes at work.[69] Derived from the illustrations on cassette boxes and other sources, these images represent a strange amalgam of Hollywood and Hong Kong imagery on the one hand and Ghanaian culture on the other. Very often, stars like Sylvester Stallone emerge on these canvases as racially indeterminate, and the suggestions of film content incorporate local traditions and beliefs. Much like the movie audiences of the 1950s, these artists, and presumably those who frequented the video dens, engaged the films they watched as cultural products to be discussed, analyzed, critiqued and reinvented. This process accelerated rapidly in the mid-1990s, with the dramatic development of indigenous video industries in Ghana and especially in Nigeria. In makeshift studios in Accra and Lagos, African filmmakers, often with very little experience, churned out hundreds of video films. With this development, local filmmakers in West Africa were for the first time reaching a mass audience, and in many cases their videos proved more popular than imports. Sharing a kinship with some of the early Hollywood directors and producers, these African producers approached filmmaking from a business perspective and saw themselves more as members of the audience than self-consciously as artists.[70] To date, there has been little study of the actual response of audiences to these ephemeral epics. With narratives that run the gamut from Christian fables to tales of cannibalism, these films represent the manifestation of the goals of the imperial filmmakers of the 1930s and 1940s to make movies with indigenous settings. It remains to be seen, however, whether these new videos will challenge imported action films, long embraced and invested with local cultural norms.

19

'Opening Everywhere'

Multiplexes and the Speed of Cinema Culture

Charles R. Acland

THE opening of a film has long held an iconic place in the imagery of American cinemagoing. Tales of Hollywood past are replete with accounts of the excitement and expectation of a film première. Histories and biographies, whether popular or scholarly, typically describe these events with reference to notable theatres, their ornamentation further adorned with red carpets and velvet ropes, and with archival photographs of the throngs of spectators waiting for admittance. Samuel Fuller reminisced that following the opening of his film *Fixed Bayonets* (1951) at the Rivoli in New York, 'we had a raucous dinner at Toots Shor's place, like in the old days, with an abundance of steaks and vodka. I don't know how I got back to my hotel that night.'[1] Whatever the circumstances and celebrations, the filmmaker's worries about critical reception, the studio's anxieties about box-office receipts, and the audiences' thrill in seeing the freshest instalment of movie culture all converge at the launch of a film. Confirming the extremes of Hollywood's glamour and spectacle, the romanticism of the première runs high.

In more quotidian contexts, the routines of commercial cinemagoing also include the pleasure—or frustration—of the opening weekend crowds. Who among us has not looked forward to seeing the new work of a treasured filmmaker or star, and considered the extra delight of watching with a gathering of similarly enthralled patrons? And who, conversely, has not waited impatiently for crowds to clear in order to enjoy a more intimate cinematic experience? The contemporary American motion picture industry relies upon opening weekends as a source of rapidly accumulated revenue and as a predictor of future economic success; in 1997, those films given wide releases, meaning 600 or more screens, earned an average of 37.3% of their total box office during their first week.[2] The opening weekends for wide released films accounted for 24.7% in 1999, 29.5% in 2001, and 30.3% in 2003 of total box office, on average.[3] The reliance on immediate box-office return rests on a broad acceptance of the value of such openings among cinemagoers. Some on-line and telephone ticketing services offer the purchase of tickets forty-five days in advance to allow customers to secure seats at the most expectantly awaited premières. Religious groups booked entire theatres in advance of the release of *The Passion of the Christ* (Mel Gibson, 2004), and some have attributed the startling early financial success of the film to this phenomenon. Exhibitors and audiences both note, often with consternation, the uneven distribution of cinemagoing throughout the week, an inequality that initial release dates accentuate further. Since they tend to be the most crowded and the most expensive of cinemagoing occasions, one is tempted to wonder why more people do not avoid opening weekends. Many do, but not enough to alter this dominant industry strategy.

Although the promotional festivities of a première at, for example, Grauman's Chinese Theater in Hollywood are a world away from the more pedestrian launches at a local multiplex, the two share a relationship with the 'new' in film culture. Wherever it is located, a première requires the circulation of some prior knowledge about coming attractions. The film itself cannot account for all of the intensity of pre-launch interest. Building expectation for and awareness of a new movie is a key goal of film advertising. For this promotion to have any consequence, there must be something especially appealing about the freshness of these new arrivals. Most obviously, the opening's added sign-value involves a sense of being up-to-date, inviting people to be the first on the scene. This supplementary value is time-sensitive and fades as the initial release date passes.

The valorisation of the 'new' is a familiar quality of consumer culture in general, but with motion pictures, patrons are attending more than a new film. Theatres play a special role as a point of initiation in the life of cultural commodities, and the release of a major motion picture into commercial cinemas is also the introduction of a set of commodities and artefacts—a soundtrack, a website, a magazine issue, a new star, a re-released book or comic, a video game, a music video, action figures and other merchandise. Audiences expect the films themselves to mutate into videos, DVDs, and television content. Because films can be viewed and experienced in multiple formats, one now hears the previously unnecessary marketing claim 'only in theatres.' Films also become fodder for posters, becoming books, and amusement park rides. There is no fixed trajectory to these transformations; there are frequent instances of films based on theme park rides and graphic novels. Moreover, fully re-mediated texts, running the gamut of all media forms, may account for only a small number—the most highly visible—of films. This multiple incarnation of related and successive texts does, however, mean that the massive amount of promotion accompanying a new blockbuster is also selling all the other artefacts that appear according to their own flexible schedules. Whether the availability of these variously mediated commodities is bundled together or staggered, these new blockbusters are selling a timeline for cultural practice and consumption.

In addition to their association with new cultural works, opening weekends provide the material and sensory experience of a shared community. The desirability of this feature varies according to taste, genre, and mood. Moviegoers may identify some films as ideally suited to the din and distraction of the full house, best seen with other spectators. Some consider the belly laughs of comedy and the embarrassing involuntary yelps of horror to be realized better in crowds than in solitary viewing situations. Although this aspect of communality may characterize much cinemagoing, queues are customary at film premières; people attend them precisely to be with strangers and, at the same time, to be part of a knowing first-on-the-scene crowd. A thin gathering at an opening weekend screening gives off a whiff of morbidity, and may instantly conjure up a sense of failure for the film in question.

Those sitting in neighbouring seats are only the most literal and visible of opening weekend cinemagoers. Significantly, the current coordination of release dates across the US, Canada and beyond, fosters an imagined and temporally bound sense of similar crowds elsewhere *Lord of the Rings: Two Towers* (Peter Jackson, 2002) opened in Germany one week, in the US, Canada, UK, Ireland, and Spain the next week, and then in Australia and Korea. The increasingly rapid circulation of new films is evident even for those that do not receive saturation release. *Gangs of New York* (Martin Scorsese, 2002) appeared first in Japan, then the US. and Canada the following week, and Italy five weeks later.[4] *The Matrix Revolutions* (Wachowski Brothers, 2003) may be an extreme instance of wide international release, but it is also a harbinger of a trend toward simultaneity. Within the first week of its release, its 10,013 prints had premièred in 107 territories, and on 18 IMAX screens. Reportedly, co-producers Warner Bros. and Village Roadshow coordinated many of the premières to begin at exactly the same time.[5]

The avoidance of piracy is a convenient excuse for this synchronization and, certainly, revenue can be siphoned off when there is a temporal lag in a film's availability; all that is needed is an enterprising individual willing to copy and distribute faster and cheaper, and to take on the associated legal risks.[6] In 2003, this prospect prompted the Motion Picture Association of America (MPAA) to ban the delivery of DVD screening copies of Academy Award nominated films to voting members.[7] Synchronization of releasing responds to more than the piracy threat, however. It is no secret that, for some blockbusters, international audiences are more important than the US. domestic market, and their distributors can make use of economies of scale in advertising and promotion to build a global time-sensitive momentum in awareness and expectation. Promotional material can travel faster across national borders than the motion pictures themselves, and a quicker release can capitalize on this. Furthermore, there are a number of industrial conditions that make this accelerated circulation feasible. To pull off their remarkable global launch, the last two *Matrix* films made full use of two producing corporations (Warner Bros. and Village Roadshow), that also act as distributors and operate large international theatre chains. The industrial rationale of piracy avoidance, economics of scale, and corporate ownership structure together equally create the conditions for an imagined transnational popular movie scene. One effect has been a widely dispersed sense of the current or the 'new' in cinema culture as well as a sense of communality among moviegoers across continents. Put differently, the coordination of one stratum of film culture offers a 'felt internationalism' to be shared by cultural consumers.

Research on the globalization of film has tended to focus on either film texts or film financing. The former examines the consequences of internationally salient conventions, as evident in art film circuits or popular movie genres. The latter considers the internationalization of the ownership of media corporations and the moves toward co-production financing. The best of this scholarship has prompted a reconsideration of so-called national cinemas.[8] Scant attention has so far been given to the internationalization of exhibition and distribution, despite the fact that operations in this part of the film business have radically altered in recent years, creating a greater coordination of openings over a wider geographical expanse.[9] The need for larger numbers of screens for saturation openings means that films are pushed aside faster, bumped from a limited number of theatrical venues to make room for newer releases. This coordination has shuffled the parameters of what is understood as being the *current cinema* by bundling the appearance of some, accelerating the arrival and departure of releases, and leaving a greater waiting period for others. The category of the 'current cinema' is a conceptual necessity in light of the fact that American cinema culture occupies multiple sites and formats, all of which have different temporalities; it designates a temporally defined slate of films characterized by their newness: that is, those movies 'in theatres now.' With the exception of the increasingly marginal repertory cinemas (especially in Canada, U.S., and the UK) theatres offer new films for a short period of time. At the same time, videotape and DVD sales and rentals offer a growing back catalogue of films, giving long-term availability to works that would have disappeared in the past. This trend introduces a modified sense of scarcity to cinemagoing: if you want to see a film on a theatrical screen, you may have but a matter of weeks to do so. Otherwise, you have the rest of your life to see it at home.

A crucial factor facilitating the speeded-up circulation of current cinema has been the building of ever more extensive theater chains on several continents through the 1990s. Crucially, the internationalization of exhibition has had the effect of exporting certain kinds of cinema spaces, most distinctively large multiplex or 'megaplex' cinemas, along with the modes of cinemagoing associated with the expanded media and leisure activities offered at these new complexes. Although the wide international opening is a feature of select highly visible movies, it is a powerful defining characteristic of contemporary cinemagoing. It is worth remembering that the history of the national 'breakout' of major films is still a fairly recent development, which film historians tend to date from the rising saturation releases of *Jaws* (Steven Spielberg, 1975), *Star Wars* (George Lucas, 1977) and the less frequently acknowledged *Breakout* (Tom Gries, 1975). Twenty years later, Canadian distributor Alliance opened *Scream 2* (Wes Craven, 1997) in Iqaluit, Nunavut, on the same day as it opened in other cities to the south. This was the first time that this northern capital had witnessed such coordination with Ottawa and New York.[10] The crowds at such synchronous openings are not solely an indication of the loss of will to consumer agendas. While indisputably representing a consumerist 'being in the world,' the crowded theatrical opening is also a means of 'being in the know' about contemporary cultural life. Just as saturation release calls forth an imagined collectivity of moviegoers in other suburbs and cities across the country, and at times across international borders, it equally emphasizes the gap between such productions and the timed appearances of more marginal contributions to the current cinema.

It is important to keep in mind the added sign-value of the film opening, for it reminds us of the practices and meanings built around the act of cinemagoing. Even as economic forces structure the cinemagoing space and event, ordinary cultural life does not simply become a static construct, in which people are programmed to exchange money, sit quietly, and leave promptly. Yet, some exemplary work continues tacitly to offer a limited view of the cultural life of cinemagoing. In an essay on digital cinema, for instance, John Belton expresses scepticism about the revolution of digital delivery and projection, and effectively debunks the myth that it is the most significant innovation since the arrival of sound. He argues that even if complete conversion transpires, 'digital projection does not offer audiences a *new experience* in the theater.'[11] Several significant changes to the experience of cinema can, however, be expected from digital delivery, many of which stem from digital cinema's reversal of the current skyrocketing expenses associated with the wider opening of films. Once the projection hardware is in place, and without the familiar, expensive and heavy film reels, digital distribution and exhibition will give an incentive to even wider openings and even faster replacement of films. Digital delivery could make routine the one-time only screenings and programmes of non-feature films with which some exhibitors have already been experimenting. Digital delivery and projection will, therefore, in all probability accelerate the temporality of the current cinema.[12] The full impact of this has yet to be imagined, let alone unfold.

While Belton's dismissal of digital delivery is a welcome response to the fever that now typically surrounds arrival of new media, it is also symptomatic of some of the conceptual blindspots that inhibit us from examining cinematic experience beyond the root definition of sound and light in the dark. Too often, media scholars define cinema culture as involving only a narrow band of activities. To emphasize how unimpressed he is with the 'digital revolution,' Belton sardonically asserts that the only substantive change in the film experience in the last forty years has been stadium seating, which he sees as window-dressing that has not truly altered the film experience.[13] If, however, we think of cinemagoing as the raw fact of gathering bodies in a designated location for a specified audiovisual performance, then any alteration to the material boundaries of this event, whether spatial or temporal, has radiating effects upon the structure and experience of that cultural practice. What at first glance appear to be trivial elements may in fact be salient components of the experience for a moviegoing population. In newly opened megaplexes and refurbished auditoria, audiences are now confronted with cupholders, expanded concessions, high-tech arcades, more leg room, longer and more varied audiovisual advertising displays before features, and, yes, stadium seating. Among these supposed trivialities are material indicators of efforts to situate the movie experience in relation to other sites, including the home, the workplace, the theatre, and the arena. Some cinemas expand access to parents with infants, to children's parties, to summer camps, to people in wheelchairs, and to corporate meetings. These features and uses are not inconsequential. They are ripples on the surface of cultural life, giving us access to what Siegfried Kracauer called the Ratio of the time.[14] If cupholders and party rooms had been part of the ornamentation of Weimer Berlin movie palaces, I believe Kracauer would have written about them. After all, he actually did comment upon stadium seating.[15]

What I am addressing here is the incorporation of the everyday into our critical tool-kit. Doing this means we must pay heed to the organization of ordinary cultural life, including those so-called trivialities that are easy to overlook. Rita Felski evocatively describes the conceptual challenge as follows: 'At first glance, everyday life seems to be everywhere, yet nowhere. Because it has no clear boundaries, it is difficult to identify. Everyday life is synonymous with the habitual, the ordinary, the mundane, yet it is also strangely elusive, that which resists our understanding and escapes our grasp. Like the blurred speck at the edge of one's vision that disappears when looked at directly, the everyday ceases to be everyday when it is subject to critical scrutiny.'[16] We might ask, then, why this 'blur' has been so well considered with other media—television, for instance—and not so with film? There has been some notable work on film audiences, in particular Miriam Hansen's sustained investigations of the making of audiences as standardized industrial components, Janet Staiger's delineations of audience historiography, as well as the edited collections of Melvyn Stokes and Richard Maltby that have rescued studies of film spectatorship from both textual universalism and anecdotal ethnography.[17] Works of this kind have begun to expand the borders of cinema scholarship to encompass everyday life and such research deserves to be broadened.

One explanation for the comparatively slow 'take up' of film and the everyday might be the apparent rhetorical collapse in the distinction between the everyday and the domestic; in much scholarship, the latter term appears as a powerful trope of the former. For example, no matter how ordinary film is, TV is seen as more so. One consequence of this presumption has been the absenting of a myriad of other extra-domestic manifestations of everyday-ness, unfortunately encouraging a rather literal understanding of the everyday. In effect, the abstractions of the everyday are reduced to daily occurrences, and the presumed status of film as more of an 'event'—something less frequently attended—marks its break from the everyday. This crude binary opposition is a philosophically untenable proposition, encouraging unproductive digressions about how often does the 'everyday' have to occur. Henri Lefebvre cautioned against such evaluations, encouraging the investigation of different orders of repetition, and pointing

370

to the uneven development of the everyday, one aspect of which is the way in which apparent breaks from the ordinary work to construct the ordinary.[18] Thus, Lefebvre observed, 'leisure appears as the non-everyday in the everyday.'[19]

In considering the everyday nature of audio-visual media, the economic and cultural interrelationship of film and videotape, DVD, broadcasting, cable, radio, soundtracks and the Internet renders strict boundaries around their cultural consumption either misguided or nostalgic, and should wash away any remaining fixations about stable and isolated media qualities. It is more advantageous to map the routines of use, addressing the place and occasion of cinemagoing in light of these inter-media meldings. There exists an assortment of paths through the world of videotape, DVD, and web-based non-theatrical viewing possibilities. This changing materiality of moving image culture, from airplane screenings to home video libraries, renders cinemagoing a special practice. We might think of this as a call for the study of *cultural occasions*. Whereas Michel de Certeau characterizes 'the procedures of everyday creativity,'[20] I want to emphasize the *parameters*, which include the routines, habits, paths, spaces and times that constitute the patterns of cultural engagement. Accordingly, as I detail industrial investments, I am attempting to portray the context for the activity surrounding the films and the practices appended to these industrial commodities, that is, the field on which the occasions for cinema culture play themselves out.

Cinema culture is woven variously into daily life: marquees adorn our cities; video rental outlets dot local malls; star interviews and production news inhabit our television schedules; film posters decorate bedrooms, offices and construction sites; promotional t-shirts are worn; entertainment sections occupy space in newspapers; favourite movies take up semi-permanent residence in home video libraries; celebrity gossip underpins some ordinary forms of sociability; and stars' faces hail us in commercial venues. Although the act of cinemagoing might occur for many people only once every few months—and the rates of attendance are one of the more pronounced features of differentiation among cinemagoing populations—cinemagoing is only one type of occasion, that is, one enactment of the structure and experience of cinema culture, one detail in the pattern. Such patterns, comprised of historically specific configurations of artefacts, spaces, times, designs, activities, bodies, and representations, constitute the ordinary and the routine of cultural life. Part of any such pattern is that cinemagoing does not involve only film viewing, a fact that the advent of megaplex cinemas has only accented differently. The public film experience involves other forms of media consumption, and even if we confine our focus to the contemporary structure of cinemagoing, the social activities of cinema culture that extend beyond film consumption must still be kept in mind.

Few periods in cinema history saw as much alteration to the cinemagoing context as the 1990s. Some locations experienced unprecedented investment in cinema building and refurbishment, as exhibition companies blindly followed a business strategy beyond economic rationality until the complete, if temporary, destabilization of U.S. exhibition was brought about with the bankruptcies of 2000. During the 1990s, this investment reshaped the spatial and temporal parameters of cinemagoing in a reconfiguration that maintained an eye on international markets. Warner's international success with *Batman* (Tim Burton, 1989) is often cited as an indicator of the contemporary turn to global marketing and releasing.[21] Comparable globalizing turns have been a feature of other eras of cinema history, but this instance, evidenced by swelling international film rentals and ancillary markets for the Hollywood majors, was substantial enough for trade publications to call globalization the 'gospel of the 1990s.'[22] An early sign of the transnationalization of exhibition was the first Cinema Expo International, held in 1992 in Brussels expressly for the film industry's 'extended global marketplace,' after which it became an annual event with steadily rising attendance over the years.[23]

Following the return to exhibition of several Hollywood majors in the mid-1980s, the 1990s witnessed growing investments in theatrical exhibition in international locations.[24] *Variety* reflected the ruling spirit, stating that global distribution was 'entering a new golden age unlike anything seen since World War II.'[25] United International Pictures (UIP) president Michael Williams-Jones, whose company handled international sales for Universal, Paramount and MGM/UA films, claimed in 1995 that 'within five years ... the current B.O. ratio between domestic and foreign for Hollywood films of around 50–50 will swing to 30–70 in foreign's favor.'[26] This highly exaggerated estimate would not come close to being realized, but it nevertheless typified the globalizing consciousness of the day.

In 1992, Millard Ochs of United Cinemas International (UCI), a theatre chain jointly owned by Paramount and Universal, commented that the internationalization of exhibition followed the saturation of the U.S. domestic market.[27] Both he and Peter Ivany of Australian exhibitor Hoyts wrote assessments on costs and issues involved with the international building of theatre chains on the occasion of the joint ShoWest/National Association of Theater Owners (NATO) meeting in 1992, encouraging unparalleled attention to this trend.[28] Intercontinental chains had some presence in earlier periods. In the 1930s, for example, Paramount and Loews had both had theatres in England and France, and Twentieth Century-

Fox had ownership interests in England's Gaumont and Australia's Hoyts, as well as cinemas in New Zealand and South Africa.[29] Thomas Guback records a failed post-World War II attempt to build theatres in West Germany, but all these efforts pale in comparison to the building and buying boom of the 1990s.[30]

What distinguished this period was not just the level of investment, but the kinds of facilities that were being constructed. This was specifically a 'multiplex building boom' with U.S.-based corporations providing much of the capital and direction for the expansion, and some commentators attributing the rise in global box office simply to 'the construction and acceptance of multiplexes.'[31] For others, the boom represented the "Americanization" of moviegoing, a term that implied a strengthened relation between shopping and cinema as manifest in multiplexes. For *Boxoffice*, the 'multiplex invasion' of Europe was a suburban American idea that was 'just now revolutionizing exhibition practices along the rues, strasses and calles of Europe.'[32] Throughout the 1990s, cinema refurbishment and construction occurred in most European countries, including Austria, Belgium, Denmark, Germany, Finland, Ireland, Italy, the Netherlands, Portugal, Spain, Turkey, and the U.K.[33] More cautious multiplex construction took place in Eastern Europe, particularly in the Czech Republic, Hungary, Poland, Slovakia and Russia.[34] With the exception of France, where multiplexing was relatively slow to take off, this Europe-wide development resulted in a rise in the number of screens per site.[35] Multiplexing did not hit Europe alone. A Sony Cinema Products vice president proclaimed that Latin America had the highest building rate of new cinemas in the world.[36] There was also an 'explosion' of new multiplex theatres in Southeast Asia.[37]

The involvement of US.-based interests in these markets was an impetus to investment by national concerns Loews Cineplex Entertainment built 175 screens in Spain through a joint venture with Yelmo Films.[38] In Italy, UCI made plans for a circuit with department-store chain Rinascente. UCI Central Europe, in conjunction with a European-based investment group, developed a multiplex chain with cinemas in the Czech Republic, Hungary, Slovakia, and Turkey.[39] Warner Bros. invested in Japan in association with supermarket chain Nichii. Smile-UA Cineplex and Tanjung Golden Village, the latter a venture combining Malaysian, Hong Kong and Australian exhibitors, opened new theatres in Malaysian shopping malls.[40] Exhibition in India saw joint multiplex building by Modi and United Artists Theater Circuit, part of the Regal Entertainment Group (including the Regal and Edwards chains) that also operated in Hong Kong and Thailand until the bankruptcies of 2000.[41]

373

Table 19.1   Countries/territories of operation for U.S.-based
exhibitors with international circuits (and majority owners), February
2004[42]

AMC	Canada, France, Hong Kong, Japan, Portugal, Spain, and U.K.[43]
Caribbean Cinemas/Regency Caribbean Enterprises	Dominican Republic, Puerto Rico, St. Maarten, Trinidad, Virgin Islands
Cinemark (Madison Dearborn Partners)	Argentina, Brazil, Canada, Chile, Colombia, Costa Rica, Ecuador, El Salvador, Honduras, Mexico, Nicaragua, Panama, Peru, and Taiwan.
Cinemastar Luxury	Mexico
Loews Cineplex (Onex)	Canada, Mexico, Spain, and South Korea
National Amusements (parent company of Viacom)	Argentina, Chile, and U.K.
Wallace	American Samoa, Guam, Marshall Islands, Saipan, and Federated States of Micronesia
Warner Bros. International Theatres (AOL Time-Warner)	China, Germany, Italy, Japan, Portugal, Taiwan, and U.K.[44]
Ultrastar	Mexico
United Cinemas International (Viacom and Universal)	Austria, Brazil, Germany, Ireland, Italy, Japan, Panama, Poland, Portugal, Spain, Taiwan, and the U.K.

These examples of investment activity are signs of the organization of the flow of national and city economies. This organization solidifies the status and presence of certain corporate agents as they participate with larger conglomerates. What we do not see here is a culture industry cleanly divided into global and local operations; instead, we see business classes and investment elites in each country taking part in economic development, perhaps angling for their own international growth. To regard this process only as an internationalization of finance misses the national, city, and neighbourhood ramifications of this investment. These outcomes have become factors in the circulation (or non-circulation) of local fare and in the materiality of parameters of cultural practice: who sees what, where people attend, under what conditions, in relation to what other moviegoing populations, and with what economic consequences.

The multi-directionality of international cultural-economic traffic has other manifestations. Firstly, the intricacies of media conglomerates mean that decision-making power and ownership is spread across several financial capitals and involves internationally circulating business elites. Associating a corporation with a single country might identify the site of its corporate headquarters, its principal location of operation, or its majority ownership, but it might not recognize the range of its participants and facilities. In a way, the phrases 'U.S. exhibitor' or even 'Hollywood major' are references to an historical sense of presence and influence rather than to actual national affiliation. Secondly, it should be evident that U.S. exhibitors were not alone in extending their global outlook. Table II indicates that Australian exhibitors Hoyts, Village Roadshow and Greater Union had screens on several continents. Other examples include Australian Amalgamated Holdings, which owns half of Germany's Kieft & Kieft circuit, Virgin Cinemas, which built in Japan, and South African exhibitor and distributor Ster Century, which opened multiplexes in the UK and Ireland, and Eastern Europe (which they have since sold).[45]

Table 19.2 Screen count for major international chains, 2002[46]

	Africa	Asia	Australia	Latin America	North America	Western Europe	Central/ Eastern Europe	Total
AMC		90		160	3,340	134		3724
Cinemark				799	2215	17		3031
Greater Union	26		457			410		893
Hoyts			408	160	857			1425
Onex		48		361	2281	263		2953
UCI		108		122		947	168	1345
Village Roadshow		129	668	69		578	22	1466
Total								14,837

Some have argued that the 'multiplex revolution' in Europe was a result of the post-recession context coinciding with an increase in attendance, but the motor of this investment wave is more intricate than this explanation suggests. U.S. interests in international exhibition were intense enough to be characterized as a mode of competition between exhibitors who were, in effect, taking their rivalries abroad.[47] As Tino Balio has suggested, the industry accepted the assessment that '[o]utside the U.S., nearly every market was under-screened.'[48] UCI, Cinemark, General Cinema and Hoyts all focussed on Brazil, with a population of 160 million and fewer than 1600 screens.[49] Spain's film attendance decreased rapidly in the mid-1980s, leading to the closing of almost 2,000 theatres.[50] New theatres were in part a response to this 'underscreening,' even though the number of screens may in fact have been an adequate reflection of cinemagoing rates that were lower than those of U.S. audiences. Additionally, distributors had long been complaining of the decrepitude of some countries' cinemas. For instance, many Italian cinemas were owned by small chains lacking the capital for refurbishment. Many were zoned to protect historic buildings, making such changes difficult.[51] As might be expected, stories of international corporate giants insensitive to historical value accumulated as the forces of global capital collided with local concerns.[52]

Even an industrial discourse of underdevelopment, however, explains only so much. Significantly, this investment spree helped to restructure existing distributor/exhibitor agreements. As one commentator put it in 1995, 'The boom is breaking down the old cozy and restrictive relationships between distrib[utor]s and the traditional circuits, and bringing family audiences back to the cinema. It is contributing to the wider release of major titles in Europe and an increase in marketing budgets.'[53] Several of the most active chains—UCI, National Amusements, Warner Bros., and for a time Loews Cineplex—were part of conglomerates that produced and distributed films. Other exhibitors formed distribution arms where domestically they had none; for instance, AMC elected to distribute its own films in Japan instead of relying on locals.[54] The new organization of chains, and the new deals struck between local and international investors, prepared exhibition for a higher degree of coordination across a vast geographical expanse. The push toward global film commodities encouraged distributors to adopt more harmonized international releasing strategies, which could mean similar or successive opening dates and promotional campaigns.[55] In effect, the exportation of the multiplex served as a beachhead for globalizing distribution.[56]

The international management of the spaces and economies of cinemagoing includes products and services as well as films. In 2003, UCI and Warner entered into a joint procurement deal for cinema concessions. With this agreement, the ordering of food, beverages and containers for their respective cinemas has the bargaining advantage of these corporations operating in tandem. They also have the power to grant global procurement contracts, of which they had eight, totaling $100 million, in 2003.[57] Notwithstanding some national differences—German tastes for sweet popcorn against Spanish preferences for salty—concessions have become more standardized, with the same soft drink and sweet selection available in a chain's theatres across continents.

For several years after the destabilization of exhibition in 2000, chains continued to change hands. Moving into Mexico, Onex acquired a share of Cinemex in 2002. Cinemark continued expansion in Mexico, Chile and Costa Rica during 2003.[58] These developments have helped make Mexico one of the top ten most lucrative markets for the Hollywood majors. In the same period, Hoyts backed away from its some of its international ambitions, particularly in the U.S. and Latin America. In order to concentrate more upon film production, Village Roadshow shut half its screens throughout Asia, although it still remained the largest chain in the region. Onex, AMC and UCI continued to develop on that continent.[59] The aftermath of the bankruptcies demonstrated the uncertainty of joint ownership of distribution and exhibition, suggesting that not all conglomerates are equally inclined to concern themselves with the nitty-gritty of ticket-taking and popcorn sales. As a consequence of its shaky financial status, French-U.S. Vivendi Universal backed away from its participation in UCI in 2002, and sold its share of Loews to Canadian Onex in 2001.[60] Onex in turn put its chain on the market in 2004, with some expectation that AMC would act upon its previous interest in buying it.[61] Viacom's continued obsession with exhibition contrasted with both Vivendi's on-again-off-again commitment to that aspect of the film business and Disney's staunch lack of interest in buying theatre chains. Even so, such broad character profiles invariably conceal more intricate positions. For example, in 1993 Disney joined with Gaumont forming Gaumont Buena Vista International to distribute films in France; Gaumont itself subsequently built multiplexes.

For theatrical exhibition, the multi-directionality of cultural flow does not describe a universe of equal economic participation. What we witness is the fortification of paths of cultural and economic circulation and a delimitation of who benefits. By 2001, exhibitors based in just four countries owned the majority of all European screens: France (32.4%), the U.S. (19.4%), Australia (18.8%), and the U.K. (17.6%).[62] The investment wave was so dramatic that, at the end of 2002, 44 per cent of European screens were in multiplexes. In Belgium, Spain, Austria, and Ireland that figure is more than 50 per cent. At 66 per cent of all screens, the U.K. is the most multiplexed European country.[63] Even when confronted with local recession, currency instability and ongoing economic hardship, situating multiplexes in 'secure shopping malls popular with the middle and upper classes' can apparently assure resounding financial success, as is the experience of international exhibitors in South America.[64]

While trade sources may give the impression of unfettered expansion, reports of struggles against this form of transnational influence have surfaced as well. Minor attempts to claw back some riches for local production, like Mexico's one peso surcharge for each admission ticket or Brazil's tax on international film distributors, sends shudders of nervousness through U.S.

industry investors and prompts the MPAA to flex its lobbying might.[65] Excluding Canada and the U.S., Brazil and Mexico accounted for 78 per cent of the Americas' remaining box office revenue in 2002, making their cultural policies obvious targets for the industry's lobbying attentions.[66]

By the end of the 1990s, the intercontinental expansion of popular cinema circuits meant the redrawing of financial commitments internationally and the realignment of selective cooperation among the majors as they pooled resources for international operations. Importantly, when we speak of the international dominance of U.S. motion pictures, the above realities alert us to the fact that globalization concerns not only the supply of films to existing domestic chains. It also involves the construction and operation of cinema spaces, and the capitalization of theatre building and reconstruction on the part of major entertainment corporations.

Hidden beneath the tales of growth and corporate acquisition during the 1990s and early 2000s are the accompanying closures and demolitions of cinemas. As sites rise and fall, cinemagoing reconfigures to suit new arrangements of cultural life. According to *Screen Digest*, the total number of world screens was 165,774 in 2002, down from 166,440 in 2001, but both still a far cry from the total of 400,107 for 1988 prior to the multiplex boom.[67] Among the material repercussions of these changes in exhibition are the spatial reformations of cities, reinvigorating certain zones at the expense of others, building new meeting places for cultural consumption and abandoning older ones. The legacy of the multiplex boom has been the installation of more screens at fewer sites in select, but dominant, locations, thus assuring those cities' participation in one version of international film culture. These venues have expanded the start-times of films and the media encountered on-site. Concurrently, the coordination that followed has changed the temporality of the arrival and departure of films, that is, which films are shared by whom for how long. Just as these changes reinforce a particular formation of an international film culture, they also mould the shape of the cinema occasion itself.

These characteristics of the coordinated life cycle of films lie behind the adoption of the digital projection and delivery of motion pictures to theatres. The logic motivating the rise of international chains is also directly responsible for the emergence of lower-resolution e-cinema and the high-resolution d-cinema, as it supports a willingness to invest in exhibition and to experiment with the temporality of the current cinema. Digital formats, using disk delivery, satellite relay or fibre-optic transmission to get moving images and sounds to theatres, dispense with the transportation of film canisters.[68] Although most industry and scholarly discussions focus on the quality of the projected image, it is the mode of delivery that is most innovative and unsettling to reigning understandings of theatrical cinematic events. Digital systems, with cheaper delivery of any video or televisual text, offer the possibility of one-time audiovisual performances for specialized audiences.

Although a broadcast-cinema concept has been simmering at least since the 1940s, a renewed enthusiasm for conversion to e-cinema and d-cinema arose at the end of 1998, before quickly becoming bogged down in debates about who would pay for it.[69] Exhibitor bankruptcies of 2000 slowed down the pace of change even further. Not to be deterred, seven Hollywood majors cooperated to form Digital Cinema Initiatives (DCI), charging it with smoothing the way for d-cinema, including making recommendations for industry-wide technical specifications, conversion financing and security standards. The DCI questioned whether 2,000 lines of resolution was an acceptable standard, as had been thought in 1998. Some argued for 4,000 lines of resolution as a more suitable goal for the industry. In the summer of 2005, DCI's long awaited report on technical standards appeared, supporting both 2K and 4K systems.[70] It did not pass unnoticed that, as a creature of the majors and in a position to have significant influence over the standards to which non-majors and exhibitors might have to adhere, DCI seemed to be a form of 'cartel behaviour.'[71]

Far from there being a sudden rejection of existing practices, by early 2003 there were only 143 commercial sites, serving 161 screens, equipped with state-of-the-art digital projectors for feature films.[72] Even the jump to 328 digital screens in 2004 does not represent more than a miniscule percentage of the total world screens.[73] China has been moving to digital projection and delivery faster than any other country, with plans for 100 cinemas before 2005, and 2,500 e-cinema venues by 2009.[74] Notwithstanding the financial and technological roadblocks to development, exhibitors have experimented with less advanced projector systems and with events other than feature films, including live sports, popular music, operas, ballets, Broadway musicals, and television programs, not to mention the now fairly common rental of facilities for corporate events.[75] Three Brazilian art film circuits have jointly developed an e-cinema network, using the technology's lower operating costs to help promote less mainstream feature fare.[76] Seeing revenue generating possibilities, U.S. exhibitor Regal has been aggressive in its establishment of pre-show e-cinema as part of its film performances By February 2003, its division Regal CineMedia had networked installations in 158 theaters, serving 2000 screens. Replacing pre-screening slide shows, these facilities present a 20-minute pre-show distributed to theatres via satellite transmission, of which one third is advertising. For this pre-show, Regal signed NBC and Turner to provide both content and advertisements.[77]

Landmark Theaters, noted for its independent and international films, set about adding digital projection to all of its fifty-three theaters, although they were not networked, each instead having its own computer.[78] Outside the U.S., the U.K. Film Council made similar investments in nearly 150 cinemas, thinking that digital cinema's reduced cost of distribution may be a boon for independent and art cinema, and Arts Alliance opened a seven screen digital projection and delivery network in 2003.[79]

When we consider this rising industrial adoption of both d- and e-cinema, it becomes clear that a reduction in the costs of distribution provides an added incentive to replace audiovisual packages faster, further reinforcing the drift toward the rapid turnover of films in cinemas. As the growing number of alternative presentations indicates, moving away from celluloid allows distributors to provide new slates of programming, from the 'live' sporting event and concert to the networked preview package. In many ways these experiments in programming begin to resemble the schedules of television broadcasters. The simultaneity of the current cinema is entrenched further, and 'opening everywhere' simultaneously remains the ever-present promise. In short, these changes amount to temporal experiments as much as tests of the acceptability of the projected digital image. Conversion is not just a technological or financial issue; it is one of procedures, genres, and practices. We might ask how we need to re-think the specificity of the cultural activity at the motion picture theatre in light of such developments. To the existing tendency for rapidly revised runs and openings we can expect to see the sense of immediacy and the 'liveness' of performance return to the movie house. While they are marginal at the moment, live event screenings should push us to reconsider our understanding of theatrical exhibition as bound by feature films, just as film studies has had to acknowledge and take seriously, however reluctantly, the reality that films are themselves not bound by theatres and have a life elsewhere.

The temporality of the cinema culture continues to accelerate in other arenas, altering the life cycle of audiovisual materials. In 2003, Disney became the last major to move to simultaneous video and DVD releasing for rental and retail markets. Their films also began to appear on pay-per-view three, rather than four, months after theatrical release.[80] At times this acceleration has been intensified as a result of poor box office performance. Such was the case of the early fall releasing of DVD and videos for the 2003 summer blockbusters, an unusual number of which were seen as disappointments by investors.[81] The timeline of the releases in successive formats, however, can create curious circumstances between countries. For example, *28 Days Later* (Danny Boyle 2002) opened in the U.K. in October, then in June 2003 in Canada and the U.S. By that time, the DVD was already available in Britain, with an alternative, more pessimistic ending. Word of the availability of a less uplifting finale traveled across the Atlantic, and drew the attention of fans. The appeal of the darker conclusion was substantial enough for the film's distributor, Fox Searchlight, to release into domestic theaters a revised version of the film that included the two endings only a month after the initial release.[82] Thus, a DVD release in one country prompted the alteration of a theatrical release in another. Or consider the innovative promotion for *Dawn of the Dead* (Zack Snyder 2004), the remake of the 1978 George Romero horror classic. On Monday, 15 March 2004, four days before its scheduled opening, USA Network presented 'the terrifying first 10 minutes of this major motion picture exactly as you'll see it on the big screen.'[83] Capitalizing on the cross-mobility of television and film audiences and their genre preferences, the promotion interrupted a broadcast of the popular horror film, *Final Destination* (James Wong 2000). More than an extended trailer, this was a first-look sneak-peek at an excerpt of a film shown in a location to which it would return some months later.

The preceding documentation of investments and experiments remain but a partial portrait, pertaining to just a fraction of the globe. The global reorganization of screen traffic has been in actuality an extraordinarily selective process, one that involves a reinforcement of the centre of gravity for the flow of transnational film culture. Thus, while one stratum of highly visible texts may be simultaneously released on a continental or global scale, others may now take longer to arrive, if they ever do. This application of international cultural power leads some to the point of grotesque celebration. *Variety* commented, triumphantly, 'in contrast to Europe, the region [Latin America] saw Hollywood's supremacy remain untroubled by domestic hits in most arenas,' as 'Mexican production sank to its lowest level since the 1930s.'[84] Such blatant imperialistic pride extended even to cinemagoing practices, as 'Even the less well-off Costa Ricans and Peruvians are getting the mall 'n' movie habit.'[85]

As control over a national cinema culture is wrested away from a domestic industry, there are supplementary consequences for cinema culture. For one, these conditions alter the disposition of cinemagoers, in whom a material and imagined sense of the 'everywhere' of the current cinema has been fostered, as is evident in the many trailers promising this ubiquity. As a result, there is a corresponding realignment of the very idea of the timeliness of cinema and of a viewer's affiliation with an international community of cinemagoers. To reiterate, cinemas are now locations for experiencing new cultural texts; there is no backlog, as would be found in videotape/DVD rental outlets or CD stores. Commercial cinemas are not just becoming more like closed-circuit broadcasting venues with e-cinema; they are also becoming more analogous to magazine and newspaper stands in the short-lived currency of their products. Films age elsewhere, but not at cinemas. We may conceptualise this era of exhibition and distribution as an effort to maintain tighter control over the economic value at the front end, the point of introduction of a film, with the expectation of increasingly looser control throughout its lifecycle as it mutates into ever more mobile, cheaper and more reproducible forms.

The 1990s multiplex building boom, much of which was jointly financed by transnational entertainment conglomerates and local national development firms, presents us with an extensive network of landing pads for a current cinema that jets its way across the world. Although this process is a product of business practices and ownership structures, its consequences extend to the very 'structure of feeling' of everyday life in a global context. As Raymond Williams powerfully argues: '... *no mode of production and therefore no dominant social order and therefore no dominant culture ever in reality includes or exhausts all human practice, human energy, and human intention*'[86] Treating the spatial and temporal determinations of film points us to the specificities of location and practice, and thus to outcomes beyond the sameness of the films.[87] The sheer volume of cinema spaces has escalated in some areas and contracted in others, reorganising where, when and how people participate in contemporary cinema culture and in 'new' audiovisual culture. It becomes important to note what kinds of spaces are being exported, and to consider what it means to 'get the mall 'n' movie habit.' These spaces are chains, literally and figuratively drawing links to other cinema spaces in other cities and to cinema culture in other countries, and conversely leaving other places out of the circuit. Here, one must recognize this as yet another instance of modernity's uneven development. The chain-links of cultural practice shift our attention from films, images, sounds and narratives, which studies of global culture tend to focus on. Instead, one becomes aware of the material and experiential dimensions resulting from an increasing involvement of internationally operating major chains.

The international multiplex manufactures zones of global cultural traffic, zones almost exclusively associated with the life of a contemporary city. As Bruce Robbins might put it, cinemas are places to be and feel global.[88] This is not to suggest that there is some global everyday; in fact, we need more work on national, city, and neighbourhood manifestations of the tendencies and sensibilities to which I have alluded. The forces documented in this chapter reshape and reinforce the flow of culture. They selectively alter city and suburban life and re-organize the relations among media and cultural practices. This fuels the alteration of the cinemagoing experience, regardless of the effect upon the look and sound of motion pictures themselves.

'Cinema Comes to Life at the Cornerhouse, Nottingham'

'American' Exhibition, Local Politics and Global Culture in the Construction of the Urban Entertainment Centre

Mark Jancovich

C INEMA has acquired a major significance in accounts of globalisation. Films feature prominently in negotiations over free trade, while the standard icons of globalisation are those of food, drink and 'Hollywood movies': what John Tomlinson refers to as 'hamburgers, Mickey Mouse and Coca-Cola.'[1] As well as the films themselves, their modes of exhibition have come to symbolise global culture. In his account of the multiplex, Stuart Hanson argues:

> Multiplexes are a clue to the process which the American sociologist George Ritzer calls 'McDonaldisation' ... 'by which the principles of the fast-foot restaurant are coming to dominate more and more sectors of American society as well as the rest of the world.'[2]

'McDonaldisation' is seen as a form of 'capitalist efficiency' specific to 'large transnational business' organisations.[3]

The multiplex, often seen as a product of American cultural imperialism and globalisation is, as Tomlinson demonstrates, often seen as little more than the result of a process of 'Americanisation.'[4] As Duncan Webster has pointed out, debates about Americanisation often present it as a three stage process through which American culture invades another culture, colonises it and final homogenises it, or else transforms it into a bland and uniform culture indistinguishable from America itself.[5] For critics from Herbert Schiller to E.W. Herman and Robert W. McChesney, American cultural products or 'homogenised North Atlantic cultural slop' are seen as the 'new missionaries of global capitalism,' whose exportation to other countries simply converts those cultures to the ethos and values of American capitalism and consumerism.[6]

There are a number of problems with this position. Firstly, as Tomlinson points out, it 'makes a leap of inference from the simple presence of cultural goods to the attribution of deeper cultural or ideological effects.'[7] The presence of American cultural goods does not determine how they are understood or consumed within a specific cultural context. Secondly, it typically conflates American culture, capitalism and consumerism, using an 'Imaginary America' as a scapegoat for capitalism. Christopher Bigsby, writing about an earlier period, observed that 'complaints about Americanisation have often amounted to little more than laments over a changing world ... where "Americanisation" frequently means little more than the incidence of change.'[8] Accusations of Americanisation often serve to deflect and disavow social problems: violence in Britain is not a product of social tensions but caused by the influence of American music, films or television programming; contemporary consumerism is not a product of specific forms of capitalist organisation but the diffusion of perverse American values such as greed and acquisitiveness; and exploitation in the work place is not a product of inherent inequalities within the structure of capitalist relations but the product of the evil business practices of American corporations such as McDonalds.[9]

Discourses of Americanisation thus involve an 'Othering' of America in which America comes to stand for all that is problematic, and other identities, particularly national identities, are absolved from blame. Identity is central to many fears of Americanisation and globalisation. Critics of globalisation frequently claim that it results in both a loss of identity *between* cultures and a loss of diversity *within* them. As Martin Woolacott puts it: 'What will it be like when all the globe is Disneyland?'[10] Identity is therefore presented as an obvious and uncontested value while conformity is presented as an obvious and uncontested threat.

This opposition is, however, based on specific classed and gendered dispositions, and is more frequently associated with certain cultural forms than others.[11] As the references to 'homogenised North Atlantic cultural slop' and 'Disneyland' make clear, popular culture almost invariably bears the brunt of the attack. On the one hand, the popular forms of the

MacDonalds meal and the genre film seem to offer the most potent images of reproducibility, with their promise of the same experience everywhere in the world.[12] On the other, the association between globalisation and popular culture also works to produce the same kind of conflations and elisions discussed above, implicitly condemning certain aspects of American culture while absolving others. This not only reproduces cultural distinctions, through which the popular is associated with the homogeneous and inauthentic and high culture is associated with diversity and authenticity, but it thereby enables certain cultural values to be seen as unproblematically universal. Those who condemn the exportation of popular culture often vocally support the global diffusion of high culture or, at least, the enforcement of human rights.

Among its reported ill effects, globalisation is often seen as having disastrous implications for our sense of place. Theorists such as Joshua Meyrowitz have claimed that global media are increasingly creating a culture in which people have 'no sense of place,' while others, such as Marc Augé, argue that global culture leads to the erosion of local identities and the emergence of 'supermodern non-places': airports, supermarkets, motorway service stations and cash-dispensers, in which interactions between individuals are increasingly replaced by instructions on monitors.[13] Many of these 'non-places' depend on and facilitate movement or travel. Within them, individuals are isolated, silent and anonymous while the environment itself lacks a sense of location and could be anywhere. Augé's vision is also related to a more general anxiety that, in global culture, 'there is nowhere to go but to the shops,' a fear that everyday life has become increasingly commodified. It is claimed that social activities have been reduced to consumerism and that the world has simply become a place to shop and 'all the globe is Disneyland.'[14] The multiplex is often associated with these non-places, but such responses tend to come most often from those social groups who rarely use these cinemas. Those who do use multiplexes are more likely to describe them in very different terms.

As Tomlinson points out, one problem with Augé's account of non-places such as Roissy Airport is that he describes only the experience of the consumers: 'what he does not account for ... is the entirely different experience of Roissy that belongs to its more permanent denizens—the check-in clerks, baggage handlers, cleaners, caterers, security staff, and so forth who work there. For these people the non-place of the terminal is clearly a "real" place—their workplace.'[15] Even for consumers, a non-place can acquire different meanings: people who use the same supermarket regularly build up familiarity with specific cashiers; run into friends who are also doing their shopping; and start to recognise other customers who use the store at the same times. The non-place starts to look a lot like a 'real' place.

Many criticisms of the regeneration of places such as Times Square in New York make similar accusations that the area has been 'Disneyfied,' converted from a 'real' place into a commercial non-place.[16] This particular regeneration was, however, specifically designed to regenerate the city by attracting tourism. If places such as Times Square, Fisherman's Wharf in San Francisco and Quincy Market in Boston are really global non-places containing the same shops and goods, it is difficult to see how they are supposed to attract tourists. Given that global non-places are associated with travel, one has to ask why people bother to travel if the world has really become homogeneous and undifferentiated.

Ulf Hannerz has argued that tourists do not really want difference, but 'home plus' some exotic extra: 'Spain is home plus sunshine, India is home plus servants, Africa is home plus elephants and tigers.'[17] Hannerz emphasises sameness in his attempt to distinguish the tourist from the true cosmopolitan, but one could equally choose to emphasise difference, or else acknowledge that all travellers need some stable points of reference, without which we are all adrift, unable to feel secure and unable to predict the consequences of our actions.[18] We might equally acknowledge that people's differing perceptions of threat are, at least in part, socially defined.[19] The attachment to the domestic, which is so often used to denigrate lower middle-class women, is related to their sense of insecurity within public space, while the social position of the middle-class male critics who celebrate public space enables them to feel relatively secure, confident and assertive within it.[20]

In his account of the multiplex, Tomlinson describes an imaginary couple on a night out:

> since the new multiplex arrived in the 1980s they go to the cinema more, and this in itself is an oddly deterritorialised experience. The cinema complex is an 'out-of-town' site on the edge of a business park and trading estate and so surrounded, as they arrive in the twilight, by dark warehouses rather than the pubs and shops and restaurants around the old city-centre Odeon or Gaumont. But it is, of course, so much easier—and safer—to park here. Once inside, the sense that this is an environment that has been artificially 'placed into' the locality continues—this is clearly an *American* cinema, evident from the transatlantic voice-overs in the trailers and the slightly jarring terms in the screened announcements ('candy', 'please deposit trash') to the giant buckets of popcorn being consumed.[21]

Although Tomlinson describes this imaginary night out as if he is discussing an abstract and generalised multiplex that could be located anywhere, the multiplex with which he, as a resident of Nottingham, would be most familiar does not conform to his description. The Nottingham Showcase may be located in an out of town site, but its immediate surroundings are not occupied by factories but rather by a series of other leisure facilities: bars, nightclubs, restaurants and a bowling alley.

The 'old city centre cinemas' such as Nottingham's Odeon, built in the 1930s and originally called the Ritz, did not try to blend into their locality but were spectacular and exotic buildings that were seen by the local press as evidence that the city was not a provincial backwater but fully modern and cosmopolitan. Many of the cinemas that opened during the cinema building boom of the 1930s closed in the late 1940s and 1950s, by which time they were seen as old, traditional buildings representing a dying way of life. They were, however, not much older when they went out of business than the 'new' multiplex that Tomlinson, writing in 1999, describes.

While Tomlinson's account concerns the insertion of cinemas into the everyday life of the city, he deduces the experience of visiting the multiplex from a description of the cinema rather than an examination of the processes through which it was placed into the locality. Nonetheless, his account does begin to suggest a key factor when he notes that it is 'easier—and safer—to park' at the multiplex than in the town centre. In Britain and elsewhere, the multiplex was a response to the crime, traffic and social problems associated with city centres during the 1970s and 1980s.[22]

Many accounts of the multiplex actually conflate two different phenomena: the multiplexes built on the outskirts of cities in the 1980s and early 1990s, and the subsequent wave of Urban Entertainment Centres built in city centres from the mid-1990s onwards.[23] While the multiplex was the product of a flight from the inner city, the UEC was the product of a concerted effort by national and local government to regenerate the city centres. By focusing on the supposedly American origins of the multiplex and the UEC, most accounts have failed to see the significant differences between them, differences that result from the different contexts within which they are located. The form and meaning of cultural goods are not simply shaped by their point of origin but are also indigenised within the specific contexts within which they are consumed,[24] and these contexts can reshape and change their meaning, a point of which developers are well aware:

> The vast majority of films screened are from Hollywood, and many of the shops and restaurants are either American or are selling American-style goods and services. But this does not mean that,

from a property point of view, all the developments are alike. The problems posed by projects in Spain are different from those in Northern Europe, for example.[25]

Indeed, as Paul Grainge has shown, different UECs have very different characters from each other, as a result of the specific local conditions within which they are developed.[26]

During the 1990s, concern about the decline of city centres led to calls for policies to regenerate them. One government response was the introduction of Planning Permission Guideline 6 (PPG 6) which required authorities 'to determine planning applications in such a manner that the city centre must be considered before an out of town site.'[27] Developers turned their attention to city centres. According to *Estates Gazette Interactive*,

> The explanation of this shift is simple: PPG6. As Steve Weiner, chief executive of Cine UK, comments: 'It's not difficult to get planning permission for out-of-town leisure schemes. It's impossible.'
>
> A stream of rejected planning applications has forced many operators to rethink their acquisition plans. Mark Atkins at Jones Lang Wootton says: 'Cinema operators want space as quickly as possible. They won't abide being seen to struggle to get planning permission. Deliverability is the key and "town centre" is deliverable.'[28]

The UEC was, therefore, the product of a pragmatic response by developers who wanted to enhance their chances of obtaining planning permission, but also hoped that by addressing current policy objectives they would obtain favourable terms from local government and so 'see planning and the market working in harmony.'[29]

While the Urban Entertainment Centre is often associated with the cinema chain housed in it, it is not usually the case that the exhibition company owns or runs the building; rather it is one of a number of different companies who occupy its space. The buildings have usually been the creation of local developers who either rent out space or sell a completed building development on to other companies. In the case of the development that became the Nottingham Cornerhouse, for example, the original developer, Forman Hardy Holdings, did not build the eventual centre, but simply obtained planning permission for the development. Having increased the value of their property, they sold the land to another developer, Wilson Bowden, at a considerable profit. That company built the site and then sold it on to a pension company, which managed the site, renting units out to shops, bars and restaurants.

Because the regeneration of city centres was seen as both socially beneficial and financially advantageous to councils, individual UEC developments have also been shaped by the agendas of local political organisations. Such developments have had the potential not only to increase the rateable value of city centre property but also to attract businesses to regions and so increase their general prosperity. Places of leisure and consumption were recognised as being particularly important in this regard; in Nottingham, for example, it was claimed that 'a multi-screen cinema should have a knock-on effect in the city centre with more people visiting the local bars and restaurants after watching a film.'[30]

The UEC in Nottingham was not simply designed to regenerate the city centre in general but also a specific section of that centre. The council supported the venture because it was to be built next to Trinity Square, 'a part of town' that 'has been terribly neglected and any development should be welcome.'[31] The centre, it was hoped, would 'revitalise" the area, attract consumers to the businesses already located there and attract new businesses to the area. The UEC site was also directly opposite the Theatre Royal and the Concert Hall, so that the development would be located 'in an established leisure circuit of the city.' Adding to the existing amenities, it was argued that the UEC 'will turn that part of Nottingham into the cultural quarter.'[32]

This strategy was particularly important to Nottingham, which has historically lacked heavy industry and has depended on leisure and consumption for its affluence.[33] It has therefore worked hard to maintain its image as the regional centre for shopping, bars and, clubs, and also 'culture,' which attracts affluent consumers to whom the other facilities do not necessarily appeal. The UEC was therefore seen as 'a unique opportunity to create a leisure scheme which will complement and enhance the existing leisure and cultural facilities within the city centre' and would therefore 'ensure Nottingham's continuing prominence as the principal regional centre.'[34] Plans for the cinema announced that it would have 'leather reclining seats' at which customers would be served 'gourmet foods' such as 'champagne and sushi.'[35] Tickets were to be as much as £10 per head, about twice that of any other cinema in the region at the time. The programming would also be different, with screens that 'aim to attract a different crowd [from the traditional multiplex audience] by showing foreign, arthouse and cult films.'[36] In addition to the cinema, the building would also house a restaurants, bars and clubs, and its 'pedestrianised front and its proximity to the Theatre Royal' would give the area a continental feel that would appeal to Nottingham's 'very cultured population ... There is definitely a market.'[37]

Like earlier cinemas in Nottingham's history, the building was therefore supposed to emphasise the city's image as a regional centre by presenting it as an affluent and cosmopolitan centre of culture rather than a provincial backwater. Neither its developers, the council nor the press viewed the centre as the product of an invasion by a foreign colonising force, threatening to destroy the city's identity and sense of place. On the contrary, their descriptions emphasised that it was a unique object, only possible because of the city's own special character. While these claims were in part local boosterism, councillors supported the venture because it would enhance the city's image and attract consumers, not by creating a homogeneity in which the city lost its identity but by distinguishing the city, at least at a regional level.

To be successful, the UEC had to attract global brands to promote the city, proving Nottingham's distinctiveness by its ability to attract such businesses. Rather than signifying homogeneity, brands such as Warner Village are used by cities such as Nottingham as assets that signify the health of the city's economy and cultural life and themselves attract yet more businesses. For example, the inward investment pages of Nottingham city council's website claim: 'The leisure market, too, has seen a great expansion, with the number of bars, clubs and pubs increasing from 209 in 1995 to 368 last year [1997], offering a combined capacity of 111,000. The recently opened Cornerhouse is a tangible sign of the confidence in this sector, with a multi-screen cinema and top restaurant chains like TGI Fridays and Wagamama.'[38] Rather than invading localities, global brands are often actively courted by these localities.

The plans for Nottingham's UEC certainly met with opposition from the start, but this opposition was not motivated by a fear of American cultural imperialism. It was not the new building itself that was opposed, but rather the demolition of the *Evening Post* building that it was to replace. In this campaign, the elderly were the most vocal protestors. They clearly identified with the building and saw its proposed demolition as representative of attitudes that defined them as irrelevant. As one protestor complained, 'we seem determined to be rid of a part of the city's history ... It's as though we are going through the 1960s syndrome "Out with the old, in with the new."'[39]

This campaign was couched not in terms of a loss of local identity brought about by American cultural imperialism, but in resistance to certain forms of local politics. It revealed a profound sense of alienation from the political process. One letter complained that the city council behaved as if they were 'omniscient' and 'omnipotent':

Having been appointed by an elected body they are no longer under its control. They make a decision, they then listen to opinions, they careful consider them, and then continue with the plan they intended to impose.[40]

Others claimed that 'the opinions of taxpayers don't seem to matter to the planners,'[41] and that: 'as a resident of Nottingham and a pensioner, I've sadly watched the city being sold to the highest bidders, whose only interest seems to be tearing down beautiful buildings and replacing them with modern monstrosities no one wants.'[42] Although English Heritage had already declared the newspaper building 'was not sufficiently architecturally or historically important' to be designated as a listed building, by the time that the plans came before the planning committee, a petition to preserve the exterior of the building had acquired 11,000 signatures.[43] The building had become symbolic of the destruction of a way of life and of a sense of political powerlessness among certain sections of the Nottingham population. As has often been pointed out, modernity, and particularly urban geography in modernity, involves a continual process of demolition and renewal.[44] In this process, the elderly often witness successive transformations, through which the city literally becomes alien to them. One Nottingham resident, for example, described driving around the city with her parents, who did not actually see or experience the city before them but rather the absence of the city they once knew.[45] In this situation, the elderly experience alienation, estrangement and a loss of security.

These responses to the demolition of the *Evening Post* building were not, however, the whole story; the new building was read very differently by its various consumers—who include the businesses renting space in the complex as well as the general public who purchase goods and services there. It is important to remember that the UEC is more than a cinema. At the Cornerhouse, the cinema occupies most of the top two floors of a five-story building. The rest of the space is rented out to other companies. From the developers' perspective, the cinema is there not to make money in itself but to deliver customers to the other companies in the building, and it was given favourable leasing terms by the owners for that reason. The UEC has been seen as 'a scaled down theme park' in which the cinema is a 'magnet for traffic, benefiting both retailers and other leisure operators.'[46] The disadvantage of cinemas for such complexes is that they do not turn over customers fast enough. Most complexes would ideally 'average a £100 spend' per car and a 'two hour turnaround,' but with cinema attendance 'the spend is low.' As a result, the 'sums don't justify having a cinema in the centre' in themselves, and it is only through their ability to 'attract extra customers' to the centre that they are seen to 'add to the value.'[47]

Factors such as these led to a transformation of the building. While the council had hoped that it would attract affluent consumers and help produce a cultural quarter within the city centre, the various companies that rented space in the centre gradually changed its image and the clientele that it attracted. Wagamama, a chain of Japanese-style noodle bars, stated that it had been attracted to the centre by 'the large and lively student population, [and] an increasing inner-city residential sector.'[48] Both of these groups are largely young and single, and the centre became increasingly directed to these groups. In transforming the meaning of the area, the centre also confirmed certain aspects of its character, consolidating its image, at least in the minds of some residents, as a potentially dangerous place at night. One letter writer asked, 'What do the police think of another nightclub and ten-screen cinema?'[49]

Concerns over the supposedly 'American' character of the entertainment emerged only very late in the day, and were clearly limited to a specific section of the Nottingham population. Predictably, these attacks focused on the lack of 'real' choice at the cinema, which, it was claimed, would 'favour the big money blockbusters over the more thoughtful independent and foreign language films.'[50] Gill Henderson, head of Nottingham's regional film theatre, the Broadway, argued that 'it might mean you can choose to go to the same film at three different cinemas. That's fine if one of them does your favourite flavour of popcorn, and you want to see the latest blockbuster there.'[51] This was, however, hardly a disinterested comment. Although art cinemas have criticised multi-screen venues for their lack of diversity, they are equally concerned that if these new venues do show art films, they will come into direct competition with their own business.

The focus on American cultural imperialism obscures the extent to which UECs have actually offered more diversity than is commonly acknowledged. The Cornerhouse has been concerned not only to stress that it would show 'a wide selection of non-mainstream movies along with the blockbusters that one would expect' but it also placed special emphasis on its 'weekly Bollywood presentation.' These screenings proved so successful that the cinema massively expanded this strand of programming and employed Ravinder Panaser, 'a Bollywood expert, to commission their range of features.'[52] Critics of the supposedly global homogeneity of multiplex entertainment rarely acknowledge the existence of such programming, but the Cornerhouse has used its promise of 'the best in Asian films' as evidence of its commitment to the local community.

The dynamics of globalisation are far more complex than is often acknowledged. Cinemas seek to prove their commitment to local communities by showing films produced on the other side of the world, and the claim that these cinemas are products of Americanisation disguises the diversification of mainstream programming, or its Bollywoodisation. As cultural goods and services move from one context to another, they are subject to a complex series of negotiations and reinterpretations. As John Tomlinson observes, while globalisation has often been seen as a Westernisation of the world,

> an acceptance of the technological-scientific culture of the West, of its economic rationality and even some aspects of its consumerism may well coexist with a vigorous rejection of its secular outlook, along with its sexual permissiveness, attitudes towards gender and the family relations, social use of alcohol and so on—as is common in different mixes in many Islamic societies."[53]

Globalisation is neither a process of homogenisation nor a one-way process. It is an uneven process of interaction and exchange in which there are 'no guarantees that the geographical patterns of dominance established in early modernity—the elective affinity between the interests of capitalism and of the West—will continue.'[54]

Notes

Introduction

1. For an overview, see Sumiko Higashi *et al.*, 'In Focus: Film History, or a Baedeker Guide to the Historical Turn,' *Cinema Journal* 44:1 (Fall 2004), pp. 94–143.
2. Colin MacCabe, 'Preface' to Slavoj Žižek, *The Fright of Real Tears: Krzysztof Kieslowski between Theory and Post-Theory* (London: British Film Institute, 2001), p. vii, quoted in David Bordwell, 'Slavoj Žižek: Say Anything' (April 2005), http://www.davidbordwell. net/zizek-say-anything.htm (accessed 26 August 2006).
3. Toby Miller, Nitin Govil, John McMurria, Richard Maxwell and Ting Wang, *Global Hollywood 2* (London: British Film Institute, 2004), p. 31.
4. Miller *et al*, *Global Hollywood 2*, p. 45.
5. James Hay, 'Piecing Together What Remains of the Cinematic City,' in David B. Clarke (ed.), *The Cinematic City* (London: Routledge, 1997), pp. 210–12.
6. Kate Bowles and Nancy Huggett, 'Cowboys, Jaffas and Pies: Researching Cinemagoing in the Illawarra,' in Richard Maltby and Melvyn Stokes (eds), *Hollywood Abroad: Audiences and Cultural Exchange* (London: British Film Institute, 2004), pp. 64–77.
7. Georg G. Iggers, *Historiography in the Twentieth Century* (Middletown, CT: Wesleyan University Press, 1997), p. 103.
8. Carlo Ginzburg, 'Checking the Evidence: The Judge and the Historian,' *Critical Inquiry* 18:1 (Autumn 1991), pp. 89–90.
9. E.P. Thompson, *The Making of the English Working Class* (London: Gollanz, 1963), p. 13. We take the term 'undistinguished' from Hamilton Holt (ed.), *The Life Stories of Undistinguished Americans As Told By Themselves* (New York: Routledge, 1990). First published in 1906, Holt's book collected sixteen of the seventy-five 'autobiographies of undistinguished American men and women' published in *The Independent* magazine over the previous four years. In an introductory note to the book, Holt described the aim of each autobiography as being 'to typify the life of the average worker in some particular vocation, and to make each story the genuine experience of a real person.' (p. xxix).
10. Thompson, *Making of the English Working Class*, p. 13; Vivian Sobchack, 'What is Film History?, or, the Riddle of the Sphinxes,' in Christine Gledhill and Linda Williams, (eds), *Reinventing Film Studies* (London: Arnold, 2000), p. 303.
11. Leo Lowenthal, quoted in Lee Grieveson, 'Mimesis at the Movies,' in Lee Grieveson and Haidee Wasson (eds), *Inventing Cinema Studies* (Duke University Press, forthcoming). The history of the 'disciplinarization' of film studies, and in particular its establishment as a critically based humanities subject and its divorce from earlier connections to the

social sciences and communication studies, is traced in several essays in *Inventing Cinema Studies*, and in particular in Lee Greiveson and Haidee Wasson's 'Introduction: on the Histories of Studying Cinema.'

12. David Bordwell, 'Contemporary Film Studies and the Vicissitudes of Grand Theory,' and Noël Carroll, 'Prospects for Film Theory: A Personal Assessment,' both in David Bordwell and Noël Carroll (eds), *Post Theory: Reconstructing Film Studies* (Madison, WI: University of Wisconsin Press, 1996).

13. Lawrence Stone, 'History and Postmodernism,' *Past and Present* 135 (May 1992), p. 194.

14. Emilie Altenhoh, 'A Sociology of the Cinema: the Audience,' trans. Kathleen Cross, *Screen* 42:3 (Autumn 2001), pp. 249–93.

15. Gregory A. Waller, 'Hillbilly Music and Will Rogers: Small-town Picture Shows in the 1930s,' in Melvyn Stokes and Richard Maltby (eds), *American Movie Audiences: From the Turn of the Century to the Early Sound Era* (London: BFI Publishing, 1999), pp. 164–79.

16. In 1948, one million American households already had their own movie cameras. Robert C. Allen, 'From Exhibition to Reception: Reflections on the Audience in Film History' *Screen* 31:4 (Winter 1990), p. 350.

17. Motion Picture Association Worldwide Market Research, 'US Entertainment Industry: 2005 MPA Market Statistics,' p. 7. Viewed at http://www.mpaa.org/researchStatistics. asp.

18. 16mm film survived for many years as the preferred gauge for schools, churches, libraries and universities.

19. 'What is Being Done for Motion Pictures,' statement by Will H. Hays, London, 5 October 1923, p. 8, in Douglas Gomery (ed.), The Will Hays Papers (microfilm, Frederick, MD: University Publications of America, 1986), part 1, reel 12, frame 813.

20. Richard Kuisel, *Seducing the French: The Dilemma of Americanization* (Berkeley, CA: University of California Press, 1993), p. 237.

21. Victoria de Grazia, *Irresistible Empire: America's Advance Through 20th-Century Europe* (Cambridge, MA: Harvard University Press, 2005), p. 3.

22. U.S. Supreme Court, *Joseph Burstyn, Inc. v. Wilson*, 343 U.S. 495 (1952).

23. For summaries and critiques of this agenda, see Jonathan Freedman, *Media Violence and Its Effect on Aggression: Assessing the Scientific Evidence* (Toronto: University of Toronto Press, 2002); Martin Barker and Julian Petley (eds), *Ill Effects: The Media/Violence Debate* (London: Routledge, 1997).

24. Reporter's transcript, Board meeting, Association of Motion Picture Producers, 10 February 1930, Motion Picture Association of America Archive, 1930 AMPP file, p. 14.

25. Herbert Blumer and Philip Hauser, *Movies, Delinquency and Crime* (New York: Macmillan, 1933), pp. 134–35.

26. Richard Maltby, '"A Brief Romantic Interlude": Dick and Jane Go to Three-and-a-Half Seconds of the Classical Hollywood Cinema,' in Bordwell and Carroll (eds), *Post-Theory*, pp. 434–59.

27. This manuscript is published as part of Garth S. Jowett, Ian C. Jarvie and Kathryn H. Fuller, *Children and the Movies: Media Influence and the Payne Fund Controversy* (New York: Cambridge University Press, 1996).

28. Paul G. Cressey, 'The Motion Picture Experience as Modified by Social Background and Personality' *American Sociological Review* Vol. 3:4 (August 1938), p. 522.

29. Cressey, 'The Motion Picture Experience,' p. 518.

30. David Buckingham, 'Electronic Child Abuse? Rethinking the Media's Effects on Children,' in Barker and Petley (eds), *Ill Effects*, p. 26.

31. Stephen Kline, 'Media Effects: Redux or Reductive?'—A Reply to the St Louis Court Brief,' *Particip@tions* Volume 1, Issue 1 (November 2003), http://www.participations.org/volume%201/issue%201/1_01_kline_reply.htm.

32. Graham Murdock, 'Reservoirs of Dogma: An Archaeology of Popular Anxieties,' in Barker and Petley (eds), *Ill Effects*, pp. 69, 77, 83; Cressey, 'The Motion Picture Experience,' pp. 518–19.

33. Cressey, 'The Motion Picture Experience,' pp. 518–19.

34. See, for example, Gregory D. Black, *Hollywood Censored: Morality Codes, Catholics, and the Movies* (Cambridge: Cambridge University Press, 1994); Gregory D. Black, *The Catholic Crusade Against the Movies, 1940–1975* (Cambridge: Cambridge University Press, 1998); James M. Skinner, *The Cross and the Cinema: The Legion of Decency and the National Catholic Office for Motion Pictures, 1933–1970* (Westport, CT: Greenwood Press, 1993); Frank Walsh, *Sin and Censorship: The Catholic Church and the Motion Picture Industry* (New Haven, NJ: Yale University Press, 1996).

35. Richard Ellis, 'American Studies at the Millennium—Some Thoughts,' *American Studies in Britain* (Autumn/Winter 1999), p. 7; Janice Radway, 'What's in a Name' *American Quarterly* (March 1999), pp. 1–32.

36. Richard White, *The Middle Ground: Indians, Empires, and Republics in the Great Lakes Region, 1650–1815* (Cambridge and New York: Cambridge University Press, 1991), pp. x, 52, 456.

37. Jean-Marie Colombani, editorial, *Le Monde*, 13 September 2001.

38. Nataša Ďurovičová, 'Translating America: The Hollywood Multilinguals, 1929–1933,' in Rick Altman (ed.), *Sound Theory, Sound Practice* (London: Routledge, 1992), p. 141.

39. Philip Rosen, 'Reformulating Hollywood as Global Cinema,' paper given at the Flinders Humanities Symposium on 'Hollywood as Global Cinema,' Flinders University, Adelaide, South Australia, December 2002, p. 6.

40. Jennifer Holt, 'In Deregulation We Trust: The Synergy of Politics and Industry in Reagan-Era Hollywood,' *Film Quarterly* 55:2 (Winter 2001–02), pp. 22–29.

41. Richard Maltby, *Hollywood Cinema* (2nd edn, Oxford: Blackwell, 2003), pp. 189–223.

42. De Grazia, *Irresistible Empire*, p. 446.

43. Simon N. Patten, *The New Basis of Civilization* (New York: Macmillan, 1907), p. 9.

44. De Grazia, *Irresistible Empire*, p. 100.

45. Carlo Ginzburg, *The Cheese and the Worms: The Cosmos of a Sixteenth-Century Miller* (Baltimore, MD: Johns Hopkins University Press, 1980).

46. Emanuel Le Roy Ladurie, *Montaillou: The Promised Land of Error* (New York: Braziller, 1978).

Chapter 1: Race, Religion, and Rusticity: Relocating U.S. Film History

1. Walker Percy, *The Moviegoer* (New York: Noonday Press, 1960), pp. 73–5.

2. Sumiko Higashi, 'In Focus: Film History, or a Baedeker Guide to the Historical Turn,' *Cinema Journal* 44:1 (Fall 2004), pp. 94–100.

3. Georg Simmel, 'The Metropolis and Mental Life,' in Kurt H. Wolff (ed.), *The Sociology of Georg Simmel* (New York: Free Press, 1950), p. 410, quoted in Ben Singer, 'Modernity, Hyperstimulus, and the Rise of Popular Sensationalism,' in Leo Charney and Vanessa Schwartz (eds), *Cinema and the Invention of Modern Life* (Berkeley, CA: University of California Press, 1995), p. 73.

4. *Thirteenth Census of the United States (1910), Abstract of the Census—Population* (Washington, DC: Government Printing Office, 1913), p. 59.

5. Frank Hobbs and Nicole Stoops, *Demographic Trends in the 20th Century*, U.S. Bureau of the Census (Washington, DC: U.S. Government Printing Office, 2002), pp. 37–38.

6. U.S. Bureau of the Census, *Historical Statistics of the U.S., Colonial Times to 1970*, Pt. 1 (Washington, DC: U.S. Government Printing Office, 1975), Series A 57–72: Population in Rural and Urban Territory By Size of Place, 1790–1970.

7. Richard Maltby, 'Sticks, Hicks and Flaps: Classical Hollywood's Generic Conception of Its Audiences,' in Melvyn Stokes and Richard Maltby (eds), *Identifying Hollywood's Audiences* (London: BFI, 1999), pp. 23–41.

8. Timothy J. Gilfoyle, 'White Cities, Linguistic Turns, and Disneylands: The New Paradigms of Urban History,' *Reviews in American History* 26:1 (1998), pp. 175–204.

9. Steven Hahn and Jonathan Prude, 'Introduction,' in Steven Hahn and Jonathan Prude (eds), *The Countryside in the Age of Capitalist Transformation: Essays in the Social History of Rural America* (Chapel Hill, NC: University of North Carolina Press, 1985), p. 6.

10. Gerald W. Creed and Barbara Ching, 'Recognizing Rusticity: Identity and the Power of Place,' in Barbara Ching and Gerald W. Creed (eds), *Knowing Your Place: Rural Identity and Cultural Hierarchy* (New York: Routledge, 1997), pp. 1–38.

11. *Motion Picture Herald*, 28 May 1938, quoted in Martin Johnson, '"See[ing] Yourself As Others See You" in the Films of H. Lee Waters,' M.A. Thesis, University of North Carolina at Chapel Hill, 2005, pp. 24–25.

12. See Jacquelyn Dowd Hall, James Leloudis, Robert Korstad, Mary Murphy, Lu Ann Jones, and Christopher B. Daly, *Like a Family: The Making of a Southern Cotton Mill World* (New York: Norton, 1989), pp. 5–13.

13. Miriam Hansen, *Babel and Babylon: Spectatorship in American Silent Film* (Cambridge, MA: Harvard University Press, 1991), pp. 90–118.

14. *Thirteenth Census of the United States (1910), Abstract of the Census—Population*, p. 80. Between 1860 and 1910 the percentage of the population made up by immigrants fluctuated between 13.2 and 14.7 per cent. Even though the total number of immigrants to the U.S. increased by more than one million between 1890 and 1900, the proportion of the total population they represented actually fell—from 14.7 to 13.6 per cent.

15. Concord *Evening Tribune*, 29 January 1908, p. 4.

16. Terry Lindvall, 'Sundays in Norfolk: Toward a Protestant Utopia Through Film Exhibition in Norfolk, Virginia, 1906–1926,' chapter three below.

17. Hansen, *Babel and Babylon*, pp. 60–61.

18. U.S. Bureau of the Census, *Historical Statistics of the U.S., Colonial Times to 1970*, Pt. 1 (Washington, DC: U.S. Government Printing Office, 1975), Series A 43–56: Number of Places in Urban and Rural Territory by Size of Place, 1790–1970.

19. *Fourteenth Census of the United States Taken in the Year 1920*, Volume I–IV, Population (Washington, D.C.: Government Printing Office, 1921–23), p. 59.

20. Jacqueline Najuma Stewart, *Migrating to the Movies: Cinema and Black Urban Modernity* (Berkeley, CA: University of California Press, 2005), pp. 1–94.

21. Stewart, *Migrating to the Movies*, p. 106.

22. *Thirteenth Census of the United States (1910), Abstract of the Census—Population*, pp. 92–95.

23. *Demographic Trends in the 20ᵗʰ Century*, Table 8, Population by Race for the United States, Regions, and States: 1900–1990, Part B Black Population, p. A–21; Table 3–1, Ten States with the Highest Percents Black, American Indian, and Alaska Native, and Asian and Pacific Islander: 1900, 1950, and 2000, p. 93.

24. *Plessy v. Ferguson*, 163 U.S. 537 (1896).

25. For a discussion of the desegregation of Southern movie theatres, see Thomas Doherty's chapter in this volume.

26. John David Smith, 'Segregation and the Age of Jim Crow,' in John David Smith (ed.), *When Did Southern Segregation Begin?* (Boston, MA: Beford/St. Martin's, 2002), p. 34.

27. Smith, 'Segregation and the Age of Jim Crow,' pp. 34–25. Grace Elizabeth Hale calls

segregation one of the 'spatial mediations of modernity.' See Hale, *Making Whiteness: The Culture of Segregation in the South, 1890–1940* (New York: Pantheon Books, 1998). The term 'panoramic perception' comes from Wolfgang Schivelbusch's *The Railway Journey: Trains and Travel in the 19th Century*, translated by Anselm Hollo (New York: Urizen Books, 1979). Lynne Kirby discusses the relationship between the 'perceptual paradigm' of train travel and that of cinema spectatorship in *Parallel Tracks: The Railroad and Silent Cinema* (Durham, NC: Duke University Press, 1997), p. 7. The expression 'racing of space' is adapted from Barbara Young Welke's *Recasting American Liberty: Gender, Race, Law, and the Railroad Revolution, 1865–1920* (Cambridge: Cambridge University Press, 2001), p. 306. 'Jim Crow,' Welke writes, 'raced space.'

28. Zygmunt Bauman, *Modernity and the Holocaust* (Ithaca, NY: Cornell University Press, 1992), pp. 61–2.

29. See Gregory A. Waller, 'Another Audience: Black Moviegoing, 1907–16,' *Cinema Journal* 31:2 (Winter 1992), pp. 3–25; Charlene Regester, 'From the Buzzard's Roost: Black Moviegoing in Durham and Other North Carolina Cities During the Early Period of American Cinema,' *Film History* 17 (2005), pp. 113–24. Waller's research on black theaters and audiences in Lexington, Kentucky, also features in his *Main Street Amusements: Movies and Commercial Entertainment in a Southern City, 1896–1930* (Washington, DC: Smithsonian Institution Press, 1995), especially chap. 7, 'Another Audience: Black Moviegoing from 1907 to 1916,' pp. 161–79.

30. Smith, 'Segregation and the Age of Jim Crow,' p. 8.

31. Barbara Welke, 'When All the Women Were White, and All the Blacks Were Men,' in Smith (ed.), *When Did Southern Segregation Begin?*, pp. 133–54. The quote is from p. 148.

32. Quoted by Leon Litwack in 'Trouble in Mind: Black Southerners in the Age of Jim Crow,' in Smith (ed.), *When Did Southern Segregation Begin?*, pp. 153–64. Quote is on p. 157.

33. Erle Stillwell Collection, Henderson County Public Library, Hendersonville, NC.

34. Robin Payne, '"We Enjoy Movies Too!" *Porgy and Bess*, the Citizens Committee for "Open" Movies, and the Desegregation of the Chapel Hill Movie Theatres, 1959–62,' unpublished seminar paper, American Studies, University of North Carolina at Chapel Hill, 2005, p. 23. She cites the following sources for the desegregation of the Carolina Theater in the fall of 1961: 'Carolina's Limited Integration Plan Accepted Calmly as One Step Forward,' *The Chapel Hill Weekly*, 24 August 1961, 4B; 'Carolina Theater Initiates Limited Integration Plan,' *The Chapel Hill Weekly*, 21 August 1961, pp. 1, 8; 'Negro Students May Attend Theater: Desegregation Moves Along in Town,' *The Daily Tar Heel*, 19 September 1961, p. 5; and 'Two Break Movie Color Bar: Chapel Hill House Opens to Race at UNC,' *The Carolina Times*, 26 August 1961, pp. 1, 3A.

35. 109 U.S. 3 (1883).

36. Max W. Turner and Frank R. Kennedy, 'Exclusion, Ejection, and Segregation of Theatre Patrons,' 32 Iowa L. Rev. 634 1947. The Tennessee law is Tenn. Code Ann. 5262 (Michie 1938).

37. 273 U.S. 418 (1927), quoted in Turner and Kennedy, 'Exclusion. Ejection and Segregation,' p. 629.

38. Nicholas K. Blomley, *Law, Space, and the Geographies of Power* (New York: The Guilford Press, 1994), pp. 45–46.

39. Charlene Regester's work is an exception here.

40. Robert J. Landry, 'Negro Only: Hazy Outlook,' Variety, 14 August 1963, p. 5. Quoted in Thomas Doherty, "Race Houses, Jim Crow Roosts, and Lily White Palaces: Desegregating the Motion Picture Theater," in this volume.

41. See Douglas Gomery, *Shared Pleasures: A History of Movie Presentation in the United States* (Madison, WI: University of Wisconsin Press, 1992), pp. 155–70; '232 Negro

Theatres 1½% of All Houses, Motion Picture Herald,' 24 April 1937, p. 78, quoted in Johnson, 'See[ing] Yourself As Others See You,' p. 24. Stewart acknowledges that most of the black theaters in Chicago were owned by whites (p. 162). In her *Film History* article, Charlene Regester discusses several notable exceptions to this generalization, in particular the theaters owned by the black exhibitor Frederick King Watkins in the 1910s and 1920s.

42. Quoted in Regester, 'From the Buzzard's Roost,' p. 116. The cartoon appeared in the Baltimore *African American*, 22 March 1930, p. 8.

43. Janna Jones, *The Southern Movie Palace: Rise, Fall and Resurrection* (Gainesville, FL: University Press of Florida, 2003), p. 59.

44. Cheryl I. Harris, 'Whiteness as Property,' 106 *Harv. L. Rev.* 1707 1993.

45. Thomas Cripps, 'The Myth of the Southern Box Office,' in James Curtis and Lewis Gould (eds), *The Black Experience in America* (Austin, TX: University of Texas Press, 1970), pp. 116–44.

46. Monroe Day (ed.), *Family Expenditures for Education, Reading, Recreation, and Tobacco: Five Regions* (Washington: D.C.: Government Printing Office, 1941), cited in Gregory A. Waller, 'Free Talking Picture—Every Farmer is Welcome: Non-theatrical Film and Everyday Life in Rural America during the 1930s,' in this volume.

47. As Greg Waller details in his study of moviegoing in Lexington, Kentucky, in the silent era, religious opposition to the movies in many towns and small cities took the form of sabbatarianism, and attracted support from both fundamentalist and more mainstream Protestant clergy. Attempts by both black and white ministerial associations and the 'Moral Improvement League' to prohibit or restrict the showing of movies on Sundays continued for a decade in Lexington. Waller notes that similar sabbatarian campaigns in other Kentucky towns produced a variety of outcomes—from outright rejection of such calls to closure of all theaters not only on Sunday evenings but on Wednesday evenings as well. In the western Kentucky town of Owensboro, a 1916 municipal ordinance closed white theaters on Sundays, but allowed 'colored' shows to stay open, on the theory that 'negroes would be better off at the picture house than ... frequenting dives.' See Waller, *Main Street Amusements*, p. 134.

48. J. Melville White, 'The Motion Picture: Friend or Foe?' *Christianity Today* (22 July 1966), pp. 9–11. Changes in the evangelical stance toward the movies in the 1960s and 1970s are discussed by Shanny Luft in his unpublished 2004 paper, 'To Discern Between Good and Evil: *Christianity Today* and the Movies.'

49. Annette Kuhn, *An Everyday Magic: Cinema and Cultural Memory* (London: I.B. Taurus, 2002). The U.S. edition is: *Dreaming of Fred and Ginger: Cinema and Cultural Memory* (New York: New York University Press, 2002).

50. James Hay, 'Piecing Together What Remains of the Cinematic City,'x in David B. Clarke (ed.), *The Cinematic City* (London: Routledge, 1997), pp. 209–29. Quote is from p. 216.

Chapter 2: Tri-racial Theaters in Robeson County, North Carolina, 1896–1940

1. Lee Grieveson, 'Woof, Warp, History,' *Cinema Journal* 44:1 (Fall 2004), p. 124.

2. For similar tales of lingering resentments, this time in a larger Southern town (Durham, North Carolina), see 'The Discursive Past' in Jenna James' *The Southern Movie Palace: Rise, Fall and Resurrection* (Gainesville, FL: University of Florida Press, 2003), particularly pp. 205–208.

3. These changes have most recently been marked both by the election of a Lumbee mayor in Lumberton, and by the efforts of Senator Elizabeth Dole to secure full federal recognition of the Lumbee tribe.

4. Karen I. Blu, *The Lumbee Problem: The Making of an American Indian People* (Lincoln, NE: University of Nebraska Press, 2001), pp. 2–4.

5. Lumbee history is shrouded in mysteries. While Lumbees probably pre-dated European or African immigration to America, their precise lineage is undocumented. Since their culture generally lacks a distinctive religion, language, or set of social and/or leisure customs setting them apart from European settlers, and because they were never in open military conflict with the United States government, and subsisted primarily as a farming rather than a nomadic people, they tended to remain under the cultural radar, somewhat to their detriment, since they have not yet received complete recognition for their Native American heritage from the federal government.

6. Lumbee identity is itself primarily a social construction. As Lumbee ethnologist Karen Blu has noted, the foundation of Lumbee-ness for Lumbees consists of the confluence of a network of family ties, a shared sense of an identifiable 'home' region for families in several counties in southeastern North Carolina, and from what amounts to a group judgment, or a self-determination, of who is a Lumbee and who is not. As Blu argues, you are a Lumbee if other Lumbees say you are.

7. Blu, *The Lumbee Problem*, p. xii.

8. Michael Johnson, *Macmillan Encyclopedia of Native American Tribes* (2nd U.S. edn, New York: Macmillan Library Reference USA, 1999), p. 516.

9. Robert C. Allen, 'Decentering Historical Audience Studies: A Modest Proposal,' paper given at the Duke University/University of North Carolina conference, 'Local Color: A Conference on Moviegoing in the American South,' January 2002. See also Chapter 1 of this volume.

10. Gerald M. Sider, *Lumbee Indian Histories: Race, Ethnicity, and Indian Identity in the Southern United States* (New York: Cambridge University Press, 1993), p. xv.

11. To be consistent with the historical labels used at least until mid-century in Robeson County, at times in this study Caucasians will be termed 'white,' Native Americans 'Indian,' and African Americans 'colored,' 'black,' or 'Negro.' These labels were used with precision and historical consistency in Robeson County. As early as 1900, for example, its telephone directory was divided into sections for 'white,' 'colored,' and 'Croatan.' The latter term, which allegedly linked the Lumbees to Sir Walter Raleigh's 'Lost Colony,' has fallen into severe disfavor with the Lumbee community, and is now considered a highly derogatory term. For this reason, it will generally not be used in this chapter.

12. The general timeline for the development of various motion picture houses in Robeson has been constructed almost exclusively from a detailed review of microfilms of the local newspaper, the *Robesonian*, from 1896 until mid-1940. While a fire in the *Robesonian*'s offices in 1900 destroyed virtually all of the issues published since the paper's inception in 1877, sporadic issues were later preserved on microfilm.

13. 'Improvements at the Opera House,' *Robesonian* 18 September 1908, p. 3.

14. Few Indians lived in or near Lumberton at this time. Karen Blu notes that as late as 1970, Lumberton's Indian population stood at 342, or only 2.2 per cent of the town's population, while its 4,128 blacks accounted for 27 per cent. Blu, *The Lumbee Problem*, p. 13.

15. Ruth Dial Woods, 'Growing up Red: The Lumbee Experience,' Ph.D. dissertation, University of North Carolina at Chapel Hill, 2001, pp. 20, 115.

16. Because such announcements tended to distinguish the advantages of one house over another, this may imply that one or both of the other two houses in town—the Opera House and the Pastime Theatre—may have served non-whites. Certainly the 1908 changes in the Opera House lend credence to this idea. But there is no absolute proof that the Pastime did, or even was willing, to accommodate non-whites until possibly

1918, when an advertisement for a war propaganda film entitled 'My Four Years in Germany' announced separate showing for whites, blacks, and Indians. Even so, we have no proof that the shows advertised did, in fact, occur. See 'At the Movies,' *Robesonian* 29 November 1915, p. 5 and the movie notice from *Robesonian* 29 August 1918, p. 1. Similarly, we know that in 1915, for example, a public health initiative to reduce mosquito infestations co-sponsored by the Pastime Theatre provided free movie tickets to boys who collected and turned in tin cans. However, a second advertisement in the newspaper clarified the eligibility requirements: tickets would be provided to 'white' boys only. *Robesonian* 14 June 1915, p. 5.

17. This building was eventually donated to a local historical preservation group, Historic Robeson, Incorporated, and is now part of a town museum, but is not identifed as a site that once housed a 'colored' movie house.

18. See untitled local news items in the *Robesonian*, 3 September 1914, p. 2; 19 October 1914, p. 1; and 18 December 1919, p. 1. Charley Morrisey had a long career as a local entertainer and was responsible for organizing and performing in a series of musical shows in local sites (both black and white) in the 1920s. Ironically, he would become the janitor at the Carolina Theater when it opened in June 1928—apparently, the only non-white member of the staff.

19. See untitled local news items in the *Robesonian*, 23 June 1919, p. 1 and 11 September 1919, p. 1. Unfortunately, at this time there is no evidence to suggest how many non-whites, or whites for that matter, ever attended these sites. No other information about their exhibition or attendance policies or statistics is known.

20. 'Community Service Pictures' (editorial), *Robesonian* 18 March 1920, p. 4; 'Free Health Campaign in Robeson,' *Robesonian* 13 September 1920, p. 1; 'Health Campaign Among Colored Folks,' *Robesonian* 7 October 1920, p. 5; 'Community Service Play Hours,' *Robesonian* 27 February 1922, p. 8; 'Community Meetings,' *Robesonian* 13 April 1922, p. 9.

21. 'Educational Motion Pictures Begin Sept. 9,' *Robesonian* 1 September 1919, p. 1.

22. The letter was signed 'Indian Union Chapel.' *Robesonian* 15 September 1919, p. 8. On 16 October 1919, the Editor replied by pointing out in exasperation how 'some one got excited over the supposed statement […] that a moving picture show "for colored" people would be held at Union Chapel. That news item distinctly classified Union Chapel as Indian' (p. 4). The editor was not concerned about the need for racial classification of the CSP shows; he accepted it as part of his paper's duty, and defended his staff for having followed procedure correctly.

23. Karen Blu claims that the Riverside 'reportedly hired an Indian youngster to point out "his people" to the manager, so that racial mistakes might be minimized.' Karen I. Blu, '"We People": Understanding Lumbee Indian Identity in a Tri-Racial Situation,' Ph.D. dissertation, University of Chicago, 1972, pp. 135–36.

24. Personal correspondence between Henry A. McKinnon and the author. As an adult, McKinnon would eventually marry the daughter of Dr. Bowman, the second co-founder of the Carolina, after which he presumably had little trouble being shown a seat in the main auditorium.

25. Guy B. Johnson, 'Personality in a White-Indian-Negro Community,' *American Sociological Review* 4:4 (August, 1939), p. 518.

26. To my knowledge, these advertisements represent the first published attempt to target Indian moviegoing patrons in Robeson County. *Robesonian* 12 July 1934, p. 1; 19 July 1934, p. 8; 'Pastime Theatre Opens Saturday,' *Robesonian* 16 August 1934, p. 8; 20 August 1934, p. 8.

27. *Robesonian* 13 September 1934, p. 8.

28. See Ernest Dewey Hancock, 'A Sociological Study of the Tri-Racial Community in

401

Robeson County, North Carolina,' Masters Thesis, University of North Carolina at Chapel Hill, 1935, see pp. 39 and 41 for Lumberton figures for 1930.

29. Indians in particular may have been unwilling to coexist. In a contemporary commentary, Johnson, for example, noted that an Indian was quite willing to deny himself cinematic pleasures, preferring to conduct himself 'in such a way that the unpleasant reality [of co-equal treatment with blacks] is negated' by avoiding 'theatres where his only choice is to sit with Negroes,' even if such sites represented one's only moviegoing options. Johnson, p. 521.

30. 'Indians Crowded Out of Pastime Theatre,' *Robesonian* 1 October 1934, p. 4.

31. Wishart had been the longtime foreman of the *Robesonian*'s composing room prior to his entry into vaudeville and motion picture management around 1909. The editor of the paper, Jack A. Sharpe, appears to have been a good friend of Wishart's, and Wishart himself remained a regular contributor to newspapers in Lumberton and elsewhere during his long life. He is as responsible for the adoption of motion picture entertainment by the Robeson County public as any other individual. Beginning his career in entertainment at the age of fifty as manager of the Lumberton Opera House, Wishart later opened the Pastime, and subsequently managed both the Star and the Lyric theaters before leaving Lumberton to become a theater manager in several other towns in the general vicinity. Returning to Lumberton, he wound up his career at the Carolina, where he was still on the job at age 80 when the Riverside opened in 1939.

32. Hancock, 'A Sociological Study,' p. 101.

33. 'Rowland Theatre to Open Monday,' *Robesonian* 29 October 1937, p. 8; 'Rowland Theatre Packs 'Em In For Opening Program,' *Robesonian* 3 November 1937, p. 6; 'New Theatre for Rowland Opens,' *Robesonian* 29 November 1937; *Robesonian Historical, Agricultural and Industrial Edition*, Section 3, p. 1.

34. 'Carlyle Property Is Purchased for a New Theatre Site,' *Robesonian* 12 December 1938, p. 1; 'Riverside Theatre To Open New Building Here Tonight,' *Robesonian* 3 April 1939, pp. 1, 3, 6. The building that housed the Riverside eventually became the home of the *Robesonian*'s printing press, and although the interior of the movie-house was largely gutted, remnants of the three entrances and ticket booths still remain, as do the separate staircases running into the non-white sections (which, however, no longer contain the barriers used to distinguish 'Indian' from 'colored' sections). The other remaining early Lumberton theatre, founded as the Carolina but now restored as the Carolina Civic Centre, no longer retains any vestiges of its earlier segregationist apparatus.

35. For example, ads for 'The Home of Better Pictures' on 11 September carried this 'special notice' (*Robesonian* 11 September 1939, p. 2). Also see Maud Thomas, *Away Down Home: A History of Robeson County, North Carolina* (Charlotte, NC: Distributed by Historic Robeson, Inc., 1982), pp. 249–50.

36. Mary Carbine, 'The Finest Outside the Loop: Motion Picture Exhibition in Chicago's Black Metropolis, 1905–1928,' *Camera Obscura* 23 (May 1990), pp. 9–41.

37. Maggie Valentine, *The Show Starts on the Sidewalk: An Architectural History of the Movie Theatre, Starring S. Charles Lee* (New Haven, CT: Yale University Press, 1994), p. 3.

Chapter 3: The White in the Race Movie Audience

1. Carolyn Steedman, *Dust: The Archive and Cultural History* (New Brunswick, NJ: Rutgers University Press, 2002).

2. Jane Gaines, *Fire and Desire: Mixed Race Movies in the Silent Era* (Chicago, IL: University of Chicago Press, 2001).

3. Gregory A. Waller, *Main Street Amusements: Movies and Commercial Entertainment in a Southern City: 1896—1930* (Washington, DC: Smithsonian Institution Press, 1995).

For pioneering studies of black moviegoing, see Mary Carbine, '"The Finest Outside the Loop": Motion Picture Exhibition in Chicago's Black Metropolis, 1905–1928,' *Camera Obscura* 23, reprinted in Richard Abel (ed.), *Silent Film* (New Brunswick, NJ: Rutgers University Press, 1996) and Gregory A. Waller, 'Another Audience: Black Moviegoing, 1907–1916,' *Cinema Journal* 31: 2 (1992), pp. 3–24.

4. See, for example, Matthew Bernstein, 'Oscar Micheaux and Leo Frank: Cinematic Justice Across the Color Line,' *Film Quarterly* 57, no. 4 (Summer 2004), pp. 8–21; Pearl Bowser, Jane Gaines, and Charles Musser (eds), *Oscar Micheaux and His Circle: African American Filmmaking and Race Cinema of the Silent Era* (Bloomington, IN: Indiana University Press, 2001); Jane Gaines, 'In and Out of Race: The Story of Noble Johnson,' *Women and Performance* 29: 5:1 (2005), pp. 33–52; J. Ronald Green, *Straight Lick: The Cinema of Oscar Micheaux* (Bloomington, IN: Indiana University Press, 2000); idem, *With a Crooked Stick: The Films of Oscar Micheaux* (Bloomington, IN: Indiana University Press, 2004).

5. Steedman, *Dust*, p. 128.

6. Ibid., p. 127.

7. Jacquelyn Dowd Hall, '"The Mind that Burns in Each Body": Women, Rape, and Racial Violence,' in Ann Snitow, Christine Stansell and Sharon Thompson (eds), *Powers of Desire: The Politics of Sexuality* (New York: Monthly Review Press, 1983), pp. 328–49.

8. Dan Streible, 'The Harlem Theater: Black Film Exhibition in Austin, Texas: 1920–1973,' in Manthia Diawara (ed.), *Black American Cinema* (New York: Routledge, 1993), p. 227.

9. Oscar Micheaux, 'The Negro and the Photo-Play,' *Half-Century*, 9 May 1919, p. 9, reprinted in Anna Everett, *Returning the Gaze: A Geneology of Black Film Criticism, 1909–1949* (Durham, NC: Duke University Press, 2001), p. 133.

10. Gaines, *Fire and Desire*, p. 270.

11. Palace Theatre to George P. Johnson, 31 May 1919, in George P. Johnson Collection, Young Research Library, University of California, Los Angeles, hereafter GPJC. Gaines, *Fire and Desire*, p. 102.

12. Henry T. Sampson suggests that Micheaux's rationale for including whites in his films, producing the 'mistaken racial identity theme' went back to the advice he had from a white friend who told him that whites bought his novel, *The Homesteader*, because of the young white female character. Henry T. Sampson, *Blacks in Black and White: A Source Book on Black Films*, (Metuchen, NJ: The Scarecrow Press, 2nd edn, 1995), p. 158.

13. Pearl Bowser and Louise Spence, *Writing Himself into History: Oscar Micheaux, His Silent Films, and His Audiences* (New Brunswick, NJ: Rutgers University Press, 2000), p. 27.

14. In my own thinking I am indebted to Miriam Hansen who in her discussion of the kinds of female spectatorship in the silent era says that it 'cannot be measured in any empirical sense,' but that their 'conditions of possibility can be reconstructed.' Miriam Hansen, *Babel and Babylon: Spectatorship in American Silent Film* (Cambridge, MA: Harvard University Press, 1991, p. 125). Before this, Judith Mayne called attention an earlier imbalance between the empirical and the theoretical spectator in her remark that she had the 'sneaking suspicion that theorists of the subject have left aside the problem of the relationship between constructions and contradictory people by discarding the people.' Judith Mayne, *Cinema and Spectatorship* (London and New York: Routledge, 1993), p. 5.

15. Clarence Muse and David Arlen, *Way Down South* (Hollywood, CA: David Graham Fischer, 1932), pp. 49–50, quoted in Bowser and Louise Spence, *Writing Himself into History*, p. 81. On Jim Crow, also see Elizabeth Abel, 'Bathroom Doors and Drinking Fountains: Jim Crow's Racial Symbolic,' *Critical Inquiry* 25 (Spring 1999), pp. 435–81.

16. Charlene Regester, 'From the Buzzard's Roost: Black Moviegoing in Durham and Other

North Carolina Cities During the Early Period of American Cinema,' paper delivered at the Local Color: Moviegoing in the American South Conference, Duke University, January, 2002. For another local exploration of moviegoing in North Carolina, see John Chappell, 'A History of Motion Picture Exhibition in Greensboro, North Carolina 1908—1928' (Master's Thesis, University of North Carolina, Chapel Hill, 1978).

17. Dana F. White, "A Landmark in Negro Progress": The Auditorium Theater, 1914–1925,' *Marquee* 34:4 (2002), p. 16.

18. Douglas Gomery, *Shared Pleasures: A History of Movie Presentation in the United States* (Madison, WI: University of Wisconsin Press, 1992), p. 157.

19. Muse and Allen, *Way Down South*, p. 61. The 81 Theatre was white-owned and it was the main competition for black theatre owners in Atlanta. White, 'A Landmark in Negro Progress,' p. 16.

20. Bowser and Spence, *Writing Himself into History*, p. 81. According to Sampson, the Attucks Theatre was managed and owned by Twin City Amusement Corporation, Robert Cross and Rufas Byers. Byers was a long time exhibitor in the Washington-Virginia area. Sampson, *Blacks in Black and White*, p. 649. The white owner of the Interstate Theatre circuit in Austin, Texas, offered 'colored midnight shows' during the 1930s. Streible, 'The Harlem Theater,' p. 224, Barbara Stones confirms that these shows were popular into 1930s and 1940s and more Southern than Northern. Barbara Stones, *America Goes to the Movies: 100 Years of Motion Picture Exhibition* (North Hollywood, CA: National Association of Theater Owners, 1993), p. 208.

21. Lillian Smith, *Killers of the Dream* (New York: W.W. Norton, 1978, first pub. in 1949), p. 89.

22. Susan Gilman has recently demonstrated that Mark Twain was more interested in the race question than scholars had previously thought, going beyond the concerns evidenced in his fiction, *Huckleberry Finn* and especially *Pudd'nhead Wilson*. Susan Gilman, *Blood Talk: American Race Melodrama and the Culture of the Occult* (Chicago, IL: University of Chicago Press, 2003).

23. Donald Bogle, 'Introduction,' in John Kisch and Edward Mapp (eds), *A Separate Cinema: Fifty Years of Black Cast Posters* (New York: Farrar, Straus and Giroux, 1992), p. xvii.

24. Esther Newton, *Mother Camp: Female Impersonators in America* (Chicago, IL: University of Chicago Press, 1979), p. 106.

25. Noël Carroll, 'Notes on the Sight Gag,' in *Theorizing the Moving Image* (Cambridge: Cambridge University Press, 1996), p. 149.

26. Jacqueline Stewart, *Migrating to the Movies: Cinema and Black Urban Modernity, 1893–1920* (Berkeley, CA: University of California, 2004).

27. Eric Lott, *Love and Theft: Blackface Minstrelsy and the American Working Class* (New York and Oxford: Oxford University Press, 1993), p. 6.

28. Lott, *Love and Theft*, p. 4.

29. Norman Mailer, *The White Negro: Superficial Reflections on the Hipster* (New York: City Lights Books, 1957); Lott, *Love and Theft*, p. 5.

30. Milton 'Mezz' Mezzrow and Bernard Wolfe, *Really the Blues* (New York: Random House, 1946) For a discussion of the 1920s hipster, see Alison Griffiths and James Latham, 'Film and Ethnic Identity in Harlem, 1896–1915,' in Melvyn Stokes and Richard Maltby (eds), *American Movie Audiences: From the Turn of the Century to the Early Sound Era* (London: British Film Institute, 1999), pp. 46–63.

31. Mab Segrest, *Memoirs of a Race Traitor* (Boston, MA: South End Press, 1994).

32. Barbara M. Benedict, *Curiosity: A Cultural History of Early Modern Inquiry* (Chicago, IL: University of Chicago Press, 2001), pp. 2–3, 14.

33. See Jane Gaines, 'Everyday Strangeness: Robert Ripley's International Oddities as Documentary Attractions,' *New Literary History* 33:4 (2002), pp. 789–92; Tom Gunning,

'An Aesthetic of Astonishment: Early Cinema and the [In] Credulous Spectator,' in Linda Williams (ed.), *Viewing Positions: Ways of Seeing Films* (New Brunswick, NJ: Rutgers University Press, 1995), p. 129.

34. I am indebted to Arthur Knight for this point, which he discusses in relation to the popularity of the black musical film. Arthur Knight, *Disintegrating the Musical: Black Performance and American Musical Film* (Durham, NC: Duke University Press, 2002).

35. Knight, *Disintegrating the Musical*, p. 21.

36. Bowser and Spence, *Writing Himself Into History*, pp. 69–70. The *Chicago Defender* (19 January 1918), described Noble Johnson as 'supported by' Eddie Polo; the *Chicago Whip* (11 October 1919) announced that Johnson was 'still starring with Eddie Polo in their great serials.' The article noted that Johnson was given more heavy parts than anything. Cuing black viewers to look for him on the screen: 'Johnson's light complexion fools some people who follow the screen light but he is colored all right, and we trust that some day he will be allowed to play a stellar role.'

37. In *Migrating to the Movies*, Jacqueline Stewart stresses the pressure put upon Universal by white owners of the Black Belt theatres in Chicago where the Lincoln films were drawing business away from the theatres playing his Universal films. In other words, the pressure put on Noble Johnson to resign would have been an effect of the competition between black and white theatre owners in an extremely competitive neighbourhood. This adds to my earlier reading of Universal's 1918 contract with Noble, which effectively asserted Universal's exclusive rights to the actor's image and prohibited any new advertising of his Lincoln films. Gaines, *Fire and Desire*, pp. 99–100.

Chapter 4: Sundays in Norfolk: Toward a Protestant Utopia Through Film Exhibition in Norfolk, Virginia, 1910–1920

1. 'Sunday Hurts in K.C.' *Variety* 5 May 1916, pp. 1, 3.

2. 'Afraid of Bill Sunday' *Variety* 17 November 1916, p. 3.

3. In October 1925, *Variety* reported that evangelist George Wood Anderson attracted 'considerable daily space in the newspapers and has been responsible' for a drop in theatre attendance in Connecticut. 'Conn. Evangelist Killing Theatre Biz: Draws 3,000 Nightly at So. Norwalk—Record Low Grosses for Theatres,' *Variety* 21 October 1925, p. 1.

4. William A. Sunday, 'Amusements,' *The Papers of William Ashley and Helen Amelia Thompson Sunday: 1882 [1888–1957]* 1974; n.d. (Microfilm collection by a joint effort of the Billy Graham Center at Wheaton College, Wheaton, Illinois and Grace College and Theological Seminary, Winona Lake, Indiana, 1978), reel 11, p. 3.

5. *Motion Picture News* 21 and 23 November 1912, p. 14.

6. John Tibbetts, *His Majesty the American: The Cinema of Douglas Fairbanks*. (Cranbury, NJ: A.S. Barnes, 1977), p. 43.

7. William Gerald McLoughlin, *Billy Sunday Was His Real Name* (Chicago, IL: University of Chicago Press, 1955), p. 221.

8. Russell Merritt, 'Nickelodeon Theaters 1905–1914: Building an Audience for the Movies,' in Tino Balio (ed.), *The American Film Industry* (Madison, WI: University of Wisconsin Press, 1976), pp. 59–79.

9. Robert C. Allen, 'Motion Picture Exhibition in Manhattan, 1906–1912: Beyond the Nickelodeon,' *Cinema Journal* 19:2 (Spring 1979).

10. I discuss the theatres of Norfolk and the Wells brothers in 'Movie Gate to the South: Silent Film Exhibition in Norfolk, Virginia, 1906–1921' in Kathy Fuller and George Potamianos (eds), *Beyond the Bowery: The Cinema and Mass Entertainment in Small town America* (Berkeley, CA: University of California Press, forthcoming).

11. 'Colonial Theatre: Results and Reasons,' 17 October 1909, p. 3.

12. Carl D. Wells, 'The Motion Picture Versus the Church,' *Journal of Applied Sociology* (July–August 1932), pp. 540–46.
13. I have tried to show a trajectory of changing relations between the church and moving picture in my *Silents of God: Selected Issues and Documents in Silent American Film and Religion, 1908–1925* (London: Scarecrow Press, 2001).
14. William Uricchio, and Roberta E. Pearson, 'Constructing the Audience: Competing Discourses of Morality and Rationalization During the Nickelodeon Period,' *Iris* 17 (Fall 1994), p. 11, fn. 53.
15. Gregory A. Waller, *Main Street Amusements: Movies and Commercial Entertainment in a Southern City, 1896–1930* (Washington, DC: Smithsonian Institution Press, 1995).
16. 'Race Population in Portsmouth and Norfolk is 66,719,' *Norfolk Journal and Guide* 29 January 1921, p. 1.
17. 'Nobody Agreed at Meeting on Sunday Movies,' *Virginian-Pilot* (subsequently designated as *VP*) 25 March 1919, p. 2.
18. Thomas C. Parramore, *Norfolk: The First Four Centuries* (Charlottesville, VA: University Press of Virginia, 1999), p. 256; Carroll Walker, *Norfolk: A Pictorial History* (Virginia Beach, VA: Donning Company, 1975), p. 268.
19. *Norfolk and Portsmouth Virginia 1910 Directory* XLIII (Norfolk, VA: Hill Directory Company, 1911), p. 1122 and *Norfolk and Portsmouth Virginia 1920–21 Directory* LXXIII (Norfolk, VA: Hill Directory Company, 1920–21), p. 1454.
20. *Norfolk and Portsmouth 1920–21 Directory*, p. 1456.
21. Parramore, *Norfolk*, p. 258.
22. Charles Musser, 'Passions and the Passion Play: Theatre, Film, and Religion in America, 1880–1900' *Film History* 5 (December 1993), p. 447.
23. 'Aldermen Adopt Anti-Phonograph Ordinance,' *VP* 10 July 1907, p. 1; 'Show People to Fight Ordinance,' *VP* 11 July 1907, p. 3.
24. Tom Gunning, 'From the Opium Den to the Theatre of Morality: Moral Discourse and the Film Process in Early American Cinema' *Art and Text* 30 (September–November 1988), pp. 30–41.
25. 'Mass Meeting for Women at Colonial Next Sunday,' *VP* 23 March 1919, p. 7; 'Salvation Army to Distribute Gifts at the Majestic,' *VP* 21 December 1915, p. 4.
26. *Variety* identified a significant decline in box office revenues during Lent and Holy Week. 'Easter Week Brings Boost Followed by Another Slump' *Variety* 28 April 1922, p. 44; 'Business Minimum Holy Week At Loop's Picture Houses' and 'Week and Weather Hit Buffalo Hard: Saturday Was Worst Day' *Variety* 5 April 1922, p. 30; 'Holy Week Hits Frisco Houses Hard'; 'Lent's Bad Business Held Up Until Last: Holy Week Gave Light Business to Picture House' *Variety* 23 April 1924, p. 18. Thomas Doherty has recounted how, when potential Roman Catholic patrons celebrated Lent, box-office revenues dropped off sharply in what exhibitors dubbed the 'Lenten slump.' Thomas Doherty, 'This Is Where We Came In: The Audible Screen and the Voluble Audience of Early Sound Cinema' in Melvyn Stokes and Richard Maltby (eds), *American Movie Audiences: From the Turn of the Century to the Early Sound Era* (London: British Film Institute, 1999), p. 148.
27. 'Bishop Strange to Large Audience,' *VP* 17 March 1911, p. 10; 'Large Attendance at Noon-Day Services,' *VP* 7 March 1911, p. 4; 'Good Attendance at Monday Services,' *VP* 9 March 1911, p. 5. The next year, a Bishop Tucker appealed to a packed theater of businessmen at the Granby in an evangelistic sermon. 'Larger Crowds at Noon Services,' *VP* 23 February 1912, p. 7. The following week, the Episcopal Bishop Strange delivered a lecture on 'Love for Christ' in the same theater. 'Another Big Crowd Hears Bishop Strange,' *VP* 29 February 1912, p. 3.
28. 'Noon-day Services in the Granby Begin Today,' *VP* 1 March 1911, p. 3; 'Noonday

Lenten Series with Prominent Preachers,' *VP* 8 March 1915, p. 2; 'Large Crowd Hear Bishop Strange: Wonderland Theatre Packed to Capacity,' *VP* 16 February 1910, p. 4.

29. Even conservative Baptists held a major unification meeting in the Academy. 'Extension Rally Early in New Year,' *VP* 2 December 1908, p. 3. See also 'Large Attendance at Noon-Day Service,' *VP* 11 March 1909, p. 6; 'Noonday Services at the Wonderland,' *VP* 16 March 1909, p. 3. Such practices continued throughout the decade: 'Dr. Bell speaks during Holy Week at the American Theatre,' *VP* 16 April 1919, p. 10; 'Episcopal Church Congress Will Convene in Norfolk,' *VP* 30 April 1916, p. 3.

30. 'The Fall of Babylon: How? When? Why?,' *VP* 12 January 1918, p. 2.

31. 'To Lecture On World, War, and Bible,' *VP* 20 January 1918, p. 4.

32. 'Theatre Service Tomorrow Night,' *VP* 29 October 1911, p. 8. Norfolk and Portsmouth Baptists held revival services in the Orpheum as well. 'Theatre Meeting to Be Held Sunday,' *VP* 3 November 1916, p. 10.

33. 'Methods to Attract Worshippers,' *VP* 12 July 1908, p. 16; 'Pictures Lure for Non-Churchgoers,' *VP* 3 December 1911, p. 44.

34. 'Col. Dean to Speak at Arcade Toda,' *VP* 19 September 1915, p. 7; 'Rain Interferes With Revival,' *VP* 8 October 1915, p. 4.

35. 'Increased Interest in Baptist Revival,' *VP* 7 October 1915, p. 3.

36. 'YMCA Meeting Today,' *VP* 19 January 1908, p. 5; '"Self Control" Theme of Rev. G.E. Booker,' *VP* 31 March 1908, p. 5.

37. 'At Barton's Theatre Tuesday,' *VP* 25 April 1908, p. 2; 'Barton on Bended Knee, Seeks Blessings of God,' *VP* 29 April 1908, p. 7.

38. 'Will Operate Movie Theatre for Charity,' *VP* 4 January 1920, pp. 2:1, 6.

39. 'Will Operate Movie Theatre for Charity,' *VP* 4 January 1920, pp. 2:1, 6; 'Matinee at Academy Net Many Gifts for Tuberculosis Cases,' *VP* 23 December 1920, p. 2.

40. 'At the American,' *VP* 18 April 1915, p. 7.

41. Kathryn H. Fuller, *At the Picture Show: Small Town Audiences and the Creation of Movie for Culture* (Washington D.C.: Smithsonian Institutution Press, 1996).

42. 'Edison Moving Pictures,' *VP* 31 January 1906, p. 8.

43. Rev. Henry W. Dowd illustrated his preaching on 'The Life of St. Paul.' 'First Congregational Church,' *VP* 5 January 1908, p. 21.

44. 'The Passion Play,' *VP* 30 October 1907, p. 9.

45. 'Passion Play Pictures and Big Boys' Choir,' *VP* 11 December 1907, p. 10; 'Impressive Passion Play,' *VP* 12 December 1907, p. 10; 'Story of the Passion Play,' *VP* 13 December 1907, p. 10.

46. 'China in Moving Pictures,' *VP* 2 May 1908, p. 8.

47. 'Illustrated Lecture on Great White Plague,' *VP* 15 May 1908, p. 9.

48. 'Moving Pictures Show Heathen Religious Rites,' *VP* 11 January 1910, p. 5.

49. 'Dr. Adams Tells of Heathen Lands: Illustrated Lecture Was Interesting to Audience,' *VP* 12 January 1910, p. 4.

50. 'Go to Church Sunday,' *VP* 7 March 1914, p. 8; '"Movie" Films to Save Souls: Pictures Presenting the Story of Human Development as Told in the Bible, Four Weeks' Program for the Wells Theatre,' *VP* 15 May 1914, p. 8.

51. Richard Alan Nelson, 'Propaganda for God: Pastor Charles Taze Russell and the Multi-Media *Photo-Drama of Creation* (1914),' in Roland Cosandey, Andre Gaudreault and Tom Gunning (eds), *Une Invention du Diable? Cinema des Premiers Temps et Religion* (Lausanne: Editions Payot, 1992), p. 234.

52. 'City Churches to Use Movies: Educators and Religious Workers Complete Plans for an Extended Service,' *VP* 21 June 1914, p. 16; 'Cumberland Street Methodist Church's "Moving Pictures and Music",' *VP* 1 March 1916, p. 12; 'Will Use Moving Pictures in Church,' *VP* 12 August 1920, p. 4.

53. 'Moving Pictures to be Used in Church,' *VP* 31 December 1915, p. 8.
54. 'New Plans of a Venerable Church,' *VP* 13 February 1916, p. 7.
55. 'Feature Films of Life of Christ,' *VP* 13 February 1916, p. 18.
56. 'Norfolk's Christ, St. Luke's designated Va. historic landmark' *The Ledger-Star* 7 April 1979, A–4; 'Christ Church to Have Modern Parish House,' *VP* 24 April 1918, p. 1.
57. 'Christ Church Parish House Opened,' *VP* 11 December 1919, p. 3.
58. 'Entertainment Tonight,' *VP* 6 May 1921, p. 9; 'Picture Series to Begin Tonight,' *VP* 14 November 1921, p. 7.
59. 'Give Movies Sunday for Greek Church,' *VP* 10 December 1921, p. 14; '"Life of Moses" Will Be Shown in Pictures,' *VP* 27 August 1921, p. 10; 'Religious News: Motion Pictures at Epworth,' *VP* 10 December 1920, p. 7; 'Movies Tonight on Church Lawn,' *VP* 7 July 1922, p. 18.
60. 'Films Show Work of Catholics in War; At Colonial,' *VP* 2 May 1920, p. 3:6; 'Catholic Council War Work Shown on the Screen,' *VP* 3 May 1920, p. 3; 'Movies in Prayer Meeting,' *VP* 27 May 1920, p. 7; 'Federation's Moving Picture Program,' *VP* 23 June 1920, p. 7; 'Summer Prayer Meetings at Epworth Methodist,' *VP* 16 June 1920, p. 7; 'Religious Film is Shown at Armory,' *VP* 26 June 1920, p. 2.
61. 'Sing the Messiah at the Academy,' *VP* 30 December 1909, p. 12; 'Elks' Benefit at Granby,' *VP* 7 January 1910, p. 14; 'Sacred Concert at Academy Tuesday,' *VP* 13 February 1915, p. 3. See also Frank Burch Brown on the assimilationist sense of sacred space in his *Good Taste, Bad Taste, and Christian Taste* (Oxford: Oxford University Press, 2000).
62. 'Church or Devil to Entertain Young of This Century,' *VP* 21 August 1909, p. 5.
63. 'Using Moving Pictures to Illustrate Sermon,' *VP* 6 July 1914, p. 3.
64. 'Using Moving Pictures to Illustrate Sermon,' *VP* 6 July 1914, p. 3; 'Pictures on Liquor Evil,' *VP* 7 July 1914, p. 5.
65. 'Idle Wives' Film Sermon at Fotosho,' *VP* 8 July 1917, p. 18.
66. 'The Eternal Magdalene at the Colonial,' *VP* 5 February 1916, p. 12.
67. 'Want Movies Used to Benefit Public,' *VP* 1 December 1918, p. 8C.
68. '"The Miracle Man" Is Unusual Photodrama,' *VP* 15 October 1919, p. 9; 'After Visit to Granby Writes His Appreciation of "the Miracle Man"' *Ledger-Dispatch* 18 December 1919, p. 5; 'George Loane Tucker's "The Miracle Man",' *VP* 14 December 1919, p. 1:10.
69. 'Use Movies to Draw People to Church,' *VP* 1 February 1920, p. 5:10.
70. 'Lois Weber's Latest, "The Blot," Appears at Granby,' *VP* 11 September 1921, p. 5:3.
71. 'Private Showing Will be Made of "The Blot",' *VP* 2 October 1921, p. 6:5. See also 'The Faith Healer,' *VP* 25 September 1921, p. 5:4.
72. 'Harold Lloyd's Comedies Commended By Minister,' *VP* 22 July 1923, p. 3:10.
73. 'Censorship for Motion Pictures,' *VP* 4 May 1920, p. 15.
74. See C.H. Jack Linn, 'The Movies—The Devil's Incubator: Can a Christian go to Movies?' *Flirting With the Devil* (Oregon, WI: Hallelujah Print Shop, 1923).
75. 'Kansas City Crusade Against Sunday Theatre,' *VP* 17 October 1907, p. 1; 'N. Y. Theatres to Close on Sunday,' *VP* 5 October 1907, p. 1; 'Blue Law Lid Fits Tight on Gay New York; Kansas City Also Adopts Same Process,' *VP* 8 December 1907, p. 1. Every form of amusement, including Y.M.C.A. entertainment, fell under this 'literal enforcement of an old, but not seriously regarded statute.' Most major denominations joined the bandwagon. See 'Presbyterians Oppose Divorces: Sunday Amusements and Need of Religious Education Discussed,' *VP* 22 May 1909, p. 1; 'Methodist Preachers on Sunday Observance,' *VP* 8 June 1909, p. 4.
76. See Lindvall, *The Silents of God*, pp. 100–16.
77. 'Praise God Every Day: Sunday Protected by Divine Command' *Norfolk Virginian* 24 October 1895, p. 1.

78. *New York Times* (*NYT*) 14 October 1907; 'Pastors Open War on Sunday Shows,' *NYT* 19 January 1909, p. 8; 'Hearing on Sunday Pictures,' *NYT* 13 March 1909, p. 5.
79. '[Police Chief] Kizer Put Sunday Selling Up to the Courts,' *VP* 22 May 1909, p. 4. W. Stephen Bush culled and marshaled statistics on Sunday showings in 120 large and small cities, and their effects on public order and decorum, arguing as an editor of moving picture trade periodical that 'The advocates of rational enjoyment after church hours on Sunday are not proposing or favoring a new thing. On the contrary the right of people to innocent pastimes and healthful recreations after church hours on Sundays is almost as old as Christianity itself and exists today in every part of the Christian world with the sole exception of the British Isles.' W. Stephen Bush (ed.), *Motion Pictures on Sunday: A Collection of Facts and Figures* (Cincinnati, OH: The Billboard Pub. Co., c. 1923), p. 3.
80. 'Methodists Are Asked to Stay Out of Theatres,' *VP* 10 May 1910, p. 3; 'Conference Pays Tribute: Condemn Desecration of Sabbath,' *VP* 29 July 1910, p. 7.
81. 'Nothing Harmful in 'Traffic in Souls,' *VP* 13 January 1914, p. 4.
82. 'Better Observance of Sabbath,' *VP* 28 March 1911, p. 4; 'Better Observance of Sabbath Day,' *VP* 23 April 1911, p. 7.
83. 'A Man's Sins Will Find Him Out, Says Rev. Dr. Shelton,' *VP* 24 March 1919, p. 2.
84. 'Church Opposes Sunday Movies in Resolutions,' *VP* 24 March 1919, p. 5.
85. 'Nobody Agreed at Meeting on Sunday Movies,' *VP* 25 March 1919, p. 2.
86. Musser, 'Passions and the Passion Play,' p. 447.
87. 'Removal of Ban on Amusements Recommended: Bishops Declare Church Law Prohibiting Dancing, Card Playing Gambling, and Theatre Going Is Obsolete,' *VP* 4 May 1912, p. 1.
88. 'This Observing Preacher Sees Many Things More Interesting Than Sermon to His Flock,' *VP* 19 December 1920, p. IV: 1.
89. 'Entertainment at Spurgeon Memorial,' *VP* 25 September 1917, p. 10; 'Enlisted Men Entertained at Cumberland St. Church,' *VP* 28 September 1917, p. 4; 'Park View Church to Entertain Men,' *VP* 2 October 1917, p. 7.
90. 'Pictures at Church Entertain Sailors: Big Audience Attends Screen Show at Cumberland Street Methodist Church,' *VP* 14 September 1917, p. 7.
91. 'Orphans Invited to Free Entertainment: "Pilgrim's Progress" will be shown at Cumberland St. Church Tonight,' *VP* 18 October 1917, p. 4; 'Pilgrim's Progress and Parsifal in Pictures,' *VP* 17 November 1917, p. 7.
92. 'Oppose Moving Picture Shows on Sunday,' *VP* 10 February 1909, p. 4; 'Oppose Free Movies on Sunday Evenings,' *VP* 24 August 1914, p. 9; 'Baptist Church Puts Ban on Sunday Movies,' *VP* 27 August 1914, p. 14.
93. 'Sailors to Have Own Theatre,' *VP* 13 January 1918, p. 20; 'Naval Base Theatre Attractive Playhouse,' *VP* 30 June 1918, p. 3:1.
94. A resolution provided that the armory may be used on Sundays for the illustrating of travel talks, lectures on health, and other educational topics. It was the 'desecration of the Sabbath' that would have a tendency to lower the moral standards of the community. 'No Movies For Enlisted Men on Sundays, Citizens Committee Decides Illustrated Lectures And Travel Talks Sufficient,' *VP* 28 March 1919, p. 4; 'This Episcopal Divine Favors Liberal Sunday,' *VP* 27 July 1919, p. 5:6; 'Sunday Movies in Elizabeth City: Children and Grown-Ups Will Be Given Opportunity to See Historical Film,' *VP* 24 November 1921, p. 11.
95. '"Movie Is Poor Man's Book of Travel and Sunday Fun," Lord Beaverbrook Argues,' *VP* 17 April 1921, p. 5:2.
96. 'Nobody Agreed at Meeting on Sunday Movies,' *VP* 25 March 1919, p. 2; 'Colored Ministers Protest,' *VP* 27 March 1919, p. 6.

97. 'S.R.O. Sign Out for Sunday Movie Show of Bible Films,' *VP* 14 March 1922, p. 5; 'Those Sunday "Blues",' *VP* 6 December 1920, p. 6; 'English Liberals View With Smile "Pussyfoot Sunday" Agitation in U.S.,' *VP* 19 December 1920, p. 3:16; 'Is it Lawful to Pull Automobile Out of Ditch on Sunday?,' *VP* 30 December 1920, p. 2; Briggs, 'Movie of a Man Reading of the Blue Law' (cartoon) *VP* 3 December 1920, p. 14.

98. 'Billy Sunday Sways Audience With His Famous Sermon on "Amusements",' *VP* 7 February 1920, p. 9.

99. 'God Help Poor Girls—Says Billy Sunday,' *VP* 19 March 1922, p. 2:8; 'The Reverend Billy Sunday Says,' *VP* 30 September 1917, p. 10.

100. William T. Ellis, *"Billy" Sunday: The Man and His Message* (Philadelphia, PA: John C. Winston Company, 1914), pp. 138–39.

101. Peter Bogdanovich, *Allan Dwan: The Last Pioneer* (New York: Praeger Publishers, Inc., 1971), p. 40.

102. Elijah P.D.D. Brown, *The Real Billy Sunday: The Life and Work of Rev. William Ashley Sunday, D.D. The Baseball Evangelist* (New York: Fleming H. Revell Company, 1914), p. 217.

103. 'Says Mothers Shimmy Set Bad Example'—'While the children are at the moving picture shows, their fifty year old mothers are at the dances learning how to "shimmy"' *NJG* 29 July 1922, p. 1.

104. 'Pastor Has Novel Plan for Sermons' *NJG* 16 September 1922, p. 1; 'Church Vote Acquits Theatre Goers of Sin' *NJG* 23 September 1922, p. 1.

105. 'Bishop Ward to Open Crusade at Attucks Sunday' *NJG* 5 February 1927, p. 8.

Chapter 5: Patchwork Maps of Moviegoing, 1911–1913

1. I want to thank Virginia Wright Wexman for inviting me to present a version of this essay at the Chicago Film Seminar, 4 December 2003. Thanks also to Scott Curtis's incisive response and the discussion that followed.

2. These fictional women are based on a study of three generations of immigrant working women in Central Falls—Louise Lamphere, *From Working Daughters to Working Mothers: Immigrant Women in a New England Industrial Community* (Ithaca, NY: Cornell University Press, 1987).

3. See the New Pastime, Star, and Music Hall ads, *Pawtucket Times* (14 September 1912), p. 5.

4. Emilie Altenloh, 'A Sociology of the Cinema: the Audience,' trans. Kathleen Cross, *Screen* 42.3 (Autumn 2001), pp. 249–93. See also 'Editorial,' *Screen*, 42.3 (Autumn 2001), pp. 245–48.

5. Altenloh, 'A Sociology of the Cinema,' pp. 257–58.

6. Altenloh, 'A Sociology of the Cinema,' p. 255.

7. Altenloh, 'A Sociology of the Cinema,' p. 255.

8. Altenloh, 'A Sociology of the Cinema,' p. 256.

9. 'Nickels for Theatres vs. Nickels for Bread,' *New York Morning Telegraph* (12 May 1912), pp. 4.2, 2. In late 1909, David Hulfish offered far more conservative hours, '11:00 a.m. until 9:00 p.m.' for a typical moving picture theater in a downtown shopping district; by 1913, he changed that to '9 A.M. until 11 P.M.' for the 'large exclusive picture house'—see Hulfish, 'Economy in Picture Theater Operation,' *Nickelodeon* (1 January 1910), p. 15; and Hulfish, *Cyclopedia of Motion-Picture Work* (Chicago, IL: American Technical Society, 1914 [c. 1911]), p. 25.

10. Such 'special program nights' in theaters offering a variety program of daily changed films were common at least through the summer of 1913—see John B. Rathburn, 'Motion Picture Making and Exhibiting,' *Motography* (26 July 1913), p. 72.

11. W.W. Winters, 'With the Picture Fans,' *Nickelodeon* (1 September 1910), pp. 123–24. See also 'Spectator's' Comments,' *New York Dramatic Mirror* (7 August 1912), p. 24.

12. See also Eileen Bowser, *The Transformation of Cinema, 1907–1915* (New York: Scribner's, 1990), pp. 126–28.

13. Quoted from an unpaginated twenty-page booklet on the Bijou Theatre printed in early 1911.

14. F.H. Madison, 'In the Northwest,' *Moving Picture World* (7 September 1912), p. 994.

15. It should not be forgotten that the downside of this increase in leisure time, especially for young working women, was 'a state of affairs wherein the world's labour market [had] actually come to depend on the work of women outside the home'—see Clara E. Laughlin, *The Work-A-Day Girl: A Study of Some Present-Day Conditions* (New York: Fleming H. Revell, 1913), p. 53 A source that remains unexamined is *Mother's Magazine* (November 1912), which included four articles on motion pictures—see 'Mothers, Children and Pictures,' *Motography* (7 December 1912), pp. 419–20.

16. Frederic C. Howe, 'Leisure,' *Survey* 31 (3 January 1914), p. 415; F.H. Richardson, 'Women and Children,' *Moving Picture World* (21 February 1914), p. 962. One report claimed that 'nine out of every ten persons that enter the moving picture shows ... are women,' but this must have been exaggerated, coming from the Minneapolis Board of Home Missions and Church Extension—'Blames the Women,' *New York Morning Telegraph* (2 June 1912), 4.2: 3.

17. Alan Havig, 'The Commercial Amusement Audience in Early 20th-Century American Cities,' *Journal of American Culture* 5.1 (1982), pp. 7–8. This seems remarkable, given the Massachusetts statistics revealing that many young working women (not living at home) were paid less than $6.00 a week, far less than the estimated required budget of $10.60—see Laughlin, *The Work-A-Day Girl*, pp. 160–63. Several studies of young working women in New York City all noted that moving pictures were second only to dance halls as a preferred amusement, even if the theaters they frequented may have been in their own neighborhoods—see Robert Wood and Albert J. Kennedy (eds), *Young Working Girls* (Boston, MA: Houghton Miflin, 1913), pp. 106–107, 112–13; Ruth S. True, *The Neglected Girl* (New York: Survey, 1914), pp. 66–67; and Harriet McDougal Daniels, *The Girl and Her Chance* (New York: Fleming H. Revell, 1914), p. 71.

18. Cited in Roy Rosenzweig, *Eight Hours For What We Will: Workers and Leisure in an Industrial City, 1870–1920* (Cambridge: Cambridge University Press, 1983), p. 201. See also the more general comment about how 'clerks, stenographers, etc. employ their noon hour,' in Jos. F. Hennegan, 'Music and the Picture Show,' *Billboard* (3 February 1912), p. 13.

19. See the *Providence Sunday Journal* article (ca. 1910) reproduced in Roger Brett, 'Temples of Illusion,' *The Golden Age of Theaters in an American City* (Providence, RI: Brett Theatrical, 1976), pp. 162–65.

20. 'The Great Child Problem,' *Providence News* (15 February 1912) n.p.—Nickel Theatre and Bijou Theatre Clippings Book, Series IV, Keith-Albee Collection, Special Collections, University of Iowa Library, Iowa City, Iowa. I thank Rick Altman for drawing my attention to this and other clippings books, along with the Star Theatre's accounts book, in the Keith-Albee Collection. William Trufant Foster, *Vaudeville and Motion Picture Shows: A Study of Theaters in Portland, Oregon* (Portland: Reed College, 1914), pp. 17, 27, 28. Other surveys from Ipswich (Massachusetts) to Springfield (Illinois) and the Quad Cities (Iowa/Illinois) are summarized in Daniel J. Czitrom, *Media and the American Mind: From Morse to McLuhan* (Chapel Hill, NC: University of North Carolina Press, 1982), pp. 42–43.

21. Foster, *Vaudeville and Motion Pictures*, pp. 17, 22. Summarizing other surveys in large cities from this period, Havig concludes that 'youth and young adults ranging in age

from 15 to 25 years constituted the bulk of the movie audience in the years before World War I': in cities as different as Milwaukee, Kansas City, and Detroit, for instance, they made up 50 per cent of the audience—Havig, 'The Commercial Amusement Audience in Early 20th-Century American Cities,' p. 9.

22. Robert O. Bartholomew, 'Report of Censorship of Motion Pictures and of Investigation of Motion Picture Theatres of Cleveland, 1913'—cited in David Nasaw, 'Children and Commercial Culture: Moving Pictures in the Early Twentieth Century,' in Elliott West and Paula Petrik (eds), *Small Worlds: Children and Adolescents in America, 1850–1950* (Lawrence, KS: University of Kansas Press, 1992), p. 18.

23. Frank H. Madison, 'In the Mississippi Valley,' *Moving Picture World* (15 June 1912), p. 1051.

24. Lynn's population increased 30 per cent from 1900—see 'Population of Individual Cities,' *Thirteenth Census of the United States: Abstract of the Census* (Washington, DC: Government Printing Office, 1913), p. 64. Of those 90,000, the 1910 census listed slightly more than 30 per cent as 'foreign-born white' (with the greatest numbers coming from Canada, Ireland, and Russia), somewhat lower than the 35 per cent in Boston and substantially lower than the 40 per cent in Lowell and nearly 50 per cent in Lawrence—see 'Country of Origin,' *Thirteenth Census of the United States*, p. 212.

25. For a summary history of Lynn, see Keith Melder, *Life and Times in Shoe City: The Shoe Workers of Lynn* (Salem, MA: Essex Institute, 1979), pp. 2–9.

26. Earlier, the Dreamland and Comique also competed for customers with contests, respectively, for 'the most popular employees for local retail stores' and 'the most popular female employees of the local shoe factories'—see Henry, 'New England,' *Moving Picture World* (27 April 1912), p. 348; Henry, 'New England,' *Moving Picture World* (1 February 1913), p. 478.

27. Of the 170,000 people in Toledo, the 1910 census listed more than 30,000 as 'foreign-born white,' with nearly half coming from Germany and the next largest numbers, from Russia, Poland, Hungary, and Canada—see 'Population—Ohio,' *Thirteenth Census of the United States*, pp. 363, 398.

28. For a summary history of Toledo's commercial districts and ethnic communities, see Charles N. Glaab and Morgan J. Barclay, *Toledo: Gateway to the Great Lakes* (Tulsa: Commercial Heritage Press, 1982), pp. 66, 68, 71, 95, and 99. For the number of picture theaters in Toledo, see the city directories as well as 'The Moving Picture Situation in Toledo, O.,' *Billboard* (28 January 1911), p. 6.

29. See the Hart ads, *Toledo Union Leader* (10 December 1912), p. 6, and (23 May 1913), p. 2. Toledo had 'relatively strong unions' during this period—see Glaab and Barclay, *Toledo: Gateway to the Great Lakes*, p. 62.

30. The first of these contest announcements appeared in the *Toledo Blade* (18 February 1911), p. 1. They continued daily for the following week and then once or twice a week thereafter, through March 10.

31. 'Here Are Prize Winning Moving Picture Criticisms,' *Toledo Blade* (4 March 1911), p. 24; 'Picture Show Critics Do Better This Week,' *Toledo Blade* (11 March 1911), p. 12; and 'Last Moving Picture Prizes Won by Girls,' *Toledo Blade* (18 March 1911), p. 13.

32. This accounts book can be found in Box 10, Series III, of the Keith-Albee Collection.

33. 'Theatres,' *Pawtucket Chronicle and Gazette* (26 November 1909), p. 8. Annual city taxes for the Star Theatre's personnel came to $1,500 during this period; annual taxes on the theater itself were only $24.75—see *the Pawtucket Tax Book* (1911–1914).

34. 'Population of Individual Cities,' *Thirteenth Census of the United States*, p. 64. Of those 50,000, the 1910 census listed 18,000 or 35 per cent as 'foreign-born white,' with the greatest numbers coming from Great Britain, Ireland, and French Canada—'Country of Origin,' p. 213. Specifically, the city was known for producing calico, wadding, plush

fabric, and woolen goods—see *American Newspaper Annual and Directory* (Philadelphia, PA: N.W. Ayer & Son, 1914), p. 866. For information on nearby Providence's picture theaters, most of which were controlled by Charles Lovenberg, see Henry, 'New England,' *Moving Picture World* (16 December 1911), p. 916 and (1 February 1913), p. 479.

35. The earliest temple was located in a tenement on North Main Street, not far from the Star Theatre—*Pawtucket, Rhode Island* (1978), p. 52.

36. Lamphere, *From Working Daughters to Working Mothers*, p. 109.

37. This information is gathered from the Star Theatre and Bijou Theatre Clippings Books, Series IV, in the Keith-Albee Collection.

38. Weather may have been a factor because, the previous summer and fall, the *Durbar in Kinemacolor* had played for a record five months at the Tremont Temple in Boston— 'Correspondence: New England,' *Moving Picture World* (26 October 1912), p. 357.

39. Star Theatre and Bijou Theatre Clippings Books, Series IV, Keith-Albee Collection.

40. One of those less profitable weeks included the 4 July holiday (on a Saturday); another included the unusual expense of a new Simplex projector; and a third may have been due to bad weather (in late February).

41. For a more focused analysis of early Famous Players distribution practices, see Michael Quinn, 'Distribution, the Transient Audience, and the Transition to the Feature Film,' *Cinema Journal* 40.2 (2001), pp. 35–56.

42. The Star may well exemplify the claim, published in the *New York Dramatic Mirror*, that 'a motion picture audience, save in rare instances, [was] drawn from the population living within walking distance of the theater'—Film Man, 'Comments and Suggestions,' *New York Dramatic Mirror* (16 October 1912), p. 25.

43. That the Star may not have catered to Jewish audiences specifically is suggested by the scheduling of Kay-Bee's *The Man They Scorned* (in which a Jewish army recruit plays an unlikely western hero) on Thanksgiving weekend in 1912; although receipts were quite high, as might be expected, on the holiday, they were below normal on Friday and particularly Saturday.

44. 'Resolutions Passed by the Civic Theatre Committee of Pawtucket and Central Falls, RI, June 2, 1913,' *Moving Picture World* (2 August 1913), p. 8. See also 'Pawtucket Has Civic Theater,' *Moving Picture World* (20 March 1915), p. 1752. The resolutions specifically mention the need for translating film stories and intertitles in such languages as Polish, Italian, Syrian, and Hebrew or Yiddish.

45. 'Moving Picture Shows Capture the State,' *Providence Sunday Journal* (3 April 1910), p. IV.5.

46. This pattern of weekly attendance may well have been established prior to the fall of 1912, during the period of MPPC programs and multiple-reel specials, and perhaps then was solidified by the opening of the Pastime, one of whose weekly program changes occurred on Friday.

47. This quote comes from 'Mrs. W.H. Bryant, head worker of the Neighborhood House, 906 Galapago Street, Denver, in 'Nickels for Theatres vs. Nickels for Bread,' *New York Morning Telegraph* (12 May 1912), pp. 4.2, 2.

Chapter 6: Next Year at the Moving Pictures: Cinema and Social Change in the Jewish Immigrant Community

1. 'An Unexploited Field and Its Possibilities,' *Views and Films Index*, 6 October 1906.

2. Ben Singer, 'Manhattan Nickelodeons: New Data on Audiences and Exhibitors,' *Cinema Journal* 34:3 (Spring 1995), p. 22.

3. Abraham Cahan (1871–1951) was one of the most prominent intellectuals of the

immigrant generation: editor of the *Forward* from 1901 until his death, literary and theater critic for both English and Yiddish periodicals, and writer of short stories and a novel about life in New York's Jewish 'ghetto.'

4. The number of articles on the nickelodeon boom compared poorly to the attention paid a few years earlier to the Yiddish music hall boom. Then the *Forward* devoted over a dozen articles to the Yiddish vaudeville business within less than a few months (December 1905–March 1906).

5. 'Der unglik oyf rivington strit,' editorial, *Forward*, 15 December 1908.

6. E.g. 'Vu zaynen ahingekumen di yidishe myuzik hols?,' *Forward*, 24 May 1908; 'Vu zaynen ahingekumen di yidishe myuzik hol "stars"?,' ibid., 26 November 1908; 'Der "trost" oyf di yidishe muving piktshur "shous,"' ibid., 16 December 1908; 'Di ekelhafte shmuts fun gevise muving piktshur pletser,' ibid., 15 March 1909.

7. In 1910, AFL delegates urged local unions to 'use all legitimate means ... to discourage the exhibition of such moving pictures that falsely pretend to represent instances in connection with our movement.' Quoted in Steven J. Ross, 'The Revolt of the Audience: Reconsidering Audiences and Reception during the Silent Era,' in Melvyn Stokes and Richard Maltby (eds), *American Movie Audiences: From the Turn of the Century to the Early Sound Era* (London: BFI Publishing), p. 96. For a detailed analysis of labor and radical film production, see Steven J. Ross, *Working-class Hollywood: Silent Film and the Shaping of Class in America* (Princeton, NJ: Princeton University Press, 1998).

8. Andrew Heinze, *Adapting to Abundance: Jewish Immigrants, Mass Consumption and the Search for American Idenity* (New York: Columbia University Press, 1990), p. 150.

9. 'Der muving piktshur trost,' *Tageblatt*, 6 January 1909; 'Muving piktshurs in lebens-farben,' ibid., 17 December 1909.

10. *Tageblatt*, 14, 24, 25, 27, 28, 29 and 31 December 1908, 6 and 24 January 1909; *Morgen zhurnal* 21, 23, 24, 25, 27, 28, 29, 30 and 31 December 1908, and 7 January 1909.

11. It should be emphasized in this context that neither the *Tageblatt* nor the *Morgen zhurnal* were subject to pressure from local film exhibitors, who might have used advertising as leverage to produce favorable publicity. Movie theaters rarely advertised in the Yiddish press before 1913–14.

12. 'Golden rul theater iz zikher,' *Tageblatt*, 16 December 1908.

13. 'Der unglik oyf rivington strit,' editorial, *Forward*, 15 December 1908.

14. 'Di muving piktshur frage,' editorial, *Tageblatt*, 20 March 1911.

15. *Boston Advocate* 7:5 (10 April 1908), p. 8, quoted in David Kaufman, *Shul with a Pool: The 'Synagogue-Center' in American-Jewish History* (Hanover, NH: University Press of New England, 1999), p. 124.

16. Louis Marshall, 'The Need of a Distinctly Jewish Tendency in the Conduct of Jewish Educational Institutions,' (May 1908), quoted in Kaufman, *Shul with a Pool*, p. 125.

17. On the subject of Jewish labor and socialism, see Irving Howe, *The World of Our Fathers: The Journey of the East European Jews to America and the Life They Found and Made* (New York: Harcourt Brace Jovanovich, 1976; repr: New York, Schocken, 1990), pp. 287–324; Gerald Sorin, *A Time for Building: The Third Migration, 1880–1920* (Baltimore, MD: Johns Hopkins University Press, 1992), pp. 109–35.

18. Richard Abel, 'The Perils of Pathé or the Americanization of Early American Cinema,' in Leo Charney and Vanessa R. Schwartz, *Cinema and the Invention of Modern Life* (Berkeley, CA: University of California Press, 1995, pp. 183–223, especially pp. 200–207.

19. See Judith Thissen, 'Jewish Immigrant Audiences in New York City, 1905–1914,' in Melvin Stokes and Richard Maltby (eds), *American Movie Audiences: From the Turn of the Century to the Early Sound Era* (London: BFI Publishing, 1999), pp. 21–23 (quote p. 23), and Thissen, 'Charlie Steiner's Houston Hippodrome: Moviegoing on New York's Lower East Side, 1909–1913,' in Gregg Bachman and Thomas Slater, *American Silent Film:*

Discovering Marginalized Voices (Carbondale and Edwardsville, IL: Southern Illinois University Press, 2002), pp. 27–47, in particular pp. 43–47. For a somewhat different view on Yiddish vaudeville, see Nina Warnke, 'Immigrant Popular Culture as Contested Sphere: Yiddish Music Halls, the Yiddish Press, and the Processes of Americanization, 1900–1910,' in *Theatre Journal* 48 (1996), pp. 321–35.

20. 'Grend theater thut zikh on in di bgodim fun muving piktshurs,' *Warheit*, 5 September 1909.

21. 'Adler, miler un kompani,' *Forward*, 8 September 1909.

22. 'Vos thut zikh in theater?,' *Tageblatt*, 19 November 1910.

23. According Leo Rosten's lexicon of Yinglish words 'Alrightniks are materialists; they parade their money; they lack modest, sensitive, *edel* qualities. They talk loudly, dress garishly, show off ... Above all, they are not learned, nor devoted to learning—hence cannot be really respected.' Leo Rosten, *The Joys of Yiddish* (1968; London: Penguin Books, 1971), p. 13.

24. For a detailed analysis, see Thissen, 'Charlie Steiner's Houston Hippodrome,' p. 46.

25. For example, 'Durkh muving piktshurs beganvenen zey a hoyz,' *Forward*, 11 January 1910; 'Lernt zikh ganvenen durkh muving piktshurs,' ibid., 6 June 1910; 'Kinder veren banditen fun muving piktshurs, ibid., 11 June 1910.

26. 'Lazt nit ayere kinder gehn aleyn in di muving piktshur pletser,' *Forward*, 13 May 1910. See also '2 yidishe boys fershikt in sing-sing als kadeten,' *Forward*, 31 January 1910; 'maydlekh ferfihrt in a muving piktshur plats,' ibid., 23 December 1910; 'Vider di gefahr fun di muving piktshurs,' ibid., editorial, 2 February 1911. For the general context in which these concerns about movies and white slavery were articulated, see Janet Staiger, *Bad Women: Regulating Sexuality in Early Cinema* (Minneapolis, MN: University of Minessota Press, 1995), pp. 44–52, 99–103, 120–28.

27. 'Muving piktshurs un di kinder,' *Tageblatt*, 30 January 1911.

28. 'Interesante kleynigkayten vegn muving piktshurs,' *Forward*, 9 January 1914. After a few weeks, the column was re-titled 'Interesante fakten vegen muving piktshurs,' ibid., 16 February 1914.

29. *Moving Picture World*, 30 May 1914, p. 1218.

30. *Moving Picture World*, 22 August 1914, p. 1146 and 29 August 1914, p. 1248.

31. *Moving Picture World*, 30 January 1915, p. 757 and 6 February 1915, p. 809.

32. Advertisement Grand Theater, *Forward*, 21 October 1914; 'A varnung fun yakob p. adler zum publikum,' Advertisement People's Theater, *Forward*, 24 October 1914.

33. Warnke, 'Immigrant Popular Culture as Contested Sphere,' pp. 325–26.

34. Over the last decade, important contributions to the debate about the image-ban have been made by Moshe Halbertal and Avishai Margalit in *Idolatry* (Cambridge, MA: Harvard University Press, 1992); Loinel Kochan, *Beyond the Graven Image: A Jewish View* (New York: New York University Press, 1997), and Kalman P. Bland, *The Artless Jews: Medieval and Modern Affirmations and Denials of the Visual* (Princeton, NJ: Princeton University Press, 2000).

35. See for instance, Barbara Kirshenblatt-Gimblett and Jonathan Karp (eds), *The Art of Being Jewish in Modern Times* (Philadelphia, PA: University of Pennsylvania Press, 2007).

36. The wish 'Next year in Jerusalem' is also expressed at Yom Kippur, but there is no doubt that the cartoons refers to *Pesach*, because it appeared less than two weeks before the start of this eight day festival. As matter of fact, it is no coincidence that Marcus Loew opened his new theater around this time, because *Pesach* was not only a religious festival but also marked a highpoint in the Yiddish theatrical season. On the first two and final two days of the holiday, thousands of immigrants flocked to the theaters on the Lower East Side for special matinees and evening performances, billed '*lekoved peysekh*'—in honor of Passover.

37. In addition to the original text, I used R.J. Zwi Werblowsky and Geoffrey Widoger (eds) *The Oxford Dictionary of the Jewish Religion* (New York and Oxford: Oxford University Press, 1997).
38. Ibid., p. 199 (Deuteronomy).
39. Bland, *The Artless Jew*, p. 60.
40. Michael Steinlauf, 'Fear of Purim: Y.L. Peretz and the Canonization of Yiddish Theater,' *Jewish Social Studies* 1: 3 (Spring 1995), p. 55. The formula 'bread and circuses' occurs in Tractate *Avodah zarah* (idolatrous worship) 18 b.
41. Michael Steinlauf, 'Purimshpil to Yiddish Theater: Re-exploring the Connections,' unpublished paper presented at the Center For Judaic Studies Seminar, Philadelphia, 24 January 2001. I wish to thank Michael for sharing this paper with me.
42. Significantly, Purim is the only Jewish holiday that commemorates events that are entirely set in the Diaspora. Moreover, the scroll of Esther is a purely secular narrative which, unlike other text in the Jewish canon, does not contain the word of God even once. Steinlauf, 'Purimsphil to Yiddish theater.' See also Michael Steinlauf, 'The fear of Purim: Y.L. Peretz and the Canonization of Yiddish Theater,' *Jewish Social Studies* 1:3 (Spring 1995), p. 56.
43. Steinlauf, 'Fear of Purim,' p. 56.
44. Warnke, 'Immigrant Popular Culture as Contested Sphere,' p. 323.
45. Bernard Gorin, *Di geshikhte fun yidishen theater* (New York: Literarisher verband, 1918), vol. 2, p. 189.
46. Jacob Gordin, 'The Yiddish Stage,' *Yearbook of the University Settlement Society of New York* (1901), p. 28.
47. Typically, the *loyfer* declaimed a prologue including a demand for money from the audience and introducing the actors with the formula 'arayn, arayn ... du mayn.' In the cartoon, the two functions of the prologue are condensed in the sentence: 'aher, aher, yiden! bilig bilig bilig! ale stars un starikes far tsehn cent!' [This way, this way, Jews! Cheap, cheap, cheap! all stars for ten cents!].
48. Steinlauf, 'Fear of Purim,' p. 55; idem, 'Purimshpil to Yiddish theater,' pp. 11–12.
49. See Hadassa Kosak, *Culture of Opposition: Jewish Immigrant Workers, New York City, 1881–1905* (Albany, NY: State University of New York Press, 2000), especially chapters five and six.

Chapter 7: 'Four Hours of Hootin' and Hollerin'': Moviegoing and Everyday Life Outside the Movie Palace

1. My deepest thanks to Mary Annese, Richard McBride and Rita Soplop for their generous and indispensable contributions to this study. Douglas Gomery, *Shared Pleasures: A History of Movie Presentation in the United States* (Madison, WI: University of Wisconsin Press, 1992), *passim*; Lary May, *Screening Out the Past: The Birth of Mass Culture and the Motion Picture Industry* (Chicago, IL: University of Chicago Press, 1983), *passim*; Russell Merritt, 'Nickelodeon Theaters, 1905–1914: Building an Audience for the Movies,' in Tino Balio (ed.), *The American Film Industry* (Madison, WI: University of Wisconsin Press, 1985), pp. 83–102; Steven J. Ross, *Working-class Hollywood: Silent Film and the Shaping of Class in America* (Princeton, NJ: Princeton University Press, 1998), pp. 173–211.
2. Douglas Gomery offers a useful baseline definition of a movie palace as 'a large theater built to screen films and to accommodate live shows, seating over 1,500 people, constructed with a fan shaped auditorium and much non-functional decoration.' Gomery, 'The Picture Palace: Economic Sense or Hollywood Nonsense?', *Quarterly Review of Film Studies* 3.1 (1978), p. 24.

3. Peter Stead, *Film and the Working-class: The Feature Film in British and American Society* (London: Routledge, 1989), p. 18.

4. Richard Testa, 'Movie Exhibition Practices and Procedures During the Hollywood Studio Era in Providence Rhode Island,' Ph.D. dissertation, University of Maryland, 1992, pp. 177–78. The term 'moron' was not uncommon in the discourse of reformers and cultural elites at the time and, as Richard Maltby has found, was 'widely used to refer indirectly to the immigrant working class.' Maltby, 'The Production Code and the Hays Office,' in Tino Balio (ed.), *Grand Design: Hollywood as a Modern Business Enterprise 1930–1939* (New York: Charles Scribner's Sons, 1993), p. 45.

5. Stuart Ewen and Elizabeth Ewen, *Channels of Desire: Mass Images and the Shaping of American Consciousness* (New York: McGraw-Hill, 1982), p. 103.

6. Testa, 'Movie Exhibition Practices and Procedures,' p. 173.

7. Gomery, *Shared Pleasures*, pp. 34–56.

8. Ewen and Ewen, *Channels of Desire*, p. 104.

9. Maggie Valentine, *The Show Starts on the Sidewalk: An Architectural History of the Movie Theater* (New Haven, CT: Yale University Press, 1994), p. 89.

10. Richard Koszarski, *An Evening's Entertainment: The Age of the Silent Feature Picture 1915–1928* (New York: Charles Scribner's Sons, 1990), pp. 9–10; Miriam Hansen, *Babel and Babylon: Spectatorship in American Silent Film* (Cambridge, MA: Harvard University Press, 1991), p. 100.

11. Roy Rosenzweig, *Eight Hours for What We Will: Workers and Leisure in an Industrial City, 1870–1920* (Cambridge, MA: Cambridge University Press, 1983), p. 212. The limited mixing of social classes in industrial cities may not have been confined only to a downtown palace versus neighborhood theater split. In addition, it is possible patrons from different classes self-selected into attendance at entirely different movie palaces, or into different blocks of seats within a single palace, largely due to cost factors and/or taste preferences. For an empirical study exploring this possibility, see Jeffrey Klenotic, 'Class Markers in the Mass Movie Audience: A Case Study in the Cultural Geography of Moviegoing, 1926–1932,' *The Communication Review* 2.4 (1998), pp. 468–73, 487–89.

12. Thomas Doherty, 'This is Where We Came In: The Audible Screen and the Voluble Audience of Early Sound Cinema,' in Melvyn Stokes and Richard Maltby (eds), *American Movie Audiences: From the Turn of the Century to the Early Sound Era* (London: BFI Publishing, 1999), pp. 143–63; Lizabeth Cohen, *Making a New Deal: Industrial Workers in Chicago, 1919–1939* (Cambridge, MA: Cambridge University Press, 1990); Mary Carbine, 'The Finest Outside the Loop: Motion Picture Exhibition in Chicago's Black Metropolis, 1905–1928,' *Camera Obscura* 23 (May 1990), pp. 8–41. The question of how deep into the 1930s any given neighborhood theater remained a vital center of social activity remains an open one. Steven Ross, for instance, argues that working-class patrons quickly grew to prefer the movie palace over the local, the latter being attended only during the week and even then with some distaste. As Ross rightly observes, 'we should not romanticize the neighborhood theater' given its often run-down architecture, uncomfortable seats, narrow aisles, poor film prints, lack of ushers, and status as hangout for 'juvenile delinquents, loose women, and exceedingly loud children' (Ross, *Working-class Hollywood*, p. 192). Still, whatever questions exist over how to characterize or periodize the neighborhood theater (not to mention the even more fundamental question of whether we can do so without essentializing this type of theater), the larger theoretical issue at stake remains crucial. Namely, that practices carried out under the sign 'moviegoing' are part of a process of social communication and bear the property of multi-accentuality. If juvenile delinquents, 'loose' women, and loud children attended certain neighborhood theaters, and if some patrons defined these groups' attendance as undesirable, this underscores the point that the meaning

of moviegoing—the meaning we make of our attendance as well as the meaning made of our attendance by others—is open to competing definitions. The scenario Ross describes also reminds us that however disreputable or distasteful the practices of neighborhood theaters looked to some at the time, the movie palace was not the only form of reception operative during the 1920s and 1930s. For an excellent overview of moviegoing practices at many neighborhood theaters during the 1930s, see Richard Butsch, 'American Movie Audiences of the 1930s,' *International Labor and Working-Class History* 59 (Spring 2001), pp. 106–120.

13. Hansen, *Babel and Babylon*, p. 88. In addition to the abovementioned work on industrialized cities, recent studies documenting moviegoing in rural and small town settings also suggest the diversity in film exhibition and audience formation both during and after the period of early cinema. See Kathryn H. Fuller, *At the Picture Show: Small Town Audiences and the Creation of Movie Fan Culture* (Washington, DC: Smithsonian Institution Press, 1996); Gregory A. Waller, 'Another Audience: Black Moviegoing, 1907–1916,' *Cinema Journal* 31.2 (1992), pp. 3–25; Gregory A. Waller, 'Hillbilly Music and Will Rogers: Small-town Picture Shows in the 1930s,' in Melvyn Stokes and Richard Maltby (eds), *American Movie Audiences: From the Turn of the Century to the Early Sound Era* (London: BFI Publishing, 1999), pp. 164–79.
14. See Pierre Bourdieu, *Distinction: A Social Critique of the Judgement of Taste*, trans. Richard Nice (Cambridg, MA: Harvard University Press, 1984), p. 6.
15. See V.N. Volosinov, *Marxism and the Philosophy of Language* (New York: Seminar Press, 1973).
16. See Janet Staiger's work for an excellent example of this 'reading formation' approach to studying the historical conditions of film reception. Staiger, *Interpreting Films: Studies in the Historical Reception of American Cinema* (Princeton, NJ: Princeton University Press, 1992).
17. Drawing from Bourdieu, I discuss one way moviegoing might be conceptualized as both open to cultural agency and structured in relations of social and economic power in my essay, 'Class Markers.' That essay also provides a fuller discussion of the theoretical framework through which moviegoing can be understood as a stage in a process of social communication.
18. These theaters have been identified through Price and Lee's *Springfield City Directory* as well as an exhaustive reading of Springfield's three daily newspapers. It is difficult to determine when Price and Lee collected information for each year's directory, so it is possible a theater listed in a given year was actually out of business by the start of that year if Price and Lee based their listings on information gathered from the year before. Seat capacity figures should also be considered approximate, since these capacities often changed during this period of intense theater renovation.
19. 'State Theater Opens,' *Springfield Sunday Republican*, 6 September 1931, p. 5C.
20. The reduction in seats at Fox-Poli's Palace was due to renovations, particularly installation of larger seats designed for greater comfort.
21. Gomery, *Shared Pleasures*, p. 56.
22. For a more detailed discussion of the changing history of theater ownership in Springfield, see Jeffrey Klenotic, 'A Cultural Studies Approach to the Social History of Film: A Case Study of Moviegoing in Springfield, Massachusetts,' Ph.D. dissertation, University of Massachusetts at Amherst, 1996.
23. See H. Paul Douglass, *The Springfield Church Survey: A Study of Organized Religion with Its Social Background* (New York: George H. Doran, 1926).
24. Michael H. Frisch, *Town into City: Springfield Massachusetts and the Meaning of Community* (Cambridge, MA: Harvard University Press, 1972).
25. Springfield City Planning Board, *A City Plan for Springfield, Massachusetts: Report by the*

Planning Board, 1923 (Springfield, MA: Springfield Printing and Binding Company, 1923).

26. Population figures drawn from Douglass's *Springfield Church Survey*, Price and Lee's *Springfield City Directory* (1926–1932), and the Springfield City Planning Board's *A City Plan for Springfield*.

27. Douglass, *Springfield Church Survey*, pp. v–vi. Given the significance of Douglass's survey to this study, it is necessary to address its status and use as an historical document. Trained as a social scientist, Douglass helped start the Committee on Social and Religious Surveys, founded in 1921 in New York City. A year later the Committee became the Institute of Social and Religious Research. The Institute was charged to study 'organized religion with its social background,' and sought to generate empirical research that could help Protestantism adapt to rapidly changing patterns of social demography and geographic mobility. To this end, the Institute collaborated with local churches and civic organizations to fund and develop extensive protocols and data bases with which to survey the social and religious geography of a given site, with Douglass serving as field director.

In the case of Springfield, the Institute employed a variety of methods to map the city's social and cultural geography during the 1920s into areas distinguished by 'natural boundaries and homogeneity of population' (p. 263). In the end, the survey divided Springfield into eleven districts that it believed accurately captured the cultural contours of the city as it was lived. The delineation of these eleven districts in some cases shadowed the boundaries of the eight wards of the city, but overall the survey's identification of social and cultural fault lines was more organic, nuanced and fine-grained than what ward boundaries typically allow. To draw out social dimensions of each district, the survey amalgamated data from, among other sources, a door-to-door census of more than 16,000 residents undertaken as part of the survey itself, federal census records including data at the enumeration district level, city school censuses, local polling records, court and police records, charitable relief records, and extant records indicating the zoning and location of city industries.

The survey was not, however, a neutral or unbiased document. Its purpose was to evaluate each district according to an index of 'social quality' that formed the basis of 'popular distinctions between 'desirable' and 'undesirable' sections of the city' (p. 265). As the survey described its measure of 'social quality': 'It is assumed that a district with a large population of foreign birth or foreign antecedents, many Negroes, a high degree of industrialization and congestion of housing, with many children at work, much illiteracy, juvenile delinquency and charity, represents a less desirable combination of human fortunes than one in which opposite conditions exist, and that the ranking of districts on this basis approximately places their people in the scale of human welfare' (pp. 265–66). Given the cultural orientation behind this measure of social quality and neighborhood status, it is unsurprising that the survey maintains its results 'demonstrate conclusively that Protestantism has also a strong affinity for more desirable sections of the city [and that] ... the largest proportion of Protestants and the best social quality go together' (p. 274).

The bias in the survey does not undermine its usefulness as an historical document. On the contrary, when read against the grain, the survey reveals the anxiety of a dominant group confronting the reality of urban transformation, and it stands as a record of this group's attempt to map this transformation for the purpose of asserting control over it. Whatever we think of 'social quality' rankings, the survey remains useful precisely because it gives access to an elite perception of the changing city. This perception can then be held in tension against non-elite visions of city space, such as those gleaned here through oral histories.

28. On the development of Springfield's commercial and industrial base, see Donald J. D'Amato, *Springfield—350 years: A Pictorial History* (Norfolk, VA: The Donning Company, 1985); Michael Konig and Martin Kaufman (eds), *Springfield 1636–1986* (Springfield, MA: Springfield Library and Museums Association, 1987), pp. 146–83; and Frank Bauer, *At the Crossroads: Springfield, Massachusetts 1636–1975* (Springfield, MA: U.S.A. Bicentennial Committee of Springfield, 1975), pp. 88–101.

29. Women constituted 28.6 per cent of employed labor and worked in clerical occupations (clerks, stenographers, bookkeepers) and domestic/personal service occupations (domestic servants, waitresses, housekeepers, nurses), and as school teachers. Douglass, *Springfield Church Survey*, pp. 78–79.

30. *Springfield City Directory* (New Haven, CT: Price & Lee, 1920–1933).

31. Douglass, *Springfield Church Survey*, pp. 64, 78, 405.

32. Douglass, *Springfield Church Survey*, p. 65.

33. Douglass, *Springfield Church Survey*, p. 65; Michael H. Frisch, 'Town into City: A Reconsideration on the Occasion of Springfield's 350th Anniversary,' in Konig and Kaufman (eds), *Springfield 1636–1986*, p. 114.

34. Frisch, 'Town into City: A Reconsideration,' p. 113.

35. See Bauer, *At the Crossroads*.

36. Studio publicity for the grand opening of the Paramount was enormous, tracking construction of the theater for months and culminating with a full ten-page special section in the *Springfield Daily Republican*. 'Paramount Theater,' *Springfield Daily Republican*, 29 September 1929, pp. 1G–10G. By comparison to the cost of the Franklin, the Paramount's air-cooling system alone was estimated at $100,000. 'Air Cooling Plant of Modern Type,' *Springfield Sunday Republican*, 29 September 1929, p. 2G; 'New Paramount Theater Largest, Most Modern in Western Massachusetts,' *Springfield Sunday Republican*, 29 September 1929, p. 2G. The cost to construct the Franklin is taken from the theater's building permit, 'Application for Permit to Build,' No. 22609, Ward 2, which is archived at the Connecticut Valley Historical Museum, Springfield, Massachusetts.

37. The North End had been without its own theater since 1925 when the Globe, a vaudeville and motion picture house, closed after fourteen years.

38. Douglass, *Springfield Church Survey*, pp. 265–67.

39. Douglass, *Springfield Church Survey*, pp. 265, 407.

40. Douglass, *Springfield Church Survey*, p. 265.

41. Douglass, *Springfield Church Survey*, p. 410.

42. Mary Annese, personal interview, 13 July 1994. Annese is a second generation American of Polish and Italian heritage. Her family moved to Springfield, and to the North End, in 1926. She was seven. Her father worked on the railroad. Her mother worked in textile mills before coming to Springfield. Mary lived in the same house in the North End, less than 500 feet from the Franklin Theater, for 34 years. A long time resident of the North End, she directly participated in the culture of everyday life described in this study, and witnessed many changes to her former neighborhood at first hand. She knew the Semanie family that built the Franklin Theater, as they lived in the same neighborhood, though not on the same street. Although Mary lived near the Franklin, she acknowledged being in the theater only 'about a half-a-dozen times, because I wasn't much of a movie-goer. I was one that always went to the girls club.' When the Franklin sold at public auction in 1940, it was demolished and replaced by the new home of the Springfield Girls Club, where Mary worked for ten years. Annese's interview, like the other interviews for this study, was done face-to-face, recorded on tape with the participant's permission, transcribed, and excerpted as close to verbatim as possible (without sacrificing coherence) from those transcripts. In keeping with an 'ethno-historical' approach to social film history, I have tried to be reflexive in my use of interviews, understanding these not as

unproblematic pipelines into the past but as forms of discourse with their own unique social and psychological contexts of production. See Annette Kuhn, 'That Day *Did Last Me All My Life: Cinema Memory and Enduring Fandom,*' in Melvyn Stokes and Richard Maltby (eds), *Identifying Hollywood's Audiences: Cultural Identity and the Movies* (London: BFI Publishing, 1999), pp. 135–46.

43. Douglass, *Springfield Church Survey*, p. 265.

44. Richard McBride is a second generation American of Irish and French Canadian heritage who was born in Springfield and lived in the North End throughout his childhood and early adulthood. His mother was a homemaker and his father worked as a night supervisor at a downtown restaurant. Richard lived in a multi-family home about one-half mile north of the Franklin Theater, and would regularly walk to movies there. He was seven in 1926 and remembers attending the Franklin at least once a week (Saturdays), often more, throughout the early 1930s. He did not often attend many theaters outside the North End. As he says, 'We who were in the smaller group, the less affluent group, we'd wait 'til they came to our theaters, ones we could walk to. It would be rare for us to go to a big one.'

45. Richard McBride, personal interview, 21 October 1994.

46. Richard McBride, personal interview, 21 October 1994.

47. Douglass, *Springfield Church Survey*, p. 265.

48. These industries included, among numerous others, F.M. West Box Company and Lumber Yard, Cheney Biglow Wire Works, Hampden Brass Company, E.S. Decker Lumber Yard, Davitt Iron Foundry and Iron Works, Walsh Boiler and Iron Works, Springfield Breweries Company, and H.W. Carter Paper Company.

49. Douglass, *Springfield Church Survey*, pp. 407–08.

50. Mary Annese, personal interview, 13 July 1994.

51. Hansen, *Babel and Babylon*, p. 92.

52. Details drawn from the theater's building permit, as well as from a photograph of the building.

53. 'Congress Street Vice is the Chief Issue Says Louis,' *Springfield Daily News*, 14 October 1929, p. 2.

54. Rita Soplop, personal interview, 30 June 1995.

55. Preliminary genealogical information on the Semanie family (whose name may formerly have been Assemani) was obtained via a message board discussion posted to the web-based family history service Ancestry.com.

56. *Springfield City Directory* (New Haven, CT: Price & Lee, 1920–1933); Mary Annese, personal interview, 13 July 1994.

57. Franklin Advertisements in *Springfield Daily News*, 15 October 1929, p. 2; *Springfield Daily News*, 21 October 1929, p. 6; *Springfield Daily News*, 25 October 1929, p. 2; *Springfield Evening Union*, 24 October 1931, p. 7.

58. 'Special Notice,' *Springfield Daily News*, 25 October 1929, p. 2.

59. Klenotic, 'Class Markers,' pp. 482–83.

60. For more on the Knights of Labor, see Holly Allen, 'Gender, The Movement Press, and the Cultural Politics of the Knights of Labor,' in William S. Solomon and Robert W. McChesney (eds), *Ruthless Criticism: New Perspectives in U.S. Communication History* (Minneapolis, MN: University of Minnesota Press, 1993), pp. 122–50.

61. Bauer, *At the Crossroads*, pp. 91–92.

62. Paul Seale, 'A Host of Others: Toward a Nonlinear History of Poverty Row and the Coming of Sound,' *Wide Angle* 13.1 (1991), pp. 93–94.

63. Richard Maltby offers an excellent discussion of Hollywood's classification of film audiences between 1929 and 1933 'into a series of overlapping binary distinctions between "class" and "mass", "sophisticated" and "unsophisticated", "Broadway" and "Main Street."'

Richard Maltby, 'Sticks, Hicks and Flaps: Classical Hollywood's Generic Conception of Its Audiences,' in Melvyn Stokes and Richard Maltby (eds)," *Identifying Hollywood's Audiences: Cultural Identity and the Movies* (London: BFI Publishing, 1999), p. 25.

64. 'Seed Coming to Franklin Theater,' *Springfield Evening Union*, 24 October 1931, p. 6.

65. Richard McBride, personal interview, 21 October 1994.

66. Bourdieu, *Distinction*, p. 4.

67. Roland Marchand, *Advertising the American Dream: Making Way for Modernity 1920–1940* (Berkeley, CA: University of California Press, 1985), pp. 132–40.

68. Mary Annese, personal interview, 13 July 1994; Richard McBride, personal interview, 21 October 1994.

69. Richard McBride, personal interview, 21 October 1994.

70. Richard McBride, personal interview, 21 October 1994.

71. For more on the activities of child audiences at neighborhood theaters, and the attempt to reform these activities, see the case study presented in Jeffrey Klenotic, '"Like Nickels in a Slot": Children of the American Working-classes at the Neighborhood Movie House,' *The Velvet Light Trap* 48 (Fall 2001), pp. 20–33.

72. Richard McBride, personal interview, 21 October 1994.

73. Richard McBride, personal interview, 21 October 1994.

74. Richard McBride, personal interview, 21 October 1994.

75. Mary Annese, personal interview, 13 July 1994.

76. Richard McBride, personal interview, 21 October 1994.

77. Mary Annese, personal interview, 13 July 1994.

78. Richard McBride, personal interview, 21 October 1994.

Chapter 8: Cinemagoing in the United States in the mid-1930s: A Study Based on the *Variety* Dataset

1. The number of cinemas varied slightly because some of the smaller venues reported irregularly. Also, cities came and went. For example, New Orleans was included in 1934 but then dropped from the reports in 1935.

2. 'Bank nights' were lotteries that an audience member entered by buying an admission ticket. 'Giveaways' typically offered customers a piece of crockery for the price of admission.

3. The cities reported in the tables were Birmingham, Boston, Brooklyn, Buffalo, Chicago, Cincinnati, Denver, Detroit, Indianapolis, Kansas City (Missouri), Los Angeles, Minneapolis, Montreal, New Haven, New York, Philadelphia, Pittsburgh, Portland, Providence, St Louis, San Francisco, Seattle, Tacoma, and Washington, D.C. Reports from a further six cities are included in the text of *Variety*, but not in the monthly tables, and so these cities are not included here. They are Baltimore, Cleveland, Lincoln, Louisville, Newark and Omaha.

4. Films included in the sample are those whose principal billing, as reported in *Variety*, was during the twenty-five months between 4 October 1934 and 29 October 1936. The records of films released before 4 October 1934 but exhibited predominantly during and after this month will be included. Likewise included are the records of films released during October 1936 and receiving subsequent exhibitions in November and December 1936.

5. A 'single' bill could include a live stage show. The 'single' aspect indicates the presence of only one feature film on the programme.

6. The figure of 18 per cent is likely to be an underestimate. This is because the tables in some instances do not report on live acts, and it has not been possible to review all of the weekly text reports. Future studies, in this respect, will need to make more extensive use of the text reports.

7. *The International Motion Picture Almanac, 1936–37* (New York, 1937), p. 992.

8. Ibid.

9. *International Motion Picture Almanac*, 1946–7 (New York, 1947). The populations of the cities from which the sample set of cinemas is drawn sum to just under 26 million, out of a total U.S. population of 128 million for the mid-1930s. U.S. Department of Commerce, Bureau of the Census, *U.S. Historical Statistics: Colonial Times to 1970* (Washington, DC, 1975), Appendix One.

10. Gomery states that in some large cities there could be as many as eleven runs. Douglas Gomery, *The Hollywood Studio System* (London: Macmillan, 1986), p. 17.

11. John Sedgwick, *Popular Filmgoing in 1930s Britain: A Choice of Pleasures* (Exeter: University of Exeter Press, 2000).

12. Richard Maltby, 'Sticks, Hicks and Flaps: Classical Hollywood's Generic Conception of its Audiences', in Melvyn Stokes and Richard Maltby (eds), *Identifying Hollywood's Audiences: Cultural Identification and the Movies* (London: BFI, 1999), pp. 25–29.

13. Mark Glancy, 'MGM Film Grosses, 1924–48: The Eddie Mannix Ledger', *The Historical Journal of Film, Radio and Television*, 12 (1992), pp. 127–144; Mark Glancy, 'Warner Bros. Film Grosses, 1921–51: The William Schaefer Ledger,' *The Historical Journal of Film, Radio and Television*, 15 (1995), pp. 55–74; Richard Jewell, 'RKO Film Grosses, 1929–51: The C.J. Tevlin Ledger,' *The Historical Journal of Film Radio and Television*, 14 (1994), pp. 37–51.

14. John Sedgwick, 'Product Differentiation at the Movies: Hollywood, 1945–65,' *Journal of Economic History*, 62 (2002), pp. 682–83.

15. *Variety*, 25 October 1934, p. 8.

16. *Variety*, 30 October 1935, p. 8.

17. *Variety*, 2 April 1936, p. 8.

18. *Variety*, 31 October 1935, p. 12.

19. *Variety*, 11 December 1934, p. 11; and *Variety*, 18 December 1934, p. 11.

20. Birmingham was the only city in the deep South that *Variety* covered. This has been attributed to the poor box-office returns of the region. See Thomas Cripps, 'The Myth of the Southern Box-Office: A Factor in Racial Sterotyping in American Movies, 1920–40,' in J.C. Curtis and L.L. Lewis (eds), *The Black Experience in America: Selected Essays* (Austin, TX and London, 1970), pp. 116–44.

21. In Birmingham, for example, Temple's *Dimples*, *The Littlest Rebel* and *The Little Colonel* placed among the 20 top earning films during this period; and one of the city's leading cinemas, the Strand, regularly offered week-long engagements to low budget Westerns of stars such as Richard Dix, George O'Brien and Randolph Scott.

22. *The Barretts of Wimpole Street* was declared to be 'too snooty,' 'too stylish' and 'too highbrow' for Birmingham audiences, and it lasted only one week at the Alabama Theatre, where it earned $6,500. The week before, Will Rogers' *Judge Priest* had earned $8,500 in the same venue. *Variety*, 30 October 1934, p. 8. *Modern Times* earned a remarkable $230,500 during the six weeks it played New York's Rivoli Theatre, but this proved to be 38 per cent of its total earnings, indicating that its success elsewhere was not so great.

23. The house, said to be worth $16,000, also included home insurance and groceries for a full year. The lottery took place in Denver and four first-run cinemas participated. Denver's Orpheum, which is included in the sample, was one participant. *Variety*, 4 September 1935, p. 4.

24. The Louis-Schmeling fight film was reported to be a significant attraction in Boston, Denver, Detroit, Indianapolis, Los Angeles, Minneapolis, Montreal, Portland, San Francisco and St Louis. See *Variety*, 25 June 1936.

25. *Variety*, 23 October 1935, p. 9.

26. Earnings for *Cleopatra* reached a moderately successful $415,500, but this was below the level of earnings reached by other costume dramas. The grosses for *The Crusades* and *The Last Days of Pompeii* were much lower, at $212,900 and $186,400, respectively.

27. See, for example, Nick Roddick, *A New Deal in Entertainment: Warner Brothers in the 1930s* (London: BFI, 1983); Peter Roffman and James Purdy, *The Hollywood Social Problem Film: Madness, Despair and Politics from the Depression to the 1950s* (Bloomington, IN: Indiana University Press, 1981); and Colin Shindler, *Hollywood in Crisis: American Cinema and Society, 1929–39* (London: Routledge, 1996).

28. Brian Taves, 'The B Film: Hollywood's Other Half', in Tino Balio (ed.), *Grand Design: Hollywood as a Modern Business Enterprise 1930–1939* (New York: Scribner's, 1993), p. 321.

29. The 'Spanish' films were actually Spanish-language films, and many of these came from Mexico and South American countries, but the report does not categorise them in this way. See *Variety*, 1 January 1936, p. 43.

30. The discrepancy in running times is between the time listed for the original British release and the (shorter) time listed for the American release. For example, *Evergreen* was cut from 92 to 82 minutes; *First a Girl* from 93 to 78 minutes, *Things to Come* from 110 to 96 minutes, *Scrooge* from 78 to 72 minutes; and *Man of Aran* from 80 to 70 minutes.

31. For further analysis of London Films and the American market, see Sarah Street, *Transatlantic Crossings: British Feature Films in the USA* (London: Continuum, 2002), chap. two.

32. For further analysis of Gaumont-British's efforts in the USA, see Sedgwick, *Popular Filmgoing*, chap. ten; the American release of *The 39 Steps* is considered in Glancy, *The 39 Steps: A British Film Guide* (London: I.B. Tauris, 2002).

33. One exception to this was the British and Dominions film *Escape Me Never*, which earned $189,950, but the company's other films had very few engagements and earnings levels far below this.

34. Taves, 'The B Film,' pp. 318–20.

35. This method does under represent those very strong 'A' films, such as *San Francisco*, that occasionally played on double bills with much less popular films. This is an unavoidable problem, but also a slight one. As we have seen, the major 'A' films were actually the least likely to appear on double bills.

36. Douglas Gomery, *Shared Pleasures: A History of Movie Presentation in the United States* (Madison, WI: University of Wisconsin Press, 1992), p. 77.

37. *Variety*, 25 September 1934, p. 9.

38. To give one example, when MGM's *It's in the Air* was paired with Universal's *Fighting Youth* at the Broadway in Portland, the report commented that audiences were coming 'chiefly for *Air*.' *Variety*, 30 October 1935, p. 9.

39. Polling was reported to have included 725,824 people. *Variety*, 12 August 1936, p. 5.

40. For example, it was said that while one of the films might be 'suitable for children, the second feature generally is not' *Variety*, 12 August, 1936, p. 34.

41. *Variety*, 8 July 1936, p. 5.

42. *Variety*, 12 August 1936, p. 34.

43. *Variety*, 16 October 1934, p. 49.

44. *Variety*, 1 January 1935, p. 115.

45. *Variety*, 4 September 1935, p. 17.

46. *Variety*, 1 April 1936, p. 20.

47. *Variety*, 13 November 1934, p. 17. Of course, such reports suggest that the earnings of *The Scarlet Empress* and other films that played with prominent live acts should perhaps be altered to take account of another significant attraction on the programme. However, there is no clear and obvious method of doing this. Instead, we have chosen to draw

attention to the presence of live acts when reporting box-office grosses. See Tables One, Three, Four and Five and Appendix One for examples of this.

48. *Variety*, 22 January 1935, p. 49.

49. Gregory Waller, 'Hillbilly Music and Will Rogers: Small Town Picture Shows in the 1930s,' in Melvyn Stokes and Richard Maltby (eds), *American Movie Audiences: From the Turn of the Century to the Early Sound Era* (London: BFI, 1999), p. 171. See also Richard B. Jewell, 'Hollywood and Radio: Competition and Partnership in the 1930s,' *The Historical Journal of Film, Radio and Television*, 4 (1984), pp. 125–51.

50. The Roxy Theatre, for example, paid $6,000 for the Bowes stage show to support the Republic film *Laughing Irish Eyes*. *Variety* declared that this was a 'fair gamble' given the 'weak picture.' The week's earnings, at $24,000, were twice as high as the film earned in any other engagement. *Variety*, 8 April 1936, p. 19.

51. *Variety*, 1 April 1936, p. 6.

Chapter 9: Race Houses, Jim Crow Roosts, and Lily White Palaces: Desegregating the Motion Picture Theater

1. Variously reported in 'Atty. Gen' Kennedy on Desegregation,' *The Film Daily*, 29 October 1963, p. 3; 'Kennedy Calls for Theatres to Lead Desegregation Fight,' *Motion Picture Herald*, 13 November 1963, p. 22; and Abel Green, 'Levine, Hub's Biggest Bean,' *Variety*, 30 October 1963, pp. 7, 22. *Variety* later noted that 'many exhibs expressed embarrassment and annoyance about that booing after Attorney General Robert F. Kennedy's theater desegregation speech.' 'TOA: Take Over Americana,' *Variety*, 6 November 1963, p. 20.

2. Though not forbidden by law from entering race houses, white moviegoers 'for reasons of caste snobbery … wouldn't be seen at [such] houses.' 'Negroes-Only House in Carolina Has Own Separate But Equal Ideas; Sues for Same Dates as Whites,' *Variety*, 26 June 1957, p. 3.

3. The touchstone source on motion picture exhibition in America is Douglas Gomery, *Shared Pleasures: A History of Movie Presentation in the United States* (Madison, WI.: University of Wisconsin Press, 1992).

4. 'Southern Theatre,' *Motion Picture Herald*, 12 October 1957, p. 6.

5. 'Drops Jim Crow Policy,' *The Crisis* (March 1953), p. 161.

6. See, however, 'Movie Theaters for Black Americans,' in Gomery, *Shared Pleasures*, pp. 155–70.

7. Robert J. Landry, 'Negro Only: Hazy Outlook,' *Variety*, 14 August 1963, p. 5.

8. On 23 September 1952, in a brutal contest that boxing aficionados laud as one of the greatest fights of all time, Italian-American challenger Rocky Marciano stepped into the ring to challenge African American champion 'Jersey Joe' Walcott for the heavyweight crown. In the first round, Walcott landed a devastating right hook that dropped Marciano to the canvas for the first time in forty-three fights. By the twelfth round, ringside scorecards put Walcott well ahead on points. In the thirteenth round, Marciano rallied and knocked out Walcott with a roundhouse right cross.

9. 'Negro-White Theatre in Memphis Nixed By Binford on Walcott Pix,' *Variety*, 8 October 1952, pp. 3, 27. Binford was notorious for his 'weirdly capricious' decisions, as *Variety* noted upon the forced retirement of the eighty-eight year-old censor in 1955. See 'Memphis Powders Blue Nose,' *Variety*, 14 December 1955, p. 5.

10. John Lewis, with Michael D'Orso, *Walking with the Wind: A Memoir of the Movement* (New York: Simon and Schuster, 1998), p. 48.

11. Antoinette S. Demond, 'On Sitting,' *The Crisis* (November 1955), p. 525.

12. 'Segregated Theater Cracking,' *Variety*, 2 June 1954, pp. 1, 63.

13. 'Kick Virginia Law But Circuit Meanwhile Ends Separate Negro Areas,' *Variety*, 3 July 1963, p. 16.
14. See Abel Green, 'Show Biz: Pain-in-the-Brain,' *Variety*, 8 January 1958, p. 56. This article also marks the first time *Variety*'s annual year-end wrap-up of motion picture trends included an extensive discussion of racial issues.
15. Marian A. Wright, 'Integration Trends in the South,' *The Crisis* (March 1959), pp. 137–46.
16. 'Unsegregated Cinema,' *The Crisis* (April 1954), pp. 221–22.
17. 'So. Carolina Negroes "Trespassed" On Theater, Fined $1, Take Appeal,' *Variety*, 8 May 1963, p. 25; 'Sidewalk Sitting By Negroes,' *Variety*, 5 May 1963, p. 25.1.
18. 'So. Carolina Negroes "Trespassed" On Theatre, Fined $1, Take Appeal,' *Variety*, 8 May 1963, p. 25.
19. 'Klansman in Front of Theatre; Remembrance of Griffith's "Nation,"' *Variety*, 6 November 1963, p. 6.
20. "Dixie Widely Picketed," and "Racial Pickets Multiply in Dixie," Variety, February 15, 1961: 14.
21. 'Negro Collegians Plot Stand-Ins Vs. Dixie Theaters,' *Variety*, 15 February 1961, p. 14.
22. 'Duke U. Studes Give Segregated House Hard Time,' *Variety*, 28 March 1962, p. 18.
23. 'Double Dose of Theatre Bias for Sit-Ins,' *The Chicago Defender*, 21 April 1961, p. 18.
24. 'White Student Jailed for Sitting in Balcony,' *Variety*, 7 March 1962, p. 17.
25. Abel Green, 'Megatons and Moody Mirth,' *Variety* 10 January 1962, p. 52.
26. 'College Faculty Pickets Theaters,' *The Chicago Defender*, 15 April 1961, p. 12.
27. 'Negroes in Boycott,' *The New York Times*, 30 April 1957, p. 23; 'Urge Negroes to Boycott "10 Commandments" Under Segregated N.C. Set-up,' *Variety*, 8 May 1957, p. 3.
28. 'Whites-with-Negroes Still Testing As Interstate Rigidly Segregated,' *Variety*, 13 December 1961, p. 22.
29. 'Negroes in Louisville Can't See "Porgy" Film,' *Variety*, 13 January 1960, p. 14; 'Negro Junket to "Porgy" (Indpls) When Downtown L'ville Bans Attendance,' *Variety*, 8 February 1960, p. 2.
30. 'Ozoners' Big Negro Draw,' *Variety*, 3 August 1949, p. 4.
31. Franklin H. Williams, 'Sunshine and Jim Crow,' *The Crisis* (April 1954), p. 206.
32. Odie Anderson, 'Reluctant Race Reforms,' *Variety*, 18 October 1963, p. 18.
33. 'Negro Motorists Seek Drive-In Entrance,' *Variety*, 1 August 1962, p. 63.
34. 'Atlanta to Admit Negroes,' *Variety*, 4 April 1962, pp. 7, 13.
35. 'Washington Segregation,' *The Crisis* (April 1953), p. 226.
36. Maggie Dent, 'Art, Campus, and Racial Policy,' *Variety*, 12 June 1963, pp. 7, 11.
37. 'Anti-Segregationists Picket Theatres,' *Motion Picture Herald*, 18 February 1961, p. 6.
38. Robert J. Landry, 'Nashville Quietly De-Races,' *Variety*, 20 December 1961, pp. 20,.
39. Lewis, *Walking With the Wind*, p. 129.
40. 'Negroes Arrested in Nashville Demonstrations,' *Motion Picture Herald*, 4 March 1961, p. 6.
41. Robert J. Landry, 'Nashville Quietly De-Races,' *Variety*, 20 December 1961, pp. 3, 20.
42. 'Only Negro Balcony in Atlanta Closed; City Stands as 100% Segregated,' *Variety*, 13 December 1961, p. 22.
43. 'Quietly, Downtown Atlanta Theaters Admit Negroes,' *Variety*, 23 May 1962, pp. 3, 63.
44. Ibid.
45. For accounts of variations on the theme, see 'Charlotte Latest Dixie Community to Desegregate,' *Variety*, 3 July 1963, p. 16; 'Dallas Opens All Seats to Negroes,' *Variety*, 10 July 1963, p. 16; 'Controlled Integration Leading to Open Door Starts in Durham, N.C.,' *Variety*, 24 July 1963, p. 1; 'Negro-Only Site Now Admits Whites,' *Variety*, 14

August 1963, p. 5; Odie Anderson, 'Reluctant Race Reforms,' *Variety*, 18 October 1963, pp. 1, 18.

46. E.H. Kahn, 'Theater Desegregation Makes Progress in the South,' *Motion Picture Herald*, 29 April 1964, pp. 13, 24.

47. Robert J. Landry, 'Nashville Quietly De-Races,' *Variety*, 20 December 1961, pp. 3, 20.

48. 'Atlanta to Admit Negroes,' *Variety*, 4 April 1962, p. 13.

49. Odie Anderson, 'Reluctant Race Reforms,' *Variety*, 16 October 1963, p. 18.

50. 'Progress of U.S. Negroes,' *Variety*, 9 January 1963, p. 52. This was the first time *Variety* devoted a special sidebar to the issue of theater desegregation in its annual review of the show business highlights.

51. 'Close Negro Part,' *Variety*, 15 February 1961, p. 14.

52. 'Negroes Go In at $5 Per Ticket; Arrest Pickets,' *Variety*, 7 August 1963, p. 11.

53. 'Village Showman's Race Dilemma,' *Variety*, 3 July 1963, p. 16.

54. 'Theatres and the Race Issue,' *Motion Picture Herald*, 26 June 1963, p. 5.

55. 'Kennedy's "Desegregate!" Plea,' *Variety*, 29 May 1963, p. 3; 'Dixie's Hesitation Waltz,' *Variety*, 29 May 1963, pp. 3, 19.

56. 'Step-Up in Theatre Desegregation Sought,' *Motion Picture Herald*, 12 June 1963, pp. 38–39.

57. Harry Lando, 'Exhibs Told to Desegregate,' *The Film Daily*, 28 May 1963, pp. 1, 13.

58. 'Step-Up in Theatre Desegregation Sought,' *Motion Picture Herald*, 12 June 1963, pp. 38–39.

59. Harry Landon, 'JFK in Huddle With 30 on Segregation,' *The Film Daily*, 4 June 1963, pp. 1, 8; Harry Lando, 'Theaters Desegregating Fast,' *The Film Daily*, 5 June 1963, pp. 1, 6.

60. Harry Lando, 'Theaters Desegregating Fast,' *The Film Daily*, 5 June 1963, pp. 1, 6.

61. 'Desegregate,' *Variety*, 5 June 1963, p. 3.

62. In 1958, Robert J. Landry discerned 'a growing tendency among Hollywood producers to "cater" to [the African American] market.' '"Race": Boxoffice But Booby-Trapped,' *Variety*, 8 January 1958, p. 15. See also, 'Of Entertainment Market Interest: Big Rise in Dixie Negro Income,' *Variety*, 16 January 1963, p. 12.

63. 'Desegregation Progress in Dixie,' *Variety*, 26 June 1963, p. 7.

64. Odie Anderson, 'Reluctant Race Reforms,' *Variety*, 18 October 1963, p. 18.

65. Robert J. Landry, 'Negro Only: Hazy Outlook,' *Variety*, 14 August 1963, p. 5.

66. 'Theatre Desegregation Surveyed in 10 Cities,' *Motion Picture Herald*, 7 August 1963, p. 33.

67. Martin Quigley, Jr., 'President Kennedy and Exhibition,' *Motion Picture Herald*, 11 December 1963, p. 5.

68. 'New Orleans Last Big Dixie Key With "Jim Crow" Policy,' *Variety*, 13 November 1963, p. 1.

69. 'New Orleans Takes on Civil Rights in Stride,' *Variety*, 8 July 1964, p. 1.

70. 'Theaters in South Comply with new Civil Rights Act,' *Motion Picture Herald*, 22 July 1964, p. 14.

Chapter 10: The Reel of the Month Club: 16mm Projectors, Home Theaters and Film Libraries in the 1920s

1. See for instance Gregory Waller, *Main Street Amusements: Movies and Commercial Entertainment in a Southern City, 1896–1930* (Washington, DC: Smithsonian Institution Press, 1995); Kathryn Fuller, *At the Picture Show: Small-town Audiences and the Creation of Movie Fan Culture* (Washington, DC: Smithsonian Institution Press, 1996); Shelley Stamp, *Movie Struck Girls: Women and Motion Picture Culture After the Nickelodeon*

(Princeton, NJ: Princeton University Press, 2000); and Melvyn Stokes and Richard Maltby (eds), *American Movie Audiences: From the Turn of the Century to the Early Sound Era* (London: BFI, 1999).

2. Charles Acland, *Screen Traffic: Movies, Multiplexes and Global Culture* (Durham, NC: Duke University Press, 2003). See also Richard Maltby, '"Nobody Knows Everything": Post-Classical Historiographies and Consolidated Entertainment,' in Steve Neale and Murray Smith (eds), *Contemporary Hollywood Cinema* (London: Routledge, 1998), pp. 21–44.

3. For an engaging discussion of the changing dynamics of screen size and dimension, as well as film gauge standardization see John Belton, *Widescreen Cinema* (Cambridge, MA: Harvard University Press, 1992).

4. Barbara Klinger, 'The New Media Aristocrats: Home Theater and the Domestic Film Experience,' *The Velvet Light Trap* 42 (Fall 1998), pp. 4–19. An expanded version of this article is reprinted in Klinger, *Beyond the Multiplex: Cinema, New Technologies, and the Home* (Berkeley and Los Angeles, CA: University of California Press, 2006), pp. 17–53.

5. Klinger, 'The New Media Aristocrats.' See also Barbara Klinger 'The Contemporary Cinephile Film Collecting in the Post-Video Era,' in Melvyn Stokes and Richard Maltby (eds), *Hollywood Spectatorship: Changing Patterns of Cinema Audiences* (London: BFI Publishing, 2001), pp. 133–51; Charles Tashiro, 'The Contradictions of Video Collecting,' *Film Quarterly* 50 (Winter 1996–7); Anthony Slide, *Before Video: A History of Non-Theatrical Film* (Westport, CT: Greenwood Press, 1992); Ben Singer, 'Early Home Cinema and the Edison Home Projecting Kinetoscope,' *Film History* 2 (1988), pp. 37–69; Chris Anderson, *Hollywood TV* (Chicago, IL: University of Illinois Press, 1994); Charles Acland, 'Cinemagoing and the Rise of the Megaplex,' *Television and New Media* 1.4 (2000), pp. 375–402.

6. President's Research Committee on Social Trends, *Recent Social Trends in the United States* (New York: McGraw-Hill Book Co., 1933), pp. 210–11.

7. Moya Lucket usefully explores similar issues in relation to general ideas about home movie systems, focusing on movie making with some attention to related ideas about what she terms domestic spectatorship. Her discussion concentrates on questions of gender, middle-class ideas about film reform, and a generalized nostalgia for Victorian domestic values. Her study is not gauge specific and focuses on select discourses circulating primarily in the teens. See Moya Lucket, 'Filming the Family: Home Movie Systems and the Domestication of Spectatorship,' *The Velvet Light Trap* 36 (Fall 1995), pp. 21–32.

8. 'Ganz: Highlights From the News' [advertisement], *Amateur Movie Makers*, 2.7 (1927), p. 4. For brief historical details on Ganz, see Anthony Slide, *Before Video*, p. 9.

9. For the most thorough discussion of the history of amateur moviemaking see Patricia R. Zimmerman, *Reel Familes: A Social History of Amateur Film* (Bloomington, IN: University of Indiana, 1995), esp. chaps 2 and 3. Though Zimmerman's book focuses on filmmaking and the paired concepts of amateur and professional, her overview and analysis of these areas remains invaluable. For an examination of the parallel developments in television, see William Boddy, 'The Amateur, the Housewife and the Salesroom Floor: Promoting Postwar US Television,' *International Journal of Cultural Studies* 1.1 (1998), pp. 129–42; and in radio, see Michelle Hilmes, *Radio Voices: American Broadcasting, 1922–1952* (Minneapolis, MN: University of Minnesota, 1997), esp. chap. 2.

10. Lucket and others have argued that discourses about movies in the home existed from the beginnings of the medium. Lucket rightly identifies a growing vogue for home movie systems during the 1910s, evident in publications such as the Sears Catalogue, and magazines such as *Literary Digest*, *Scientific American*, and *Outlook* ('Filming the Family', p. 31). One of the key differences between the 1910s and 1920s is the aggressive entry

of Kodak into the home cinema market. Kodak was one of the world's most formidable advertising powerhouses, building an empire on its clever transformation of photography from clumsy machine to easy everyday activity. With the standardization of the 16mm format, the company promptly expanded the venues in which its own home systems were being sold, piggybacking on its strategies for snap-shot photography. Thus the venues for home movie ads grew to include a vast range of newspapers and the emergent generation of picture magazines, visual education journals, and, important for our purposes here, mass distributed women's magazines. Also pivotal was the internationally distributed magazine entitled *Amateur Movie Makers* (later shortened to *Movie Makers*) which began publishing in 1926, a prominent site for advertising a whole range of home movie systems and film rental services. For more on the history of Kodak's advertising see Nancy Martha West, *Kodak and the Lens of Nostalgia* (Charlottesville, VA: University Press of Virginia, 2000), esp. chap. 1.

11. For an overview of early developments in this equipment, see Alan D. Kattelle, *Home Movies: A History of the American Industry, 1897–1979* (Nashua, NH: Transition Publishing, 2000).

12. Zimmerman, 'Reel Familes'; Brian Winston, *Technologies of Seeing: Photography, Cinema, Television* (London: BFI, 1996). See also Moya Lucket "Filming the Family.".

13. Pathé already had a well established extra-theatrical rental system in place, which used its own 28mm and, as of 1922, a 9.5mm gauge. Yet 16mm proved so successful so quickly that even Pathé began to issue its films in the new gauge. For more on these early film libraries see David Pierce, 'Silent Movies and the Kodascope Libraries,' *American Cinematographer* (January 1989), pp. 36–40; and 'The Legion of the Condemned—Why American Silent Films Perished,' *Film History* 9 (1997), pp. 5–22. See also Ben Singer, 'Early Home Cinema and the Edison Home Projecting Kinetoscope,' *Film History* 2 (1988), pp. 37–69.

14. Kodascope had secured the rights to films featuring Felix the Cat, Mickey Mouse, Charlie Chaplin, Gloria Swanson, Constance Talmadge, Douglas Fairbanks, Pola Negri, Emil Jannings and many other stars of the silent screen.

15. Pierce notes that Kodak often edited their films in order to fit them on a minimum number of reels. As it was, most available projectors could only hold a maximum of one 400 ft reel. Depending on projection speed, this resulted in a running time of between 11 and 15 minutes per reel. While most films seem to have been edited for length rather than content, there is some evidence that 'racy' scenes were eliminated. It seems that Kodak actively tailored their films for 'wholesome' audiences. David Pierce, 'Silent Movies,' p. 40.

16. 'Political Story' [Pathégrams advertisement], *Movie Makers* 3.9 (1928), p. 565.

17. 'Cinegraphs' [advertisement], *Amateur Movie Makers* 2.7 (1927), p. 30.

18. Eastman Kodak, Inc., *Kodak Cinegraphs* [catalogue] (Rochester, NY: Eastman Kodak, Inc., n.d.), inside front cover.

19. 'World War Movies' [Cinegraphs advertisement], *Amateur Movie Makers* 2.11 (1927): inside back cover. Advertisements for the *War* films also clearly tried to appeal to a certain desire for 'being there-ness.' They advertised: 'Taken in action. Made under actual service conditions in France. Compiled and edited by military experts. A film in which you, yourself, or someone near and dear to you were probably one of the actors.' 'Cinegraphs: "World War Movies"' [advertisement], *Amateur Movie Makers* 2.10 (1927): inside back cover.

20. Donald Crafton, The *Talkies: American Cinema's Transition to Sound, 1926–1931* (Berkeley, CA: University of California Press, 1997), p. 15. For more on the cross-media interests of Hollywood during the 1920s and 1930s, see Michelle Hilmes, *Hollywood and Broadcasting: From Radio to Cable* (Chicago, IL: University of Illinois Press, 1990).

21. The idea of connecting the home to the world was not limited to news events but also to Hollywood. Show-at-Home Film Library, supported by Universal Pictures, advertised a 'new era in motion pictures for the home.' They promised to bring 'the World's Greatest Stars to the Home,' guaranteeing 'the best and only the best for the American Home.' With no substantial theatrical holdings of its own, Universal early on marketed its films and its stars to these expanded cinematic stages. 'Show-at-Home Film Library' [advertisement], *Amateur Movie Makers* 2.10 (1927), p. 3.

22. 'Talkers in 2,000,000 Homes Confidently Looked for in Future by Device Makers,' *Variety* 98.12 (2 April 1930), p. 3. A few weeks later *Variety* exclaimed that a 'moving film in radio cabinet' was expected to garner $1,000,000,000 a year in film rentals and equipment sales. As such, 'the picture industry is seriously set for the first time to invade thousands of American homes.' 16mm was deemed to be the gauge of choice. 'Moving Film in Radio Cabinet,' *Variety* 99.3 (30 April 1930), pp. 1, 60.

23. '48 Brands of Home Talker Sets by Xmas,' *Variety* 100.2 (23 July 1930), p. 5. The featured unit in this article was a 'three way home show' that contained 'A television, camera and recording attachment where by a family can shoot its own pictures and do its own recording, plus the expected radio and phonograph.' Also important for the entry of Hollywood into the home was the design of a continuous sound-on-film reduction printer by Victor-RCA in 1933. This was some six years before the first sound cameras, emphasizing the importance of 16mm exhibition and its distinct impact on exhibition as opposed to production.

24. John Archer, 'Suburbia and the American Dream House,' in Daniel R. Rubey and Barbara McKelly (eds), *Redefining Suburban Studies: Searching for a New Paradigm* (New York: Greenwood Press, 2003); Gwendolyn Wright, *Building the Dream: A Social History of Housing in America* (Cambridge, MA: MIT Press, 1981) and Gail Radford, *Modern Housing for American; Policy Struggles in the New Deal Era* (Chicago, IL: University of Chicago Press, 1996).

25. For the key analysis of these trends see Ruth Cowan Schwartz, *More Work for Mother: The Ironies of Household Technology from the Open Hearth to the Microwave* (New York: Basic Books, 1983).

26. These women's magazines are a hitherto untapped source for work on home film entertainment. Hollywood studios also advertised their films regularly in these same venues. Celebrities frequently endorsed products sold in these magazines. Phonographs and radios appeared with equal regularity. It was also in such magazines that public officials published treatises on the 'Better Homes Movement' and the importance of the home for national prosperity, suggesting the relevance of this particular readership to emergent federal policies. This also indicates rich links between cultures of domesticity and cultures of cinema. For a more specific discussion of women's magazines with an emphasis on *Ladies Home Journal's* relationship to gender politics see Sally Stein, 'The Graphic Ordering of Desire: Modernization of a Middle-class Women's Magazine, 1919–1939,' in Richard Bolton (ed.), *The Contest of Meaning: Critical Histories of Photography* (Cambridge, MA: MIT Press, 1992), pp. 145–62.

27. It is crucial to note that images of watching movies at home published in women's magazines were inseparable from the marketing campaigns enacted by Kodak to sell home movie cameras. The screens necessary for showing home movies were simultaneously linked to an expanded complement of films made outside of the home yet appropriate for in-home audiences. This link between early home movie theaters and home movie-making is, I think, key to future work on the history of home theaters generally. It provides a material and ideological connection between self-imaging and images of the world, both intended to affirm not just the bourgeois self but also the bourgeois family.

28. For example, in 1928 the Kodascope B Projector was listed as $300 ($3,648.00 in 2007 dollars). Projectors ranged in price from $60.00 to $450 ($729.60 to $5,472.00 in 2007 dollars). According to the U.S. Bureau of the Census, 65 per cent of families reported income less than $1,999.00 and 82 per cent of families reported income less than $2,999.00 for the year 1929. This suggests that the most expensive projector unit designed for the home would require well over 10 per cent of most family budgets, an unlikely if not impossible purchase. The least expensive units constituted a minimum of 2 per cent of total family income for 82 per cent of American families, still a formidable expense (*Historical Statistics of the United States, Colonial times to 1970, Bicentennial Edition, part 1*. Washington, DC, 1975).

29. This survey also announced that on average owners of home movie equipment retained three or more servants, far above the average even for the paper's clearly affluent readership. J. Walter Thompson, Co. 'Eastman Kodak Survey, December 1930,' Reel #198, J. Walter Thompson Collection, Hartman Center for Sales, Advertising and Marketing History, Duke University), 8.

30. One could imagine a very different study that co-articulated tool ownership, fishing pole equipment and hunting paraphernalia with camera acquisition. For an excellent analysis of masculinized contemporary discourses see Barbara Klinger, 'The New Media Aristocrats.'

31. See Janice Radway, *A Feeling for Books: the Book-of-the-Month Club, Literary Taste, and Middle-class Desire* (Chapel Hill, NC: University of North Carolina Press, 1997); see also Joan Shelley Rubin, *The Making of Middlebrow Culture* (Chapel Hill, NC: University of North Carolina Press, 1992).

32. See, for instance, Klinger, *Beyond the Multiplex*.

Chapter 11: Early Art Cinema in the U.S.: Symon Gould and the Little Cinema Movement of the 1920s

1. Anne Morey would like to acknowledge generous support for the research for this chapter from the Melbern G. Glasscock Center for Humanities Research and a College of Liberal Arts Faculty Research Enhancement Grant at Texas A&M University. National Board of Review materials are quoted courtesy of National Board of Review of Motion Pictures, Records, Manuscripts, and Archives Division, The New York Public Library, Astor, Lenox, and Tilden Foundations. David Bordwell, 'The Art Cinema as a Mode of Film Practice' *Film Criticism* 4.1 (Fall 1979), p. 56.

2. Steve Neale, 'Art Cinema as Institution' *Screen* 22.1 (1981), p. 15.

3. Daniel Czitrom, 'The Redemption of Leisure: The National Board of Censorship and the Rise of Motion Pictures in New York City, 1900–1920' *Studies in Visual Communication* 10 (Fall 1984), p. 4.

4. Mike Budd, 'The National Board of Review and the Early Art Cinema in New York: *The Cabinet of Dr. Caligari* as Affirmative Culture' *Cinema Journal* 26.1 (Fall 1986), p. 5.

5. Francis G. Couvares, 'Hollywood, Main Street, and the Church: Trying to Censor the Movies before the Production Code,' in Couvares (ed.), *Movie Censorship and American Culture* (Washington: Smithsonian Institution Press, 1996), p. 139.

6. David H. Pratt, '"Fit Food for Madhouse Inmates": The Box Office Reception of the German Invasion of 1921' *Griffithiana* 48/49 (October 1993), p. 101.

7. Pratt, 'Fit Food', p. 101.

8. Budd, 'The National Board of Review,' p. 4.

9. Ibid.

10. Ibid., p. 6.

11. Wilton Barrett to A.W. Newman, 1 November 1927, The National Board of Review

of Motion Pictures Records, Manuscripts and Archives Division, The New York Public Library, Astor, Lenox and Tilden Foundations, 'Subjects Correspondence—Little Theatre Movement' folder.

12. I am indebted to Janet Staiger for bringing this reference to my attention.

13. Howard Thompson Lewis, 'Century Theater,' *Cases on the Motion Picture Industry* Harvard Business Reports, volume 8 (New York: McGraw-Hill Book Co., 1930), p. 543.

14. Lewis, 'Century Theater,' p. 543.

15. Symon Gould circular to delegates of the Second National Better Films Conference, January 1926, National Board of Review Records, 'Film Alliance-Film Exchange' folder.

16. Lewis, 'Century Theater,' p. 544.

17. Lewis, 'Century Theater,' p. 544.

18. Symon Gould press release, 9 February 1927, National Board of Review Records, 'Film Alliance–Film Exchange' folder.

19. Herman G. Weinberg, typescript of 'The Film Arts Guild,' National Board of Review Records, 'Film Alliance–Film Exchange' folder, p. 5.

20. *The New York Telegram*, 8 June 1926, reprint of 'Round the Town' column by Symon Gould, National Board of Review Records, 'Film Alliance–Film Exchange' folder.

21. Harry Alan Potamkin, 'The Ritual of the Movies' *The National Board of Review Magazine* 8.5 (May 1933), p. 3.

22. Lenox Little Theatre circular, National Board of Review Records, 'Lenox Little Theatre' folder.

23. Alfred Kuttner to Montgomery Evans, 24 August 1928, National Board of Review Records, 'John Milligan' folder.

24. Anne Friedberg, 'Introduction: Reading *Close Up*, 1927–1933,' in James Donald, Anne Friedberg, and Laura Marcus (eds), *Close Up, 1927–1933: Cinema and Modernism* (Princeton, NJ: Princeton University Press, 1998), p. 12.

25. Film Arts Guild press release, 19 January 1926, National Board of Review Records, 'Film Alliance-Film Exchange' folder.

26. *The New York Telegram*, 8 June 1926, reprint of 'Round the Town' column by Symon Gould, National Board of Review Records, 'Film Alliance-Film Exchange' folder.

27. Symon Gould to Wilton Barrett, 14 August 1929, National Board of Review Records, 'Film Alliance-Film Exchange' folder.

28. Film Arts Guild circular, 20 November 1929, National Board of Review Records, 'Film Alliance-Film Exchange' folder.

Chapter 12: Free Talking Picture—Every Farmer is Welcome: Non-theatrical Film and Everyday Life in Rural America during the 1930s

1. Thanks to Jason McEntee and Anna Froula for their work as research assistants, and to Brenda Weber for so many conversations that helped shape this project. "Directory of Agricultural Films," *Educational Screen* 11 (1932), p. 178.

2. For background on the development of 16mm for industrial and educational uses and a general overview of non-theatrical film during this period, see Anthony Slide, *Before Video: A History of the Non-Theatrical Film* (New York: Greenwood Press, 1992), pp. 19–43. Arthur Edwin Krows' 'Motion Pictures—Not for Theatres,' an invaluable, fact- and anecdote-filled chronicle of the history of non-theatrical film up to the late 1930s, ran in fifty-eight monthly instalments in *Educational Screen* from September 1938 through June 1944.

3. My focus in this chapter is on the 1930s and, to a lesser extent, the 1920s. An area for future research is the role of agricultural film in the development of the non-theatrical

film industry in the United States during the 1910s. In 1915 alone, the relevant material in the *Moving Picture World* includes descriptions of screenings intended specifically for farmers (for example, at Henderson, Kentucky [*Moving Picture World*, 27 February 1915, p. 1320]), the use of film by schools of agriculture in Minnesota, Wisconsin, and Nebraska (*Moving Picture World*, 25 September 1915, p. 2209), farm-related 'industrialogs' like International Harvester's *The Dawn of Plenty* (*Moving Picture World*, 30 October 1915, p. 831), and the marketing of a portable projector to 'rural community clubs and county farm bureaus' (*Moving Picture World*, 25 September 1915, p. 2220).

4. As Anne B. Effland argues, '"rural" isn't synonymous with "agricultural," which, in turn, is distinct from the "agrarian ideal."' She calls for historians to examine the 'full texture of rural experience.' Effland, 'When Rural Does Not Equal Agricultural,' *Agricultural History* 74:2 (2000), p. 500.

5. See, for example, 'Hillbilly Music and Will Rogers: Small-Town Picture Shows in the 1930s,' in Gregory A. Waller (ed.), *Moviegoing in America: A Sourcebook in the History of Film Exhibition* (Malden, MA: Blackwell, 2002), pp. 175–88; idem, 'Imagining and Promoting the Small-Town Theater,' *Cinema Journal* 44:3 (Spring 2005), pp. 3–19; and *At the Picture Show*, my 1993 documentary on moviegoing in Campbellsville, Kentucky from the 1920s through the 1940s. For material on the small-town theaters in the late silent era see, in particular, Kathryn H, Fuller, *At the Picture Show: Small-Town Audiences and the Creation of Movie Fan Culture* (Washington, DC: Smithsonian Institution Press, 1996).

6. J.H. Kolb and Edmund de S. Brunner, 'Rural Life,' in *Recent Trends in the United States: Report of the President's Research Committee on Social Trends* (New York: McGraw-Hill, 1933), pp. 511, 508, 497, 523–25. Significantly, when de S. Brunner returned to the subject with Irving Lorge in *Rural Trends in Depression Years: A Survey of Village-Centered Agricultural Communities, 1930–1936* (New York: Columbia University Press, 1937), they found more indications that rural villages were marked by the 'spread of urban services' in, for example, the number of beauty parlors, drugstores, tourist camps, and liquor stores (p. 103). They also discovered what was for them a much more encouraging populist development: the flowering of 'rural community theaters' that 'have in them nothing of the commercial. They are the voices of the men and women who have struggled through drought, thaw, drifts, impassable roads, dust, and hail storms' (p. 196). Meanwhile, the movie theater—along with a strong bank or a government office—remained one way for the agricultural village to generate trade (p. 107).

7. Monroe Day (ed.), *Family Income and Expenditure: Five Regions: Part 2, Family Expenditures* (Washington, DC: Government Printing Office, 1941), pp. 330–31. Mary Neth offers a more nuanced argument focusing on farm youths, placing 'town-centered' moviegoing in the context of both commercial and non-commercial forms of recreation. Neth, 'Leisure and Generational Change: Farm Youths in the Midwest, 1910–1940,' *Agricultural History* 67:2 (1993), pp. 163–84.

8. *Family Income and Expenditure*, p. 3.

9. *Family Income and Expenditure*, p. 6.

10. Monroe Day (ed.), *Family Expenditures for Education, Reading, Recreation, and Tobacco: Five Regions* (Washington, DC: Government Printing Office, 1941), pp. 3, 39–40.

11. *Family Income and Expenditures*, p. 195.

12. *Family Income and Expenditures*, pp. 286–95. Surprisingly, an article entitled 'Farmers Go to the Movies' in *Rural America* 16 (September 1938), p. 9, could declare that 'when farm families look for entertainment, one of the favorite diversions is "going to the movies."'

13. See Nicholas Peter Sargen, *'Tractorization' in the United States and Its Relevance for the Developing Countries* (New York: Garland, 1979); Robert C. Williams, *Fordson, Farmall, and Poppin' Johnny: A History of the Farm Tractor and Its Impact on America* (Urbana, IL:

University of Illinois Press, 1987); Alan L. Olmstead and Paul W. Rhode, *The Diffusion of the Tractor in American Agriculture: 1916–1960* (Cambridge, MA: National Bureau of Economic Research, 2000); R. Douglas Hurt, *American Agriculture: A Brief History* (West Lafayette, IN: Purdue University Press, rev. edn 2002); and Deborah Fitzgerald, *Every Farm a Factory: The Industrial Ideal in American Agriculture* (New Haven, CT: Yale University Press, 2003). After the 'tractor wars' of the 1920s and early 1930s (which involved extensive advertising campaigns that included moving pictures), by 1936 International Harvester, Allis-Chalmers, and John Deere accounted for almost 80 per cent of the farm equipment market. See Wayne G. Broehl, *John Deere's Company: A History of Deere & Company and Its Times* (New York: Doubleday, 1984), p. 528.

14. Cited in Kolb and de Brunner, 'Rural Life,' p. 538.
15. *Winamac*[Indiana*] Republican*, 25 June 25 1936, pp. 2–3.
16. *Winamac* [Indiana] *Republican*, 21 July 1938, p. 8.
17. *Park City Daily News* [Bowling Green, Kentucky], 23 January 1935, p. 6.
18. *Park City Daily News* [Bowling Green, Kentucky], 4 February 1936, p. 2.
19. *Park City Daily News* [Bowling Green, Kentucky], 21 January 1936, p. 3.
20. *Park City Daily News* [Bowling Green, Kentucky], 24 January 1938.
21. *Taylor County* [Kentucky] *News-Journal*, 28 January 1938, p. 4; 12 December 1940.
22. *Adair County News* [Columbia, Kentucky], 23 February 1938.
23. *Winamac* [Indiana] *Republican*, 27 May 1937, p. 8.
24. According to *1000 and One: The Blue Book of Non-Theatrical Films* (Chicago, IL: Educational Screen, 4th edn 1926).
25. Williams, *Fordson, Farmall, and Poppin' Johnny*, p. 54.
26. Slide, *Before Video*, p. 48.
27. *Blue Book of Non-Theatrical Films* (1926).
28. *Motion Pictures of the United States Department of Agriculture* (Washington, DC: Government Printing Office, 1927), p. 17.
29. *Blue Book of Non-Theatrical Films* (1926), p. 18. A different sort of tribute to the heavy machinery industry and its extensive use of motion pictures for promotional purposes came from one of America's most widely circulated magazines, the *Saturday Evening Post*, which published William Hazlett Upson's long-running series of comic stories concerning the misadventures of Alexander Botts, a traveling sales representative for the Earthworm Tractor Company. (Botts was brought to the screen by Joe E. Brown in the 1937 comedy, *Earthworm Tractors*.) Upson's stories cast a broad satiric net: the highly competitive agricultural machinery business, the Hollywood way of moviemaking, and the tactics of the advertiser all merit comic deflation. In 'More Trouble with the Expense Account' (17 September 1932), for example, Botts concocts a successful scheme to acquire a high-quality tractor film by allowing a motion-picture company on location to use an Earthworm tractor for a spectacular chase scene; in exchange, the Hollywood crew agrees to film additional footage of the tractor hauling a load of stone up a mountain. In later stories, like 'Good News' (29 June 1935) and 'Hollywood is Wonderful, but—' (31 August 1935), the ever-hustling tractor salesman actually goes to Hollywood, where he makes the most of product placement possibilities and almost convinces a studio head to back a whole series of heavy-machinery-laden melodramas.
30. For information on innovations in tractor design and the state of the highly competitive farm equipment industry in the 1920s and, particularly, in the 1930s, see, in addition to works already cited, in-house histories and case studies such as Wayne G. Broehl, *John Deere's Company: A History of Deere & Company and Its Times* (New York: Doubleday, 1984), pp. 468–543; and Walter Fritiof Peterson and C. Edward Weber, *An Industrial Heritage, Allis-Chalmers Corporation* (Milwaukee, WI: Milwaukee County Historical Society, 1978), pp. 237–79. Williams's *Fordson, Farmall, and Poppin' Johnny* offers an

extremely thorough bibliography of the literature on tractors in specialized and more popular periodicals through the mid-1980s.

31. 'Who Is the Most Extensive Commercial User of Motion Pictures?' *Educational Screen*, 11 (1932), p. 272.

32. 'Industrial Subjects,' *Educational Screen* 15 (1936), p. 318. In 1934, DeVry Corporation announced the sale of nineteen sound portable 16mm projectors to the Armstrong Cork Company, sixty to Firestone, and 150 portable 35mm sound projectors to Ford ('Unprecedented Orders from Big Business for "Talkie Units,"' *Educational Screen* 13 [1934] p. 198).

33. Information about International Harvester's films in the mid-1930s comes from *1000 and One: The Blue Book of Non-Theatrical Films* (Chicago, IL: Educational Screen, 10th edn 1934), p. 123. See also Arthur Edwin Krows, 'Motion Pictures—Not for Theatres,' *Educational Screen*, 23 (1943), pp. 200, 223.

34. 'Industrial Pictures for Selling Programs,' *Educational Screen* 13 (1934), p. 216. *Partners* was actually made by Ray-Bell Films (based in St. Paul, Minnesota) under contract to John Deere. Promotional material rarely indicates exactly who made the films produced by farm equipment companies, though a notice in *Educational Screen* from 1937 indicates that Ray-Bell would continue to produce a diverse array of industrials, including films for John Deere, Ford, and International Harvester ('Ray-Bell Film-Ad Productions,' *Educational Screen*, 16 [1937] p. 170.) Krows claims that Ray-Bell 'possibly holds a record for the production of agricultural subjects, notably for the John Deere companies' ('Motion Pictures—Not for Theatres,' *Educational Screen* 19 [1940] p. 195).

35. 'Reaper Most Widely Used Industrial,' *Educational Screen* 10 (1931), p. 217.

36. *Chesterton Tribune*, 12 February 1931. I found this ad reprinted on a family genealogy webpage: http: worldconnect.rootsweb.com.cigin/igm.cgi?op=GET&db=tetzloff&id=1831.

37. A.P. Hollis, *Proceedings and Addresses, Eight Session National Conference on Visual Education and Film Exhibition and Year Book of Visual Education* (Chicago, IL: DeVry Foundation, 1936), pp. 150, 152, 182, 230. See also Slide, *Before Video*, p. 26.

38. Hollis, *Proceedings and Addresses*, pp. 95, 97.

39. An apparently earlier International Harvester foray into motion pictures was *Romance of the Reaper*, which was mentioned in the *Moving Picture World*, 10 (October 7, 1911), p. 60 as an 'educational entertainment' about 'implement making.'

40. Hollis, *Proceedings and Addresses*, p, 13. See Slide, *Before Video*, pp. 49–50, for more information concerning this 1912 production, which he identifies as *Back to the Old Farm*. The *Lexington [Kentucky] Leader* reported on 11 February 1925, that *Back to the Farm* was screened for students at a local school, suggesting how long this particular 'industrial' stayed in circulation.

41. Broehl, *John Deere's Company*, p. 543.

42. Christiana Campbell, *The Farm Bureau and the New Deal: A Study of Making of National Farm Policy, 1933–40* (Urbana, IL: University of Illinois Press, 1962), p. 3.

43. Krows also notes that AFBF's two-reel *The Homestead* was produced, as was *My Farm Bureau* (1924), by Homestead Films, located in Chicago ('Motion Pictures—Not for Theatres,' *Educational Screen* 19 [1940] p. 193).

44. 'Motion Pictures—Not for Theatres,' *Educational Screen* 18 (1939), p. 192.

45. Nancy K. Berlage, 'Organizing the Farm Bureau: Family, Community, and Professionals, 1914–1928,' *Agricultural History* 75 (2001), pp. 420, 436. See Verna L. Hatch, 'Social and Educational Ideals,' *Hoosier Farmer*, 15 March 1928, pp. 3, 42–43, for a contemporary statement of this ideology.

46. *American Farm Bureau Community Handbook* (Chicago, IL: Home and Community Department, American Farm Bureau Federation, 1928), p. 15. Berlage discusses these

'highly organized social events,' which 'offered traditional as well as new forms of entertainment for members and non-members alike—picnics, Fourth of July celebrations, plowing matches, chicken-calling contests, baseball leagues, showings of bureau-produced films, and community plays and "sings"' ('Organizing the Farm Bureau,' pp. 429–30).

47. *American Farm Bureau Community Handbook*, p. 120.

48. 'Farm Bureau Film Activities,' *Educational Screen* 11 (1932), p. 74. The 4-H Club was a youth organization, sponsored by the USDA, providing education in agriculture and home economics.

49. 'Farm Bureau Film Activities,' p. 74; see also Campbell, *Farm Bureau*, p. 4.

50. 'Farm Bureau Film Activities,' p. 74.

51. 'Farm Bureau Film Activities,' p. 74. This preference for actors over non-actors came at time when national firms were developing advertising campaigns for magazines like *Country Gentleman* featuring 'real' farmers, such as the Erdman family of Jefferson, Wisconsin, satisfied users of Lava Soap (*Country Gentleman*, February 1934, p. 34), and the Mullinnix family of Lone Tree, Iowa, who appeared in a testimonial ad for John Deere tractors (*Country Gentleman*, February, 1936, p. 36).

52. 'Farm Bureau Film Activities,' p. 74. For information on the Atlas Educational Film Company of Chicago, see Krows, 'Motion Pictures—Not for Theatres,' *Educational Screen* 19 (1940), p. 193.

53. 'Farm Bureau Film Activities,' p. 74.

54. 'Farm Bureau Film Activities,' p. 74.

55. 'Two American Farm Bureau Productions,' *Educational Screen* 10 (1931), p. 159. This same review also praised *All in the Same Boat*, a 2-reel AFBF film made in cooperation with Armour and Company, which 'in story form ... treats interestingly and vividly the economic causes of fluctuations in the price of meat—cold storage facilities, feast days, employment conditions, etc.'

56. *Blue Book of Non-Theatrical Films* (1934), p. 22.

57. 'County Agent Wins Motion Picture Contest,' *Hoosier Farmer*, July 1934, p. 25.

58. De Brunner and Lorge, *Rural Trends in Depression Years*, pp. 189–90. See also Ethel W. Gardner, 'Rural Recreation,' *Rural America* 15 (September 1937), pp. 12–13, which is indicative of the programs promoted in *Rural America*, the monthly journal of the American Country Life Association.

59. C.R. Hoffer, 'The Home and Leisure Time,' *Rural America* 12 (January 1934), p. 12.

60. See my essay, 'Hillbilly Music and Will Rogers,' and documentary film, *At the Picture Show*, which describe live performances in a rural small-town theaters, particularly during the Depression.

61. Department of Commerce, *Composite List of Non-Theatrical Film Sources* (Washington, DC: Government Printing Office, 1935).

62. The information about Venard is drawn from *Blue Book of Non-Theatrical Film*, (1941).

63. Alan E. Fusonie, 'The Heritage of Original Art and Photo Imaging in USDA: Past, Present and Future,' *Agricultural History* 64:2 (Spring 1990), pp. 300–18, describes color illustrations and photographs in the USDA archives, but makes no mention of motion pictures as 'original art' produced by the USDA.

64. For background on the formation and subsequent development of the USDA film unit, see Slide, *Before Video*, pp. 47–48; Richard Dyer MacCann, *The People's Film: A Political History of U.S. Government Motion Pictures* (New York: Hastings House, 1973), pp. 52–55; and Krows, 'Motion Pictures—Not for Theatres,' *Educational Screen* 21 (1942), pp. 33–34.

65. See *List of Technical Workers in the Department of Agriculture and Outline of Department Functions* (Washington, DC: Government Printing Office, 1935), p. 2.

66. *Blue Book of Non-Theatrical Film* (1926), p. 18.

67. Information on individual titles from *Motion Pictures of the United States Department of Agriculture* (1926).

68. *Motion Pictures of the United States Department of Agriculture* (Washington, DC: Government Printing Office, 1931), pp. 4, 18.

69. See *Blue Book of Non-Theatrical Film* (1934), p. 127.

70. 'Music by Service Bands in New Motion Pictures,' *Educational Screen* 13 (1934), p. 76; 'New U.S. Agriculture Films,' *Educational Screen* 11 (1932), pp. 301–02.

71. 'New Directory Lists Seventeen New Pictures,' *Educational Screen* 18 (1939), p. 214.

72. *Motion Pictures of the United States Department of Agriculture* (1935), pp. 1–7.

73. 'New U.S. Dept. of Agriculture Films,' *Educational Screen* 12 (1933), p. 278.

74. Brian Winston, *Claiming the Real: The Documentary Film Revisited* (London: British Film Institute, 1995), p. 70. See, for example, Erik Barnouw, *Documentary: A History of the Non-Fiction Film* (New York: Oxford University Press, 1993), pp. 114–21.

75. Raymond Evans, 'The Motion Picture Policy of the United States Department of Agriculture,' *Educational Screen* 16 (1937), pp. 283–84.

76. Cited in Hollis, *Proceedings and Addresses*, pp. 57–58. Hearon's remarks were also delivered to an audience at New York University in February 1938 and published as 'The Motion-Picture Program and Policy of the United States Government,' *Journal of Educational Sociology* 12:3 (November 1938), pp. 147–62.

77. See William Stott's influential account of this debate in *Documentary Expression and Thirties America* (New York: Oxford University Press, 1973).

78. Evans, 'Motion Picture Policy,' p. 284.

79. *Blue Book of Non-Theatrical Films* (1941), pp. 13, 18.

80. MacCann, *People's Film*, pp. 53–54.

81. Cline M. Koon, *Motion Pictures in Education in the United States: A Report Compiled for the International Congress of Educational and Instructional Cinematography* (Chicago, IL: University of Chicago Press, 1934), p. 33.

82. Arthur Edwin Krows, 'Motion Pictures—Not for Theatres,' *Educational Screen* 21 (1942), p. 14.

83. United States Department of Agriculture, *Use of Motion Pictures in Agricultural Extension Work* (Washington, DC: Government Printing Office, 1926), p. 2.

84. 'U.S. Agriculture Film Record,' *Educational Screen* 10 (1931), p. 298.

85. *Use of Motion Pictures in Agricultural Extension Work*, p. 2.

86. Koon, 'Motion Pictures in Education,' p. 34.

87. Raymond Evans, 'Motion Picture Activities of the U.S. Department of Agriculture,' *Educational Screen* (1932), pp. 268. In like manner, the U.S. Bureau of Mines had its own preferred network of non-theatrical screening sites, distributing its 400 reels 'on mineral and allied industries' primarily to schools, but also to 'engineering and scientific organizations, civic and business associations, clubs, churches, miners' local unions and the various service schools of the Army and Navy' ('Bureau of Mines Motion Picture Film Collection Continues to Grow,' *Educational Screen* 10 [1931] p. 78).

88. This proviso, which occurs in all the USDA motion picture catalogues for this period, suggests that farm films were frequently vehicles for 'commercial advertising matter.'

89. *Lexington* [Kentucky] *Herald*, 4 June 1924, p. 3; *Lexington [Kentucky] Leader*, 29 October 1924, p. 1.

90. *Lexington* [Kentucky] *Herald*, 28 April 1922.

91. Don Carlos Ellis and Laura Thornborough, *Motion Pictures in Education: A Practical Handbook for Users of Visual Aids* (New York: Thomas Y. Crowell, 1923, pp. 29–30; E.J. Giering, Jr., 'Motion Pictures as an Aid in Agricultural Extension Work,' *Educational Screen* 16 (1937), pp. 90–91, 94. What is needed is more research on the circulation of agriculture films in the 1910s; the exhibitor columns in the *Moving Picture World* are

one important source. See, for example, 'Farmers' Films,' an account of a screening in Henderson, Kentucky (*Moving Picture World*, 27 February 1915, p. 1320) and accounts of *Bumper Harvest*, a film shot in North Dakota (*Moving Picture World*, 9 October 1915, p. 203; 30 October 1915, p. 830).

92. *Use of Motion Pictures in Agricultural Extension Work*, pp. 12–14.
93. For a discussion of the program in the 1930s, see Eric Smoodin, *Animating Culture: Hollywood Cartoons from the Sound Era* (New Brunswick, NJ: Rutgers University Press, 1993), pp. 44–70.
94. Ruth Hogeland, 'Personality and Personalities,' *Country Gentleman* 105 (November 1935), p. 68.
95. This particular phrase comes from a Lux soap ad, *Country Gentleman*, 108 (April 1938), p. 71.
96. Goodrich ad, 'The Surrender of Old Man Winter—A Newsreel Short,' *Country Gentleman*, 106 (February 1936), p. 39; Lava soap ad, 'A Lava Soap Movie with Real People,' *Country Gentleman* 103 (September 1933), p. 45.
97. Wolverine Shell Horsehide work shoes ad, *Country Gentleman*, 106 (June 1936), p. 85. Of course, moviegoing could also serve as the epitome of unwholesome urban excess. An illustration for a 1934 story about a married couple who move to the city after striking it rich when oil is discovered on their farm shows the wife getting a manicure and explains that she is 'growing fat and soft. She went to the movies too often, and to the beauty parlor too often' (*Country Gentleman*, 104 [May 1934] p. 12).
98. 'Farm Bureau Film Activities,' p. 74.
99. 'Insuring the Future,' *Country Gentleman*, 105 (August 1935), p. 20.
100. Ben Highmore, *Everyday Life and Culture Theory: An Introduction* (New York: Routledge, 2002); and Ben Highmore (ed.), *The Everyday Life Reader* (New York: Routledge, 2002).

Chapter 13: Cinema's Shadow: Reconsidering Non-Theatrical Exhibition

1. This description is paraphrased from FilmAidInternational.org.
2. The film and radio adaptations are available on the DVD special edition of *Rebecca*.
3. Ibid. The site reports that 1.2 million Afghanis lost their homes in 2001 and approximately 2 million fled to camps across the border in Pakistan. A northern city in Afghanistan for the internally displaced, Gardez, is the world's largest refugee camp.
4. Connie Billips and Arthur Pierce, *Lux Presents Hollywood: A Show-by-Show History of the Lux Radio Theatre and the Lux Video Theatre, 1934–1957* (Jefferson, NC: McFarland & Company, Inc., 1995). Other Hitchcock titles adapted for 'Lux' were *Suspicion* (1941), *Mr. and Mrs. Smith* (1941), *Shadow of a Doubt* (1943), *Lifeboat* (1944), *Spellbound* (1945), *Notorious* (1946), and *The Paradine Case* (1948).
5. As Michele Hilmes points out, despite advantages to both parties, the relationship between film and radio was not without controversy and contentiousness. See Hilmes, *Hollywood and Broadcasting: From Radio to Cable* (Urbana and Chicago: University of Illinois Press, 1990), especially 26–77.
6. FilmAidInternational.org.
7. Ben Singer, 'Early Home Cinema and the Edison Home Projecting Kinetoscope,' *Film History* 2 (1988), pp. 42, 44–45.
8. For more on the importance of family home entertainment, including cinema, to families in the late nineteenth and early twentieth centuries, see Moya Luckett, '"Filming the Family": Home Movie Systems and the Domestication of Spectatorship,' *The Velvet Light Trap* 36 (1995), pp. 21–32.
9. Singer, 'Early Home Cinema,' pp. 44–48; Anthony Slide also discusses the early non-

theatrical distribution of films in *Before Video: A History of the Non-Theatrical Film* (Westport, CT: Greenwood Press, 1992).

10. Toby Miller *et al.*, *Global Hollywood* (London: BFI Publishing, 2001), p. 8.

11. Patrick R. Parsons and Robert M. Frieden, *The Cable and Satellite Television Industries* (Needham Heights, MA: Allyn and Bacon, 1998), pp. 199, 244.

12. See Hilmes, *Hollywood and Broadcasting*, pp. 78–115 for a more detailed analysis of the structure of a 'Lux' presentation of a Hollywood film.

13. Slide, *Before Video*, pp. 96–97. See also Eric Smoodin, '"The Moral Part of the Story was Great": Frank Capra and Film Education in the 1930s,' *Velvet Light Trap* 42 (Fall 1998), pp. 20–35. In his study of the film education movement in the 1930s, Smoodin shows how common the conversion of feature films into pedagogical tools was, as film appreciation and other courses stressing the art and morality of cinema to young people grew across the nation.

14. Douglas Gomery, *Shared Pleasures: A History of Movie Presentation in the United States* (Madison, WI: University of Wisconsin Press, 1992), pp. 3–17; Gregory A. Waller, *Main Street Amusements: Movies and Commercial Entertainment in a Southern City, 1896–1930* (Washington and London: Smithsonian Institution Press), pp. 23–64. See, also, a 58-part series of essays by Arthur Krows, 'Motion Pictures—Not for Theaters,' that appeared in *Educational Screen* from 1938 to 1944.

15. Anna McCarthy, *Ambient Television* (Durham, N.C. and London: Duke University Press, 2001), pp. 1–2.

16. Raymond Williams, *The Sociology of Culture* (New York: Schocken Books, 1982), pp. 130–31.

17. Ella Shohat and Robert Stam, 'From the Imperial Family to the Transnational Imaginary: Media Spectatorship in the Age of Globalization,' in Rob Wilson and Wimal Dissanayake (eds), *Global/Local: Cultural Production and the Transnational Imaginary* (Durham, N.C. and London: Duke University Press, 1996), p. 161.

18. For pioneering scholarship that focuses on the power cultural displacement exercises on media interpretation and consumption, see Hamid Naficy, *The Making of Exile Cultures: Iranian Television in Los Angeles* (Minneapolis, MN: University of Minnesota Press, 1993) and Marie Gillespie, *Television, Ethnicity, and Cultural Change* (London and New York: Routledge, 1995).

19. Kerry Segrave, *Movies at Home: How Hollywood Came to Television* (Jefferson, NC: McFarland & Company, Inc., 1999), p. 92.

20. Peter Krämer, 'The Lure of the Big Picture: Film, Television, and Hollywood,' in John Hill and Martin McLoone (eds), *Big Picture, Small Screen: Relations between Film and Television* (Luton: University of Luton Press, 1996), pp. 9–46.

21. Roy Rosenzweig, 'From Rum Shop to Rialto: Workers and Movies,' in Gregory A. Waller (ed.), *Moviegoing in America* (Oxford: Blackwell Publishers, 2002), p. 33; Janet Staiger, 'Writing the History of American Film Reception,' in Melvyn Stokes and Richard Maltby (eds), *Hollywood Spectatorship: Changing Perceptions of Cinema Audiences* (London: British Film Institute, 2001), pp. 20–26.

22. Uma Dinsmore-Tuli, 'The Pleasures of "Home Cinema," or Watching Movies on Telly: An Audience Study of Cinephiliac VCR Use,' *Screen* 41: 3 (Autumn 2000), pp. 315–27.

23. Charles Musser, 'The Early Cinema of Edwin Porter,' *Cinema Journal* 19:1 (Fall 1979), p. 23.

24. André Bazin, 'Adaptation, or the Cinema as Digest,' in James Naremore (ed.), *Film Adaptation* (New Brunswick, NJ: Rutgers University Press, 2000), p. 26.

Chapter 14: Changing Images of Movie Audiences

The analysis in this chapter is developed further in Richard Butsch, *The Citizen Audience: Crowds, Politics and Individuals* (New York: Routledge, 2007).

1. Paul Gilje, *Rioting in America* (Bloomington, IN: Indiana University Press 2000).
2. Eric Hobsbawm, *Primitive Rebels* (New York: Norton, 1959), pp. 7, 110ff; E.P. Thompson, 'The Moral Economy of the English Crowd in the Eighteenth Century,' *Past and Present*, 50, February 1971. For a critique of Thompson, see John Bohstedt, *Riots and Community Politics in England and Wales, 1790–1810* (Cambridge, MA: Harvard University Press, 1983).
3. Richard Butsch, *The Making of American Audiences, from Stage to Television, 1750–1990* (Cambridge: Cambridge University Press, 2000), chaps 1–3.
4. Likewise the emerging industrial working class, organized at work, began also to organize outside work and preferred the permanence of unionization to momentary riot. Hobsbawm, *Primitive Rebels*, p. 124.
5. Marc Baer, *Theatre and Disorder in Late Georgian London* (Oxford: Oxford University Press, 1992).
6. Gilje, *passim*; Butsch, *American Audiences*, chaps 4–5.
7. Bruce McConachie, 'Pacifying Theatrical Audiences,' in Richard Butsch (ed.), *For Fun and Profit* (Philadelphia, PA: Temple University Press, 1990), pp. 47–70.
8. J. Albert Brackett, *Theatrical Law* (Boston, MA: C.M. Clark Publishing, 1907), pp. 232–33.
9. Joel Prentiss Bishop, *A Treatise on Criminal Law* (Indianapolis, IN: Bobbs-Merrill, 1923), pp. 248–49.
10. Anon, 'Americans at the theatre,' *Every Saturday*, 18 May 1871, p. 451.
11. Butsch, *American Audiences*, chap. 8.
12. John Collier, 'Cheap Amusements,' *Survey*, 11 April 1908, p. 74; Mary Heaton Vorse, 'Some Picture Show Audiences,' *Outlook*, 24 June 1911, p. 445; Sherman Kingsley, 'The Penny Arcade and the Cheap Theatre,' *Charities and the Commons* 8 June 1907, p. 295; Barton Currie, 'The Nickel Madness,' *Harper's Weekly*, 24 August 1907, p. 1246; see also Judith Mayne, 'Immigrants and Spectators,' *Wide Angle* 5:2 (1982), pp. 32–40; Elizabeth Ewen, 'City Lights: Immigrant Women and the Rise of the Movies,' in Catharine R Stimson *et al.* (eds), *Women and the American City* (Chicago, IL: University of Chicago Press, 1981), pp. 42–63; Roy Rosenzweig, *Eight Hours for What We Will: Workers and Leisure in an Industrial City, 1870–1920* (Cambridge: Cambridge University Press, 1983); Miriam Hansen, *Babel and Babylon* (Cambridge, MA: Harvard University Press, 1991). On crowds as masses in cities see Eugene Leach, '"Mental Epidemics": Crowd Psychology and American Culture, 1890–1940,' *American Studies* 33:1 (1992), pp. 5–29; Mary Gabrielle Esteve, 'Of Being Numerous: Representations of crowds and anonymity in late nineteenth century and early twentieth century urban America," Ph.D. dissertation, University of Washington, 1995. During this period, fear of movies stirring audiences to act collectively was revealed by censorship of strike scenes in early movies. See Steven J. Ross, *Working-class Hollywood: Silent Film and the Shaping of Class in America* (Princeton, NJ: Princeton University Press, 1998).
13. Jaap Van Ginneken, 'Crowds, Psychology and Politics, 1871–1899,' Academisch Proefschrift, University of Amsterdam, 1989; Robert A. Nye, *The Origins of Crowd Psychology: Gustave Le Bon and the Crisis of Mass Democracy in the Third Republic* (London: Sage 1975); see also Eugene Leach and Mary Gabrielle Esteve on the twentieth-century evolution of crowd psychology into theories of masses of isolated individuals typical in these stories of audiences.

440

14. Lee Grieveson, *Policing Cinema: Movies and Censorship in Early Twentieth Century America* (Berkeley, CA: University of California Press, 2004), pp. 63–64, and Jeffrey Sconce, *Haunted Media: electronic presence from telegraphy to television* (Durham, NC: Duke University Press, 2000), discuss some of these connections.

15. Gustave Le Bon, *The Crowd* (New York: The Viking Press, 1960, first pub. in 1898), pp. 31–36, 39–40, 117–18, 158. Also see Nye, *Origins of Crowd Psychology*; Erika G. King, *Crowd Theory as a Psychology of the Leader and the Led* (Lewiston, NY: E. Mellen Press, 1990), pp. iii–v, 25–33, 56–68, 110–23.

16. Reverend H.A. Jump, 'The Social Influence of the Moving Picture,' New York: Playground and Recreation Association of America, 1911; Maurice Willows, 'The Nickel Theater,' *Annals of the American Academy of Political and Social Science*, July 1911, pp. 95–99; Jane Addams, *The Spirit of Youth and the City Streets* (New York: Macmillan, 1912), p. 76.

17. *Harpers Weekly*, 18 January 1913, p. 22; C.H. Claudy, *Photo Era*, March 1909, p. 121. These stories refer to 'youth' as distinct from children; the term 'teenager' was not yet coined Copy-cat theory can be traced back at least to Goethe, when a novel of his allegedly influenced many German youth to commit suicide. See Ray Surette (ed.), *The Media and Criminal Justice Policy: Recent Research and Social Effects* (Springfield, IL: C.C. Thomas, 1990), pp. 63, 88–89).

18. George Elliot Howard, 'Social Psychology of the Spectator,' *American Journal of Sociology*, July 1912, pp. 33–50.

19. Hugo Münsterberg, *The Photoplay: A Psychological Study* (New York: Arno Press, 1970, first pub. in 1916), p. 95; also see Allan Langdale (ed.), *Hugo Munsterberg on Film* (New York: Routledge, 2002); on Sidis see Eugene Leach, 'Mental Epidemics,' *American Studies* 33:1 (1992), pp. 14–15.

20. Matthew Hale, *Human Science and Social Order: Hugo Münsterberg and the Origins of Applied Psychology* (Philadelphia, PA: Temple University Press, 1980), pp. 60–63, 186; Phyllis Keller, *States of Belonging: German-American Intellectuals and the First World War* (Cambridge, MA: Harvard University Press, 1979), p. 36; Münsterberg, *The Photoplay*, pp. 96, 98–99.

21. Poffenberger from Robert E. Davis, *Response to Innovation: A Study of Popular Argument About New Mass Media* (New York: Arno Press, 1976), p. 263; Ross quote in Norman Denzin, *Symbolic Interactionism and Cultural Studies* (Oxford: Blackwell, 1992), p. 104; Burgess quoted by Henry Forman, *Our Movie Made Children* (New York: Macmillan, 1933), pp. 5–6.

22. *Christian Century*, 15 January–12 February 1930.

23. Garth Jowett, Ian Jarvie and Katherine H. Fuller, *Children and the Movies: Media Influence and the Payne Fund Studies* (Cambridge: Cambridge University Press, 1996).

24. *Motion Pictures and Youth* (New York: Macmillan, 1933; e.g. Ruth Peterson and Louis Thurstone, *Motion Pictures and the Social Attitudes of Children* (New York: Macmillan, 1933), pp. 14–15; Frank Shuttleworth and Mark May, *The Social Conduct and Attitudes of Movie Fans* (New York; Macmillan, 1933), p. 85; Forman, *Our Movie Made Children*; see also Jowett, Jarvie, and Fuller, *Children and the Movies, passim*. Blumer became one of the most important figures in American sociology. His graduate students became particularly well-known for their research on the urban working class.

25. Blumer, *Movies and Conduct* (New York: Macmillan, 1933), p. 74.

26. Blumer, *Movies and Conduct*, pp. 127, 193, 197. Also see Norman Denzin, *Symbolic Interactionism*, pp. 106–12; Patricia Clough, 'The Movies and Social Observation: Reading Blumer's *Movies and Conduct*,' *Symbolic Interaction* 11:1 (1988), pp. 85–97.

27. The work of Paul Cressey, in a Payne Fund study entitled 'Boys, Movies, and City Streets,' represents an exception to this, but Cressey's manuscript was unfinished, and

remained unpublished until 1996, when it was published as 'The Community—A Social Setting Study for the Motion Picture,' in Jowett, Jarvie, and Fuller, *Children and the Movies*. See also Richard Maltby, 'Why Boys Go Wrong: Gangsters, Hoodlums, and the Natural History of Delinquent Careers,' in Lee Grieveson, Esther Sonnet and Peter Stanfield, eds., *Mob Culture: Hidden Histories of the American Gangster Film* (New Brunswick, NJ: Rutgers University Press, 2005), pp. 41–66.

28. James B. Gilbert, *A Cycle of Outrage: America's Reaction to the Juvenile Delinquent in the 1950s* (New York: Oxford University Press, 1986), p. 75; Thomas Doherty, *Teenagers and Teenpics: The juvenilization of American movies in the 1950s* (Philadelphia, PA: Temple University Press, rev. edn, 2002).

29. David Jobes *et al.*, 'The Kurt Cobain Suicide Crisis,' *Suicide and Life Threatening Behavior* 26:3 (Fall 1996), pp. 260–69; Michel Marriott, 'A Thin Line between Movie and Joystick,' *New York Times*, 20 February 2003, G1, p. 8.

30. Timothy Hickman, 'Drugs and Race in American Culture: Orientalism in the turn-of-the-century discourse of narcotic addiction,' *American Studies* 41:1 (Spring 2000), pp. 71–91; Jill Jonnes, *HepCats, Narcs and Pipe Dreams* (Baltimore, MD: Johns Hopkins University Press, 1996); David Musto, *The American Disease: Origins of Narcotics Control* (New York: Oxford University Press, 1987).

31. Samantha Barbas, *Movie Crazy: Fans, Stars and the Culture of Celebrity* (New York: Palgrave, 2001), pp. 160, 168, 173, 175; Margaret Thorp, *America at the Movies* (New Haven, CT: Yale University Press, 1939), p. 5. Caricatures of soap opera fans have been even more extreme. See James Thurber, *The Beast in Me and Other Animals* (New York: Harcourt Brace, 1948), pp. 151–61; Tania Modoleski, *Loving with a Vengeance: Mass-Produced Fantasies for Women* (Hamden, CT: Arcon Books, 1982), pp. 85–109; Ellen Seiter, Hans Borchers, Gabriele Kreutzner, and Eva-Maria Warth, '"Don't treat us like we're so stupid and naïve": Toward an ethnography of soap opera viewers,' in *Remote Control: Television, Audiences and Cultural Power* (New York: Routledge, 1989), pp. 241–47.

32. Joli Jensen, 'Fandom as Pathology: The consequences of characterization,' in Lisa Lewis (ed.), *Adoring Audience: Fan Culture and Popular Media* (New York: Routledge, 1992); Henry Jenkins, *Textual Poachers: Television Fans and Participatory Culture* (New York: Routledge, 1992).

33. Jane Gaines, 'Political Mimesis,' in Gaines and Michael Renov (eds), *Collecting Visible Evidence* (Minneapolis, MN: University of Minnesota Press, 1999), pp. 90–91.

34. Linda William, 'Film Bodies: Gender, genre and excess,' *Film Quarterly* 44:4 (Summer, 1991), pp. 2–13.

35. Psychologist Hadley Cantril compared speakers and radio to make a similar argument about radio's influence in the 1930s. See Butsch, 'Class and Audience Effects: a history of research on movies, radio and television,' *Journal of Popular Film and Television* 29:3 (Fall 2001), pp. 112–20.

36. Miriam Hansen, *Babel and Babylon: Spectatorship in American Silent Film* (Cambridge, MA: Harvard University Press, 1991).

37. Jürgen Habermas, *The Structural Transformation of the Public Sphere*, trans. by Thomas Burger (Cambridge, MA: MIT Press, 1989), esp. chap. 3.

38. Butsch, 'American Theater Riots and Class Relations, 1754–1849,' *Theatre Annual*, 48 (1995), pp. 41–59.

39. Butsch, *American Audiences*, pp. 118–10, 126–38.

40. Butsch, *American Audiences*, pp. 54–56, 78.

41. The continued belief in this image of audiences is testified by the popularity of Robert D. Putnam's work, *Bowling Alone: The Collapse and Revival of American Community* (New York: Simon and Schuster, 2000).

42. A related argument on this point was made about everyday resistances of working class African Americans in Robin Kelly, '"We are not what we seem": rethinking black working class opposition in the South,' *Journal of American History* 80:1 (June 1993), p. 76. Kelly emphasized the collective nature of these resistances.

Chapter 15: 'Healthy Films from America': The Emergence of a Catholic Film Mass Movement in Belgium and the Realm of Hollywood, 1928–1939

1. Pope Pius XI, extract from the Encyclical Letter on the Motion Picture, *Vigilanti Cura*, given at Rome, 29 June 1936. The complete text of the Encyclical can be found on the Vatican website. See: http://www.vatican.va/holy_father/pius_xi/encyclicals/documents/hf_p-xi_enc_29061936_vigilanti-cura_en.html.
2. For research on the Legion of Decency see Gregory Black, *Hollywood Censored: Morality Codes, Catholics and the Movies* (Cambridge: Cambridge University Press, 1994), James Skinner, *The Cross and the Cinema: The Legion of Decency and the National Catholic Office for Motion Pictures, 1933–1970* (Westport, CT: Praeger, 1993), and Frank Walsh, *Sin and Censorship: The Catholic Church and the Motion Picture Industry* (New Haven, CT: Yale University Press, 1996). For wider work on the influence of the Legion and Catholic figures demanding self-censorship in the USA, see Lea Jabobs' discussion and book review of Black's *Hollywood Censored*, in *Historical Journal of Film, Radio and Television*, 16: 1 (1996), pp. 103–7.
3. See e.g. Roland Cosandey, André Gaudreault & Tom Gunning (eds), *Une Invention du Diable? Cinéma des Premiers Temps et Réligion* (Laval: Presses de l'Université Laval, 1992).
4. The *OCIC* (Office Catholique International du Cinématographe) was founded during a conference in The Hague (23–25 April 1928), bringing together organizations from 15 different nations. During a decisive conference in Brussels (29 September–1 October 1933) the OCIC decided to reorganize the network and to locate its central office in Brussels. See OCIC, *L'Office Catholique International du Cinématographe* (Brussels: OCIC, 1937).
5. See, for example, the letter on the film problem by Cardinal Pacelli, later Pope Pius XII, ('Lettre de S.E. le Cardinal Pacelli au Président de l'OCIC') sent on 27 April 1934 to the Belgian OCIC president Brohée. In this very important letter, the future Pope Pius XII praises OCIC for 'the work already done, as well as the action programme it proposes for the near future' The letter was published in different languages and formats, including a special OCIC brochure in French (*Lettre de S.E. le Cardinal PACELLI au Président de l'Office Catholique international du Cinématographe*, Louvain: OCIC, 1934) and articles in Catholic newspapers and magazines (for instance in German: *Ecclesiastica*, 29 December 1934; Italian: *Osservatore Romano*, 18 May 1934).
6. John T. Trumpbour, *Selling Hollywood to the World: U.S. and European Struggles for Mastery of the Global Film Industry, 1920–1950* (Cambridge: Cambridge University Press, 2002), p. 11. See also Rutger Penne, *Veertig jaar christelijke filmcultuur* (Leuven: dissertation, 1987).
7. Trumpbour, *Selling Hollywood*, p. 213.
8. For a similar argument on France, see C. Bonnafoux, *Les Catholoques français devant le cinéma entre désir et impuissance* (paper for the 4th International Symposium of History and Film, Madrid, 27–29 November 2002).
9. This paper is part of the research project 'Forbidden Images: the history of controversial movies, the official and Catholic film censorship in Belgium' (Scientific Research Council, 2003–6).
10. For an overview, see Marc Reynebeau, 'Mensen zonder eigenschappen', pp. 13–73 in R. Gobbyn & W. Spriet (eds), *De Jaren '30 in België* (Gent: Ludion/ASLK).

11. Ivo Blom, *Jean Desmet and the Early Dutch Film Trade* (Amsterdam: Amsterdam University Press, 2003).

12. Before World War I, there were approximately 650 cinemas in the Kingdom for a population of 7.5 million; see Guido Convents, 'Les Catholiques et le Cinéma en Belgique (1895–1914),' pp. 21–43 in Roland Cosandey, André Gaudreault & Tom Gunning (eds), *Une Invention du Diable? Cinéma des Premiers Temps et Réligion* (Laval: Presses de l'Université Laval, 1992). Compared to other European countries with quite similar population sizes and socio-economic contexts, Belgium had a wide film exhibition sector. By the beginning of the 1930s, Belgium counted 740 theaters, the Netherlands 266 and Switzerland 330. See Ian Jarvie, *Hollywood's Overseas Campaign: The North Atlantic Movie Trade, 1920–1950* (Cambridge: Cambridge University Press, 1992), p. 141.

13. See *Film Year Book 1929* (New York: J. Alicoate, 1929), p. E.

14. See the various editions of Jack Alicoate's *Film Year Books;* Trumpbour, *Selling Hollywood*, pp. 213, 222.

15. Mike Walsh, 'Options for American Film Distribution: United Artists in Europe, 1919–1930,' in Andrew Higson and Richard Maltby (eds), *'Film Europe' and 'Film America': Cinema, Commerce and Cultural Exchange 1920–1939* (Exeter: University of Exeter Press, 1999), p. 142.

16. *Film Year Book 1929*, pp. 1049–56; *Film Year Book 1930* (New York: J. Alicoate, 1930), pp. 1051–56.

17. *Film Year Book 1924* (New York: J. Alicoate, 1924), p. 391.

18. *Film Year Book 1928* (New York: J. Alicoate, 1928), p. 948.

19. *Film Year Book 1934* (New York: J. Alicoate, 1934), p. 1014.

20. *Film Year Book 1938* (New York: J. Alicoate, 1938), p. 1175.

21. Jozef Van Haver, *Voor U Beminde Gelovigen: Het Rijke Roomse Leven in Vlaanderen* (Lannoo: Tielt, 1995), pp. 249–50.

22. Convents, p. 31.

23. Felix Morlion, 'Even nadenken na het volksverzet tegen de "Heldhaftige Kermis,"' *De Standaard* (14.2.1936).

24. The Catholic film movement operated in the language of both major cultural communities in Belgium: Dutch in Flanders and Brussels, and French in Wallonia and Brussels. For the sake of clarity, we will only use Dutch-language abbreviations. 'Een algemene vergadering te Brussel. Katholieke filmactie,' *De Standaard* (27.9.1928).

25. Felix Morlion, *Filmleiding* (Leuven: Davidsfonds, 1932), p. 7.

26. Jean-Pierre Wauters, '50 jaar K.F.A. in België,' *Film en Televisie*, vol. 25, no. 282 (1980), pp. 21–43.

27. In Flanders, the daily press has long been highly dominated by Catholic newspapers.

28. Father Lunders claims that DOCIP articles and lists of movies appear in sixty newspapers and magazines. *De Film, Moderne Grootmacht* (Roeselare: Hernieuwen-uitgaven, 1937), p. 59.

29. Morlion, *Filmleiding*, p. 15. In another article, Morlion claimed that by September 1934 'the press agency DOCIP covered all Catholic newspapers in country, organizing quicker than foreseen newspapers in Luxembourg, Saarland, Alsace and France.' F. Morlion, *De les uit Amerika*, in *De Standaard* (28.9.1934).

30. This Catholic censorship board was another initiative by Father Morlion. See internal document 'Commission de Censure Catholique' (20.4.1932, KADOC/KFA box 39, Louvain). The board was recognized as a separate service within the film movement in 1931, but only reached its full role in 1932. The board mainly classified movies according to their moral and religious value, but it soon also looked at the artistic and commercial value of them as well. The censorship board produced standard questionnaires for the priests, lay men and women, who were engaged in classifying movies. These

questionnaires were sent to the Brussels headquarters, where the central censorship board (KFK), headed by priests, gave a final classification. The results of this rather bureaucratic process were publicized through leaflets, posters, DOCIP film reviews, etc. See internal document 'Directives de la Commission Catholique de Sélection' (July 1934, KADOC/KFA box 40, Louvain).

31. Internal document, 'Commission de Censure Catholique' (20.4.1932, KADOC/KFA box 39, Louvain). [My translation].

32. Wauters, '50 jaar K.F.A. in België,' p. 23; Morlion, *Filmleiding*, p. 18; Brohée & Cartuyvels, *Het Middenbestuur der Katholieke Filmaktie* (Brussels: KFA, 1933), p. 25.

33. After World War II, Morlion, an enigmatic figure, became the founder of the Vatican Intelligence organization 'Pro Deo.'

34. Morlion, *Filmleiding*, p. 19 [my translation].

35. Brohée & Cartuyvels, *Het Middenbestuur*, p. 8. See also: Undated internal document 'De Katholieke filmliga naar eigen productie' (probably May/June 1933, KADOC/KFA box 43).

36. The future Pope wrote to Brohée that OCIC should arouse the interest of 'good people' in the industry for 'the production of high class films,' which 'protect good manners' *Lettre de S.E. le Cardinal PACELLI au Président de l'Office Catholique international du Cinématographe*, 1934, p. 4.

37. For a case study, see D. Biltereyst & S. Van Bauwel, 'Emerging regional cinema, folk art and nationalism: the case of *De Witte* (1934),' in E. Mathys, *Cinema in the Low Countries* (London: Wallflower, 2004).

38. Felix Morlion mentioned the start of the KFL in his booklet *Filmleiding*, pp. 21–24. See also Wauters, '50 jaar K.F.A. in België,' p. 23.

39. See the literal reference in Lunders, *De Film, Moderne Grootmacht*, p. 59.

40. Lunders, *De Film, Moderne Grootmacht*, pp. 59–60; Wauters, '50 jaar K.F.A. in België,' p. 24.

41. Wauters, '50 jaar K.F.A. in België,' p. 24.

42. More research needs to be done on the international orientation of such organizations as DOCIP, but several sources indicate that this information, documentation and propaganda machinery did not limit its range of action to the Belgian press and media only. It seems that, in the wake of OCIC's move to Brussels, DOCIP played a supra-national role in bringing together data from Belgian and foreign Catholic press releases, film information and censorship data. It seems that in the mid- and later 1930s, French and Swiss Catholic newspapers and magazines also used DOCIP film articles, censorship data and information. A major archival problem deals with the confiscation (and probably destruction) of pre-war DOCIP material when the Gestapo came in Brussels in 1940. Wauters, '50 jaar K.F.A. in België,' p. 23.

43. For information on the interwar Catholic film movements in the Netherlands, see Ansje Van Beusekom, *Kunst en Amusement* (Haarlem: Arcadia, 2001), pp. 268–75; and Bert Hogenkamp, *De Nederlandse documentaire film 1920–1940* (Amsterdam: Van Gennep, 1988), pp. 67–80; for France, see C. Bonnafoux, *Les Catholoques français devant le cinéma entre désir et impuissance* (paper for the 4th International Symposium of History and Film, Madrid, 27–29 November 2002); and Colin Crisp, *The Classic French Cinema 1930–1960*, (Bloomington, IN: Indiana University Press, 1993), pp. 255–63.

44. Lunders, *De Film, Moderne Grootmacht*, p. 44; Reynebeau, 'Mensen zonder eigenschappen,' p. 66; Van Haver, *Voor U Beminde Gelovigen*, pp. 249–53.

45. Brohée & Cartuyvels, *Het Middenbestuur der Katholieke Filmaktie*, p. 19.

46. Undated internal report, 'Legion of Decency,' KADOC/KFA box 42, probably 1934.

47. Felix Morlion, 'Het Filmvraagstuk voor de Katholieke Pers' (undated internal document, KADOC/KFL box 44, probably 1935, pp. 4–5).

48. Felix Morlion, 'Hollywood huivert, zuivert ... huichelt', *De Standaard*, 17 August 1934.

49. Undated internal report, Legion of Decency, KADOC/KFA box 42, p. 1.

50. Undated internal report, Legion of Decency, KADOC/KFA box 42, p. 1.

51. See Higson and Maltby, *'Film Europe' and 'Film America,'* pp. 7–16.

52. J.B., 'De Vlaamsche Katholieken tegenover het Filmprobleem,' *De Standaard*, 29 January 1929 and 5 February 1929.

53. A.J. Nuyens, *Waarheen met de film?* (Antwerp: Geloofsverdediging, 1932), pp. 17–18.

54. Nuyens, *Waarheen met de film?*, pp. 20–22.

55. J.B., 'De Vlaamsche Katholieken tegenover het Filmprobleem.'

56. Felix Morlion, 'La conscience devant le cinéma,' KADOC/KFA box 37, p. 1.

57. Felix Morlion, 'De Grondlagen van de Kommunistische Film?,' *De Standaard*, 3 March 1934; Morlion, 'De Kommunistische mirakelfilm en wij,' *De Standaard*, 4 May 1934. See also Van Beusekom, *Kunst en Amusement*, p. 270.

58. Morlion, 'La conscience devant le cinema,' KADOC/KFA box 37, p. 2.

59. Morlion, 'La conscience devant le cinema,' KADOC/KFA box 37, p. 4.

60. Morlion, 'Het Filmvraagstuk voor de Katholieke Pers,' p. 2.

61. See KADOC/KFA box 31.

62. Crisp, *The Classic French Cinema*, pp. 258–60.

63. Felix Morlion *De Fransche Film*, in *De Standaard*, 14 September 1934; F.M. Grootheid en ellende van de Fransche Film, in *De Standaard*, 12.10.1934.

64. Morlion, *Filmleiding*, p. 17; Paul Léglise, *Histoire de la Politique du Cinéma Française* (Paris: Pichon & Durand-Auzias, 1970), p. 247; Crisp, *The Classic French Cinema*, pp. 259–60.

65. Throughout the 1930s, Belgium lived through a period of intense conflicts of varying kinds. The kingdom saw the rise and success of more extremist political formations on the left and right, often associated with linguistic and nationalist aspirations. In a highly polarized society, these conflicts were unsurprisingly interwoven with questions on the role of the state, trade unions and the church. See K. Deprez & L. Vos (eds), *Nationalism in Belgium* (London: Macmillan Press, 1999).

66. Felix Morlion, 'Even nadenken na het volksverzet tegen *"Heldhaftige Kermis,"'* *De Standaard* 14 February 1936. For a more extended discussion of the public debate on *La Kermesse Héroïque*, see Benoît Mihaïl, *'La Kermesse héroïque*, un hommage à la Flandre? La polémique autour du film de Jacques Feyder en Belgique (janvier–mars 1936),' *BEG*, 10:1 (2002), pp. 43–78.

67. *Filmliga*, 4: 6 (November 1936), p. 4.

68. 'Filmnieuwtjes,' *De Standaard*, 3 August 1934.

69. Jeanne De Bruyn, 'De Film en het Katholieke Leven,' *Nieuw Vlaanderen*, 19 September 1936, p. 22. See also Crisp, *The Classic French Cinema*, p. 258.

70. Ruth Vasey, *The World According to Hollywood, 1918–1939* (Exeter: Exeter University Press, 1997).

71. Ian Jarvie, review of Vasey, *The World According to Hollywood*, *Historical Journal of Film, Radio and Television*, 18:2 (1998), pp. 302–304.

Chapter 16: The Child Audience and the 'Horrific' Film in 1930s Britain

1. This chapter is considerably extended from '"Horrific" films, cinema memory and constructions of childhood,' *Screen* Studies Conference, Glasgow, June 2000; and 'Children, "horrific" films and censorship in 1930s Britain,' *Historical Journal of Film, Radio and Television*, 22:2 (2002). My thanks to Ian Conrich for his very helpful feedback and comments.

2. For a summary of the international position in the mid-1910s, see National Council of Public Morals, Cinema Commission of Inquiry, *The Cinema: Its Present Position and Future Possibilities* (London: Williams and Norgate, 1917), pp. 313–31. For a résumé covering the period to the mid-1920s, see Sarah J. Smith, *Angels With Dirty Faces: Children, Cinema and Censorship in 1930s Britain*, Ph.D. thesis, University of Strathclyde, 2001, pp. 43–48.
3. PRO/HO45/11008, Report of Bradford MOH, 1917; report on a deputation of educationalists, 29 May 1916.
4. *The Times* (London), 5 January 1915.
5. National Council of Public Morals, Cinema Commission of Inquiry, *The Cinema: Its Present Position and Future Possibilities.* On the involvement of discourses of 'social purity' and 'social hygiene' in early debates on cinema in Britain and on social class issues motivating concerns about the cinema audience, see Annette Kuhn, *Cinema, Censorship and Sexuality, 1909 to 1925* (London: Routledge, 1988), especially chaps 6 and 7.
6. In 2002, responsibility for the BBFC was moved from the Home Office to the Department of Culture, Media and Sport.
7. United Kingdom. Home Office, 'The censorship of cinematograph films,' 6 July 1923. For a brief account of the BBFC's history, see Annette Kuhn, 'British Board of Film Censors/Classification,' in Derek Jones (ed.), *Censorship: A World Encyclopedia* (London: Fitzroy Dearborn, 2001).
8. United Kingdom. Home Office, 'The Cinema and Children,' 16 December 1929.
9. Fawcett Library, National Vigilance Association Archive, S.1s, Cinema Censorship; Public Record Office (PRO), HO45/14731, local ban upheld by justices, January 1931; Richard Ford, *Children in the Cinema* (London, 1939), p. 92.
10. PRO, HO45/14731, Report on questionnaire findings, October 1931. See Smith, *Angels With Dirty Faces*, pp. 74–76, for a summary of the report's findings.
11. British Film Institute Special Collections (BFI), BBFC Verbatim Reports, 1930–31 bound volume, Deputation to BBFC from London PMC, 3 April 1930; BFI, BBFC Verbatim Reports, 1930–38 folder, Deputation from Parliamentary Film Committee to Home Secretary, 15 July 1930; PRO, HO45/14275, NCW report of visit to Home Office, July 1930. Verbatim reports were commissioned by an anxious BBFC.
12. BFI, BBFC Verbatim Reports, bound volume 1930–31, Notes on a meeting convened by Birmingham Cinema Inquiry Committee, 7 November 1930; also PRO, HO45/14275.
13. PRO, HO45/14276, circular letter from BBFC, 1 January 1931.
14. Birmingham Cinema Inquiry Committee, *The Influence of Cinema on Children*, April 1930-May 1931; PRO, HO45/14276, Deputation from BCIC, 8 May 1931; PRO, HO45/15206, Deputation from BCIC, 6 April 1932.
15. PRO, HO45/14731, Sheffield Social Survey Committee inquiry into children's cinema matinees, July 1931; Birkenhead Vigilance Committee, *A Report of Investigations, June–October 1931* (Birkenhead, 1931); PRO, HO45/14277, National Council of Women, 'Report of an Inquiry into Film Censorship', May 1931, PRO, HO45/14277, Mothers' Union, 'Moral Influence of Cinema Films', July 1931.
16. PRO, HO45/14275, BCIC deputation, 7 November 1930.
17. See PRO, HO45/14276 and PRO, HO45/14276 for details of BCIC deputation, 8 May 1931; BFI, BBFC verbatim report of BCIC deputation, 8 May 1931; PRO, HO45/14276, reply to BCIC request for public inquiry, 10 July 1931.
18. PRO, HO45/14275, Summary of proceedings of LPMC private conference, 12 January 1931; also in BFI, BBFC Verbatim Reports, bound volume 1930–31.
19. PRO, HO45/14277, National Council of Women, 'Report of an Inquiry into Film Censorship', May 1931.
20. PRO, HO45/14276, Proposed consultative committee, February 1931; PRO, HO45/15208, notes on first meeting of FCCC, 26 November 1931.

21. BFI, BBFC Verbatim Reports, 1932–35 bound volume, BCIC National Conference on Problems Connected with the Cinema, 27 February 1932.
22. PRO, HO45/15208, Minutes of 4th meeting of FCCC, 4 April 1932.
23. PRO, HO45/15208, Minutes of 7th meeting of FCCC, 10 October 1932.
24. PRO, HO45/17036, FCCC report to Home Office on Children and 'A' Films, 21 December 1932; United Kingdom. Home Office, 'Children and "A" Films,' 6 March 1933.
25. PRO, HO45/17036, LCC minutes, 20 June 1933.
26. For memories of frightening films in the 1930s, see Annette Kuhn, *An Everyday Magic/ Dreaming of Fred and Ginger: Cinema and Cultural Memory* (London: I B Tauris, and New York: New York University Press, 2002), pp. 66–80. Bad dreams caused by films was one of the issues investigated in the early 1930s in the U.S. Payne Fund Studies of young people's cinemagoing: see W.W. Charters, *Motion Pictures and Youth* (New York: MacMillan, 1933); S. Renshaw and others, *Children's Sleep* (New York: MacMillan, 1933).
27. For examples, see *Kinematograph Weekly*, 7 September 1933 (Birmingham); *Kinematograph Weekly*, 16 November 1933 (St Helens); *Today's Cinema*, 1 November 1935 (London County Council, Middlesex County Council); *Today's Cinema*, 2 November 1935 (Devon, Cornwall); *Kinematograph Weekly*, 7 November 1935 (Exeter); *Today's Cinema*, 4 December 1935 (Surrey County Council); *Today's Cinema*, 13 January 1936 (Torquay); *Today's Cinema*, 22 January 1936 (Margate); *Daily Film Renter*, 7 December 1936 (Essex County Council); *Today's Cinema*, 19 December 1939 (Margate).
28. 'Film Censorship Today,' speech to CEA, 24 June 1936; *Today's Cinema*, 31 July 1936, 8 August 1936, 23 September 1936. The introduction of the 'H' certificate is relatively well documented: see, for example, Tom Johnson, *Censored Screams: the British Ban on Hollywood Horror in the 1930s* (Jefferson, NC: McFarland, 1997); Frank J. dello Stritto, 'The British "ban" on horror films of 1937,' *Cult Movies*, 14 (1995), p. 26.
29. From a note in the MPPDA case file on *Son of Frankenstein*, cited in David Skal, *The Monster Show: a Cultural History of Horror* (London: Plexus, 1993), p. 205.
30. For a list of films given the advisory 'H' label (1933–36) and the 'H' certificate (1937–50), see James C. Roberstson, *The British Board of Film Censors: Film Censorship in Britain, 1896–1950* (London: Croom Helm, 1985), pp. 183–84.
31. Earlier inquiries into children's film preferences include London County Council Education Committee, 'School Children and the Cinema' (London: London County Council, 1932); John MacKie, 'The Edinburgh Cinema Enquiry: Being an investigation conducted into the influence of the film on schoolchildren and adolescents in the city' (Edinburgh: Edinburgh Cinema Enquiry Committee, 1933). See also William Farr, 'Films for children—plea for co-operation,' *Cinematograph Times*, no. 12, September (1936); British Film Institute, 'Report of the Conference on Films for Children, November 20th and 21st, 1936,' in *Films for Children* (London: British Film Institute, 1936).
32. British Film Institute, 'Films for Children: a First List of Films Recommended for Special Performances for Children in Cinema' (London, 1937); PRO, HO45/21118, Odeon Theatres report on children and the cinema, October 1938; William Farr, 'Analysis of questionnaire to adolescents 14–18 years' (London: British Film Institute, [1939]).
33. Richard Ford's 1939 book, *Children in the Cinema*, encapsulates this new way of thinking. For a discussion of these developments in terms of shifting conceptualisations of childhood, see Kuhn, *An Everyday Magic/Dreaming of Fred and Ginger*, pp. 81–84.
34. See Ellen Wartella and Byron Reeves, 'Historical trends in research on children and the media, 1900–1960,' *Journal of Communication*, 35:2 (1985), for an overview of research on children's use of film, radio and television.

35. Quoted in ibid., pp. 130–31.

Chapter 17: Hollywood in Vernacular: Translation and Cross-Cultural Reception of
American Films in Turkey

1. Miriam Hansen, 'The Mass Production of the Senses: Classical Cinema as Vernacular
Modernism,' *Modernism/Modernity* (1999) 6:2, p. 60.
2. Will H. Hays cited by Ruth Vasey, *The World According to Hollywood 1918–39* (Exeter:
University of Exeter Press, 1997), p. 21.
3. Victoria de Grazia, 'Mass Culture and Sovereignty: The American Challenge to
European Cinema, 1920–1960,' *Journal of Modern History* (1989), pp. 61, 79–81; Armand
Mattelart, C.X. Delcourt and M. Mattelart, *International Image Markets: In Search of an
Alternative Perspective* (London: Comedia, 1984), pp. 94–98.
4. See Thomas Guback, *The International Film Industry: Western Europe and America Since
1945* (Bloomington, IN: Indiana University Press, 1969); David Bordwell, Janet Staiger
and Kristin Thompson, *The Classical Hollywood Cinema: Film Style and Mode of Production
to 1960* (London: Routledge, 1985); Kristin Thompson, *Exporting Entertainment: America
in the World Film Market 1907–34* (London: BFI, 1985); de Grazia, 'Mass Culture and
Sovereignty'; Mattelart *et al.*, *International Image Markets*.
5. Jacques Malthête, 'Méliès et le conférencier,' *Iris* (1996), pp. 122–23.
6. Hansen, 'Mass Production of the Senses,' p. 68.
7. The Production Code of 1930 stated that 'the history, institutions, prominent people,
and citizenry of other nations shall be represented fairly.' Donald Crafton, *The Talkies:
American Cinema's Transition to Sound 1926–1931* (New York: Charles Scribner's Sons,
1997), p. 437.
8. For a wider conception of cinema as vernacular modernism see Kaveh Askari and Joshua
Yumibe, 'Cinema as 'Vernacular Modernism' Conference, University of Chicago, 18 May
2002,' *Screen* (2002) 43:4 pp. 432–37.
9. Hansen, 'Mass Production of the Senses,' p. 68.
10. Ironically, after the First World War, the movie theatre was renamed the *Russo-
Americain* in 1920. Mustafa Gökmen, *Eski İstanbul Sinemaları* (Istanbul: İstanbul
Kitaplığı Yayınları, 1991), p. 221.
11. Attila İlhan, 'Seyirci'yi "Yüceltmek" mi, "Kullanmak" mı?,' *Cumhuriyet* 1 January
2001.
12. *World Trade In Commodities*, VI:4, no. 21, p. 2.
13. Even before its release the movie was promoted as an epic on 'Turkish' (!) heroism.
Paramount invited a journalist from Turkish film magazine *Holivut* [sic] to the
filming. The conversation between journalist İsmet Sırrı and director Cecil de Mille is
revealing:.

Sırrı: 'This is a film made for Christian audiences; I hope you do not misrepresent
the heroism of Turkish leader Salahaddin.

de Mille: 'I want to assure you that the real hero of this film is Salahaddin. I did
not hesitate to represent Richard Coeur de Lion's inferior position.'

See Ismet Sırrı, 'Atatürk'ün ünü Hollywood stüdyolarında,' *Holivut* 5:26 (1935), pp. 8–9;
idem., 'Salahattin-i Eyyubinin Kılıncı,' *Holivut* 5:27 (1935), p. 7.
14. Robert Stam, *Subversive Pleasures: Bakhtin, Cultural Criticism, and Film* (Baltimore, MD:
Johns Hopkins University Press, 1989), p. 74.
15. For more information on movie programmes see Behzat Üsdiken, 'Beyoğlu'nun
Eski Sinemaları-I,' *Toplumsal Tarih* (1995) 4:22 pp. 12–18; idem, 'Beyoğlu'nun Eski

Sinemaları-II,' *Toplumsal Tarih* (1995) 4:23 pp. 12–18; Atilla Dorsay, *Benim Beyoğlum* (Istanbul: Çağdaş Yayıncılık, 1991); and Giovanni Scognamillo, Cadde-i Kebir'de Sinema (Istanbul: Metis Yayınları, 1991).

16. See *Yıldız*, 15 October 1946 (16:185), pp. 8–9.
17. Dorsay, *Benim Beyoğlum*, p. 84.
18. Kerry Segrave, *American Films Abroad: Hollywood Domination of the World's Movie Screens from the 1890s to the Present* (Jefferson, NC: McFarland, 1997), p. 197.
19. Alim Şerif Onaran, *Sinematoğrafik Hürriyet* (Ankara: İçişleri Bakanlığı Tetkik Kurulu Yayınları, 1968), p. 179.
20. According to the Istanbul Film Censorship Commission, 68 dubbed foreign films were released in 1947, and 116 in 1948. Onaran, *Sinematoğrafik Hürriyet*, p. 176.
21. Hülya Arslanbay, 'Faruk Kenç,' *Antrakt* 24 (1993), p. 25; Mediha Sağlık, 'Sinemamızın İlk Yılları: Faruk Kenç İle Söyleşi,' *Kurgu* 14 (1996), p. 100.
22. *Holivut* 4:49 (1934), p. 5.
23. Miriam Bratu Hansen, 'Early Cinema, Late Cinema: Transformations of the Public Sphere,' in Linda Williams (ed.), *Viewing Positions: Ways of Seeing Film* (New Brunswick, NJ: Rutgers University Press), p. 139.
24. Segrave, *American Films Abroad*, pp. 202–203.
25. Gökhan Akçura, *Aile Boyu Sinema* (Istanbul: Yapı Kredi Yayınları, 1995), pp. 59–60.
26. Gökmen, *Eski İstanbul Sinemaları*, p. 61.
27. Mücap Ofluoğlu, *Bir Avuç Alkış* (Istanbul: Çağdaş Yayınları, 1985), p. 65.
28. Gökhan Akçura, 'Dublaj Tarihimizde Yeri Doldurulamayan Bir Efsane: Ferdi Tayfur-1,' *Antrakt* 5 (1992), p. 43.
29. Memet Fuad, *Gölgede Kalan Yıllar* (Istanbul: Adam Yayınları, 1997), p. 298.
30. Cited by Gökhan Akçura, *Aile Boyu Sinema* (Istanbul: Yapı Kredi Yayınları, 1995), p. 170.
31. Martine Danan, 'Hollywood's Hegemonic Strategies: Overcoming French Nationalism with the Advent of Sound,' in Andrew Higson and Richard Maltby (eds) *'Film Europe' and 'Film Americ': Cinema, Commerce and Cultural Exchange 1920–1939* (Exeter: University of Exeter Press, 1999), p. 231.
32. Tim Bergfelder, 'Reframing European Cinema—Concepts and Agendas for the Historiography of European Film,' *Lähikuva* 4 (1998), p. 13.
33. Agah Özgüç, *Başlangıcından Bugüne Türk Sinemasında İlk'ler* (Istanbul: Yılmaz Yayınları, 1990), p. 46.
34. Charles Musser, 'Ethnicity, Role-playing, and American Film Comedy: From *Chinese Laundry Scene* to *Whoopee* (1894–1930),' in Lester D. Friedman (ed.), *Unspeakable Images: Ethnicity and the American Cinema* (Urbana and Chicago, IL: University of Illinois Press, 1991), p. 56.
35. Musser, 'Ethnicity,' p. 62.
36. E.g. *Il medico dei pazzi* (Eduarda Scarpetta, 1954, Turkish title: *Toto Tımarhanede*) (Scognamillo, *Cadde-i Kebir'de Sinema*, p. 74).
37. Ofluoğlu, *Bir Avuç Alkış*, p. 140.
38. Ian C. Jarvie, 'Stars and Ethnicity: Hollywood and the United States, 1932–51,' in Lester D. Friedman (ed.), *Unspeakable Images: Ethnicity and the American Cinema* (Urbana and Chicago, IL: University of Illinois Press, 1991), pp. 82–111.
39. Mark Betz, 'The Name above the (Sub)Title: Internationalism, Coproduction, and Polyglot European Art Cinema,' *Camera Obscura*, 16:1 (2001), p. 34.
40. Antje Ascheid, 'Speaking Tongues: Voice Dubbing in the Cinema as Cultural Ventriloquism,' *The Velvet Light Trap* 40 (1997), pp. 39–40.
41. Instead of censorship the officials preferred the more 'neutral' term of control.
42. A former member of the commissions reports that, an officer from the Army's First

Division permanently joined the commission in Istanbul which censors foreign films. Onaran, *Sinematoğrafik Hürriyet*, p. 153.

43. Oğuz Makal, 'Le cinema et la vie politique: le jeu s'appelle "vivre avec la censure,"' in Mehmet Basutçu (ed.), *Le Cinema Turc* (Paris: Centre Georges Pompidou, 1996), p. 134.

44. Nijat Özön, *Karagözden Sinemaya: Türk Sineması ve Sorunları*, vol. 2 (Ankara: Kitle Yayınları, 1995), p. 316.

45. The films were banned in 1953, 1962, 1966 and 1962 respectively. The decision on *The Ten Commandments* was overturned by the Court of Appeals and the film was later released. Özkan Tikveş, *Mukayeseli Hukukta ve Türk Hukukunda Sinema Filmlerinin Sansürü* (Istanbul: İstanbul Üniversitesi Yayınları, 1968), p. 177.

46. These two movies could only be screened during the 1990s on television.

47. Özön, *Karagözden Sinemaya* and Tikveş, *Mukayeseli Hukukta ve Türk Hukukunda Sinema Filmlerinin Sansürü*.

48. Onaran, *Sinematoğrafik Hürriyet*, p. 174.

49. 25.1.1962, File: 91123/901.

50. 11.3.1966.

51. 8.10.1971, File no: 91123/983. I would like to thank Dilek Kaya Mutln for letting me use the censorship committee's reports. For a thorough analysis of these reports see Nezih Erdoğan and Dilek Kaya, 'Institutional Intervention in the Distribution and Exhibition of Hollywood Films in Turkey,' *Historical Journal of Film, Radio and Television* 22:1 (2002), pp. 47–59.

52. Özkan Tikveş, *Mukayeseli Hukukta ve Türk Hukukunda Sinema Filmlerinin Sansürü* (Istanbul: İstanbul Üniversitesi Yayınları, 1968).

53. Annette Kuhn, *Cinema, Censorship and Sexuality, 1909–1925* (London and New York: Routledge, 1988), p. 127.

54. Daniel Lerner, *The Passing of Traditional Society: Modernizing the Middle East* (New York: The Free Press, 1964), p. 25.

55. Lerner, *Passing of Traditional Society*, p. 119.

56. R.D. Robinson, cited by Lerner, *Passing of Traditional Society*, p. 120.

57. Lerner, *Passing of Traditional Society*, p. 28.

58. For an insightful critic of Lerner's study see Reşat Kasaba, 'Kemalist Certainties and Modern Ambiguities,' in Sibel Bozdoğan and Reşat Kasaba (eds), *Rethinking Modernity and National Identity in Turkey* (Seattle and London: University of Washington Press, 1997).

Chapter 18: Cowboy Modern: African Audiences, Hollywood Films, and Visions of the West

1. J.M. Burns, *Flickering Shadows: Cinema and Identity in Colonial Zimbabwe* (Athens, OH: Ohio University Press, 2002), pp. 53–54.

2. A.R. Baeta, 'The Two Worlds,' *Sight and Sound* 17 (1948), pp. 5–8.

3. Baeta, 'The Two Worlds', p. 5.

4. Baeta, 'The Two Worlds', p. 5.

5. Burns, *Flickering Shadows*, esp. pp. 37–59.

6. I developed this argument in 'Popular Films and Colonial Audiences: The Movies in Northern Rhodesia,' *American Historical Review* 106 (2001), pp. 81–105.

7. Baeta, 'The Two Worlds', p. 7.

8. Richard Maltby, 'Introduction,' in Melvyn Stokes and Richard Maltby (eds), *Identifying Hollywood's Audience: Cultural Identity and the Movies* (London: British Film Institute, 1999), p. 3.

9. Charles Ambler, 'Mass Media and Leisure in Africa,' *International Journal of African Historical Studies* 35 (2002) pp. 119–36.
10. Note Thelma Gutsche, *The History and Social Significance of Motion Pictures in South Africa: 1895–1940* (Cape Town: Howard Timmins, 1972, first pub. in 1946); and Brian Larkin, 'The Materiality of Cinema Theaters in Northern Nigeria,' in Faye D. Ginsburg, Lila Abu-Lughod and Brian Larkin (eds), *Media Worlds: Anthropology on New Terrain* (Berkeley, CA: University of California Press, 2002), pp. 319–36.
11. Robert Donald, 'Films and the Empire,' *The Nineteenth Century*, 100: 596 (1926), pp. 497–510, quote p. 498.
12. Donald, 'Films and the Empire,' p. 499.
13. Donald, 'Films and the Empire,' p. 499.
14. Lawrence Levine, 'The Folklore of Industrial Society: Popular Culture and its Audiences,' *American Historical Review* 97 (1992), p. 1396.
15. Catherine M. Cole, *Ghana's Concert Party Theatre* (Bloomington, IN: Indiana University Press: 2001), p. 72.
16. Cole, *Ghana's Concert Party Theatre*, p. 72.
17. Cole, *Ghana's Concert Party Theatre*, pp. 73–77.
18. Catherine M. Cole, '"This is Actually a Good Interpretation of Modern Civilisation": Popular Theatre and the Social Imaginary in Ghana, 1946–66,' *Africa* 67 (1997), p. 371.
19. Cameron Duodu, *The Gab Boys* (Bungay, Suffolk: Fontana Books, 1969, [1967]), p. 54.
20. Steve Salm, '"Rain or Shine, We Gonna Rock": Dance subcultures and identity construction in Accra, Ghana,' in Toyin Falola and Christine Jennings (eds), *Sources and Methods in African History: Spoken, Written, Unearthed* (Rochester, NY: University of Rochester Press, 2003).
21. Ambler, 'Popular Films and Colonial Audiences,' p. 100.
22. Hortense Powdermaker, *Copper Town: Changing Africa: The Human Situation on the Rhodesian Copperbelt* (New York: Harper and Row, 1962), pp. 254–72.
23. Harry Franklin, Director of Information, Northern Rhodesia, quoted in James Burns, 'Watching African Watch Films: Theories of Spectatorship in British Colonial Africa,' *Historical Journal of Film, Radio and Television* 20 (2000), p. 208.
24. Robert Stem and Louise Spence, 'Colonialism, Racism and Representation: An Introduction,' *Screen* 24 (1983), pp. 4–20.
25. Though see Douglas Gomery's book, *Shared Pleasures: A History of Movie Presentation in the United States* (Madison, WI: University of Wisconsin Press, 1992); Melvyn Stokes and Richard Maltby (eds), *American Movie Audiences: From the Turn of the Century to the Early Sound Era* (London: British Film Institute, 1999); Melvyn Stokes and Richard Maltby (eds), *Identifying Hollywood's Audiences: Cultural Identity and the Movies* (London: British Film Institute, 1999); and Janet Staiger, *Interpreting Films: Studies in the Historical Reception of American Cinema* (Princeton, NJ: Princeton University Press, 1992).
26. Burns, *Flickering Shadows*, esp. pp. 37–59.
27. Fifth Report from the Select Committee on Estimates (1950) quoted in Peter Morton-Williams, *Cinema in Rural Nigeria: A Field Study of the Impact of Fundamental-education Films on Rural Audiences in Nigeria* (Ibadan: Federal Information Services, 1953), p. vi.
28. Morton-Williams, *Cinema in Rural Nigeria*, p. vi–vii.
29. Morton-Williams, *Cinema in Rural Nigeria*, pp. vi–vii.
30. Morton-Williams, *Cinema in Rural Nigeria*, Introduction and pp. 1–7.
31. Morton-Williams, *Cinema in Rural Nigeria*, pp. 4–6.
32. Morton-Williams, *Cinema in Rural Nigeria*, p. 3.
33. Morton-Williams, *Cinema in Rural Nigeria*, p. 45.
34. Morton-Williams, *Cinema in Rural Nigeria*, pp. 29–30, 79, 122.

35. Morton-Williams, *Cinema in Rural Nigeria*, pp. 35, 37.
36. Roan Antelope Mine Welfare Office, Annual Report, 1952–1953, Zambia Consolidated Copper Mines, Archives. This screening is examined in greater depth in Ambler, 'Popular Films and Colonial Audiences,' p. 98.
37. Morton-Williams, *Cinema in Rural Nigeria*, p. 42.
38. Morton-Williams, *Cinema in Rural Nigeria*, p. 58.
39. Gutsche, *History and Social Significance of Motion Pictures in South Africa*, p. 379. Also, Ambler, 'Popular Films and Colonial Audiences,' pp. 81–82.
40. Shimmer Chinodya, *Harvest of Thorns* (Harare: Baobab Books, 1989), p. 78.
41. I explored this issue at some length in Ambler, 'Popular Films and Colonial Audiences,' pp. 83–87. Even James Burns's important new book, *Flickering Shadows*, focuses largely on the production and reception of propaganda films. An important exception to the generalization is Rob Nixon, *Homelands, Harlem and Hollywood: South African Culture and the World Beyond* (New York: Routledge, 1994).
42. Sembene Ousman, *God's Bits of Wood* (Oxford: Heinemann, 1986 [1960]), p. 154.
43. P.E.H. Hair, 'The *Cowboys*: A Nigerian Acculturative Institution (ca. 1950),' *History in Africa* 28 (2001), pp. 83–93.
44. Peter Fraenkel, *Wayaleshi* (London: Weidenfeld & Nicolson, 1959), p. 78.
45. Fraenkel, *Wayaleshi*, p. 148.
46. J.A.K. Leslie, *A Survey of Dar es Salaam* (London: Oxford University Press, 1963), pp. 112–13.
47. Phyllis Martin, *Leisure and Society in Colonial Brazzaville* (Cambridge: Cambridge University Press, 1995), p. 86; and Bill Nasson, '"She Preferred Living in a Cave with Harry the Snake-catcher": Towards an Oral History of Popular Leisure and Class Expression in District Six, Cape Town, c.1920s–1950s,' in Philip Bonner et. al. (eds), *Holding their Ground: Class, Locality and Culture in Nineteenth and Twentieth Century South Africa* (Johannesburg: Ravan Press, 1989), p. 286.
48. David J. Gainer, '"Man, the People would Really Go Wild Then": The Bioscope and Cape Town Audiences,' African Studies Association, Annual Meeting, Washington, DC, December 2002, p. 22.
49. Nasson, 'Towards an Oral History of Popular Leisure,' pp. 286–94.
50. Gainer, 'The Bioscope and Cape Town Audiences,' pp. 1, 6.
51. Gainer, 'The Bioscope and Cape Town Audiences,' pp. 6, 13–14, 21; Modikwe Dikobe, *The Marabi Dance* (London: Heinemann, 1973), pp. 72, 109; and Ezekiel Mphahlele, *Down Second Avenue* (London: Faber and Faber, 1971 [1959]), p. 96.
52. Judith Thissen, 'Jewish Immigrant Audiences in New York City, 1905–14," in Melvyn Stokes and Richard Maltby (eds), *American Movie Audiences: From the Turn of the Century to the Early Sound Era* (London: British Film Institute, 1999), pp. 15–28.
53. Gainer, 'The Bioscope and Cape Town Audiences,' pp. 10–12.
54. Dan Mattera, *Sophiatown: Coming of Age in South Africa* (Boston, MA: Beacon Press, 1989 [1987]), p. 75.
55. Godfrey Moloi, *My Life: Volume One* (Johannesburg: Ravan Press, 1987), pp. 27–30, 73–75.
56. Powdermaker, *Copper Town*, pp. 255–56.
57. Powdermaker, *Copper Town*, p. 270.
58. Powdermaker, *Copper Town*, p. 264.
59. I address the discourse of censorship in relationship to gender, class, and race in 'Popular Films and Colonial Audiences,' pp. 89–94.
60. Powdermaker, *Copper Town*, p. 258.
61. Powdermaker, *Copper Town*, pp. 260–61.
62. Powdermaker, *Copper Town*, p. 262.

63. Powdermaker, *Copper Town*, p. 263.
64. Powdermaker, *Copper Town*, p. 267. In fact, censors were probably more concerned about such negative judgements than they were about the possible impact of film imagery and narrative on African behavior. Ambler, 'Popular Films and Colonial Audiences,' p. 100.
65. Charles Ambler, 'Mass Media and Leisure in Africa,' *International Journal of African Historical Studies* 35 (2002), pp. 119–36.
66. Ernie Wolfe, III, 'Adventures in African Cinema, 1975–1998,' in Wolfe (ed.), *Extreme Canvas: Hand-Painted Movie Posters from Ghana* (New York: Dilettante Press, 2000), pp. 17–33.
67. For a study of the role of video in reinforcing the seclusion of Muslim women on the Kenya coast, see Minou Fuglesang, *Veils and Videos: Female Youth Culture on the Kenyan Coast* (Stockholm: University of Stockholm, 1994).
68. 'Mortal Combat Rages, but "Mortal Kombat" Rules,' *New York Times*, 10 June 2003.
69. Wolfe, *Extreme Canvas*.
70. Jonathan Haynes (ed.), *Nigerian Video Films* (Athens: Ohio University Press, rev. edn, 2000); Ola Balogun, 'Africa's Video Alternative' (www.unesco.org/courier/1998); Norimitsu Onishi, 'Step Aside, L.A. and Bombay, for Nollywood,' *New York Times*, 16 September 2002.

Chapter 19: 'Opening Everywhere': Multiplexes and the Speed of Cinema Culture

Acknowledgement. The author thanks Peter Lester for research assistance.

1. Samuel Fuller, *A Third Face: My Tale of Writing, Fighting, and Filmmaking* (New York: Knopf, 2002), p. 277.
2. 'EDI Box Office News: More Shelf Space for Films,' *Variety*, 5–11 January 1998, p. 30.
3. Nielsen/EDI, 'Box Office News,' *Variety*, 16–22 February 2004, p. 23.
4. '*Variety* Box Office,' *Variety*, 24 February–2 March 2003, p. 21; '*Variety* International Box Office,' *Variety*, 24 February–2 March 2003, p. 23.
5. Don Groves, '"The Matrix" Takes Over the World,' *Variety*, 17–23 November 2003, p. 17. Doing so resulted in an extraordinary box office gross of $204 million in 96 countries in the first five days of release. Laura M. Holson, 'An Elf and a Bear Trip up the final "Matrix,"' *New York Times*, 10 November 2003, C2.
6. Sharon Waxman, '"Rings" Shows Trend toward Global Premiers,' *New York Times*, 22 December 2003, E1.
7. Some, including the U.S. Federal courts, saw this policy as detrimental to non-major distributors whose films are not easily available otherwise, leading the MPAA to reverse its stance.
8. Mette Hjort and Scott MacKenzie (eds), *Cinema and Nation* (New York: Routledge, 2000).
9. Important exceptions include Tino Balio, '"A Major Presence in All of the World's Important Markets": The Globalization of Hollywood in the 1990s,' in Steve Neale and Murray Smith (eds), *Contemporary Hollywood Cinema* (New York: Routledge, 1998), pp. 58–73; Toby Miller, Nitin Govil, John McMurria, and Richard Maxwell, *Global Hollywood* (London: BFI Publishing, 2001); Toby Miller, Nitin Govil, John McMurria, Richard Maxwell, and Ting Wang, *Global Hollywood 2* (London: BFI Publishing, 2005); Mark Jancovich and Lucy Faire, 'The Best Place to See a Film: The Blockbuster, the Multiplex, and the Contexts of Consumption,' in Julian Stringer (ed.), *Movie Blockbusters* (New York: Routledge, 2003), pp. 190–201; and Melvyn Stokes and Richard Maltby

(eds), *Hollywood Abroad: Audiences and Cultural Exchange* (London: BFI Publishing, 2004).

10. 'Screaming into Iqaluit,' *Globe and Mail*, 9 December 1997, A15.

11. John Belton, 'Digital Cinema: A False Revolution,' *October* 100, spring 2002, p. 114.

12. Cf. Charles R. Acland, *Screen Traffic: Movies, Multiplexes, and Global Culture* (Durham, NC: Duke University Press, 2003), pp. 213–23.

13. Belton, 'Digital Cinema,' p. 105.

14. Siegfried Kracauer, 'The Mass Ornament,' in ed. and trans., Thomas Y. Levin, *The Mass Ornament: Weimar Essays* (Cambridge, MA: Harvard University Press, 1995, originally published in 1927), pp. 75–86. Kracauer defined 'the Ratio of the capitalist economic system' as an abstracted form of reasoning that did not encompass the organically human. In this essay, he used the concept to compare the mechanised division of factory labour under Taylorism to the performance and consumption of manufactured visual spectacle, using the regimented patterns created by the Tiller Girls dance troupe as his example: 'The ratio that gives rise to the ornament [spectacle] is strong enough to invoke the mass and to expunge all life from the figures constituting it … it is the rational and empty form of the cult, devoid of any explicit meaning, that appears in the mass ornament' (p. 84).

15. Kracauer, 'The Mass Ornament,' p. 76.

16. Rita Felski, 'The Invention of Everyday Life,' *New Formations* 39 1999, p. 15.

17. Miriam Hansen, *Babel and Babylon: Spectatorship in American Silent Film* (Cambridge, MA: Harvard University Press, 1991); Janet Staiger, *Interpreting Films: Studies in the Historical Reception of American Cinema* (Princeton, NJ: Princeton University Press, 1992); Melvyn Stokes and Richard Maltby (eds), *Identifying Hollywood's Audiences: Cultural Identity and the Movies* (London: BFI Publishing, 1999); Melvyn Stokes and Richard Maltby (eds), *American Movie Audiences: From the Turn of the Century to the Early Sound Era* (London: BFI Publishing, 1999); Melvyn Stokes and Richard Maltby (eds), *Hollywood Spectatorship: Changing Perceptions of Cinema Audiences* (London: BFI Publishing, 2001).

18. Cf. Henri Lefebvre, 'The Everyday and Everydayness,' *Yale French Studies* 73 (1987), pp. 7–11.

19. Henri Lefebvre, *Critique of Everyday Life, Volume I*, 2nd edn, trans. John Moore (New York: Verso, 1958).

20. Michel de Certeau, *The Practice of Everyday Life*, trans. Steve Rendall (Berkeley, CA: University of California Press, 1984), p. xiv.

21. Amy Dawes, 'Global Batmania Lifts Warners to Foreign Mark; Success Mirrors 1989 U.S. Results; Firm Cites Euro Screen Proliferation,' *Variety*, 28 February 1990, pp. 7, 16.

22. Richard Gold, 'Globalization: Gospel for the '90s,' *Variety*, 2 May 1990, S–1, S–104.

23. Larry Leventhal, 'Cinema Trade Show Makes Euro Debut,' *Variety*, 29 June 1992, pp. 61, 62.

24. Janet Wasko, *Hollywood in the Information Age* (Austin, TX: University of Texas Press, 1994); Acland, *Screen Traffic*, pp. 85–106.

25. Don Groves, 'Prexy Predicts Global Golden Age,' *Variety*, 11–17 September 1995, p. 56.

26. Ibid. In actuality, by 2000, the split for box office rental was 55.6 per cent domestic and 44.4 per cent international. Don Groves, 'B.O. World is Flat; Local Pix, Strong Dollar Hurt Yanks o'seas,' *Variety.com*, 11 June 11 2002, last accessed 25 June 2002.

27. Millard L. Ochs, 'Cost Considerations in Developing the International Market,' *Boxoffice*, February 1992, SW-16, SW-18.

28. Peter A. Ivany, 'The Development of the International Market,' *Boxoffice*, February 1992, SW-17, SW-19.

29. Douglas Gomery, *The Hollywood Studio System* (New York: St. Martin's Press, 1986), pp. 35, 58, 84.
30. Thomas Guback, *The International Film Industry* (Bloomington, IN: Indiana University Press, 1969), pp. 130–31.
31. Leonard Klady, 'Locals Boost B.O.: Plexes, Homegrown Heroes Pump Global 100,' *Variety*, 9–15 February 1998, p. 30; Don Groves, 'New Multiplex Building Boom May Reshape Euro Film Biz,' *Variety*, 13 June 1990, pp. 1, 20, 21.
32. Kim Williamson, 'A Small World After All,' *Boxoffice*, July 1994, p. 26.
33. 'Euro screen growth: Multiplex Boom Continues,' *Variety*, 23–29 June 1997, p. 53; Stephen Mackey, 'Foreign Exhibs Fuel Boom,' *Variety*, 15–21 June 1998, p. 71; Stephen Mackey, 'Madrid's Megaplex Mania,' *Variety*, 20–26 April 1998, p. 33; Don Groves, 'TW Announces Co-ventures for European Hardtops,' *Variety*, 27 May 1991, pp. 35, 39; John Nadler, 'Cineplex Enters Turkey,' *Variety*, 27 April–3 May 1998, p. 16; John Nadler, 'Multiplex Mania Strikes Exhib Biz,' *Variety*, 18–24 May 1998, p. 64; 'Multiplex Mania Hits Exhibitors,' *Variety*, 26 September–2 October 1994, p. 55.
34. Rick Richardson, 'Underscreened Market Soldiers On,' *Variety*, 15–21 June 1998, p. 78; John Nadler, 'More Multis Mean More Magyar Moviegoers,' *Variety*, 15–21 June 1998, p. 82; Cathy Meils, 'Arthouses Hopping in Prague,' *Variety*, 15–21 June 1998, p. 82; Tom Birchenough, 'Slow Progress for Soviets,' *Variety*, 15–21 June 1998, p. 86; Cathy Meils, 'Politics Plays Havoc with Plexes,' *Variety*, 15–21 June 1998, p. 86.
35. Nancy Tartaglione, 'Arthouse Exhibs Fight Back,' *Variety*, 15–21 June 1998, p. 49.
36. Andrew Paxman, 'Southern Renaissance: Corporate Ventures Multiply Region's Booming Multiplexes,' *Variety*, 23–29 March 1998, p. 43.
37. 'Exhibition explodes in Asia,' *Variety*, 3 May 1993, p. 37; 'Exhibs gear for multiplex era,' *Variety*, 22–28 August 1994, p. 41; Cathy Meils, 'Austria's Plexes Target Small-town Expansion,' *Variety*, 5–11 January 1998, p. 26
38. Martin Peers, 'Loews Lines up World: Shugrue tapped to lead exhib in global moves,' *Variety*, 15–21 June 1998, p. 12.
39. UCI backed away from this venture, and the new owners renamed it Palace Cinemas in 1999.
40. Baharudin Latif, 'Chan, Godzilla battle it out on Malaysian Screens,' *Variety*, 30 November–6 December 1998, p. 36.
41. Don Groves, 'Multiplying Multiplexes,' *Variety*, 12–18 June 1995, p. 42.
42. 'Special Report: Giants of exhibition,' *Boxoffice*, February 2004, http://www.boxoffice.com/index.html, last accessed 15 March 2004.
43. AMC planned to divest its Swedish cinemas (not included here) claiming that film policy there gave local chains advantages in acquiring hit films. Should this transpire, it would be an example of what happens when a chain is *not* able to influence local policy to its own advantage. 'AMC to exit Swedish Exhibition Sector,' *Screen Digest*, December 2003, p. 374.
44. In early 2004, WBIT announced their intention to get out of the Taiwan market. Don Groves, 'WB, Village eye exit of Taiwan exhib'n,' *Variety.com*, 3 March 2004, last accessed 15 March 2004.
45. Don Groves, 'Teuton Exhibs follow Many Yankee Missteps,' *Variety*, 3–9 March 2003, A8; Jon Herskovitz, 'Japanese Biz Thriving in Face of Economic Troubles,' *Variety*, 30 November–6 December 1998, p. 32; Bryan Pearson, 'South African Exhib Builds on Euro Stake,' *Variety*, 30 August–5 September 1999, p. 45. UCI Central Europe acquired some of Ster Century's European screens, though the antimonopoly office of Slovak Republic did not approve this acquisition as it would limit competition. Decision No. 2003/FH/3/1/007, 23 January 2003, www.antimon.gov.sk, last accessed 15 March 2004.

46. 'Major Consolidation in Global Exhibition Sector; Acquisitions shrink number of international players,' *Screen Digest*, July 2003, p. 198. Note that this source did not provide a breakdown for what countries appeared in each of these tallies. It is highly likely that several do not conform to accepted geographical standards; for instance, Mexico probably appears in the Latin America count and not the North American one.

47. Don Groves, 'Exhib Battle Goes Global,' *Variety*, 26 July 1993, pp. 23, 32.

48. Balio, "'A Major Presence,'" p. 60.

49. Marcelo Cajuiero, 'Cinemark Targets Brazil with 6 Plexes,' *Variety*, 6–12 April 1998, p. 17.

50. Linda Moore, 'Spain: The multiplex pick-me-up arrives late but strong,' *Variety*, 29 June 1992, p. 62.

51. Jennifer Clark, 'Italy: Setting houses in order after decades of neglect,' *Variety*, 29 June 1992, p. 62.

52. See Mark Jancovich's chapter in this book for a discussion of a comparable instance in Britain.

53. Adam Dawtrey, 'Euros Go on Screen-building Spree,' *Variety*, 6–12 February 1995, p. 1.

54. Gwen Robinson, "Plexes Proliferate amid Downward Box Office Trend,' *Variety*, 6–12 March 1995, p. 49.

55. Richard Gold, 'U.S. Pix Tighten Global Grip: Major studios speed up their foreign openings to synch with U.S. push," *Variety*, 22 August 1990, pp. 1, 96.

56. The degree of coordination of interests can be seen in the cross-membership of boards of directors. To take one example, in 2002 Isaac Palmer, Senior VP of Corporate Development for Viacom Entertainment Group, was on the board of UCI (Asia, Europe and South America), Famous Players (Canada) and WF Cinema Holdings LLP (U.S.), which owns and runs the Mann Theater chain. Each of these chains operates in different territories, and functions as a distinct corporate entity, and yet, they are ultimately accountable to some identical members on their governing boards. The history of WF Cinema Holdings is instructive in itself. In the major studios' rush back into exhibition in the mid-1980s, Warner and Paramount entered a joint venture with the chain Cinamerica. Seen as too intimate a corporate relationship, they divested themselves of this operation in 1997, selling it for $165 million to WestStar Holdings, which already included the Mann Theater circuit. WestStar filed for Chapter 11 bankruptcy protection in 1999, at which point Warner and Paramount (now owned by Viacom, itself owned by the National Amusement chain), bought it back for $91 million, creating WF Cinema Holdings with 54 theaters and 357 screens. Most of these screens were shut, until only 123 remained at some 21 theatres in 2004. When all is said and done, Warner's participation in WF Cinema Holdings gives them a U.S. domestic chain to complement their international ones. And, in fact, the corporate unit that oversees these domestic U.S. theatres is Warner Bros. International Cinemas. Isaac Palmer promotion, http://www.writenews.com/2002/101102_soundbytes.htm, last accessed 15 March 2004; 'Business Brief—WF Cinema Holdings LP: Assets of WestStar Cinemas to be bought for $91 million,' *Wall Street Journal*, 13 January 2000, p. 1; 'WestStar Cinemas: Viacom and Warner Bros. to Acquire Assets,' January 2000, http://bankrupt.com/TCR_Public/000114.MBX, last accessed 15 March 2004.

57. 'Two Become One,' *Food Chain Magazine: The Business of Food and Drink*, November/December 2003, www.foodchain-magazine.com, last accessed 15 March 2004.

58. 'Cinemark Pushes Deeper into Latin America,' *Screen Digest*, July 2003, p. 193.

59. 'Major Consolidation in Global Exhibition Sector,' p. 198; Don Groves, 'Screen Surge Submerged by Saturation in Global Market,' *Variety*, 3–9 March 2003, A2.

60. 'New Major Strips down by Selling Exhibitor,' *Screen Digest*, April 2002, p. 103.
61. Andrew Willis, 'Onex Puts Loews Cineplex on Sales Block,' *Globe and Mail*, 13 March 2004, B3. At the same time, Cinemark sold its 296 theaters to investment concern Madison Dearborn for $1.5 billion in 2004. 'Theater Chain plans $1.5 Billion Merger,' *New York Times*, 14 March 2004, p. 16.
62. 'Uneven Pace of European Cinema Development: Circuit consolidation as multiplexes spread,' *Screen Digest*, September 2001.
63. 'Half of all European Screens are Multiplexed,' *Screen Digest*, November 2003, p. 324.
64. Mary Sutter, 'Auds Flock to Theaters despite Area's Recession,' *Variety*, 3–9 March 2003, A10.
65. Sutter, 'Auds Flock to Theaters,' A10.
66. 'Global Cinema Exhibition Markets,' *Screen Digest*, October 2003, p. 299.
67. 'Global Cinema Exhibition Markets,' p. 298; 'World Cinema Fails to Keep up with U.S.A.; Global spending now close to $17 billion,' *Screen Digest*, September 1999, p. 22.
68. Henri-Pierre Penel, 'Deux innovations pour une révolution,' *Science et Vie* Avril 2000, p. 128; Michel Marriott, 'Digital projectors use flashes of light to paint a movie,' *New York Times*, 27 May 1999, G7; 'Major Studios Agree to Set Digital Standards,' *Globe and Mail*, 4 April 2002, R2.
69. Cf. William Boddy, *Fifties Television: The Industry and its Critics* (Champaign, IL: University of Illinois Press, 1990).
70. Digital Cinema Initiatives, *Digital Cinema System Specifications*, 20 July, Hollywood: Digital Cinema Initiatives, LLC, 2005.
71. The coalition was said to have been responsible for blocking Boeing's rising power in d-cinema, leading them to put their Boeing Digital Cinema division up for sale. 'Profile—Working towards digital cinema—year 4—limbo, not launch,' *Screen Digest*, February 2003, p. 54; 'Boeing to sell its digital cinema division,' *Screen Digest*, December 2003, p. 375.
72. 'Profile—Working towards digital cinema,' p. 55.
73. 'Hot Number,' *Variety*, 21–27 March 2005, p. 6.
74. 'Profile—Working towards digital cinema,' p. 53; Tim Lee Master, 'China's Digital Dreams,' *Far Eastern Economic Review*, 17 April 2003, p. 50; 'China Plans Large-scale e-cinema Network,' *Screen Digest*, February 2004, p. 51.
75. Some of the chains active in these tests are Famous Players (Canada), UCI (UK, Germany and Brazil), Odeon (UK), Emagine Entertainment (US), and Network Event Theatres (US). 'Exhibitors Eye Alternative Revenue Streams,' *Screen Digest*, October 2003, p. 291.
76. Marcelo Cajueiro, 'Arthouse Circuits win Digital Race,' *Variety*, 2–8 August 2004, pp. 11, 13.
77. 'Regal e-cinema Network Half-way Completed,' *Screen Digest*, February 2003, p. 37.
78. 'Microsoft e-cinema Network Expands,' *Screen Digest*, April 2003, p. 100.
79. 'U.K. Film Council Funds Art-house Digital Cinema,' *Screen Digest*, August 2003, p. 242; 'First Digital Cinema Chain for UK Launched,' *Screen Digest*, October 2003, p. 314.
80. 'Disney Abolishes Video Rental Window,' *Screen Digest*, October 2003, p. 306.
81. 'Summer Cinema Titles for Early Video Release,' *Screen Digest*, September 2003, p. 283.
82. A.O. Scott, 'Even later, "28 Days" hedges its ending," *New York Times*, 21 July 2003, B1, B4.
83. Newspaper advertisement for *Dawn of the Dead*, *New York Times*, 14 March 2004, AR12.

84. Andrew Paxman, 'Latin B.O. Surges 13%: Regional revs up but stock market blasts Brazil,' *Variety*, 19–25 January 1998, p. 21; 'The multiplexing of Latin America,' *Variety*, 23–29 March 1998, p. 68.

85. Paxman, 'Southern Renaissance,' p. 43.

86. Raymond Williams, *Marxism and Literature* (New York: Oxford University Press, 1977), p. 125. Italics are in the original.

87. Some theorists who have pointed the way here are Kevin Robins, *Into the Image: Culture and Politics in the Field of Vision* (New York: Routledge, 1996); Anne Friedberg, *Window Shopping: Cinema and the Postmodern* (Berkeley, CA: University of California Press, 1993); and James Hay, 'Piecing Together What Remains of the Cinematic City,' in David B. Clarke (ed.), *The Cinematic City* (New York: Routledge, 1997), p. 212.

88. Bruce, Robbins, *Feeling Global: Internationalism in Distress* (New York: New York University Press, 1999).

Chapter 20: 'Cinema Comes to Life at the Cornerhouse, Nottingham': 'American' Exhibition, Local Politics and Global Culture in the Construction of the Urban Entertainment Centre

1. John Tomlinson, *Globalisation and Culture* (Cambridge: Polity, 1999), p. 80. See also Toby Miller, Nitin Govil, John McMurria and Richard Maxwell, *Global Hollywood* (London: BFI, 2001).

2. Stuart Hanson, 'Spoilt for Choice? Multiplexes in the 90s,' in Robert Murphy (ed.), *British Cinema of the 90s* (London: BFI, 2000), p. 51.

3. Hanson, 'Spoilt for Choice?', p. 51.

4. Tomlinson, *Globalisation and Culture*, *passim*.

5. Duncan Webster, *Looka Yonder! The Imaginary America of Populist Culture* (London: Routledge, 1988), *passim*.

6. Herbert I. Schiller, 'Electronic Information Flows: New Basis for Global Domination,' in Philip Drummond and Richard Paterson (eds), *Television in Transition* (London: BFI, 1985), p. 19; E.S. Herman and R.W. McChesney, *The Global Media: The New Missionaries of Global Capitalism* (London: Cassell, 1997).

7. Tomlinson, *Globalisation and Culture*, p. 84.

8. Christopher Bigsby, *Superculture: American Popular Culture and Europe* (London: Paul Elek Books, 1975), p. 6.

9. Duncan Webster, '"Whodunnit? America Did": Rambo and the Post Hungerford Rhetoric,' in *Cultural Studies* 3:2 May 1989, pp. 173–93.

10. Martin Woolacott, 'The Mouse that Soared,' *The Guardian* 19 August 1985, p. 12.

11. For further discussion, see Joanne Hollows, *Feminism, Femininity and Popular Culture* (Manchester: Manchester University Press, 2000); Andreas Huyssen, 'Mass Culture as Woman: Modernism's Other,' in Tania Modleski (ed.), *Studies in Entertainment: Critical Approaches to Mass Culture* (Bloomington, IN: Indiana University Press, 1986); and Mark Jancovich and Lucy Faire with Sarah Stubbings, *The Place of the Audience: Cultural Geographies of Film Consumption* (London: BFI, 2003).

12. This promise or brand guarantee is not total, however. McDonalds meals and Starbucks coffees are not identical in every location, as customer complaints testify. Similarly, American films have to be re-edited and re-recorded for different markets.

13. See Joshua Meyrowitz, *No Sense of Place* (Oxford: Oxford University Press, 1985); Marc Augé, *Non-Places: Introduction to an Anthropology of Supermodernity* (London: Verso, 1995).

14. Jean Baudrillard, quoted in Tomlinson, *Globalisation and Culture*, p. 88.

15. Tomlinson, *Globalisation and Culture*, pp. 111–12.

16. See, for example, Sharon Zukin, *The Culture of Cities* (Oxford: Blackwells, 1991); and John Hannigan, *Fantasy City: Pleasure and Profit in the Postmodern Metropolis* (London: Routledge, 1998).

17. Ulf Hannerz, 'Cosmopolitans and Locals in World Culture,' in Mike Featherstone (ed.), *Global Culture: Nationalism, Globalisation and Modernity* (London: Sage, 1990), p. 241.

18. Nicolas Garnham, *Capitalism and Communication: Global Culture and the Economics of Information* (London: Sage, 1990).

19. See for example, Annette Hill, *Shocking Entertainment: Responses to Violent Movies* (Luton: University of Luton Press, 1997).

20. Hollows, *Feminism, Femininity and Popular*.

21. Tomlinson, *Globalisation and Culture*, p. 118.

22. For an extended discussion, see Jancovich and Faire with Stubbings, *The Place of the Audience, passim*.

23. For example, in his account of the multiplex, Stuart Hansen refers to 'the star site in Birmingham [that] will incorporate a 50,000 shopping and restaurant complex' although he acknowledges that it is 'technically in the inner city.' Hanson, 'Spoilt for Choice', p. 50.

24. See, for example, Arjun Appadurai, *Modernity at Large: Cultural Dimensions of Globalization* (Minneapolis, MN: University of Minnesota Press, 1996); and David Morley and Kevin Robins, *Spaces of Identity: Global Media, Electronic Landscapes and Cultural Boundaries* (London: Routledge, 1995).

25. *Estates Gazette*, 8 March 1997, p. 132.

26. Paul Grainge, 'The World is Our Audience: Warner Village, Brand Space and the Local Everyday,' in Richard Maltby (ed.), *Hollywood in the World* (forthcoming). See also Doreen Massey, *Space, Place and Gender* (Cambridge: Polity, 1994).

27. *Nottingham Evening Post* (hereafter *NEP*), Nottingham Commercial Property Weekly, 12 April 1998.

28. *Estates Gazette Interactive*, 6 December 1997, http://www.egi.co.uk/.

29. John Lett, the London Planning Advisory Committee, quoted in *Estates Gazette*, 4 July 1998, p. 113.

30. *NEP*, 24 July 1997.

31. *NEP*, 17 April 1998.

32. *NEP*, 25 August 1998.

33. See John Beckett (ed.), *A Centenary History of Nottingham* (Manchester: Manchester University Press, 1997).

34. *NEP*, Commercial Property Weekly, 21 April 1998.

35. *NEP*, 20 November 1998.

36. *NEP*, 20 November 1998.

37. *NEP*, Commercial Property Weekly, 24 November 1998, *NEP*, 20 November 1998.

38. Information from Nottingham City Council's Inward Investment Team, http://www.nottinghamcity.gov.uk/busin/default.asp.

39. Letter to *NEP*, 28 April 1998.

40. Letter to *NEP*, 7 May 1998.

41. Letter to *NEP*, 8 May 1998.

42. Letter to *NEP*, 8 May 1998.

43. *NEP*, 4 July 1996.

44. See, for example, David Harvey, *The Limits of Capital* (Oxford: Blackwell, 1982); and *The Urbanization of Capital* (Oxford: Blackwell, 1985).

45. Sharon, 37, lecturer. This article is based upon the findings for an AHRB funded research project that involved archival research and the collection and analysis of questionnaires and oral histories.

46. *Estates Gazette*, 8 March 1997, p. 131.
47. *Estates Gazette*, 4 July 1998, p. 83.
48. *NEP*, 18 August 2000.
49. Letter to *NEP*, 8 May 1998.
50. *NEP*, 23 February 2001.
51. *NEP*, 15 March 1997.
52. *NEP*, 23 February 2001.
53. Tomlinson, *Globalisation and Culture*, p. 96.
54. Tomlinson, *Globalisation and Culture*, p. 96.

Index